MW01052352

Easy Cooking with Brand Names

Easy Cooking WITH Brand Names

A LORRAINE GREEY BOOK

CHARTWELL
BOOKS, INC.

ALL RIGHTS RESERVED

Copyright © 1987, 1992 by Lorraine Greey Publications Limited, Toronto, Canada. All recipes and photographs are the property of the respective food companies and have been reproduced here with their permission. No part of this work may be reproduced or used in any form or by any means—graphic, electronic or mechanical, including photocopying, recording, taping or information storage and retrieval systems—without the prior written permission of the copyright holder.

Tabasco is the registered trademark of McIlhenny Company. Uncle Ben's Converted is the registered trademark of Effem Foods Ltd. ANGEL FLAKE, BAKER'S, CATALINA, CERTO, CHEEZ WHIZ, COOL WHIP, CRACKER BARREL, CRYSTAL LIGHT, DE LUXE, DREAM WHIP, JELL-O, KRAFT, KOOL-AID, MAXWELL HOUSE, MINUTE RICE, MIRACLE WHIP, PARKAY, PHILADELPHIA BRAND, POST, POST BRAN FLAKES, QUENCH, SHAKE'N BAKE, SINGLES, TANG, THICK'N SPICY, and VELVEETA are registered trademarks of Kraft General Foods Canada Inc. **Similarly, all other brand names in this cookbook are the registered trademarks of the food companies that have provided the recipes.**

Published by
Lorraine Greey Publications Limited
Suite 303, 56 The Esplanade
Toronto, Ontario, Canada
M5E 1A7
and
Ottenheimer Publishers, Inc.
10 Church Lane
Baltimore, Maryland 21208

Specially produced for

CHARTWELL BOOKS, INC.
A Division of **BOOK SALES, INC.**
P.O. Box 7100
Edison, New Jersey 08818-7100

Introduction: Lise O'Brien
Front cover photograph: Mark Heayn

Printed and bound in Canada.
CB641B

Contents

24 BISCUITS 400g
Weetabi
WHOLE WHEAT
NABISCO
100%
Bran
New Recipes
Nouvelles
Uncle Ben's
Rice
Florenti
Green Giant
White and Wild Rice
in a seasoned sauce
NESCAFÉ
Rich Blend
Minute Rice
HERSHEY'S
Chocolate syrup
Wasa
Crispbread
Realemon
LEMON JUICE
FROM CONCENTRATE
What a difference whole eggs make!
HP
Carnation
2%
FIRST FOODS
BANANAS
Gerber
COW BRAND
baking soda
SODIUM BICARBONATE U.S.P.
Hunt's
tomato paste
ALL VEGETABLE
TOUT VÉGÉTAL
Crisco
LAWRY'S
TOBLERONE
SWISS MILK CHOCOLATE WITH ALMOND AND HONEY NOU
MADE BY FABRIQUÉ PAR Chocolat Tobler LTD. BERNE/SWITZERLAND S.A. BERNE/SUISSE
Green Giant
NIBLETS
WHOLE KERN

Foreword

Our most precious memories sometimes involve food. Perhaps it is the recollection of a steaming bowl of Grandma's homemade soup that warmed you on a cold winter's day. Or the elegant meal you shared the night you fell in love. It could be that special dessert that you thought you could never make but tried anyway; they loved it and you felt like you had just conquered the world.

Easy Cooking with Brand Names is full of recipes like the ones those memories are made of.

In these pages, you'll find a wealth of wonderful recipes newly created for you by the makers of the products you have known and trusted all your life. And because we know a classic when we've tasted one, you'll find some of their all-time favorites, too.

You'll also discover recipes made with delightful new specialty products from around the world which are now available right in your local supermarket.

Our recipes are both budget-wise and easy to prepare. We've used plain and simple language—no confusing "insider" terms—because we know that a recipe doesn't have to be complicated to be appealing.

Each chapter features recipes designed with today's tastes in mind, as well as preparation methods employing the latest appliances. For your convenience, we have used easy-to-read symbols, ▭ and ▥, where microwave and barbecue methods of cooking are included.

It has been said that a picture is worth a thousand words and we believe the photographs you'll find throughout this book are both a delight to look at and a helpful source of serving and presentation ideas. They represent the work of some of the world's finest food photographers.

From quick and easy-to-prepare appetizers to elegant main dishes, from the wholesome simplicity of our soups, stews and breads to some of the most scrumptious desserts you've ever tasted, we'll show you how to achieve the kind of results you will be proud of.

Whether you're planning a full-course meal or a simple snack. Whether it's for the entire gang, a special guest or your own family, you'll find our recipes delightful, sometimes daring, always delicious...and a joy to prepare.

We hope **Easy Cooking with Brand Names** will help you create some very special memories of your own.

—Lise O'Brien

EDITOR'S NOTE

All reasonable care has been taken to ensure that the foods used in **Easy Cooking with Brand Names** are available in both Canada and the United States of America. However, certain brands may not be available in every region and we regret any inconvenience this may cause our readers.

American weights and measures have been used throughout this cookbook. To assist you in finding equivalent package sizes where only metric measure is sold, we have prepared this conversion chart for the most common sizes.

WEIGHTS	FLUID MEASURES
1 oz. = 28 grams	4½ fl. oz. = 128 mL
2 oz. = 57 grams	5½ fl. oz. = 156 mL
3 oz. = 85 grams	6 fl. oz. = 170 mL
3½ oz. = 100 grams	7 fl. oz. = 199 mL
4 oz. = 113 grams	7½ fl. oz. = 213 mL
5 oz. = 142 grams	8 fl. oz. = 227 mL
6 oz. = 170 grams	10 fl. oz. = 284 mL
6½ oz. = 184 grams	12 fl. oz. = 341 mL
7 oz. = 198 grams	13½ fl. oz. = 385 mL
7½ oz. = 213 grams	14 fl. oz. = 398 mL
8 oz. = 227 grams	16 fl. oz. = 455 mL
10 oz. = 284 grams	19 fl. oz. = 540 mL
12 oz. = 340 grams	28 fl. oz = 796 mL
14 oz. = 397 grams	48 fl. oz. = 1.36 L
15 oz. = 425 grams	
16 oz. = 454 grams	
1½ lb. = 680 grams	

microwave method included
barbecue recipe or barbecue method included

APPETIZERS

Tempting to the eye and teasing to the taste buds, appetizers are artful dishes meant to stimulate rather than satisfy the palate. They are an integral part of any special menu, therefore selecting them carefully to harmonize with the rest of your meal is an important part of your preparations.

By using contrasts in color, texture and shape, the imaginative cook can transform some very ordinary ingredients into delectable little delights. There is almost no limit to the kinds of meat, poultry, fish, cheese, vegetables and fruit you can use.

So show a little innovation, have a little fun, relax. . . and let the party begin.

Here's to some great beginnings!

Crabmeat Canapés with Anchovy and Yogurt Canapés (see page 3)

Chicken Hors d'Oeuvres

CHICKEN HORS D'OEUVRES

1 10-oz. can **Campbell's Condensed Cheddar Cheese Soup**
1 5-oz. can chunk white chicken or 1 7-oz. can tuna, drained and flaked
1 egg, slightly beaten
½ cup Italian flavored fine dry bread crumbs
2 tbsp. finely chopped green pepper
2 tbsp. finely chopped green onions
¼ tsp. hot red-pepper sauce
salad oil
¼ cup sour cream
generous dash crushed tarragon leaves

In bowl, mix thoroughly ¼ cup soup, chicken, egg, bread crumbs, green pepper, green onions and hot red-pepper sauce. Shape into 40 small (½") chicken meatballs, roll in additional bread crumbs. Half-fill deep fryer or large saucepan with oil; preheat to 350°F. Fry meatballs, a few at a time, in hot oil until browned. Drain; keep warm. Meanwhile, in saucepan, combine remaining soup, sour cream and tarragon. Heat; stir occasionally. Serve with meatballs.
Makes 40 appetizers

SPANISH DIP

1 10-oz. can **Campbell's Condensed Cream of Celery Soup**
1 8-oz. package cream cheese, softened
2 tbsp. chopped green pepper
2 tbsp. chopped ripe olives
2 tbsp. finely chopped onion
¼ tsp. Worcestershire sauce
generous dash hot red-pepper sauce

With electric mixer or rotary beater, gradually blend soup into cream cheese. Add remaining ingredients; chill. Serve with crackers or chips.
Makes 2 cups

LOBSTER STARTER

1 5-oz. can lobster
2 10-oz. cans **Campbell's Condensed Consommé**, chilled
lemon wedges
parsley

Drain lobster and cut into bite-sized pieces. Fold lobster into jellied consommé. Serve in seafood cocktail glasses and garnish with lemon and parsley.
Serves 6

CHILI SHRIMP DIP

1 10-oz. can **Campbell's Condensed Cream of Shrimp Soup**
1 8-oz. package cream cheese, softened
¼ cup finely chopped celery
2 tbsp. chili sauce
1 tbsp. finely chopped onion
dash Worcestershire sauce

With electric mixer or rotary beater, gradually blend soup into cream cheese. Beat just until smooth (overbeating makes dip thin). Stir in remaining ingredients and chill 4 hours or more. Serve as a dip with crackers or chips.
Makes 2 cups

COCKTAIL MEATBALLS

1 lb. ground beef
2 tbsp. bread crumbs
1 egg, slightly beaten
½ tsp. salt
½ cup finely chopped onion
⅓ cup finely chopped green pepper
2 tbsp. butter or margarine
1 10-oz. can **Campbell's Condensed Tomato Soup**
2 tbsp. brown sugar
1 tbsp. vinegar
1 tbsp. Worcestershire sauce
1 tsp. prepared mustard
dash hot red-pepper sauce

Mix beef, bread crumbs, egg and salt; shape into 50 small meatballs (½"). Place in shallow baking pan (13" x 9" x 2") and broil until browned; turn once. Spoon off fat. Meanwhile, in saucepan, cook onion and green pepper in butter until tender. Stir in remaining ingredients. Pour over meatballs. Cover; bake at 350°F for 20 minutes.
Makes 50 meatballs

IDEAL CRISPBREAD CHEESE ROLLS

2 cups soft cream cheese
10 crushed **Ideal Crispbread**

Roll cream cheese into small balls and cover with crushed Ideal Crispbread. Stick a toothpick into each one.
Makes approximately 24

YOGURT CREAM PUFFS WITH CHICKEN

1 cup water
½ cup butter
½ tsp. salt
1¼ cups flour
4 eggs
⅓ cup **Delisle Plain Yogurt**
¼ cup sesame seeds
2 cups chopped cooked chicken
3 tsp. dill
3 tbsp. mayonnaise
2 tbsp. **Delisle Plain Yogurt**
1 tbsp. mustard
salt and pepper

Heat water, butter and salt in a small saucepan. When water is boiling and butter melted, add flour all at once. Cook 2 minutes stirring vigorously. Remove from heat and let stand 2 minutes. Add eggs, one at a time, beating after each addition. Add ⅓ cup yogurt and sesame seeds. Drop by spoonfuls onto a lightly greased cookie sheet. Bake at 425°F about 12 minutes. Lower temperature to 350°F and continue baking 5-10 minutes. Remove from oven and place on cooling racks. Combine chicken, dill, mayonnaise, Delisle Yogurt, mustard, salt and pepper. Cut a slice off each puff and remove any moist dough. Fill each puff with chicken mixture. Replace tops and serve.

Makes 40 small puffs

CRABMEAT CANAPÉS

15 slices bread
8 oz. crabmeat, flaked
1 small onion, finely chopped
1 cup grated **Delisle Cheddar Cheese**
½ cup **Delisle Yogurt**
½ cup mayonnaise
1 tsp. curry powder
½ tsp. salt

Remove crusts from bread slices. Stir together the crabmeat, onion, cheese, yogurt, mayonnaise, curry powder and salt. Cut bread slices in 4 and spread some of the crabmeat mixture on each canapé. Broil until golden.

Makes 60 canapés

ANCHOVY AND YOGURT CANAPÉS

3 oz. anchovy fillets
3 oz. cream cheese
1 green onion, minced
½ cup **Delisle Plain Yogurt**
pinch curry powder
1 tsp. chopped parsley
⅛ tsp. paprika

Mash anchovies. Cream the cheese, add green onion, yogurt, curry powder and anchovies. Spread mixture on crackers or toast. Sprinkle with parsley and paprika.

Makes 18-24 canapés

IDEAL HORS D'OEUVRES

Caviar and Cream: Top **Ideal Crispbread** with caviar, chopped onion and crème fraîche.

Shrimp and Avocado: Fry shrimp or prawns in oil and curry. Place sliced avocado on **Ideal Crispbread** and top with shrimp or prawns.

Yogurt Cream Puffs With Chicken

Mornay Cheese Dip

MORNAY CHEESE DIP

2 tbsp. margarine
1 cup milk
¼ tsp. salt
pinch nutmeg
¼ cup **Veloutine Light**
¼ cup grated Swiss cheese
1 tbsp. grated Parmesan cheese
assorted fresh vegetables, apple wedges or ham cubes

In small saucepan combine margarine, milk, salt and nutmeg. Bring to boil; sprinkle in Veloutine, stirring constantly. Boil 1 minute. Stir in cheeses until melted. Keep warm over candle warmer or on a hot tray and serve with raw vegetables, ham or apple for dipping. Sauce variation: Use only 3 tbsp. Veloutine and serve over cooked vegetables, crêpes or poached eggs.

DOUBLE-DANISH CHEESE AND NUT DIP

1 lb. **Danish Natural Cream Cheese with Herbs and Spices**
6 tbsp. water
½ cup sour cream
½ cup crumbled **Danish Blue Cheese**
½ cup chopped nuts or seeds (pistachios, almonds, cashews, pumpkin, sunflower or combination)
apples and pears, sliced

Cube cream cheese. Transfer to food processor or mixing bowl. Gradually add water and mix until smooth and creamy. If using processor, transfer to mixing bowl. Fold in sour cream, blue cheese and nuts or seeds. Spoon onto serving platter or into wide, shallow bowl. If dip is made ahead of time, keep in mixing bowl and refrigerate until ready to serve. Slice fruits and tuck into dip just before serving. To prevent fruit from browning, dip slices into salt water or ascorbic acid solution immediately after cutting. Let stand a few minutes, then remove and drain well on paper towels.
Makes about 2½ cups

DANISH COUNTRY LIVER AND CHEESE PÂTÉ

1½ lb. liver (pork, beef or calves')
4 eggs, lightly beaten
2 tbsp. flour
1 lb. coarsely ground pork shoulder
¾ lb. **Danish Fontina** or other mild **Danish Cheese**, diced (about 2 cups)
½ lb. mushrooms, chopped and sautéed
¼ cup finely chopped yellow onion
1 garlic clove, mashed
2 tsp. salt
1 tsp. pepper
½ tsp. dried leaf thyme
½ cup brandy (optional)

With sharp knife cut away veins in liver. Chop coarsely with knife or in food processor. Set aside. In mixing bowl whisk eggs and flour. Blend in liver and remaining ingredients. Turn into 2 5-cup buttered molds. Cover with foil. Place in baking pan. Pour boiling water into pan to come halfway up on molds. Bake in preheated 350°F oven for 1¼ hours. Remove foil. Bake 30-40 minutes more, or until center is firm and done (internal temperature should be 160°F). Cool molds on rack. Garnish with sprig of fresh herb. Serve lukewarm or cool with fresh crusty bread.
Makes 2 2-lb. pâtés

MUSSELS VOL-AU-VENTS

1 package frozen Vol-au-Vents cases
1½ oz. butter
1½ oz. flour
1¾ pints milk
seasoning
1 jar or tin **Marina Mussels in Brine**
lemon, sliced

Prepare Vol-au-Vents as directed on package. Make a white roux sauce (melt butter, add flour and cook for 2 minutes; gradually stir in the milk to form a thick, white sauce; season to taste). Drain mussels and add to sauce. When Vol-au-Vents are cooked, cut out the tops and scoop out any uncooked pastry. Fill with mussel sauce and serve hot. Garnish with slices of lemon.
Makes 20 small or 10 large

Vegetable Dip

VEGETABLE DIP

1 pouch **Lipton 7 Vegetable Recipe, Soup and Dip Mix**

2 cups sour cream

Combine above ingredients. Chill for at least 2 hours to allow flavors to blend.

Vegetable Yogurt Dip: Replace 1 cup sour cream with plain yogurt.

Vegetable Cheese Dip: Add either ¼ cup grated Parmesan cheese or 1 cup grated Cheddar cheese.

Ginger and Nut Dip: Add ¼ cup chopped almonds and ½ tsp. ground ginger or 1 tsp. finely chopped fresh ginger.

Calico Seafood Dip: Add 1 cup finely chopped cooked shrimp or crabmeat. Also excellent served on avocado halves as an appetizer.
Makes 2 cups

DANISH FETA MORSELS

Crumble **Danish Feta** and blend with softened **Danish Cream Cheese with Herbs and Spices**. Spread a layer on crackers, toast or baguette slices. Decorate with a strip of red or green pepper and a slice of black olive. Surround hors d'oeuvres tray with raw vegetables, halved mushrooms, slices of jicama, green pepper rings and assorted crackers. Garnish with a bouquet of watercress.

DANISH CAMEMBERT DELIGHT COCKTAIL SNACK

¼ lb. **Danish Camembert** in tins

flour

egg whites, lightly beaten

fine bread crumbs

cooking oil

butter

The cheese must be cold. Cut the cold Camembert into small wedges. Coat with flour, lightly beaten egg whites and fine bread crumbs. Coat again with egg whites and bread crumbs, then refrigerate. Remove from refrigerator when required and sauté in hot oil and butter until golden on all sides. Do not overcook. Drain on paper towels. Serve hot as a cocktail snack or as a light dessert with toast and black currant jam.

One variation uses whole **Danish Camembert**. Coat the whole Camembert as directed above. Place in freezer for 30 minutes. Arrange on greased foil in baking pan. Drizzle with melted butter. Bake in preheated 400°F oven for 10 minutes. Remove to serving plate. Let stand 10 minutes. Cut into small wedges and serve as described above.

DANISH FETA SPREAD

1 cup (4 oz.) crumbled **Danish Feta Cheese**

3 oz. **Danish Cream Cheese with Herbs and Spices**, softened

1 garlic clove, crushed

2 tbsp. olive oil

¼ cup coarsely chopped walnuts

8 Italian olives, pitted and chopped

In mixing bowl, combine feta and cream cheese. Beat to blend. Stir in remaining ingredients. Spoon into an attractive glass dish. Serve with crackers, raw vegetables or chips.

DANISH HERBED FETA HORS D'OEUVRES

Roll **Danish Feta** chunks in minced fresh herbs. Parsley, oregano, dill and basil are favorites.

DANISH BLUE CHEESE CRUNCHY PECAN DIP

½ cup mayonnnaise

1 cup sour cream

1 tbsp. dry sherry

½ cup **Danish Blue Cheese**, crumbled, loosely packed

½ cup finely chopped pecans

Blend together mayonnaise, sour cream and sherry. Gently fold in blue cheese and pecans. Chill for about 1 hour.
Makes 2 cups

Danish Blue Cheese Crunchy Pecan Dip (left), Danish Blue Cheese Mermaid Dip (center) and Danish Blue Cheese Watercress Dip

DANISH BLUE CHEESE MERMAID DIP

½ cup mayonnaise

1 cup sour cream

¼ tsp. dillweed

½ tsp. dried tarragon, crumbled

dash cayenne

1 cup chilled cooked salmon, cut into small pieces

⅓ cup finely diced **Danish Samsoe** or **Havarti Cheese**

Blend together mayonnaise, sour cream, herbs and cayenne. Fold in salmon and cheese. Chill for about 1 hour.
Makes 2 cups

DANISH BLUE CHEESE WATERCRESS DIP

½ cup mayonnaise

1 cup sour cream

1 garlic clove, pressed

½ tsp. salt

1 tbsp. fresh lemon juice

⅓ cup finely chopped watercress

½ cup **Danish Blue Cheese**, crumbled, loosely packed

Blend together mayonnaise, sour cream, garlic, salt and lemon juice. Gently fold in watercress and blue cheese. Chill for about 1 hour.
Makes 2 cups

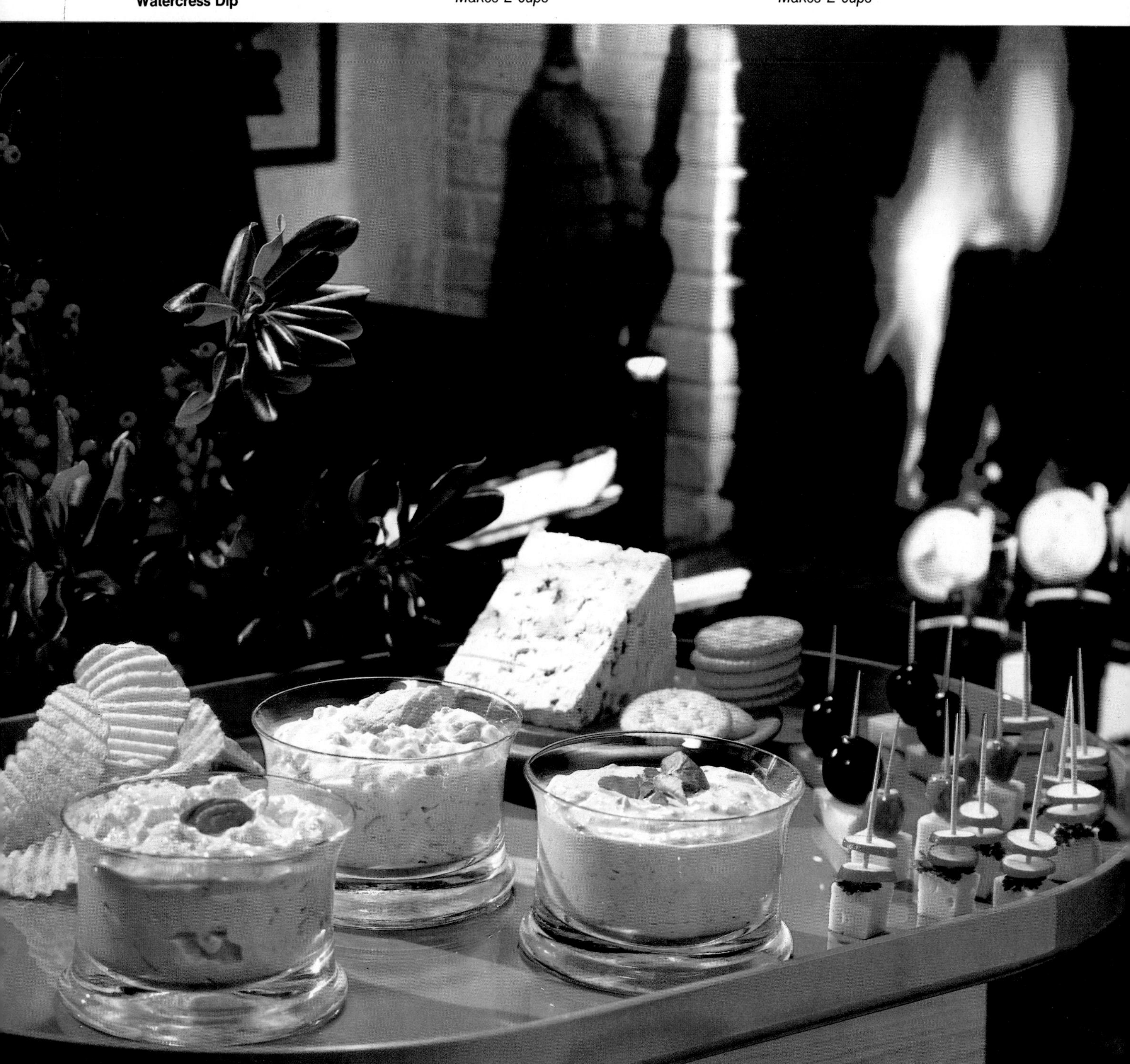

"DARE TO BE DIFFERENT" DIP

½ cup **Skippy Super Chunk Peanut Butter**

4 oz. cream cheese

½ cup grated carrot (1 medium carrot)

⅓ cup orange juice

Beat all ingredients together until smooth and well blended. Serve with assorted vegetables or crackers.
Makes 1½ cups

STUFFED CHICKEN-BREAST ROLL-UPS

2 2-lb. whole chicken breasts, skinned, boned and halved

1 garlic clove, pressed

1 tbsp. fresh thyme or rosemary, minced

½ cup chopped green onion with some of the green stem

salt and freshly ground pepper

1 large bunch watercress, stemmed, or 4 leaves Swiss chard

8 3" x ½" sticks **Danish Fontina or Havarti Cheese**

parsley sprigs as garnish

Pound each chicken breast half between sheets of waxed paper or plastic wrap into a rectangle about 7" x 5" and ¼" thick. Place each breast on 12" square of foil, pushing meat together, if necessary, to reshape. Rub with garlic and sprinkle with herb. Top with onion. Season with salt and pepper. Blanch watercress or Swiss chard in boiling water until limp. Drain well, then pat dry with paper towels. Divide leaves among breasts, arranging in an even layer over chicken. Top each with 2 pieces of cheese placed end-to-end in center of chicken. Bring one edge of chicken over cheese, then using foil as an aid, roll evenly pinwheel-style to form a log. Bring lengthwise edges of foil together, then fold over to encase roll tightly. Turn up ends of foil to seal. Arrange slightly apart on baking sheet. Bake in preheated 450°F oven for 12 minutes. Let packets cool on rack. Refrigerate at least 2 hours or overnight. To serve, unwrap chicken and cut into slices ½" thick. Arrange cut-side-up on tray and garnish with parsley.

For a savory variation, add a thin layer of sautéed chopped mushrooms before adding cheese.
Makes 4 rolls, about 10 slices per roll

"Dare to be Different" Dip

BAKED-IN-THE-CAN DANISH CAMEMBERT HORS D'OEUVRES TRAY

4 4½-oz. cans **Danish Camembert**, at room temperature

melted butter

Open cans; discard lids and remove cheeses. Unwrap and set aside. Using a pastry brush, waxed paper or fingers, completely coat inside of cans with melted butter, avoiding sharp edges. Flavor as desired using any of the four variations that follow. Preheat oven to 350°F. Place cans on baking sheet and bake 10 minutes. Remove from oven. Invert cans onto serving tray. Let stand 10 minutes before serving. Garnish with fruit and serve with crackers.

Almond-Coated Camembert: Sprinkle sliced almonds inside cans. Return cheese to cans. Top with additional almonds. Drizzle with melted butter.

Herbed Camembert: Sprinkle minced fresh herbs in cans. Return cheese to cans. Coat top of cheese with melted butter and sprinkle generously with additional herbs.

Mustard-and-Herb Coated Camembert: Sprinkle mixed herbs in cans. Return cheese to cans. Brush Dijon mustard generously over top of cheese. Top with additional chopped herbs.

Camembert with Danish Blue Topping: Dip cheese in beaten egg, then into crumbs. Return to cans. Bake as directed. Top with crumbled blue cheese immediately after removing from cans.

DANISH CAMEMBERT AND CREAM CHEESE APPETIZER

1 4½-oz. can **Danish Camembert** or **Brie Cheese**

4 oz. **Danish Natural Flavored Cream Cheese, Peach, Pineapple** or **Herb and Spice**, at room temperature

sliced almonds, chopped green onions, peach, pineapple or radish slices for garnish

Slice Danish Camembert or Brie in half to make two layers. Mound half of softened cream cheese on bottom layer of Camembert or Brie. Cover with top half of Camembert or Brie and remaining cream cheese. Firmly press almond slices on top and sides of fruit flavored cheeses or green onions on herb flavored. Garnish peach flavor with sliced peaches, pineapple flavor with slices of pineapple and herb flavor with radish slices.

CRABMEAT APPETIZERS

2 tbsp. butter
2 tbsp. minced green onions,
2 tbsp. minced green peppers
2 tbsp. minced celery
1 recipe, White Sauce
1 tsp. prepared mustard
½ tsp. dry mustard
1 tsp. Worcestershire Sauce
½ tsp. paprika
salt and pepper to taste
¼ cup lemon juice
8 oz. crabmeat, shredded
½ stick butter, melted for fillo
½ lb. **Krinos Fillo Leaves**

White Sauce:

¾ cup milk
2 tbsp. flour
2 tbsp. butter
½ tsp. salt
⅛ tsp. pepper

Prepare White Sauce. Brown flour, salt and pepper in butter in a small skillet. At the same time, heat the milk in a saucepan. Add the butter and flour mixture to the milk (it is best to stir a little of the milk into the butter and flour first to avoid lumps). Bring to a boil, stirring constantly. Boil for 1 minute. Remove from heat and set aside. Combine crabmeat and lemon juice in a bowl and set aside. In a large skillet, sauté first four ingredients for 5 minutes. Turn off heat, then add White Sauce and mix well. Blend in all seasonings and lastly add crabmeat and lemon juice. Prepare fillo leaves according to directions on package and fold to shape desired. Make variations such as triangles, rolls, small squares (5 leaves on bottom, 2 on top), or make them pizza style using a shallow pizza pan. Bake in preheated 400°F oven for 15 minutes.

ROLLED DANISH FRANK APPETIZERS

2 jars Danish franks
1 lb. **Krinos Fillo Leaves**
½ lb. butter, melted

Prepare fillo according to package directions. Place one Danish frank on a fillo strip. Roll, butter and bake in a preheated 375°F oven for 20 minutes or until golden brown.

GREEK MEAT PIE

2 medium onions, chopped
2 tbsp. butter, melted
1-1½ lb. ground beef, lamb or pork
¼ tsp. garlic powder or
1 garlic clove, minced
1 tsp. chopped parsley
pinch oregano
salt and pepper to taste
½ cup crumbled feta cheese
¼ cup bread crumbs
4 eggs, beaten
1 lb. **Krinos Fillo Leaves**
½ lb. butter, melted for fillo

Sauté onions in 2 tbsp. butter or margarine. Add meat and brown. Add garlic, parsley, oregano, salt and pepper and simmer for 15 minutes. Remove from heat and cool. Combine cheese, bread crumbs and eggs. Add to cooled meat mixture and mix well. Prepare fillo according to package directions and shape into rolls, triangles or squares. Bake in preheated 375°F oven for 20 minutes.

CHICKEN LIVERS AND MUSHROOMS

4 tbsp. butter
½ lb. mushrooms, sliced
1 medium onion, sliced and then finely chopped
1 lb. chicken livers, in bite-sized pieces
salt and pepper to taste
½ cup red wine
½ cup beef stock or bouillon
2 tbsp. chopped fresh parsley
2 tbsp. cornstarch
½ lb. **Krinos Fillo Leaves**
½ stick butter, melted for fillo

In a large skillet, sauté mushrooms and onion in butter until limp. Add the chicken livers and continue to sauté. Once browned, add salt and pepper, wine, stock and parsley. Simmer 5 minutes. Put the cornstarch in a cup and slowly pour off some of the juices into it, meanwhile stirring to make a smooth paste. Add this paste to the chicken liver mixture stirring constantly, thus making a smooth gravy. Prepare fillo leaves according to package directions and make either crêpes, triangles or rolls. Once made, bake at 375°F for 20 minutes.

GREEK VEGETABLE PIE

1 lb. **Krinos Fillo Leaves**
½ lb. butter, melted for fillo
1 medium onion, chopped
¼ cup olive oil
1 bunch scallions, chopped (less if desired)
2 cups chopped celery
1 tsp. garlic powder or 1 garlic clove, minced
2 tbsp. chopped parsley
1½ cups cooked rice
1 lb. mushrooms, cooked and chopped
2 eggs, beaten
salt and pepper to taste

Sauté onion in olive oil. Add scallions, celery, garlic, parsley and cook until tender. Remove from heat and cool. To cooled mixture add rice, mushrooms and eggs. Mix well. Prepare as desired in fillo rolls, triangles or squares, preparing fillo according to package directions. Bake in preheated 375°F oven for 20 minutes.

GREEK CHICKEN PIE

1 medium onion, chopped
½ stick butter, melted
1 cup chopped celery
4 cups cooked and chopped chicken or turkey
4 eggs, beaten
½ cup bread crumbs or cooked rice
1 tsp. salt
pepper to taste
1 lb. **Krinos Fillo Leaves**
½ lb. butter, melted for fillo

Sauté onion in butter, add celery and cook until tender. Remove from heat. Add chicken, eggs, bread crumbs, salt and pepper. Mix well and prepare as desired in rolls, triangles or squares, preparing fillo according to package directions. Bake in preheated 350°F oven for 35 minutes or until golden brown.

Party Potato Slices

PARTY POTATO SLICES

6 **KRAFT DE LUXE Process Cheddar Cheese Slices**, quartered

2 large potatoes

garnishes: sliced black olives and cherry tomatoes, chopped chives and crumbled cooked bacon

Cut 2 large baking potatoes into ½" slices. Place on well-greased cookie sheet. Bake at 450°F for 25-30 minutes until lightly browned on both sides, turning halfway. Top with quartered cheese slices. Continue baking until cheese melts. Garnish with sliced black olives, cherry tomato slices, chopped chives and crumbled cooked bacon.

Makes 24 appetizers

LIVER AND BACON APPETIZERS

½ lb. **Krinos Fillo Leaves**

1 stick butter, melted for fillo

½ lb. bacon

½ lb. chicken livers, cut in bite-sized pieces

½ cup finely chopped onion

¼ cup chopped fresh parsley

salt and pepper to taste

Cook bacon in large skillet. Remove from heat. Save drippings in the pan. Chop the cooked bacon into fine pieces and set aside. Brown chicken livers in bacon drippings. Add onion, parsley, salt and pepper and sauté until onion is tender. Blend in bacon pieces. Remove from heat and drain all excess fat and liquid. Prepare fillo according to directions on package and fold into triangles. Bake in preheated 375°F oven for 20 minutes or until golden brown.

KRINOS EGG SALAD

½ lb. **Krinos Fillo Leaves**

½ stick butter, melted for fillo

4 eggs, hard cooked and chopped

¼ cup chives

1 tsp. garlic salt

½ tsp. pepper

1 tsp. dry mustard

½ tsp. thyme

½ cup cream of celery soup

Mix all ingredients except fillo leaves and butter. Spoon onto prebuttered Krinos Fillo Leaves. Fold up into triangles, squares or rolls. Bake at 350°F for 20 minutes.

DIP AND DUNK CHICKEN

1 lb. boneless chicken, cut in 1" pieces
1 egg
½ cup water
½ cup flour
2 tbsp. sesame seeds
½ tsp. salt
¼ tsp. pepper
1 cup **Mazola Corn Oil**

Dill Sauce:

½ cup **Hellmann's or Best Foods Real Mayonnaise**
¼ cup sour cream
1 tsp. dried parsley flakes
1 tsp. dried dillweed
½ tsp. dry mustard

Tomato Sauce:

½ cup ketchup
¼ cup sweet relish
1 tsp. horseradish
½ tsp. Worcestershire sauce
½ tsp. dried oregano leaves
½ tsp. dried basil leaves

Beat together egg, water, flour, sesame seeds, salt and pepper. Pour oil into large skillet and heat to medium-high. Dip chicken pieces in batter and fry, one half at a time, 3-4 minutes per side depending on thickness. Drain and serve with dunking sauces. To prepare the sauces, just mix together the ingredients for each sauce.

CANTERBURY CHEESE BALL

8 oz. cream cheese, at room temperature
¼ cup (about 2 oz.) blue cheese
2 tbsp. butter, at room temperature
5 tsp. **Lea & Perrins Worcestershire Sauce**
1 large garlic clove, minced
¼ cup chopped parsley
¼ cup chopped walnuts or pecans

Combine cheeses, butter, Lea & Perrins and garlic; beat until smooth. Spoon mixture onto a piece of plastic wrap. Shape into a ball, using plastic wrap to assist. Chill, wrapped, until firm. Then unwrap ball, smooth surface and roll in chopped parsley or chopped nuts, or a combination of both. Serve surrounded by crackers.

Party Dip: Beat 2 tbsp. milk into cheese mixture. Serve at room temperature, surrounded by assorted crisp vegetables.

Stuffed Tomatoes: Spoon or pipe cheese mixture into 30-35 cherry tomatoes, hollowed and drained. Chill.

Ham Pinwheels: Spread cheese mixture evenly over six 4" x 6" ham slices. Roll each, beginning along the 4" side. Chill. At serving time, cut each roll into 5 or 6 slices.

Stuffed Snow Peas: Spoon or pipe cheese mixture into about 60 snow peas that have been blanched, chilled and slit open along the straight side. Chill.

Mini Cheese Balls: Form chilled mixture into about 40 small balls, about ¾" in diameter. Roll in chopped parsley or nuts. Chill.

FRENCH'S HOT AND TANGY CHICKEN WINGS

2 lb. chicken wings or pieces
¾ cup ketchup
2 tbsp. **French's Worcestershire Sauce**
½ cup **French's Horseradish Mustard**
¼ cup honey
2 tbsp. bread crumbs
1 tbsp. chopped green onion
2 tbsp. **French's Parsley Flakes**
pinch **French's Cayenne Pepper**

In a medium-sized bowl combine all ingredients except chicken wings. Place chicken wings in a baking dish and spread sauce over wings. Bake in a preheated 400°F oven for 40 minutes, turning once.

Serve as appetizer or main course for 4-6

KRINOS HAM SALAD

½ lb. **Krinos Fillo Leaves**
½ stick butter, melted for fillo
2 cups chopped, cooked ham
¼ cup relish
½ cup cream of mushroom soup (or celery soup)
salt and pepper to taste

Mix all ingredients except fillo leaves and butter. Spoon onto prebuttered Krinos Fillo Leaves. Fold up into triangles, squares or rolls. Bake at 350°F for 20 minutes.

Dip and Dunk Chicken

POTTED CHEESE SPREAD

2 cups (8 oz.) grated old Cheddar
4 oz. cream cheese, softened
¼ cup **Heinz Chili Sauce**
2 tbsp. dry sherry
½ tsp. dry mustard

Blend all ingredients until smooth. Pack into a crock or serving dish. Chill several hours. (May be stored in refrigerator up to a week.) Serve with crackers or apple slices.
Makes 1¾ cups

CHEESE FILLED FILLO

½ lb. **Krinos Fillo Leaves**
½ stick butter, melted for fillo
1 cup cheese, melted (Cheddar or Velveeta)
½ cup chopped black olives
2 tbsp. pimento, cut in strips

Mix cheese, olives and pimento together. Spoon onto prebuttered Krinos Fillo Leaves. Fold up into triangles, squares or rolls. Bake at 350°F for 20 minutes.

CAVIAR PIE

6 hard-cooked eggs, chopped
3 tbsp. mayonnaise
1 large sweet onion, finely chopped
8 oz. cream cheese, softened
⅔ cup sour cream
1 3½-oz. jar **Château Thierry Whitefish Caviar** (about 7 tbsp.)
lemon wedges and parsley for garnish

Grease bottom and sides of an 8" square springform pan. In a mixing bowl, combine eggs and mayonnaise until well blended. Spread in bottom of pan to make an even layer. Sprinkle with onion. Combine cream cheese and sour cream. Beat until smooth. By spoonfuls, drop onto onion. With wet table knife, spread gently to smooth. Cover and chill at least 3 hours or overnight. At serving time, top with a layer of caviar, distributing it to the edges of the pan. Run a knife around sides of pan. Loosen and lift off sides. Arrange lemon wedges in open pinwheel. Fill center with parsley sprigs. Serve with small slices of pumpernickel bread.
Serves 10-12

Potted Cheese Spread

ARTICHOKE SPREAD

1 cup **MIRACLE WHIP Salad Dressing**
1 cup **KRAFT Grated Parmesan Cheese**
1 14-oz. can artichoke hearts, drained and chopped
1 baguette, sliced

Combine salad dressing, cheese and artichoke hearts. Spread 1 tbsp. on each slice of bread. Place on cookie sheet; broil 2-3 minutes until hot and bubbly.
Makes 3 dozen

FRENCH'S HOT CRAB DIP

1 7-oz. can crabmeat
4 oz. cream cheese
1 tbsp. **French's Horseradish Mustard**
1 tbsp. lemon juice
½ tbsp. **French's Worcestershire Sauce**
freshly ground **French's Whole White Pepper**
2 tbsp. freshly grated Parmesan cheese

In a small ovenproof dish, mix together the crabmeat, cream cheese, horseradish mustard, lemon juice, Worcestershire sauce and white pepper. Sprinkle with Parmesan cheese and bake in a preheated oven at 375°F for approximately 25 minutes or until hot and bubbly.

Potato Pakoras (top) and Vegetable Samosas

POTATO PAKORAS

- 4 oz. gram flour or plain flour
- 1 tsp. salt
- ½ cup water
- 4 medium potatoes, boiled and roughly mashed
- 1 small onion, finely chopped
- 4 tsp. **Sharwood's Medium Hot Curry Powder**
- 1 tsp. puréed fresh ginger (optional)
- 1 tbsp. chopped fresh coriander (optional)
- 2 green chiles, chopped (optional)
- oil for deep frying

Blend the flour and salt with sufficient water to make a smooth batter, beat well, then set aside. Mix potato, onion, curry powder, ginger, coriander and chiles. Divide filling into approximately 14 balls. Dip into the batter and fry in moderately hot oil a few at a time for 5-10 minutes until golden brown. For variety add 1 tbsp. curry powder to the batter and use to coat a selection of vegetables: peppers, cauliflower and eggplant. Deep fry as above.

VEGETABLE SAMOSAS

- ½ package **Sharwood's Chapati Paratha & Puri Mix**
- water

Filling:

- 2 oz. butter
- 2 tsp. **Sharwood's Mild** or **Hot Curry Paste**
- 1 lb. potatoes, cooked and diced
- 4 oz. frozen peas
- 1 tbsp. chopped fresh coriander (optional)
- ½ tsp. salt
- 1 tsp. plain flour mixed with a little water
- oil for shallow frying

Fry the curry paste, potatoes, peas, coriander and salt gently in butter for 10 minutes. Make up Chapati Mix according to the package instructions, cut each in half. To shape samosas, fold over ⅓, paste to top ⅓ with flour and water paste, fold over next ⅓ on top to form a cone; place a small quantity of filling into the cone; use paste to seal the top flap of the cone. Repeat until all are filled. Fry the samosas in hot oil until golden brown. Serve hot or cold, with **Sharwood's Green Label Mango Chutney**.

MARINATED MUSHROOMS IN WINE

- ½ cup **Mazola Corn Oil**
- ¼ cup red wine vinegar
- 2 shallots or 1 small onion, diced
- 1 garlic clove, minced
- ½ tsp. dried tarragon leaves
- ½ tsp. dried thyme leaves
- ½ tsp. salt
- ⅛ tsp. pepper
- 1 lb. mushrooms, halved if large
- ¼ cup red wine

Combine oil, vinegar, shallots, garlic, tarragon, thyme, salt and pepper in small saucepan. Bring to boil. Pour over mushrooms in shallow pan. Stir in red wine. Marinate 3-4 hours. Remove mushrooms with slotted spoon and serve on toothpicks. *Makes 5 cups*

RUSSIAN MOUSSE

- 1 English cucumber, peeled
- 1 tsp. salt
- 12 hard-boiled eggs
- 6 green onions
- ⅓ cup warm water
- 2 tbsp. lemon juice
- 1 package unflavored gelatin
- ¾ cup mayonnaise
- 1 cup sour cream
- 1 tsp. Dijon mustard
- 1 jar **Château Thierry Whitefish Caviar**

Cut part of the cucumber into small pieces and the other slice evenly for garnish. Sprinkle with salt and allow to rest for 30 minutes. Drain well. Mash eggs. Transfer to a large bowl and reserve ⅓ cup for garnish. Chop green onions. Reserve ⅓ for garnish. Combine the rest with the chopped eggs. Pour water and lemon juice into heavy saucepan. Sprinkle with gelatin. Allow it to soften for 5 minutes. Let it dissolve over low heat. Put ¾ cup of mayonnaise into a bowl and add ½ of the sour cream, 1 tsp. of mustard and gelatin. Blend, then combine with eggs and cucumber mixture. Pour into a springform pan or an alternative (greased quiche dish, for example). Refrigerate for about 2 hours. Unmold mousse into serving platter lined with lettuce leaves. Spread top with other half of sour cream and arrange caviar in the center. Ring with a border of chopped eggs, green onions and cucumber. Serve with pumpernickel bread.

Ham Appetizer Crescents

HAM APPETIZER CRESCENTS

1 6½-oz. can flaked ham

½ cup **Hellmann's or Best Foods Real Mayonnaise**

1 tbsp. finely chopped onion

1 tbsp. lemon juice

1 tsp. Dijon mustard

1 tsp. horseradish

1 tsp. dried parsley flakes

⅛ tsp. pepper

2 cups biscuit mix

½ cup cold water

Break up ham with fork. Mix ham, mayonnaise, onion, lemon juice, mustard, horseradish, parsley and pepper. Stir biscuit mix and water together, with a fork, to make a soft dough. Roll out to a 14" circle. Spread with ham mixture. Cut into 30 wedge-shaped sections. Roll up beginning at wide end. Shape into crescents. Bake on greased cookie sheet at 425°F 12-15 minutes, until lightly browned.
Makes 30 rolls

PARTY TIDBITS

½ cup finely chopped onion

⅓ cup finely chopped green pepper

2 tbsp. butter or margarine

1 10-oz. can **Campbell's Condensed Tomato Soup**

1 tbsp. vinegar

1 tbsp. Worcestershire sauce

1 tsp. prepared mustard

dash hot red-pepper sauce

1 lb. wieners, cut into 1" pieces

In 1½-quart glass casserole, combine onion, green pepper and butter. Cook in microwave oven for 4 minutes or until vegetables are tender, stir once. Add remaining ingredients. Cover with waxed paper; cook 8 minutes or until hot, stir twice. Let stand 5 minutes. Stir before serving.
Makes 50 appetizers

HOT ARTICHOKE SPREAD

1 cup **Hellmann's or Best Foods Real Mayonnaise**

½ cup Parmesan cheese

1 garlic clove, chopped

1 tsp. Worcestershire sauce

½ tsp. dried oregano leaves

⅛ tsp. pepper

1 6-oz. jar marinated artichoke hearts, chopped

2 tbsp. Parmesan cheese

Combine mayonnaise, ½ cup cheese, garlic, Worcestershire sauce, oregano and pepper. Blend in chopped artichokes. Pour into small casserole dish and top with remaining cheese. Bake at 350°F 15 minutes. Serve immediately with assorted crackers.
Makes 1½ cups

CHEESY CORN DIP

3 cups shredded sharp orange Cheddar cheese
½ cup sour cream
½ cup salad dressing or mayonnaise
¼ cup finely chopped green onion
¼ cup chopped pimento or red pepper
1 12-oz. can **Green Giant Niblets Whole Kernel Corn**, drained

Bring cheese to room temperature. In large bowl, mash cheese with a fork or blend in food processor. Blend in remaining ingredients except corn; stir in corn. Cover; chill several hours or overnight. Serve with raw vegetables or crackers.
Makes 3½ cups

TWO-MINUTE SMOKED OYSTER PÂTÉ

1 3-oz. tin smoked oysters
4 oz. cream cheese
1 tbsp. **Honeycup Mustard**
2 whole green onions, coarsely sliced

Rinse drained smoked oysters with cold water and pat dry. Place well dried oysters in a food processor fitted with the metal blade. Add remaining ingredients. Purée using an on-and-off motion until mixture is fairly smooth. Pack into a small attractive serving or pâté dish. Cover and refrigerate at least until cold or overnight. Serve sprinkled with chopped parsley surrounded with melba toast or thin slices of crusty bread rounds.
Makes ¾ cup

Hot Crab Dip

CHEESY CRESCENT NACHOS

1 8-roll can **Pillsbury Refrigerated Crescent Dinner Rolls**
¼ cup cornmeal
½ cup chopped green pepper
2 tbsp. finely chopped hot pickles (optional)
1 cup grated old Cheddar cheese
1 cup grated Mozzarella cheese
⅓ cup taco sauce
½ tsp. chili powder

Heat oven to 350°F. Separate dough into 4 rectangles. Sprinkle half of cornmeal in bottom of ungreased 13" x 9" pan. Place dough in pan; press over bottom and ½" up sides to form crust. Sprinkle with remaining cornmeal, green pepper and hot pickles (optional). Combine cheeses; sprinkle over green pepper. Drizzle with nacho or taco sauce and sprinkle with chili powder. Bake for 25-28 minutes or until crust is golden brown. Cool 5 minutes; cut into triangles or squares.
Makes 24 nachos

SPINACH AND PARMESAN DIP

1 small package frozen spinach
½ cup Parmesan cheese
1 small onion, finely chopped
2 tbsp. lemon juice
½ tsp. ground nutmeg
1 cup **Hellmann's or Best Foods Real Mayonnaise**

Thaw spinach, squeeze to remove as much water as possible and chop. In medium bowl combine spinach with cheese, onion, lemon juice and nutmeg. Stir in mayonnaise and blend thoroughly.
Makes 1¾ cups

HOT CRAB DIP

8 oz. cream cheese, softened
¼ cup **Heinz Chili Sauce**
1 tsp. **Heinz Worcestershire Sauce**
½ tsp. salt
1 6-oz. can crabmeat, drained
2 green onions, sliced
1 tbsp. sliced almonds

Blend cream cheese, chili sauce, Worcestershire sauce, salt until smooth. Add crabmeat, green onions. Spoon into small greased ovenproof crock. Sprinkle with almonds. Bake at 375°F 15-20 minutes until lightly browned. Serve hot with crackers.

SPINACH FILLO APPETIZERS (SPANAKOPITA)

1 lb. **Krinos Fillo Leaves**
1-2 sticks butter, melted
2 lb. fresh spinach
1 onion, finely chopped
4 tbsp. butter
5-6 eggs, beaten
1 cup feta cheese, finely crumbled
salt and pepper to taste
dash nutmeg

Wash spinach and discard stems. Dry as thoroughly as possible on absorbent paper and cut into small pieces. Sauté onion in butter until soft. Add spinach and sauté a few minutes longer. Cool. Add eggs, cheese, salt, pepper and nutmeg. Mix well. Prepare fillo according to package directions and fold into triangles or rolls. Bake in preheated 350°F oven for 20 minutes or until golden brown.

MARNI'S SEAFOOD SHELLS

1 10-oz. can cream of celery soup
¼ cup milk
1 egg, beaten
1 tsp. **McCormick Lemon & Pepper Seasoning**
1 tbsp. **McCormick Fines Herbes**
1 tsp. **McCormick Shellfish Seasoning**
2 tbsp. grated Parmesan cheese
½ lb. fresh cooked shrimp or 1 4-oz. can large shrimp
½ lb. fresh cooked crabmeat or 1 4.2-oz. can crabmeat
1 10-oz. can button mushrooms

Topping:
2 tbsp. butter or margarine, melted
1 tbsp. grated Parmesan cheese
¼ cup bread crumbs

Combine cream of celery soup, milk, egg, seasonings and cheese in a medium saucepan. Over medium heat, stir constantly until slightly thickened. Remove from heat; add shrimp, crab and mushrooms. Stir gently; transfer to six seashell serving dishes. Mix together ingredients for topping and sprinkle over seafood mixture. Bake in 350°F oven for 20 minutes.
Serves 6

CHILI CHEESE APPETIZER FONDUE

1 tbsp. butter or margarine
1 small onion, chopped
1 large tomato, chopped
2 tsp. **Club House Chili Powder**
¼ tsp. **Club House Crushed Red Pepper**
¼ tsp. salt
1½ cups shredded Cheddar cheese
1 tbsp. all-purpose flour
½ cup light cream
Assorted Dippers: Tortilla chips, corn chips, fresh vegetables (mushrooms, broccoli and cauliflower flowerets, green peppers, carrots, celery sticks)

In small saucepan, melt butter over medium heat. Sauté onion for 2 minutes. Add tomato, chili powder, crushed red pepper and salt. Cook over low heat, uncovered, 10 minutes, stirring occasionally. Gradually add cheese. Heat and stir until melted. Dissolve flour in cream. Add to cheese mixture. Cook and stir until slightly thickened. Serve warm in fondue pot over low heat. Arrange assorted dippers around pot.
Makes about 2 cups

HUMPTY DUMPTY CONFETTI DIP FOR CHIPS

3 eggs, beaten
3 tbsp. sugar
3 tbsp. vinegar
1 tsp. butter
½ lb. cream cheese
¼ tsp. salt
a few drops hot red-pepper sauce
1 small onion, chopped
1 sweet red pepper, chopped
1 green pepper, chopped

Combine eggs, sugar and vinegar. Cook over hot water, stirring until mixture thickens. Add butter. Add cream cheese. Beat until smooth. Add other ingredients. Keep refrigerated. Serve with **Humpty Dumpty Potato Chips**.
Serves 12

CHICKEN LIVER PÂTÉ

1 tbsp. **Mazola Corn Oil**
1 tbsp. butter
2 medium onions, chopped
1 garlic clove, chopped
1 lb. chicken livers
1 cup sliced mushrooms
½ cup **Hellmann's or Best Foods Real Mayonnaise**
3 tbsp. brandy
½ tsp. salt
½ tsp. ground nutmeg
½ tsp. ground allspice
¼ tsp. ground cloves
⅛ tsp. pepper
½ cup toasted almonds

In large skillet, sauté onions and garlic in butter and oil over medium heat, until softened. Add chicken livers and sauté until they are no longer pink, about 5 minutes. Add mushrooms and cook 5 minutes longer. Spoon all into blender or food processor. Add remaining ingredients except almonds. Blend until smooth. Spoon into serving dish and chill thoroughly. Garnish with toasted almonds.
Makes 3 cups

HOT AND FIERY CHICKEN WINGS

12 chicken wings
salt and pepper
ground celery seed
½ jar **Emelia Hot and Fiery Jalapeno Pepper Jelly**

Preheat oven to 375°F. Dry chicken wings. Sprinkle on all sides with salt, pepper and ground celery seed. Roast for 30 minutes. Brush on Jalapeno Pepper Jelly and continue roasting another 15-20 minutes until wings are nicely glazed with the jelly. Serve with cold vegetable sticks: celery, carrots, raw zucchini, etc., with a blue cheese dip. For hotter wings, add ½ tsp. cayenne to the jelly.

Breaded Fingers

BREADED FINGERS

1 pouch **Lipton Golden Onion Recipe and Soup Mix**

½ cup dry bread crumbs

1 lb. veal scallopini, pounded boneless chicken or lean pork

2 eggs, well beaten

¼ cup oil for frying

Combine Golden Onion Soup Mix with bread crumbs. Cut meat or poultry into thin strips. Dip strips into egg; coat well with bread crumbs. Heat oil in large frypan, cook strips about 5-10 minutes until golden brown and tender.

PARTY MEATBALLS WITH SHERRIED MUSHROOM SAUCE

1½ lb. ground beef

¾ cup **Quaker Oats**, uncooked

½ cup finely chopped onion or green pepper

½ cup tomato sauce or ketchup

1 egg, beaten

½ tsp. salt

¼ tsp. pepper

Sherried Mushroom Sauce:

1 10-oz. can cream of mushroom soup

2 tsp. sherry

Heat oven to 400°F. Combine all ingredients; mix well. Shape into 1" balls. Place on rack in shallow baking pan. Bake 18-20 minutes. Serve with your favorite spaghetti sauce or Sherried Mushroom Sauce. For Mushroom Sauce, heat soup, stirring occasionally. Add sherry just before serving. Serve warm with meatballs.

Makes about 3 dozen

FRIED CAMEMBERT

2 3½-oz. packages **President Camembert**

milk or water

bread crumbs

vegetable fat for frying

2 bunches parsley

cranberry sauce

We recommend the use of 2 saucers. In one pour a little water or milk, in the other the bread crumbs. Moisten Camembert in milk or water and turn in bread crumbs. Press mixture firmly into cheeses, then allow to steep several minutes. Repeat procedure until coating covers entire Camembert. Then fry the breaded cheeses in vegetable fat until golden brown (approximately 5 minutes in a deep fat fryer at 340°F; about 4 minutes each side in a frypan at medium heat). Garnish with deep-fried parsley bouquets and cranberries. Serve with bread and beer or wine.

Serves 2

STUFFED MUSHROOM APPETIZERS

1 lb. medium mushrooms
¼ cup chopped onion
¼ cup chopped green pepper
3 tbsp. butter
1½ cups dried and crumbled **Krinos Fillo Flakes**
½ tsp. salt
½ tsp. thyme
¼ tsp. pepper
1 tbsp. butter

Cut stems from mushrooms. Finely chop enough stems to measure ⅓ cup. Set mushroom caps aside. Cook and stir chopped mushroom stems, onion and green pepper in 3 tbsp. butter until tender, about 5 minutes. Remove from heat. Stir in Krinos Fillo crumbs, salt, thyme and pepper. Heat 1 tbsp. butter in a shallow baking dish until melted. Fill mushroom caps with stuffing mixture. Place mushrooms, filled-sides-up, in baking dish. Bake in preheated 350°F oven for 15 minutes. Set oven to broil. Make sure rack in oven is 3"-4" from heat. Broil for 2 minutes. Serve hot.

ANTIPASTO CATALINA

½ cup **CATALINA Dressing**
1 small onion, finely chopped
1 clove garlic, minced
½ medium head cauliflower, cut into small pieces
1 carrot, diced
1 stalk celery, chopped
½ red pepper, chopped
½ green pepper, chopped
¼ lb. fresh mushrooms, chopped
8 pitted, small black olives, sliced
1 6½-oz. can flaked tuna, drained (optional)
hot pepper sauce

In large skillet, mix dressing with all ingredients except olives, tuna and pepper sauce. Bring to boil; cover and reduce heat. Let simmer 15 minutes or until vegetables are tender. Stir once during cooking. Add sliced olives and tuna, if desired. Stir in pepper sauce to taste. Serve cold with crackers as an appetizer.
Makes about 3 cups

SWEET POTATO CHIPS

1 large sweet potato
Crisco Shortening for frying
salt (plain, onion, garlic or seasoned)

Pare potato with vegetable peeler, then pull vegetable peeler down length of potato making long, thin strips. Heat a 1½" layer of Crisco to 365°F in a deep heavy saucepan. Add about 1 cup of potato strips to hot Crisco. Fry for 1 minute or until light golden brown. Remove strips from Crisco with a slotted spoon and drain on paper towels. Sprinkle with desired salt before serving.

Serves 4

BUENOS NACHOS

⅓ cup chopped tomato, drained
¼ cup chopped green pepper
3 tbsp. minced onion
2 garlic cloves, minced
¾ tsp. **Tabasco** brand pepper sauce
18 round tortilla chips
¾ cup guacamole (recipe follows)
½ cup shredded sharp Cheddar cheese

Preheat broiler. In small bowl combine tomato, green pepper, onion, garlic and Tabasco pepper sauce. Arrange tortilla chips in single layer on baking sheet. Place small dollop of tomato mixture in center of guacamole. Sprinkle with cheese. Broil 3 minutes or just until cheese is melted. Serve immediately.
Makes 18 appetizers

GUACAMOLE

1 ripe medium avocado, seeded and peeled
1 tbsp. lemon or lime juice
½ tbsp. finely chopped onion
½ tsp. seasoned salt
¼ tsp. **Tabasco** brand pepper sauce
¼ tsp. garlic powder

In medium bowl, mash avocado. Add lemon juice, onion, salt, Tabasco pepper sauce and garlic powder; mix well. Chill thoroughly to blend flavors.
Makes ¾ cup

FINN CRISP HORS D'OEUVRES

Lettuce, Ham and Tomato: Butter **Finn Crisp** and top with sliced tomatoes, ham, lettuce and parsley.

Cheese and Apple: Butter **Finn Crisp** and top with a slice of cheese and pieces of apples.

Peanut Butter: Spread peanut butter on **Finn Crisp** and sprinkle with peanuts.

Fruit and Cheese: Place slices of Roquefort cheese, slices of canned peaches and green grapes on **Finn Crisp**.

DECADENT CHEESE TOAST

¾ cup **PARKAY Margarine**
1 cup grated **CRACKER BARREL Cheddar Cheese**
½ cup grated **KRAFT Mozzarella Cheese**
½ cup **KRAFT Grated Parmesan Cheese**
1 tsp. garlic salt
½ tsp. pepper
1 loaf French bread, cut into 1" slices

Cream margarine until light. Add cheeses and seasonings, blending until well mixed. Spread onto both sides of bread slices. In a non-stick frypan, sauté until brown, turn and brown other side. If bread sticks, lift pan from heat for a few seconds before turning.
Serves 4-6

SUE'S SPICY FOREST CITY CHICKEN WINGS

1 lb. chicken wings, each wing split in half
1 cup plain barbecue sauce
⅓ cup white vinegar
1 tsp. **McCormick Ground Turmeric**
1 tsp. **McCormick Ground Coriander**
½ tsp. **McCormick Ground Cumin**
1-2 tsp. **McCormick Crushed Red Pepper**
1-2 tsp. **Gilroy Crushed Garlic** or 1-2 fresh garlic cloves, crushed

Broil or barbecue wings until brown and crispy. Set aside to cool. Mix all remaining ingredients. Preheat oven to 325°F. Line baking sheet with foil and spray with a non-stick coating. Dip wings in barbecue sauce mixture, shaking off excess sauce. Place on baking sheet in a single layer. Bake 20-30 minutes until sauce adheres well to wings. Turn once while baking.
Serves 5

SOUPS

Cool and refreshing or steamy and comforting, today's soups are more flavorful than ever before.

There's just something special about a good soup, whether it be a clear bouillon, a delicate creamy purée or a thick and wholesome meal-in-a-bowl.

With the help of modern kitchen appliances as well as new brand-name ingredients, today's soups require much shorter preparation and cooking times. The results are simply outstanding and the varieties nearly endless. Read on for some favorite brand-name recipes and ideas that are easy to prepare, affordable, nutritious and absolutely mouth watering.

Best-Ever Vegetable Beef Soup (see page 23)

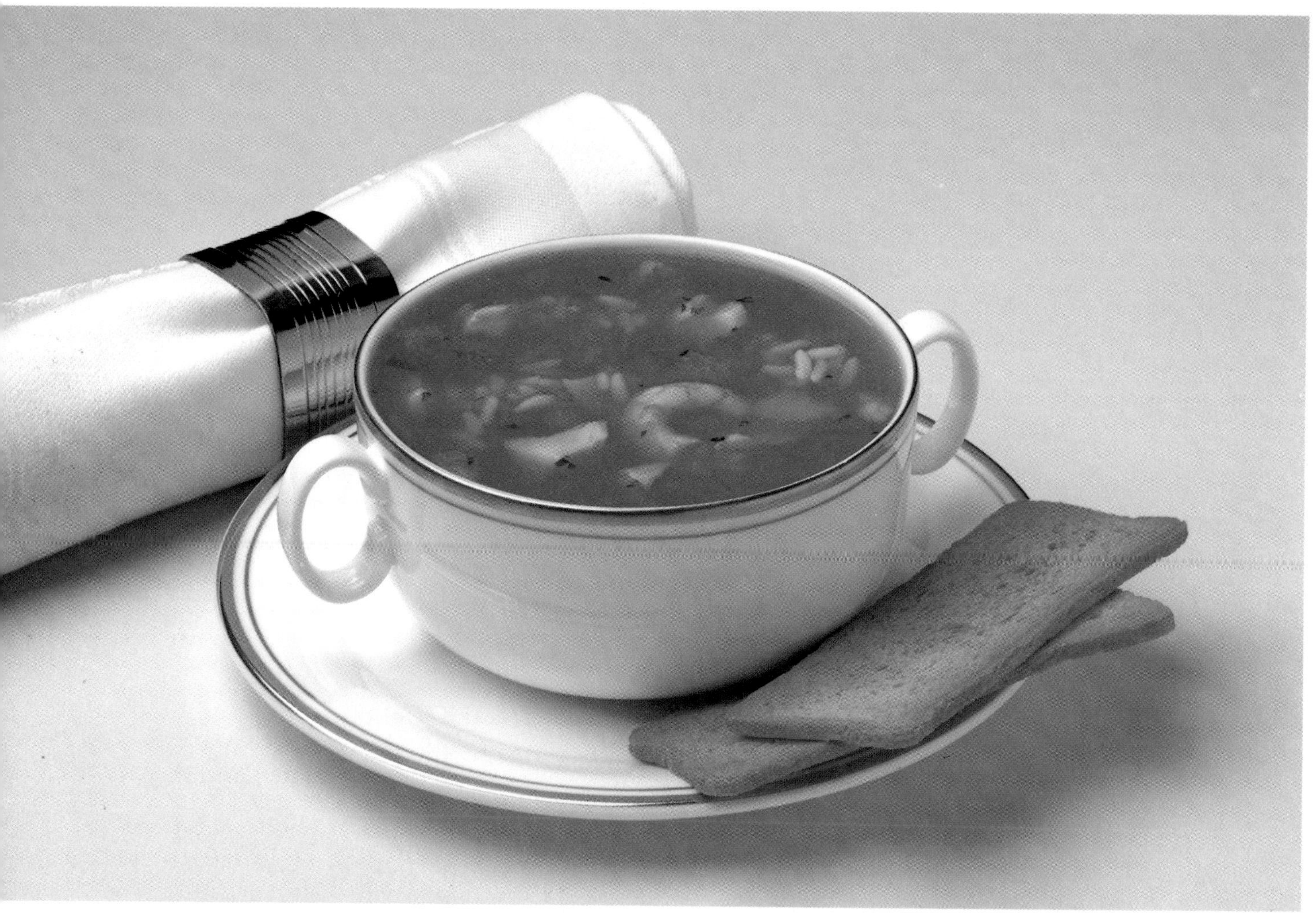

CREAMY CORN-CLAM CHOWDER

1 tbsp. butter
3 slices bacon, chopped
1 large onion, chopped
4 large potatoes, diced
2 5-oz. cans clams
1 bay leaf
1 14-oz. can **Green Giant Cream Style Corn**
1 12-oz. can **Green Giant Niblets Whole Kernel Corn**
1½ cups milk
½ cup table cream (18%)
1 tsp. salt
chopped parsley

In a large heavy saucepan, cook bacon in butter until softened. Add onion and sauté until tender. Stir in potatoes; brown lightly. Drain clam juice into a measure; add water to make 2 cups; stir liquid into potato mixture. Add bay leaf. Bring to a boil; reduce heat, cover and simmer 10 minutes or until potatoes are just tender. Stir in clams, cream style corn, whole kernel corn, milk and cream. Stir over medium heat until thoroughly heated. Season to taste with salt and parsley. Discard bay leaf. Serve hot, garnished with additional chopped parsley.
Serves 6-8

SWEETLETS EGG DROP SOUP

4 cups chicken broth
1½ cups **Green Giant Frozen Sweetlet Peas**
2 eggs, slightly beaten
¼ tsp. salt
⅛ tsp. pepper
2 green onions, finely chopped

Prepare chicken broth in a large saucepan and bring to a boil. Add peas and simmer for 1 minute. Combine eggs, salt and pepper. Pour the eggs slowly into the chicken broth. Stir constantly until the eggs form thin threads in the broth. Serve in soup bowls and sprinkle with chopped green onion.
Serves 4

Seafood Rice Chowder

SEAFOOD RICE CHOWDER

¾ cup **Uncle Ben's Converted Brand Rice**
1½ lb. seafood (haddock, shrimp, clam, crab, etc.), cut into bite-sized pieces
¾ cup diced celery
1½ cups chopped onion
4 cups vegetable or tomato juice
3 cups water
¼ cup chopped fresh parsley
2 tsp. salt
½ tsp. pepper
1 tsp. basil leaves
1 garlic clove, minced

Prepare seafood for use (clean, shell, devein, etc.). Cut into bite-sized pieces. Combine all ingredients, except rice, in a large stockpot. Bring to a boil over high heat. Reduce heat to medium-low and simmer slowly for 20 minutes. Stir occasionally. Add rice; cover and simmer 20 minutes longer. Serve piping hot with crackers.
Makes 14 ¾-cup portions

COLD DANISH CHEESE SOUP

2 10¾-oz. cans Vichyssoise (semi-condensed)

1 3½-oz. package **Danish Natural Cream Cheese with Herbs and Spices**

½ cup light cream

sour cream, chopped chives and crumbled **Danish Blue Cheese** as garnish

crescent rolls

Put soup, cream cheese and cream in blender. Blend until smooth. Pour into 4 oz. soup bowls. Chill. Just before serving, top with a dollop of sour cream. Sprinkle with chives and crumbled Danish Blue Cheese. Serve at once with crescent rolls.
Serves 4

DUTCH CHOWDER AND DUMPLINGS

1½ cups cooked pork, cut in strips

¼ cup chopped onion

2 tbsp. butter or margarine

2 10-oz. cans **Campbell's Condensed Green Pea Soup**

15 oz. water

1 10-oz. package frozen mixed vegetables, cooked and drained

¼ tsp. ground nutmeg

generous dash salt

½ cup biscuit mix

2 tsp. chopped parsley

3 tbsp. milk

In saucepan, brown pork and cook onion in butter until tender. Add soup; gradually blend in water. Add vegetables, nutmeg and salt; bring to boil. Meanwhile, combine biscuit mix, parsley and milk; drop by teaspoonful into simmering soup. Cook 5 minutes. Cover; cook 5 minutes more or until done.
Makes 6½ cups

DANABLU SOUP

1½ tbsp. butter

2½ tbsp. flour

4 cups boiling water

4 chicken bouillon cubes

1½ cups crumbled **Danish Blue Cheese**

2 cups half and half cream

Topping:

½ cup whipping cream, whipped

1 tbsp. finely chopped parsley

In large saucepan, melt butter and blend in flour. Remove from heat and stir in boiling water, a little at a time. Bring to a rolling boil. Add bouillon cubes and stir to dissolve. Add crumbled blue cheese, stirring as cheese is added to dissolve. Return to boiling and boil 10 minutes. Reduce heat to medium and add the half and half cream, stirring constantly. Heat just to boiling and serve piping hot, adding a spoonful of the topping to each individual serving.
Serves 6-8

5-MINUTE DANISH GOURMET SOUP

2 cups chicken or beef broth (ready to serve)

1 10-oz. package frozen leaf or chopped spinach (or 1 12-oz. bunch fresh spinach)

6 oz. **Danish Natural Cream Cheese with Herbs and Spices**, cubed

sour cream

parsley

In saucepan, bring broth to a boil. Cut frozen spinach into 4 pieces; then drop into broth. (If using fresh spinach, trim stems from leaves and discard.) Return to boil, stirring occasionally. Simmer 2 minutes. Carefully pour into blender or food processor fitted with steel blade. Add cream cheese and process until smooth. Pour into warm soup bowls and garnish with dollops of sour cream and chopped parsley. Or chill and reheat at serving time, over low heat or in a double boiler. This soup is also good served chilled.
Serves 4-6

Dutch Chowder and Dumplings

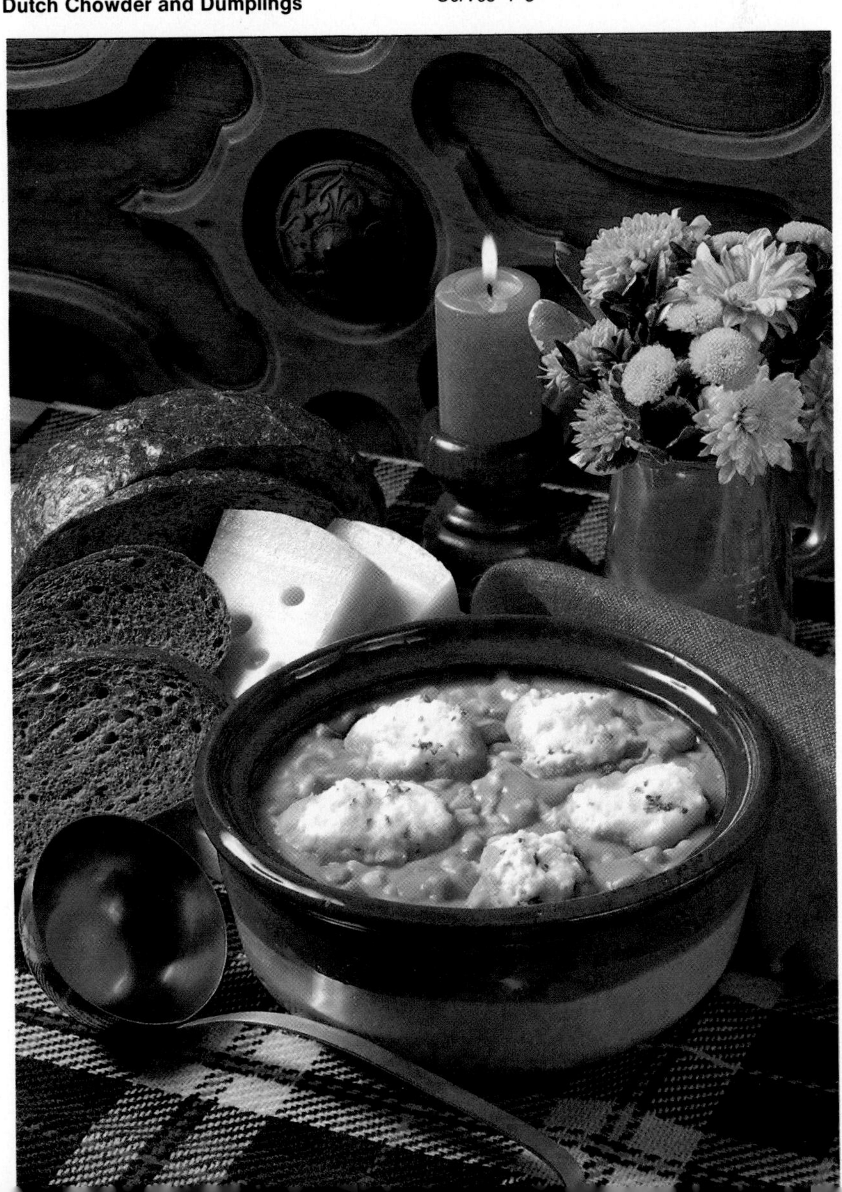

DANISH CHEESE AND VEGETABLE SOUP

3 cups water
2 10-oz. cans chicken broth
2 cups diced celery
2 cups thinly sliced carrots
2 cups broccoli flowerets
1 cup thinly sliced leeks or onions
2 tbsp. butter
2 tbsp. flour
2 cups shredded **Danish Creamy Havarti**, **Danish Fontina**, **Danbo**, **Tybo** or **Svenbo Cheese** (for fuller flavor, **Esrom** or **Havarti**)
½ cup whipping cream
dash ground red pepper
2 egg yolks
fresh parsley or chives, chopped

In a large saucepan, combine water and broth and bring to a boil over high heat. Add vegetables and cook over medium heat until just tender, about 10 minutes. Strain, set vegetables aside, return liquid to pan and bring to boil. Blend butter with flour to make a smooth paste; stir into liquid, mixing well. Reduce heat, add cheese, cream and red pepper and stir constantly until smooth and creamy. Blend a small amount of hot liquid into egg yolks, then gradually stir into soup. Add vegetables and heat through but do not boil. Put into tureen or ladle into bowls and sprinkle with parsley or chives.
Serves 4-6

CREAM OF ZUCCHINI SOUP

1 small onion, coarsely chopped
1 tbsp. butter
3 medium zucchini, coarsely chopped
1 medium potato, coarsely chopped
3 cups chicken stock
1 tsp. **McCormick Rosemary Leaves**
½ tsp. **McCormick Thyme Leaves**
½ tsp. **McCormick Basil Leaves**
1½ cups half and half cream
½ tsp. **McCormick Ground Black Pepper**

In large saucepan or Dutch oven, sauté the onion in butter until soft. Add the zucchini and potato; cook 5 minutes. Add stock and cook until vegetables are tender. Add rosemary, thyme and basil. Transfer to a food processor or a blender and process until smooth. Return to saucepan and add cream and ground black pepper. Season with salt to taste. Reheat gently and serve.
Serves 4

ITALIAN RICE AND BEAN SOUP

4 tsp. olive oil
2 stalks celery, diced
2 carrots, cleaned and diced
2 cloves garlic, minced
1 onion, chopped
¼ tsp. hot pepper flakes
1 cup chopped, drained, canned plum tomatoes
½ tsp. salt
¼ tsp. crumbled rosemary
¼ tsp. dried sage
1 19-oz. can Romano beans, drained and rinsed
¾ cup **Uncle Ben's Converted Brand Rice**
8 cups low-salt chicken broth
pepper
chopped parsley
freshly grated Parmesan cheese

In large saucepan, heat oil and cook celery, carrots, garlic, onion and hot pepper flakes over medium-low heat for 10 minutes, stirring often. Stir in tomatoes, salt, rosemary and sage; cook, uncovered, for 10 minutes. Add beans and rice; cook for 3 minutes, stirring often. Stir in broth; bring to boil, reduce heat, cover and cook 20 minutes. Add pepper to taste and salt if necessary. Serve immediately, sprinkled with parsley and Parmesan cheese. (Soup becomes very thick upon sitting. Thin any leftovers with additional broth or water.)
Serves 6-8

FRANKLY CORNY CHOWDER

1¼ cups water
2 carrots, thinly sliced
1 large potato, diced
½ green pepper, diced
1 10-oz. can cream style corn
1 cup **CHEEZ WHIZ Process Cheese Spread**
6 wieners, sliced
chopped parsley

Combine water, carrots, potato and green pepper in a large saucepan. Bring to a boil. Cover and simmer 10 minutes until vegetables are tender. Stir in corn, cheese spread and wieners; heat thoroughly, stirring occasionally. Sprinkle with parsley.
Serves 4-6

LEMONY TURKEY AND RICE SOUP

6 cups low-sodium chicken broth
2 carrots, sliced
1 onion, chopped
1 stalk celery, sliced
1 clove garlic, minced
½ cup **Uncle Ben's Wholegrain Brown Rice**
12 oz. raw turkey, cubed
1 tsp. grated lemon rind
1 bay leaf
¼ tsp. each salt and pepper
¼ cup chopped parsley
2 tbsp. fresh lemon juice
½ tsp. ground cumin

In large saucepan, combine broth, carrots, onion, celery and garlic. Bring to boil. Stir in rice, turkey, lemon rind, bay leaf, salt and pepper. Return to boil, reduce heat, cover and simmer about 25 minutes or until turkey and rice are tender. Remove bay leaf. Stir in parsley, lemon juice and cumin. Taste and adjust seasoning if necessary.
Serves 4-6

DHAL SOUP

4 oz. Masoor Dhal (lentils)
1" piece fresh ginger (optional)
2 cups water
3 tbsp. **Sharwood's Vegetable Ghee**
2 bay leaves or curry leaves
1 tsp. black mustard seeds
1 medium onion, finely chopped
1 tsp. **Sharwood's Garlic Purée**
2 tsp. **Sharwood's Hot Curry Powder**
1 tsp. turmeric

Place dhal, ginger and water in a pan, cook over a very low heat until the dhal is soft, approximately 20 minutes, discard ginger. Liquidize, beat or sieve dhal to a smooth consistency, leave to one side. Heat ghee, add leaves and mustard seeds, fry until the mustard seeds pop, add the onion and garlic, fry until onion is golden brown, add curry powder and turmeric, cook for a further 2 minutes. Add the dhal mixture to the fried ingredients. Water may be added to adjust the consistency, bring to boil and serve.

BEST-EVER VEGETABLE BEEF SOUP

1 lb. ground beef
2 cups chopped onion
1 cup chopped celery
1 cup thinly sliced carrots
6 cups water
3 tbsp. beef bouillon powder
1 28-oz. can tomatoes, undrained, cut up
1 7½-oz. can tomato sauce
½ cup pasta stars
2 bay leaves
2 tsp. basil
2 tsp. chili powder
1 tsp. salt
⅛ tsp. pepper
2 14-oz. cans **Green Giant Kitchen Sliced Cut Green Beans**, drained

In a large heavy saucepan, brown ground beef; drain off fat. Add onion, celery and carrots; stir and cook 5 minutes. Add remaining ingredients, except green beans, and bring to a boil. Reduce heat, cover and simmer 50 minutes. Stir in green beans; cook until heated through or until vegetables and pasta are tender. Discard bay leaves; serve hot.
Serves 6-8

BOUILLABAISSE

8 oz. fresh or frozen lobster tail
¼ lb. fresh or frozen fish fillets
4 clams in shells
1 10-oz. can **Campbell's Condensed Tomato Soup**
1 cup water
½ cup dry white wine
1 medium onion, cut up
2 sprigs parsley
1 garlic clove, minced
1 bay leaf
½ tsp. salt
½ tsp. dried thyme, crushed
¼ tsp. coriander, crushed
dash pepper
French bread

Partially thaw lobster and fish (if frozen). Split lobster tail in half lengthwise, then cut in half crosswise to make 4 portions. Cut fish fillets into 1" pieces. Thoroughly wash clams and cover with salted water (3 tbsp. salt to 2 quarts cold water). Let stand 15 minutes and rinse; repeat twice. In medium saucepan combine tomato soup, water, wine, onion, parsley, garlic, bay leaf, salt, thyme, coriander and pepper. Simmer, covered, for 30 minutes. Strain the tomato mixture and discard vegetables and herbs. Bring the strained mixture to boil; add lobster, fish and clams. Cook about 5 minutes or until fish flakes easily and clams open. Serve with French bread.
Serves 2

OLD FASHIONED VEGETABLE SOUP

1 10-oz. can **Campbell's Condensed Beef Broth**
1 10-oz. can **Campbell's Condensed Vegetable Soup**
20 oz. water
2 cups cabbage, cut in long thin shreds
1 cup cubed cooked beef
1 cup cut up tomatoes
½ cup uncooked small shell macaroni
1 medium onion, sliced
2 tbsp. grated Parmesan cheese
1 medium garlic clove, minced
½ tsp. caraway seed

In large saucepan, combine ingredients; bring to boil; reduce heat. Simmer 30 minutes or until done; stir occasionally.
Makes 8 cups

Old Fashioned Vegetable Soup

Watermelon and Yogurt Soup

WATERMELON AND YOGURT SOUP

1 watermelon
2 cups sweet white wine
2 tbsp. brown sugar
1 tsp. ground allspice
1 tbsp. grated lemon rind
1 cup **Delisle Yogurt**

Cut watermelon in half, remove seeds and peel. Put watermelon in a saucepan, add wine, brown sugar, allspice and lemon rind. Bring to a boil stirring constantly. Lower heat and simmer 20 minutes. Put in a food processor or blender and purée. Let cool completely, then add yogurt. Refrigerate at least 1 hour.
Serves 4

CAVIAR AND CONSOMMÉ RAMEKINS

10-oz. can consommé
8 oz. cream cheese
2 oz. **Marina Lumpfish Caviar**
parsley, garnish

Blend consommé and cream cheese. Pour into 6 ramekin dishes and set in fridge for 2 hours. Garnish with 1 tsp. Marina Caviar and parsley and serve with thinly sliced bread and butter.
Serves 6

CREAM À LA REINE

1 2⅜-oz. package **Le Gourmet Bresse Noodle Soupmix, Chicken Flavor**
3½ cups cold water
1 cup cream
2 egg yolks, well beaten
a few pieces cooked chicken meat, thinly sliced

Empty contents of Noodle Soupmix into the cold water. Bring to a boil. Simmer for 7 minutes. In another dish, mix cream and egg yolks. Pour into soup. Add chicken slices and serve.
Serves 6

CHICKEN SOUP NEW ORLEANS

1 cup diced cooked ham
½ cup chopped onion
dash thyme
generous dash poultry seasoning
1 tbsp. butter or margarine
3 10-oz. cans **Campbell's Condensed Chicken Gumbo Soup**
30 oz. water
1 cup cubed cooked chicken
1 10-oz. package frozen asparagus, cooked and drained

In large pan, lightly brown ham and cook onion with thyme and poultry seasoning in butter until tender. Add remaining ingredients. Heat; stir occasionally.
Serves 6

DUTCH POTAGE

1 cup shredded cabbage
¼ cup shredded carrot
¼ tsp. caraway seeds
1 tbsp. butter or margarine
1 10-oz. can **Campbell's Condensed Cream of Potato Soup**
1 cup milk
½ cup sour cream

In saucepan, cook cabbage, carrot and caraway in butter until vegetables are tender; add remaining ingredients. Heat; stir occasionally. Chill 4 hours or more; thin to desired consistency with milk. Serve in chilled bowls.
Serves 2-3

CRAB BISQUE

½ cup diagonally sliced celery
¼ tsp. crushed chervil
2 tbsp. butter or margarine
1 10-oz. can **Campbell's Condensed Cheddar Cheese Soup**
1 10-oz. can **Campbell's Condensed Cream of Chicken Soup**
15 oz. milk
¼ cup sherry
2 7-oz. packages crab, thawed and drained (about 1½ cups)
⅓ cup sliced water chestnuts

In saucepan, cook celery with chervil in butter until tender. Stir in remaining ingredients; heat, stir occasionally. Cubed, cooked lobster may be substituted for crab.
Serves 4

CREAMED AVOCADO SOUP

2 tbsp. sliced green onion
2 tbsp. butter or margarine
1 10-oz. can **Campbell's Condensed Chicken Broth**
1 avocado, peeled and cubed
1 tsp. lemon juice
½ cup light cream
½ cup milk
lemon slices

In saucepan, cook onion in butter until tender. Add broth, avocado and lemon juice. Pour into electric blender or food processor; blend until smooth. Return mixture to saucepan; stir in cream and milk. Heat; stir occasionally. Garnish with lemon slices.
Makes 3 cups

CHICKEN MULLIGATAWNY SOUP

1 2½ lb. whole chicken, cut up
1 medium onion, chopped
1 carrot, sliced
1 stalk celery, chopped
1 bouquet garni
pinch pared lemon rind
pinch salt
3 tbsp. salad oil
2 heaped tsp. **Sharwood's Madras Curry Powder**
1 tsp. ground ginger
pinch chili powder (optional)
1 tbsp. all-purpose flour
4 tsp. applesauce
bunch watercress for garnish

Place chicken pieces in a large saucepan with onion, carrot, celery, bouquet garni, lemon rind and salt. Cover with 4½ cups of water, bring to boil, cover and simmer over a low heat for 25 minutes or until chicken is tender. Strain and reserve stock and cut meat from the chicken bones. Heat oil and lightly cook curry powder, ginger, chili powder and flour for 2-3 minutes. Blend in gradually the reserved chicken stock. Bring to boil, stir in applesauce and chicken meat. To serve, garnish with a few watercress leaves.
Serves 4-6

GARDEN PATCH SOUP

2 28-oz. cans tomatoes, divided
1½ cups chopped English cucumber, divided
1 garlic clove
¾ cup chopped green pepper
1 tsp. salt
¾ cup **KRAFT Real Mayonnaise** or **KRAFT Light Mayonnaise**

Drain tomatoes, reserving 1 cup of juice. In blender, purée half of the tomatoes, half of the cucumber and the garlic clove. Break up remaining tomatoes in large bowl. Add remaining cucumber, green pepper, salt and puréed mixture. In small bowl, whisk reserved tomato juice into mayonnaise. Stir mayonnaise mixture into vegetable mixture. Heat gently over medium heat (do not boil). Soup may also be served chilled.
Serves 6

Upper Canada Pumpkin Soup

CAULIFLOWER SOUP GRUYÈRE

2 tbsp. chopped onion
2 tbsp. butter or margarine
1 10-oz. can **Campbell's Condensed Cream of Chicken Soup**
1 cup cooked cauliflower
dash dry mustard
dash white pepper
1 cup milk
¼ cup shredded process Gruyère cheese

In saucepan, cook onion in butter until tender. Add soup, cauliflower, mustard and pepper. Pour into electric blender or food processor; blend until smooth. Return mixture to saucepan; gradually stir in milk and cheese. Heat until cheese melts, stir often.
Serves 4

UPPER CANADA PUMPKIN SOUP

¼ cup finely chopped onion
2 tbsp. butter or margarine
1 10-oz. can **Campbell's Condensed Cream of Chicken** or **Mushroom Soup**
1 cup canned or mashed cooked pumpkin
10 oz. milk
generous dash ground nutmeg
dash pepper

In saucepan, cook onion in butter until tender. Add remaining ingredients. Heat; stir occasionally. Garnish with parsley.
Serves 2-3

BREADS AND MUFFINS

There's nothing quite like the rich aroma of fresh baked bread and muffins. Bread making was one of the first culinary arts practiced, and is still found by many to be a satisfying and pleasurable pastime.

Many countries have developed recipes for bread which are unique to their own cultural heritage. In North America, where no one particular recipe is followed, we have welcomed the traditions of various countries.

Among the recipes that follow, we've included some quick-to-mix (and quick-to-disappear) breads and muffins. There are recipes for every occasion.

From the basic goodness of whole wheat loaves and cornmeal muffins to breads bursting with fruits, nuts and spices, you'll discover a world of tempting creations.

Chelsea Bun Breakfast Ring (see page 29)

CORN-FETTI BREAD

- 1½ cups all-purpose flour
- ½ cup yellow cornmeal
- 2 tbsp. sugar
- 1 tbsp. baking powder
- 1 tsp. salt
- ½ tsp. dry mustard
- ½ cup milk
- ⅓ cup butter or margarine, melted
- 3 eggs, beaten
- ¼ cup finely chopped onion
- ¼ cup finely chopped green pepper
- ¼ cup finely chopped sweet red pepper (optional)
- 1 12-oz. can **Green Giant Niblets Whole Kernel Corn**, drained
- ½ cup grated Cheddar cheese

Heat oven to 425°F. Grease 9" square pan. Lightly spoon flour into measuring cup; level off. In medium bowl, combine flour, cornmeal, sugar, baking powder, salt and dry mustard. Stir in milk, butter and eggs. Add onion, green pepper, red pepper and corn; stir until mixed. Spoon batter into prepared pan. Bake for 30-35 minutes or until a toothpick inserted in center comes out clean. Immediately after removing from oven, top with grated cheese, if desired. Serve warm. Store tightly covered in refrigerator.
Serves 4-6

IRISH SODA BREAD

- 4 cups sifted all-purpose flour
- 1 tbsp. sugar
- 1½ tsp. **Cow Brand Baking Soda**
- 1 tsp. salt
- 1 tsp. baking powder
- ¼ cup butter or margarine
- 1 cup seedless raisins
- 1½ cups buttermilk

Sift together flour, sugar, baking soda, salt and baking powder into large bowl. Cut in butter until crumbly. Stir in raisins. Add buttermilk and stir to make a soft dough. Turn onto lightly floured board and knead to form a smooth ball. Pat by hand on greased baking sheet to 1¼" thickness. With sharp knife score into 4 sections. Bake in 350°F oven 1 hour or until bread is browned and a toothpick inserted in the center comes out clean. Serve warm with butter.
Makes 1 loaf

BAKING SODA BISCUITS

- 2 cups sifted all-purpose flour
- ½ tsp. **Cow Brand Baking Soda**
- ½ tsp. salt
- ¼ cup vegetable shortening
- ¾ cup buttermilk

Sift together flour, baking soda and salt into large bowl. Cut in shortening until mixture resembles coarse meal. Make a well in center of flour mixture; add all the buttermilk at one time. Stir to make a soft dough. Turn onto lightly floured board and knead about 30 seconds. Pat or roll to ½" thickness. Cut with floured 2" biscuit cutter. Place on ungreased baking sheet. Bake in 450°F oven 12 minutes or until lightly browned.
Makes about 12 biscuits

BREAKFAST MUFFINS

- 1¾ cups sifted all-purpose flour
- 2 tbsp. sugar
- 1 tsp. baking powder
- ½ tsp. **Cow Brand Baking Soda**
- ½ tsp. salt
- 1 cup buttermilk
- 1 egg, slightly beaten
- 3 tbsp. butter or margarine, melted

Sift together flour, sugar, baking powder, baking soda and salt into large bowl. Combine buttermilk, egg and butter; add to flour mixture and stir just until all ingredients are moistened. Fill greased 2¾" muffin cups about ⅔ full. Bake in 400°F oven 20-25 minutes. Serve warm with butter or preserves.
Makes about 1 dozen

BARBECUE PRETZELS

- 1 8-oz. package **Pillsbury Refrigerated Buttermilk** or **Sweetmilk Biscuits**
- 1 tbsp. flour
- 10 sticks of wood, with bark peeled off
- 2 tbsp. sesame seeds or coarse salt (optional)

Separate dough into 10 pieces. Flour hands and a flat surface. Roll each piece of dough into a 10" rope. Wind each dough rope around a stick, leaving space between spirals and pinching dough together tightly at each end. If desired, roll in salt or sesame seeds, pressing coating into dough. Bake over coals, turning to bake and toast evenly (about 4 minutes per pretzel). To remove from stick, twist pretzel counter clockwise, then turn clockwise and pull off. Serve with Tangy Barbecued Beans *(see Vegetables and Side Dishes).*
Makes 10

Corn-fetti Bread

CHELSEA BRANS

1 tsp. granulated sugar
¼ cup warm water (100°F)
1 envelope **Fleischmann's Fast Rising Active Dry Yeast**
¾ cup milk
1 tsp. lemon juice
¼ cup **Blue Bonnet Margarine**
1 egg, beaten
3 cups all-purpose flour
1 cup **Nabisco 100% Bran Cereal**
⅓ cup granulated sugar
1 tsp. salt
3 tbsp. **Blue Bonnet Margarine**, melted
½ cup granulated sugar
1 tsp. cinnamon
½ cup chopped walnuts
½ cup raisins
½ cup chopped glacé cherries

Stir 1 tsp. sugar in water. Stir in yeast and let stand 10 minutes, then stir well. Heat milk, lemon juice and margarine. Cool to lukewarm. Add egg. Stir in 1 cup flour, cereal, ⅓ cup sugar and salt; beat until smooth. Add yeast mixture and stir well. Gradually add enough additional flour to make a soft dough. Turn out onto floured surface and knead until smooth and elastic, about 8-10 minutes. Place in a greased bowl, turning to grease top. Cover and let rise in a warm place until doubled in bulk, about 1 hour. Grease a 13" x 9" baking pan. Cover bottom with 2 tbsp. melted margarine. Mix together ½ cup sugar and cinnamon. Punch dough down; turn out onto lightly floured surface. Roll or pat dough into a rectangle about 16" x 9". Spread with remaining 1 tbsp. melted margarine. Sprinkle with sugar and cinnamon mixture, reserving 2 tbsp. Sprinkle nuts, raisins and cherries evenly over surface. Roll up as for jelly roll, seal edge well. Cut into 12 equal pieces with a sharp knife. Dip bottom of each piece in reserved sugar and cinnamon and then place in prepared baking pan. Cover and let rise in a warm place until doubled in bulk, about 1 hour. Bake at 375°F 30-35 minutes or until done. Remove from pan and let cool on a wire rack.

Makes 12 buns

Chelsea Brans

CHELSEA BUN BREAKFAST RING

¼ cup butter
½ cup brown sugar
2 tbsp. corn syrup
¼ tsp. ground cinnamon
½ cup pecan halves
12 maraschino cherries, cut in halves
1 8-oz. package **Pillsbury Refrigerated Buttermilk** or **Sweetmilk Biscuits**

Combine butter, brown sugar, corn syrup and cinnamon in an 8" or 9" glass pie plate. Microwave at high power (100%) for 30 seconds to 1 minute. Stir mixture and spread over bottom of plate. Place a glass or custard cup, right-side-up, in center of plate. Arrange pecans and cherries (cut-side-up) over mixture. Arrange biscuits, with sides overlapping, over mixture in plate. Microwave at medium power (50%) for 5-6 minutes. (Cooking time may vary with oven.) Remove glass and invert ring onto serving platter. Leave plate over rolls for 5 minutes or until syrup becomes sticky. Serve warm.

Serves 4-6

Apricot Almond Coffee Cake (top) and Orange and Honey Pull-Apart Loaf

ALPEN LOAF

½ cup margarine
2 eggs
¾ cup sugar
rind and juice of 1 lemon
1 cup all-purpose flour
1 tsp. baking powder
1 cup **Alpen Mixed Cereal**
2 tbsp. milk

Soften margarine with a wooden spoon. Beat in all ingredients until well mixed. Place mixture in loaf pan. Bake at 350°F for approximately 45-50 minutes.
Makes 1 loaf

BILLY BEE WHOLE-WHEAT MUFFINS

2 cups whole-wheat flour
2 tsp. baking powder
½ tsp. salt
1⅓ cups milk
½ cup **Billy Bee Honey**
¼ cup vegetable oil
1 egg, beaten

Combine flour, baking powder and salt. In separate bowl mix milk, honey, oil and egg. Stir liquid ingredients into dry ingredients just until flour is moistened. Spoon batter into greased muffin tins. Bake in preheated 400°F oven for 20-25 minutes.
Makes 12 muffins

APRICOT ALMOND COFFEE CAKE

2 8-roll cans **Pillsbury Refrigerated Crescent Dinner Rolls**
½ cup dried apricots, finely chopped
2 tbsp. sugar
2 tbsp. poppy seed
Topping:
¼ cup apricot or peach jam
1 tbsp. finely sliced almonds
1 tsp. poppy seed, if desired

Heat oven to 375°F. Grease 9" round cake pan. Unroll crescent dough into 4 long rectangles; firmly press perforations to seal. In a small bowl, combine apricots, sugar and poppy seed; spread mixture evenly over each of the 4 rectangles. Starting at longest side of rectangle, roll up; press edges to seal. Wind dough into greased pan, beginning at outer edge and coiling inward. Seal ends of dough. Bake for 20-24 minutes or until golden brown. Remove cake from pan. Spread jam over top; sprinkle with almonds and poppy seed. Serve warm.
Serves 6

ORANGE AND HONEY PULL-APART LOAF

18-roll can **Pillsbury Refrigerated Crescent Dinner Rolls**
2 tbsp. butter or margarine, melted
2 tbsp. honey
½ tsp. finely grated orange peel

Heat oven to 350°F. Remove crescent dough from can; do not unroll. Place section seam-side-down on ungreased cookie sheet. With a serrated knife, partially cut roll into 12 slices (being careful not to cut through to bottom). Fold slices, alternating from left to right to form a loaf. Bake for 20-25 minutes or until deep golden brown. To prepare honey glaze, combine butter, honey and orange peel; brush over warm loaf. Serve warm.

Herb Glazed Pull-Apart Loaf: Follow recipe as indicated above omitting honey glaze. To make herb glaze, combine 2 tbsp. butter or margarine, ¼ tsp. basil leaves, ¼ tsp. oregano leaves and ⅛ tsp. garlic powder. Brush over warm loaf. Serve warm.
Serves 4

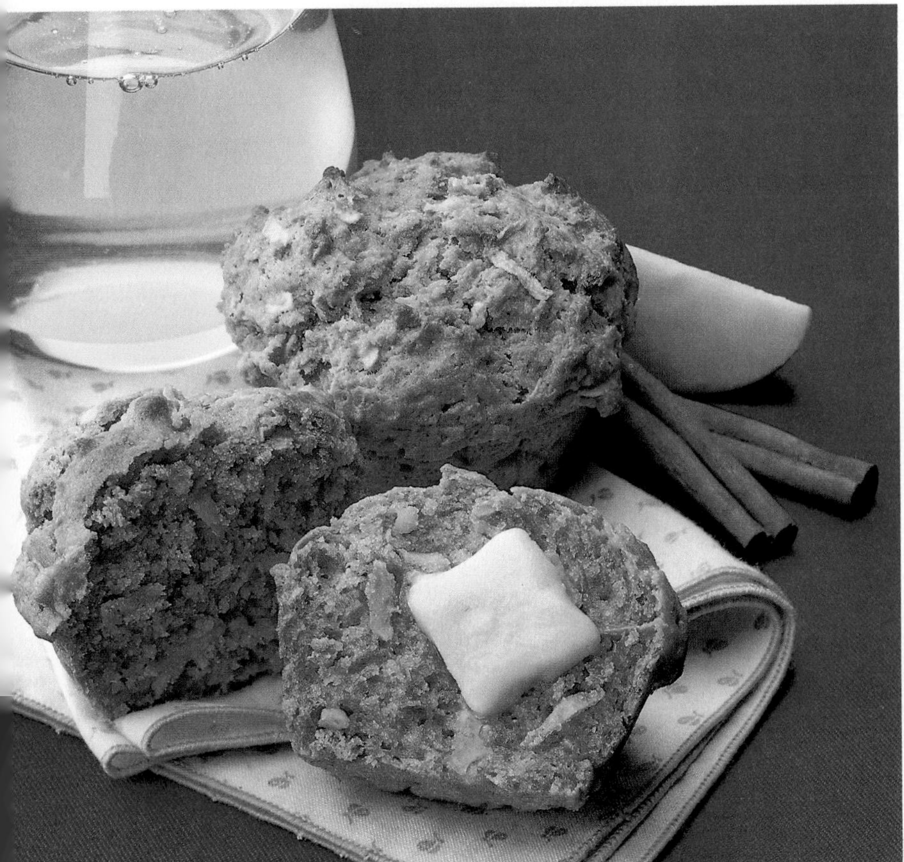

APPLECRISP MUFFINS

1 egg
1¼ cups milk
½ cup **Blue Bonnet Margarine**, melted
⅓ cup liquid honey
1½ cup **Honey Maid Graham Crumbs**
1½ cups all-purpose flour
1 tbsp. **Magic Baking Powder**
1 tsp. cinnamon
½ tsp. salt
1 cup grated peeled apple (1 medium)

Grease large muffin tins or line with paper baking cups. Beat egg in bowl with a fork. Blend in milk, margarine and honey. Stir in crumbs. Combine flour, baking powder, cinnamon and salt in large bowl. Stir liquid mixture into dry ingredients, stirring just until moistened. Fold in grated apple. Spoon batter into muffin cups, generously filling each to the top. Bake at 400°F for about 20 minutes or until done. Cool. Store in airtight container.
Makes 12 large muffins

PORK AND BEAN BREAD

⅓ cup raisins
⅓ cup boiling water
1 egg
⅓ cup oil
1 cup sugar
1 tsp. vanilla
1 8-oz. can **Libby's Deep-Browned Beans**
1⅓ cup flour
1 tsp. cinnamon
½ tsp. baking powder
½ tsp. baking soda
¼ tsp. salt
⅓ cup chopped walnuts

Mix raisins with boiling water, stir and set aside. Beat egg, oil, sugar, vanilla and Libby's Deep-Browned Beans until beans are broken. Add flour, remaining ingredients, including raisins and water. Mix well. Pour batter into a well greased 9" x 5" x 2¾" loaf pan. Bake at 325°F for 60-70 minutes. This recipe is also great baked as muffins. Makes 6 large muffins. Bake at 325°F for 40-45 minutes.

Applecrisp Muffins (top)
Pork and Bean Bread (bottom)

Swirly Danish Cheese Bread

SWIRLY DANISH CHEESE BREAD

- 2 cups milk
- 2 tbsp. sugar
- 1 tbsp. salt
- 2 tbsp. butter
- ½ cup warm water (110-115°F)
- 2 packages active dry yeast
- 5 cups unbleached flour
- 2 cups rolled oats
- 3 cups (¾ lb.) shredded **Danish Cheese** (**Tybo**, **Samsoe**, **Fontina** or **Creamy Havarti**)
- 1 egg white
- 2 tsp. poppy seeds

Scald milk. Stir in sugar, salt and butter. Cool to lukewarm. Pour warm water into large mixing bowl. Sprinkle in yeast; stir until dissolved. Add milk mixture, then flour and oats, mixing well with beater or wooden spoon. Turn out onto floured board. Knead until smooth and elastic (about 10 minutes). Place in greased bowl, turning dough to grease top. Cover with damp towel. Let rise in warm place until doubled in bulk (45-60 minutes). Punch down, cover and let rest 10 minutes. Divide dough in half. Roll each piece to a rectangle twice the length of the pan (about 18" x 6"). Reserving ½ cup of the cheese for tops of loaves, arrange remaining cheese on dough, dividing evenly. Roll up dough from short side, jelly-roll fashion, sealing edge and ends. Place seam-side-down in 2 greased 9" x 5" loaf pans. Cover and let rise in warm place until doubled in bulk, about 45 minutes. Brush gently with lightly beaten egg white. Sprinkle reserved cheese and poppy seeds on top. Bake in preheated 375°F oven for 30-35 minutes, or until golden brown. For additional crustiness, remove loaves from pans. Return to oven rack for 5 minutes. Cool on racks. This bread is nice served reheated, or sliced and toasted.
Makes 2 loaves

CLOVER TEA ROLLS

- 2 cups sifted all-purpose flour
- ¼ cup sugar
- ¾ tsp. **Cow Brand Baking Soda**
- ½ tsp. salt
- ⅓ cup vegetable shortening
- ½ cup milk
- 3 tbsp. lemon juice

Sift together flour, sugar, baking soda and salt into large bowl. Cut in shortening until mixture resembles course meal. Combine milk and lemon juice; quickly stir into flour mixture to form a soft dough. Turn onto lightly floured board; knead slightly. Form into small balls about the size of marbles. Put three balls into each greased muffin cup (about 2¾" diameter). Bake in 450°F oven 15 minutes or until lightly browned.
Makes about 1 dozen

BROWN RICE MUFFINS

1¼ cups **Uncle Ben's Perfected Brown Rice**, uncooked
2½ cups water
1 tbsp. butter or margarine
4 cups whole wheat flour
4 cups all-purpose flour
¼ cup baking powder
1 tbsp. salt
6 cups milk
1⅔ cups vegetable oil
6 large eggs, beaten
3 cups firmly packed brown sugar

Topping:

1½ cups brown sugar
2 tbsp. cinnamon
1 cup chopped nuts (if desired)

Combine rice, water and butter in a saucepan. Bring to a boil over high heat. Stir well, cover and reduce heat to medium-low. Simmer until most of the water has been absorbed, about 20 minutes. Remove from heat, cover and chill several hours. Note: If using already prepared rice (i.e.: leftover extra rice) this recipe requires 4 cups cooked and chilled rice. Combine flours, baking powder and salt. Mix using a wire whisk. Stir in cooked and chilled rice. Combine milk, oil, eggs and brown sugar. Stir until well blended. Pour into center of flour mixture. Stir just enough to moisten flour; mixture will be lumpy. Fill well-greased muffin tins ⅔ full; sprinkle with topping mixture. Bake at 400°F for about 12-15 minutes. Muffins can be frozen and reheated.
Makes 4 dozen large muffins

MCVITIE'S DIGESTIVE STUFFING

2 oz. bacon
1 oz. butter
1 small onion, finely chopped
4 oz. **McVitie's Digestive Biscuits**, crushed
1 tbsp. chopped parsley
grated rind of 1 small or ½ a large lemon
salt and pepper
1 egg, beaten

Chop the bacon finely. Melt the butter in a saucepan and fry the bacon and onion until soft. Remove the pan from the heat, add all the remaining ingredients and mix thoroughly. This is a good stuffing for meat, especially pork or poultry.

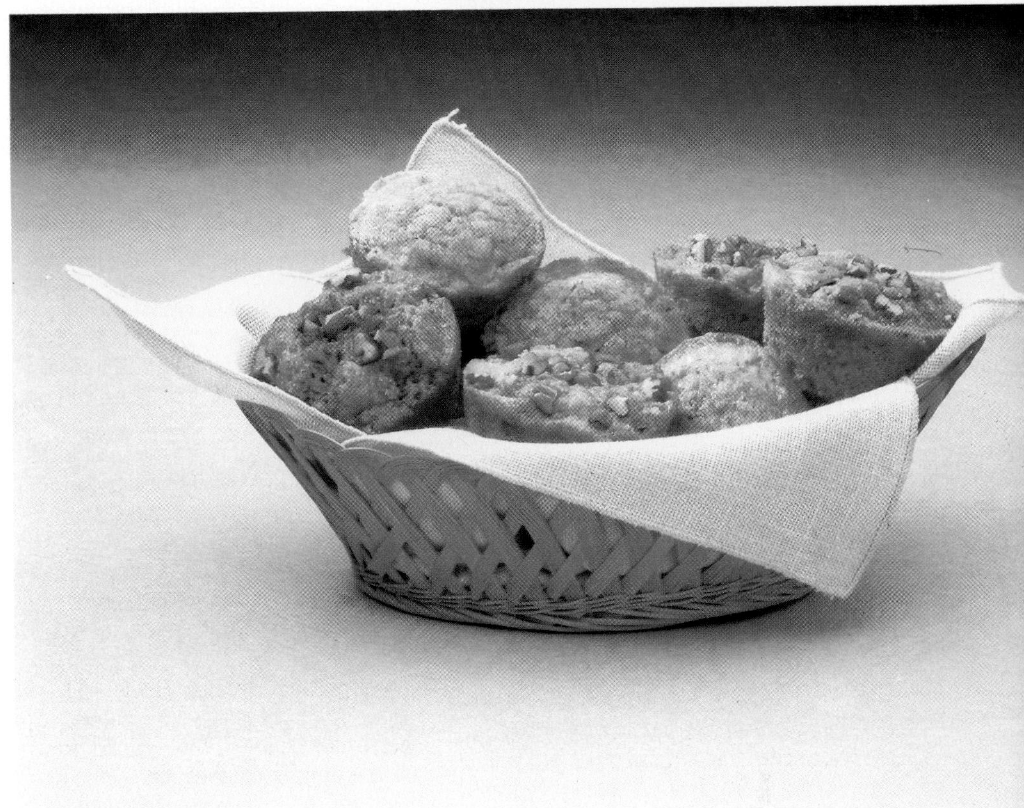

Brown Rice Muffins

DATE-NUT BREAD

2½ cups sifted all-purpose flour
1¼ tsp. **Cow Brand Baking Soda**
1 tsp. salt
1 cup chopped dates
2 eggs
5 tbsp. white vinegar
¾ cup milk
½ cup firmly packed light brown sugar
¼ cup vegetable shortening, melted
¾ cup chopped nuts

Sift together flour, baking soda and salt into large bowl. Stir in chopped dates. In separate bowl, beat eggs; add vinegar and milk. Stir in brown sugar. Add melted shortening. Pour egg mixture into flour mixture all at one time. Stir only until all flour is dampened: then add nuts and mix lightly. Turn into a greased 9" x 5" loaf pan and bake in 350°F oven for 1 hour or until toothpick inserted in center comes out clean. Remove from pan and cool several hours or overnight before slicing.
Makes 1 loaf

BLACKCURRANT QUICK BREAD

1 cup **Lynch Blackcurrant Topping**
1 cup brown sugar
3 cups flour
2 tsp. baking powder
2 tsp. baking soda
1 tsp. salt
1 egg
1½ cups sour cream
5 tbsp. vegetable oil
½ cup milk

Sift together dry ingredients in a large bowl and set aside. Mix egg, sour cream, oil and milk together and stir into dry ingredients. Starting with batter, layer batter and topping into a greased and floured loaf pan and bake for approximately 1 hour at 350°F.
Makes 1 loaf

BASKET BREAD

- 1 cup milk
- 1 tsp. sugar
- 2 packages active dry yeast
- 1 cup beer, at room temperature
- 1 cup (4 oz.) shredded **Danish Creamy Havarti Cheese** (or **Esrom** or **Danish Tilsit** for a more pronounced cheese flavor)
- 3 tbsp. caraway seed
- 1 cup rye flour
- 4½ cups all-purpose flour
- 1 tsp. salt
- vegetable oil
- flour
- 10" x 3" round straw or wicker basket

Heat milk in small saucepan until warm (110°F). Pour into large bowl. Add sugar, then sprinkle with yeast and let stand without stirring until slightly foamy, about 5 minutes. Stir to mix. Blend in beer, cheese, caraway seed, rye flour, 4 cups of the all-purpose flour and salt. Beat well with wooden spoon. Turn out onto lightly floured surface and knead until smooth and elastic, about 5 minutes, adding remaining flour as necessary. Using pastry brush, lightly but thoroughly oil inside of basket; then sprinkle generously with flour. Thoroughly sprinkle surface of dough with additional flour. Place in basket and cover with a lightly floured cloth. Let rise in warm, draft-free area until dough almost fills basket, about 40 minutes. Preheat oven to 400°F. Generously oil baking sheet. Set atop basket and carefully invert dough onto baking sheet. Bake until golden brown, about 40 minutes. Transfer to rack and let cool completely before slicing.
Makes 1 round loaf

BRAIDED EGG BREAD

- 2 tsp. sugar
- ½ cup warm water (105-115°F)
- 2 packages active dry yeast
- 1½ cups milk
- 3 tbsp. sugar
- 2 tsp. salt
- ¼ cup butter or margarine
- 2 eggs, beaten
- 6½-7 cups **Robin Hood All-Purpose Flour**
- 1 egg yolk
- 2 tbsp. water
- 2 tbsp. sesame or poppy seeds

Dissolve 2 tsp. sugar in warm water in large bowl. Sprinkle in yeast. Let stand 10 minutes, then stir well. Heat milk to lukewarm. Stir in sugar, salt, butter and eggs. Add milk mixture and 2 cups flour to dissolved yeast mixture. Beat with wooden spoon or electric mixer until smooth and elastic. Stir in 4½ cups of remaining flour gradually. If necessary, add more flour to make a soft dough which leaves sides of bowl. Turn out onto floured board. Round up into a ball. Knead dough, adding more flour as necessary, until it is smooth, elastic and no longer sticky (about 10 minutes). Place in lightly greased bowl. Turn dough to grease top. Cover with greased waxed paper and tea towel. Let rise in warm place (75-85°F) until doubled (1-1½ hours). Punch down. Turn out onto lightly floured board and divide into 2 equal portions. Round up each portion. Cover and let rest for 10 minutes. Roll 1 portion into 9" x 14" rectangle. Cut lengthwise into 3 equal strips. Fold each strip lengthwise in half and seal edges together. With seam-side-down, braid the 3 strips together. Repeat with remaining dough. Place each braid on greased baking sheet. Tuck ends under to make neat-looking loaves. Cover with tea towel and let rise in warm place until doubled (about 45 minutes). Brush loaves with egg yolk beaten with 2 tbsp. water. Sprinkle with sesame or poppy seeds. Bake at 350°F for 25-30 minutes. Remove from baking sheets immediately and cool on wire racks.
Makes 2 loaves

DILLY CHEESE BREAD

- 1 tsp. sugar
- ½ cup warm water (105-115°F)
- 1 package active dry yeast
- 1 cup creamed cottage cheese
- 2 tbsp. dried onion flakes
- 2 tbsp. dill seed
- 1 tbsp. oil
- 1 tsp. salt
- ¼ tsp. baking soda
- 1 egg
- 2½-3 cups **Robin Hood All-Purpose Flour**

Dissolve sugar in warm water in blender or food processor container. Sprinkle in yeast. Let stand 10 minutes, then blend for 1 minute. Add remaining ingredients except flour and blend 1 minute. Measure 2½ cups flour into large bowl. Add blender contents. Stir well. Knead dough on lightly floured board adding more flour as necessary, for 5 minutes. Dough will be slightly sticky. Place in greased bowl. Turn dough to grease top. Cover with greased waxed paper and tea towel. Let rise in warm place (75-85°F) until doubled (1½-2 hours). Turn out dough onto lightly floured board. Knead 3 minutes. Shape into a ball. Place dough into greased 1½-quart casserole. Cover with tea towel. Let rise in warm place until dough is 1½" above top of casserole (1½-2 hours). Bake at 350°F on lower oven rack for 40-45 minutes or until done. Remove from casserole immediately and cool on wire rack.
Makes 1 loaf

BASIC WHITE BREAD

- 1 tsp. sugar
- ½ cup warm water (105-115°F)
- 1 package active dry yeast
- 1 cup milk
- ¼ cup butter, margarine or shortening
- 3 tbsp. sugar
- 2 tsp. salt
- ½ cup warm water
- 5-6 cups **Robin Hood All-Purpose Flour**

Dissolve 1 tsp. sugar in ½ cup warm water in large bowl. Sprinkle in yeast. Let stand 10 minutes, then stir well. Heat milk to lukewarm. Stir in butter, sugar, salt and ½ cup warm water. Add milk mixture and 2 cups flour to dissolved yeast mixture. Beat with wooden spoon or electric mixer until smooth and elastic. Stir in 3 cups of remaining flour gradually. If necessary, add more flour to make a soft dough which leaves sides of bowl. Turn out on floured board. Round up into a ball. Knead dough, adding more flour as necessary, until dough is smooth, elastic and no longer sticky (about 10 minutes). Place in lightly greased bowl. Turn dough to grease top. Cover with greased waxed paper and tea towel. Let rise in warm place (75-85°F) until doubled (1-1½ hours). Punch down. Turn out onto lightly floured board and divide into 2 equal portions (or follow instructions for one of the variations below). Cover and let rest 10 minutes. Shape each portion into a loaf. Place seam-side-down in greased 8½" x 4½" x 2¾" loaf pans. Cover with tea towel. Let rise in warm place until dough rises 1½" above top of pan in center and corners are filled (1-1½ hours). Bake at 400°F on lower oven rack for 35-45 minutes. Remove from pans immediately. Brush top crust with butter if soft crust is desired. Cool on wire racks.

Whole Wheat Bread: Prepare Basic White Bread as recipe directs except substitute up to half the amount of Robin Hood All-Purpose Flour with **Robin Hood Whole Wheat Flour**.
Makes 2 loaves

HONEY WHEAT-GERM BREAD

1 tsp. sugar
½ cup warm water (105-115°F)
2 packages active dry yeast
1½ cups milk
¼ cup liquid honey
2 tsp. salt
2 tbsp. butter, margarine or shortening
1 egg, beaten
1 cup **Kretschmer Wheat Germ**
5-5½ cups **Robin Hood All-Purpose Flour**

Dissolve sugar in warm water in large bowl. Sprinkle in yeast. Let stand 10 minutes, then stir well. Heat milk to lukewarm. Stir in honey, salt, butter and egg. Add milk mixture and 2 cups flour to dissolved yeast mixture. Beat with wooden spoon or electric mixer until smooth and elastic. Stir in wheat germ with wooden spoon. Add 3 cups of remaining flour gradually. If necessary, add more flour to make a soft dough which leaves sides of bowl. Turn out onto floured board. Round up into a ball. Knead dough, adding more flour as necessary, until it is smooth, elastic and no longer sticky (about 10 minutes). Place in lightly greased bowl. Turn dough to grease top. Cover with greased waxed paper and tea towel. Let rise in warm place (75-85°F) until almost doubled (1-1½ hours). Punch down. Turn out onto lightly floured board and divide into 2 equal portions. Round up each portion. Cover and let rest 10 minutes. Shape each portion into a loaf. Place seam-side-down in greased 8½" x 4½" x 2¾" loaf pans. Cover with tea towel. Let rise in warm place until dough rises 1½" above top of pan in center and corners are filled (1-1½ hours). Bake at 375°F on lower oven rack for 35-40 minutes. Cover with foil during last 15 minutes if crust browns too quickly. Remove from pans immediately. Brush top crust with butter if a soft crust is desired. Cool on wire racks.
Makes 2 loaves

MINCEMEAT MUFFINS

2 cups all-purpose flour
3½ tsp. baking powder
½ tsp. salt
2 tbsp. granulated sugar
1 egg
2 tbsp. melted shortening or oil
¾ cup milk
1 cup **Lynch Olde Style Mincemeat**

Preheat oven to 425°F. Sift together flour, baking powder, salt and sugar. Combine egg, shortening, milk and mincemeat. Quickly stir liquid ingredients into flour mixture until just moistened. Spoon into 12 lightly greased muffin pans. Bake approximately 25 minutes until golden brown. Serve warm with butter and applesauce.
Makes 12 medium muffins

FRESH CRANBERRY NUT MUFFINS

¾ cup **MIRACLE WHIP Salad Dressing** or **MIRACLE WHIP Light Dressing**
¼ cup orange juice concentrate, thawed, undiluted
2 eggs, beaten
2 cups fresh or frozen whole cranberries
2 cups all-purpose flour
¾ cup sugar
½ cup chopped nuts
2 tsp. grated orange rind
1 tsp. each baking powder and baking soda

Combine salad dressing, orange juice, eggs and berries. In separate bowl, combine remaining ingredients. Stir wet mixture into dry ingredients. Fill 12 greased or paper-lined muffin cups. Bake at 350°F for 20-25 minutes. Let stand 10 minutes; remove from pan.
Makes 12 muffins

Fresh Cranberry Nut Muffins

CINNAMON-SWIRL RAISIN BREAD

1 tsp. sugar
¾ cup warm water (105-115°F)
1 package active dry yeast
½ cup milk
2 tbsp. butter or margarine
1 tbsp. sugar
1 tsp. salt
3¼-3½ cups **Robin Hood All-Purpose Flour**
½ cup raisins
¼ cup sugar
1 tsp. cinnamon

Dissolve 1 tsp. sugar in warm water in large bowl. Sprinkle in yeast. Let stand 10 minutes, then stir well. Heat milk to lukewarm. Stir in butter, 1 tbsp. sugar and salt. Add milk to mixture and 1 cup flour to dissolved yeast mixture. Beat on medium speed of electric mixer for 1 minute. Gradually add 1¼ cups more flour, beating on medium speed for 3 minutes. Add raisins. Gradually stir in almost all the remaining flour, using enough flour to make a soft dough which leaves sides of bowl forming a ball. Knead dough, adding more flour as necessary, until dough is smooth, elastic and no longer sticky (about 10 minutes). Place dough in lightly greased bowl. Turn dough to grease top. Cover with greased waxed paper and tea towel. Let rise in warm place (75-85°F) until doubled (1-1½ hours). Punch down. Turn out onto lightly floured surface and let rest for 10 minutes. Roll dough into rectangle 12" x 9" of uniform thickness. Brush lightly with water. Combine ¼ cup sugar and cinnamon. Sprinkle evenly over rectangle. Roll up dough jelly-roll fashion, beginning with short side. Seal seam and ends well. Place in a greased 9" x 5" x 3" loaf pan. Cover with tea towel and let rise in warm place until doubled (40-60 minutes). Bake at 375°F on lower rack for 50 minutes or until done. Cover top of loaf with foil during last 15 minutes if becoming too brown. Remove from pan immediately and cool on wire rack.
Makes 1 loaf

BASIC SWEET DOUGH

1 tsp. sugar
½ cup warm water (105-115°F)
1 package active dry yeast
⅔ cup milk
¼ cup sugar
1 tsp. salt
¼ cup butter or shortening
1 egg
3¾-4 cups **Robin Hood All-Purpose Flour**

Dissolve 1 tsp. sugar in warm water in large bowl. Sprinkle in yeast. Let stand 10 minutes, then stir well. Heat milk to lukewarm. Stir in ¼ cup sugar and salt. Add lukewarm milk mixture, butter, egg and 1 cup flour to dissolved yeast mixture. Beat for 3 minutes. Stir in about 3 cups remaining flour gradually. If necessary, add more flour to make a soft dough which leaves sides of bowl. Turn out onto lightly floured board. Knead dough, adding more flour as necessary, until dough is smooth, elastic and no longer sticky (about 5 minutes). Place in lightly greased bowl. Turn dough to grease top. Cover with greased waxed paper and tea towel. Let rise in warm place (75-85°F) until doubled (about 1 hour). Punch down. Turn out onto lightly floured board and round up into a ball. Cover and let rest 10 minutes. Shape and prepare according to one of the following variations.(These variations can also be made with Basic White Bread dough.)

Dinner Rolls: Divide each portion of prepared dough into 16-24 equal pieces depending on size of buns desired. Shape into balls and flatten slightly. Place on greased baking sheet or in muffin cups. Cover with a tea towel and let rise in warm place until doubled (about 30 minutes). Bake at 375°F for 12-15 minutes or until golden. Brush with melted butter, if desired, for soft shiny crust.

Pan Rolls: Divide each portion of dough into 16 equal pieces. Shape into balls. Place balls, almost touching, in rows, in a greased 8" square pan. Cover and let rise as above. Bake at 375°F for 25-30 minutes.

Twin Rolls: Divide each portion of dough into 12 equal pieces; then divide each piece in half. Shape into balls. Place 2 balls in each of 12 greased muffin cups. Cover, let rise, and bake as for Dinner Rolls.

Cloverleaf Rolls: Divide each portion of dough into 12 equal pieces; then divide each piece into thirds. Shape into balls. Place 3 balls in each of 12 greased muffin cups. Cover, let rise, and bake as for Dinner Rolls.

Crescents: Divide each portion of dough in half. Roll each piece to a 9" circle. Brush with melted butter. Cut each circle into 8 wedges. Roll up each wedge from wide end to point. Place on greased baking sheet, point-side-down, curving slightly to form a crescent. Cover, let rise, and bake as for Dinner Rolls.

Parkerhouse Rolls: Roll dough to ¼" thickness. Cut into 2½" circles or press small ball of dough into circle. Crease just off-center with a knife. Fold over with wider half on top. Press down and seal edges. Place on greased baking sheet. Cover, let rise and bake as for Dinner Rolls.

Fan Tans: Roll each portion of dough into 9" x 14" rectangle. Brush with melted butter. Cut lengthwise into 6 strips. Stack strips. Cut into 9 pieces. Place cut-side-down in greased muffin cups. Cover with a tea towel and let rise in warm place until doubled (about 30 minutes). Bake at 375°F for 12-15 minutes or until golden. Brush with butter, if desired, for a soft shiny crust.

Knots: Shape dough into ropes. Tie with a loose knot. Place on greased baking sheet. Cover, let rise and bake as for Fan Tans.

Swirls: Roll dough into a rectangle about ½" thick. Brush with melted butter and cut into 1"-wide strips. Twist each strip if desired. Holding one end of a strip firmly on greased baking sheet wind dough around to form a coil. Tuck end under firmly. Swirls can also be shaped and placed in greased muffin cups. Cover, let rise and bake as for Fans Tans.

Posies: Divide each portion of dough into 16 equal pieces. Shape into balls and flatten slightly. Make 6 ¼" cuts around edge. Place on greased baking sheet. Cover, let rise, and bake as for Fan Tans.

CHOCOLATE-GLAZED YEAST DOUGHNUTS

1 tsp. sugar
½ cup warm water (105-115°F)
2 packages active dry yeast
⅓ cup sugar
¼ cup milk
¼ cup shortening
1 tsp. salt
2 eggs
3½-4 cups **Robin Hood All-Purpose Flour**
oil or shortening for deep frying

Chocolate Glaze:

2 cups sifted icing sugar
¼ cup milk
2 squares semi-sweet chocolate, melted
1 tsp. vanilla

Dissolve 1 tsp. sugar in warm water in large mixing bowl. Sprinkle in yeast. Let stand 10 minutes, then stir well. Heat ⅓ cup sugar, milk, shortening and salt together to lukewarm. Add milk mixture, eggs and 1½ cups flour to yeast mixture. Beat at low speed of electric mixer ½ minute, scraping bowl often. Beat 3 minutes at high speed. Stir in enough remaining flour to make a soft dough. Turn out onto lightly floured board. Knead dough, adding more flour as necessary, until dough is smooth, elastic and no longer sticky (3-5 minutes). Shape into a ball. Place in lightly greased bowl. Turn dough to grease top. Cover with greased waxed paper and tea towel. Let rise in warm place (75-85°F) until doubled (1-1¼ hours). Punch down. Turn out onto lightly floured board and divide into 2 equal portions. Cover and let rest 10 minutes. Roll each portion to ½" thickness. Cut with floured doughnut cutter. Re-roll leftover dough and cut again. Place on tray or baking sheet. Cover with tea towel and let rise until very light (45-60 minutes). Heat oil to 375°F. Carefully add 2 or 3 doughnuts. Fry 1 minute on each side or until golden. Drain well. Dip tops of warm doughnuts into Chocolate Glaze, cinnamon-sugar or icing sugar. Place on rack set over waxed paper to catch glaze which can be reused. Cool. To prepare Chocolate Glaze, combine all ingredients together, mixing until smooth.
Makes 18 doughnuts

"To Your Health" Muffins

"TO YOUR HEALTH" MUFFINS

1 cup whole wheat flour
1 cup natural bran
½ cup brown sugar
1 tsp. baking soda
½ tsp. salt
½ tsp. cinnamon
1 cup grated carrots (about 4)
½ cup raisins
1 cup buttermilk or sour milk
¼ cup **Mazola Corn Oil**
1 egg
1 tsp. vanilla

Blend together in large bowl flour, bran, brown sugar, baking soda, salt, cinnamon, carrots and raisins. In second bowl, beat buttermilk, oil, egg and vanilla. Add liquid ingredients to dry ingredients and mix just until moistened. Spoon into 12 greased or paper-lined muffin cups. Bake at 375°F for 20 minutes. (To sour milk, put 1 tbsp. vinegar into 1 cup measure. Fill with milk. Let stand 5 minutes.)

BANANA AND PEANUT BREAD

2 cups all-purpose flour
1 tsp. baking powder
½ tsp. baking soda
½ tsp. salt
1 egg
1 cup **Delisle Plain Yogurt**
1 cup brown sugar
2 tbsp. peanut butter
1 cup unsalted chopped peanuts
1 cup mashed banana

Sift and measure flour, add baking powder, soda and salt. Beat egg, add yogurt, brown sugar and peanut butter. Coat peanuts with some of the flour. Fold remaining flour into yogurt mixture alternately with mashed banana. Add peanuts. Pour into a greased 9" x 5" x 3" loaf pan. Bake at 350°F 1-1¼ hour. Remove from pan and let cool.
Makes 1 loaf

FRY'S APPLE NUT BREAD

2 cups all-purpose flour
1¼ cups sugar
⅓ cup **Fry's Cocoa**
1 tsp. baking soda
¼ tsp. salt
1 tsp. ground cinnamon
½ tsp. ground nutmeg
2 eggs, beaten
½ cup milk
¾ cup butter, melted
2 cups peeled and diced apples
1 cup chopped walnuts

Sift together flour, sugar, cocoa, baking soda, salt, cinnamon and nutmeg. Combine eggs, milk and butter; add to dry ingredients; stir just until moistened. Stir in apples and nuts. Pour into a greased 6-cup loaf pan. Bake in preheated 350°F oven 70-80 minutes or until done. Cool 10 minutes in pan. Turn out of pan; cool.
Makes 1 loaf

LIGHT RYE BREAD

1⅓ cups milk
¼ cup brown sugar
2 tsp. salt
2 tbsp. shortening
1 tsp. sugar
½ cup warm water (105-115°F)
1 package active dry yeast
2⅓ cups dark rye flour
2¾-3¼ cups **Robin Hood All-Purpose Flour**
1 egg white, lightly beaten

Scald milk. Pour into large bowl and add brown sugar, salt and shortening, stirring until shortening melts. Cool to lukewarm. Dissolve sugar in warm water. Sprinkle in yeast. Let stand 10 minutes, then stir well. Stir into milk mixture. Add rye flour. Beat vigorously by hand or with electric mixer until smooth. Add 2¾ cups all-purpose flour gradually, beating in with a spoon. Work in enough more flour to make a soft dough which leaves sides of bowl. Turn out onto floured board. Knead dough, adding more flour as necessary, until dough is smooth and elastic (about 10 minutes). Place in lightly greased bowl. Turn dough to grease top. Cover with greased waxed paper and tea towel. Let rise in warm place (75-85°F) until doubled (1-1½ hours). Punch down. Turn out onto lightly floured board and divide into 2 equal portions. Roll each portion into a 10" x 8" rectangle. Roll up tightly, jelly-roll fashion, starting at long edge. Seal seam and ends well. Taper ends by rolling gently between hands. Place seam-side-down on greased baking sheet. Cover with tea towel and let rise until doubled (30-45 minutes). Slash top of loaves diagonally with sharp knife or razor blade. Bake at 400°F for 20 minutes. Brush loaves with egg white and continue baking 10-15 minutes longer or until golden. Cool on wire rack.
Makes 2 loaves

BACHELOR BREAD

1 tbsp. brown sugar
⅓ cup warm water (105-115°F)
1 package active dry yeast
⅔ cup warm milk
½ cup grated Parmesan cheese (optional)
2 tbsp. oil
½ tsp. salt
1 cup **Robin Hood Whole Wheat Flour**
1 cup **Robin Hood All-Purpose Flour**

Dissolve sugar in warm water in large bowl. Sprinkle in yeast. Let stand 10 minutes, then stir well. Add warm milk, cheese (if desired), oil and salt. Mix well. Stir in flours. Dough will be sticky. Pour dough into a well-greased 1-lb. coffee can. Place lid on loosely or cover with greased foil. Let rise in a warm place (75-85°F) just until dough reaches lid (about 30 minutes). Remove lid or foil. Bake uncovered at 350°F for 45-50 minutes. Remove bread from can immediately and cool on wire rack.
Makes 1 loaf

BLACK BREAD (PUMPERNICKEL)

2 cups water
1 square unsweetened chocolate
¼ cup cider vinegar
¼ cup dark molasses
2 tbsp. caraway seed
2 tsp. instant coffee powder
1 tbsp. salt
1 tbsp. sugar
½ cup warm water (105-115°F)
2 packages active dry yeast
4 cups dark rye flour
1 cup natural bran
2½-3 cups **Robin Hood All-Purpose Flour**
1 egg white, lightly beaten
1 tbsp. cold water

Combine first 7 ingredients in saucepan. Cook over medium heat, stirring occasionally until mixture reaches 110-115°F. If mixture becomes too warm, cool to correct temperature. Dissolve sugar in warm water in large mixing bowl. Sprinkle in yeast. Let stand 10 minutes, then stir well. Stir in chocolate mixture. Add rye flour, bran and 2 cups all-purpose flour. Mix well. Stir in enough remaining flour to make a soft dough. Turn out on floured board. Knead, adding more flour as necessary, until dough is smooth and elastic (about 10 minutes). Place dough in greased bowl. Cover with greased waxed paper and tea towel. Let rise in warm place (75-85°F) until doubled (about 1½ hours). Punch down. Turn out onto lightly floured board and divide into 3 equal portions. Shape each portion into a round loaf. Place on greased baking sheets. Cover with tea towel and let rise until doubled (about 1½ hours). Brush dough lightly with a mixture of egg white and water. Bake at 350°F for 25 minutes. Brush again with egg-white mixture and continue baking 15-20 minutes longer. Cool on wire rack.
Makes 3 round loaves

SPICED FRUIT BREAD

2 tsp. sugar
2 cups warm water (105-115°F)
2 packages active dry yeast
½ cup brown sugar
⅓ cup granulated sugar
2 tsp. salt
½ tsp. cinnamon
½ tsp. nutmeg
¼ tsp. allspice
¼ tsp. ginger
¼ tsp. ground cloves
2 tbsp. soft butter
6-7 cups **Robin Hood All-Purpose Flour**
1 cup raisins
1 cup chopped walnuts
1 cup candied cherries, chopped

Dissolve 2 tsp. sugar in warm water in large bowl. Sprinkle in yeast. Let stand 10 minutes, then stir well. Add sugars, salt, spices, butter and 2 cups flour to dissolved yeast mixture. Beat with wooden spoon or electric mixer until smooth and elastic. Stir in raisins, walnuts and cherries. Stir in 4 cups of remaining flour gradually. If necessary, add more flour to make a soft dough which leaves sides of bowl. Turn out onto floured board. Round up into a ball. Knead dough, adding more flour as necessary, until it becomes smooth, elastic and no longer sticky (about 10 minutes). Place in lightly greased bowl. Turn dough to grease top. Cover with greased waxed paper and tea towel. Let rise in warm place (75-85°F) until doubled (1½-2 hours). Punch down. Turn out onto lightly floured board and divide into 2 equal portions. Round up each portion. Cover and let rest 10 minutes. Shape each portion into a loaf. Place in well-greased 8½" x 4½" x 2¾" loaf pans. Cover with tea towel and let rise in warm place until dough rises 1½" above the top of pan in center and corners are filled (1-1½ hours). Bake at 350°F on lower oven rack for about 1 hour. Remove from pans immediately. Brush top crust with butter if a soft crust is desired. Cool on wire racks.

Makes 2 loaves

CRUMPETS

1 tsp. sugar
½ cup warm water (105-115°F)
1 package active dry yeast
1 cup warm water
1 cup warm milk
2 tbsp. oil
3 cups **Robin Hood All-Purpose Flour**
1 cup **Robin Hood Velvet Cake & Pastry Flour**
1 tbsp. salt
½ tsp. baking soda
¼ cup warm water

Dissolve sugar in ½ cup warm water. Sprinkle in yeast. Let stand 10 minutes, then stir well. Add 1 cup warm water, warm milk and oil. Stir well. Mix flours and salt in large mixing bowl. Stir in yeast mixture. Beat at medium speed of electric mixer for 2 minutes. Cover with greased waxed paper and let rise in warm place until mixture has risen and is bubbly. Dissolve soda in ¼ cup warm water. Stir into the batter. Let rise in very warm place 90°F for 30 minutes. Stir lightly. Heat a griddle or frypan to 350°F. Grease pan lightly and grease inside of 4" crumpet rings (if you don't have crumpet rings, salmon or tuna cans opened at both ends work well). Place rings on griddle. Pour batter into rings filling half full. Cook until bubbles break on surface and top is almost dry (about 10 minutes). Serve warm with butter and maple syrup.

Makes about 18 crumpets

EVE'S FAVORITE APPLE LOAF

1 cup whole wheat flour
¾ cup all-purpose flour
1 tsp. baking powder
1 tsp. baking soda
½ tsp. cinnamon
¼ tsp. salt
¾ cup applesauce
¾ cup **Skippy Super Chunk** or **Creamy Peanut Butter**
½ cup brown sugar
1 egg
½ cup milk

Combine first 6 ingredients in large bowl. In second bowl, beat together remaining ingredients. Add liquid ingredients to dry ingredients and blend thoroughly. Pour into greased 8" x 4" loaf pan. Bake at 325°F for 40 minutes.

Makes 1 loaf

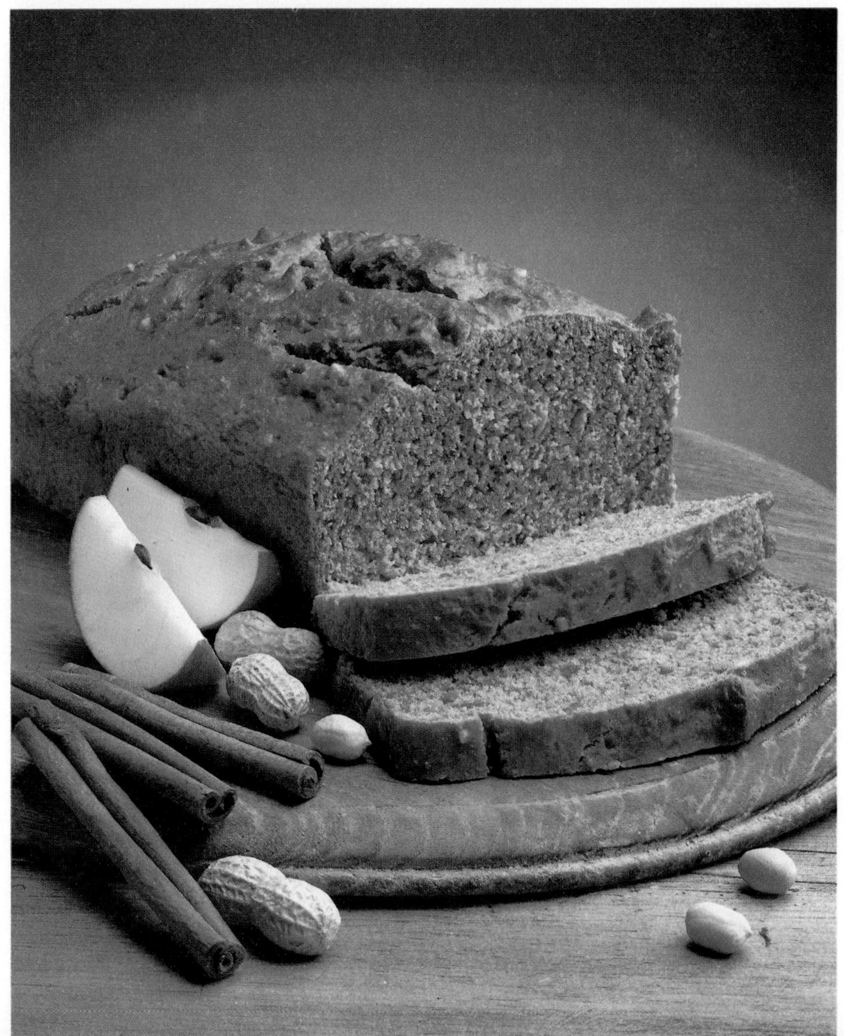

Eve's Favorite Apple Loaf

ENGLISH MUFFINS

1 tsp. sugar
½ cup warm water (105-115°F)
2 packages active dry yeast
1½ cups milk
2 tbsp. sugar
2 tbsp. shortening
2 tsp. salt
5-5½ cups **Robin Hood All-Purpose Flour**
cornmeal

Dissolve 1 tsp. sugar in warm water in large mixing bowl. Sprinkle in yeast. Let stand 10 minutes, then stir well. Heat milk, 2 tbsp. sugar, shortening and salt in saucepan, stirring constantly, until shortening melts. Cool to lukewarm. Stir into yeast mixture. Add 2 cups flour. Beat at low speed of electric mixer until combined, then at high speed for 3 minutes. Stir in enough remaining flour until dough forms a ball that leaves sides of bowl. Turn out onto lightly floured surface. Knead in enough remaining flour to make a moderately stiff dough that is smooth and elastic (6-8 minutes). Place dough in greased bowl. Cover with greased waxed paper and let rise in warm place (75-85°F) until doubled (about 1 hour). Punch down. Cover and let rest 10 minutes. Roll out dough on lightly floured surface to about ¼" thickness. Cut with 4" round cutter. Dip in cornmeal to coat both sides. Place on tray or baking sheet. Cover with tea towel and let rise until very light (about 30 minutes). Cook on medium heat on ungreased griddle or frypan about 25 minutes or until golden. Turn frequently during cooking. Cool. To serve, split and toast. Serve warm with butter, honey, jam or as desired.
Makes about 16 muffins

QUAKER CORN MEAL MUFFINS

1 cup **Quaker Corn Meal**
1 cup sifted all-purpose flour
⅓ cup sugar
½ tsp. salt
4 tsp. baking powder
1¼ cups milk
1 egg
¼ cup shortening, at room temperature

Sift dry ingredients together into medium-sized bowl. Add milk, egg and shortening. Beat with rotary egg beater until smooth, about 1 minute (do not over beat). Fill muffin cups ¾ full, bake in preheated oven at 425°F approximately 20 minutes.
Makes 1 dozen

RED RIVER PUMPERNICKEL

3 cups **Monarch Red River Cereal**
1 cup whole wheat flour
2 tsp. baking soda
1 tsp. salt
½ cup molasses
3 cups hot water (almost boiling)

In a large bowl, combine Monarch Red River Cereal, whole wheat flour, baking soda and salt. Blend together molasses and hot water. Add liquid to dry ingredients and stir together. Let stand at least 2 hours or overnight. Turn into greased 9" x 5" x 3" loaf pan. Cover with foil. Bake in preheated 275°F oven for 3 hours or until firm.
Makes 1 loaf

QUAKER OAT BRAN MUFFINS

1¼ cups all-purpose flour
½ cup brown sugar
¾ cup **Quaker Oat Bran**
¼ cup sugar
2 tsp. baking powder
½ tsp. salt
¼ tsp. cinnamon
1 egg, slightly beaten
1 cup milk
¼ cup vegetable oil
¼ cup honey

Combine all dry ingredients and add egg, milk, oil and honey, mixing just until blended. Grease muffin pans or line with paper muffin cups. Fill muffins cups ⅔ full and bake at 400°F for 20-22 minutes.
Makes 1 dozen

PEAR AND LEMON MUFFINS

1 cup **Emelia Pear and Lemon Marmelo with Ginger**
½ cup softened butter
1½ cups buttermilk
¾ cup unbleached all-purpose flour
2 tsp. baking flour
2 tsp. baking powder
½ tsp. baking soda

Preheat oven to 375°F. Blend Pear and Lemon Marmelo with Ginger with butter. Add buttermilk. Combine dry ingredients and add, stirring just enough to moisten flour. Pour into muffin cups. Bake for 20 minutes. Serve hot with fresh butter. (To sour milk, add 1 tbsp. lemon juice to 1 cup milk.)
Makes 16 muffins

RED RIVER CEREAL BREAD

2 cups **Monarch Red River Cereal**
¼ cup shortening
3 cups boiling water
2 tsp. sugar
1 cup lukewarm water (100°F)
2 envelopes active dry yeast
⅔ cup molasses
4 tsp. salt
8-8½ cups all-purpose flour, divided

Measure Monarch Red River Cereal and shortening into a large bowl. Add boiling water, stirring until shortening melts. Let stand for 20 minutes, stirring occasionally. Meanwhile, dissolve sugar in warm water. Sprinkle yeast over top. Let stand 10 minutes. Stir briskly with a fork. Add softened yeast to lukewarm cereal mixture together with molasses and salt. Stir. Add 2½ cups all-purpose flour. Beat vigorously by hand or with electric mixer. Gradually beat in with a wooden spoon an additional 5½-6 cups all-purpose flour. Work in last of flour with a rotating motion of the hand. Turn dough onto a lightly floured surface and knead 8-10 minutes. Shape into a smooth ball and place in a greased bowl, rotating dough to grease surface. Cover with a damp cloth and let rise until doubled in volume (about 1½ hours). Keep in a warm place. Punch down and shape into 4 loaves. Place in greased 8½" x 4½" loaf pans. Cover with greased waxed paper and a damp cloth. Let rise again until doubled (about 1-1½ hours). Bake in preheated 400°F oven for 30-35 minutes.
Makes 4 loaves

PESHWARI NAAN

1 package **Sharwood's Naan Bread Mix**
1 oz. flaked almonds
2 tsp. fennel seeds
1 oz. desiccated coconut
1 oz. raisins

Make up bread mix as instructed on the package. Divide dough into 4 pieces. Mix together all other ingredients. Roll out each piece of dough into an oval shape measuring 9" x 4". Place a small amount of mixture down the center of the dough, leaving 2" from the edge. Fold the long edges together over the mixture to form a seal. Turn the bread over and lightly roll out to form a tear shape, approximately 9" x 4". Grill on a baking sheet for 1½ minutes until lightly scorched and browned.

Scottish Scones

SCOTTISH SCONES

1⅓ cups all-purpose flour (or use 1 cup all-purpose flour and ⅓ cup whole wheat flour)
2 tbsp. sugar
2 tsp. baking powder
¼ tsp. salt
½ cup butter or margarine
1 egg yolk
1 egg
⅓ cup milk
1 cup **Post Grape-Nuts Flakes Cereal**
¼ cup raisins
1 egg white, slightly beaten
sugar or cinnamon-sugar

Mix flour with 2 tbsp. sugar, baking powder and salt. Cut in butter. Combine egg yolk, egg and milk; add to flour mixture with cereal and raisins. Stir until soft dough is formed. Turn out on lightly floured board and knead until smooth. Divide dough into 4 parts. Pat or roll each into a circle ½" thick. Cut into quarters and place on ungreased baking sheets. Brush tops lightly with egg white; sprinkle with sugar. Bake at 450°F for about 10 minutes or until lightly browned. Serve warm.

Makes 16 small scones

CRANBERRY ORANGE MUFFINS

Mix:
10 cups sifted all-purpose flour
⅓ cup baking powder
¼ cup sugar
1 tbsp. salt
2 cups **Crisco Shortening**

Filling:
½ cup sugar
1 tbsp. grated orange peel
1 egg
½ cup milk
½ cup orange juice
1 cup fresh or frozen cranberries

For mix: Combine flour, baking powder, sugar and salt in a large bowl. Cut in shortening with pastry blender until mixture resembles coarse crumbs. (Mix may be stored in covered container up to 6 weeks at room temperature, or frozen for longer storage.) For filling: Combine 3 cups Mix, sugar and orange peel in a bowl. Beat egg, milk and orange juice together with a fork. Add to dry ingredients; stir only until dry ingredients are moistened. Carefully fold in cranberries. Spoon batter into 12 medium-sized muffin cups greased with Crisco. Bake at 400°F for 18-22 minutes or until browned.

Makes 12 muffins

POPPY CHEDDAR STICKS

1 cup hot milk (about 120°F)
¼ cup **Crisco Shortening**
1 tbsp. sugar
1 tsp. salt
2½ cups all-purpose flour
1 package quick-rise active dry yeast
½ cup grated sharp Cheddar cheese
1 egg
2 tbsp. water
2 tbsp. poppy or sesame seeds

Combine milk, Crisco, sugar and salt. Set aside and cool slightly. Combine flour, yeast and cheese in a large bowl. Stir in milk mixture until well blended. Turn onto a slightly floured surface. Knead for 5 minutes until smooth and elastic. Let rest for 10 minutes. Cut dough into 4 equal portions; divide each portion into 9 equal pieces. Roll pieces into 1" x 8" strips. Place on cookie sheet greased with Crisco. Combine egg and water, brush onto breadsticks. Sprinkle with poppy or sesame seeds, cover with tea towel. Let rest for 30 minutes. Preheat oven to 300°F. Bake for 40 minutes or until golden brown. Cool on racks.

Makes 3 dozen

CRÊPES AND PANCAKES

Variations of the basic pancake are found throughout the world, but whether you call them blintzes or waffles, griddle cakes or crêpes, the key word is delicious.

While the traditional pancake has become a breakfast staple, more and more people are discovering how versatile pancakes really are. By using a pancake to envelope your favorite meat, cheese or fruit filling you can create a hearty meal or a light and delicate dessert.

Flambé them, dust them lightly with sugar, or stack them high with butter and real maple syrup. Pancakes, crêpes and waffles are a treat that can be enjoyed any day.

Rice Waffles with Tropical Fruit Salsa (see page 46)

ZUCCHINI CRÊPES

6 small zucchini
2 tbsp. olive oil
2 tbsp. butter
2 scallions, chopped
¼ lb. mushrooms, chopped
¼ cup **Krinos Fillo**, dried and crumbled for fillo flakes
2 tbsp. chopped fresh parsley
1 medium tomato, finely chopped
½ cup tomato juice
2 tbsp. grated Parmesan cheese
salt and pepper to taste
½ lb. **Krinos Fillo Leaves**
½ stick butter, melted

Topping:

1 tbsp. butter
2 tbsp. bread crumbs
2 tbsp. Parmesan cheese

Clean and lightly scrape the outside of the zucchini. Cut off ends. Cut in half lengthwise and scoop out the seeds and a little pulp. Put 2 tbsp. of olive oil in a large skillet and sauté the zucchini quickly in the oil, turning over once or twice. Remove from pan and put them in salted boiling water to cover and cook for 10 minutes, or until just tender. Then cut into bite-sized pieces. While zucchini are cooking, add 2 tbsp. butter to the oil in the skillet and sauté the chopped scallions and mushrooms for 3-4 minutes. Add fillo flakes, stir a few times, then add chopped parsley and tomato. Add tomato juice and cook until it thickens. Add the cheese and salt and pepper. Drain the zucchini and spoon a portion on a prepared fillo crêpe *(see instructions for making crêpe shells in Chicken and Egg Crêpes)*. This filling will make 12 pieces. Spoon mushroom and tomato sauce on the zucchini pieces. Close the crêpes with the seams up. Brush tops of crêpes with butter and sprinkle with cheese and crumbs. Bake in a preheated 375°F oven for 20 minutes or until golden brown.

CHICKEN AND EGG CRÊPES

Filling:

1 cup chopped cooked chicken
2 eggs, hard boiled
2 tbsp. chopped scallions (green part only)
¼ cup chopped fresh mushrooms
1 cup cheese sauce
1 tsp. salt
½ tsp. pepper
1 tbsp. thyme
1 tbsp. lemon juice

Cheese Sauce:

1 cup milk
2 tbsp. butter
2 tbsp. flour
½ tsp. salt
¼ tsp. pepper
3 slices processed cheese

Crêpes:

¼ cup melted butter
6 **Krinos Fillo Leaves**

To make Cheese Sauce: Heat milk in double boiler to prevent scorching. Do not boil. In a small frypan, melt butter until it bubbles. Add flour, salt and pepper. Stir until it becomes a smooth mixture. Add this mixture to the warm milk, stirring constantly. Bring the milk to a boil. Boil for 1 minute. Remove from heat. Add the cheese and stir until all the cheese is melted. Chicken and Egg Filling: Premeasure all filling ingredients. Eggs should be mashed with a fork. In medium-sized bowl, combine chicken, eggs, scallions and mushrooms. Add cheese sauce and mix well. Add salt, pepper, thyme and lemon juice. Mix entire mixture thoroughly. (Optional: scallions and mushrooms can be sautéed in 1 tbsp. oil if tender texture is desired.) Divide mixture into equal portions depending upon desired size of crêpe. Place on waxed paper. To make Crêpes: Preheat oven to 400°F. Prepare crêpe shells 2 at a time to prevent fillo from drying out. (Fold fillo leaf in half lengthwise, then in half again to form a square. Fold corners in or cut them off to form a circle.) Butter the crêpe and spoon portions of filling on the middle of the crêpe. Fold ⅓ of the crêpe over the filling. Fold the other ⅓ of the crêpe over the filling. Place crêpe seam-side-up on greased shallow baking pan and brush with butter. Bake in oven for 15-20 minutes or until browned.

MEXICAN FILLO CRÊPES

Sauce:

1 large onion, chopped
1 tbsp. vegetable oil
3 garlic cloves, crushed
3 small serrano chiles, chopped
2 8-oz. cans tomato sauce
3 tbsp. chili powder
¾ lb. lean ground beef, browned and drained

Other ingredients:

½ lb. **Krinos Fillo Leaves**
1½ cups sour cream
½ lb. sharp Cheddar cheese, grated

To prepare sauce: Sauté onion and add remaining sauce ingredients except for meat. Simmer for 1 hour. Divide sauce in half and pour in 2 separate bowls. Add the meat to 1 bowl and leave the other meatless. Prepare fillo crêpe shells *(see Chicken and Egg Crêpes for folding directions)*. Spoon on meat sauce and then the sour cream. Fold up and place in a greased baking pan and bake in a preheated 350°F oven for 25-30 minutes or until golden brown. Five minutes before they are done, place grated cheese on crêpes and allow to melt. Serve while hot along with the extra meatless sauce.

CHILI FILLO CRÊPES

1 lb. ground beef
1 cup chopped onion
2 garlic cloves, crushed
1 16-oz. can whole tomatoes
¾ cup chopped celery
2-3 tbsp. chili powder
2 tsp. salt
pepper to taste
1 tsp. sugar
1 tbsp. Worcestershire sauce
1 15-oz. can kidney beans, drained
½ lb. **Krinos Fillo Leaves**
1 stick butter

Sauté beef, onion and garlic. Add next 7 ingredients and simmer for 1 hour. Add beans and bring to a boil. Simmer for 15 minutes. Make fillo crêpe shells and spoon mixture in crêpes *(see instructions for making crêpe shells in Chicken and Egg Crêpes)*. Bake in preheated 375°F oven for 20 minutes or until fillo is golden brown. Garnish with fresh green and red peppers for added color.

CRÊPES SUZETTE WITH GRAND MARNIER

Crêpes:

1 cup all-purpose flour

¼ tsp. salt

2 eggs

1¼ cup milk

1 tbsp. sugar

2 tbsp. melted butter

1 tbsp. **Grand Marnier**

Orange Sauce:

2 seedless oranges

¼ cup sugar

1 cup butter

½ cup **Grand Marnier**

¼ cup **Cognac Marnier-Lapostolle**

Combine all crêpes ingredients in a bowl, using a wire whisk or an electric hand mixer to beat the batter until smooth and creamy. Batter should be consistency of heavy cream. Add ¼ cup milk, if necessary. Crêpes will be more tender if batter is allowed to stand 1 hour before using. Rub the crêpe pan with a little melted butter. Spoon 2-3 tbsp. batter into pan and swirl pan around until bottom is evenly coated. Cook briefly until crêpe starts to brown on bottom. Turn crêpe and cook a few seconds on the other side. Turn out on waxed-paper-covered rack. Continue in this way until all the batter is used. To make Orange Sauce: Peel oranges and cut peel into very thin slivers. Squeeze oranges to get about ½ cup juice. Cream the slivered peel with sugar and ½ cup butter. Melt the remaining butter in a skillet or chafing dish. Add orange peel mixture and simmer 5-6 minutes. Stir in orange juice and ¼ cup Grand Marnier. Keep mixture hot over very low heat. Use a spoon to spread some sauce on unbrowned side of each crêpe. Roll crêpes, or fold into triangles. Arrange crêpes in pan or skillet, spooning sauce from pan over them. Place pan in a hot 400°F oven, bake for 5 minutes. Sprinkle with 1 tbsp. sugar and pour ¼ cup Grand Marnier and ¼ cup Cognac Marnier-Lapostolle. Ignite, and while flaming, ladle sauce over crêpes until flame dies.

Makes 12-24 crêpes

Crêpes Suzette with Grand Marnier

BEEF BURGUNDY CRÊPES

1½ lb. lean beef (round or sirloin), cut into bite-sized pieces

¼ cup vegetable oil

1 medium onion, thinly sliced and broken into pieces

¼ cup chopped parsley

½ lb. mushrooms, sliced

1 tsp. thyme

salt and pepper to taste

1 cup beef bouillon

½ cup red wine

3 tbsp. cornstarch

8 **Krinos Fillo Leaves**

1 stick butter

In a large skillet, brown beef in vegetable oil for 12-15 minutes. While the beef is browning, sauté onion, parsley and mushrooms in another skillet until tender. Add thyme, salt and pepper, beef bouillon and red wine. Simmer for 5 minutes. Add to beef. Pour out ¼ cup liquid from skillet into a bowl. Add cornstarch and make a smooth paste. Add to skillet to make a gravy. Stir and bring to a boil. Remove from heat and let cool 10 minutes. Prepare Krinos fillo for crêpes *(see Chicken and Egg Crêpes)*. Place in baking pan and then spoon mixture into crêpes and butter them. Keep seam-side-up. Bake in preheated 400°F oven for 15-20 minutes or until golden brown. (Optional: This can also be made into squares if crêpes are not preferred, using the same amount of fillo. Use 6 leaves on the bottom of the pan and 2 on top, covering the entire Beef Burgundy. Bake. Be sure to sprinkle each layer with bread crumbs or fillo flakes after buttering.)

GRIDDLE CAKES

2 cups sifted all-purpose flour

1 tbsp. sugar

1 tsp. **Cow Brand Baking Soda**

1 tsp. salt

2 eggs

2 cups buttermilk

2 tbsp. vegetable shortening, melted

Sift together flour, sugar, baking soda and salt. In large bowl, beat eggs until light and fluffy; stir in buttermilk and melted shortening. Add dry ingredients to liquid, beating until smooth. Pour a scant ¼ cup batter for each griddle cake onto hot griddle. (For thin griddle cakes, spread batter with spoon.) Turn griddle cakes as soon as they are puffed and full of bubbles but before bubbles break. Bake other side until golden brown. Serve immediately with butter and hot maple syrup.

Makes about 2 dozen 4" cakes

PANCAKES FLAMBÉES WITH GRAND MARNIER

½ pint milk
pinch salt
1 oz. sugar
2 eggs
4 oz. flour
1 oz. butter, melted
3½ oz. butter
sugar
5 tbsp. **Grand Marnier**

Pancake batter: Pour ⅔ of the milk into a bowl; add salt, sugar, eggs and flour and beat until the batter is smooth. Use as much of the remaining milk as needed to obtain the consistency required. Add the lukewarm melted butter. Fry each pancake in butter, sprinkle with sugar and fold in 4. Lay the pancakes on a buttered metal dish and put over gentle heat. Pour over the Grand Marnier and wait until it is warm before setting alight. Batter would be improved, with more aroma, by adding 1½ tbsp. Grand Marnier.
Makes 12 pancakes

GINGER PEACHY PINWHEEL PANCAKES

1 14-oz. can peach slices, reserve juice for syrup
1½ cups **Aunt Jemima Complete Pancake Mix**
¼ tsp. ground ginger
1 cup water
8 maraschino cherries
Peachy Syrup:
reserved peach juice
1 cup **Aunt Jemina Original Syrup**

Drain peaches well, reserving juice; set aside. In a bowl, combine pancake mix and ginger. Add water and stir until batter is fairly smooth. For each pancake pour about ¼ cup batter on hot, lightly greased griddle. On each pancake arrange 5 or 6 peach slices in a pinwheel with a cherry in the center. Gently push peach slices and cherries into batter. Turn pancakes carefully when edges look cooked. Turn only once. Serve with warm Peachy Syrup: combine reserved peach juice and 1 cup Aunt Jemima Original Syrup in a saucepan. Stir over medium heat until warm.
Makes 8

RICE PANCAKES OR WAFFLES WITH TROPICAL FRUIT SALSA

Tropical Fruit Salsa:
2 kiwi, peeled and diced
1 mango, peeled and diced
1 banana, peeled and diced
½ cup quartered red grapes
¼ cup granulated sugar
¼ cup lime juice
Rice Pancakes:
1¼ cups all-purpose flour
1 tbsp. granulated sugar
1 tbsp. baking powder
½ tsp. salt
1 cup cooked **Uncle Ben's Converted Brand Rice**, cooled
¼ cup butter, melted
2 eggs, lightly beaten
2 cups milk

For Tropical Fruit Salsa, stir fruit, sugar and juice together in small bowl. Set aside while preparing pancakes. To make pancakes, in large bowl, stir together flour, sugar, baking powder and salt with fork. Stir in rice. In small bowl, stir together butter, eggs and milk. Stir into dry ingredients until just barely moistened, ignoring lumps. Drop batter in ¼-cup batches onto hot, non-stick heavy skillet sprayed with cooking spray. Cook 2-3 minutes until top is bubbly. Turn and cook until bubbly side is well-browned. Serve immediately with salsa and yogurt.
Makes about 14 pancakes

Rice Waffles: For rice waffles, separate eggs; mix yolks in with butter and milk, but beat whites and fold into finished batter. Bake in seasoned waffle iron according to manufacturer's directions.
Makes 8-10 waffles

ALPEN FLAPJACKS

¼ cup margarine
1 tbsp. sugar
2 tsp. honey
1 cup **Alpen Mixed Cereal**

Melt margarine, sugar and honey in top of double boiler. Pour in Alpen and mix well. Pour mixture into greased shallow tin and press down well. Bake in 350°F oven for 15-20 minutes, until golden brown. Cut into fingers while still hot. Remove from tin when cold.

CINNAMON PANCAKES WITH BLUEBERRY SYRUP

Blueberry Syrup:
1 tbsp. **Club House Minute Tapioca**
⅓ cup water
½ cup maple syrup
1 10-oz. package frozen blueberries
Pancakes:
1 cup **Club House Rice Flour**
2 tsp. baking powder
1 tsp. **Club House Ground Cinnamon**
½ tsp. baking soda
½ tsp. salt
2 eggs
1¼ cups buttermilk or sour milk*
¼ cup butter or margarine, melted

For Blueberry Syrup, combine tapioca and water in small saucepan. Let stand 5 minutes. Stir in maple syrup and blueberries. Bring to boil; simmer over low heat for 5 minutes, stirring frequently until slightly thickened. To make pancakes, combine rice flour, baking powder, cinnamon, baking soda and salt. Beat eggs lightly; add buttermilk and melted butter. Stir into flour mixture, just until blended. Heat lightly greased frypan or griddle over medium-high heat. Pour about ¼ cup batter onto pan for each pancake. Cook until bubbles form on surface. Turn and brown other side. Serve with warm syrup.
*To sour milk, place 1 tbsp. white vinegar in measuring cup. Add milk and let stand a few minutes.
Makes about 12 pancakes or 4 servings

WAFFLES

2 cups sifted all-purpose flour
1 tbsp. sugar
1 tsp. **Cow Brand Baking Soda**
½ tsp. salt
2 eggs, separated
2 cups buttermilk
¼ cup vegetable shortening, melted

Sift together flour, sugar, baking soda and salt. In large bowl, beat together egg yolks, buttermilk and shortening; beat in dry ingredients until smooth. Beat egg whites until stiff; fold into batter. Pour batter from cup or pitcher onto center of hot waffle iron. Bake about 6 minutes or until steaming stops and waffle is lightly browned. Remove waffle carefully. Serve immediately.
Makes 3 9" square waffles

LOBSTER CRÊPES

½ cup flour
salt
2 eggs
½ cup milk
½ cup **Delisle Plain Yogurt**
1 tbsp. oil
Filling:
1 onion, chopped
1 bay leaf
1 cup milk
2 tbsp. butter
2 tbsp. flour
2 tbsp. dry sherry
1 tsp. Worcestershire sauce
1 tsp. dry mustard
½ cup **Delisle Plain Yogurt**
¼ cup Parmesan cheese
salt and pepper
½ lb. lobster meat

For crêpes, put flour and salt in a bowl. Make a well in the center, add eggs, milk, yogurt and oil. Mix thoroughly. Refrigerate at least 1 hour. For filling, put onion, bay leaf and milk in a small saucepan. Bring to boil; remove from heat and let rest 30 minutes to develop flavor. Melt butter, add flour and cook. Remove from heat, add strained milk. Return to heat and cook, stirring until thickened. Add sherry, Worcestershire sauce, mustard and yogurt, ½ the Parmesan cheese, salt and pepper. Put lobster in a bowl; add ½ the sauce; mix thoroughly and adjust the seasoning. Fill and roll crêpes and sprinkle with remaining Parmesan cheese. Bake at 425°F 8-10 minutes or until hot.

Serves 8

BACON CHEDDAR PANCAKES

1⅓ cups **Aunt Jemima Complete Pancake Mix**
1 cup shredded Cheddar cheese
5 slices bacon, cooked and crumbled
1 cup water
Poached Apple Slices in Syrup:
1 medium apple
2 cups **Aunt Jemina Original Syrup**

In a bowl combine pancake mix, cheese and crumbled bacon. Add water and stir until fairly smooth. For each pancake pour about ¼ cup batter onto a hot, lightly greased griddle. Turn pancakes when edges look cooked. Turn only once. Top each serving of two pancakes with Poached Apple Slices in Syrup: Core and quarter 1 medium apple (do not peel). Slice apple into a saucepan. Add 2 cups syrup. Cook over medium heat until syrup comes to a boil. Reduce heat and simmer until apples are just crisp on the outside.

Lobster Crêpes

SPINACH CRÊPES

8 8″ crêpes
¼ cup finely chopped onion
¼ cup butter or margarine
2 tbsp. **ReaLemon Reconstituted Lemon Juice**
1 tsp. salt
¼ tsp. pepper
1 10-oz. can condensed cream of chicken, celery or mushroom soup, undiluted
3 eggs, beaten
½ cup grated Parmesan and Romano cheese
2 10-oz. packages frozen chopped spinach, thawed and drained
Hollandaise Sauce
toasted slivered almonds to garnish (optional)

Preheat oven to 350°F. In large saucepan, cook onion in butter until transparent; stir in ReaLemon, salt, pepper, soup, eggs and cheese. Cook and stir about 5 minutes. Stir in spinach; heat thoroughly. Place about ½ cup spinach mixture on each crêpe; roll up and place seam-side-down in 13″ x 9″ baking dish. Bake 10-15 minutes or until hot. Serve with Hollandaise Sauce; garnish with almonds. Refrigerate leftovers.

Makes 8 crêpes

GINGER AND BANANA PANCAKES

Batter:
1 cup all-purpose flour
pinch salt
1 egg
1¼ cups milk
Filling:
3 bananas
1 tbsp. heavy cream
3 pieces **Sharwood's Stem Ginger**, chopped
confectioners' sugar
3 tbsp. brandy (optional)

Mix batter ingredients together and use to make a batch of pancakes. To prepare filling: Mash bananas together with the cream. Stir in the stem ginger. Divide this mixture between the pancakes and roll up each one. Dredge pancakes with confectioners' sugar. Set alight brandy and pour it over.

Makes 6-8 pancakes

EGG DISHES

Appealing morning, noon or night, eggs have a versatility and nutritional value matched by few foods.

Fragile as they may be, eggs are a powerful source of vital nutrients such as protein, iron and lecithin. They are a year-round favorite and are always affordable.

Fluffy omelets, light-as-air soufflés and sophisticated quiches are just a few of the imaginative egg dishes you'll find in the recipes ahead.

Omelette Flambée au Grand Marnier **(see page 52)**

CHILE RELLENO QUICHE

2 9″ deep-dish pie shells
2 12-oz. packages bulk pork sausage
1 onion, chopped
1 14-oz. can **Hunt's Tomato Sauce**
1 package taco seasoning mix
5 eggs
½ cup milk
3 tbsp. flour
2 4-oz. cans green chiles, diced
3 cups grated Jack cheese
1 2.2-oz. can ripe olives, sliced

Prebake pie shells at 400°F 15-20 minutes. Brown pork; drain fat. Add onion, tomato sauce and taco seasoning; simmer 10 minutes. Beat together next 3 ingredients. Layer chiles, pork mixture, cheese, olives and egg mixture in pie shells. Bake at 325°F 25-30 minutes. Let stand 10 minutes. May be frozen after cooking.
Each quiche serves 4-6

MINI CHEESE AND CORN SOUFFLÉS

2 tbsp. butter or margarine
2 tbsp. finely chopped onion
2 tbsp. flour
1 cup milk
¼ tsp. salt
dash garlic powder
dash cayenne pepper or hot red-pepper sauce
2 tbsp. grated Parmesan cheese
1 cup grated Cheddar cheese
2 eggs, separated
1 12-oz. can **Green Giant Niblets Whole Kernel Corn**, drained

Heat oven to 350°F. In medium saucepan, melt butter or margarine. Sauté onion; add flour. Gradually stir in milk and cook over medium heat until thickened. Stir in salt, garlic powder, cayenne, Parmesan and Cheddar cheese until melted. Remove from heat; stir in egg yolks and corn. Beat egg whites until stiff but not dry. Fold into cheese mixture. Pour into 6 buttered custard dishes. Place cups in baking dish. Bake for 25-30 minutes.
Serves 6

CURRIED QUICHE

1 8″ pie shell
Filling:
1 tbsp. butter or margarine
1 small onion, sliced
4 strips bacon
2 cups mushrooms, sliced
1 heaped tsp. **Sharwood's Madras Curry Powder**
3 eggs, beaten
⅔ cup plain yogurt
1 tbsp. tomato purée
parsley for garnish

Bake pastry shell for approximately 10 minutes. For filling, melt fat and pan fry onion, bacon and mushrooms. Add curry powder and cook for a further few minutes. Place this mixture in baked pastry shell. Beat together eggs, yogurt and tomato purée and pour over bacon mixture. Bake at 400°F for 25 minutes or until set. Garnish with sprig of parsley.
Serves 4

CHEESE LOAF

4 eggs, hard cooked and chopped
2 cups shredded Cheddar cheese
10 stuffed olives, chopped
8 small pickles, chopped
1 tbsp. chopped chives
1 tsp. **Sharwood's Mustard**
3 tbsp. mayonnaise
3 tbsp. heavy cream
salt and pepper

Mix together the eggs, cheese, olives, pickles and chives, reserving a few olives and pickles for garnish. Combine the mustard, mayonnaise and cream and blend this with the cheese mixture. Season to taste. Line a 9″ x 5″ loaf pan with foil, leaving sufficient foil at the sides to lift out. Pile the mixture into the pan and smooth the surface. Leave to chill for about 1 hour or until firm. Lift out from pan and carefully remove the foil. Garnish the top of the loaf with the reserved olives and pickles.
Serves 6 as a starter with toast or use as a sandwich spread

OMELET COPENHAGEN

4 large eggs
¼ tsp. salt
¼ tsp. white pepper
1 tbsp. water
2 tbsp. butter
½ cup diced avocado
1 cup (about 4 oz.) shredded **Danish Havarti**, **Creamy Havarti**, **Tybo** or **Samsoe Cheese**
¾ cup finely diced cooked turkey
sliced avocado, green pepper rings and parsley for garnish

In a medium mixing bowl, beat eggs with salt, pepper and water until well mixed, but not frothy. Heat an 8″ x 9″ omelet pan or heavy skillet over medium-low heat. Add butter, heating until it begins to sizzle. Tilt pan to coat bottom and sides with butter. Add eggs all at once to pan. With spatula, gently lift sides of omelet to let uncooked egg run underneath. When egg is set, spoon avocado, ½ cup cheese and turkey over half of omelet. Loosen edges with spatula, fold in half and quickly turn out onto serving plate. Sprinkle remaining ½ cup shredded cheese on top and garnish with sliced avocado, green pepper rings and parsley.
Serves 2

MUSHROOM QUICHE WITH BROWN RICE CRUST

1½ cups **Instant Brown MINUTE RICE**
1¼ cups water
4 eggs
1 10-oz. can cream of asparagus soup or cream of mushroom soup
⅓ cup milk
1 cup each diced **CRACKER BARREL Cheddar Cheese**, diced cooked chicken and sliced mushrooms
½ teaspoon rosemary

Bring water to boil in medium saucepan. Stir in rice; return to boil. Cover, reduce heat and simmer 5 minutes. Remove from heat. Let stand 5 minutes. Mix in 1 beaten egg, then press into greased 9″ pie plate. Beat soup, milk and remaining eggs. Stir in remaining ingredients; pour over prepared crust. Bake at 350°F for 50 minutes or until filling is set.
Serves 6-8

CAJUN-STYLE BRUNCH EGGS

1 tbsp. **PARKAY Margarine**

1 small onion, diced

1 19-oz. can stewed tomatoes (if desired, use a flavored variety such as Cajun or Italian)

4 eggs

1 cup grated **CRACKER BARREL Light Cheese**

In medium skillet, sauté onion in margarine until tender. Add tomatoes; bring to boil. Reduce heat; break eggs into pan. Cover and cook until eggs are almost set. Sprinkle with cheese; replace cover. Let stand to melt cheese.

Microwave Method: In a 2-quart microwaveable covered casserole, melt margarine on low for 30 seconds. Add onion. Cook on high 1-2 minutes until onions are soft. Add tomatoes. Cover and cook on high for 5-7 minutes until tomatoes boil. Break eggs over tomatoes. Pierce yolks. Cover and cook on high 3-5 minutes until eggs are desired doneness. Remove cover. Sprinkle with cheese. Cook on high 1 minute to melt cheese.

Serves 4

CHEESY DEVILLED EGGS

8 eggs, hard-cooked, peeled and halved

¼ cup **MIRACLE WHIP Salad Dressing**

¼ cup **CHEEZ WHIZ Process Cheese Spread**

pepper

Mix egg yolks, salad dressing and cheese spread until well blended and smooth. Season to taste with pepper. Pipe or spoon filling into egg halves.

Makes 16 hors d'oeuvres

CRISPY BAKED EGGS

1¼ cups grated **CRACKER BARREL Cheddar Cheese**

1¼ cups **POST BRAN FLAKES**

1½ tsp. melted **PARKAY Margarine**

4 eggs

salt and pepper

Combine 1 cup of the cheese with cereal. Pour margarine over cereal mixture and toss lightly to mix. Form a nest in four greased custard cups, or in four greased sections of a muffin pan. Break eggs carefully, slipping one into each nest. Sprinkle with salt and pepper. Bake at 325°F for 15 minutes. Top with reserved cheese and return to oven for about 5 minutes longer just to melt cheese.

Down-Home Garden Eggs

DOWN-HOME GARDEN EGGS

12 eggs

¼ cup water

salt and pepper, to taste

1 tbsp. **PARKAY Margarine** or butter

¼ lb. mushrooms, sliced

4 green onions, sliced

½ green pepper, coarsely chopped

½ sweet red pepper, coarsely chopped

1 small zucchini, coarsely chopped

1 medium tomato, coarsely chopped

¾ cup **CHEEZ WHIZ Light Pasteurized Cheese Product**, melted

Beat eggs and water. Season with salt and pepper. Melt ½ tbsp. margarine in non-stick frypan and add egg mixture. Scramble just until moist. Place in large oven-proof dish and keep warm in oven. Melt remaining margarine in frypan and sauté all vegetables until tender-crisp. Spoon over eggs. Drizzle cheese spread over top of eggs. Serve with toast or fresh homemade muffins.

Serves 6

Cheesy Broccoli Eggs Benedict

CHEESY BROCCOLI EGGS BENEDICT

1 8-oz. package **Green Giant Frozen Cut Broccoli in Cheese Sauce**

2 slices toasted bread or 1 English muffin, split and toasted

2 slices cooked ham, heated

2 poached eggs

Prepare Broccoli in Cheese Sauce as directed on package. Place toast or English muffin on serving plates; top each with a ham slice and poached egg. Divide Broccoli in Cheese Sauce into 2 equal portions; spoon over eggs. Serve each with a wedge of lemon.
Serves 2

OMELETTE FLAMBÉE AU GRAND MARNIER

4 eggs

⅛ tsp. salt

¼ cup unsalted butter

3 tbsp. **Grand Marnier**

1 cup orange marmalade
(or ¾ cup canned fruit salad)

6 tbsp. confectioners' sugar

In a bowl, whip the eggs with the salt. Melt the butter in a frypan. Pour in the eggs and cook like an ordinary omelet. Warm a serving dish. Warm the Grand Marnier. Slide the omelet onto the serving dish. Spread a layer of orange marmalade or fruit salad on and fold the omelet. Sprinkle with sugar. Pour the Grand Marnier immediately over the omelet and ignite it.
Serves 4

CREAMED EGGS

1 10-oz. can **Campbell's Condensed Cream of Celery**, **Chicken** or **Mushroom Soup**

⅓ cup milk

4 hard-cooked eggs, sliced

2 tbsp. chopped pimento

4 slices toast

In saucepan, blend soup and milk. Heat. Gently stir in eggs and pimento. Add extra milk if necessary; serve on toast.

Eggs Goldenrod: Omit pimento, separate cooked egg yolks and whites; chop whites coarsely; force yolks through a fine sieve. Blend soup and milk; heat and pour over toast. Arrange chopped egg whites in a ring on top of toast and soup; pile sieved egg yolks in center.
Serves 4

PIZZA QUICHE

pastry for a single-crust 9" pie *(see Crisco Pastry in Pies and Tarts)*

¾ lb. hot Italian-style pizza sausage

3 eggs

1¾ cups hot milk

2 cups shredded Mozzarella cheese

¼ cup finely chopped canned green chiles

Preheat oven to 400°F. Line 9" pie plate with pastry. Crumble sausage, removed from casing, if necessary. In skillet, cook sausage until browned, breaking up with fork; drain well. Beat eggs and stir in milk, sausage, cheese and chiles. Turn into pastry shell. Bake for 40-45 minutes or until knife inserted off center comes out clean. Let stand about 10 minutes before serving.
Serves 6

EGGS FOR TWO

2 small potatoes, chopped

1 tbsp. bacon drippings

2 tbsp. chopped onion

1 tbsp. chopped green chiles

1 tomato, chopped

½ tsp. salt

¼ tsp. pepper

½ tsp. ground coriander

5 **Krinos Fillo Leaves**

½ stick butter, melted for fillo

4 eggs, beaten

hot red-pepper sauce (optional)

In a skillet, sauté potatoes in bacon drippings until tender. Add chopped onion, chiles, tomato, salt, pepper and coriander. Sauté until tender. Remove from heat. Grease and layer a 9" x 9" baking pan with 5 fillo leaves. Butter each layer. Roll the edges in toward the rim of the pan to finish off the fillo and butter the edged rim. Pour the potatc mixture in the fillo-lined pan. Pour beaten eggs over this mixture. Bake in preheated 450°F oven for 10 minutes; lower heat to 350°F and bake for 20 minutes. The dish will be done when the eggs are firm and the fillo is golden brown.

SPANISH EGGS

½ cup chopped onion

¼ cup chopped green pepper

1 medium garlic clove, minced

1 tbsp. chili powder

2 tbsp. butter or margarine

1 10-oz. can **Campbell's Condensed Tomato Soup**

⅓ cup water

¼ cup sliced ripe olives

8 eggs

salt and pepper

shredded Cheddar cheese

tortillas

In saucepan, cook onion and green pepper with garlic and chili in butter until tender. Stir in soup, water and olives. Cook over low heat 15 minutes; stir occasionally. Pour half of soup mixture into a 2-quart shallow baking dish; break eggs into sauce. Spoon remaining soup mixture over eggs. Salt and pepper to taste. Bake eggs at 350°F for 10-15 minutes or until set. Garnish with cheese; serve with tortillas.
Serves 4

QUICHE LORRAINE

2 cups light cream

4 eggs, slightly beaten

¾ tsp. salt

¼ tsp. pepper

7 **Krinos Fillo Leaves**

½ stick butter, melted for fillo

12 slices bacon, crisply fried and crumbled

1 cup shredded Gruyère or Swiss cheese (or 2 cups if bacon is omitted)

⅓ cup finely chopped onion

Preheat oven to 450°F. Beat together cream, eggs, salt and pepper. Place fillo on greased 10" pie plate, in different directions, buttering each layer. (Bread crumbs can also be placed between each layer for a thicker bottom crust.) Trim edges and turn under toward rim of pie plate; butter fillo. Sprinkle bacon, cheese and onion in fillo-lined pie plate. Pour egg mixture into pie plate. Cook uncovered for 15 minutes. Reduce oven temperature to 325°F and bake 20-30 minutes or until knife inserted halfway between center and edges comes out clean. Let stand 10 minutes before cutting.

DOWN EAST SCRAMBLE

½ cup chopped green pepper

¼ cup chopped onion

2 tbsp. butter or margarine

1 10-oz. can **Campbell's Condensed New England Clam Chowder**

8 eggs, slightly beaten

dash pepper

In 10" frypan, cook green pepper and onion in butter until tender. In bowl, stir soup until smooth; gradually blend in eggs and pepper. Pour into frypan; cook over low heat; do not stir. As mixture begins to set around edges, gently lift cooked portions with large turner so that thin, uncooked portion can flow to the bottom. Continue gently lifting cooked portions until eggs are completely set, but still moist (about 8 minutes).
Serves 4

EGGS SUBLIME

1 10-oz. can **Campbell's Condensed Cream of Mushroom Soup**

4 softly poached eggs

2 tbsp. butter or margarine

⅓ garlic clove, finely chopped

2 tbsp. flour

⅓ cup milk

½ cup grated sharp Cheddar cheese

2 eggs, separated

Put ½ cup of the mushroom soup in the bottom of each of 4 individual au gratin dishes and place a poached egg on each. Melt butter in a small saucepan and sauté garlic briefly. Add flour, cook a minute or two, then add milk, slowly stir until smooth and thickened. Add grated cheese, stir, remove from heat, add egg yolks, blend well. Fold in stiffly beaten egg whites. Pile gently on top of the poached egg and mushroom mixture, spread lightly to the edges. Put in a 350°F oven 25-30 minutes or until the top puffs up and springs back when lightly touched.
Serves 4-6

Cheese Lovers' Crescent Quiche

CHEESE LOVERS' CRESCENT QUICHE

1 8-roll can **Pillsbury Refrigerated Crescent Dinner Rolls**

½ cup Swiss cheese (cut in ½" cubes)

½ cup Mozzarella cheese (cut in ½" cubes)

1 cup orange Cheddar cheese (cut in ½" cubes)

1 cup cooked ham (cut in ½" cubes)

1 small onion, chopped

2 eggs

dash cayenne pepper

2 tbsp. grated Parmesan cheese

Heat oven to 375°F. Separate crescent dough into 8 triangles. Place 5 triangles in a pie plate or quiche dish, pressing together to form a crust. (Reserve 3 triangles for top crust.) Combine Swiss cheese, Mozzarella cheese, Cheddar cheese, ham cubes and onion in a bowl. Arrange mixture in crust. In small bowl, beat eggs and add cayenne pepper; pour over pie. Press 2 remaining triangles together to form a rectangle. Cut rectangle and remaining triangle into ½" strips; criss-cross over filling to form lattice top. Tuck ends under bottom crust. Sprinkle with Parmesan cheese. Bake at 375°F for 25-30 minutes or until egg mixture is set in center. Let stand 5 minutes before serving.
Makes 1 quiche

EGGS IN CHEESE SAUCE

1 10-oz. can **Campbell's Condensed Cream of Celery** or **Mushroom Soup**

½ cup milk

½ cup shredded sharp Cheddar cheese

4 hard-cooked eggs, sliced

4 slices toast

chopped parsley, if desired

Combine soup, milk and cheese. Cook over low heat until cheese melts; stir often. Add eggs. Serve on toast, rice or asparagus; garnish with parsley.
Serves 2-3

EGGS FLORENTINE

2 cups chopped, cooked spinach or 2 10-oz. packages frozen, drained

6 eggs

1 10-oz. can **Campbell's Condensed Cream of Celery Soup** or **Mushroom Soup**

1 cup shredded mild processed cheese

Cover bottom of shallow baking dish 10" x 6" x 2" with cooked spinach; break eggs and place on top. Pour soup around eggs completely covering spinach; sprinkle with cheese. Bake in a 350°F oven 25-30 minutes or until eggs are done.
Serves 6

QUICK EGG CURRY

1 10-oz. can **Campbell's Condensed Cream of Mushroom Soup**

⅓ cup milk

1 tsp. curry powder

4 hard-cooked eggs, sliced

4 slices bread, toasted

shredded coconut, toasted slivered almonds, chutney or raisins

Stir soup until smooth; blend in milk and curry powder. Heat; stir often. Add eggs. Serve over toast with coconut, almonds, chutney or raisins.
Serves 4

MAKE-AHEAD BACON'N CHEDDAR STRATA

12 slices egg bread, crusts removed and cubed
12 slices crisply cooked bacon, crumbled
½ red pepper, chopped
3 green onions, sliced
4 cups grated **CRACKER BARREL Old Cheddar Cheese**
6 eggs
3 cups milk
½ tsp. salt
½ tsp. dry mustard
¼ tsp. pepper

Place half of cubed bread on bottom of greased 13″ x 9″ x 2″ baking dish. Cover bread with half the bacon, red pepper, onion and Cheddar cheese. Repeat layers again. In a small bowl, beat together eggs, milk and seasonings. Pour over bread mixture. Let stand in refrigerator for at least 3 hours or overnight before baking. Bake, uncovered, at 350°F for 45-55 minutes until knife inserted in center comes out clean. Let stand 10 minutes.
Serves 8-10

MIRACLE STRATA

8 slices white bread, cubed, divided
2 cups diced cooked ham
⅔ cup **MIRACLE WHIP Salad Dressing**
1 onion, chopped
1 celery stalk, chopped
1 green pepper, chopped
2 cups grated **CRACKER BARREL Cheddar Cheese**
4 eggs, well beaten
1½ cups milk

Cover bottom of greased 8″ x 12″ baking dish with half of the bread cubes. Combine salad dressing, ham, onion, celery and green pepper; spoon over bread. Sprinkle cheese over salad dressing mixture. Sprinkle rest of bread over cheese. Combine eggs and milk and pour over top. Refrigerate overnight. Heat oven to 350°F. Bake 45 minutes to 1 hour. Let stand 10 minutes before serving.
Serves 6

WILD SCRAMBLED EGGS

1 box **Uncle Ben's Long Grain & Wild Rice**
1 dozen large eggs, beaten
2 tbsp. butter or margarine
⅓ cup finely chopped onion
1 cup sliced mushrooms
¾ cup thinly sliced celery
⅓ cup diced green pepper
1 cup diced fresh tomato

Prepare rice according to package directions. Meanwhile, melt 1 tbsp. butter or margarine in a large frypan. Add eggs and hard scramble. Remove from pan when done and keep warm. Add remaining butter to pan and stir in onions and mushrooms. Cook over medium heat until onion is tender. Stir in celery and green pepper. Cook 5 minutes longer, then add tomato. Combine vegetables with hot rice. Coarsely chop scrambled eggs and fold into rice mixture.
Makes 8 1-cup portions

HERB OMELET

2 eggs
1 tbsp. fresh parsley, chopped
1 tsp. fresh chives, chopped
¼ tsp. tarragon, dried
⅛ tsp. **Tabasco** brand pepper sauce
1 tbsp. unsalted butter or margarine

In small bowl, combine eggs, parsley, chives, tarragon and Tabasco pepper sauce. Melt butter in a non-stick 7″ or 8″ omelet pan or skillet; heat until bubbly. Pour egg mixture into heated pan; let set around edges. Gently lift edges with spatula as eggs set, tilting pan to allow uncooked portion to run underneath. Shake pan occasionally to keep omelet moving freely. Continue to cook until center is almost set. Fold in half. Slide omelet onto serving plate.
Serves 1

EASY EGGS CELESTINE

2 tbsp. butter or margarine
2 tbsp. all-purpose flour
¼ tsp. curry powder
1 10-oz. can **Campbell's Condensed Chicken Broth**
½ cup milk
½ tsp. salt
¼ tsp. pepper
1 cup asparagus tips, drained and cut into pieces
4 hard-cooked eggs, sliced
toast points

In a frypan over medium heat, melt butter and stir in flour and curry powder until blended. Gradually stir in chicken broth and milk; cook, stir until thickened. Stir in salt, pepper, asparagus and eggs; heat. Serve over toast.
Serves 2

"CROWD-SERVIN" CHEESY OMELET BAKE

12 slices bread, crusts removed
2 cups cubed ham
1 package frozen broccoli, thawed and chopped
⅓ cup finely chopped onion
8 **KRAFT DE LUXE Process Cheddar Cheese Slices**, halved
6 eggs
½ tsp. salt
½ tsp. pepper
½ tsp. dry mustard
3 cups milk

Place 6 slices of bread on bottom of greased 13″ x 9″ x 2″ baking dish. Cover bread with half of the ham, broccoli, onions and cheese. Repeat layers again, omitting cheese layer. Beat eggs and seasonings in a bowl. Gradually blend in milk. Pour over ham mixture. Refrigerate 3 hours or overnight. Bake uncovered at 350°F for 45 minutes. Place remaining cheese on top and bake 10-15 minutes longer or until cheese is melted. Let stand 10 minutes before serving.
Serves 8-10

SANDWICHES

When we think of sandwiches we often think of the traditional luncheon creations. The not-so-humble sandwich, however, can also make a star appearance as a dainty hors d'oeuvre or canapé, an ingenious open-faced creation, a crispbread snack or a hot or cold main dish.

While filling or topping combinations are limited only by your imagination, a good, fresh bread is essential to making any truly great sandwich. Why not experiment a little? French, Italian, pumpernickel, potato, egg, raisin, rye, whole wheat, crispbreads, fruit breads, hard rolls, even croissants offer some excellent alternatives to the old standby, enriched white.

In this chapter you'll find imaginative sandwich ideas that are sure to please.

Wasa Crisp Sandwiches (see page 58)

WASA CRISP SANDWICHES

On buttered **Wasa Crisp**, try the following combinations of ingredients for individual sandwiches: Salami and onions, grated cheese, paté and sliced cucumbers, sliced tomatoes and lettuce, pastrami and thinly sliced cooked chicken, fish roe, sliced hard-cooked eggs and sardines, or Havarti cheese.

FRENCH TOASTED HAM AND CHEESE

1 6½-oz. can flaked ham
¼ cup **Hellmann's or Best Foods Real Mayonnaise**
2 tbsp. sweet pickle relish
1 tsp. prepared mustard
¼ tsp. dried oregano leaves
⅛ tsp. pepper
12 slices rye bread
6 Mozzarella cheese slices
3 eggs
¾ cup milk
2 tbsp. **Mazola Corn Oil**

Sauce:

1 garlic clove, finely chopped
2 tbsp. **Mazola Corn Oil**
½ cup **Hellmann's or Best Foods Real Mayonnaise**
2 tbsp. milk
1 tsp. prepared mustard

Mash ham with fork. Mix in mayonnaise, relish, mustard, oregano and pepper. Spread evenly on 6 slices of bread. Cut cheese slices to fit bread and place on top of ham. Top with remaining bread slices. Beat together eggs and milk. Pour into shallow pan. Place sandwiches in egg mixture and dip. Turn sandwiches to coat second side. Cook sandwiches in 2 tbsp. oil in skillet until browned on both sides and cheese begins to melt. Keep warm. In small saucepan, soften garlic in remaining oil over medium heat. Remove from heat and whisk in mayonnaise, milk and mustard. Serve over sandwiches.
Makes 6

IDEAL CRISPBREAD WARM SANDWICHES

On **Ideal Crispbread**, spread butter and add 1 or more of the following combinations for individual open-face sandwiches. Place in 500°F oven for 5 minutes.

Paprika, cucumber, tomato and cheese.
Boiled ham and tomato, topped with cheese.
Caviar, whipped egg whites, grated cheese and chives.
Mustard, sausage, tomato ketchup and cheese.
Minced meat mixed with onions, capers and beet-root, tomato ketchup and cheese.
Herrings, leeks and cheese.
Sardines, chopped pickles and cheese.
Mushrooms and cheese.
Seafood and cheese.
Scrambled eggs, anchovies and cheese.

IDEAL CRISPBREAD COLD SANDWICHES

With **Ideal Crispbread**, you can make delicious sandwiches with combinations of the following ingredients: Goat cheese, cooked and sliced potatoes, pickled herring, chives, cod roe, chopped onion, minced meat, caviar, tuna fish, mayonnaise, paté, bacon, pickles, leeks, crème fraîche, cottage cheese, grated cheese, grated carrots, orange marmalade, salami, pieces of fruit, etc.

OPEN-FACE RUEBEN SANDWICH

1 lb. sliced cooked corned beef
8 slices rye bread, toasted
3 cups prepared coleslaw
4 slices (about 4 oz.) Swiss cheese, cut in half
1 10-oz. can **Campbell's Condensed Cream of Onion Soup**
½ cup milk
¼ cup ketchup
2 tbsp. mayonnaise
2 tbsp. sweet pickle relish
dash hot red-pepper sauce

On baking sheet, arrange half of corned beef on bread slices. Top with coleslaw and remaining corned beef. Cover; bake at 400°F for 15 minutes or until hot. Top with cheese; bake uncovered until cheese melts. Meanwhile, combine remaining ingredients. Heat; stir occasionally. Serve over sandwiches.
Makes 8 open-face sandwiches

CLUB-ON-A-BUN

1 cheese or onion bun
1 tbsp. **MIRACLE WHIP Salad Dressing**
lettuce
1 tomato, thinly sliced
2 slices turkey or ham
4 slices **KRAFT SINGLES Process Cheese Food**
3 slices crisply cooked bacon

Cut bun into three slices horizontally. Place sliced bun on baking sheet; bake at 350°F for 5 minutes until lightly toasted. Spread one side of each slice with salad dressing. Place lettuce, tomato, turkey and 2 cheese slices on bottom slice of bun; top with middle slice. Repeat layers using bacon instead of turkey; top with top slice of bun.
Makes 1 sandwich

WHOLESOME PITA SANDWICHES

2 large whole wheat pita rounds, cut in half
¼ cup **MIRACLE WHIP Light Salad Dressing**
fresh spinach leaves
4 **KRAFT SINGLES Light Slices**
red onion rings

For each sandwich, spread inside of bread with salad dressing, add spinach leaves, cheese slices and onion rings.
Serves 4

CRAB MUSHROOM CROISSANTS

1 5-oz. can crabmeat, drained
½ cup **Hellmann's or Best Foods Real Mayonnaise**
1 tbsp. chopped green onion
½ tsp. dried marjoram leaves
⅛ tsp. pepper
4 croissants or English muffins, split and buttered
2 tomatoes, sliced
1 cup sliced mushrooms
2 tbsp. melted butter
¼ tsp. dried marjoram leaves
½ cup grated Swiss cheese

Mix crabmeat, mayonnaise, green onion, ½ tsp. marjoram and pepper. Spread on croissants. Place tomato slices on crabmeat and then top with sliced mushrooms. Stir ¼ tsp. marjoram into melted butter and brush on mushrooms. Top with cheese. Broil sandwiches until cheese is bubbly, about 5 minutes.
Makes 8 sandwiches

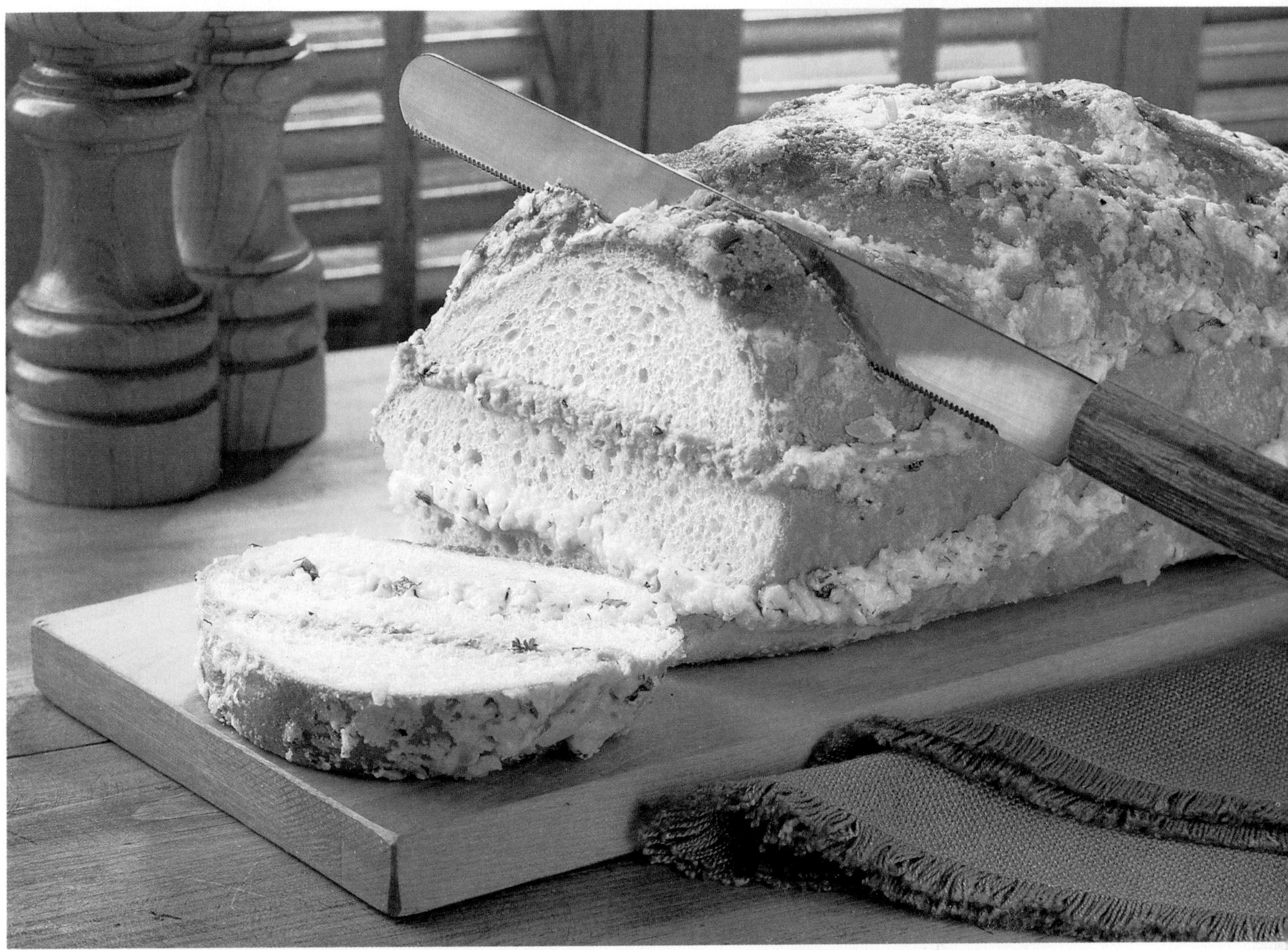

Triple Treat Hot Sandwich Loaf

TRIPLE TREAT HOT SANDWICH LOAF

1 loaf French bread, unsliced

½ cup **Hellmann's or Best Foods Real Mayonnaise**

Egg Filling:

3 hard-cooked eggs, chopped

⅓ cup **Hellmann's or Best Foods Real Mayonnaise**

2 tbsp. chopped green onions

½ tsp. dried dillweed

salt and pepper to taste

Salmon Filling:

1 7¾-oz. can salmon, drained

¼ cup **Hellmann's or Best Foods Real Mayonnaise**

1 tbsp. lemon juice

1 tbsp. chopped parsley

1 tsp. basil leaves

⅛ tsp. pepper

Topping:

½ cup butter

¼ cup **Hellmann's or Best Foods Real Mayonnaise**

½ cup grated Cheddar cheese

¼ cup grated Parmesan cheese

1 tbsp. finely chopped green onion

¼ tsp. tarragon leaves

¼ tsp. basil leaves

¼ tsp. garlic powder

Make 2 lengthwise cuts through bread and spread with mayonnaise. Prepare fillings and topping. Spread egg mixture on bottom slice. Top with middle slice of bread. Spread salmon mixture on top of middle slice and top with remaining bread slice. Spread topping over loaf. Wrap and chill 2 hours. Unwrap and bake at 350°F for 20 minutes.

FRUIT-AND-CHEESE-FILLED TUNA SANDWICHES

½ cup mayonnaise

½ cup sour cream

1 tbsp. fresh lemon juice

¼ tsp. curry powder

⅛ tsp. dried thyme

⅛ tsp. salt

1 7-oz. can tuna, drained and flaked (water packed, light)

2 cups **Danish Havarti** or **Creamy Havarti Cheese**, diced

1 cup seedless grapes, halved

1 cup fresh apple, diced

Blend together mayonnaise, sour cream, lemon juice and spices. Fold in tuna, cheese, grapes and apples. Serve on toasted French bread or whole grain bread. Garnish with fresh fruit.

Serves 6

GREEK SPICED LAMB PITAS

1 lb. boneless lamb shoulder or leg roast, thinly sliced
4 pita breads
Marinade:
3 tbsp. olive oil
1 tbsp. lemon juice
rind of 1 lemon, finely grated
1 tbsp. chopped parsley
1 tsp. **Sharwood's Madras Curry Powder**
1 small onion, minced
2 garlic cloves, minced
Salad:
lettuce
green pepper
black olives
tomatoes
3 tbsp. lemon juice

Mix together the marinade ingredients. Toss the lamb in the marinade and leave for 1 hour. Meanwhile, prepare salad and toss in lemon juice. Warm the pita breads. Broil lamb for 10-15 minutes, turning frequently and brushing with marinade. Slit pita breads open and pile some lamb and salad into each. If preferred, the lamb may be served with rice allowing 1½ cups of uncooked rice for 4 servings.
Serves 4

MUSSEL TOASTIES

1 tin **Marina Mussels in Brine**
1 package white sauce mix
3 oz. Cheddar cheese
4 slices bread
lettuce
1 tomato, cut in wedges

Drain mussels. Make up sauce mix as directed on the package. Stir in mussels. Grate cheese, stir into sauce. Toast 1 side of the slices of bread. Turn over and butter the untoasted sides. Spread on mussel mixture and grill for 5 minutes. Serve on a bed of shredded lettuce, garnished with tomato wedges.
Serves 4

MEXICAN SLOPPY JOES

1 lb. ground beef
1 cup chopped onion
1 cup chopped celery
1 tsp. chili powder
½ tsp. salt
dash pepper
1 tbsp. shortening
1 10-oz. can **Campbell's Condensed Tomato Soup**
6 buns, split and toasted

Brown beef with onion, celery and seasonings in shortening. Stir to break up meat. Add soup; simmer to blend flavors. Serve on buns.
Serves 6

FLORENTINE CROISSANTS

1 small package frozen chopped spinach
¼ cup minced onion
2 tbsp. butter
2 cups milk
¼ tsp. ground nutmeg
½ tsp. salt
½ cup **Veloutine Light**
2 tsp. lemon juice
8 large croissants, split and warmed
½ cup **Hellmann's or Best Foods Real Mayonnaise**
8 hard-cooked eggs, peeled and sliced

Cook spinach; drain well, squeezing out extra moisture. Sauté onion in butter until limp. Add milk, nutmeg and salt; bring just to boil. Sprinkle in Veloutine, stirring constantly. Boil 1 minute. Add drained spinach and lemon juice. Spread each croissant with mayonnaise and then spread bottom halves with ⅓ cup of spinach mixture. Arrange sliced egg over spinach mixture. Put tops of croissants in place.
Serves 8

Florentine Croissants

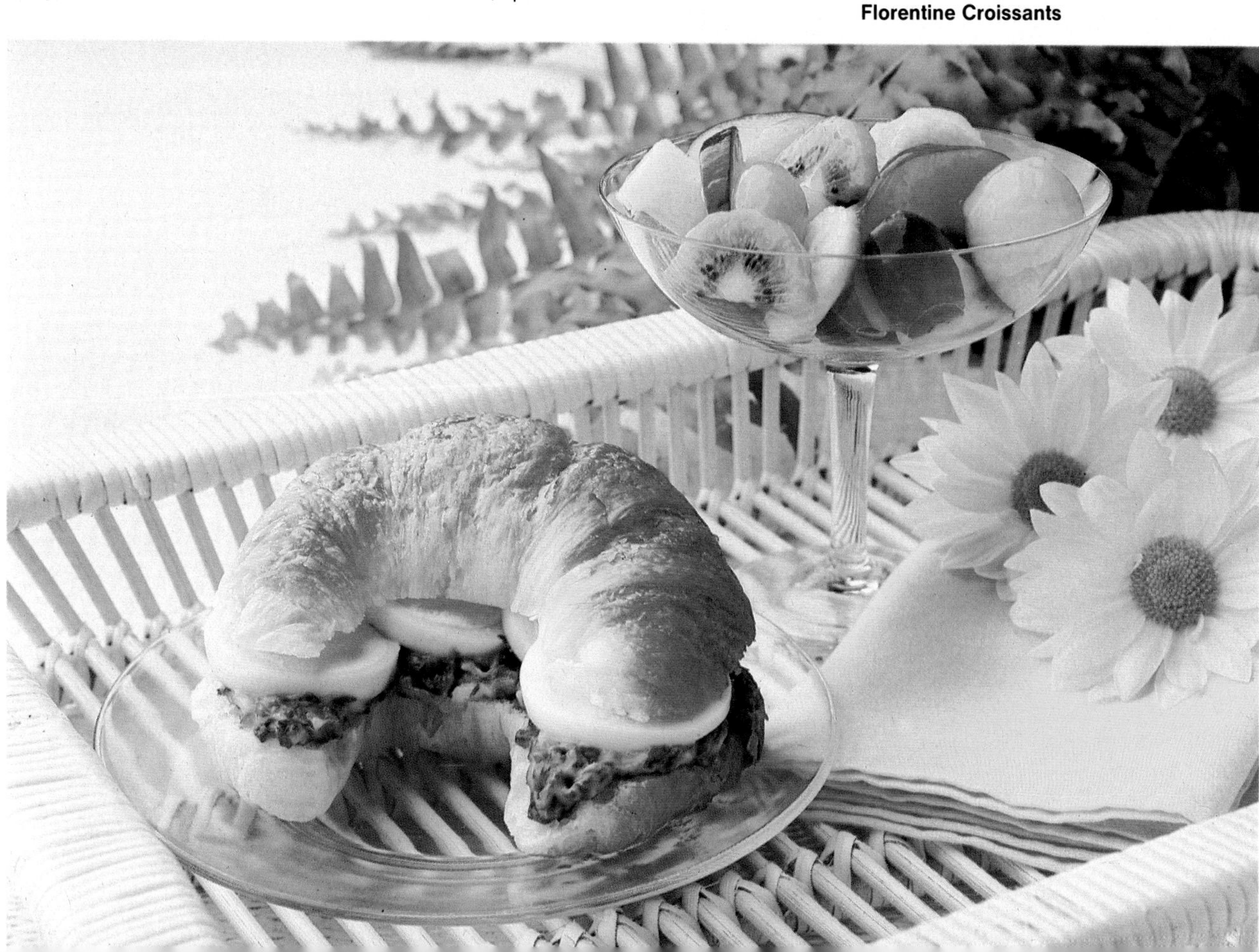

HEARTY SALAD ROLLS

- 2 cups diced cooked turkey or chicken
- 2 cups diced cooked ham
- 6 slices bacon, cooked and crumbled (optional)
- 1 cup shredded Cheddar or Swiss cheese
- 1½ cups diced green pepper
- 1 cup chopped **Bick's Sweet Mixed Pickles**
- 1 cup mayonnaise
- ¼ cup chopped green peppers
- 8 cheese buns or crusty rolls
- lettuce (optional)

Combine first 8 ingredients. Mix well. Season to taste. Split buns. Butter if desired. Line bottom with lettuce leaf. Spoon on salad filling. Cover with bun tops.
Makes 8 sandwiches

FROM THE BEEF INFORMATION CENTRE

SPICY BEEF PITA SANDWICHES

- ½ lb. cooked roast beef, sliced ⅛″ thick
- ¾ cup **KRAFT Zesty Italian Dressing**
- 2 green onions, sliced
- 2 medium red or green peppers, cut into julienne strips
- ¼ lb. **KRAFT Swiss Sliced Cheese**, cut into ¼″ strips
- ⅓ cup **KRAFT Real Mayonnaise**
- 6 pita pocket breads, cut in half

Cut beef into julienne strips. Combine dressing, onions, roast beef and peppers; cover and chill several hours or overnight. Drain beef mixture, reserving dressing. Add cheese to drained beef mixture. Combine mayonnaise with reserved dressing. Fill pita bread with beef and cheese mixture and top with mayonnaise mixture.
Makes 12 sandwich halves

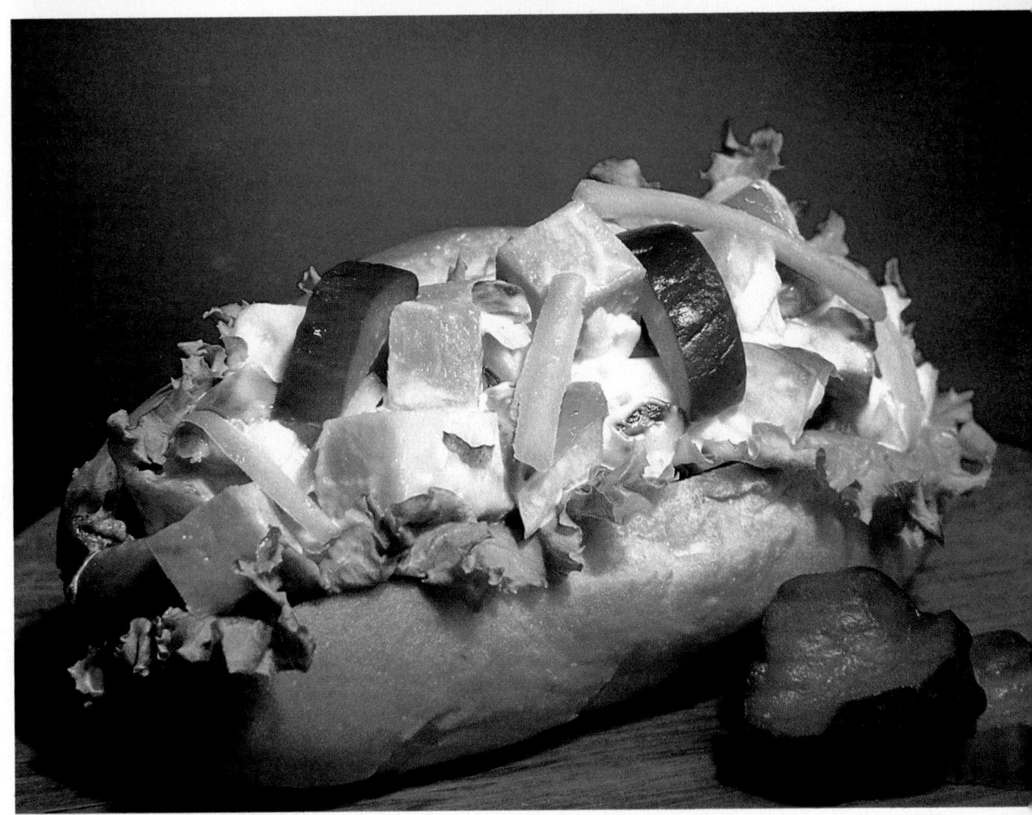

Ham-Cheese Spread Deluxe (top)
Hearty Salad Rolls (bottom)

HAM-CHEESE SPREAD DELUXE

- 1 8-oz. package cream cheese, softened
- ½ cup chopped **Bick's Yum Yum Pickles**
- ¼ cup grated carrots
- ¼ cup chopped walnuts
- 1 tbsp. mayonnaise
- 12 thin slices of ham or corned beef
- 4-6 bagels or kaiser buns, split

Combine first 5 ingredients. Mix well. Layer ham on bottom halves of buns and spread cheese mixture on cut surface of tops. Sandwich together.
Makes 4-6 sandwiches

SALADS AND DRESSINGS

We live in a contradictory age. On one hand we strive to eat right and develop healthy lifestyles; on the other, we strive to get ahead. Considering the time pressures placed on us daily, "fast foods" can look very tempting. But why not opt for the healthy alternative that many North American fast-food giants are discovering? Salads...they can be the quickest, easiest and most nutritious "fast foods" around. With today's emphasis on health and fitness, more and more people are making salads a major part of their diet.

Not just made of lettuce anymore, salads can take a variety of forms...from exotic seafood creations to imaginative cheese, pasta, vegetable or fruit combinations, from crisp appetizers to more satisfying light meals.

Many salads require special dressings...and choosing the right one to complement your ingredients is key. Use only high-quality oils and vinegars and the freshest herbs and spices, because only the best is good enough for your great salad.

Marinated Summer Salad (top), Apple Valley Salad (center) and Capri Salad **(see page 64)**

Hot Dilled Bean Salad

MELLOW GARDEN ASPIC

3 envelopes unflavored gelatin

1 28-oz. bottle **E.D. Smith Garden Cocktail**

1 tsp. salt

½ tsp. **Lea & Perrins Worcestershire Sauce**

⅔ cup water

1 8-oz. package cream cheese, softened

1 cup mayonnaise

2 tbsp. sugar

2 tbsp. lemon juice

½ tsp. salt

1 cup coarsely grated unpeeled cucumber

¼ cup finely chopped green onion

¼ cup chopped parsley

In a medium saucepan, sprinkle 2 envelopes gelatin over 1 cup Garden Cocktail. Heat to dissolve. Stir in remaining Garden Cocktail, salt and Lea & Perrins. Pour into an 8-cup jelly mold or fluted tubepan. Chill until firm. In a small saucepan, sprinkle 1 envelope gelatin over ⅔ cup water. Heat to dissolve. Beat cream cheese. Gradually add gelatin mixture, beating until smooth. Fold in remaining ingredients. Pour over firm aspic layer; chill. Unmold onto a lettuce lined serving platter.
Serves 12

HOT DILLED BEAN SALAD

¼ cup water

3 green onions, finely chopped

2 tsp. finely chopped fresh dill

1 tomato, peeled and chopped

1 14-oz. can **Libby's Deep-Browned Beans**

dash hot red-pepper sauce

salt and pepper to taste

In a medium saucepan, cook onions, dill and tomato in ¼ cup water until onions are just tender. Blend in beans and seasonings. Heat mixture thoroughly. Serve warm over lettuce as a hot salad. This salad may also be served chilled.
Serves 6-8

SENSATIONAL SALAD DRESSING

1 garlic clove, minced

3 tbsp. freshly grated Parmesan cheese

2 tbsp. lemon juice

1 tbsp. red wine vinegar

1 tsp. **Lea & Perrins Worcestershire Sauce**

½ tsp. salt

½ cup olive oil

salad greens

Combine all ingredients; whisk to blend. Serve with assorted salad greens.
Makes ¾ cup

APPLE VALLEY SALAD

1 package **Wish-Bone Italian Salad Dressing Mix** or ½ cup **Wish-Bone Italian Salad Dressing**

4 cups shredded cabbage

2 medium apples, quartered, cored and diced

¼ cup chopped green onion

½ medium green bell pepper, slivered

1 tsp. sugar

1 tsp. **Lawry's Seasoned Salt**

¼ tsp. **Lawry's Seasoned Pepper**

Prepare Italian Dressing according to package directions if using mix. Chill dressing. Toss cabbage, apples, green onion and green pepper. Sprinkle with sugar, Seasoned Salt and Seasoned Pepper. Add ½ cup prepared dressing and toss.
Serves 6

CAPRI SALAD

1 head cauliflower, broken into flowerets

1 onion, sliced in rings

3 zucchini, thinly sliced

1 green pepper, diced

½ cup diced celery

1 cup pitted ripe olives, drained

1 cup prepared **Wish-Bone Caesar Dressing Mix** or **Wish-Bone Caesar Salad Dressing**

Combine vegetables in large bowl. Heat Caesar Dressing but do not boil. Add hot dressing to vegetables; toss. Cover and refrigerate at least 4 hours, tossing several times.
Serves 10-12

MARINATED SUMMER SALAD

1 package **Wish-Bone Italian Salad Dressing Mix** or 1 cup **Wish-Bone Italian Salad Dressing**

1 bunch broccoli

1 red onion, diced

1 large tomato, diced

1 cup grated Cheddar cheese

Prepare Italian Dressing according to package direction if using mix. Use only the buds and uppermost part of broccoli stalk and chop. Add remaining ingredients to dressing and marinate overnight.
Serves 10

CAESAR SALAD DRESSING

3 tbsp. red wine vinegar
1 tsp. lemon juice
1 garlic clove, minced
salt and pepper to taste
1 tsp. Dijon mustard
½ cup **Mazola Corn Oil**

Stir together vinegar, lemon juice, garlic, salt, pepper and mustard. Slowly beat in corn oil. Serve with crisp torn romaine lettuce and toss with Parmesan cheese.
Makes ¾ cup

CHEF'S SECRET DRESSING

¾ cup sugar
½ cup ketchup
1 tbsp. finely chopped onion
1½ tsp. salt
1½ tsp. celery seed
1½ tsp. paprika
1½ cups **Mazola Corn Oil**
½ cup cider vinegar

Stir together sugar, ketchup, onion, salt, celery seed and paprika. Alternately beat in oil and vinegar slowly. Serve with crisp tossed salad.
Makes 2 cups dressing

ORIENTAL CABBAGE SALAD

1 green cabbage, sliced in ¼" strips
2 cups fresh spinach leaves, washed and sliced in strips
¾ cup **KRAFT French Dressing**
¼ cup brown sugar
3 tbsp. soy sauce
1 tbsp. lime juice
½ tsp. ground ginger
2 green onions, thinly sliced
2 tbsp. sesame seeds, toasted

In large bowl, toss together cabbage and spinach. Whisk together remaining ingredients except green onions and sesame seeds. Pour half the dressing over cabbage and spinach. Sprinkle with green onions and sesame seeds. (Remaining dressing can be refrigerated for later use. Recipe can be halved.) Chill.
Serves 8

Four Bean Salad

FOUR BEAN SALAD

1 14-oz. can **Libby's Deep-Browned Beans**, drained
1 cup **Libby's Red Kidney Beans**, drained
1 cup green beans, cooked, cut into 2" pieces
1 cup wax beans, cooked, cut into 2" pieces
1 small onion, finely chopped
½ cup chopped green pepper
½ cup chopped celery
¼ cup drained and chopped pickled beets
⅓ cup Italian dressing
salt and pepper to taste

In a large bowl, gently toss all ingredients together. Chill for at least 1 hour. Serve on lettuce.
Serves 12

ZESTY MAILLE VINAIGRETTE

¾ cup virgin olive oil
¼ cup **Maille Red Wine Vinegar**
3 tbsp. **Maille Mustard with Tarragon**
1 tsp. salt
⅛ tsp. pepper
1 medium garlic clove, crushed
½ tsp. sugar
2 tbsp. water

Combine all ingredients in blender or processor. Blend until smooth. Pour over salads or vegetables to enhance their flavor.

DOUBLE-DANISH PASTA SALAD

4 oz. pasta (medium shells, bow ties, elbow macaroni, etc.)
2 6-oz. jars marinated artichoke hearts
4 oz. **Danish Natural Cream Cheese with Herbs and Spices**
6 tbsp. milk
dash ground red pepper
3 oz. cooked Danish ham, cubed
½ cup frozen peas, thawed
6 oz. **Danish Fontina Cheese**
round loaf of French or Italian Bread (optional)
crisp salad greens (optional)

Cook pasta according to package directions until just tender (al dente). Drain but do not rinse. Transfer to large mixing bowl. Add artichokes and marinade and toss well. Let cool. Meanwhile, prepare dressing by blending cream cheese, milk and red pepper until smooth. Combine dressing with pasta, ham and peas. Chill about 1 hour, if desired. Just before serving, cut Fontina into 1" x ¼" sticks. Add to salad and toss gently. Hollow out bread to make salad bowl, or serve in regular salad bowl and garnish with a few crisp greens.
Serves 6

Carrot and Raisin Rice Salad (top)
Kumquat Salad (bottom)

HONEY TARRAGON SALAD DRESSING

1¼ cups **Hellmann's or Best Foods Real Mayonnaise**
2 tbsp. red wine vinegar
1 tbsp. honey
1 tsp. dried tarragon leaves
½ tsp. dried thyme leaves
½ tsp. paprika
½ tsp. salt
⅛ tsp. pepper

Whisk all ingredients together and serve over assorted salad greens.
Makes 1½ cups dressing

KUMQUAT SALAD

1 cup chopped fresh pineapple
1 cup minced candied kumquats
½ cup green grapes, cut in 2 and seeded
Dressing:
1 cup **Delisle Plain Yogurt**
½ tsp. dried tarragon
1 tbsp. lemon juice
salt and pepper
6 lettuce leaves

Mix pineapple, kumquats and grapes. Combine dressing ingredients and stir into fruit salad. Refrigerate. Just before serving, arrange lettuce leaves on 6 individual plates. Spoon fruit salad onto lettuce.
Serves 6

CARROT AND RAISIN RICE SALAD

½ cup **Uncle Ben's Converted Brand Rice**
1⅓ cups water
1 tsp. butter or margarine
1½ cups coarsely shredded carrots
⅓ cup diced celery
½ cup seedless raisins
4 tsp. finely chopped onion
⅓ cup mayonnaise
⅓ cup sour cream
½ tsp. lemon juice

Combine rice, water and butter or margarine in a large saucepan. Bring to a boil. Cover; reduce heat to medium-low and boil gently for 20-25 minutes until most of the water is absorbed. Remove from heat. Makes approximately 1½ cups cooked rice. Cover and chill several hours or overnight. Combine carrots, celery, raisins and onion and add to chilled rice. Toss lightly to mix. Combine mayonnaise, sour cream and lemon juice and stir into rice mixture. Cover and chill until ready to serve.
Makes 6 ½-cup portions

SPINACH SALAD WITH HOT BACON DRESSING

1 10-oz. package spinach, cleaned
½ lb. mushrooms, sliced
4 slices bacon
2 tbsp. minced onion
¾ cup water
¼ cup vinegar
1 tbsp. sugar
¼ tsp. salt
⅛ tsp. black pepper
3 tbsp. **Veloutine Dark**

Tear spinach into bite-sized pieces. Combine with mushrooms in large salad bowl. Cook bacon in skillet until crisp. Remove bacon and crumble. Add onion to bacon drippings; sauté 1-2 minutes. Gradually stir in water, vinegar, sugar, salt and pepper; bring to boil. Sprinkle in Veloutine; stirring constantly. Boil 1 minute. Pour over bacon, spinach and mushrooms; toss and serve at once.

SESAME-ZUCCHINI RICE SALAD

1 box **Uncle Ben's Long Grain & Wild Rice Blend**
2 cups water
1 tbsp. margarine or butter
1/3 cup sesame seeds
1/2 cup Italian salad dressing
1 1/2 cups zucchini, with seeds removed and cut into strips about 2" long
1/2 cup thinly sliced radishes
1/3 cup finely diced carrots
2 tsp. lemon juice
2 tsp. coarsely grated lemon rind
2 tbsp. sesame seeds, toasted

In a large saucepan, combine the seasoning packet and water. Bring to a boil over high heat. Meanwhile, combine the rice and sesame seeds with the margarine (or butter) in a large frypan. Sauté the mixture until lightly browned. Add to the seasoned water. Bring the mixture to a boil; stir well. Cover and reduce heat to medium-low. Simmer until most of the water has been absorbed (about 20 minutes). Remove from heat. Stir in Italian salad dressing. Chill for several hours. Before serving, combine cold rice mixture with zucchini, radishes, carrots, lemon juice and rind. Place in serving dish, sprinkle with toasted sesame seeds and serve.
Makes 8 1/2-cup portions

LUNCHEON TOSTADA SALAD

1 lb. ground beef
1 package **MexiCasa Taco Seasoning Mix** or **Lawry's Taco Seasoning Mix**
3/4 cup water
3/4 tsp. **Lawry's Seasoned Salt**
1 14-oz. can red kidney beans, drained
4 tomatoes, cut in wedges
1 avocado, peeled and cut in thin slices
1 package nacho chips
1 head lettuce, torn in small pieces
2 cups grated Cheddar cheese
1 cup chopped onion
3/4 cup **MexiCasa Taco Relish** or **Lawry's Chunky Taco Sauce**

Brown ground beef; drain fat. Add Taco Seasoning Mix, water, Seasoned Salt and beans. Bring to boil, reduce heat, cover and simmer 10 minutes. Reserve some tomato wedges, avocado slices and nacho chips for use as a garnish. Combine all remaining ingredients in a large salad bowl; add hot ground beef mixture and lightly toss all ingredients. Garnish with reserved tomato, avocado and chips. Serve immediately.
Serves 6-8

Luncheon Tostada Salad (top)
Sesame-Zucchini Rice Salad (bottom)

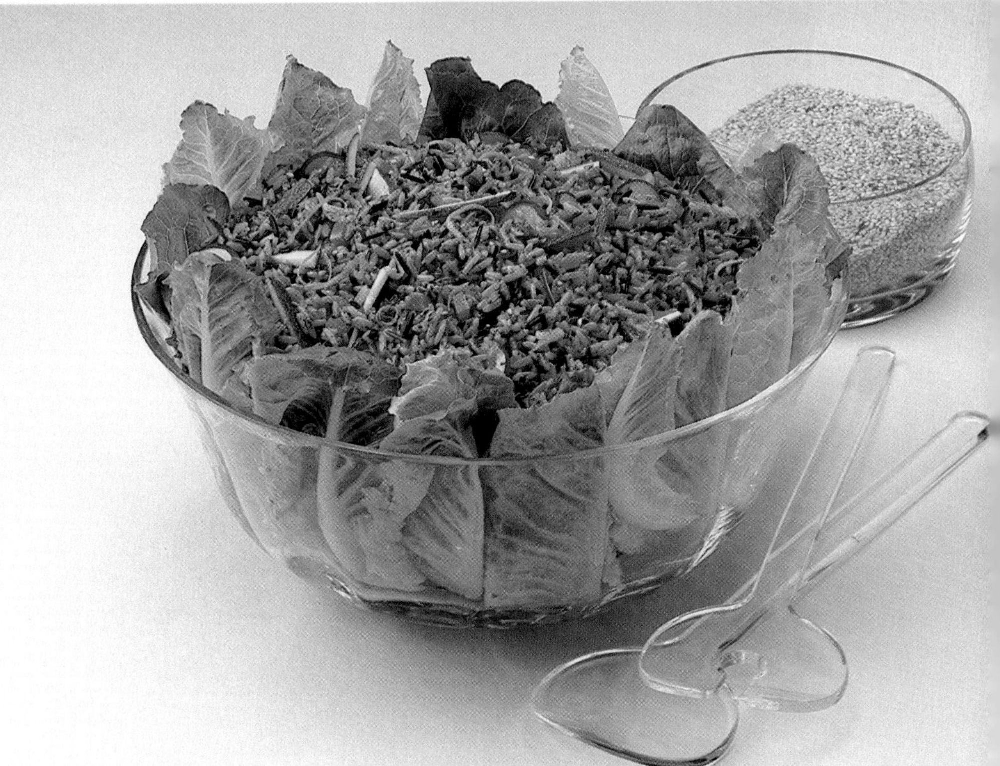

RED AND GREEN COLESLAW

2 cups shredded red cabbage
2 cups shredded green cabbage
2 cups diced, unpeeled apples
3/4 cup **Hellmann's or Best Foods Real Mayonnaise**
2 tbsp. cider vinegar
1/4 cup chopped onion
1 tsp. dried oregano leaves
1/2 tsp. salt
1/8 tsp. pepper
1/2 cup walnut pieces

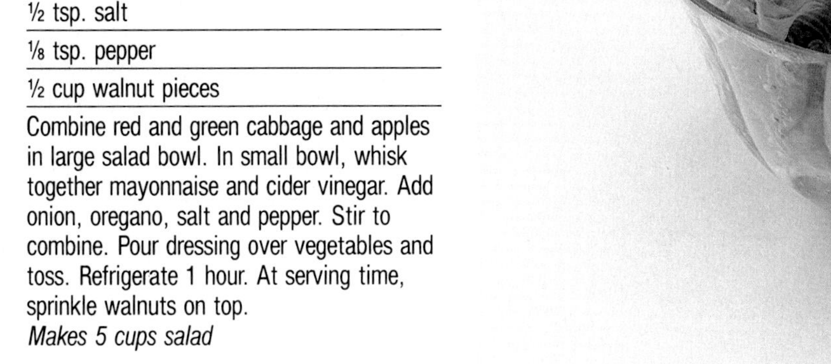

Combine red and green cabbage and apples in large salad bowl. In small bowl, whisk together mayonnaise and cider vinegar. Add onion, oregano, salt and pepper. Stir to combine. Pour dressing over vegetables and toss. Refrigerate 1 hour. At serving time, sprinkle walnuts on top.
Makes 5 cups salad

BASQUE SALAD

6 cups new potatoes, cooked and diced (about 6 medium)

1 small package frozen whole green beans, cooked and drained

1 package **Wish-Bone Italian Salad Dressing Mix** or 1 cup **Wish-Bone Italian Salad Dressing**

lettuce leaves

1 tsp. **Lawry's Seasoned Salt**

3 tbsp. minced green onion

1 tbsp. sliced ripe olives

1 tomato, cut in wedges

1 cup julienne ham or 1 7½-oz. can crabmeat (optional)

Combine potatoes and green beans (while warm) in a shallow dish. Prepare Italian Dressing Mix according to directions if using mix. Pour dressing over vegetables, cover and marinate overnight in refrigerator. Line a salad bowl with lettuce leaves; arrange potato-bean mixture over greens and sprinkle with Seasoned Salt. Add green onions and ripe olives; garnish with tomato wedges. Add ham or crabmeat if desired. Toss before serving.
Serves 8

TOMATO SHRIMP BASKETS

1 10-oz. can **Campbell's Condensed Cream of Chicken Soup**

¼ cup mayonnaise

½ tsp. salt

dash crushed tarragon leaves

2 cups cut up cooked shrimp or cubed cooked chicken

2 hard-cooked eggs, chopped

½ cup chopped celery

½ cup chopped green pepper

2 tbsp. thinly sliced green onions

6 medium tomatoes

salt

pepper

In bowl, blend soup, mayonnaise, ½ tsp. salt and tarragon. Stir in shrimp, eggs, celery, green pepper and onions; chill. Place tomatoes stem-end-down. With knife, cut each tomato almost to stem end, making 5 or 6 sections; spread apart slightly. Season with salt and pepper; fill with shrimp mixture. Arrange on salad greens.
Serves 6

Basque Salad

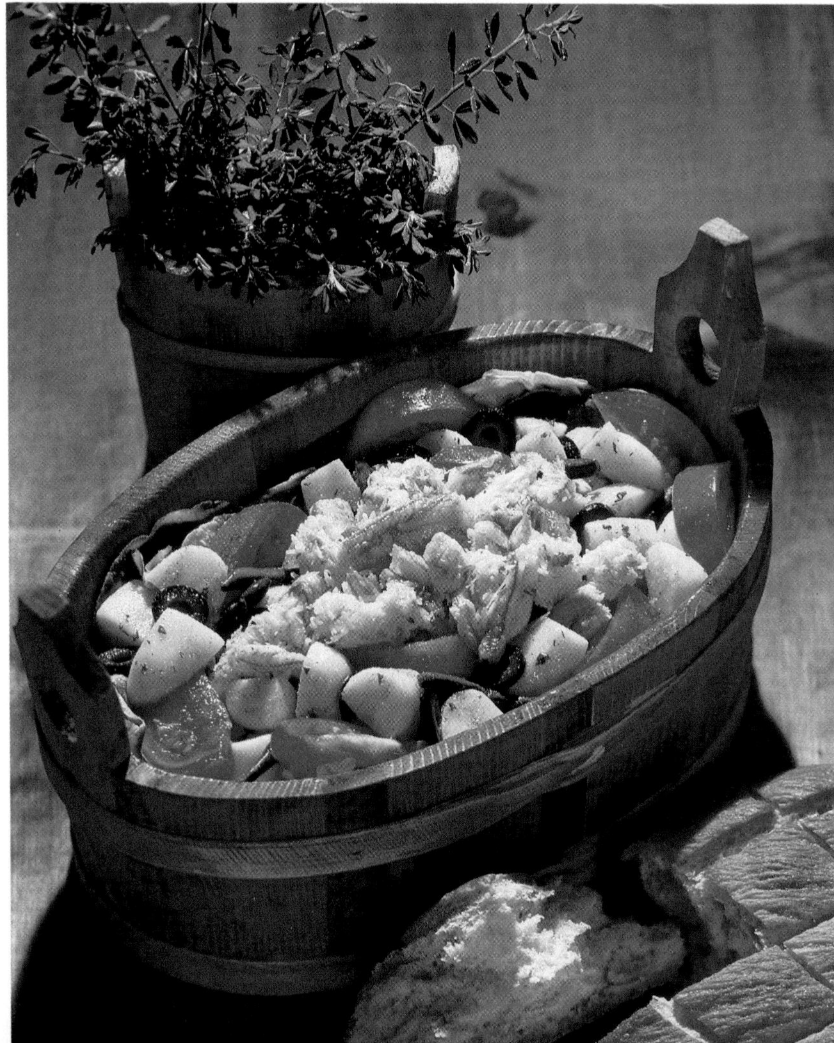

SPINACH SALAD À LA RUSSE

1 10-oz. can **Campbell's Condensed Tomato Soup**

½ cup sour cream

¼ cup milk

2 tsp. prepared horseradish

8 cups spinach, torn in bite-sized pieces

4 hard-cooked eggs, sliced

2 3¼-oz. cans sardines, drained

1 cup sliced cucumber

½ cup sliced red onion

½ cup sweet gherkin pickles, cut in strips

To make dressing, blend soup, sour cream, milk and horseradish; chill. In large bowl, layer remaining ingredients. Serve with dressing.
Serves 4

CRUNCHY CUCUMBER SALAD

1 10-oz. can **Campbell's Condensed Cream of Celery Soup**

½ cup sour cream

2 tbsp. finely chopped onion

¼ cup chopped radishes

generous dash pepper

4 cups thinly sliced cucumbers (about 4 medium)

Combine soup, sour cream, onion, radishes and pepper. Add cucumbers; chill. Serve on salad greens; garnish with parsley and additional radishes.
Makes 4 cups

CUCUMBERS IN SOUR CREAM DRESSING

1 10-oz. can **Campbell's Condensed Cream of Celery Soup**

½ cup sour cream

2 tbsp. finely chopped dill pickle

2 tbsp. finely chopped onion

2 tbsp. finely chopped radishes

generous dash pepper

4 cups thinly sliced cucumber (about 4 medium)

lettuce

parsley

Mix soup, sour cream, pickle, onion, radish and pepper; add cucumber. Chill; serve on lettuce; garnish with parsley and additional radishes.
Serves 6-8

Chef's Salad Pacifica

CHEF'S SALAD PACIFICA

4 cups torn romaine lettuce
2 medium heads butter lettuce, torn into bite-sized pieces
cucumber slices
julienne strips of chicken or turkey and ham
crisp crumbled bacon
julienne strips of Swiss cheese
artichoke halves or quarters, cooked and cooled
sliced fresh mushrooms
asparagus tips, cooked and cooled
hard-cooked eggs, chopped
croutons
1 tsp. **Lawry's Seasoned Salt**
½ tsp. **Lawry's Seasoned Pepper**
1 cup prepared **Wish-Bone Salad Dressing Mix** or **Wish-Bone Salad Dressing** (any flavor)

Combine romaine and butter lettuce in large bowl. Choose any or all of the next 9 ingredients and arrange them over lettuce. Sprinkle with Seasoned Salt and Seasoned Pepper. Add your favorite dressing and toss.
Serves 8

CRAB LOUIS

1 10-oz. can **Campbell's Condensed Tomato Soup**
¼ cup mayonnaise
½ cup chopped green pepper
¼ cup chopped dill pickle
¼ cup finely chopped onion
3 tbsp. prepared horseradish
2 tbsp. lemon juice
1 tbsp. Worcestershire sauce
1 lb. (about 2 cups) well-drained cooked Alaskan king crabmeat
3 medium avocados, cut in half

Blend soup and mayonnaise. Add green pepper, pickle, onion, horseradish, lemon juice, Worcestershire and crab; chill. Spoon into avocado halves. Arrange on salad greens; garnish with lemon wedges.
Makes 4½ cups

SUMMER SUPPER SALAD

1 10-oz. can **Campbell's Condensed Cream of Mushroom Soup**
¼ cup chopped celery
¼ cup chopped onion
¼ cup chopped green pepper
½ tsp. prepared mustard
dash hot red-pepper sauce
dash pepper
¼ tsp. rosemary
2 cups cooked macaroni
2 cups diced cooked ham
tomatoes, cut in wedges

Combine soup, celery, onion, green pepper, mustard, hot red-pepper sauce, pepper and rosemary. Add macaroni and ham; chill. Serve with tomato wedges.
Serves 4

AVOCADOS WITH CONSOMMÉ

2 10-oz. cans **Campbell's Condensed Consommé**
½ cup sherry
3 avocados
lemon juice
pepper
6 tbsp. sour cream

Add sherry to consommé, chill and jell in square or loaf pan. Halve and seed avocados, season with lemon juice and pepper. Unmold jellied consommé, cut into cubes, fill hollows of avocados. Garnish with sour cream.
Serves 6

HAM AND MACARONI TOSS

1 10-oz. can **Campbell's Condensed Cream of Chicken Soup**
¼ cup chopped celery
¼ cup chopped onion
2 tbsp. chopped green pepper
½ tsp. prepared mustard
dash hot red-pepper sauce
dash pepper
2 cups cooked macaroni
1½ cups diced cooked ham
tomatoes, cut in wedges

Combine soup, celery, onion, green pepper, mustard, hot red-pepper sauce and pepper. Add macaroni and ham; chill. Serve with tomato wedges.
Serves 4

RICE AND LENTIL SALAD

3 cups cooked **Uncle Ben's Converted Brand Rice**
1 19-oz. can lentils, drained and rinsed
1 cup sliced celery
½ cup diced red onion
½ cup unpeeled cucumber
½ cup roasted red peppers
¼ cup chopped fresh coriander or parsley
¼ cup fresh lemon juice
3 tbsp. olive oil
2 tbsp. red wine vinegar
salt and pepper
thin unpeeled cucumber slices

In large bowl, gently stir together rice, lentils, celery, onion, diced cucumber, red peppers and coriander. In measuring cup, stir together lemon juice, olive oil, vinegar and salt and pepper to taste. Pour over rice mixture and toss gently to coat. (Salad can be prepared, covered and refrigerated for up to 1 day ahead; add more lemon juice if necessary to moisten it after it sits.) To serve, mound on large platter and surround with circle of overlapping thin cucumber slices.
Serves 8

Carrot and Pineapple Salad

SIMPLE CAESAR

1 head romaine lettuce, washed and dried
4 croutons
1 large clove garlic, minced
3-4 drops Worcestershire sauce
1 tsp. Dijon mustard
1 egg yolk (optional)
3 tbsp. lemon juice
½ cup olive oil
croutons for garnish
salt and pepper to taste
¼ cup **KRAFT Grated Parmesan Cheese**

In a bowl, mash 4 croutons into crumbs with a wooden spoon. Add garlic, Worcestershire sauce, mustard and egg yolk (if desired) and blend into a thick paste. Whisk in lemon juice. Add oil very slowly, drop by drop, whisking until smooth and thick. If mixture seems too thick, add more lemon juice. Toss romaine leaves with dressing to coat. Place on serving plates and sprinkle with Parmesan.
Serves 4

RAISIN COLESLAW

1 10-oz. can **Campbell's Condensed Cream of Asparagus Soup**
¼ cup mayonnaise
5 cups shredded cabbage
1 cup grated carrot
½ cup raisins

In large bowl, mix soup and mayonnaise. Add remaining ingredients; toss gently to mix well. Cover; refrigerate 2-4 hours.
Makes 4 cups

CARROT AND PINEAPPLE SALAD

2 cups grated carrots
1 cup diced celery
1 14-oz. can pineapple chunks
½ cup chopped dates
salt
1 cup **Delisle Plain Yogurt**
lettuce

Mix together the carrots, celery, pineapple and dates. Chill. At serving time, salt and add yogurt. Serve on lettuce.
Serves 6

SCALLOP AND MUSHROOM SALAD

¾ cup dry white wine
½ tsp. **McCormick Shellfish Seasoning**
1 lb. sea scallops
2 green onions, thinly sliced
1 cup sliced mushrooms
lettuce
Dressing:
⅓ cup mayonnaise
¼ cup sour cream
1 tbsp. lemon juice
½ tsp. **McCormick Shellfish Seasoning**
1 tsp. **McCormick Parsley Flakes**

In saucepan, bring wine and shellfish seasoning to a boil. Add scallops and simmer 2-3 minutes or until tender. Drain scallops, reserving 2 tbsp. liquid. Chill. Combine mayonnaise, sour cream, lemon juice, ½ tsp. shellfish seasoning, parsley flakes and reserved cooking liquid. Toss with chilled scallops, onions and mushrooms. Serve on lettuce.
Serves 4

ORANGE ROMAINE SALAD

¼ cup vegetable oil
1 tbsp. lemon juice
1 tbsp. mayonnaise
1 tsp. **McCormick Lemon & Pepper Seasoning**
¼ tsp. salt
1 head romaine lettuce, torn into bite-sized pieces
1 small red onion, sliced and separated into rings
1 10-oz. can mandarin orange segments, drained
¼ cup slivered almonds, toasted*

In jar with tight fitting lid, combine oil, lemon juice, mayonnaise, lemon & pepper seasoning and salt. Shake well until smooth; chill until serving time. In large bowl, combine romaine, onion, oranges and almonds. Toss with dressing just before serving.
*To toast almonds, place on baking sheet. Bake at 350°F about 5 minutes.
Serves about 6

CHEESE-STUFFED PEAR SALADS

- 4 Anjou or Bosc pears
- lemon juice
- 1 cup shredded **Danish Fontina**, **Tybo**, **Elbo** or **Milk Havarti** (chill cheese well before shredding)
- ¼ cup chopped cashew nuts
- 2 tbsp. mayonnaise
- salad greens
- fresh strawberries
- French dressing

Halve and core pears. Brush cut sides with lemon juice. Combine shredded cheese and cashew nuts. Toss with mayonnaise. Arrange 2 pear halves on each of 4 salad plates lined with greens. Fill centers with cheese mixture. Garnish plates with fresh strawberries. Accompany with choice of favorite French dressings.
Serves 4

PEAR SHRIMP SALAD

- 4 Anjou or Bosc pears
- lemon juice
- ½ lb. cooked shrimp
- ¼ cup chopped celery
- ¼ cup chopped green pepper
- 1 tbsp. chopped green onion
- 1 tbsp. chopped pimento

Creamy Danablu Dressing:

- ¼ lb. **Danablu (Danish Blue) Cheese**
- ½ cup sour cream
- juice of ½ lemon
- 2 tsp. grated onion
- ¼ tsp. salt
- ⅛ tsp. paprika
- dash sugar

Prepare dressing by crumbling cheese and combining with remaining dressing ingredients; chill 1 hour to blend flavors. Core pears and cut into wedges. Dip in lemon juice to keep bright. Arrange, spoke fashion alternating skin-side-up and down, in 4 salad bowls. Combine shrimp, celery, green pepper, green onion and pimento. Toss with enough dressing to coat lightly. Spoon shrimp mixture in center of pear wedges. Serve remaining dressing on the side.
Serves 4

PEAR CHEESE PINWHEEL SALADS

- 3 Anjou or Bosc pears
- lemon juice
- **Danish Esrom Cheese**
- prosciutto
- grapes
- clear French dressing

Core pears and cut each into 8 wedges. Dip pear wedges in lemon juice to prevent discoloration. Slice cheese into small sticks. Wrap half of pear wedges in thin slices of prosciutto. Arrange pear wedges and cheese sticks, alternating in spoke fashion, on each of 4 salad plates. Place small cluster of grapes in center. Serve with clear French dressing.
Serves 4

CREAMY DANABLU AVOCADO DRESSING

- ½ ripe avocado
- ½ cup sour cream
- ⅓ cup dry white wine
- 2 tbsp. lemon juice
- 1 tbsp. finely chopped green onion
- 1 garlic clove, mashed
- dash cayenne pepper
- salt to taste
- ½ cup **Danish Blue Cheese**, crumbled

In small bowl, mash avocado with a fork. Blend in sour cream, then add wine, lemon juice, green onion, garlic, cayenne pepper and salt to taste. Fold in the blue cheese, cover and chill to allow flavors to blend.
Makes 1¾ cups

Cheese-Stuffed Pear Salads (left), Pear Cheese Pinwheel Salads (center) and Pear Shrimp Salad

COPENHAGEN DRESSING

1½ cups Danish French Dressing
¼ cup **Danish Blue Cheese**, crumbled
½ cup mayonnaise
½ cup sour cream
½ cup watercress leaves
3-4 tender parsley leaves
2 green onions, cut in several pieces with a bit of the green

Prepare the recipe for Danish French Dressing in electric blender. Add blue cheese, mayonnaise, sour cream, watercress, parsley and green onions. Blend at medium speed for about 40 seconds until light and creamy and a delicate shade of green. The watercress and parsley leaves should be in fine pieces. Store in refrigerator several hours before serving, or overnight.
Makes approximately 3 cups

DANISH FRENCH DRESSING

⅓ cup red wine vinegar (or white wine vinegar or half wine vinegar and half lemon juice)
⅓ cup olive oil
⅓ cup salad oil
1 tsp. salt
⅛ tsp. white pepper
dash paprika
dash cayenne pepper
1 tsp. sugar
1 garlic clove, crushed
½ cup **Danish Blue Cheese**, crumbled

Combine all ingredients except cheese in a jar with a tight fitting lid and shake well to blend. Add crumbled Danish Blue Cheese and shake to blend.
Makes 1½ cups

Copenhagen Dressing (left), Creamy Danablu Dressing (center) and Danish French Dressing

CREAMY DANABLU DRESSING

¼ lb. **Danablu (Danish Blue) Cheese**
½ cup sour cream
juice of ½ lemon
2 tsp. grated onion
¼ tsp. salt
⅛ tsp. paprika
dash sugar

Crumble cheese. Combine with remaining ingredients. Chill 1 hour to blend flavors.
Makes 1 cup

CREAMY DANABLU DRESSING WITH BUTTERMILK

½ cup **Danish Blue Cheese**
½ cup mayonnaise
½ cup sour cream
⅓ cup buttermilk
1 tsp. lemon juice
¼ tsp. onion powder
¼ tsp. garlic powder
freshly ground pepper

In a small bowl, crumble blue cheese with a fork. Blend in mayonnaise, sour cream and remaining ingredients. Refrigerate several hours or overnight for flavors to blend.
Makes 2 cups

SUNSHINE FIESTA SALAD

3 cups cooked rice
½ cup diced red and green pepper
½ cup chopped celery
½ cup chopped walnuts
1 10-oz. can mandarin orange sections
½ cup **Hellmann's or Best Foods Real Mayonnaise**
¼ cup **Mazola Corn Oil**
2 tbsp. white vinegar
2 tbsp. finely chopped onion
½ tsp. salt
¼ tsp. dried marjoram leaves
⅛ tsp. pepper

Combine rice, red and green pepper, celery and walnuts. Drain mandarin orange sections reserving ¼ cup juice. Stir together this juice and mayonnaise. Add to rice mixture and mix well. Marinate 1 hour. In small jar, shake together oil, vinegar, onion, salt, marjoram and pepper. Stir into rice mixture at serving time. Fold in drained orange sections.
Makes 4 cups salad

CALIFORNIA CAESAR SALAD

½ cup vegetable oil
⅓ cup **ReaLemon Reconstituted Lemon Juice**
1 egg, beaten
2 garlic cloves, crushed
2 medium heads romaine lettuce, torn into bite-sized pieces
2 medium tomatoes, diced
1 ripe avocado, sliced
1 cup seasoned croutons
⅓ cup grated Parmesan cheese
¼ cup sliced green onions
¼ cup bacon bits

Combine oil, ReaLemon, egg and garlic; mix well. Refrigerate for at least 1 hour. Combine remaining ingredients in large salad bowl. Toss with dressing just before serving.
Serves 6-8

TANGY THOUSAND ISLAND DRESSING

1 cup mayonnaise or salad dressing
½ cup chili sauce
¼ cup **ReaLemon Reconstituted Lemon Juice**
2 tsp. sugar
½ tsp. salt
2 hard-cooked eggs, finely chopped
½ cup finely chopped green pepper
¼ cup finely chopped onion
3 tbsp. pickle relish

In medium bowl, combine mayonnaise, chili sauce, ReaLemon, sugar and salt; mix well. Stir in remaining ingredients. Refrigerate.
Makes 2½ cups

TARRAGON FRENCH DRESSING

¾ cup **Crisco Oil**
¼ cup tarragon vinegar
1 tsp. sugar
¾ tsp. salt
¼ tsp. paprika
¼ tsp. dry mustard
¼ tsp. pepper
1 garlic clove, halved
¼ tsp. Worcestershire sauce
⅛ tsp. thyme

Combine all ingredients in a screw-top jar. Cover tightly and shake vigorously to blend well. Store covered in refrigerator. Shake well before using.
Makes 1 cup

California Caesar Salad

FRESH SPINACH SALAD

1 lb. fresh spinach
¼ lb. bacon, fried crisp and crumbled
1 hard-cooked egg, diced
1 small red Italian onion, separated into rings

Wash and pat dry spinach. Add bacon, diced egg and Italian onion. Pour Red Wine Vinegar Dressing over all and toss lightly to coat evenly.
Serves 4-6

MUSTARD DRESSING

3 egg yolks
2 tbsp. prepared yellow or brown mustard
1 tbsp. lemon juice
2 tsp. cider vinegar
2 tsp. sugar
1 tsp. seasoned salt
3-4 drops hot red-pepper sauce
1½ cups **Crisco Oil**

Place egg yolks in medium mixing bowl. Beat at high speed until thick and lemon colored. Add mustard, lemon juice, vinegar, sugar, seasoned salt and hot red-pepper sauce. Beat at low speed until blended. Add Crisco Oil and beat until mixture thickens. Cover and store in refrigerator. Stir before serving.
Makes 2 cups

RED WINE VINEGAR DRESSING

½ cup **Crisco Oil**
¼ cup red wine vinegar
1 tsp. salt
freshly ground pepper
⅛ tsp. oregano

Combine all ingredients in a screw-top jar. Cover tightly and shake vigorously to blend well. Store covered in refrigerator. Shake well before using.
Makes ¾ cup

HONEYED ITALIAN DRESSING

¾ cup vegetable oil
½ cup **ReaLemon Reconstituted Lemon Juice**
¼ cup grated Parmesan cheese and Romano cheese
¼ cup honey
½ tsp. oregano leaves
¼ tsp. salt
dash pepper

In 1-pint jar with tight-fitting lid, combine ingredients; shake well. Chill to blend flavors. Refrigerate.
Makes 1½ cups

CHICKEN SALAD ROYALE

2 cups chopped cooked chicken
1 10-oz. can water chestnuts, sliced
1 6-oz. jar marinated artichokes, chopped
½ cup chopped celery
2 tbsp. chopped green onion
½ cup **Hellmann's or Best Foods Real Mayonnaise**
½ cup sour cream
¾ tsp. dried dillweed
½ tsp. salt
⅛ tsp. pepper
1 4-oz. can shrimp
2 tbsp. chopped parsley

Toss together chicken, water chestnuts, artichokes, celery and green onion. Mix mayonnaise, sour cream, dillweed, salt and pepper in small bowl. Pour over chicken mixture and combine gently. Add shrimp. Chill. At serving time, garnish with chopped parsley.
Makes 4 cups

MARINATED VEGETABLE POTPOURRI

3 cups cauliflowerets
3 cups broccoli flowerets
1 cup mushrooms, halved if large
1 cup carrot coins
1 red onion, thinly sliced
½ cup red pepper strips
1 cup **Mazola Corn Oil**
½ cup red wine vinegar
2 tsp. sugar
1 tsp. salt
1 tsp. dried dillweed
½ tsp. dry mustard
½ tsp. dried thyme leaves
½ tsp. paprika
⅛ tsp. pepper

Combine all vegetables in large salad bowl. Combine remaining ingredients in jar with tight-fitting lid. Shake well and pour over vegetables. Marinate 3-4 hours before serving.
Makes 8 cups

DELI SALAD

2 cups cooked medium pasta shells (1½ cups uncooked)
2 cups diced ham
1 cup cubed Cheddar cheese
½ cup chopped celery
½ cup **Mazola Corn Oil**
¼ cup yogurt
¼ cup chopped green onions
2 tbsp. lemon juice
1 tbsp. **Crown Brand** or **Karo Corn Syrup**
1 tsp. Dijon mustard
1 tsp. dried tarragon leaves
½ tsp. salt
⅛ tsp. pepper
2 cups frozen peas, thawed
2 tbsp. chopped parsley

Combine pasta shells, ham, cheese and celery in salad bowl. In blender combine oil, yogurt, green onions, lemon juice, corn syrup, mustard, tarragon, salt and pepper. Pour over salad. Marinate 1 hour. At serving time, stir in peas and parsley.
Makes 6 cups

Marinated Vegetable Potpourri (left) and Deli Salad

THE WAGONWHEEL SALAD

1 small head iceberg lettuce, torn in bite-sized pieces
1 small head romaine lettuce, torn in bite-sized pieces
½ cup garbanzo beans
1 cup cherry tomato halves
¼ cup sliced ripe olives
¼ cup shoestring beets
¼ cup sliced radishes

Have all ingredients prepared and chilled. In a large, shallow salad bowl, make a bed with lettuce and arrange toppings in wedge design. To serve, toss with your choice of prepared **Wish-Bone Salad Dressing Mix** or **Wish-Bone Salad Dressing** (Classic Caesar, Green Goddess, Original Thousand Island, Zesty Italian, Creamy French, Creamy Garden Herb).
Serves 6-8

"SUN" SALAD

2 cups diced cooked chicken
¾ cup pecans or other nuts
2 cups diced celery
2 cups orange sections
Dressing:
1½ cups orange sherbet
¾ cup **Delisle Plain Yogurt**
½ cup mayonnaise

Mix together chicken, nuts, celery and orange. Whip sherbet with Delisle Yogurt and mayonnaise. Combine the two mixtures and serve in orange or grapefruit shells or bowls.
Serves 6

RAINBOW PARTY SALAD

2 medium zucchini, sliced
1 red pepper, cut in slivers
1 green pepper, cut in slivers
2 cups shredded lettuce
1½ cups sliced mushrooms
½ cup sliced radishes
¼ cup chopped red onion
1 cup grated Cheddar cheese
1 cup **Hellmann's or Best Foods Real Mayonnaise**

Use a clear glass salad bowl. Starting with zucchini, layer vegetables in order given above, in salad bowl. Top red onion layer with ¾ cup grated cheese. Spread mayonnaise in a thick layer over all. Garnish with remaining ¼ cup cheese.
Serves 6

The Wagonwheel Salad (top)
"Sun" Salad (bottom)

VINAIGRETTE DRESSING

¾ cup **Crisco Oil**
¼ cup white wine vinegar
1½ tsp. seasoned salt
¼ tsp. pepper
1 tsp. dry mustard
¼ tsp. oregano
¼ tsp. basil

Combine all ingredients in a screw-top jar. Cover tightly and shake vigorously to blend well. Store covered in refrigerator. Shake well before using.
Makes about 1 cup

PASTA DISHES

Historians recognize Marco Polo as the explorer who opened the trade routes between Europe and the Orient. But legend has it that this adventurer also introduced the western world to pasta.

Originating in China and perfected in Italy, pasta has become a staple item in the diets of millions, from Hong Kong to Dallas.

As varied as the places where pasta is enjoyed are the ways in which it can be prepared. In this chapter we show you some new variations of popular recipes such as lasagna, hearty macaroni casseroles and even the all-time favorite, spaghetti.

Remember not to overcook pasta; cook it as the Italians say, "al dente", firm when bitten.

Garden Skillet **(see page 79)**

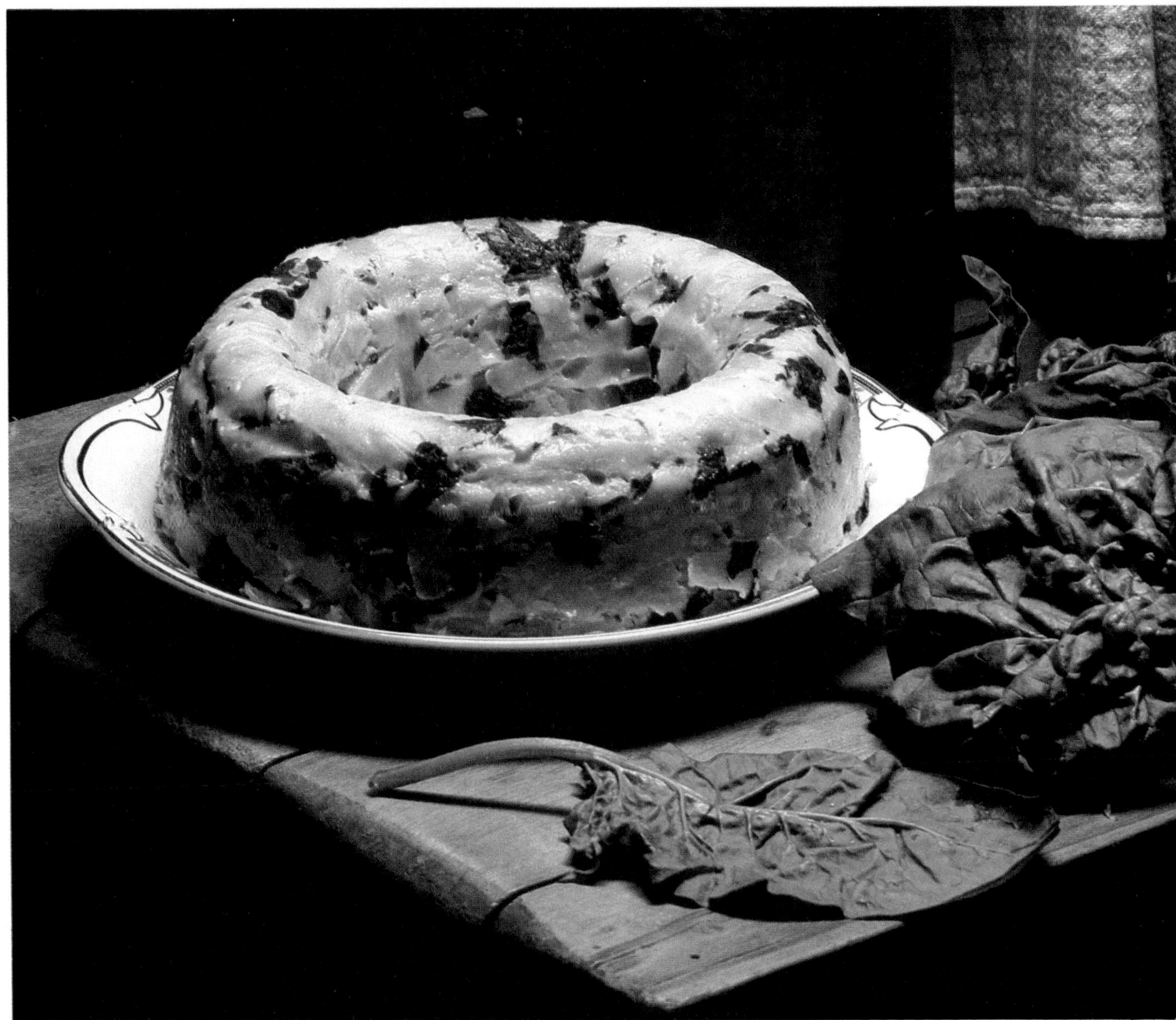

Spinach and Noodles

SPINACH AND NOODLES

½ lb. wide noodles
1 onion, chopped
½ cup butter
2 8-oz. packages spinach, chopped, cooked and drained
3 eggs, slightly beaten
1 cup **Delisle Plain Yogurt**
salt and pepper

Cook noodles in salted boiling water; drain. Sauté onion in butter. Mix noodles, onion, spinach, eggs, yogurt, salt and pepper. Pour into a 6-cup ring mold. Place mold in a pan of hot water and bake 45 minutes at 350°F. Unmold and serve at once.
Serves 6

BEEF AND MACARONI SCRAMBLE

1 cup elbow macaroni
1 large onion, chopped
1 tbsp. vegetable oil
1 lb. ground beef
1 19-oz. can **Campbell's Chunky Vegetable Soup**
1 tbsp. chopped parsley
½ tsp. seasoned salt
¼ tsp. pepper

Cook macaroni in boiling, salted water, following label directions; drain, reserve. In a large frypan, sauté onion in vegetable oil until soft. Crumble ground beef into pan, continue cooking until pink is gone from meat. Stir in vegetable soup, parsley, salt, pepper and macaroni. Heat until bubbly.
Serves 4-6

MACARONI EXPRESS

⅓ cup chopped onion
3 tbsp. butter or margarine
1 small garlic clove, minced
¼ tsp. crushed basil leaves
¼ tsp. pepper
1½ cups cubed bologna
2 15-oz. cans **Campbell's Macaroni and Cheese**
1 14-oz. can beans with pork in tomato sauce
parsley

In a 2-quart glass casserole, combine onion, butter and seasonings. Cook in microwave oven 2 minutes or until onion is tender. Add bologna. Cook 2 minutes; stir. Add macaroni and beans. Cook 10-12 minutes or until hot, stir twice. Stir before serving; garnish with parsley.
Serves 6-8

WIENERS AND NOODLES

1 lb. wieners, cut in half diagonally
½ cup chopped onion
½ tsp. crushed basil or oregano leaves
2 tbsp. butter or margarine
1 10-oz. can **Campbell's Condensed Cream of Celery** or **Mushroom Soup**
½ cup milk
½ cup chopped canned tomatoes
2 cups cooked wide noodles
2 tbsp. chopped parsley

In frypan, brown wieners and cook onion with basil in butter until tender. Stir in remaining ingredients. Heat; stirring occasionally.
Makes 4 cups

SAUSAGE LASAGNA

4 or 5 uncooked lasagna noodles
½ lb. bulk Italian sausage
2 tbsp. chopped onion
1 10-oz. can **Campbell's Condensed Tomato Soup**
1 large tomato, peeled and coarsely chopped
1 garlic clove, minced
¼ tsp. crushed dried basil
¼ tsp. crushed dried oregano
dash pepper
dash salt
1 beaten egg
½ cup ricotta or cream-style cottage cheese
2 tbsp. grated Parmesan cheese
2 tbsp. snipped parsley
¼ cup shredded Mozzarella cheese

Cook lasagna noodles according to package directions, drain. Halve noodles crosswise. In frypan cook sausage and onion until meat is brown and onion is tender, drain off fat. Combine tomato soup, chopped tomato, garlic, basil, oregano, pepper and salt, add to meat and mix well. In small mixing bowl combine egg, ricotta or cottage cheese, grated Parmesan cheese and parsley. Place half the noodles in a greased 8-cup baking dish (or place ¼ of the noodles in each of 2 greased 4-cup baking dishes). Spread half the sausage mixture over noodles. Spoon the egg-cheese mixture over sausage layer. Top with remaining noodles. Spread remaining sausage mixture over noodles; sprinkle with Mozzarella cheese. Bake, covered, in 375°F oven for 30-35 minutes. Let stand 10 minutes before serving.
Serves 2

TETRAZZINI

2 tbsp. chopped onion
1 tbsp. butter or margarine
1 10-oz. can **Campbell's Condensed Cream of Mushroom Soup**
½ cup water
½ cup shredded sharp Cheddar cheese
1 tbsp. sherry (optional)
1 cup diced cooked chicken, turkey or ham
2 tbsp. chopped pimento
1 tbsp. chopped parsley
2 cups cooked spaghetti

In saucepan, cook onion in butter until tender. Blend in soup, water, cheese and sherry. Heat until cheese melts; stir occasionally. Add chicken, pimento, parsley and spaghetti.
Serves 4

GARDEN SKILLET

2 cups diced zucchini
½ cup chopped onion
½ tsp. crushed basil leaves
2 tbsp. butter or margarine
1 10-oz. can **Campbell's Condensed Cheddar Cheese Soup**
3 cups cooked elbow macaroni
2 cups shredded sharp Cheddar cheese
2 cups chopped and well drained tomatoes
½ tsp. prepared mustard

In frypan, cook zucchini and onion in butter with basil until tender, then add remaining ingredients. Heat mixture until cheese melts, stirring occasionally.
Makes 6 cups

Wieners and Noodles

LEEK AND ZUCCHINI PASTA

2 medium leeks
2 tbsp. vegetable oil
1½ cups sliced mushrooms
1 large tomato, diced
1 medium zucchini, cut into julienne strips
¼ cup dry white wine
1 cup whipping cream
1 tsp. **McCormick Tarragon Leaves**
½ tsp. salt
3 cups penne pasta

Discard green part of leeks and slice thinly lengthwise. In large frypan, heat oil over medium-high heat. Sauté leeks, mushrooms, tomato and zucchini for 5 minutes. Add wine and simmer 5 minutes longer. Stir in cream, tarragon and salt. Bring to a boil and simmer until slightly thickened. While preparing sauce, cook pasta according to package directions. Drain well. Spoon onto plates and top with sauce.
Serves 4

STUFFED PASTA SHELLS

2 cups finely chopped cooked ham or turkey
1 cup ricotta cheese
½ cup **MIRACLE WHIP Salad Dressing**
¼ cup chopped red onion
18 jumbo pasta shells, cooked and drained
2 tbsp. cold water
¼ cup **KRAFT Grated Parmesan Cheese**
¼ cup dry bread crumbs
2 tbsp. chopped parsley
1 tbsp. **PARKAY Margarine**, melted

Combine ham, ricotta cheese, salad dressing and onions; mix lightly. Fill shells with ham mixture; place, filled side up, in shallow baking dish. Add 2 tbsp. cold water to dish; cover with foil. Bake at 350°F for 30 minutes or until thoroughly heated. Combine Parmesan cheese, crumbs, parsley and margarine; sprinkle over shells. Continue baking, uncovered, 5 minutes.
Serves 6

Pasta Primavera with Chicken

PASTA WITH GRILLED VEGETABLES

1 tsp. **McCormick Peppercorn Mélange**
3 tbsp. olive oil
3 small zucchini, sliced
12 mushrooms, quartered
1 sweet red pepper, thickly sliced
⅓ lb. fettuccine
2 tbsp. flour
1 cup milk
2 tbsp. freshly grated Parmesan cheese
½ tsp. **McCormick Peppercorn Mélange**
¼ tsp. **McCormick Italian Seasoning**

Whisk together 1 tsp. peppercorn mélange and olive oil. Toss in vegetables. Grill or broil vegetables, basting frequently, for 10-15 minutes or until tender. Meanwhile, cook fettuccine, drain and set aside. Combine flour and milk in large skillet over low heat. Cook, stirring until thickened, about 3-5 minutes. Add last 3 ingredients. Toss with pasta and grilled vegetables until all ingredients are well blended.
Serves 4

PASTA PRIMAVERA WITH CHICKEN

12 oz. uncooked spaghetti
¼ cup grated Parmesan
2 tbsp. butter
2 tbsp. vegetable oil
1 garlic clove, minced
2 chicken breasts, cut in ¼" strips
½ cup **Heinz Chili Sauce**
½ cup chicken broth
1 tsp. basil
½ tsp. salt
⅛ tsp. pepper
2 cups broccoli pieces
1 cup bias-sliced celery
2 carrots, sliced
½ cup sliced red pepper
3 green onions, cut in ½" pieces

Cook spaghetti about 10 minutes. Drain. Stir in cheese and butter. Meanwhile, heat oil in frypan. Sauté garlic and chicken until brown. Stir in remaining ingredients. Cook over low heat for 8-10 minutes. Stir occasionally. Spoon over spaghetti.
Serves 4

ALOHA MEAT BALLS

1 1-lb. 8-oz. can **Puritan Gravy & Meat Balls**
1 cup chopped onion
½ cup chopped red and green pepper
1 cup pineapple chunks, drained
2 tbsp. soy sauce
½ tsp. dry mustard
1 tbsp. vinegar
cooked noodles

In a medium saucepan, combine all ingredients. Cook, covered, stirring occasionally, 8-10 minutes. Serve with cooked noodles.
Serves 5-6

TOP-OF-STOVE MACARONI AND CHEESE

1 cup uncooked macaroni
3 cups water
1 pouch **Lipton Cheddar Cheese Recipe, Soup and Sauce Mix**
1 cup milk
¼ cup margarine or butter

In a medium saucepan, cook macaroni in boiling water about 8 minutes, drain. Add Soup Mix, milk and margarine. Cook and stir about 5 minutes until sauce thickens.
Serves 4

DANISH BAKED SPAGHETTI

2 cups loosely packed **Danish Esrom**, **Tybo**, **Fontina** or **Havarti Cheese**
1 cup chopped onion
1 cup diced celery
6 medium mushrooms, sliced
2 garlic cloves, finely minced
1 15-oz. can tomato sauce
1 28-oz. can whole peeled tomatoes, coarsely chopped
2 tsp. oregano
1½ tsp. marjoram
salt and pepper to taste
4 oz. regular spaghetti
butter or margarine for sautéeing

Shred cheese and set aside. In a large heavy saucepan, sauté first 3 vegetables and garlic in melted butter or margarine until tender. Add tomato sauce, tomatoes, herbs, salt and pepper. Bring to a boil; then reduce heat and simmer 5 minutes. Bring to full boil; then add spaghetti, broken in half. Stir well in one direction. Cover and simmer on low heat for 20 minutes, stirring once or twice. Stir in shredded cheese until melted. Before serving check for seasoning.
Serves 6

PASTA WITH GOLDEN CAVIAR

2 cups crème fraîche
¼ cup Calvados or other brandy
1 bay leaf
6 tbsp. unsalted butter, softened
1 lb. angel-hair pasta or another very fine type
1 egg yolk
14-15 oz. **Golden (Whitefish) Caviar**
salt
freshly ground pepper

Bring crème fraîche, Calvados and bay leaf to a boil over moderate heat. Reduce heat to very low; cook slowly. Meanwhile, bring a large pot of water to a boil. Add 2 tbsp. of butter and the pasta. Cook until pasta is just done, 3-5 minutes. Drain. In a large bowl, beat together egg yolk and remaining 4 tbsp. butter. Add pasta and toss gently to coat strands. Discard bay leaf and pour crème-fraîche mixture over pasta. Spoon on about ¾ of the caviar and toss gently until well mixed. Season to taste with salt and pepper. Top each portion with a heaping spoonful of the remaining caviar, and serve at once on warm plates.

Aloha Meat Balls

LITE SHRIMP AND PASTA

2 tbsp. **Kikkoman Lite in Salt Soy Sauce**

1 cup water

¾ lb. medium-sized shrimp, peeled and deveined

¼ cup unsalted butter

½ cup thinly sliced green onion and tops

3 large garlic cloves, minced

1½ tsp. cornstarch

4 tsp. lemon juice

¼ cup finely chopped fresh basil leaves, packed

2 tbsp. minced fresh parsley

½ tsp. crushed red pepper

½ lb. vermicelli, spaghettini or linguine, cooked and drained

Combine soy sauce and 1 cup water in small saucepan; bring to boil. Add shrimp and cook 2 minutes or just until shrimp turn pink. Reserving liquid, remove shrimp and keep warm. Heat butter in large skillet over medium heat. Add green onions and garlic; sauté 2 minutes. Meanwhile, combine cornstarch and lemon juice; stir into skillet with reserved shrimp liquid and basil. Bring to boil and simmer 1 minute. Add sauce, shrimp, parsley and pepper to hot pasta; toss to combine. Serve immediately.
Serves 4

Lite Shrimp and Pasta (top)
Pasta with Zucchini Meat Sauce (bottom)

PASTA WITH ZUCCHINI MEAT SAUCE

4 tbsp. **Mazola Corn Oil**

1 garlic clove, minced

½ medium onion, chopped

1 lb. frozen sausage meat, thawed, or ground beef

1 28-oz. can tomatoes

pinch nutmeg

pinch marjoram

pinch black pepper

½ tsp. salt

½ tsp. dried basil

3 small zucchini, thinly sliced

¼ lb. mushrooms, sliced

3 tbsp. **Veloutine Light**

1 lb. spaghetti or fettuccine, cooked

In a large saucepan heat ½ of the oil until hot. Add garlic, onion and meat. Stir fry until meat is cooked. Drain off any excess fat; add tomatoes, nutmeg, marjoram, pepper, salt and basil. Stir to break up tomatoes; cover and simmer 10-15 minutes. Heat remaining oil in a skillet. Add zucchini and mushrooms, stir fry just until tender-crisp and set aside. Sprinkle Veloutine into meat mixture, stirring constantly. Boil 1 minute. Add zucchini and mushrooms and serve over spaghetti.
Serves 4-6

ONE BOWL MAC'N CHEESE

½ cup chopped red and green peppers

¼ cup chopped onion

2 tbsp. **PARKAY Margarine**

1 lb. **VELVEETA Pasteurized Cheese Product**, cubed

½ cup milk

2 cups elbow macaroni, cooked and drained

KRAFT Grated Parmesan Cheese (optional)

In 2-quart casserole, microwave vegetables and margarine on high 2-2½ minutes or until tender. Stir in process cheese and milk. Microwave on high 3-4 minutes or until cheese is melted, stirring after 2 minutes. Add macaroni; toss lightly. Microwave on high 4-6 minutes or until thoroughly heated, stirring every 3 minutes. Sprinkle with Parmesan cheese, if desired.
Serves 6

Dinner Party Pasta

NOODLE AND YOGURT CASSEROLE

½ lb. uncooked noodles
1½ cups **Delisle Cottage Cheese**
1½ cups **Delisle Plain Yogurt**
1 garlic clove
1 onion, minced
1 tbsp. Worcestershire sauce
a few drops hot red-pepper sauce
salt
1½ tsp. prepared horseradish
¼ lb. bacon, cooked and crumbled
½ cup grated Parmesan cheese

Cook noodles in salted boiling water. Drain thoroughly. Mix cottage cheese, yogurt, garlic, onion, Worcestershire sauce, hot red-pepper sauce, salt, horseradish, bacon and noodles. Pour into a baking dish. Cover and bake at 350°F for 30-35 minutes. Uncover, sprinkle with Parmesan cheese and return to oven until golden.
Serves 6

DINNER PARTY PASTA

1 cup broccoli flowerets
2 tbsp. **Mazola Corn Oil**
1 small onion, chopped
1 garlic clove, chopped
2 tbsp. **Mazola Corn Oil**
2 cups sliced mushrooms
½ cup whipping cream
1 tomato, peeled and chopped
1 4-oz. can shrimp, drained
1 tsp. dried dillweed
½ tsp. salt
⅛ tsp. pepper
1 package medium noodles, cooked and drained
½ cup grated Parmesan cheese

Cook broccoli in boiling water 2 minutes. Drain and immerse in ice water 5 minutes. Drain and set aside. Sauté onion and garlic in 2 tbsp. oil. Add remaining 2 tbsp. oil to skillet. Sauté mushrooms 5 minutes. Stir in cream, broccoli, tomato, shrimp, dillweed, salt and pepper. Simmer 5 minutes. Serve over cooked pasta. Garnish with Parmesan cheese.
Serves 4

PASTA PRIMAVERA AU GRATIN

3 tbsp. butter
3 tbsp. flour
1 tsp. chicken bouillon mix
½ tsp. salt
2 cups milk
3 cups shredded **Spring Farm Cheddar Cheese** (mild, medium, old or extra old)
1 lb. uncooked linguine or spaghetti
2 tbsp. butter
1 tsp. basil leaves
4 cups hot cooked vegetables
parsley

Melt 3 tbsp. butter in saucepan. Blend in flour, bouillon mix and salt. Gradually stir in milk. Cook and stir over medium heat until mixture comes to a boil. Remove from heat. Add cheese, stir until melted. Keep warm. Cook linguine according to package directions. Drain well. Add 2 tbsp. butter, basil and hot cooked vegetables (use your family's favorites). Toss lightly to combine. Pour hot cheese sauce over each serving. Sprinkle with parsley.
Serves 4

PARISIENNE SEAFOOD SUPREME

¼ cup butter or margarine
¼ cup sliced green onions
1 small garlic clove, crushed
2 tbsp. flour
1 tbsp. **French's Dijon Mustard**
2 5-oz. cans baby clams
⅓ cup water
¼ cup dry white wine
2 tbsp. **French's Parsley Flakes**
½ tsp. **French's Basil**
¼ tsp. salt
½ lb. medium-sized shrimp, cooked
hot cooked noodles

Melt butter or margarine in medium-sized skillet; add onions and garlic and cook over medium heat for 3 minutes. Stir in flour and mustard. Add liquid from clams, water, wine, parsley flakes, basil and salt. Simmer, covered, 10 minutes, stirring occasionally. Stir in clams and shrimp; heat to serving temperature. Serve over noodles.
Serves 4

Broccoli Linguine Carbonara

SAVORY SPAGHETTI CASSEROLE

1 lb. ground beef

½ cup chopped onion

¼ cup chopped green pepper

2 tbsp. butter or margarine

1 10-oz. can **Campbell's Condensed Cream of Mushroom Soup**

1 10-oz. can **Campbell's Condensed Tomato Soup**

10 oz. water

1 garlic clove, minced

1 cup shredded sharp processed cheese

½ lb. spaghetti, cooked and drained

Cook beef, onion and green pepper in butter until meat is lightly brown and vegetables are tender; stir to break up meat. Add soups, water and garlic; heat. Blend with ½ cup cheese and cooked spaghetti in a 3-quart casserole, top with remaining cheese. Bake in a 350°F oven 30 minutes or until bubbling and hot.
Serves 4-6

NOODLE AND MUSHROOM CASSEROLE

½ cup butter

1 onion, finely chopped

1 garlic clove, minced

1 lb. mushrooms, chopped

1½ lb. ground beef

3 tbsp. lemon juice

¼ cup red wine

1½ cups beef bouillon

salt and pepper to taste

1 lb. medium noodles

1½ cups **Delisle Plain Yogurt**

chopped parsley

Heat butter, sauté onion, garlic and mushrooms. Add ground beef and cook a few minutes. Add lemon juice, red wine and beef bouillon. Salt and pepper to taste. Bring to boil, lower heat and simmer about 15 minutes. Add noodles and cook 15-18 minutes or until tender. Add yogurt, cook a few minutes but do not let boil. Sprinkle with chopped parsley.
Serves 10

BROCCOLI LINGUINE CARBONARA

8 oz. uncooked linguine or spaghetti

2 8-oz. packages **Green Giant Frozen Broccoli in Cheese Sauce**

1 cup julienne cut cooked ham (or 8 slices of crumbled bacon)

¼ cup butter or margarine

1 cup whipping cream or milk

2 eggs, beaten

¼ cup grated Parmesan cheese

Cook linguine to desired doneness according to package directions; drain. Cook broccoli pouches as directed on package. In large saucepan, combine cooked linguine, ham and butter. With wooden spoon, stir constantly over medium heat until thoroughly heated. Remove from heat; stir in Broccoli in Cheese Sauce. In small bowl combine cream and eggs; stir into linguine mixture. Return to low heat and stir gently until heated and sauce thickens. Serve immediately, sprinkled with Parmesan cheese.
Serves 4-6

ZUCCHINI PASTA TOSS

1 lb. zucchini, cut into julienne strips
1 lb. fresh spaghetti
4 eggs, lightly beaten
1 cup **KRAFT Grated Parmesan Cheese**
freshly ground black pepper

Boil zucchini and spaghetti until tender; drain well. Place in large serving bowl. Toss eggs and cheese with spaghetti mixture until eggs cook and cheese is melted. Season with pepper.
Serves 6

SALMON PENNE TOSS

2 cups penne pasta, cooked and cooled
1 cup **MIRACLE WHIP Salad Dressing**
½ cup each sliced black olives, sliced green onions and sliced celery
1 cup chopped fresh spinach
2 tbsp. Dijon mustard
¼ cup **KRAFT Grated Parmesan Cheese**
1 tbsp. lemon juice
1 7½-oz. can salmon, drained and flaked

In large bowl, combine all ingredients except salmon. Add salmon and toss lightly. Chill.

Variations: Substitute canned tuna or cooked chicken for salmon.
Serves 4-6

STUFFED SHELLS WITH TOMATO SAUCE

2 garlic cloves, minced
1 tsp. vegetable oil
2 tsp. salt
½ tsp. pepper
1 tsp. oregano
1 10-oz. can **Campbell's Condensed Tomato Soup**
2 eggs
½ cup partly skimmed ricotta cheese
8 large macaroni shells

Brown garlic in oil in saucepan. Add 1 tsp. salt, ¼ tsp. pepper, oregano and soup. Cook until sauce thickens or about 15 minutes. Mix eggs, cheese, remaining salt and pepper. Cook macaroni until slightly hard or about 7 minutes; drain well. Stuff each shell with cheese mixture. Pour tomato sauce over stuffed shells in baking dish. Bake at 350°F for 20 minutes. May be frozen.
Serves 2

Skillet Chili Olé

SKILLET CHILI OLÉ

1 lb. lean ground beef
1 small onion, chopped
2 tsp. chili powder
2½ cups water
1 package **Lipton Pasta & Sauce: Tomato & Herb Marinara**
½ cup chopped green pepper
1 cup grated mild Cheddar cheese

In medium skillet, brown ground beef and onion; drain. Stir in chili powder and water; bring to boil. Stir in Lipton Pasta & Sauce and green pepper, simmer over medium heat for 8 minutes; stir occasionally. Remove from heat. Sprinkle with cheese; let stand covered 3-5 minutes or until cheese is melted and sauce thickened.
Serves 4-5

ITALIAN PASTA SUPREME

3 cups spiral-shaped pasta (tri-colored rotini or fusilli), cooked and drained
1 cup **KRAFT Grated Parmesan Cheese**
1 cup **KRAFT House Italian Dressing**
½ red pepper, chopped
½ red onion, sliced
2 cups broccoli flowerets
½ cup black olives, sliced

Combine all ingredients in a salad bowl. Toss gently to mix. Chill.
Serves 6

PARTY TIME LASAGNA

1 lb. mild Italian sausage
½ lb. ground beef
½ cup chopped onion
2 garlic cloves, minced
1 28-oz. can whole tomatoes
1 7½-oz. can **Hunt's Tomato Sauce**
1 5½-oz. can **Hunt's Tomato Paste**
1 tbsp. chopped parsley
1½ tsp. Italian seasoning
1 tsp. salt
½ tsp. basil
¼ tsp. black pepper
½ lb. lasagna noodles, cooked and drained
1½ lb. ricotta cheese
1 lb. Mozzarella cheese
Parmesan cheese

In skillet, brown Italian sausage, ground beef, onion and garlic; drain fat. Stir in tomatoes, sauce, paste, parsley and seasonings; simmer 30 minutes. In 13" x 9" x 2" baking dish spread a thin layer of meat sauce; add a layer of half the noodles, half the ricotta, half the Mozzarella and half the sauce. Repeat layers. Sprinkle with Parmesan cheese. Bake at 350°F for 40-45 minutes. Let stand 10 minutes before cutting.
Serves 8

VEGETABLES AND SIDE DISHES

In days gone by, the availability of fresh vegetables was sometimes limited, to say the least. The selection in stores was often poor, and once out of season, even common varieties had to be painstakingly preserved. Today, however, with new growing and storage techniques, a ready and bountiful supply of fresh vegetables is always on display at nearly every local supermarket or green grocer.

This chapter helps you make the most of this year-round harvest with a variety of side and main-dish recipes.

Remember, it is generally better not to peel vegetables before cooking them unless the skin is tough or damaged, as the skin and the layer just beneath tend to be rich in fiber and nutrients. And care should be taken not to overcook vegetables since many of these nutrients can be lost in the cooking process. A crisp, crunchy and colorful vegetable is not only much better for you, it's tastier and more pleasing to the eye.

Harvest Vegetables Italiano (see page 88)

BROCCOLI WITH CASHEWS

2 tbsp. butter
½ onion, chopped
1 cup **Delisle Plain Yogurt**
2 tsp. sugar
1 tsp. vinegar
½ tsp. poppy seeds
¼ tsp. salt
½ tsp. paprika
2 ½-lb. packages frozen broccoli, cooked
1 cup chopped cashews

Heat butter and sauté onion. Remove from heat, add Delisle Yogurt, sugar, vinegar, poppy seeds, salt and paprika. Pour over cooked broccoli. Sprinkle with chopped cashews.
Serves 6-8

Broccoli with Cashews

POTATOES AU GRATIN

6 potatoes
1½ cups **Delisle Plain Yogurt**
1 cup grated Gruyère (or other cheese)
salt and pepper

Peel and slice potatoes thinly. Pour a thin layer of yogurt into a 9" x 12" ovenproof dish. Add a layer of potatoes, a layer of cheese, salt and pepper. Repeat layers until potatoes are used up. Finish with a layer of Delisle Yogurt. Cover with aluminum foil. Place dish in a pan of hot water. Bake at 350°F until potatoes are cooked, about 50-60 minutes. Check after ½ hour and add yogurt or cream if mixture appears too dry. Remove pan of water, uncover and continue baking until top is golden. Add cheese and return to oven until cheese is melted and golden.
Serves 6

HARVEST VEGETABLES ITALIANO

1 small eggplant, peeled and cubed
2 medium zucchini, cubed
1 tsp. salt
2 tbsp. **Mazola Corn Oil**
2 medium onions, halved and sliced
1 garlic clove, chopped
2 tbsp. **Mazola Corn Oil**
2 cups sliced mushrooms
1 19-oz. can tomatoes
1 tsp. dried oregano leaves
1 tsp. dried basil leaves
⅛ tsp. pepper
2 slices Mozzarella cheese

Sprinkle eggplant and zucchini with salt and leave in sieve to drain 30 minutes. In large skillet, sauté onions and garlic in 2 tbsp. oil until softened. Add eggplant and zucchini and sauté 10 minutes. Add remaining 2 tbsp. oil to skillet. Add mushrooms and sauté 5 minutes. Drain tomatoes, reserving ½ cup juice. Add tomatoes, reserved juice, oregano, basil and pepper to skillet. Simmer covered 20 minutes. Lay cheese slices on top of vegetables. Broil until cheese is melted.
Serves 6

PARSNIP PURÉE WITH YOGURT

2 lb. parsnips
salt and pepper
1 cup **Delisle Plain Yogurt**
¼ tsp. ground ginger

Peel parsnips and cut into 1" cubes. Cook in salted boiling water until tender. Drain and purée parsnips. Combine salt, pepper, yogurt and ginger. Add this mixture to parsnips. Cook over very low heat or bake at 350°F 10-15 minutes or until thoroughly heated.
Serves 8

BAKED SPINACH WITH YOGURT

2 10-oz. packages frozen spinach
2 cups **Delisle Plain Yogurt**
1 envelope onion soup mix
¼ cup bread crumbs

Thaw and chop spinach. Add yogurt and soup mix. Pour into a baking dish. Sprinkle with bread crumbs. Bake 30-35 minutes at 350°F.
Serves 6

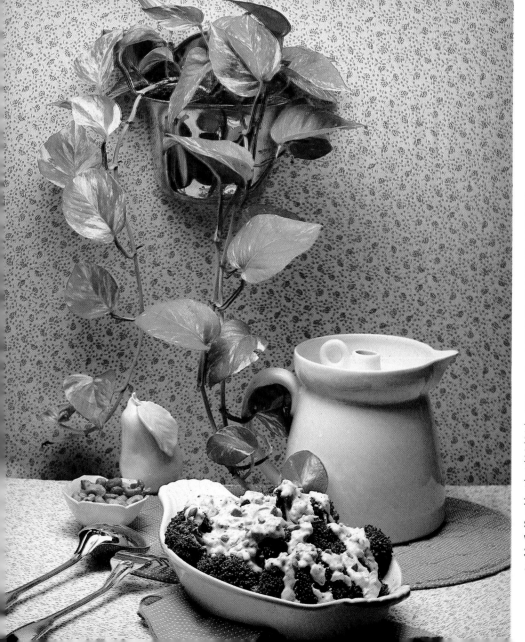

BEET PURÉE

12 medium beets
¼ cup canned pimento
salt and pepper
1 tbsp. lemon juice
½ cup **Delisle Plain Yogurt**
1 garlic clove, cut in half
bread crumbs
dabs of butter

Cook beets in boiling water until tender. Drain and add pimento. Purée in a blender or food processor. Add salt, pepper, lemon juice and Delisle Yogurt. Rub the inside of a baking dish with the garlic clove and pour in the beet mixture. Sprinkle with bread crumbs and dab with butter. Bake at 350°F for 20-25 minutes.
Serves 6-8

GREEN OR WAX BEAN CASSEROLE

1½ lb. wax or green beans
2 tbsp. butter or margarine
1 onion, chopped
2 tbsp. flour
1 cup **Delisle Plain Yogurt**
salt and pepper
½ cup grated Cheddar cheese
¼ cup bread crumbs

Trim beans and cut into ½" pieces. Cook in salted boiling water. Drain. Heat fat and sauté onion. Add flour and cook. Remove from heat, add yogurt, salt and pepper. Mix thoroughly. Return to heat and cook stirring to boiling point. Add beans. Pour into a baking dish. Sprinkle with cheese and bread crumbs. Bake at 350°F 20 minutes.
Serves 6

RED CABBAGE WITH YOGURT

1 red cabbage
1 tbsp. butter
salt and pepper
¼ tsp. nutmeg
1 cup **Delisle Plain Yogurt**

Core cabbage. Place cabbage in a saucepan, add salted boiling water. Bring to a boil, cover and simmer 15-20 minutes or until tender. Drain and chop finely. Heat butter, add chopped cabbage. Sprinkle with salt, pepper and nutmeg and cook 1-2 minutes. Remove from heat. Gradually add yogurt. Return to heat but do not boil.
Serves 6

WHITE CORN SAUTÉ

2 cups sliced zucchini
⅓ cup chopped onion
1 tbsp. butter or margarine
1 12-oz. can **Green Giant Whole Kernel White Corn**, drained
⅛ tsp. salt
⅛ tsp. pepper
1 large tomato, cut into thin wedges
1 cup grated Cheddar cheese

In medium skillet, sauté zucchini and onion in butter until tender. Stir in corn, salt, pepper, tomato wedges and cheese. Cover; heat until cheese is melted.
Serves 4

BARLEY WITH YOGURT

2 cups chicken broth
1 cup barley
2 tsp. butter and oil
1 celery stalk, chopped
½ cup chopped green pepper
¼ cup chopped green onions
¼ lb. mushrooms, chopped
2 eggs, slightly beaten
½ cup **Delisle Plain Yogurt**
salt and pepper

Heat broth, add barley, cover and cook 18-20 minutes or until tender. Stir occasionally. Drain. Heat fat and sauté celery, green pepper, green onions and mushrooms. Combine eggs, yogurt, barley, salt and pepper. Add to vegetables. Pour into a baking dish. Place the dish in a pan of water and bake at 375°F 40-50 minutes.
Serves 8

BAKED POTATOES

1 cup **Delisle Cottage Cheese**
½ cup **Delisle Plain Yogurt**
1½ tsp. margarine
½ onion (or 3 green onions), chopped
3 cups diced cooked potatoes
salt
½ cup grated cheese
paprika

Mix cottage cheese and yogurt. Heat margarine and sauté onion or green onions. Mix onion and potatoes, and add the cottage-cheese mixture. Salt. Pour into a buttered baking dish. Sprinkle with grated cheese and paprika. Bake 40 minutes at 350°F.
Serves 8

DOUBLE CORN SCALLOP

1¼ cups fine cracker crumbs
2 eggs, well beaten
1 cup milk
1 10-oz. can **Green Giant Cream Style Corn**
1 12-oz. can **Green Giant Whole Kernel White Corn**, drained
¼ cup finely chopped onion
¼ cup finely chopped green pepper
¾ tsp. salt
⅛ tsp. pepper
2 tbsp. butter or margarine, melted

Heat oven to 350°F. Combine ¾ cup cracker crumbs with remaining ingredients, except butter. Turn into a greased 8" square baking dish. Toss remaining ½ cup cracker crumbs with melted butter; sprinkle over corn mixture. Bake 35-45 minutes or until knife inserted in center comes out clean. Serve warm.
Serves 6

White Corn Sauté (top) and Double Corn Scallop

Uncle Ben's Lemon Rice Florentine

GARDEN STIR FRY

3 tbsp. **Crisco Oil**
2 medium carrots, peeled and thinly sliced
1 unpeeled zucchini, sliced
½ red pepper, cut in ¼" strips
½ green pepper, cut in ¼" strips
1 medium celery stalk, sliced
½ tsp. dried basil

Heat Crisco Oil in large pan over medium-high heat. Add vegetables, stir fry for 2½ minutes or until tender-crisp. Sprinkle with basil. Serve warm.
Makes 4 1-cup servings

VEGETABLE PULLAO

1 cup chopped onion
2 tbsp. oil
1 cup Basmati or long grain rice
1¾ cups water
¾ tsp. salt
2 tbsp. **Patak's Biryani Spice Paste**
1 cup finely chopped carrots
1 cup thinly sliced green beens

Cook onion in oil until golden brown. Add rice; cook and stir until golden brown. Stir in water, salt, biryani paste, carrots and green beans. Bring to a boil. Cover and simmer 20 minutes.
Serves 6

UNCLE BEN'S LEMON RICE FLORENTINE

1 box **Uncle Ben's Rice Florentine**
2 cups water
1 tsp. butter or margarine
2 tbsp. vegetable oil
½ cup chopped green onion
1 garlic clove, minced
½ cup coarsely chopped fresh tomato
1 tsp. lemon juice
½ tsp. coarsely grated lemon peel

In a large saucepan, combine rice, seasoning, water and butter. Bring to a boil, reduce heat to medium-low and cover. Boil gently for about 20 minutes or until most of the water has been absorbed. Sauté onions and garlic in vegetable oil. Stir in hot rice, tomatoes, lemon juice and peel. Serve immediately.
Makes 6 ½-cup portions

CHEESE LIMA BEANS

2 10-oz. packages frozen lima beans
½ lb. fresh mushrooms, sliced and sautéed briefly in 2 tbsp. butter
¼ lb. Velveeta cheese
¼ cup milk
1 tbsp. Worcestershire sauce
2 tbsp. chili powder
hot red-pepper sauce to taste
salt and pepper to taste
4 **Krinos Fillo Leaves**
½ stick butter, melted for fillo

Cook lima beans until tender. Drain and combine with sautéed mushrooms. Melt cheese in a double boiler; add milk and seasonings. Stir until smooth; pour into the beans and mushrooms. Place 4 fillo leaves in criss-cross fashion in a 9″ x 9″ square pan, buttering each leaf. Finish edges by folding over edges toward rim of pan. Pour bean mixture in pan. Bake in a preheated 350°F oven for 25-30 minutes or until golden brown.

FILLO BEAN BAKE

1 16-oz. can baked beans
1½ cups frozen corn
¼ cup ketchup
1 tbsp. prepared mustard
¼ cup chopped onion
2 tbsp. chopped pimento
salt and pepper to taste
1 tsp. chili powder (optional)
6 **Krinos Fillo Leaves**
bread crumbs
6 tbsp. butter, melted for fillo
3 hot dogs, sliced lengthwise
2 slices bacon, crisply fried
½ cup shredded Cheddar cheese

In a medium-sized bowl, mix first 7 ingredients and chili powder (optional). Place 5 fillo leaves in a greased 9″ x 13″ glass baking pan, butter and sprinkle bread crumbs after each layer. Pour bean mixture in pan. Top with hot dogs, then bacon strips, and lastly the shredded cheese. Cover with one fillo leaf, buttering top of leaf. Finish off edges by trimming thick edges and turning under toward rim of pan. Butter edges well. Bake in preheated 400°F oven for 30 minutes or until golden brown.

CHINESE GREEN BEAN BAKE

½ lb. green beans
½ cup water
1 tbsp. butter
1 can water chestnuts, sliced
1 cup chicken broth
salt and pepper to taste
2 tsp. cornstarch, dissolved in 1 tbsp. water
½ cup slivered toasted almonds (save some for garnish)
4 **Krinos Fillo Leaves**
bread crumbs
½ stick butter, melted for fillo

Cook beans in water until tender. Add remaining ingredients except fillo, bread crumbs and melted butter and blend well. Place fillo leaves in a 6″ x 10″ baking pan (butter and sprinkle with bread crumbs after each layer). Finish off edges by trimming large edges and turning trimmed edges under toward rim of pan. Butter well. Fill pan with bean mixture. Bake in preheated 400°F oven for 15-20 minutes or until golden brown. Garnish with almonds.

GRILLED SUMMER VEGGIES

1 cup **KRAFT Zesty Italian Dressing**
4 zucchini, sliced in ¼″ diagonals
3 yellow peppers, cut into pieces
3 red peppers, cut into pieces
½ cup **KRAFT Grated Parmesan Cheese**

Heat barbecue or electric grill. Grill vegetables until tender but crisp; place in large bowl. Heat dressing; toss into vegetables. Use a slotted spoon to dish vegetables onto serving plate. Sprinkle with cheese.
Serves 8-10

SAVORY BROWN RICE

1½ tbsp. **PARKAY Margarine**
2 medium onions, chopped
1 10-oz. can mushrooms pieces, drained
1 10-oz. can beef broth
½ cup hot water
2¼ cups **Instant Brown MINUTE RICE**

Melt margarine in a large frypan. Add onions and mushrooms and sauté until tender. Add broth and water; bring to boil. Stir in rice; simmer 5 minutes. Cover, remove from heat and let stand 5 minutes. Fluff with fork and sprinkle with parsley before serving.
Serves 6

SPINACH PIE (SPANAKOPITA)

2 lb. spinach, washed, drained and chopped (discard stems)
½ lb. butter, melted
4 eggs
pinch of parsley
1 lb. cheese (½ feta, ½ cottage)
salt (optional)
minced onion for flavor
1 tsp. dill
½ lb. **Krinos Fillo Leaves**
1 stick butter, melted for fillo

Mix first 8 ingredients together. Butter the bottom of a 9″ x 13″ baking pan. Place 4 fillo leaves on the bottom, buttering after each. Place half of spinach mix on fillo leaves and then place 4 more fillo leaves on top of spinach, buttering each leaf. Place remainder of spinach and place one more fillo leaf on very top. (For a thicker and flakier crust, add more fillo leaves on top.) Sprinkle with butter. Turn fillo at edges toward the rim of the pan. Bake in moderately hot 375°F oven for 30 minutes or until golden brown.

CARROT AND CAULIFLOWER CASSEROLE

1 small cauliflower, cut into small flowerets
1 lb. carrots, cut into 1″ sticks
2 tbsp. butter or margarine, melted
1 tsp. **McCormick Basil Leaves**
1 tsp. Dijon mustard
½ tsp. salt
¾ cup shredded old Cheddar cheese
½ cup soft bread crumbs
1 tsp. **McCormick Parsley Flakes**

Cook cauliflower, covered, in small amount of boiling water for 5 minutes or until tender-crisp. Cook carrots separately, covered, in small amount of boiling water for 5 minutes or until tender-crisp. Drain both vegetables and combine in greased 2-quart casserole. Combine butter, basil, mustard and salt; stir into vegetables. Combine cheese, bread crumbs and parsley flakes; sprinkle on top. Bake at 375°F for 20-25 minutes.
Serves about 8

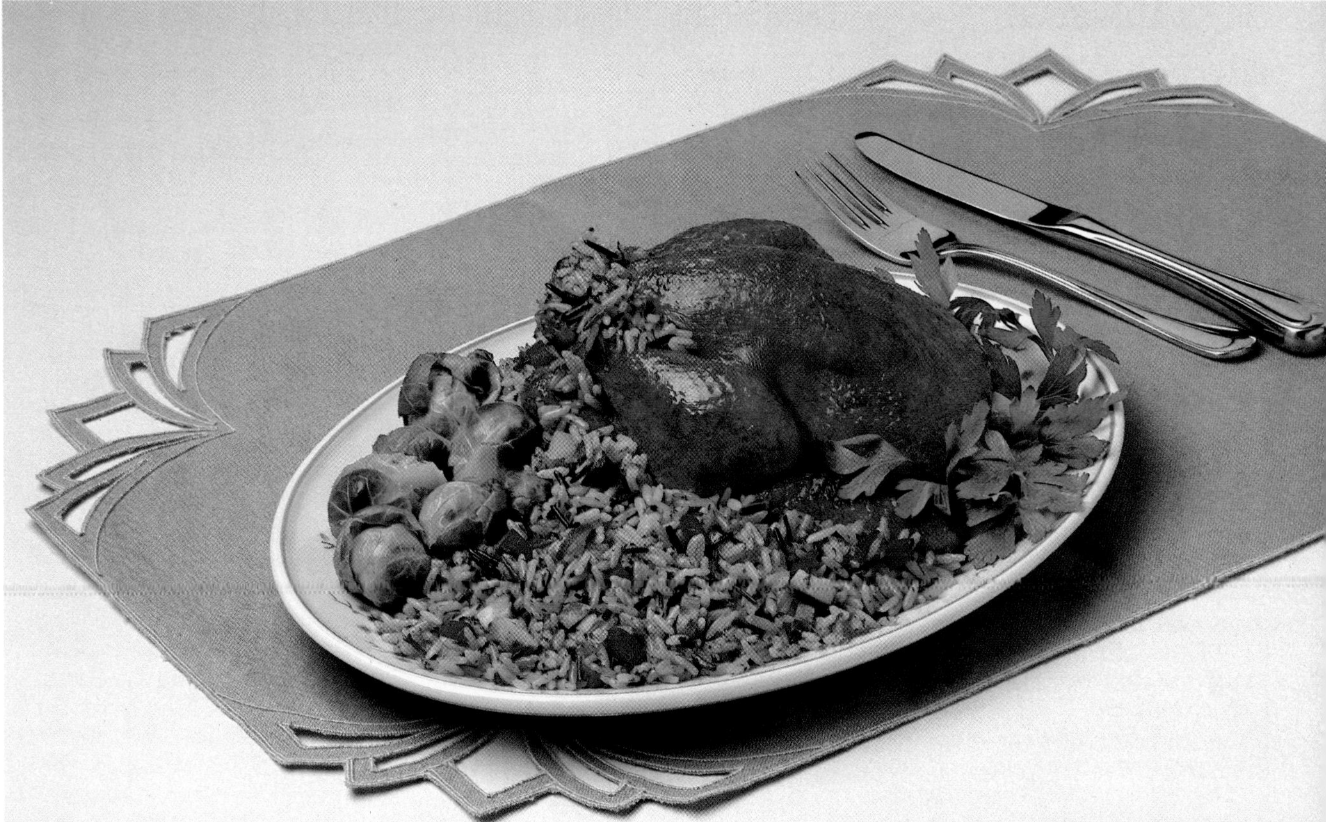

Wild Dillie Rice

WILD DILLIE RICE

1 box **Uncle Ben's Long Grain & Wild Rice Blend**
2 cups water
1 tbsp. butter or margarine
¼ cup diced red bell pepper
½ cup chopped onion
½ cup chopped celery
2 tbsp. margarine or butter
½ cup chopped dill pickles

In a large stockpot, combine rice, seasoning packet, water and margarine or butter. Bring to boil. Stir well. Cover and reduce heat to medium-low. Simmer until most of the water has been absorbed, about 20 minutes. Meanwhile, in a large frypan, sauté pepper, onion and celery in margarine until tender-crisp. Add dill pickles to mixture and cook until heated, about 3-5 minutes. Stir in prepared rice; toss gently. Serve.
Makes 8 ½-cup portions

POTATO-STUFFED CABBAGE ROLLS

8 cabbage leaves
2½ cups finely diced potatoes
½ cup finely diced carrots
2 tbsp. chopped onion
½ tsp. salt
4 tsp. **Patak's Medium Curry Paste**
2 cups water
4 tsp. chick-pea or all-purpose flour
½ tsp. sugar
1 tbsp. plain yogurt

Cook cabbage leaves in boiling water for 3 minutes until limp; drain. Combine potatoes, carrots, onion, salt and 2 tsp. curry paste. Place about ⅓ cup in center of each cabbage leaf. Fold sides of cabbage over filling; roll up. Gradually stir water into 2 tsp. curry paste, flour and sugar in medium-sized skillet. Add cabbage rolls, seam-side-down. Bring to a boil. Cover and simmer 35-40 minutes or until vegetables are tender. Remove rolls to platter. Stir yogurt into sauce; heat. Pour over rolls.
Serves 8

VEGETABLE NARRATA KORMA

1½ lb. fresh or frozen vegetables (diced cauliflower, diced carrots, green beans, peas, etc.)
1 medium onion, diced
1 10-oz. can **Patak's Korma Curry Sauce**
1 small carton light cream

Boil vegetables and onion in salt water for 5 minutes (3 minutes if frozen), drain. Add Patak's Curry Sauce and heat through. Simmer for 3 minutes. Prior to serving add cream. Serve immediately with any roast meat and potatoes. As an alternative serve with rice or bread.
Serves 4

SPICED BOMBAY POTATOES

1 lb. peeled potatoes
2 tbsp. **Patak's Mild Curry Paste**
2 tbsp. oil

Cut the potatoes and boil in salt water for 4 minutes; drain. Mix together oil and Patak's Curry Paste in a baking tray. Coat the potatoes in the oil and paste. Bake in 325°F oven for 35 minutes or until cooked. Serve with roast meat and vegetables. The degree of spiciness can be reduced by adding a little less of the paste.
Serves 4

HOT MUSHROOM CAPS

12 large fresh mushrooms
¼ cup **Crisco Shortening**
2 oz. chicken livers
1 tsp. finely chopped onion
½ cup fine bread crumbs
½ tsp. salt
pinch crushed tarragon leaves
1 chicken bouillon cube
½ cup boiling water
1 tbsp. grated Parmesan cheese

Preheat oven to 375°F. Clean mushrooms and remove stems; reserve caps. Chop mushroom stems. Melt Crisco Shortening in large pan; add mushroom stems, chicken livers, chopped onion. Cook over medium heat for 10 minutes, stirring occasionally. Remove with slotted spoon to a bowl. Chop livers. Add bread crumbs, salt, tarragon, and dissolved bouillon to bowl and mix well. Fill mushroom caps with chicken liver mixture. Arrange in a shallow baking pan (may be refrigerated, covered, at this stage). Sprinkle with Parmesan cheese. Bake for 20 minutes or until hot. Serve immediately.
Makes 1 dozen

FRIED EGGPLANT

1 cup unseasoned dry bread crumbs
¼ cup grated Parmesan cheese
1 tsp. Italian seasoning
½ tsp. salt
½ cup all-purpose flour
2 eggs
¼ cup milk
1 lb. eggplant, peeled and cut into ¼" slices
Crisco Oil for frying
grated Parmesan cheese to garnish (optional)

Mix bread crumbs, Parmesan cheese, Italian seasoning and salt in shallow dish. Place flour on sheet of waxed paper. Blend eggs and milk in another shallow dish. Dip each slice of eggplant first in flour, then in egg mixture, then in bread-crumb mixture to coat. Heat ¼" Crisco Oil in medium skillet. Fry a few slices eggplant at a time over moderate heat 4-5 minutes, or until golden brown, turning over once. Drain on paper towels. Serve immediately or keep warm in 175°F oven. Garnish with grated Parmesan cheese, if desired.
Serves 4-6

UNCLE BEN'S RICE CONFETTI

1 cup **Uncle Ben's Converted Brand Rice**, uncooked
½ cup chopped onion
¼ cup butter or margarine
½ tsp. salt
⅛ tsp. black pepper
1¾ cups chicken broth
¼ cup canned mushrooms, coarsely chopped
2 tbsp. diced pimento
2 tbsp. chopped parsley
2 tbsp. seedless raisins

Sauté rice and onions in butter or margarine over low heat until lightly browned. Add salt, pepper and broth. Bring to a boil. Cover and cook over low heat until most of the liquid is absorbed, about 20 minutes. Stir in remaining ingredients. Heat through. Transfer immediately to a shallow pan. Serve with fried, baked or broiled fish.
Makes 6 ½-cup portions

Uncle Ben's Rice Confetti

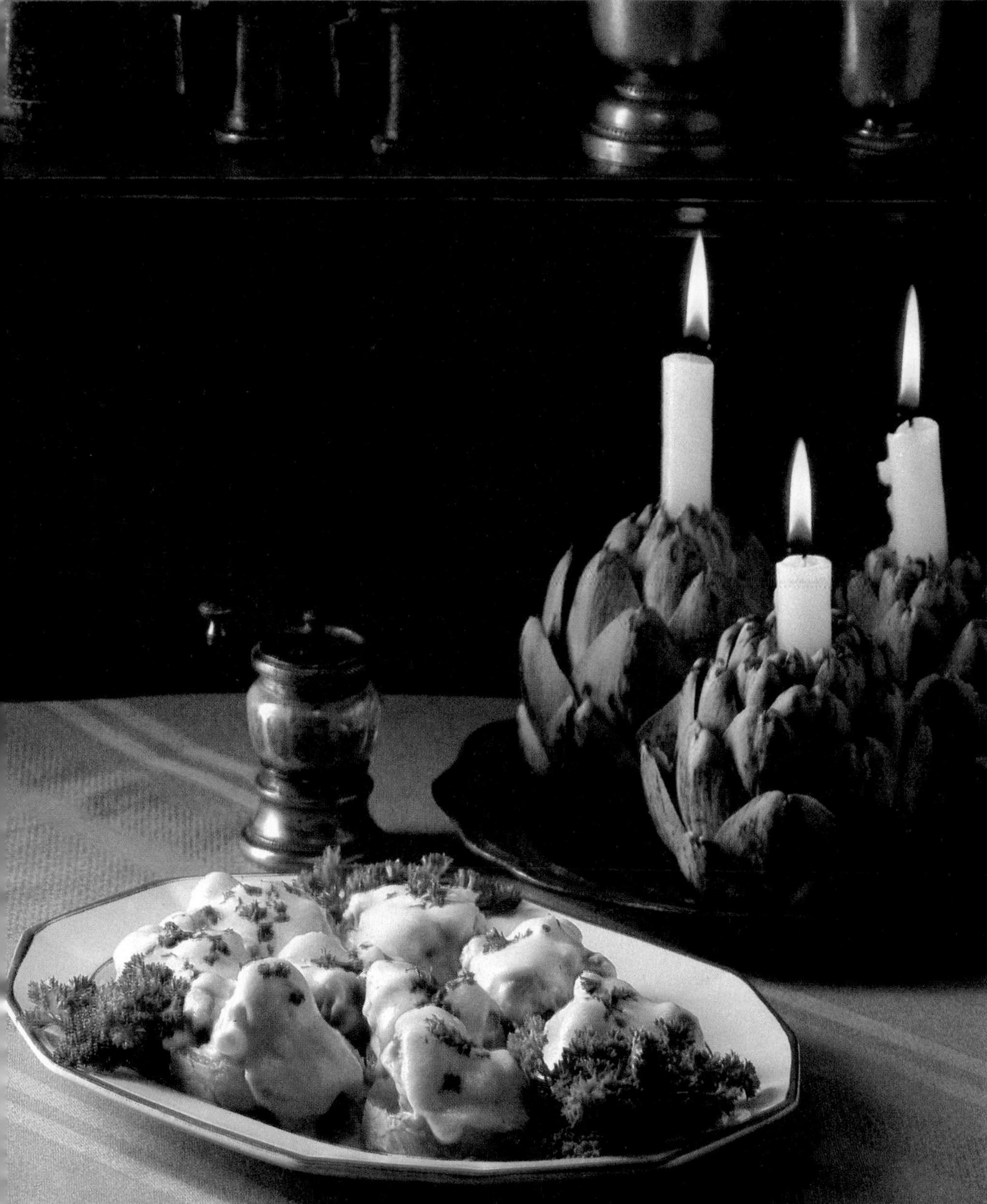

Artichoke Bottoms with Yogurt

LEMONY ZUCCHINI

4 small zucchini, sliced (about 5 cups)
¾ cup chopped onion
¼ cup butter or margarine
3 tbsp. **ReaLemon Reconstituted Lemon Juice**
1 tsp. parsley flakes

In large skillet, cook zucchini and onion in about ½" boiling salted water for about 8 minutes. Drain and place in serving dish. Melt butter in skillet; add ReaLemon and parsley. Bring to boil; pour over zucchini. Serve immediately.
Serves 6-8

SPECIAL BAKED POTATOES

¼ cup butter or margarine
1 tbsp. all-purpose flour
1 tsp. prepared horseradish
½ tsp. parsley flakes
1 cup sour cream
2 tbsp. **ReaLemon Reconstituted Lemon Juice**
6-8 medium potatoes, baked

In small saucepan, melt butter; stir in flour. Cook until smooth and bubbly. Stir in horseradish and parsley. Remove from heat; stir in sour cream and ReaLemon. Chill. Serve on baked potatoes. Refrigerate leftovers. This topping is also delicious over asparagus or broccoli.
Serves 6-8

ARTICHOKE BOTTOMS WITH YOGURT

1 tbsp. butter and oil
1 onion, finely chopped
1 1-lb. package frozen peas
1 14-oz. can artichoke bottoms, drained and cut in half
½ lb. mushrooms, chopped
salt and pepper
½ tsp. paprika
¾ cup **Delisle Plain Yogurt**

Heat butter and oil and sauté onion until transparent. Add peas, artichoke bottoms, mushrooms, salt, pepper and paprika. Reduce heat, and cook for 10 minutes, stirring. Stir in Delisle Yogurt and cook a few minutes but do not let boil. Pour into 1-quart serving dish and serve at once.
Serves 6

VEGETABLE CURRY

1 tbsp. salad oil
1 large onion, sliced
3 heaped tsp. **Sharwood's Madras Curry Powder**
⅔ cup bouillon
2 tbsp. tomato purée (optional)
1 medium-sized cauliflower, broken into flowerets
1 cup sliced carrots
½ lb. green beans, cut up
2 cups sliced mushrooms
1 16-oz. can kidney beans, drained
salt and pepper

Heat oil in a large saucepan and cook onion until soft. Stir in curry powder and cook for a further few minutes. Gradually add bouillon and tomato purée and bring to the boil. Meanwhile, cook the cauliflower, carrots and beans in boiling salted water for approximately 10-15 minutes until fork tender. Drain and add to the sauce together with the mushrooms and kidney beans. Cover and simmer gently for 15 minutes. Season according to taste.
Serves 4

OKRA CURRY

3 tbsp. salad oil
2 large onions, sliced
2 heaped tsp. **Sharwood's Madras Curry Powder**
3 tomatoes, peeled and quartered
2 tsp. lemon juice
2 10-oz. packages frozen okra, thawed

Heat oil in a saucepan and cook onions until soft. Add curry powder and cook for a further few minutes. Add tomatoes and lemon juice, cook for 5 minutes until they have softened, then add the okra and heat through.
Serves 3-4 as a side dish

SAFFRON RICE

pinch saffron threads
(or a large pinch of turmeric)
3 tbsp. oil
1 large onion, sliced
1½ cups **Sharwood's Basmati** (or regular) **Long Grain Rice**
4-6 cloves

Place saffron in a small bowl and pour 3 tbsp. boiling water over it. Leave to soak for approximately 10 minutes. (This is not necessary if using turmeric.) Heat oil in a large skillet and cook onion until soft. Add rice and cook gently for a few minutes. Add 2½ cups boiling salted water to skillet, together with cloves (and turmeric). Bring to boil, add soaked saffron and turn heat down to simmering temperature. Cover and cook for 20-25 minutes or until rice has absorbed all the liquid.
Serves 4

"E-Z" VEGETABLE STIR FRY

¼ cup **Mazola Corn Oil**
1 medium onion, halved and sliced
2 cups thinly sliced carrot coins
1 cup sliced zucchini
1 tsp. sugar
½ tsp. dried basil leaves
¼ tsp. salt
⅛ tsp. pepper

In large skillet or wok, stir fry onion in oil 2 minutes. Add carrots, zucchini, sugar, basil, salt and pepper. Stir fry 5 minutes. Cover skillet and continue to cook 3-5 minutes shaking pan frequently, until vegetables are tender crisp.
Serves 4

MUSSELS STUFFED TOMATOES

a few lettuce leaves
8 firm tomatoes
1 jar **Marina Mussels Salad Mix**
4 oz. cream cheese
parsley to garnish
½ red pepper, sliced
brown bread and butter

Wash and dry lettuce leaves and arrange on serving plates. Cut tops off the tomatoes, scoop out the seeds and allow shells to drain upside down. Fill tomatoes with drained Mussels Salad Mix and arrange on the lettuce leaves. Top each with a spoonful of cream cheese, and garnish with parsley and red pepper. Serve with brown bread and butter.
Serves 4

OKRA TAMATAR

4 tbsp. oil
8 oz. okra, cut into 1" pieces
2 fresh green chiles, finely sliced
1 can **Sharwood's Rogan Josh Curry Sauce**
salt
2 tomatoes

Fry okra and chiles together in oil. Add Rogan Josh Sauce and salt to taste. Chop the tomatoes and add to the sauce, mix well and serve.

BOMBAY POTATOES

5 tbsp. oil
1 tsp. black mustard seeds
1 medium onion, finely chopped
1 tsp. **Sharwood's Garlic Purée**
2 tbsp. **Sharwood's Medium Hot Curry Powder**
1 lb. potatoes, boiled and cubed
salt

Heat oil, fry mustard seeds, allow to pop and add onion and garlic, fry until golden brown, add the Curry Powder and fry gently for 2-3 minutes. Add potato and salt, continue frying for 5 minutes adding a little water to prevent sticking if necessary.

VEGETABLE MEDLEY SAUTÉ

¼ cup **Mazola Corn Oil**
1 garlic clove, quartered
1 cup carrot sticks
1 cup sliced celery
1 cup caulifloweretts
1 cup broccoli flowerets
⅓ cup chicken stock
½ tsp. dried dillweed
¼ tsp. salt
¼ tsp. dry mustard
⅛ tsp. pepper

In large skillet or wok, stir fry garlic in oil 2 minutes. Remove garlic and discard. Add carrots and celery and stir fry 2 minutes. Add cauliflower and broccoli and stir fry 5 minutes. Combine chicken stock, dillweed, salt, mustard and pepper. Pour over vegetables. Continue to cook until vegetables are just tender crisp.
Serves 4

VEGETABLE CHOW-MEIN

3 tbsp. salad oil
2-3 garlic cloves, minced
½ lb. carrots, cut into julienne strips
1 green pepper, deseeded and cut into julienne strips
½ lb. small mushrooms, sliced
¼ cucumber, cut into julienne strips
1 tsp. salt
3 tbsp. **Sharwood's Major Grey Chutney**
2 pieces **Sharwood's Stem Ginger**, sliced
8 oz. folded vermicelli

Heat oil in a large skillet and gently cook garlic, carrots, pepper, mushrooms, cucumber and salt for 5-10 minutes, tossing continuously. Stir in chutney and ginger. Cook vermicelli in rapidly boiling salted water for 4-5 minutes. Drain and add to the vegetables. Serve immediately.
Serves 4 as a side dish

MCVITIE'S DIGESTIVE NUT RISSOLES

2 oz. margarine
2 oz. plain flour
10 oz. water
1 tbsp. chopped fresh chives
½ tbsp. fresh marjoram
1 tsp. yeast extract (such as Marmite or Vegemite)
2 oz. chopped brazil nuts
6 oz. **McVitie's Digestive Biscuits**, crushed
1 egg, beaten
1 tbsp. oil for frying

Make sauce by melting margarine, mixing in flour and gradually blending in the water. Continue cooking until the mixture begins to thicken. Remove from the heat and stir in the chives, marjoram, yeast extract, nuts and 3 oz. of the biscuits. Place in the refrigerator for half an hour. When cool, shape the mixture into 8 rissoles. Dip the rissoles into the beaten egg and into the remaining biscuit crumbs. In a non-stick frypan, heat the oil and fry the rissoles gently until golden brown on both sides. Serve immediately.
Makes 8

Tangy Barbecued Beans (top) and Barbecue Pretzels (see page 28)

LEMON HERBED BEANS

⅓ lb. bacon
½ cup finely chopped onion
¼ cup **ReaLemon Reconstituted Lemon Juice**
¼ cup water
2 tbsp. sugar
½ tsp. thyme leaves
½ tsp. salt
2 10-oz. packages frozen French-style green beans, thawed

In large skillet, fry bacon; remove and crumble. Reserving ¼ cup bacon drippings, pour off excess. Add onion; cook slightly. Add ReaLemon, water, sugar, thyme and salt, bring to boil. Add grean beans and cook just until tender; stir in bacon.
Serves 8

LEMON ORANGE CARROTS

3 cups sliced fresh carrots
½ cup orange marmalade
2 tbsp. **ReaLemon Reconstituted Lemon Juice**
2 tbsp. butter or margarine

In large saucepan, cook carrots in small amount of water; drain. Add marmalade, ReaLemon and butter; stir to coat evenly. Heat thoroughly.
Serves 6

TANGY BARBECUED BEANS

1 lb. ground beef
1 pouch onion soup mix
2 14-oz. cans **Clark Beans with Pork in Tomato Sauce**
1 14-oz. can red kidney beans, drained
1 cup tomato sauce
½ cup cold water
2 tbsp. prepared mustard
1 tbsp. cider vinegar
1 tsp. chili powder

In large casserole or bean pot, brown meat; drain. Stir in soup mix, beans, kidney beans, tomato sauce, water, mustard, vinegar and chili powder. Cover; simmer over low heat (or over low coals on barbecue) for 20-30 minutes or until hot and bubbly. To bake in oven: Bake at 400°F for 25-30 minutes or until bubbly and thoroughly heated.
Serves 4-6

MAUI-STYLE FRIED RICE

4 frankfurters, cut in ¼" pieces
4 cups green string beans, sliced in 1" pieces
1 tbsp. oil
4 cups cooked rice
1 tbsp. chopped green onion
1 package **Noh Chinese Fried Rice Seasoning Mix**

Add 1 tbsp. oil to a large skillet. Add frankfurters and string beans. Cook until done. Add rice and stir fry. Garnish with green onion, sprinkle with Noh Fried Rice Seasoning Mix and stir fry. Shredded carrots may be used as a garnish. Serve immediately.

GLAZED CARROTS

1 lb. (about 6-8) carrots, cleaned
1 cup water
2 tbsp. butter
¼ cup brown sugar
3 tbsp. **Veloutine Light**
¼ cup chopped nuts (optional)

Cut carrots into ½" diagonal slices. In medium saucepan combine carrots, water, butter and brown sugar. Cook until just tender-crisp. Sprinkle in Veloutine, stirring constantly. Boil 1 minute; stir in nuts if desired.
Serves 4-5

ORIENTAL BEANS

- 2 tsp. cornstarch
- 2 tbsp. honey
- ⅓ cup chicken stock
- ¼ tsp. garlic powder
- 1 tbsp. dry sherry
- 2 tsp. soy sauce
- 1 14-oz. can **Libby's Deep-Browned Beans**, drained and rinsed
- ½ cup red pepper strips, 1″ lengths
- 1 green onion, 1″ pieces diagonally cut
- ¼ cup water chestnuts, sliced

Preheat oven to 350°F. In a medium saucepan, stir cornstarch into honey. Gradually mix in chicken stock. Add garlic powder, sherry and soy sauce. Stir constantly over medium heat until sauce boils and thickens. Remove from heat. In a medium-sized bowl, combine Libby's Deep-Browned Beans, red pepper, green onion, water chestnuts and thickened sauce. Place in a 2-cup casserole dish and bake, covered, for 20 minutes.
Serves 4-5

LIBBY'S-STYLE RATATOUILLE

- 2 cups canned tomatoes
- 1 garlic clove, minced
- 1 tsp. Italian herb seasoning
- 3 tbsp. tomato paste
- ½ tsp. sugar
- 1 red onion, diced
- 1 medium-sized zucchini, sliced
- ½ medium-sized eggplant, peeled and cubed
- 1 14-oz. can **Libby's Deep-Browned Beans**, drained and rinsed
- salt and pepper to taste

In a large saucepan, combine tomatoes, garlic, herb seasoning, tomato paste and sugar. Bring to a boil. Stir to break up the tomatoes. Add onion, zucchini and eggplant. Reduce heat, cover and simmer for about 10 minutes. Gently mix in Libby's Deep-Browned Beans and season with salt and pepper. Heat thoroughly.
Serves 6-7

Uncle Ben's Pepper Rice Florentine

UNCLE BEN'S PEPPER RICE FLORENTINE

- 1 box **Uncle Ben's Rice Florentine**
- 2 cups water
- 1 tbsp. butter or margarine
- ½ cup green pepper, cut into 2″ strips
- ½ cup red pepper, cut into 2″ strips
- ½ cup yellow pepper, cut into 2″ strips
- 2 tbsp. butter or margarine

In a large saucepan, combine rice, seasoning packet, butter or margarine and water. Bring to a boil. Stir well. Cover and reduce heat to medium-low. Simmer until most of the water has been absorbed (about 20 minutes). In a large skillet, sauté green, red and yellow peppers in butter or margarine until heated through, about 4-6 minutes. Pour cooked rice mixture into heated dish and stir in peppers. Serve immediately.
Makes 8 ½-cup portions

GREEN LENTIL CURRY

4 oz. green lentils, soaked in water overnight
1 can **Sharwood's Tamatar Madras Curry Sauce**
½ can water
2 tbsp. oil
1 medium onion, finely sliced
½ tsp. **Sharwood's Garlic Purée**

Drain the lentils and simmer very gently with Curry Sauce and water for 30-45 minutes until lentils are soft and most of the sauce absorbed. Fry onion and garlic in oil until the onions are browned. Stir the onions into the lentils and serve.

PARSNIP PURÉE

5-6 lb. parsnips
½ cup melted butter
½ cup **Grand Marnier**
3 tbsp. finely chopped walnuts

Boil the parsnips in water to cover until they can be pierced with a fork. Drain. When cool, peel them, cut into pieces, and put through a food mill. Combine with melted butter and Grand Marnier. Spoon the purée into a 6-cup baking dish, sprinkle with finely chopped walnuts and place in a 350°F oven for 15 minutes, or until heated through.
Serves 6

PURÉE OF CARROTS

2 lb. fairly small carrots
¼ cup **Grand Marnier**
4 tbsp. unsalted butter

Scrape the carrots and cut into slices or leave whole. Put in a pan with enough boiling salted water to cover and cook until just tender, about 20 minutes if left whole, about 10 minutes if sliced. Drain; purée in a food processor or food mill, then blend in the Grand Marnier. Spoon into a baking dish, dot with butter and heat through in a 350°F oven.

Purée of Carrots and Beets: Combine equal quantities of puréed carrots and puréed baked beets. Add 4 tbsp. butter, ¼ cup Grand Marnier and ⅛ tsp. nutmeg.
Serves 4

SAVORY STUFFED TOMATOES

a little cooking oil
1 small onion, finely chopped
1 small green pepper, finely chopped
4 oz. grated cheese
2 oz. **McVitie's Digestive Biscuits**, crushed
salt and pepper
½ tsp. cayenne pepper
2 tsp. finely chopped parsley
6 large firm tomatoes

Heat the oil in a small saucepan, add the onion and green pepper and cook gently until soft but not brown, about 5 minutes. Remove the pan from the heat and add the cheese, biscuits, seasoning and parsley. Take a slice off the top of each tomato, then using a sharp knife, scoop out all the seeds, leaving as much flesh as possible. Fill each tomato with the biscuit mixture and then put the top slice back in place. Place in an ovenproof dish with a little water around the base of each tomato and bake in a moderate 350°F oven for about 25-30 minutes until hot through and the tomatoes are soft. Serve these as a first course or as a vegetable to accompany a meat dish. They may also be served for lunch or supper; then allow 2 tomatoes per person.
Serves 6 as a first course

ONION RINGS

Crisco Oil for frying
1 large onion, cut into ½" slices and separated into rings
Batter:
¾ cup all-purpose flour
½ cup water
½ cup milk
6 tbsp. white cornmeal
1 tbsp. **Crisco Oil**
¾ tsp. seasoned salt
½ tsp. sugar
5-6 drops hot red-pepper sauce

For batter: Combine all batter ingredients in small mixing bowl. Stir until smooth. Heat 2"-3" Crisco Oil in deep-fryer or large saucepan to 375°F. Dip a few onion rings in batter. Let excess batter drip back into bowl. Fry a few at a time 2-3 minutes, or until golden brown. Drain on paper towels. Repeat with remaining onion. Serve immediately or keep warm in 175°F oven.
Serves 4-6

ASPARAGUS WITH SAUCE MALTAISE

2 lb. asparagus
Sauce Maltaise:
3 egg yolks
½ tsp. salt
1 tbsp. orange juice
8 tbsp. butter, cut into small pieces
2 tsp. orange zest
2 tbsp. **Grand Marnier**
watercress as garnish

Wash and trim the asparagus. Lay flat in a skillet. Barely cover with cold water seasoned with salt. Bring to a boil, uncovered, and boil until just tender, about 6-8 minutes. Drain. Put the egg yolks, salt and orange juice in a small pan over low heat. Beat with a wire whisk until well blended and the egg yolks have thickened to the consistency of heavy cream. Add the butter piece by piece until it has been absorbed. Blend in the orange zest and Grand Marnier. Arrange the asparagus on individual plates and spoon the Sauce Maltaise over the tips. Garnish with a sprig or two of watercress.
Serves 4

SQUASH SOUFFLÉ

3-4 lb. squash (butternut, acorn or hubbard)
¼ tsp. mace
3 tbsp. **Grand Marnier**
4 tbsp. unsalted butter
½ tsp. freshly ground black pepper
1 tsp. orange zest
5 large eggs, separated

Split the squash in half and remove the seeds. Place on a baking sheet, split-side-down, and bake in a 350°F oven for about 50-60 minutes. When tender remove from the oven and cool. Spoon the fleshy part of the squash into a food processor and process, or put through a food mill, to make a smooth purée. You should have 3 cups. Combine the purée, mace, Grand Marnier, butter, pepper, orange zest and egg yolks in the bowl of a food processor. Process until well blended. In another bowl, whisk the egg whites to the soft peak stage. Spoon a dollop of egg whites into the squash mixture to soften it and fold in the remaining egg whites. Spoon the soufflé mixture into a well buttered 1½-quart soufflé dish and bake in a 375°F oven for 30 minutes. Remove and serve at once.
Serves 4-6

FILLO PIZZA

1 6-oz. can tomato sauce
1 tbsp. sugar
1 tbsp. oregano
1 tsp. cinnamon
½ lb. **Krinos Fillo Leaves**
½ stick butter, melted for fillo
1 green scallion
¼ cup fresh chopped mushrooms
¼ cup sliced black pitted olives
½ cup shredded Mozzarella cheese

Preheat oven to 375°F. Grease a 9″ x 13″ rectangular baking or pizza pan. Combine first 4 ingredients in a bowl and set aside. Arrange 5 fillo leaves evenly over the pizza pan, buttering after each. Then place 5 more sheets on the bottom of the pan (not on the sides) to allow for more bulk. Butter again after each leaf. Bake fillo shell for 5 minutes and then take out of oven. Pour sauce evenly over fillo pizza shell. Top sauce with chopped scallion, mushrooms, olives and cheese. Bake for 25 minutes or until golden brown.

STUFFED EGGPLANT

2 medium eggplants
1 tbsp. salad oil
1 medium onion, sliced
2 garlic cloves, minced
1 heaped tsp. **Sharwood's Madras Curry Powder**
½ tsp. nutmeg
½ tsp. cinnamon
1 large potato, peeled, diced and cooked
1 large carrot, peeled, diced and cooked
2 tomatoes, peeled and chopped
1 cup frozen peas
⅔ cup bouillon

Cut eggplants in half lengthwise. Slash flesh, lightly sprinkle cut side with salt and put aside. Heat oil in a large skillet and cook onion and garlic gently until soft. Add curry powder and other spices and continue cooking for a few minutes. Add cooked potato and carrot to onion mixture together with tomatoes and peas. Remove flesh carefully from eggplants and chop the flesh roughly. Add flesh to other vegetables in the pan. Add bouillon and cook gently for 10 minutes. Blanch the eggplant skins in boiling salted water for 5 minutes. Drain well. Fill the skins with the vegetable mixture and bake for 20 minutes at 350°F.
Serves 4

MOM'S SUMMER SQUASH

2 lb. summer squash, cut in big slices
4 eggs
½ cup milk
9 oz. Monterey Jack cheese, shredded
2 tsp. salt
1½ tsp. pepper
2 tsp. baking powder
3 tbsp. flour
½ cup chopped parsley
½ stick butter, melted
½ cup bread crumbs or **Fillo Flakes**
4 **Krinos Fillo Leaves**
½ stick butter, melted for fillo

Cook squash in 2 cups water for 7 minutes at a boil. Mash, drain and cool in a bowl. Mix eggs, milk, cheese, salt, pepper, baking powder, flour, parsley and butter. Fold into squash. Place 4 leaves fillo in a 9″ x 13″ baking pan, buttering after each layer, and sprinkle bread crumbs after each layer. Pour in squash mixture and top with bread crumbs. Bake in a preheated 325°F oven for 30 minutes or until golden brown.

MEXICAN STUFFED PEPPERS

4 medium green peppers
1 14-oz. can kidney beans
½ lb. ground beef
1 tbsp. vegetable oil
1½ tsp. salt
1 tsp. chili powder
1½ cups **Minute Rice**
¾ cup grated Cheddar cheese
1 10-oz. can stewed tomatoes
½ tsp. chili powder

Cut peppers in half lengthwise and remove stems and seeds. Cook in boiling salted water for 5 minutes, or until just tender. Drain and set aside. Drain beans, reserving liquid. Add water to liquid to make 1½ cups. Brown beef lightly in oil in small frypan; add salt, 1 tsp. chili powder and the measured liquid. Bring to boil; stir in rice, cover and simmer 5 minutes. Stir in ¼ cup of cheese and spoon meat mixture into peppers. Pour tomatoes, kidney beans and ½ tsp. chili powder into frypan. Place stuffed peppers in frypan; sprinkle with remaining cheese. Cover and simmer 5 minutes.
Serves 4

Mexican Stuffed Peppers

PEPPERCORN MARINATED VEGETABLE KEBABS

⅓ cup vegetable oil
3 tbsp. lemon juice
1 tbsp. **McCormick Green Peppercorns**
1 tsp. **McCormick Thyme Leaves**
¼ tsp. salt
4 cups prepared vegetables (peppers, mushrooms, zucchini, pearl onions, cherry tomatoes)

In food processor or blender, combine all ingredients except vegetables. Process until well blended and peppercorns are crushed. Prepare vegetables: cut peppers into 1″ pieces and zucchini into ½″ slices. Leave other vegetables whole. Place in non-metallic bowl. Pour marinade over vegetables and mix well. Cover and chill several hours or overnight, stirring occasionally. Thread vegetables alternately on skewers. Barbecue or broil, brushing with marinade, for about 15 minutes or until vegetables are tender.
Serves 4

FISH AND SEAFOOD

Delicious, wholesome and easy to prepare, fish is gaining in popularity both in home cooking and on restaurant menus.

Modern methods of storage and transportation have made it possible for us to obtain a varied selection of fresh fish and seafood year round. And for the budget-conscious meal planner, there is a wide variety of reasonably priced canned and frozen fish available in our supermarkets. As fish is generally lower in calories than meats, but contains approximately the same amount of protein, it is also a wise choice for dieters. Whether you choose fish or seafood for its flavor, its excellent value or its calorie count, we hope you'll enjoy trying some of the great dishes that follow.

Crescent Seafood Cheese Melts (see page 102)

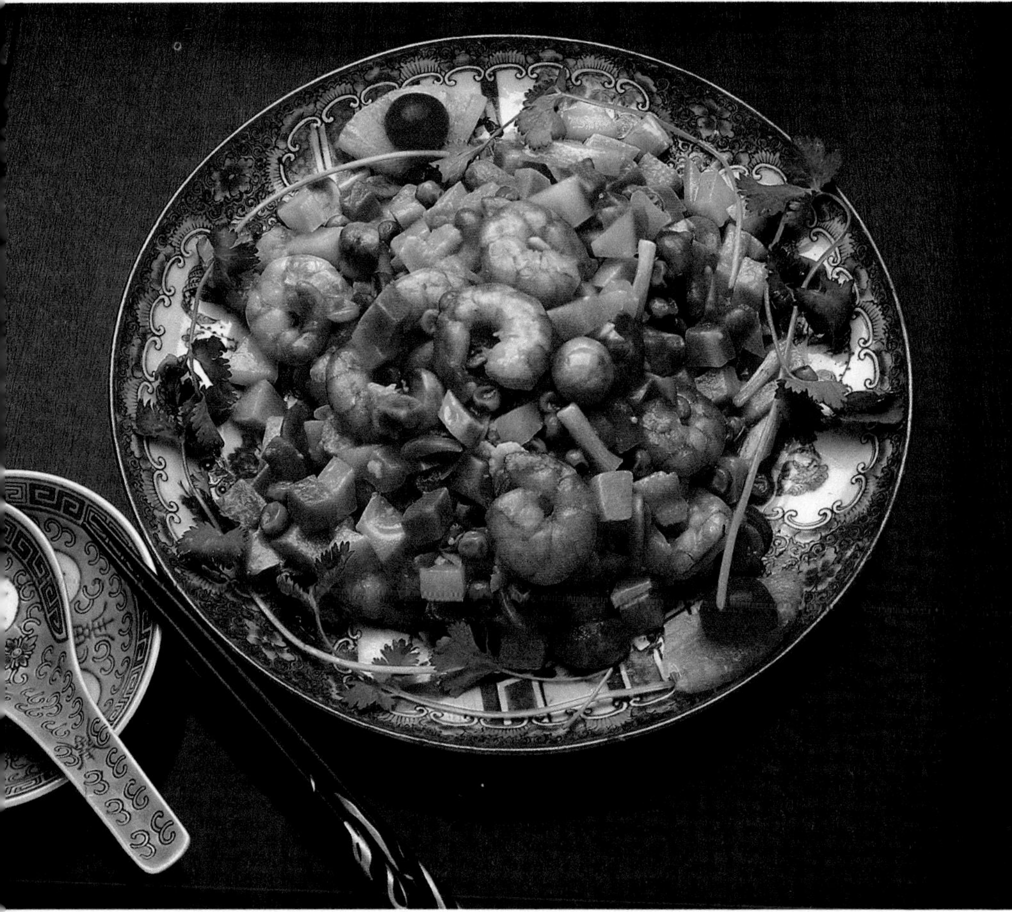

Shrimp with Cashew Nuts

SHRIMP WITH CASHEW NUTS

4 oz. small raw shrimp, shelled and deveined
½ egg white, beat until foamy
1 tbsp. cornstarch
¼ tsp. salt
1 cup oil
½ tsp. **Golden Dragon Minced Garlic**
1 green onion, cut in 1" pieces
8 slices fresh ginger
1 tbsp. **Golden Dragon Light Soy**
1 tsp. **Golden Dragon Sesame Oil**
1 tbsp. cooking wine
4 oz. roasted cashew nuts

Clean shrimp and pat dry with paper towel. Mix together egg white, cornstarch and salt; add shrimp and marinate for ½-1 hour. In a wok, heat 1 cup oil over high heat until it starts to smoke. Pour in marinated shrimp, stir fry quickly for 1 minute, remove shrimp and drain oil from wok. With 1 tbsp. of the same oil stir fry Golden Dragon Minced Garlic, green onion and fresh ginger quickly, add marinated shrimp and rest of ingredients except nuts, then stir fry quickly over high heat until thoroughly mixed. Take off heat, pour in cashew nuts and serve. For variety, at final stir-fry stage, add 1 cooked celery stalk and 1 cooked carrot, both cut diagonally into bite-sized pieces. To cook celery and carrot, heat 2 tbsp. oil over high heat until the oil starts smoking. Put in bite-sized celery and carrot and 2 oz. water. Stir and cover with a lid. Cook over high heat for 2 minutes and drain.

FRIED COD'S ROE

2 slices bread
1 tin **Marina Cod's Roe**
2 oz. butter
2 oz. **Marina Lumpfish Caviar**
lemon slices

Cut bread slices in half. Slice cod's roe thinly. Fry bread in melted butter until brown and crispy. Keep warm. Brown cod's roe slices and arrange on bread. Garnish with caviar and lemon slices.
Serves 4

CRESCENT SEAFOOD CHEESE MELTS

1 6-oz. can crabmeat or
7¾-oz. can salmon or
6½ oz. solid light tuna, well drained
⅓ cup mayonnaise
¼ cup chopped red or green pepper
⅓ cup chopped celery
2 hard-cooked eggs, chopped
1 tsp. onion flakes
1 tbsp. lemon juice
dash cayenne pepper
1¼ cups grated Colby, Brick or Mozzarella cheese
1 8-roll can **Pillsbury Refrigerated Crescent Dinner Rolls**

Heat oven to 375°F. Combine ingredients reserving ¼ cup cheese and the crescent dough. Separate crescent dough into 4 rectangles; press perforations together to seal. Divide mixture evenly into center of 4 rectangles. Roll up and press seam to seal; place seam-side-down on greased cookie sheet. Sprinkle tops of rolls with ¼ cup cheese. Bake for 16-18 minutes or until golden. Serve with a salad.
Serves 4

HERRING KEBABS

8 oz. long grain rice, cooked
1 small tin sweet corn, drained
1 tbsp. chopped parsley
3 tbsp. French dressing
1 jar **Marina Herring Fillets in Dill Sauce**, drained
½ green pepper, deseeded
1 small tin mandarin oranges, drained
4 oz. Cheddar cheese, cubed
fresh dill

Mix the rice, sweet corn, parsley and French dressing. Cut each fillet into 3 pieces and green pepper into squares. Fold herring pieces. Thread them onto skewers with pieces of orange, cheese and green pepper between them. Serve kebabs on bed of rice and sweet corn. Garnish with fresh dill.
Serves 4

Rice-Stuffed Sole with Lemon Dill Sauce

RICE-STUFFED SOLE WITH LEMON DILL SAUCE

1 8-oz. package **Green Giant Frozen Rice (White and Wild Rice**, **Rice Medley**, **French Rice** or **Rice Pilaf**)
1/3 cup chopped green onions
4-6 whole sole fillets

Glaze:

2 tsp. butter or margarine
1/2 tsp. salt
1/8 tsp. pepper
1/2 tsp. dillweed

Lemon Dill Sauce:

1/4 cup butter or margarine
1/8 tsp. dillweed
dash cayenne pepper
1/4 tsp. salt
2 egg yolks
1 tbsp. lemon juice
1/3 cup sour cream
3 tbsp. milk

Thaw rice pouch. In medium bowl, combine rice and chopped onion. Separate sole fillets; divide rice mixture evenly among fillets. Roll up and place seam-side-down in small baking dish. In small bowl, combine butter, salt, pepper and dillweed. Brush mixture over sole rolls. Bake sole in uncovered baking dish at 400° for 15-20 minutes or until fish flakes with a fork. To prepare sauce, combine butter, dillweed, cayenne pepper, salt and egg yolks in small saucepan. Stir over medium heat until thickened. Add lemon juice, sour cream and milk. Reduce heat and cover. Serve over sole rolls.
Serves 4-6

HERRING WALDORF

1 carton natural yogurt
1 jar **Marina Herring in Sour Cream**
1 red apple, cored and sliced
2 celery stalks, chopped
walnuts
watercress

Mix together yogurt and herring in Sour Cream. Reserve 2 apple slices for garnish and chop the rest. Stir into the yogurt mixture, together with celery and walnuts. Pile into serving dish and serve with whole wheat bread and butter. Garnish with apple slices dipped in lemon juice, and watercress.
Serves 3-4

HERRING IN CURRY SAUCE

1 jar **Marina Herring Fillets in Wine Sauce**
1 apple, cored and sliced
2 tbsp. mayonnaise
yogurt
2 tsp. curry powder
1/2 onion, finely chopped
8 oz. cooked rice
watercress

Drain herring fillets and cut into pieces about 1" long. Reserve 3 slices of apple for garnish and chop the rest. Mix together mayonnaise, yogurt, curry powder and onion. Stir in herring pieces and apple. Leave to marinate for 2-3 hours. Serve with a border of cold cooked rice and garnish with reserved apple slices and watercress.
Serves 3

SEAFOOD MEDLEY

1 cup frozen cut green beans
1 10-oz. can **Campbell's Condensed Cream of Mushroom Soup**
1/4 cup milk
1 tbsp. chopped pimento
1/4 tsp. crushed dried thyme
dash salt
dash cayenne pepper
1 cup cooked rice
1 7-oz. can tuna, drained and broken into chunks
1 4-oz. can shrimp, drained and deveined
1/4 cup French-fried onions

Cook green beans according to package directions, drain and set aside. In mixing bowl combine mushroom soup, milk, pimento, thyme, salt and cayenne. Stir half of the soup mixture into cooked rice, fold in tuna. Turn tuna-rice mixture into a 1-quart casserole. Spread green beans over mixture, top with shrimp. Pour remaining soup mixture over all. Bake, covered, in 350°F oven for 25-30 minutes or until heated through. Sprinkle with onions. Bake, uncovered, about 5 minutes longer.
Serves 2

SARDINE POTATO CROQUETTES

½ cup chopped onion
1 tbsp. butter or margarine
1 tbsp. vegetable oil
2 cups cooked, mashed potatoes
1 egg, beaten
½ tsp. salt
few grains pepper
3 cans **Brunswick Sardines in Soya Oil** (or **Brunswick Sardines in Spring Water** or **Brunswick Connaisseur Sardines**), drained and mashed
1 cup fine dry bread crumbs

Cook onion in butter and oil until tender. Add onion, egg and seasonings to potatoes. Whip until well blended and light. Add sardines; mix well. Chill 2 hours. Shape into flat patties ½" thick. Coat with bread crumbs. Pan fry in hot butter and oil until golden brown; turning once. Serve piping hot with tomato sauce.
Serves 6-8

SIMPLY DELICIOUS SOLE

1 lb. sole fillets
½ cup all-purpose flour
1 egg
1 tbsp. cold water
¾ cup cracker crumbs
¼ cup **Mazola Corn Oil**
Dill Butter:
¼ cup melted butter
1 tsp. dried dillweed

Coat sole with flour. Beat together egg and water. Dip sole in egg mixture. Coat with crumbs. Fry sole in corn oil about 3 minutes each side. Serve with Dill Butter, which is made by combining butter and dillweed.
Serves 4

SHRIMP CREOLE

2 garlic cloves, minced
1 green pepper, chopped
½ cup chopped onion
½ cup sliced celery
2 tbsp. oil
1½ cups water
1 5½-oz. can **Hunt's Tomato Paste**
½ tsp. salt
1 bay leaf
¼ tsp. thyme
dash hot red-pepper sauce
2 cups cooked baby shrimp
2 cups cooked rice

In large skillet, cook garlic, green pepper, onion and celery in oil until tender. Stir in water, Hunt's Tomato Paste, salt, bay leaf, thyme and hot red-pepper sauce. Simmer 15 minutes, stirring occasionally. Add shrimp and simmer until heated through. Remove and discard bay leaf before serving. Serve on rice.
Serves 4

FRENCH'S SWEET 'N TANGY SEAFOOD WRAPS

oil
4 fillets of fish
⅓ cup **French's Sweet 'n Tangy Mustard**
⅓ cup cream
4 green onions, cut into 2" lengths
¼ tsp. **French's Lemon Pepper**

Cut 4 pieces of aluminum foil into 10" squares. Brush oil on one side of each piece of foil. Season fish with Lemon Pepper, place on foil. Mix mustard and cream together; spread over each fillet. Scatter onions evenly on each fillet. Fold foil over fish and seal. Bake in preheated 325°F oven for 20 minutes or until fish flakes easily with fork.
Serves 4

HALIBUT STEAKS WITH YOGURT SAUCE

2 cups dry white wine
2 tbsp. lemon juice
1½ tsp. dill
1 onion, cut in two
6 peppercorns, crushed
salt
6 halibut steaks, 1½" thick (or salmon)
¾ cup flour
1½ tsp. paprika
salt and pepper
1 cucumber, peeled, seeded and chopped
¾ cup **Delisle Plain Yogurt**
1 tbsp. butter and oil

Mix wine, lemon juice, dill, onion, peppercorns and salt. Add halibut steaks and marinate 2-3 hours in a cool place, turning occasionally. Mix flour, paprika, salt and pepper. Dip fish in flour mixture to coat both sides. Shake to remove excess flour. Remove onion and pour marinade in a small saucepan. Add cucumber. Over moderate heat, bring to boil, stirring occasionally, and let boil until liquid is reduced to 1 cup. Remove from heat. Blend sauce in a food processor or blender. Add yogurt to sauce and return to saucepan. Cook stirring over low heat 3-4 minutes or until hot and smooth. Remove saucepan from heat and keep warm. Heat fat and cook 2 or 3 steaks at a time, 7-8 minutes on each side or until fish flakes easily with a fork. Remove fish from pan, drain them on paper towels and place them on a warm serving dish. Keep warm. Cook the other halibut steaks. Pour hot sauce over fish and serve at once.
Serves 6

CELEBRATION FISH PIE

1 6-oz. package frozen cod in parsley sauce
2 oz. peeled prawns
1 package instant potato or mashed potato
1 oz. butter
2 oz. **Marina Lumpfish Caviar**

Make up cod according to directions. Transfer to ovenproof dish and flake the fish. Add the prawns. Make up mashed potatoes and add the butter. Pipe or spoon the potato around the fish. Grill for 10 minutes until golden brown. Garnish with caviar.
Serves 2

PRAWNS IN COCONUT

2 tbsp. oil
1 small onion, chopped
½ tsp. puréed fresh ginger (optional)
2 tbsp. **Sharwood's Mild Madras Curry Powder**
2 oz. **Sharwood's Coconut Cream**
½ cup hot water
1 lb. cooked, shelled prawns
2 tomatoes, roughly chopped
1 tsp. **Sharwood's Tomato Purée**
2 tsp. lemon juice
salt to taste

Fry the onion and ginger purée in oil until the onion is golden, add curry powder and cook gently for 2 minutes. Blend the coconut with the hot water, add the prawns, coconut stock and tomatoes, stir well. Add tomato purée, lemon juice and salt to taste, simmer gently for 5 minutes.

FISH COOKED WITH YOGURT

2 tbsp. oil
3 small bay leaves
1 large onion, chopped
1 tsp. puréed fresh ginger (optional)
½ tsp. **Sharwood's Garlic Purée**
1 tsp. turmeric
2 tsp. **Sharwood's Hot Madras Curry Powder**
8 oz. natural yogurt (preferably Greek strained yogurt)
1 lb. halibut fillets, cut into bite-sized pieces
salt to taste
2 green chiles, chopped (optional)
coriander as garnish

Fry the bay leaves and onion in oil until translucent. Add ginger and garlic and continue to cook for 5 minutes. Add turmeric and curry powder and fry for a few seconds. Add yogurt and cook on a high heat until yogurt becomes thick. Add fish, salt and chiles, cook gently for 5 minutes until fish is tender. Garnish with coriander. Note: Yogurt has a tendency to separate when subjected to heat, this in no way affects the flavor but has a slight granular appearance. Greek strained yogurt has a higher fat content and will not separate on cooking.

Prawns in Coconut (left), Fish Cooked with Yogurt (center) and Mackerel with Coconut

MACKEREL WITH COCONUT

2 tbsp. oil
1 large onion, finely chopped
2 tbsp. **Sharwood's Hot Madras Curry Powder**
3 oz. desiccated coconut
2 15-oz. can mackerel fillets in brine, drained, cut each fillet in half
2 15-oz. cans tomatoes
salt to taste

Fry the onion in the oil until soft, add curry powder and coconut, fry for 2 minutes or until coconut has a toasted appearance. Add the fish pieces and tomatoes. Season, simmer until the sauce has thickened.

COASTAL FISH DINNER

1 16-oz. can tomatoes, cut up
1 green pepper, diced
3 tbsp. **Patak's Tikka Spice Paste**
1 tbsp. chick-pea or all-purpose flour
½ tsp. sugar
1½ lb. skinned haddock, cod or whitefish fillets, cut into serving-sized pieces

Combine all ingredients except fish in large skillet. Add fish. Cover and simmer 15 minutes or until fish flakes easily when pierced with a fork, spooning sauce over fish occasionally.
Serves 6

JINGHA FISH VINDALOO

1½ lb. peeled prawns or fish fillets or small whole fish
2 tbsp. oil
1 onion, finely chopped
1 large tomato
1 10-oz. can **Patak's Vindaloo Curry Sauce**

Wash prawns, sauté the onions in the oil for 5 minutes. Add tomato and cook for a further 2 minutes. Add prawns and continue cooking for 10 minutes. Add Vindaloo Curry Sauce and simmer for 20 minutes. Serve with rice, naan or pita bread. A little water may be added to obtain a gravy consistency.
Serves 4

SHRIMP CURRY

1 package **Noh Hawaiian Style Curry Sauce Mix**
1½ cups water
1 lb. medium-sized raw shrimp (shelled, deveined and cooked)

Combine Noh Hawaiian Style Curry Sauce Mix with water in a small pot; stirring constantly. Bring to boil until it thickens. Serve over cooked shrimp. Beef, chicken, turkey or meatballs may be used instead of shrimp.

MARINA PAELLA

- 2 tbsp. olive oil
- 1 onion, chopped
- 1 garlic clove, chopped
- 4 oz. bacon, chopped
- 1 red pepper, chopped
- 8 oz. long grain rice
- 1 pint chicken stock
- 8 oz. filleted white fish
- 4 oz. frozen peas
- 1 tin or jar **Marina Mussels in Brine**
- 4 oz. peeled prawns
- 6 oz. cooked chicken
- parsley to garnish

Fry onion and garlic in oil, add bacon and red pepper. Cook for 5 minutes. Add rice, cook, stir a few minutes. Add stock, bring to boil. Add fish and peas, cook for 20 minutes. Add drained mussels, prawns and chicken to rice. Heat, garnish and serve.
Serves 4

OYSTERS AND YOGURT

- ¾ cup cracker crumbs
- ½ lb. Parmesan cheese
- ¼ cup melted butter
- ½ tsp. salt
- pepper
- 6 shells or ramekins
- 2 cups cooked, drained oysters
- ¼ cup dry sherry
- ½ cup **Delisle Plain Yogurt**
- dabs of butter

Combine crumbs, cheese, melted butter, salt and pepper. Mix thoroughly. Spread half the mixture over the bottom of 6 shells or ramekins. Divide oysters between the shells or ramekins. Mix sherry and yogurt, and spoon over oysters. Sprinkle with remaining crumb mixture. Dab with butter. Place shells or ramekins on a cookie sheet and bake at 375°F 15-18 minutes or until crumbs are golden and oysters are thoroughly heated.
Serves 6

PAELLA

- 2½-3 lb. chicken pieces
- ¼ cup oil
- 1 onion, sliced
- 2 garlic cloves, minced
- 3 cups water
- 1 5½-oz. can **Hunt's Tomato Paste**
- 1 tsp. salt
- ¼ tsp. saffron
- 1 cup uncooked rice
- ½ tsp. oregano
- 1 lb. raw medium shrimp, peeled and deveined
- 1 10-oz. package frozen peas
- ½ lb. unshelled clams
- 1 4-oz. jar pimento strips, drained

In Dutch oven or paella pan, brown chicken in oil. Add onion and garlic and cook until onion is tender; drain fat. Combine 2 cups water, Hunt's Tomato Paste and salt; pour over chicken. Simmer, covered, 30 minutes. In a small saucepan bring remaining 1 cup water and saffron to boil; add to chicken. Stir in rice and oregano; simmer, covered, 25 minutes. Add remaining ingredients; cook 10 minutes longer.
Serves 8

SHRIMP CURRY

- 3 tbsp. salad oil
- 1 large onion, sliced
- 2 garlic cloves, minced
- 3 heaped tsp. **Sharwood's Madras Curry Powder**
- ¼ cup **Sharwood's Creamed Coconut**
- ⅔ cup milk, warmed
- pinch paprika
- 3 tbsp. tomato purée
- 1 lb. cooked, shelled and deveined shrimp
- 1 10-oz. package frozen spinach, thawed and coarsely chopped

Heat oil in a saucepan and lightly cook onion and garlic until soft. Add curry powder and cook for 2-3 minutes. Dissolve coconut in warmed milk, then add to onion mixture together with paprika and tomato purée. Stir in shrimp and spinach, cover pan and cook gently for 10 minutes.
Serves 4

Oysters and Yogurt

Salmon en Croute

SALMON EN CROUTE

½ lb. butter
2 cups all-purpose flour
½ tsp. salt
½ cup **Delisle Plain Yogurt**

Stuffing:

1 lb. salmon, cooked and flaked
⅔ cup **Delisle Plain Yogurt**
2 tbsp. dill
2 tbsp. chopped parsley
2 celery stalks, finely chopped
1 onion, minced
4 hard-cooked eggs, chopped
2 tbsp. lemon juice
salt and pepper
1 egg, slightly beaten

Sauce:

2½ cups **Delisle Plain Yogurt**
3 tbsp. dill
3 tbsp. lemon juice
⅓ cup mayonnaise

Cut butter into flour and salt (as for pie dough). Add yogurt and mix well. Divide dough into 2 parts, wrap and refrigerate 1 hour. Mix salmon, yogurt, dill, parsley, celery, onion, hard-cooked eggs, lemon juice, salt and pepper. Roll out dough into 2 12" x 4" rectangles. Place 1 rectangle on a cookie sheet. Spread salmon mixture over rectangle. Top with remaining rectangle. Press the edges to seal. Brush with beaten egg. Bake at 425°F 10 minutes. Lower temperature to 350°F and continue baking 30-40 minutes. Serve sliced with the sauce, which is all sauce ingredients mixed together. Canned salmon, tuna or any other fish may be substituted for the fresh salmon.

Serves 10

HADDOCK WITH FENNEL

2 lb. haddock
1½ cups **Delisle Plain Yogurt**
½ cup mayonnaise
celery salt
pepper
½ tsp. thyme
½ tsp. paprika
2 tbsp. chopped pimento
fennel sprigs
lemon wedges
parsley sprigs

Place haddock in a buttered 6-cup casserole. Mix yogurt, mayonnaise, celery salt, pepper, thyme, paprika and pimento. Pour over fish and top with fennel sprigs. Bake at 350°F 35-40 minutes or until fish flakes easily with a fork. Serve hot, garnished with lemon wedges and parsley sprigs.

Serves 12

SEAFOOD PIE

¼ cup butter
1 green onion, chopped
¼ cup flour
1¼ cup milk
⅔ cup **Delisle Plain Yogurt**
⅔ cup chicken broth (or dry white wine)
¾ lb. sole fillets, in chunks
¼ lb. scallops, diced
¼ lb. cooked shrimp
¼ lb. cooked crabmeat
salt and pepper
2 pie crusts
1 egg, beaten

Heat butter and sauté green onion. Add flour and cook a few minutes. Remove from heat, add milk, yogurt and chicken broth. Return to heat and cook stirring for about 2-3 minutes. Add sole, scallops, shrimp and crabmeat. Salt and pepper. Cool. Roll out dough and line a deep pie plate. Pour in cooled seafood mixture. Cover with top crust. Brush with beaten egg. Bake at 425°F 10 minutes. Lower temperature to 375°F and bake 20-25 minutes.

Serves 10-12

SALMON MOUSSE

1 7¾-oz. can salmon, drained
2 hard-cooked eggs, finely chopped
½ cup stuffed olives, halved
¼ cup chopped celery
¼ cup finely chopped green onions
1 tsp. dried dillweed
¼ tsp. salt
¼ tsp. pepper
1 envelope unflavored gelatin
¼ cup cold water
1 cup **Hellmann's or Best Foods Real Mayonnaise**
1 tbsp. lemon juice

Mix salmon, eggs, olives, celery, green onions, dillweed, salt and pepper. Soften gelatin in cold water. Set over hot water to dissolve. Stir together gelatin, mayonnaise and lemon juice. Combine with salmon mixture. Spoon into 3-cup mold. Refrigerate until firm.
Makes 1 3-cup mold

FILLETS OF SOLE TYROLEAN

½ cup chopped onion
1 lb. fillets of sole
2 tsp. chopped parsley
1 cup shredded Swiss cheese
1 10-oz. can **Campbell's Condensed Cream of Celery Soup**
¼ cup Chablis or other dry white wine
1 tbsp. lemon juice
2 tbsp. Italian flavored fine dry bread crumbs
paprika

In 1-cup glass measuring cup, cook onion in microwave oven 2 minutes or until tender. In 2-quart shallow glass dish (12" x 8" x 2"), arrange fish in single layer; top with cooked onion, parsley and cheese. Combine soup, wine and lemon juice. Pour over fish; top with bread crumbs and paprika. Cook 2-5 minutes or until done; giving dish ¼ turn every 1½ minutes.
Serves 4

COQUILLES OF SHRIMP MORNAY

3 10-oz. cans **Campbell's Condensed Beef Broth**
2 lb. fresh shrimp
1 10-oz. can **Campbell's Condensed Cheddar Cheese Soup**
⅓ cup water
¼ lb. mushrooms, chopped
1 tbsp. butter or margarine
pepper
1 tbsp. chopped parsley
scallop shells or ramekins
4 tsp. grated Swiss cheese

Poach shrimp in broth for 5-6 minutes; shell and devein. Heat soup and water to make sauce. Sauté mushrooms in melted butter, add pepper and parsley. Combine shrimp, mushrooms and cheese sauce; pour into scallop shells or ramekins; sprinkle each with grated Swiss cheese. Broil until surface is golden.
Serves 4

Salmon Mousse

TEMPTING SEAFOOD CASSEROLE

½ cup chopped celery
¼ cup chopped onion
2 tbsp. chopped green pepper
2 tbsp. butter or margarine
1 10-oz. can **Campbell's Condensed Cream of Mushroom Soup**
¼ cup water
2 cups diced cooked lobster or shrimp
1 tsp. lemon juice
½ cup shredded mild processed cheese
2 tbsp. buttered bread crumbs

In saucepan, cook celery, onion and green pepper in butter until tender. Add remaining ingredients except cheese and crumbs. Pour into 1-quart casserole. Bake at 350°F for 25 minutes; stir. Top with cheese and crumbs. Bake 5 minutes more or until hot.
Serves 4-5

CRAB AND ARTICHOKE BAKE

1 10-oz. can **Campbell's Condensed Cheddar Cheese Soup**
⅓ cup Chablis or other dry white wine
1 tsp. Dijon mustard
generous dash hot red-pepper sauce
1½ cups cooked Alaska king crabmeat or cut-up shrimp
1 10-oz. can artichoke hearts, cooked and drained
buttered croutons

In 1½-quart shallow baking dish, combine soup, wine, mustard and hot red-pepper sauce; add crabmeat and artichoke hearts. Bake at 400°F for 15 minutes or until hot; stir. Top with croutons, bake 10 minutes more.
Makes 3 cups

Seafood in Creamy Wine Sauce

SEAFOOD IN CREAMY WINE SAUCE

½ lb. medium shrimp or scallops, cooked
1 cup milk
2 tbsp. butter
¼ tsp. salt
½ tsp. dried dillweed or tarragon
¼ cup **Veloutine Light**
¼ cup dry white wine
hot cooked rice or patty shells

In medium saucepan combine milk, butter, salt, dillweed or tarragon. Bring just to boil; sprinkle in Veloutine, stirring constantly. Boil 1 minute; stir in wine and cooked shrimp or scallops. Heat. Serve over hot rice or in patty shells. A combination of shrimp and scallops can be used.
Serves 2

Shrimp Sukiyaki

SHRIMP SUKIYAKI

1 12-oz. package frozen raw shrimp, thawed
2 tbsp. lemon juice
dash pepper
2 chicken bouillon cubes
1½ cups boiling water
2 tbsp. soy sauce
2 tbsp. vegetable oil
2 cups thinly sliced fresh mushrooms
1½ cups fresh bean sprouts
½ cup diagonally sliced celery
½ cup sliced green onions
1 medium onion, thinly sliced
¼ cup water chestnuts, thinly sliced
2 cups fresh spinach
1½ cups **Minute Rice**

Combine shrimp and lemon juice in a bowl; sprinkle with pepper. Set aside. Dissolve bouillon cubes in water, stir in soy sauce. Set aside. Heat oil in wok or large frypan. Add mushrooms, bean sprouts, celery, onions, water chestnuts and cook stirring continuously for 2 minutes. Add bouillon mixture; bring to boil. Stir in spinach, rice and shrimp; mix well. Cover; remove from heat. Let stand 5 minutes. Stir and serve.
Serves 4

TUNA OR SALMON FILLO BAKE

2 cans tuna fish or salmon
2 onions, chopped
1 cup dry bread crumbs
1 cup warm milk
2 eggs, beaten slightly
2 tbsp. lemon juice
¼ tsp. salt
2 tbsp. minced parsley
1 tsp. minced mint leaves
¼ tsp. oregano
¾ cup celery, finely chopped
7 **Krinos Fillo Leaves**
1 stick butter, melted for fillo

Mix all ingredients except fillo and butter together and bake in greased fillo-lined pan. (Place 4 fillo leaves in a 9" x 13" baking pan, buttering and sprinkling bread crumbs after each. Place half the mixture in pan. Place 2 more fillo leaves on mixture, buttering after each. Pour in remaining mixture and top with one fillo leaf and butter. Trim edges and roll toward rim of pan. Butter edges well.) Bake in preheated 350°F oven for about 1 hour. After 30 minutes, check every so often to make sure the fillo isn't burning. If edges get too dark, place aluminum foil around them. When finished, allow to cool for 15 minutes. This mixture can also be made in rolls or triangles.

FISH FILLETS CREOLE STYLE

1 16-oz. package frozen fish fillets
2 tbsp. **Mazola Corn Oil**
1 small onion, minced
½ green pepper, minced
1 19-oz. can tomatoes
½ tsp. salt
¼ tsp. garlic powder
1 bay leaf
pinch cayenne pepper
⅛ tsp. black pepper
½ tsp. Worcestershire sauce
1 tsp. sugar
¼ cup **Veloutine Dark**
1 tbsp. minced parsley
hot cooked rice

Bake, fry, poach or microwave fish according to package directions. In medium saucepan heat oil; add onion and green pepper. Sauté 2-3 minutes. Add tomatoes, salt, garlic powder, bay leaf, cayenne, pepper, Worcestershire sauce and sugar. Stir to break up tomatoes. Cover and simmer 10 minutes. Sprinkle in Veloutine, stirring constantly. Boil 1 minute. Remove bay leaf and add parsley. Serve over cooked fish fillets. Pass any remaining sauce to spoon over rice if desired.

Microwave Method: Cook fish in microwave according to package directions. Combine oil, onion and green pepper in a 2-quart microproof casserole or bowl. Cover and microwave on high 1½ minutes. Add tomatoes, salt, garlic powder, bay leaf, cayenne, pepper, Worcestershire sauce and sugar. Cover and microwave on high for 3-4 minutes or until boiling, stirring after 2 minutes. Sprinkle in Veloutine, stirring constantly. Microwave on high 2 minutes, stirring after 1 minute. Remove bay leaf and add parsley. Serve over fish.
Serves 4

SEAFOOD KEBABS WITH RICE

1 cup chicken broth
½ cup dry white wine or water
2 green onions, sliced
¼ tsp. tarragon leaves
¼ tsp. salt
24 large shrimp, cleaned (about 1 lb.) or scallops or a combination of shrimp and scallops
2 large red peppers, cut in 1″ cubes
1½ cups **Instant Brown MINUTE RICE**
1 tbsp. **PARKAY Margarine**, melted

Mix broth, wine, onions, tarragon and salt in large shallow dish; set aside. Place shrimp and peppers alternately on 4 skewers. Place kebabs in broth mixture. Let stand 15 minutes, turning once; remove to broiling pan. Pour broth mixture into saucepan. Stir in rice; bring to boil. Reduce heat and simmer 5 minutes. Remove from heat and let stand 5 minutes. Meanwhile, brush kebabs with margarine. Broil until tender. Serve kebabs over rice.

Microwave Method: Mix broth, wine, scallions, tarragon and salt in 8″ square microwaveable dish; set aside. Place shrimp and peppers alternately on skewers. Place kebabs in broth mixture. Let stand 15 minutes, turning once; remove. Stir rice into broth mixture. Cover and cook on high 4 minutes. Place kebabs on rice mixture around edges of dish. Cover and cook 5 minutes longer.
Serves 4

SCALLOPS IN HOT SAUCE

¼ cup olive oil
5 cloves garlic, coarsely chopped
1 lb. bay scallops
¾ cup slivered red peppers
¾ cup slivered green peppers
½ cup chopped onion
½ tsp. **Tabasco** brand pepper sauce
¼ tsp. salt
2 tbsp. drained capers

In large skillet heat oil; sauté garlic until golden. Add scallops, peppers, onion, Tabasco pepper sauce and salt. Cook, stirring constantly, until scallops turn white and vegetables are tender-crisp. Stir in capers. Serve hot.
Serves 4

LIVELY LEMON ROLL-UPS

1 cup cooked rice
⅓ cup butter or margarine
⅓ cup **ReaLemon Reconstituted Lemon Juice**
2 tsp. salt
¼ tsp. pepper
1 10-oz. package frozen chopped broccoli, thawed
1 cup shredded sharp Cheddar cheese
8 fish fillets (2 lb.), fresh or frozen, thawed
paprika

Preheat oven to 375°F. In small saucepan, melt butter; stir in ReaLemon, salt and pepper. In medium bowl, combine rice, broccoli, cheese and ¼ cup ReaLemon mixture; mix well. Divide broccoli mixture equally among fillets. Roll up and place seam-side-down in shallow baking dish. Pour remaining sauce over roll-ups. Bake 25 minutes or until fish flakes with fork. Spoon sauce over individual servings; garnish with paprika.
Serves 8

BAKED PERCH WITH LEMON CELERY SAUCE

2 lb. perch fillets, fresh or frozen, thawed
1 10-oz. can condensed cream of celery soup, undiluted
¼ cup **ReaLemon Reconstituted Lemon Juice**
2 tbsp. finely chopped green pepper
paprika

Preheat oven to 400°F. Arrange fish in 13″ x 9″ baking dish. In small bowl, combine soup, ReaLemon and green pepper. Spoon over fillets; sprinkle with paprika. Cover with aluminum foil. Bake 30 minutes or until fish flakes with fork. Serve hot.
Serves 8

SEAFOOD POTATO BAKE

½ lb. sole fillets
½ cup **KRAFT Real Mayonnaise**
½ cup sour cream
3 cups frozen hash brown potatoes
4 green onions, chopped
¾ cup grated **CRACKER BARREL Cheddar Cheese**

Cover bottom of 8″ baking dish with sole. Combine mayonnaise and sour cream; fold in potatoes and onions. Cover sole with mayonnaise mixture. Sprinkle cheese over top. Bake at 375°F for 30 minutes.
Serves 3-4

FILLET OF SOLE WITH SORREL-CHEESE SAUCE

1 cup water
¾ cup dry white wine
herb bouquet (3 sprigs each thyme, parsley; 1 leaf each bay and lovage)
12 small fillets of sole (about 2 lb.) or other fillet of firm fish
salt and white pepper
juice of ½ lemon
2 tbsp. butter
1½ cups chopped vegetables (carrots, celery and leeks or onions)
4 oz. **Danish Natural Cream Cheese with Herbs and Spices**
3½ oz. fresh, finely chopped sorrel (about 1 cup)
cooked rice or crisp French bread (optional)

In pan fitted with rack and cover, bring water, wine and herb bouquet to boil, simmer 5 minutes. With skin-side-up, lightly sprinkle fish fillets with salt, pepper, lemon juice and a bit of butter and chopped sorrel. Roll up each fillet; then place on rack. Cover pan; steam over simmering water (about 5 minutes). Carefully remove fish to warm platter; keep warm. Strain broth, discarding herbs. Return broth to pan, along with 3 chopped vegetables. Bring to boil; then simmer uncovered until tender, about 15 minutes. Cool slightly. Pour vegetables and broth into blender. Whirl until smooth. Add Danish Cream Cheese; whirl again. Pour back into pan. Add sorrel; cook over very low heat for 3 minutes only. Add salt and pepper to taste. If desired thin with a little wine. To serve, arrange fish on warm platter or on 6 individual plates. Spoon hot sauce on top. Garnish with a sprig of fresh herb. Serve at once. Note: ¼ cup fresh dill, finely chopped, can be substituted for the sorrel.
Serves 6

MEAT AND POULTRY

Statistics show that we are a nation of meat eaters. Meat and poultry are often the focal point around which the rest of the meal is planned. They satisfy hungry appetites as few other foods can.

The trend today is toward poultry and the leaner cuts of meat which are high in protein while being lower in calories and fats. When choosing lean meats, marinades often become an important part of your preparations. They add moisture and flavor while tenderizing, and they can be very simple to prepare.

Eating meat every day can be costly, so among these recipes you'll find some budget-conscious recipes to help stretch your food dollar. You will find succulent kebabs, piquant barbecues and traditional roast recipes.

Several of our recipes can be used as models and adapted to other kinds of meat. Let your imagination be the limit.

Mandarin Beef Stir Fry (see page 117)

TENDER BEEF IN OYSTER SAUCE

½ lb. flank steak or top round beef
½ tsp. salt
½ tsp. baking soda
½ tsp. baking powder
½ tbsp. cooking wine
3 tbsp. water
1 tbsp. **Golden Dragon Light Soy Sauce**
¾ tbsp. cornstarch
½ tsp. oil
1 cup oil
½ tsp. **Golden Dragon Minced Garlic**
2 green onions, cut in 1" pieces
6 slices fresh ginger
2 tbsp. **Golden Dragon Oyster Sauce**
1 tbsp. **Golden Dragon Dark Soy Sauce**
1 tsp. **Golden Dragon Sesame Oil**
1 tbsp. cooking wine
¼ tsp. sugar
½ tsp. cornstarch
1 tbsp. water

Slice flank steak or top round beef against grain into thick slices. Dredge sliced beef with combination of salt, baking soda, baking powder, cooking wine, water, Golden Dragon Light Soy Sauce, cornstarch and ½ tsp oil and marinate at least 2 hours. Heat wok over high heat until it starts to smoke, add 1 cup oil, separate marinated beef and sauté until half done (about 1-2 minutes). Remove and drain. Heat 2 tbsp. of the same oil in wok. When oil starts to smoke add Golden Dragon Minced Garlic, green onion and fresh ginger. Stir fry for ½ minute, then return beef to wok. Add remaining ingredients and stir fry rapidly for 2-3 minutes until beef is done to taste. Serve hot.

CURRIED ROAST

¼ cup **Patak's Kebab Spice Paste**
2 tbsp. water
3 lb. sirloin tip or lamb roast

Combine spice paste and water in small bowl. Trim fat from surface of roast. Pierce roast with knife. Spread entire surface of roast with kebab paste mixture, rubbing into slashes. Roast on rack in shallow pan, uncovered, at 350°F for 1½-2 hours.
Serves 6

Tender Beef in Oyster Sauce

VEAL SCALLOPS

4 tbsp. unsalted butter
2 tbsp. olive oil
4-5 shallots, finely chopped
1½ lb. veal scallops, pounded until thin
1 tbsp. orange zest
¼ cup **Grand Marnier**
¼ cup port wine
2 lemons, cut into wedges, and chopped parsley for garnish

Heat the butter and oil in a heavy skillet and sauté the shallots for 2-3 minutes. Add the scallops, a few at a time, and sauté them quickly over high heat, about 3-4 minutes a side, until delicately browned. Remove to a platter as they are done and keep warm. Add the orange zest, Grand Marnier and port to the skillet and bring to a boil. Arrange the veal scallops on a platter, pour the sauce over them, and garnish with wedges of lemon and chopped parsley.
Serves 4

CHINESE FLANK STEAK

1½ lb. flank steak, cut in thin 2" strips
¼ cup vegetable oil
½ cup water
1 16-oz. can bean sprouts
1 8-oz. can water chestnuts
1 green pepper, cut into strips
1 cup beef stock
1 tbsp. soy sauce
2 tbsp. Worcestershire sauce
1 tbsp. cornstarch
8 **Krinos Fillo Leaves**
½ stick butter, melted for fillo

In a wok or large skillet, cook steak in oil and water until steak is tender. Keep wok covered. Add all remaining ingredients except fillo and butter and cook for 5 minutes stirring occasionally. Prepare fillo for crêpes and fill crêpes *(see Chicken and Egg Crêpes in Crêpes and Pancakes)* with flank steak mixture. Butter the tops of crêpes. Bake in preheated 375°F oven for 20 minutes or until golden brown.

DANISH BEEF LOAF

3 eggs
½ cup milk
2 tsp. salt
¼ tsp. black pepper
2 tbsp. finely chopped parsley
½ green pepper, finely chopped
1 cup finely chopped celery
½ cup finely chopped onion
2 tsp. Worcestershire sauce
2½ lb. ground chuck
⅓ lb. **Danish Cheese** (**Samsoe**, **Tybo**, **Havarti** or **Danish Blue**), cut in 4 slices approximately ¼" thick

In a large mixing bowl, beat eggs slightly with fork. Stir in milk, salt, pepper, parsley, green pepper, celery and onion and blend together. Add Worcestershire sauce and ground chuck to mixture and combine all ingredients, using hands, or a large mixing spoon. Divide meat in half. On platter-like ovendish mold half the meat loaf to form the base about 3-3½" wide and 7"-8" long. Indent the center slightly; divide and place the cheese down the center. Cover with remaining meat and with hands mold and round the meat to form a loaf. Place in preheated 350°F oven. Bake 45 minutes.
Serves 8

DANISH-STYLE LIVER

1 lb. calves liver, cut in thin strips
¼ cup flour
1½ tsp. salt
1 tsp. pepper
1 tsp. paprika
¼ cup butter
1 medium onion, chopped
1 green pepper, chopped
10 cherry tomatoes, cut in half
1½ cups milk
¼ cup red wine (optional)
1 cup shredded **Danish Samsoe** or **Creamy Havarti Cheese**, divided
3 cups hot fluffy rice

Sprinkle liver on all sides with a mixture of flour, salt, pepper and paprika. In a large skillet, heat butter until light brown, then fry liver over medium-high heat, turning to brown evenly. Add onion and green pepper. Cook for about 10 minutes, then add tomatoes. Simmer about 5 minutes. Add milk and wine; bring to boil. Cook, stirring, until thickened. Add ½ cup cheese and stir gently until cheese has melted. Spoon hot fluffy rice into an ovenproof serving dish. Top with liver mixture. Sprinkle with remaining ½ cup cheese. Place in a 300°F oven for about 10 minutes.
Serves 4-5

BRANDIED BEEF ROAST

3 lb. whole, well trimmed tenderloin (or eye-of-the-round roast)
3 tbsp. butter
salt and pepper to taste
¾ cup brandy

When purchasing your meat at the butcher, ask for some extra suet (fat) to place on top of the roast during cooking. Melt butter in a shallow roasting pan over high heat. Sear the meat quickly on all sides. Remove pan from heat; sprinkle meat with salt and pepper. Pour approximately ⅓ of the brandy over the roast. Roast at 325°F, without lid, for approximately 15-20 minutes per lb. for rare. (If using eye-of-the-round roast, reduce oven temperature to 275°F for approximately 40 minutes per lb.) Gradually pour remaining brandy over roast throughout cooking time. Baste frequently. If the surface of the roast appears to be drying out during cooking, cover with suet or bacon strips. When roasted to desired doneness, remove from oven, allow meat to stand 10 minutes before carving.
Serves 8-10

FROM THE BEEF INFORMATION CENTRE

Brandied Beef Roast

TERIYAKI POT ROAST

- ½ cup all-purpose flour
- ½ tsp. garlic powder
- ¼ tsp. black pepper
- 3-4 lb. beef chuck pot roast (about 2" thick)
- 1 tbsp. vegetable oil
- ½ cup **Kikkoman Teriyaki Marinade & Sauce**
- 3 medium potatoes, quartered

Combine flour, garlic powder and pepper. Coat both sides of meat with flour mixture; reserve ¼ cup mixture. Lightly brown meat slowly on both sides in hot oil in Dutch oven or large skillet. Combine teriyaki sauce and 1¼ cups water; pour over meat. Cover and simmer 1½ hours. Arrange potatoes around meat and simmer, covered, 30 minutes longer or until potatoes are tender. Meanwhile, blend ¼ cup reserved flour mixture and ½ cup water; set aside. Remove meat and potatoes to serving platter; keep warm. Pour pan drippings into large measuring cup. Skim off fat. Reserve 2½ cups of the liquid; return to pan and bring to boil. Gradually stir in flour mixture. Cook and stir until thickened. To serve, slice meat across grain and serve with gravy.
Serves 4-6

CHINESE STYLE RED-COOKED SHORT RIBS

- 3 lb. beef short ribs
- flour
- 2 tbsp. vegetable oil
- ½ cup **Kikkoman Teriyaki Marinade & Sauce**
- 1 garlic clove, minced
- ½ tsp. ground ginger
- pinch of ground cloves
- ¼ cup all-purpose flour

Coat ribs thoroughly with a small amount of flour. Brown ribs slowly on all sides in hot oil in Dutch oven or large saucepan; drain off excess oil. Combine teriyaki sauce, garlic, ginger, cloves and 1¼ cups water; pour over ribs. Cover and simmer 2 hours or until ribs are tender. Meanwhile, blend ¼ cup flour and ½ cup water. Remove ribs to serving platter; keep warm. Pour pan drippings into large measuring cup; skim off fat. Add enough water to measure 2½ cups; return to pan and bring to boil. Gradually stir in flour mixture. Cook and stir until thickened; serve with ribs.
Serves 4

Teriyaki Pot Roast (top)
Chinese Style Red-Cooked Short Ribs (bottom)

MANDARIN BEEF STIR FRY

1 lb. pre-cut beef strips or round or sirloin tip steak
¼ cup soy sauce
½ cup frozen orange juice concentrate
¼ tsp. ginger
¼ tsp. garlic powder
2 tbsp. oil
1 medium red onion, sliced
2 cups snow peas
1 cup fresh mushrooms
1 medium green pepper, sliced
1 10-oz. can mandarin oranges, drained
2 tbsp. cornstarch

For round or sirloin tip steak, pound beef lightly with meat mallet; cut into ¼″ x 2″ strips. Combine soy sauce, orange juice, ginger and garlic powder. Pour over meat; stir, leave to marinate. Prepare vegetables. Heat oil in wok or frypan. Add red onion, snow peas, mushrooms and green pepper. Cook uncovered for 2 minutes. Move vegetables to side of wok. Drain beef, reserving marinade. Stir fry beef until the color changes. Mix with vegetables. Add orange segments. Do not stir. Combine reserved marinade with cornstarch; add to wok. Heat, just to thicken. Serve immediately over rice.
Serves 5

FROM THE BEEF INFORMATION CENTRE

CHINESE BEEF TOMATO STIR FRY

1 package **Noh Beef Tomato Sauce Mix**
1 cup water
1 lb. beef, sliced into strips ⅛″ x 1½″ x 1″
1 tbsp. cooking oil
1 onion, cut into ¼″ slices
1 cup sliced celery
1 green pepper, cut into 1″ cubes
2 tomatoes, cut into 8 wedges each

Combine Beef Tomato Sauce Mix with water; blend well. Add sliced beef to marinade. Heat skillet or wok; add cooking oil and stir fry beef for 1 minute. Add onion, celery and green pepper; stir fry for 2-3 minutes. Add tomatoes and stir fry for 1 minute.

For Beef Broccoli: Use 3 cups broccoli, sliced ⅛″ diagonally. Omit the tomatoes and green pepper.

LIVER FIESTA

1 lb. thinly sliced beef liver
3 tbsp. all-purpose flour
½ tsp. salt
3 tbsp. margarine, butter or salad oil
½ cup thinly sliced onion
½ cup thinly sliced green pepper (optional)
1 14-oz. can tomatoes
⅔ cup **KRAFT Barbecue Sauce**, any flavor
MINUTE RICE

Remove heavy membranes and veins from liver. Cut liver in about 4″ x ½″ strips. (Liver can be cut more easily if it is frozen.) Dredge in flour and salt. Lightly brown in butter in frypan. Remove from frypan; keep warm. Sauté onion and green pepper until onion is transparent. Add tomatoes and barbecue sauce. Bring to boil. Add liver; heat thoroughly—about 10 minutes (overcooking will cause liver to toughen). Serve over rice.
Serves 6

PEPPER SEARED STEAK

New York strip steak or filet mignon
⅓ tsp. **Tabasco** brand pepper sauce
coarse, cracked black pepper to taste

Briskly rub Tabasco pepper sauce into both sides of steak. Sprinkle liberally with pepper and pat it in. Grill over a hot fire, searing the steak quickly on both sides before cooking it slowly over a corner of the grill. Serve medium to medium-rare.

MONGOLIAN BEEF

1 package **Noh Beef Tomato Sauce Mix**
1 cup water
1 lb. chopped steak
1 tbsp. cooking oil
1 onion, sliced in ½ moons
1 parsley sprig

Stir Tomato Sauce Mix with water. Add chopped steak to marinade. Heat skillet or wok, add cooking oil and stir fry chopped steak for 1 minute. Add onions and stir fry for 1 minute. Remove onions and place them in the center of a platter. Cover onions with steak and garnish with parsley.

BEEF BOURGUIGNON

2 lb. lean beef, cut in 1½″ cubes
1 tsp. salt
⅛ tsp. pepper
4 tbsp. butter or margarine, divided
⅓ cup diced carrot
1 cup diced onions
2 tbsp. all-purpose flour
1 garlic clove, minced
pinch of thyme
1 bay leaf
¼ cup chopped parsley, divided
1 cup beef bouillon or 1 beef bouillon cube dissolved in 1 cup water
1 cup dry red wine
2 tbsp. brandy (optional)
10 tiny white onions
10 small (or 5 large) carrots, cut in 1″ pieces
½ lb. small fresh mushrooms, stems and caps separated
MINUTE RICE

Sprinkle beef cubes with salt and pepper. Allow to stand for a few minutes. Melt 2 tablespoons of the butter in large heavy saucepan. Add beef cubes, a few at a time, and brown well on all sides. Add diced vegetables and brown lightly. Mix in flour, garlic, thyme, bay leaf and 2 tablespoons of the parsley. Stir in bouillon, wine and brandy. (Liquids should almost cover meat; add additional bouillon or wine, if necessary.) Cover and simmer for 1½ hours or until meat is tender. Meanwhile, brown onions and carrots in remaining butter in frypan; add to meat mixture. Sauté mushroom stems and caps in butter remaining in frypan. Add to meat mixture and cook 15 minutes longer or until vegetables are tender. Serve with rice. Recipe may be doubled, using 1½ teaspoons salt.
Serves 8

VEAL SCALLOPS WITH CRÈME DE GRAND MARNIER

1½ lb. veal medallions (scallops), or chicken breasts or pork tenderloin
salt and pepper to taste
all-purpose flour
8 tbsp. peanut or olive oil
Sauce:
2 oz. sweet butter
4 shallots, finely chopped
1 garlic clove, minced
⅓ cup fresh orange juice
1 tsp. fresh lemon juice
zest of 1 orange, finely chopped
½ tsp. tarragon
1 tbsp. soy sauce
⅓ cup **Crème de Grand Marnier**
chopped fresh parsley

Cut and flatten the meat; season with salt and pepper. Lightly pound scallops in flour on both sides. In a frypan, heat oil and cook the meat, turning until golden-brown and tender. Set aside on a warm serving platter; discard oil. Melt butter, sauté shallots until soft. Add garlic, orange juice, lemon juice, orange zest, tarragon, soy sauce and simmer until reduced by half (i.e., water from juices has evaporated considerably). Finally, add the Crème de Grand Marnier. Let it boil through for 1-2 minutes and pour the sauce over meat. Sprinkle with chopped parsley, decorate with orange slices.
Serves 4

WEETABIX MEATLOAF

1 onion, sliced
2 tbsp. oil
1½ lb. lean ground beef
1 egg, slightly beaten
1 **Weetabix**, crushed
salt and freshly ground pepper
garlic powder
7-10 large fresh mushrooms

Heat oil in pan and sauté onion until golden brown. Place in the bottom of a 9" loaf pan. Combine beef, egg and Weetabix. Season to taste with salt, pepper and garlic powder. Flatten mixture and shape into a rectangle. Place mushrooms along 1 side and roll into a loaf. Place in onion-lined pan and bake 1 hour at 350°F.

EASY BEEF WELLINGTON

3 lb. beef rib-eye roast
¼ cup butter
2 cups fresh mushroom slices
¼ cup chopped onion
2 tbsp. sherry
¼ cup chopped parsley
1 package frozen puff pastry or enough pastry for 2 double-crust pies
4 oz. liver sausage or liver pâté
1 egg, beaten

Preheat oven to 425°F. Place beef on a rack in an open roasting pan and cook for 50 minutes or until meat thermometer registers 120°F. Remove from oven; let stand 30 minutes. Melt butter in a frypan; sauté mushrooms and onions until tender. Add sherry and parsley. Cook until all liquid evaporates; cool. Roll pastry into an 18" x 14" rectangle, ¼" thick. Spread liver sausage or pâté over the surface leaving a 2" margin around edges. Spoon mushroom mixture down center of pastry. Place roast, top-side-down, in the middle of the pastry. Wrap meat completely with pastry, sealing edges with beaten egg. Decorate with extra pieces of pastry. Place roast, seam-side-down, on baking sheet. Brush top and sides with egg. Bake at 425°F for 30 minutes. Let cool 10 minutes before carving. Note: This may be completely prepared ahead of time and reheated at 300°F for 45 minutes to 1 hour.
Serves 6-8

FROM THE BEEF INFORMATION CENTRE

FRENCH'S FLANK STEAK WITH CREAMY HORSERADISH MUSTARD SAUCE

Flank Steak:
1 lb. flank steak
¼ cup olive oil
¼ cup soy sauce
½ cup red wine
2 tbsp. lemon juice
2 garlic cloves, crushed
Creamy Horseradish Mustard Sauce:
2 tbsp. sour cream or yogurt
¼ cup mayonnaise
2 tsp. **French's Horseradish Mustard**
1 tsp. lemon juice
freshly ground **French's Whole Black Pepper** to taste

To prepare steak: In a shallow dish, combine olive oil, soy sauce, red wine, lemon juice and garlic cloves. Place steak in marinade, turning to coat both sides. Cover and refrigerate for at least 2 hours. Preheat broiler if manufacturer recommends. Grill steak 4" from broiler turning once until medium rare. Thinly slice meat across the grain and serve with Creamy Horseradish Mustard Sauce. To make sauce: In a small bowl, combine the sour cream, mayonnaise, horseradish mustard and lemon juice. Grind pepper to taste. This will yield about ½ cup.
Serves 4

Easy Beef Wellington

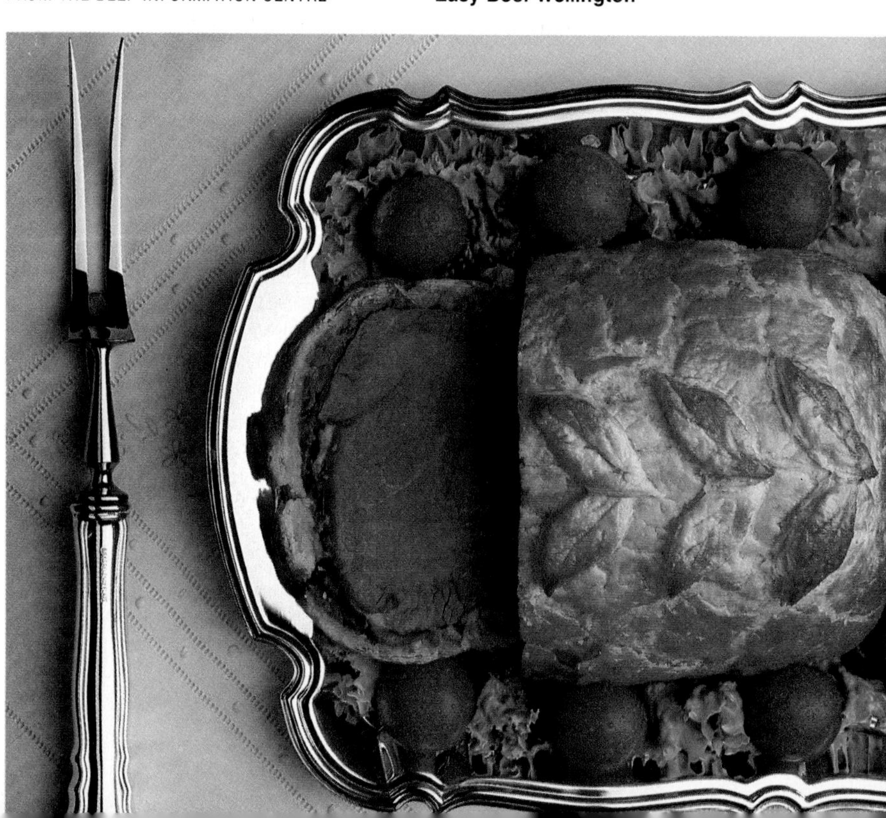

BASIC BURGERS

1 lb. medium ground beef
½ tsp. regular or seasoned salt
⅛ tsp. pepper
1 egg, beaten
¼ cup bread crumbs

Combine all ingredients in a bowl. Mix only until blended. Shape into 4-6 broad, flat patties. Broil or barbecue to desired doneness.

FROM THE BEEF INFORMATION CENTRE

MATAMBRE

2¼ lb. flank steak
½ cup wine vinegar
¼ cup oil
1 garlic clove, minced
5 oz. fresh spinach
2 carrots, blanched, cut in half lengthwise
2 hard-cooked eggs, quartered
1 sweet red pepper, sliced
1 medium onion, sliced
1 tbsp. parsley flakes
1 tsp. salt
⅛ tsp. pepper
7 cups beef stock

"Butterfly" flank steak by splitting in half lengthwise to within ½" of base to form one large steak (do not slice apart completely). Place open steak on cutting board. Pound meat to ¼" thickness. Mix vinegar, oil and garlic. Marinate steak at least 6 hours, covered, in refrigerator. Remove steak from marinade; drain. Layer spinach, carrots, eggs, pepper strips, onion, parsley and seasonings evenly across meat. Carefully roll meat jelly-roll fashion. Tie roll securely at 1" intervals, crosswise and once lengthwise. Place meat roll in roasting pan. Add beef stock to cover ⅔ of roll. (Add more stock or water if necessary.) Cover tightly and bake at 375°F for 1½ hours, or until meat is tender. Turn gently during cooking to prevent top from drying out. Let stand 10 minutes before untying strings and slicing. *Serves 4-6*

FROM THE BEEF INFORMATION CENTRE

Basic Burgers (top)
Matambre (bottom)

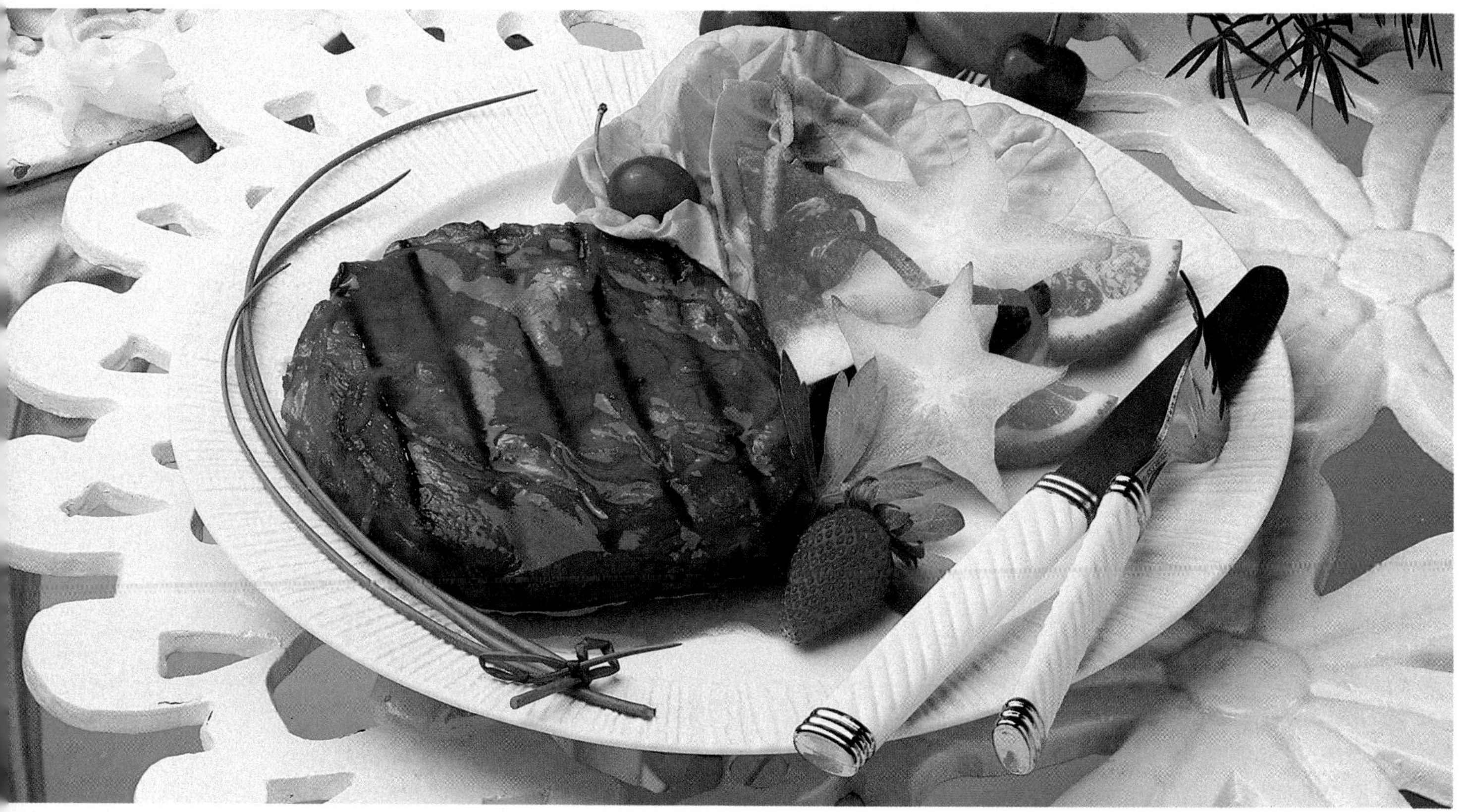

ORANGE-GLAZED BARBECUE STEAK

½ cup orange juice
⅓ cup ketchup
¼ cup lemon juice
¼ cup liquid honey
2 tsp. dry mustard
1 tsp. Worcestershire sauce
1 tsp. grated orange peel
½ tsp. paprika
1 garlic clove, minced
salt and pepper to taste
4 rib-eye, strip loin or tenderized eye-of-round steaks

Combine all ingredients except steaks in a saucepan and bring to boil. Reduce heat and simmer for approximately 10 minutes or until sauce is reduced to ¾ cup. Sear steaks over medium coals for 2 minutes on each side. Continue to cook for 5-6 minutes on each side, brushing with sauce occasionally. Reheat remaining sauce and serve with steaks, if desired.
Serves 4

FROM THE BEEF INFORMATION CENTRE

SWEET AND SOUR MEAT BALLS

Meatballs:
2 lb. lean ground meat
1 cup bread crumbs
1 onion, grated
salt and pepper to taste
1 egg, beaten
½ cup **Billy Bee Honey Bar-B-Q Sauce**
½ cup water

Sauce:
1 large onion
2 tbsp. oil
2 garlic cloves, squashed or diced
1 green pepper (optional)
1 cup **Billy Bee Honey Bar-B-Q Sauce**
½ cup **Billy Bee Honey**
2 cups water

Mix all meatball ingredients in a medium-sized bowl and form meatballs. To make sauce: In a medium-sized pot, cut up and fry onion in oil; add garlic. Add cut-up green pepper if desired. Add Billy Bee Honey Bar-B-Q Sauce, Billy Bee Honey and the water, and extra seasoning if required. Simmer sauce for 15 minutes then add the meatballs to sauce. If the meatballs are not completely covered in the sauce add water. Simmer for 1 hour and serve with rice.
Serves 6

Orange-Glazed Barbecue Steak

BEEF AND BROCCOLI

2 cups fresh broccoli flowerets
1 medium red pepper, cut into strips
1 8-oz. can water chestnuts, drained and sliced
3 tbsp. oil, divided
1 lb. flank steak, cut across grain into ¼" strips
½ cup water
3 tbsp. soy sauce
1 tbsp. sherry
1 tbsp. cornstarch
1 tsp. sugar
½ tsp. garlic powder
½ tsp. ground ginger
1½ cups **MINUTE RICE**

Cook and stir vegetables and water chestnuts in skillet in 1 tbsp. hot oil until tender-crisp, about 2 minutes; remove from skillet. Heat remaining oil in skillet; add meat and brown quickly. Combine water, soy sauce, sherry, cornstarch, sugar, garlic powder and ginger. Add to skillet; bring to boil. Stir in vegetables. Prepare rice as directed on package. Serve meat mixture over rice.
Serves 4

WOODMAN'S STEW

- 1½ lb. beef, cut into 1½" cubes
- 2 tbsp. shortening
- 1 10-oz. can **Campbell's Condensed Golden Mushroom Soup**
- ¼ cup water
- ½ cup chopped, canned tomatoes
- 1 tsp. wine vinegar
- generous dash cinnamon
- 2 whole cloves
- 1 lb. (about 16) small whole white onions

In large heavy pan, brown beef in shortening; pour off fat. Stir in remaining ingredients except onions. Cover; cook over low heat 1½ hours. Add onions; cook 1 hour more or until meat is tender. Stir occasionally.
Serves 4-6

MEATBALL STEW

- 1½ lb. ground beef
- 1 egg, slightly beaten
- 1 cup small bread cubes
- ¼ cup finely chopped onion
- 1 tsp. salt
- 2 tbsp. shortening
- 1 10-oz. can **Campbell's Condensed Beef Broth**
- 1 10-oz. can **Campbell's Condensed Tomato Soup**
- ¼ tsp. crushed thyme
- 1 14-oz. can sliced carrots, drained
- 1 19-oz. can whole white potatoes, drained
- 1 14-oz. can whole onions, drained

Mix beef, egg, bread, onion and salt; shape into 24 meatballs. Brown in shortening in frying pan; pour off fat. Add remaining ingredients. Cook over low heat 20 minutes; stir occasionally. Top with chopped parsley.
Serves 6

MOGUL MEDIUM CURRY

- 1 medium onion, chopped
- 4 tbsp. oil
- 1 lb. stewing beef, cubed
- 1 sachet **Sharwood's Mogul Medium Curry Sauce Mix**
- 1 15-oz. can tomatoes, undrained
- 2 tbsp. **Sharwood's Green Label Mango Chutney**

Fry the onion in oil until soft, add beef and brown all surfaces, add the curry sauce mix and cook for 2 minutes. Add the can of tomatoes and mix in the mango chutney. Simmer gently for 1-1½ hours or until the meat is tender. The thickness and quantity of sauce can be adjusted by adding more water or evaporating the excess liquid.

VEAL KIDNEY MADEIRA

- 3 veal kidneys
- flour
- ½ cup butter
- ½ cup Madeira
- ¼ cup **Delisle Plain Yogurt**
- salt and pepper

Skin kidneys and remove all fat and veins. Cut in thin slices. Dip kidney slices in flour. Heat butter in a large frypan; add kidneys and fry. Kidneys should cook in 3-4 minutes. Arrange kidney slices on a warm serving dish. Pour Madeira into frypan, add yogurt, heat gently over low flame, stir and add salt and pepper. Pour sauce over kidneys and serve.
Serves 6

Woodman's Stew (top) and Meatball Stew

FRUITED BAKED BRISKET

3-4 lb. beef brisket
1 garlic clove
1 medium onion, sliced
12-oz. beer
1 cup water
3 carrots, sliced
1 5½-oz. can tomato paste
2 tbsp. brown sugar
3 tbsp. onion soup mix
¾ cup dried fruit (raisins, prunes or apricots)

Place whole garlic clove in bottom of roasting pan, top with brisket and onion rings. Add 1 cup beer and 1 cup water. Cook uncovered at 425°F for 30 minutes. Remove from oven. Cover with carrots. Combine remaining beer, tomato paste, brown sugar and onion soup mix. Pour over meat. Top with fruit. Cook covered at 325°F, 2½-3 hours until tender. Carve diagonally across the grain.
Serves 8-10

FROM THE BEEF INFORMATION CENTRE

Kiwi Kebabs

GROUND BEEF PIPERADE ON RICE

1½ cups chopped celery
1 large onion, cut in wedges
1 medium green pepper, cut in strips
1 large garlic clove, minced
2 tbsp. vegetable oil
¾ lb. ground beef
⅛ tsp. pepper
2 tbsp. cornstarch
2 tbsp. soy sauce
1⅓ cups cold water
1½ cups boiling water
1½ cups **MINUTE RICE**
½ tsp. salt

In frypan, sauté celery, onion, green pepper and garlic in oil until lightly browned but still crisp. Remove from pan. Keep warm. Brown ground beef in pan, leaving meat in large chunks. Drain excess fat. Combine pepper, cornstarch, soy sauce and cold water. Add to meat; cook and stir until mixture thickens. Pour boiling water into frypan. Stir in rice and salt. Cover, remove from heat and let stand 5 minutes. Stir in vegetables a few minutes before serving.
Serves 4

KIWI KEBABS

1¼ lb. beef cubes or sirloin or inside round steak
¼ tsp. fresh pepper
¼ tsp. garlic powder
3-4 kiwi fruit, thickly sliced
4 cherry tomatoes
½ cantaloupe, cubed, or 4 apricots, halved (other firm yellow fruits may be substituted)
1 small red onion, quartered (optional)

To tenderize round steak and beef cubes, squeeze juice from ½ kiwi fruit over meat. Leave 10-15 minutes. Cut steak in 1" cubes. Season beef with pepper and garlic powder. Alternate beef with fruit and onion on skewers. Barbecue over medium-hot coals approximately 7 minutes for rare or until desired doneness. Turn once during barbecuing.
Serves 4

FROM THE BEEF INFORMATION CENTRE

BARBECUED STEAK WITH ORANGE BUTTER

½ cup softened butter
1 tbsp. grated orange rind
½ tsp. dried thyme
2 green onions, finely chopped
½ tsp. salt
4 rib eye, T-bone or wing steaks
freshly ground pepper

In a small bowl, combine butter, orange rind, thyme, green onion and salt. Blend well. Place butter mixture on a piece of waxed paper and roll into a 1" cylinder. Chill well or freeze. Rub steaks with freshly ground pepper. Sear over hot coals on both sides. Continue to barbecue over medium coals until nicely browned on the outside and a tender juicy pink inside. Serve sizzling hot topped with a slice of orange butter.
Serves 4

FROM THE BEEF INFORMATION CENTRE

CHEESEBURGERS DIJON

1 tbsp. **Maille Dijon Mustard**
1 lb. ground beef
4 cheese slices

Mix 1 tbsp. of mustard with 1 lb. ground beef before forming patties. Form the beef into 4 patties. After cooking, spread additional mustard on the burgers; top with cheese slices and broil to melt cheese.
Makes 4 ¼-lb. burgers

FONDUE KEBABS

2 lb. beef cubes or sirloin or round steak
¼ cup oil
1 tsp. Worcestershire sauce
¼ cup lime or lemon juice
½ tsp. salt
1 bay leaf

Cut steak into 1" cubes. Mix together oil, Worcestershire sauce, lime or lemon juice, salt and bay leaf. Pour over cubed steak and marinate 2 hours for sirloin and 4-6 hours for round or beef cubes. Skewer and barbecue over medium coals, approximately 10 minutes, turning and basting occasionally with one of the following dipping sauces. Make vegetable kebabs as well to serve with the fondue.

Hot Sauce:

1 cup chili sauce
1 small onion, finely chopped
1 tsp. lemon juice
1 tsp. Worcestershire sauce
2 drops hot red-pepper sauce

Combine ingredients and blend well.

Teriyaki Sauce:

½ cup soy sauce
½ tsp. ground ginger
¼ cup sugar
2 tbsp. lemon juice

Combine ingredients in a small pot. Bring to boil and stir until sugar is dissolved. Serve hot or cold.
Serves 6

FROM THE BEEF INFORMATION CENTRE

FRESH ORANGE HERB STEAK

4 oz. eye-of-the-round steak, 1" thick
¼ cup freshly squeezed orange juice
1 tsp. grated orange peel
1 tsp. red wine vinegar
¼ tsp. thyme
salt and freshly ground pepper to taste

Place steak in a small deep bowl. Combine remaining ingredients and pour over steak. Cover and marinate 6-8 hours or overnight. Drain marinade. Broil 4-6 minutes per side for rare or until desired doneness. The marinade may be heated and served as a sauce.
Serves 1

FROM THE BEEF INFORMATION CENTRE

Fondue Kebabs (top)

Fresh Orange Herb Steak (bottom)

HERBED SIRLOIN TIP ROAST

4 lb. sirloin tip roast
1 tsp. **McCormick Oregano Leaves**
1 tsp. **McCormick Thyme Leaves**
1 tsp. **McCormick Celery Seed**
1 tsp. **McCormick Marjoram Leaves**
1 tsp. **McCormick Garlic Powder**
1 tsp. **McCormick Ground Black Pepper**

Bring roast to room temperature. In a small bowl, combine all seasonings. Rub seasonings onto roast. Put roast in roasting pan and place in preheated 450°F oven for 10 minutes. Reduce heat to 350°F and cook until meat thermometer registers 125°F for rare, 140°F for medium or 160°F for well done. Remove from oven. Let roast stand for 10 minutes before carving.
Serves 8

BEEF STEAK PARMESAN

1-1¼ lb. boneless beef, sirloin, round or blade, cut ¾"-1" thick
3 tbsp. olive oil
⅓ cup dry red wine
2 tbsp. chili sauce
¼ tsp. finely chopped garlic
¼ tsp. salt
¼ tsp. pepper
½ cup finely grated Parmesan cheese

Cut beef into 4 equal servings. Combine oil, wine, chili sauce, garlic, salt and pepper; pour over beef and marinate 4 hours for sirloin or overnight for round or blade. Remove beef from marinade and drain; coat with cheese. Place steaks about 3" above hot coals; barbecue 5-6 minutes on one side, turn steaks, sprinkle generously with cheese, barbecue 5 minutes on second side for rare or to desired degree of doneness.
Serves 4

FROM THE BEEF INFORMATION CENTRE

GINGERED BEEF

1 tbsp. vegetable oil
1 medium green pepper, thinly sliced
¼ cup chopped onion
1 cup sliced mushrooms
1 lb. sirloin or inside round steak, thinly sliced
1 tbsp. water
1 tbsp. soy sauce
¼ tsp. ginger
⅛ tsp. garlic powder
1 tbsp. cold water
1 tbsp. cornstarch

Sauté vegetables in hot oil in skillet until tender-crisp. Remove vegetables from pan. Brown meat in remaining hot oil. Add water, soy sauce, ginger and garlic powder; cover and simmer for 5 minutes or until meat is tender. Stir in vegetables. Combine water and cornstarch; add to meat mixture and stir until thickened.
Serves 6

FROM THE BEEF INFORMATION CENTRE

Gingered Beef

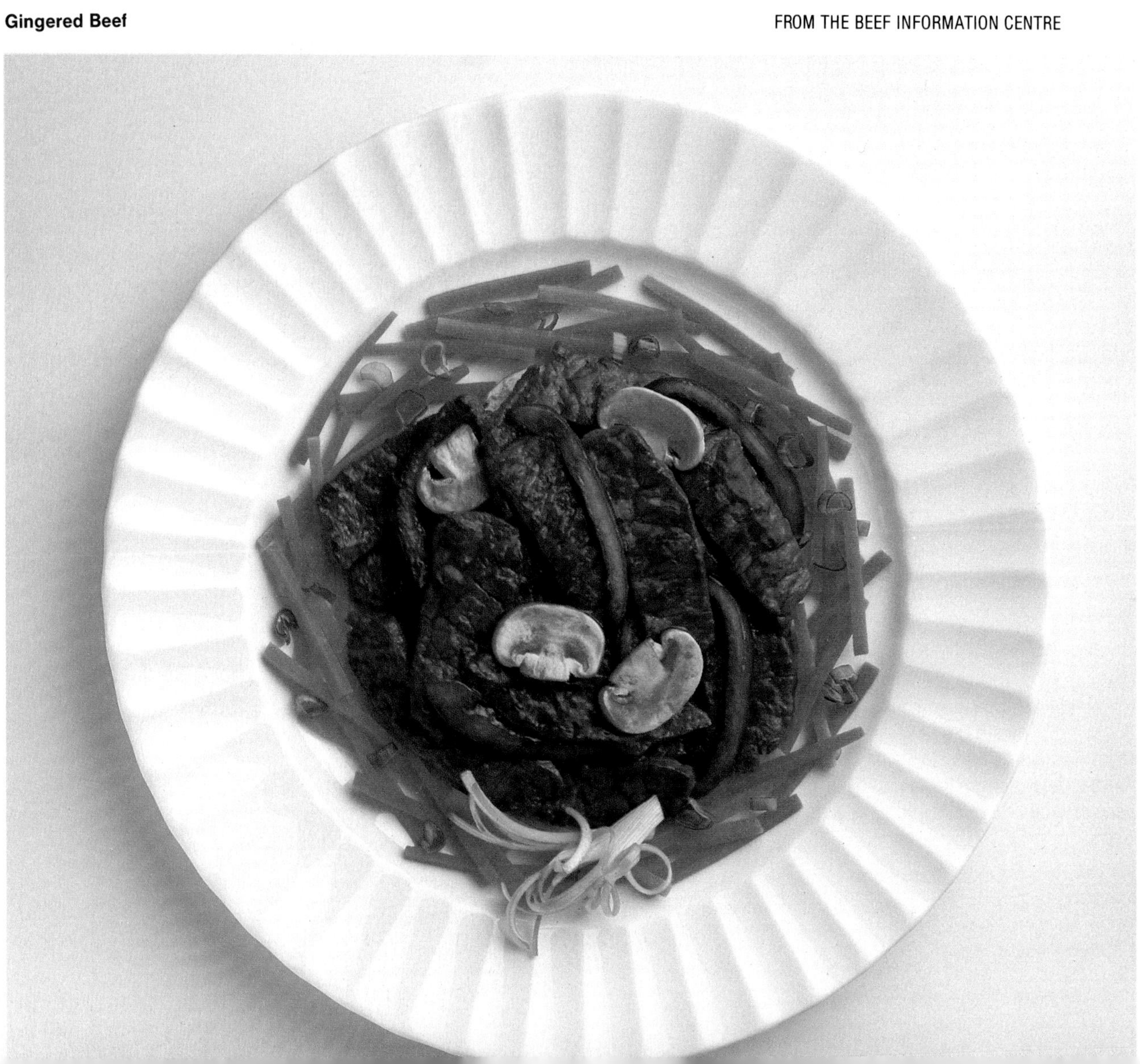

FIERY BEEF AND SNOW PEA STIR FRY

½ lb. tender beef steak
2 tbsp. cornstarch, divided
3 tbsp. **Kikkoman Soy Sauce**, divided
1 tbsp. dry sherry
1 garlic clove, minced
¼-½ tsp. crushed red pepper
6 oz. fresh snow peas
2 tbsp. vegetable oil, divided
1 medium onion, cut in chunks
salt to taste
1 medium tomato, cut in chunks

Slice beef across grain into thin strips. Combine 1 tbsp. each cornstarch and soy sauce with sherry and garlic; stir in beef. Let stand 15 minutes. Meanwhile, combine remaining cornstarch, soy sauce, red pepper and ¾ cup water. Set aside. Remove tips and strings from snow peas. Heat 1 tbsp. oil in wok or large skillet over high heat. Add beef and stir fry 1 minute; remove. Heat remaining oil in same wok. Add snow peas and onion. Sprinkle salt lightly over vegetables and stir fry 3 minutes. Add beef, soy sauce mixture and tomato. Cook and stir until mixture boils and thickens and tomato is heated through.
Serves 4

QUICK GLAZED MEATLOAF

2 eggs, beaten
⅔ cup **Kikkoman Teriyaki Baste & Glaze**
4 slices bread, cubed
1½ lb. ground beef
½ lb. ground pork
1 small onion, chopped
1 tbsp. chili powder
2 tbsp. **Kikkoman Teriyaki Baste & Glaze**

Combine eggs and Teriyaki Baste & Glaze in large bowl; stir in bread cubes. Let stand 5 minutes or until bread cubes are soft. Add ground beef and pork, onion and chili powder; mix until blended. Press firmly into 10″ glass or ceramic pie plate. Microwave on high 20 minutes turning plate once. Brush top of meat mixture with remaining 2 tbsp. Teriyaki Baste & Glaze; microwave on high 5 minutes longer. Let stand 5 minutes before serving.
Serves 6

Fiery Beef and Snow Pea Stir Fry (top)
Quick Glazed Meatloaf (bottom)

PEPPER ROAST

2 garlic cloves, cut in large pieces
5 lb. rib, rump, round or sirloin tip roast
2 tbsp. Dijon mustard
2 tsp. freshly ground pepper

Insert garlic pieces randomly around roast between outside layer of fat and meat, making cuts only if necessary. Insert barbecue spit lengthwise through center of roast. In a small bowl, combine mustard and pepper, spread mixture over roast. Insert meat thermometer into thickest part of roast. Place spit on barbecue over drip pan; cook over medium coals until meat thermometer registers 140°F for rare or 145°F for medium-rare, about 2 hours. Do not overcook. Let stand for 10 minutes before carving.
Serves 15

FROM THE BEEF INFORMATION CENTRE

FILET MIGNON WITH DIJON BRANDY SAUCE

4 filets mignon
salt and pepper
1 tbsp. butter or margarine
¼ cup brandy
2 tbsp. finely chopped fresh onion
1 cup heavy cream
¼ cup **Maille Dijon Mustard**

Sprinkle filets with salt and pepper to taste. In large skillet, melt butter. Cook filets as desired. Pour brandy over meat. Ignite carefully. When flame dies, remove meat to heated platter. Cook onion in drippings. Stir in heavy cream. Simmer until sauce slightly thickens. Mix in mustard. Serve sauce immediately over filets.
Serves 4

Pepper Roast

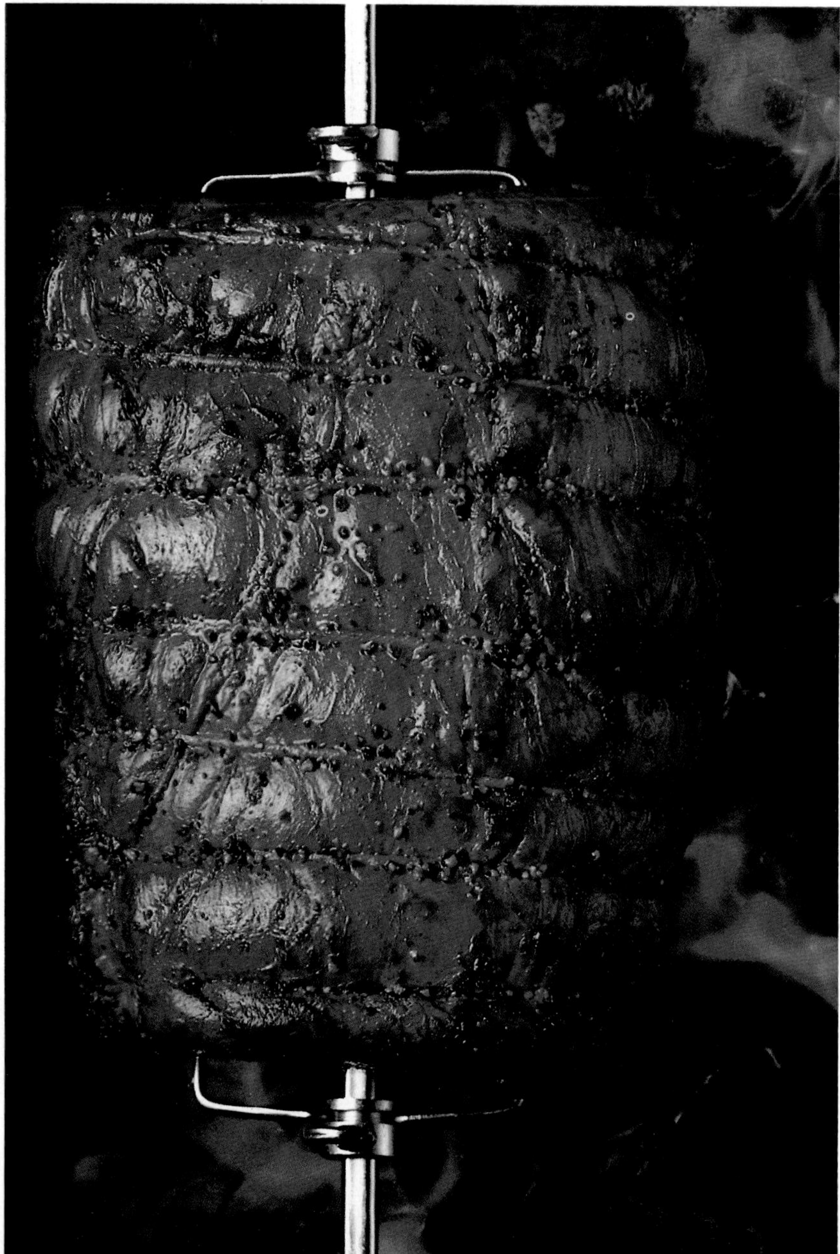

FAJITA RICE

1½ cups **Instant Brown MINUTE RICE**
¾ lb. flank steak, cut into thin strips
1 medium onion, sliced
1 medium green pepper, sliced
1 medium red pepper, sliced
1½ tsp. garlic powder
1 tbsp. oil
½ cup water
¼ cup lime juice
1 tsp. hot pepper sauce
¼ tsp. pepper

Prepare rice as directed on package, omitting margarine and salt. Meanwhile, cook and stir meat, vegetables and garlic powder in hot oil in large skillet until browned. Add remaining ingredients and bring to boil. Reduce heat and simmer 5 minutes. Serve meat mixture over rice.
Serves 4

PEPPERED FLANK STEAK

2 tbsp. Dijon mustard
1 tsp. honey
1 tsp. **Club House Black Pepper** or **Black Peppercorns**, freshly ground
½ tsp. **Club House Garlic Salt**
1 lb. flank steak

Combine mustard, honey and spices and spread on both sides of steak. Let stand 5 minutes. Broil or grill 8-12 minutes. Slice thinly to serve.
Serves 4

PRIZE-WINNING MEATLOAF

1½ lb. ground beef
1 cup tomato juice
¾ cup **Quaker Oats**, uncooked
1 egg, beaten
¼ cup chopped onion
1 tbsp. Worcestershire sauce
1 tsp. salt
¼ tsp. pepper

Heat oven to 350°F. Combine all ingredients; mix well. Press firmly into 8" x 4" loaf pan; bake 60-65 minutes. Let stand 5 minutes before slicing.
Serves 8

Oriental Skewered Beef (top) and Taco Burgers

END OF THE GARDEN JAMBALAYA

1 lb. ground beef
1 onion, chopped
1 tsp. curry powder
3 cups chopped vegetables (tomatoes, carrots, peppers, cucumber, zucchini, etc.)
1 19-oz. can tomato juice
2 cups **MINUTE RICE**
½ cup grated Mozzarella cheese (optional)

Brown beef, onion and curry powder in a large frypan. Add vegetables; stir-fry 2 minutes until tender-crisp. Pour in juice and bring to boil. Stir in rice. Cover; let stand 5 minutes. Sprinkle with cheese if desired.
Serves 4

BEEF BARBECUE

2 lb. ground beef
1½ cups ketchup
¼ cup pickle relish
2 tbsp. Worcestershire sauce
1½ tsp. **Club House Season All**

Brown ground beef and drain fat if necessary. Add remaining ingredients and simmer 10 minutes. Serve on open Kaiser buns with a tossed salad on the side.
Serves 6-8

TACO BURGERS

1 lb. medium ground beef
½ tsp. regular or seasoned salt
⅛ tsp. pepper
1 egg, beaten
¼ cup bread crumbs
1 small onion, minced
1 tbsp. chili powder
½ tsp. dried mustard
4 thin slices of Cheddar or Monterey Jack cheese
hot sauce, chopped onion and tomato to garnish

Combine all ingredients except cheese in a bowl. Mix only until blended. Shape mixture into 8 thin patties. Make rectangular patties if serving in a taco shell. Place a thin slice of Cheddar or Monterey Jack cheese on top of 4 patties. Top with remaining patties. Seal edges. Barbecue and serve in a bun or taco shell topped with hot sauce, chopped onion and tomato.

FROM THE BEEF INFORMATION CENTRE

ORIENTAL SKEWERED BEEF

2 lb. round or flank steak
¼ cup oil
¼ cup honey
⅓ cup dry sherry
½ cup soy sauce
1 garlic clove, minced
1 tsp. grated fresh ginger root (or ½ tsp. dry ginger)
4 green onions
water chestnuts

Slice beef into strips ⅛" thick diagonally across the grain holding the knife blade at 45°. Thoroughly mix together oil, honey, sherry, soy sauce, garlic, ginger and 2 finely chopped green onions. Add beef strips and marinate covered, 4 hours or longer, in refrigerator. Remove beef from marinade and thread on skewers, slipping a piece of green onion or a water chestnut between the folds of meat. Place skewers over hot coals. Turn occasionally and brush with marinade until tender and nicely browned. Accompany with steamed rice and crunchy stir-fried vegetables or a crisp oriental-style salad, including snow peas and asparagus.
Serves 4

FROM THE BEEF INFORMATION CENTRE

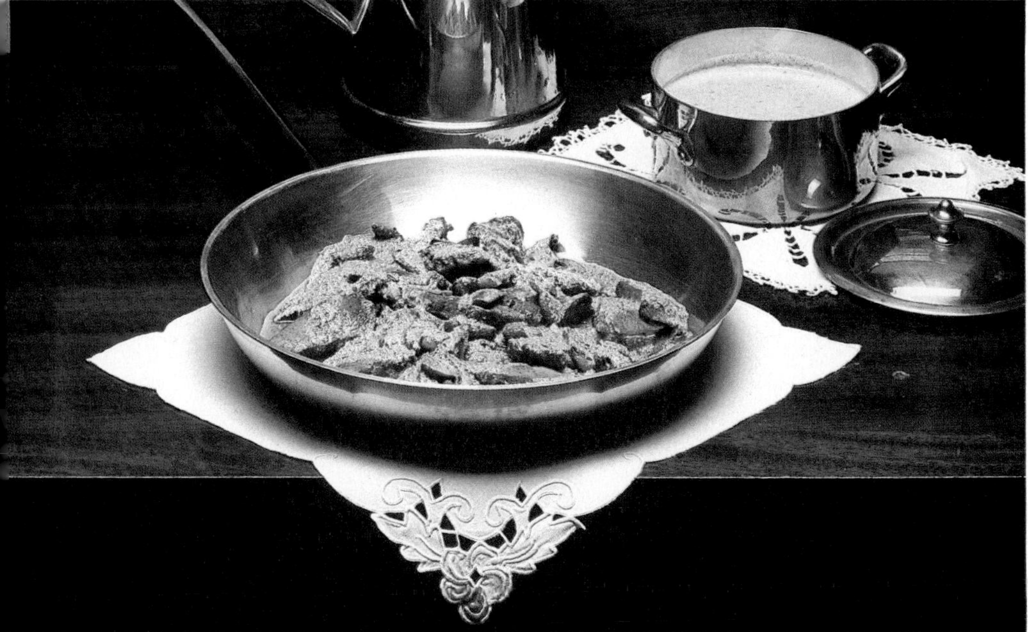

CALF LIVER IN YOGURT

2 lb. calf liver
¼ cup flour
salt and pepper to taste
¼ cup butter
1 garlic clove, minced
¼ cup beef bouillon
1 cup **Delisle Plain Yogurt**
2 tsp. fresh dill (or 1 tsp. dried)

Clean liver and cut into 1" cubes. Mix flour with salt and pepper. Coat liver cubes with flour mixture. Heat butter, sauté liver and garlic. Mix bouillon and yogurt. Over low heat, add yogurt mixture to liver, stirring gently. Taste and adjust seasoning, adding salt and pepper if needed. Add dill.
Serves 6

VEAL CUTLETS PARMESAN

4 frozen **Cardinal Breaded Veal Cutlets, Italian Style**
4 slices Mozzarella cheese

Tomato Sauce:

2 medium tomatoes, coarsely chopped (or 1 14-oz. can tomatoes)
1 small onion, finely chopped
1 small green sweet pepper, finely chopped
1 garlic clove, finely chopped
1 tsp. Worcestershire sauce
½ tsp. salt
pinch freshly ground pepper
2 tbsp. grated Parmesan cheese

Place veal cutlets on a rack in a shallow baking pan. Bake in a 350°F oven for 25 minutes or until browned. Top each cutlet with a slice of cheese and bake 5 minutes longer until cheese melts. While cutlets are baking, make tomato sauce. In a saucepan, combine tomatoes, onion, green pepper, garlic, Worcestershire sauce, salt and pepper. Cook over medium heat, stirring often, for about 15 minutes or until thickened. Place cutlets on serving platter or plate. Spoon sauce over top and sprinkle with Parmesan cheese. Serve immediately.
Serves 4

Calf Liver in Yogurt (top)
Veal Cutlets Parmesan (bottom)

SAAG GOSHT

2 oz. **Sharwood's Ghee**

2 tbsp. oil

1 large onion, chopped

1 tsp. **Sharwood's Garlic Purée**

1 lb. braising steak or lamb, cubed

3 tbsp. **Sharwood's Hot Madras Curry Powder**

1 lb. frozen spinach, defrosted

salt to taste

Heat the ghee and the oil, fry onion and garlic purée until golden. Add meat and continue frying until brown on all surfaces. Add curry powder and continue cooking for 2 minutes, add spinach and salt, combine all ingredients, cover and cook over a low heat for 1¼-1½ hours or until the meat is tender. If the mixture becomes very dry add a little water to prevent it sticking to the pan.

KEEMA MATAR

2 tbsp. oil

1 large onion, chopped

1 lb. minced beef

1 can **Sharwood's Tamatar Madras Curry Sauce**

4 oz. frozen peas

2 tsp. fresh coriander, chopped

Fry the onion in oil until soft; add the beef and brown well. Pour on the curry sauce and stir well. Add the peas and chopped coriander and simmer until the mince and peas are cooked.

BEST-EVER MEATLOAF

1 10-oz. can **Campbell's Condensed Cream of Mushroom** or **Golden Mushroom Soup**

2 lb. ground beef

½ cup fine dry bread crumbs

1 egg, slightly beaten

⅓ cup finely chopped onion

1 tsp. salt

⅓ cup water

Mix thoroughly ½ cup soup, beef, bread crumbs, egg, onion and salt. Shape firmly into 8" x 4" loaf; place in shallow baking pan. Bake at 375°F for 1 hour 15 minutes. In saucepan, blend remaining soup, water and 2-3 tbsp. drippings. Heat; stir occasionally; serve with loaf.
Serves 6-8

Best-Ever Meatloaf (top)
Saag Gosht (middle)
Keema Matar (bottom)

BEEF WITH CAJUN RICE

- 2 tbsp. oil
- 1½ tsp. chili powder
- ½ tsp. thyme leaves
- ¼ tsp. paprika
- dash cayenne
- 1 lb. flank steak, cut into thin strips
- 1 onion, chopped
- 1 green pepper, cut into strips
- 1½ cups beef broth
- 1½ cups **MINUTE RICE**

Sauté beef and onion in oil until meat is browned, about 5 minutes. Add remaining ingredients except rice; bring to boil. Stir in rice. Cover; remove from heat. Let stand 5 minutes.

Microwave Method: In a 3-quart non-metal baking dish, combine oil, chili powder, thyme, paprika and cayenne. Microwave on high power 1 minute. Add beef and onion. Microwave covered on high power 4 to 5 minutes or until meat is slightly pink, stirring once. Stir in remaining ingredients. Microwave covered on high power 5 to 6 minutes longer or until boiling. Stir. Let stand, covered, for 5 minutes.

Serves 4

COCKTAIL RICE MEATBALLS

- 1½ lb. ground beef
- 1 cup **MINUTE RICE** or **Instant Brown MINUTE RICE**
- 1 8-oz. can crushed pineapple in juice
- ½ cup finely shredded carrot
- ⅓ cup chopped onion
- 1 egg, slightly beaten
- 1 tsp. ground ginger
- ¼ tsp. salt
- ¼ tsp. pepper
- 1 8-oz. bottle **KRAFT French Dressing**
- 2 tbsp. soy sauce

Heat oven to 400°F. Mix ground beef, rice, pineapple, carrot, onion, egg, ginger, salt and pepper. Form into 1″ meatballs. Place on greased baking sheets. Bake 15 minutes or until browned. Meanwhile, mix together dressing and soy sauce. Serve meatballs with dressing mixture.

Makes 50-60 meatballs

DOUBLE CHEESE AND BEEF BAKE

- 1 lb. ground beef
- ½ onion, finely chopped
- 1 green or red pepper, coarsely chopped
- 1½ tsp. salt
- ½ tsp. pepper
- ⅛ tsp. garlic powder
- ⅛ tsp. oregano
- 1 19-oz. can stewed tomatoes
- 1 10-oz. can cream of mushroom soup
- 1 cup **MINUTE RICE**
- ¼ cup sliced black olives
- ¼ cup **KRAFT Grated Parmesan Cheese**
- 2 cups grated **KRAFT Mozzarella Cheese**

Brown beef (ground beef may be shaped into small meatballs if desired) in large frypan over high heat. Add onion and pepper. Cook over medium heat until tender. Stir in remaining ingredients, reserving 1 cup Mozzarella cheese for top of casserole. Bring to boil, reduce heat and simmer 5 minutes, stirring occasionally. Spoon into a 6-cup casserole dish. Sprinkle cheese over top. Broil until cheese melts.

Serves 5-6

BEEF AND TOMATO PASAINO

- 1 lb. ground beef
- 1 tbsp. salad oil
- ¾ cup finely chopped onion
- ½ tsp. salt
- ⅛ tsp. oregano leaves
- ⅛ tsp. garlic powder
- ⅛ tsp. thyme
- dash of pepper
- ½ small bay leaf
- 2 7½-oz. cans tomato sauce or 1 19-oz. can tomatoes or 1½ cups tomato juice (omit water)
- 1 10-oz. can cream of mushroom soup
- 1 cup **MINUTE RICE**
- 3 stuffed olives, sliced
- ½ cup water

Brown meat in oil over high heat. Add onion; reduce heat and cook over medium heat until onion is tender, but not browned. Stir in remaining ingredients. Bring to boil; reduce heat. Cover and simmer 5 minutes, stirring occasionally. Garnish with additional sliced stuffed olives, if desired.

Serves 4-6

RICE MEATLOAF

- ¾ lb. lean ground beef
- ¾ lb. lean ground pork
- ½ cup **Uncle Ben's Converted Brand Rice**, uncooked
- ½ cup milk
- ¼ cup minced onion
- 2 tbsp. ketchup
- 1 tbsp. Worcestershire sauce
- 2 eggs, slightly beaten
- ½ tsp. salt
- ½ tsp. dry mustard
- ¼ tsp. each dried marjoram, dried thyme and pepper

In large bowl, mix together all ingredients. Pack into 9″ × 5″ loaf pan, cover with foil and bake in 350°F oven for 1 hour and 15-30 minutes or until well browned and meat is cooked through with an internal temperature of 160°F, removing foil after 30 minutes. (Even when cooked through, meat will still be slightly pink because of ketchup.) Drain off fat and let rest for 5 minutes before cutting in slices to serve.

Serves 4-6

QUICK PEPPER STEAK

- 1 tbsp. cornstarch
- ¼ cup soy sauce
- 2 tbsp. oil, divided
- dash pepper
- 1 lb. lean sirloin or flank steak, cut diagonally into thin strips
- 2 garlic cloves, minced
- 1 10-oz. can beef broth
- 1½ cups **Instant Brown MINUTE RICE**
- 2 peppers, (red, green or yellow), cut into strips

Mix cornstarch, soy sauce, 1 tbsp. oil and pepper in a bowl; stir in beef. Cover and let stand at least 15 minutes to marinate. Heat remaining oil in large skillet. Add beef and garlic, reserving marinade. Cook and stir until meat is brown. Remove meat from pan and keep warm. Pour broth and reserved marinade into the skillet and bring to boil. Stir in rice and peppers. Simmer 5 minutes. Cover, remove from heat and let stand 5 minutes. Stir in beef and serve.

Serves 4

LIME SOY MARINADE FOR KEBABS

2 tbsp. lime juice, freshly squeezed
1 tbsp. low-salt soy sauce
¼ cup vegetable oil
1 tsp. **La Grille Montreal Steak Spice**
2 lb. strip loin or sirloin steak, cut into 1" cubes
bell peppers, onions, mushrooms

Combine lime juice, soy sauce, oil and La Grille Montreal Steak Spice. Mix well and pour into a plastic bag or shallow non-metallic dish. Add steak cubes and coat well. Cover and marinate for 1 hour in refrigerator. Arrange steak cubes on skewers alternately with green or red bell peppers, onions and mushrooms. Broil 4 inches from heat or barbecue, turning frequently for 5-8 minutes. While cooking, brush with marinade. Discard leftover marinade.

Makes 8-10 kebabs

QUICK ITALIAN BEEF STEW

2 tbsp. vegetable oil
1 lb. round steak, cut into thin strips
3 medium carrots, chopped
2 medium potatoes, cubed
1 medium onion, halved and sliced
1 cup sliced mushrooms
½ cup chopped celery
1 19-oz. can stewed tomatoes
1 **Club House Bay Leaf**
1 tbsp. **Club House Parsley Flakes**
1 tsp. **Club House Italian Seasoning**
½ tsp. **Club House Minced Garlic**
½ tsp. salt

In large frypan, heat oil over medium-high heat. Brown steak strips on both sides. Stir in carrots, potatoes, onions, mushrooms and celery. Sauté 5 minutes. Stir in remaining ingredients. Bring to boil. Cover and simmer over low heat for 25-30 minutes or until vegetables and meat are tender. Remove bay leaf.

Serves 4

Microwave Individual Meatloaves

MICROWAVE INDIVIDUAL MEATLOAVES

1 lb. lean ground beef
6 crushed soda crackers
1 egg, slightly beaten
1 tsp. dried parsley flakes
½ cup **KRAFT Regular Barbecue Sauce**, divided

Mix beef, crackers, egg, parsley flakes and ¼ cup barbecue sauce. Divide mixture into 6 balls. Press balls into a microwave muffin pan or 6 heat-resistant custard cups, or place balls in a circle in glass pie plate. Microwave on high 6 minutes. Drain off pan juices. Drizzle remaining barbecue sauce over meatloaves; microwave on high 3 minutes longer, or until meat is no longer pink.

Makes 6 individual meatloaves

FIESTA BURGERS

1 lb. ground beef
2/3 cup crushed corn chips
1/2 cup chili sauce
4 **VELVEETA Process Cheese Food Slices**
4 hard rolls, split
lettuce
red onion slices
guacamole
chopped tomato

Combine meat, corn chips and half of chili sauce; mix lightly. Shape into 4 patties; place on rack of broiler pan. Broil on both sides to desired doneness. Top with cheese slices; broil until cheese begins to melt. Spread rolls with remaining chili sauce. For each sandwich, cover bottom half of roll with lettuce, onion and patty. Top with remaining ingredients, additional chips and top half of roll.
Serves 4

FESTIVE MEXICAN TOSTADOS

10 large flour tortillas
vegetable oil
1 1/2 lb. lean ground beef
1/2 chopped onion
1 cup **KRAFT THICK'N SPICY Onion Bits Barbecue Sauce**
2 tsp. chili powder
2 avocados, peeled and mashed
1/2 cup **KRAFT Real Mayonnaise**
1 tsp. lemon juice
1/4 tsp. salt
1 1/2 cups grated **CRACKER BARREL Old Cheddar Cheese**
2 cups shredded lettuce
1 large tomato, seeded and chopped

Fry each tortilla in 1/2″ of hot oil until crispy and lightly browned; drain on paper towels. Brown meat and drain; add onion and cook until tender. Stir in sauce and chili powder; simmer 15 minutes, stirring occasionally. Meanwhile, mix avocados, mayonnaise, lemon juice and salt in small bowl. For each tostado, top tortilla with meat mixture, cheese, lettuce, tomato and avocado mixture.
Serves 10

MINUTE RICE MEATLOAF

Meatloaf:
1 1/2 lb. medium ground beef
3/4 cup grated **CRACKER BARREL Cheddar Cheese**
3 eggs
1/2 cup milk
3/4 cup **MINUTE RICE**
1 small onion, finely chopped
1 tsp. Worcestershire sauce
1 tsp. salt
1/4 tsp. pepper

Sauce:
1 7 1/2-oz. can tomato sauce
1/3 cup tomato ketchup
1 tsp. sugar
1/8 tsp. dry mustard
1 tsp. Worcestershire sauce

For meatloaf, combine meatloaf ingredients; mix well. For sauce, combine remaining ingredients; mix well. Divide in half. Add half sauce mixture to meatloaf; mix well. Spread into 9″ × 5″ loaf pan. Bake at 350°F for 1 1/2 hours. Heat remaining sauce and serve with meatloaf. Garnish with parsley, if desired.
Serves 4-6

CREAMY LIVER

1 lb. sliced baby beef liver
1/4 cup all-purpose flour
1 tsp. salt
1/4 tsp. pepper
3 tbsp. butter or margarine
1/4 cup chopped onion
2 garlic cloves, minced or pressed
1 cup sliced mushrooms
1 10-oz. can cream of mushroom soup
3 tbsp. chopped parsley
1 tsp. basil
3 cups prepared **MINUTE RICE**

Combine flour, salt and pepper; use to coat liver. Melt butter in frypan over medium-high heat; add liver and sauté until browned, about 2 minutes per side. Keep warm. Add onion to pan and cook until tender, then add garlic and mushrooms and cook about 1 minute. Add soup, parsley and basil. Stir, scraping pan. Return liver to pan. Heat and serve over rice.
Serves 4

GORGEOUS PORK CHOPS

6 pork chops, trimmed
2 tbsp. butter
dash cayenne
salt to taste
6 medium mushrooms, sliced
1 12-oz. package frozen spinach, thawed, (or 1 bunch fresh)

Cheese Sauce:
1 cup half and half cream
1 tbsp. flour
1 cup shredded **Danish Havarti** or **Creamy Havarti Cheese**
dash cayenne
salt to taste

In large skillet, sauté pork chops in 1 tbsp. butter over medium heat until browned on both sides and no longer pink inside. Sprinkle with salt and cayenne. Remove to ovenproof dish; set aside, reserving pan drippings. Sauté sliced mushrooms until tender in pan drippings; remove from skillet. Melt remaining butter in skillet; sauté spinach to heat through. Sprinkle with salt to taste. Arrange spinach on top of pork chops; then cover with foil and place in a 250°F oven while making Cheese Sauce. Sauce: In a small saucepan, bring cream to a slow boil over medium heat. Lightly toss flour into shredded cheese and add to cream. Cook, stirring, until sauce is smooth. Add cayenne, salt and sautéed mushrooms to sauce and pour over pork chops and spinach. Serve with crisp French bread, rice or buttered noodles.
Serves 6

SEASONED PORK ROAST

2 tsp. **Club House Garlic Salt**
1/2 tsp. **Club House Black Pepper**
1-2 lb. boneless pork roast
1/4 cup honey
1 tsp. prepared horseradish
1 tsp. **Club House Ground Ginger**

Mix together garlic salt and black pepper. Rub on boneless pork roast. Roast in 350°F oven 40 minutes per lb. In the last 30 minutes, baste pork with honey, horseradish and ground ginger.
Serves 4-6

SWEET AND SOUR PORK

½ lb. pork, fresh shoulder or loin, cut into ½" cubes
1 tsp. salt
1 tbsp. dry sherry
1 egg
1 tbsp. cornstarch
⅓ cup vegetable oil
½ cup bamboo shoots
1 green pepper, cut into thin strips
1 scallion, cut into ½" pieces
1 onion, chopped
8-10 **Krinos Fillo Leaves**
1 stick butter, melted for fillo

Sweet and Sour Sauce:

½ cup brown sugar
3 tbsp. white vinegar
1 tbsp. orange juice
1 tbsp. tomato paste
1 tbsp. soy sauce
1 tbsp. cornstarch

Combine pork, salt and sherry. Marinate for 20 minutes. Make a batter with egg and cornstarch and set aside. Make sweet and sour sauce by mixing all ingredients together except for the cornstarch. Heat until sugar is completely dissolved. Remove from heat. Coat pork pieces with egg batter. In skillet, heat vegetable oil. Add pork and stir fry for 2½ minutes. Add bamboo shoots and stir fry for 30 seconds. Remove pork and bamboo shoots and set aside. Pour off all but 1 tbsp. oil. Replace skillet over heat and add pepper, scallion and onion. Stir fry for 1 minute. Add cornstarch to sauce, blend well, and pour into skillet. Bring to a boil, then add pork and bamboo shoots. Turn off heat. Heat oven to 400°F. Prepare fillo for crêpes *(see Chicken and Egg Crêpes in Crêpes and Pancakes)*. Fill crêpes with Sweet and Sour Pork. Butter crêpes. Bake for 15 minutes or until golden brown.

HAPA HAOLE PORK

2 cups thin strips uncooked lean pork
3 tbsp. salad oil
½ garlic clove, minced
1½ cups **MINUTE RICE**
¼ tsp. salt
⅛ tsp. pepper
2 cups hot water
1½ cups shredded lettuce or spinach
2 tbsp. soy sauce

Sauté pork in oil until evenly browned; add garlic and sauté until golden brown. Add rice, salt, pepper and hot water; mix just to moisten rice. Bring quickly to boil over high heat. Then cover and remove from heat. Let stand 5 minutes. Just before serving, add lettuce and soy sauce and toss lightly to heat through.
Serves 4

TANGY HONEY BBQ SPARERIBS

5 lb. spareribs
salt and pepper to taste
½ cup water
½ cup **KRAFT Regular Barbecue Sauce**
½ cup **KRAFT Liquid Honey**
2 tbsp. soy sauce
⅓ cup finely chopped onion

Place spareribs in a large roasting pan. Season with salt and pepper. Add water and cover with foil. Bake at 350°F for 30 minutes. Remove foil and continue cooking for 15 minutes. Meanwhile, mix remaining ingredients in small saucepan and simmer 5 minutes. Heat barbecue. Carve spareribs into individual pieces and grill or broil, turning frequently and basting with barbecue sauce until tender and crisp, about 15 minutes.
Serves 4-5

Tangy Honey BBQ Spareribs

DEEP-DISH PORK PIE WITH RICE AND APPLES

1½ lb. lean ground pork
1 onion, chopped
1 clove garlic, minced
1 stalk celery, in 3 pieces
½ tsp. each dried thyme, sage and salt
¼ tsp. pepper
pinch cloves
½ cup **Uncle Ben's Converted Brand Rice**, uncooked
2 eggs
3 cups sliced peeled apples
1 tbsp. each brown sugar and lemon juice
sufficient pastry for 9″ pie shell

In medium saucepan, combine pork, onion, garlic, celery, thyme, sage, salt, pepper and cloves with 1½ cups water and bring to boil. Boil for 1 minute. Stir in rice; reduce heat. Cover and simmer for about 20 minutes or until rice is cooked. Cool; skim off any excess fat from surface, remove and discard celery; then stir in 1 of the eggs. Combine apples, sugar and lemon juice. Layer in baking dish 9″ in diameter and about 2″ deep. Spread pork mixture on top. Roll out pastry to 10″ circle and place over pork. Turn under sides and flute. Cut 3 vents in top. Beat together remaining egg with 1 tbsp. cold water; brush mixture over top of pastry. Bake in 450°F oven for 10 minutes; reduce heat to 350°F and bake for 20 minutes longer or until crust is golden brown. If freezing, cool in refrigerator, cover well with foil and freeze for up to 2 months.
Serves 6

BAVARIAN SAUSAGE AND SAUERKRAUT

1½ lb. bratwurst sausage
½ cup chopped onion
6 cups sauerkraut, drained
2 apples, pared, cored and diced
2 tbsp. brown sugar
1 cup apple cider
½ tsp. **Tabasco** brand pepper sauce

Brown sausage in Dutch oven over low heat. Add onion, sauerkraut and apples. Combine brown sugar, apple cider and Tabasco pepper sauce; pour over sausage mixture. Cover and simmer 45 minutes.
Serves 4

INDONESIAN SPARERIBS

¼ cup vegetable oil
¼ cup lime or lemon juice
¼ cup soy sauce
1 tbsp. liquid honey
1½ tsp. **McCormick Ground Coriander**
½ tsp. **McCormick Ground Ginger**
¼ tsp. **McCormick Ground Black Pepper**
3 lb. pork side spareribs, cut into serving-sized pieces

In large shallow dish, combine oil, lime juice, soy sauce, honey, coriander, ginger and pepper. Add spareribs, turning to coat both sides. Cover and marinate in refrigerator several hours or overnight, turning once. Place spareribs on rack in shallow, foil-lined pan. Bake at 325°F for 1½ hours, basting occasionally with remaining marinade.
Serves 4-6

TERIYAKI SKILLET BRAISED CHOPS

½ cup **Kikkoman Teriyaki Baste & Glaze**
2 tbsp. Dijon mustard
2 tbsp. water
4 pork chops (about ½″ thick)
1 tbsp. vegetable oil
1 small onion, thinly sliced

Combine Teriyaki Baste & Glaze, mustard and 2 tbsp. water; set aside. Brown chops on both sides in hot oil over medium-high heat in large skillet; remove from heat and drain off excess fat. Pour Baste & Glaze mixture over chops; turn over to coat both sides. Sprinkle onion slices evenly over chops. Return to heat, cover and simmer 30 minutes. Turn chops over and simmer, covered, 30 minutes longer or until tender.
Serves 4

PORK PICCATA

1 large pork tenderloin
½ cup **MIRACLE WHIP Salad Dressing**, divided
½ cup seasoned bread crumbs
2 tbsp. vegetable oil
1 tbsp. milk
1 tbsp. lemon juice

Slice pork into 8 equal slices. Place between sheets of waxed paper and pound to ¼″ thickness. Spread slices with half the salad dressing; coat with crumbs. In large frypan, cook meat in oil until golden brown. Remove from heat and keep warm. Combine the remaining dressing, milk and lemon juice in frypan. Warm gently; do not boil. Pour over pork and serve.
Serves 4

GLAZED ROAST OF PORK

1 roast of pork, shoulder, loin or crown
1 jar **Emelia Old English Spiced Apple Preserve**
6-8 large apples

Roast pork as you like it. Meanwhile, core apples and fill center with half the Preserve, reserve the other half for glazing. Bake apples for 1 hour. Glaze the roast during the last 30 minutes several times until the roast is beautifully glazed. Serve the baked spiced apples around the roast on a large platter.

Teriyaki Skillet Braised Chops

HOISIN PORK AND RICE

1½ cups **Uncle Ben's Instant Rice**
1 lb. boneless pork tenderloin
2 tbsp. peanut or vegetable oil
2 cloves garlic, minced
1 tbsp. minced fresh ginger
dash **Tabasco** brand pepper sauce
1 small head broccoli, flowerets and thinly sliced strips
1 each sweet red and yellow pepper, cut in strips
1 small onion, cut in 8 wedges
¼ cup each hoisin sauce and chicken stock
¼ cup dry-roasted peanuts

Cook rice according to package directions. Meanwhile, cut tenderloin across grain into ¼" slices; cut slices into strips. Set aside. In wok or large skillet, heat 1 tbsp. oil over high heat. Stir-fry garlic, ginger and Tabasco pepper sauce for 30 seconds. Add broccoli, peppers and onion; stir-fry for 2 minutes. Transfer vegetables to large heated platter. Wipe out wok with paper towel. Heat remaining oil over high heat. Add pork; stir-fry for 2 minutes. Return vegetables to wok; stir in hoisin sauce and chicken stock; stir-fry for 2-3 minutes or until vegetables are tender but still crisp. Sprinkle with peanuts and serve over rice.
Serves 4

ROAST PORK WITH HERBS

4-5 lb. center-cut pork loin roast
salt and **McCormick Ground Black Pepper**
1 tsp. **McCormick Rosemary Leaves**
1 tsp. **McCormick Garlic Powder**
1½ tsp. **McCormick Sage Leaves**
1½ tsp. **McCormick Oregano Leaves**
1½ tsp. **McCormick Thyme Leaves**

Wipe pork with damp towels and put on rack in roasting pan, fat side up. Season with salt and black pepper. Cut ½"-deep slits in fat between ribs. Combine seasonings and press ½ tsp. of the mixture into each slit. Rub remaining mixture over roast. Put in preheated 450°F oven; reduce heat to 325°F. Roast about 30 minutes per pound or until meat thermometer registers 185°F.
Serves 8

GINGERED PORK'N RICE

1 lb. pork tenderloin
2 tbsp. vegetable oil
2 garlic cloves, crushed
2 carrots, cut into julienne strips
1 celery stalk, cut into julienne strips
1 tbsp. cornstarch
¼ cup water
3 tbsp. Dijon mustard
2 tbsp. soy sauce
1 tbsp. brown sugar
1 tsp. ground ginger
1½ cups **MINUTE RICE**
1½ cups water

Cut pork into ½" slices. Pound into ¼" slices. Sauté pork in hot oil until lightly browned. Add garlic, carrots and celery. Cook until vegetables are tender-crisp. Combine cornstarch and ¼ cup water; mix until smooth. Add mustard, soy sauce, sugar and ginger. Bring to boil, stirring constantly until mixture thickens. Add 1½ cups water; return to boil; stir in rice. Cover; remove from heat. Let stand 5 minutes.

Microwave Method: Cut pork as in frypan method. Measure oil into a 3-quart non-metal baking dish. Microwave on high power for 1 minute. Add pork, cover and cook for 2 minutes on high power until partially cooked. Stir in garlic, mustard, soy sauce, brown sugar and ginger. Combine corn-starch and ¼ cup water; mix until smooth. Stir into meat mixture and cook for 4 to 4½ minutes (stir mixture after 2 minutes) or until mixture comes to a boil and thickens. Add rice and 1½ cups water; cook for 4 to 5 minutes on high power or until bubbles break surface of rice mixture. Let stand, covered, for 5 minutes.
Serves 4

SESAME PORK

1 tbsp. orange juice
1 tsp. honey
1 tsp. sesame oil
1-2 tsp. **McCormick Ground Ginger**
½ tsp. **McCormick Garlic Powder**
1 lb. lean boneless pork, cut in ⅛" strips
3 green onions, chopped
1 tbsp. soy sauce
1 tsp. cornstarch
1 tbsp. **McCormick Sesame Seed**, toasted*
cooked rice

Combine first 5 ingredients. Pour over pork; marinate 10 minutes. Stir-fry with green onions 8-10 minutes. Pour mixture of soy sauce and cornstarch over pork. Cook until thickened. Sprinkle with sesame seeds and serve over rice.
*To toast sesame seeds, heat in non-stick skillet over medium heat, stirring until lightly browned.
Serves 4

APPLE'N SAUSAGE SUPPER

16 pork sausages (about 1 lb.)
2 medium cooking apples, cut into 8 wedges each
1 medium green pepper, cut into thin strips
2 tbsp. sliced green onions
3 tbsp. brown sugar
2 tbsp. cornstarch
1½ cups water
½ cup apple juice
2 tbsp. soy sauce
1 tbsp. vinegar
MINUTE RICE

Cut each sausage into 3 pieces. Brown sausages. Drain off fat. Add apples, green pepper and onions and fry 1 minute. Combine brown sugar and cornstarch. Gradually stir in water, apple juice, soy sauce and vinegar; then stir sauce into sausage mixture. Bring to boil; boil 1 minute. Stir in rice. Cover; remove from heat. Let stand 5 minutes.
Serves 4

PORK STIR-FRY

½ lb. snow peas
1 lb. pork shoulder, cut into thin strips
2 tbsp. oil
1 red pepper, cut in 1″ chunks
¼ lb. mushrooms, sliced
4 green onions, cut in 1″ pieces
2 tbsp. soy sauce
½ tsp. **Tabasco** brand pepper sauce
½ cup beef stock or water
1 tbsp. cornstarch
1 tbsp. cold water

Remove strings from snow peas and blanch for 2 minutes in lightly salted boiling water. Rinse under cold water. Heat oil in large skillet, add pork and stir-fry for 5 minutes. Add vegetables, soy sauce and Tabasco pepper sauce to skillet and stir-fry another 2-3 minutes, then add stock or water. In a separate bowl, mix cornstarch and cold water. Add to pan, stirring until liquid clears and thickens.
Serves 4

Piquant Pork Roast

PORK KOFTA

1 lb. minced pork or beef
½ tsp. **Sharwood's Garlic Purée**
1 tsp. **Sharwood's Hot Madras Curry Powder**
1 tbsp. chopped fresh coriander
salt to taste
Sauce:
2 tbsp. oil
2 bay leaves
1 large onion, chopped
1 tsp. puréed fresh ginger (optional)
1 tsp. **Sharwood's Garlic Purée**
4 tbsp. **Sharwood's Mild Curry Paste**
1 15-oz. can tomatoes, undrained
1 cup water
salt

Combine the pork, garlic purée, curry powder, fresh coriander and salt. Shape into 8 balls and refrigerate while preparing sauce. Heat the oil, add bay leaves and fry for a few seconds; add onion, ginger, and garlic purée and fry until brown. Add curry paste and cook for further 2 minutes. Add tomatoes, water and salt. Place the meat balls in the sauce, cover and simmer gently for 30-40 minutes. The thickness and quantity of sauce can be adjusted by adding more water or evaporating the excess liquid.

GLAZED BAKED HAM WITH GRAND MARNIER

6-8 lb. cooked ham
2 cups dry white wine
¾ cup dry bread crumbs
1 tbsp. dry mustard
½ cup brown sugar
Grand Marnier
sprigs of parsley or mint to garnish
Grand Marnier Sauce:
½ cup port wine
½ cup **Grand Marnier**
juice of 1 orange
1 tbsp. lemon juice
½ cup orange marmalade

Put the ham, fat-side-down, in a roasting pan with the wine and cover with aluminum foil. Bake in a 350°F oven for 2 hours, basting with the liquid in the pan. Remove the ham from the oven and trim off all but ¼″ of the fat. Mix the bread crumbs and dry mustard together and press into the fat with your hand. Press the brown sugar into the crumbs and sprinkle liberally with Grand Marnier. Broil about 10″ from the broiling unit, or put in a 450°F oven until nicely glazed, watching carefully that it does not burn. Remove to a carving board while you prepare the sauce. Put the port, Grand Marnier and orange juice in a saucepan and bring to a boil. Boil briskly until reduced to ⅓ cup. Add the lemon juice and orange marmalade and stir until blended and smooth. Carve the ham into thin slices and arrange on a heated platter. Garnish with sprigs of parsley or mint and serve with the sauce.
Serves 8-10

PIQUANT PORK ROAST

¾ cup **Heinz Chili Sauce**
½ cup dry red wine
1 4½-oz. jar **Heinz Apricot Baby Food**
1 garlic clove, minced
1 tsp. salt
½ tsp. thyme
¼ tsp. pepper
3-4 lb. boned, rolled pork loin roast

Combine first 7 ingredients for marinade. Marinate pork in covered container overnight in refrigerator. Turn occasionally. Place on rack in roasting pan. Bake at 325°F for 2-2½ hours. Baste with marinade occasionally. Heat remaining marinade to serve as a sauce with pork.
Serves 8

LOIN OF PORK AU GRAND MARNIER

5 lb. loin of pork, boned, with rack reserved
glazed apple slices to garnish
Marinade:
3 garlic cloves
3 tbsp. soy sauce
1 cup **Grand Marnier**
zest of 1 orange
½ orange, cut into sections
1 tsp. freshly ground black pepper

Place the roast on its own rack in a roasting pan. Combine the garlic, soy sauce, ⅔ cup Grand Marnier, zest of orange, orange sections and freshly ground black pepper in the bowl of a food processor or in a blender. Process until well blended. Rub the loin of pork well with the marinade and allow to marinate for 2-3 hours, turning 2-3 times. Roast the loin in a 350°F oven for 1 hour and 45 minutes, basting every 20 minutes, or until the internal temperature reaches 160°F. Remove from the oven and allow to rest for 5 minutes. Place on a serving platter and garnish with glazed apple slices. Heat the remaining ⅓ cup Grand Marnier, flame, and pour over the pork before going to the table.

BEANS AND RIBS PROVENÇAL

1 14-oz. can **Libby's Deep-Browned Beans**
1 carrot, thinly sliced
1 celery stalk, chopped
1 bay leaf
1 tbsp. dried parsley
1 garlic clove, chopped
1 large onion, chopped
2 tbsp. lard or shortening, melted
1 lb. pork spareribs, separated
1 cup canned tomatoes
2 tbsp. canned tomato paste
½ tbsp. sugar
1 cup chicken stock
salt and pepper to taste

In a large saucepan, combine Libby's Deep-Browned Beans, carrot, celery, bay leaf, parsley and garlic. Simmer at medium-low heat for 20 minutes. Meanwhile, in a deep frypan, fry onions and the ribs until ribs are browned. Stir in tomatoes, tomato paste, sugar and stock. Bring the mixture to a boil. Add the ribs to the beans. Season with salt and pepper and simmer for 20 minutes until the meat is tender and liquid is thickened.

GOAN VINDALOO

2 tbsp. oil
1 onion, chopped
1 tbsp. **Sharwood's Garlic Purée**
1 lb. pork, cubed
½ jar **Sharwood's Vindaloo Curry Paste**
2 tbsp. vinegar
2 medium tomatoes, chopped
2 large potatoes, cubed

Fry onion in oil; when soft, add garlic and pork. Fry for further 5-10 minutes until brown. Add paste, vinegar, chopped tomatoes and potatoes. Simmer for approximately 30 minutes until the potato is cooked. Add water if necessary to prevent sticking to the pan.

TABASCO LAMB KEBABS

¼ cup olive oil
¼ cup yogurt
½ tsp. salt
½ tsp. **Tabasco** brand pepper sauce
½ tsp. powdered rosemary
2 lb. boneless lamb, cut into 1½" cubes
2 large mild yellow onions, cut in wedges
2 tomatoes, quartered
pitted ripe olives

In large bowl, combine olive oil, yogurt, salt, Tabasco pepper sauce and rosemary. Stir in lamb and marinate in refrigerator for 2 hours. Place meat, onion, tomato and olives on skewers alternately. Broil kebabs about 3" from heat for 10-12 minutes, brushing frequently with marinade and turning to brown evenly.
Serves 4-6

MUSTARD-CRUSTED LEG OF LAMB

6 lb. leg of lamb
2 tbsp. olive oil
½ cup Dijon mustard
2 tbsp. soy sauce
1 garlic clove, minced
¼ tsp. ginger
½ tsp. **Tabasco** brand pepper sauce
1 tsp. dried leaf thyme
½ cup bread crumbs

In medium bowl, combine all ingredients except lamb and bread crumbs. Spread mixture on lamb, sprinkle with crumbs and let stand 1 hour. Place lamb on rack in roasting pan. Roast in 350°F oven for 1½ hours.
Serves 8

LAMB À LA GRECQUE

1 lb. lamb chops (about 4-8) or 1 lb. lamb sausages, thawed
1 onion, chopped
1 garlic clove, minced
1 zucchini, cut in strips
1 10-oz. can mushrooms, drained
1 19-oz. can tomatoes
½ cup white wine (or chicken broth)
1 tsp. each rosemary and oregano
1½ cups **MINUTE RICE**

In large frypan, sauté lamb, onion, garlic and zucchini until vegetables are tender. Add mushrooms, tomatoes, wine and herbs. Bring to boil, then simmer 10 minutes until lamb is cooked. Remove lamb to serving platter. Stir rice into remaining vegetable mixture. Cover; remove from heat. Let stand 5 minutes. Serve with lamb.
Serves 4

LAMB SHISH KEBABS

⅓ cup vegetable oil
3 tbsp. white wine vinegar
2 tbsp. lemon juice
1 tbsp. **McCormick Lemon & Pepper Seasoning**
1 garlic clove, minced
2 lb. boneless, lean lamb, cut into 1" cubes
3 medium zucchini, cut in 1" pieces
1 large red pepper, cut into 1" pieces

In shallow glass dish, combine oil, vinegar, lemon juice, lemon & pepper seasoning and garlic. Stir in lamb. Cover and marinate several hours or overnight in refrigerator, turning once. Thread on skewers alternately with zucchini and red pepper. Place on barbecue over hot coals (or use broiler) and cook 6-8 minutes on each side for medium doneness, brushing occasionally with marinade.
Serves 6

CURRIED LEG OF LAMB

1 5-6 lb. leg of lamb, deboned
2 garlic cloves, finely chopped
½ jar **Emelia Spiced Kiwi Fruit Preserve**
2 tbsp. lemon juice
1 tsp. curry powder
2 tsp. coriander

Make marinade by mixing together the last 5 ingredients. Marinate meat for at least 1 hour (or overnight). Barbecue or broil until crisp on the outside and medium rare inside (15 minutes on each side). Carve against the grain. Serve with rice pilaf and a crisp green salad.
Serves 6-8

LAMB TIKKA KEBABS WITH MINT CHUTNEY

1½ lb. boneless lamb shoulder, cut into 1½" cubes
onion rings and lemon wedges to garnish

Marinade:

3 tsp. **Sharwood's Curry Paste**
⅔ cup plain yogurt
2 pieces **Sharwood's Stem Ginger**, minced
1 tbsp. lemon juice

Mint Chutney:

3 tbsp. mint sauce
2 tsp. chili powder
1 small onion, minced

Mix together the marinade ingredients. Toss lamb in marinade, ensuring that all the meat is coated, then refrigerate overnight. Skewer lamb onto 4 metal skewers and place on a greased rack in a broiling pan. Broil for 15-20 minutes or until tender, turning kebabs occasionally. To make mint chutney: Blend mint sauce, chili powder and onion. Garnish kebabs with onion rings and lemon wedges and serve with mint chutney.

BUTTERFLIED LEG OF LAMB

1 5-lb. leg of lamb, boned and butterflied

Marinade:

½ cup **HP Sauce**
½ cup dry white wine
¼ cup **Lea & Perrins Worcestershire Sauce**
2 tbsp. olive oil
1 finely chopped garlic clove

Open leg of lamb and place fat-side-down in large flat glass or enamel pan. Marinade: In a small bowl, combine HP Sauce, wine, Worcestershire sauce, oil and garlic. Mix well. Pour over lamb. Cover and refrigerate for 12 hours or overnight, turning once or twice. Keep refrigerated until 1 hour before cooking time. Drain lamb, reserving marinade. Place on lightly greased barbecue grill. Barbecue 6" from hot coals for 50-60 minutes, turning occasionally and basting with reserved marinade, until lamb is browned but still pink in center when slashed.

To Broil: Place marinated butterflied leg of lamb on foil-lined broiling rack. Broil 4"-6" from heat, basting occasionally with reserved marinade, for 30-35 minutes on each side, until lamb is browned but still pink in center when slashed.
Serves 6-8

LAMB DO-PIAZA

2 medium onions, finely chopped
4 tbsp. oil
1 tsp. puréed fresh ginger (optional)
1 tsp. **Sharwood's Garlic Purée**
3 tbsp. **Sharwood's Medium Hot Curry Powder**
1 lb. lamb, trimmed and cubed
5 oz. natural yogurt
1 large onion, sliced
salt to taste

Fry the chopped onions in oil, add the ginger and garlic purée and curry powder, fry well for a few minutes. Add the lamb and brown all surfaces. Stir and fry, very gradually incorporating the yogurt into the sauce. Lower heat and simmer for 25 minutes. Fry the sliced onion until well browned, add to the meat and season, simmer for a further 20 minutes until the meat is tender.

BRAISED LAMB SHANKS

5 lb. lamb shanks
small peas and chopped parsley to garnish

Marinade:

3 tbsp. olive oil
2 tbsp. ketchup
2 tbsp. Worcestershire sauce
1 tbsp. Dijon mustard
2 garlic cloves, finely chopped
¼ cup **Grand Marnier**

Combine all the ingredients for the marinade in a bowl or pan large enough to accommodate the lamb shanks. Allow the shanks to marinate for 5-6 hours or overnight. Remove the shanks from the marinade and place them on a broiling rack. Broil about 4" from the heat, until nicely brown, turning once. Remove to a braising pan. Spoon the marinade over the shanks and cover. Braise in a 350°F oven for 45 minutes to 1 hour. Arrange the shanks on a platter. Garnish the platter with a wreath of small peas and sprinkle with chopped parsley.
Serves 4-5

DRY SPICED ROAST LAMB

1 3-lb. leg of lamb
1 tbsp. salt
2 oz. blanched whole almonds, toasted, to garnish

Marinade:

2 tbsp. puréed fresh ginger (optional)
1 tbsp. **Sharwood's Garlic Purée**
4 green chiles, very finely chopped
½ cup natural yogurt
2 oz. almonds
3 tbsp. **Sharwood's Garam Masala**
1 tsp. ground cloves (optional)
2 tbsp. very finely chopped fresh coriander (optional)
1 tsp. ground cardamom seeds (optional)

Blend together marinade ingredients. Make regular 1" cuts into lamb, rub in salt then coat in marinade. Cover in oiled foil and refrigerate for several hours, preferably overnight. Roast on an oiled tray at 450°F for 20 minutes, reduce to 350°F for 30 minutes or until lamb is cooked and marinade is crisp. Garnish with whole almonds pushed into slits.

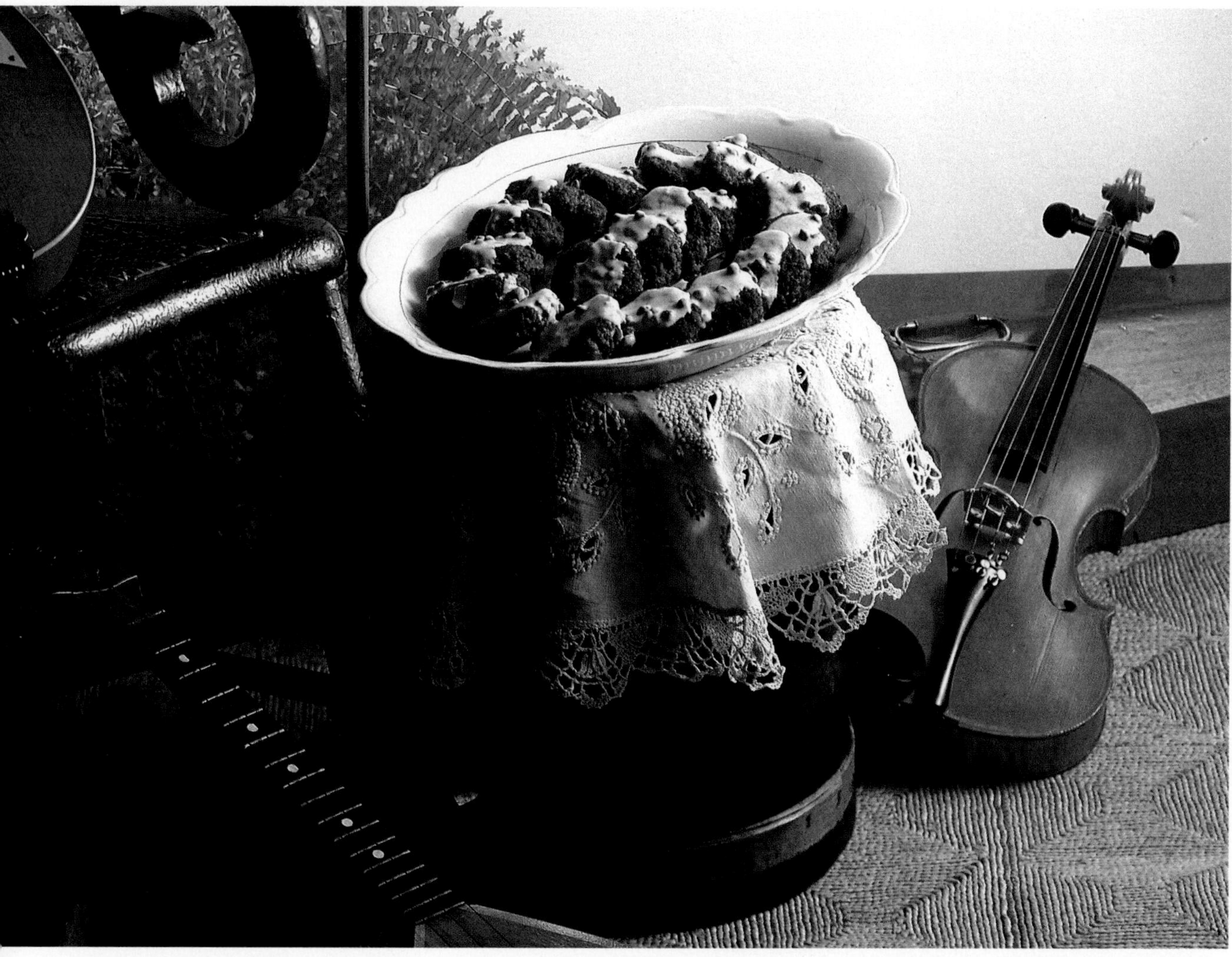

Lamb Patties with Yogurt and Caper Sauce

LAMB PATTIES WITH YOGURT AND CAPER SAUCE

2 tsp. butter and oil
1½ cups chopped onion
1 garlic clove, minced
2 lb. ground lamb
¾ cup bread crumbs
2 eggs, slightly beaten
3 tbsp. parsley
2 tbsp. dill
salt and pepper to taste
2 tbsp. butter
1½ tsp. paprika
½ tsp. thyme
¾ cup dry white wine
¾ cup chicken broth
1¼ cups **Delisle Plain Yogurt**
¼ cup capers
4 cups cooked rice or noodles

Heat fat, sauté half the onions and garlic. Remove from pan and let cool, reserving hot fat. Combine lamb with sautéed onion, bread crumbs, eggs, parsley, 1 tbsp. dill, salt and pepper. Mix thoroughly. Shape mixture into 24 balls. Flatten into small patties. Fry patties in fat about 5 minutes on each side. Remove to a warm dish. Pour off drippings from pan, add 2 tbsp. butter and sauté remaining onion. Add paprika, thyme, wine and chicken broth. Cook until liquid is reduced by half. Remove from heat and add yogurt. Return to heat and cook gently but do not let boil. Strain sauce, return to heat and add capers. Pour sauce over lamb patties. Sprinkle with remaining dill. Serve on rice or noodles.

Serves 8

Ginger Chicken and Bean Stir Fry

GINGER CHICKEN AND BEAN STIR FRY

1 lb. boneless chicken breasts
2 tbsp. vegetable oil
2 small garlic cloves, crushed
⅔ cup carrots, thinly sliced
2 large onions, quartered
2 tsp. grated fresh ginger (or 1 tsp. powdered ginger)
1 cup green or red pepper, cut in cubes
1 cup sliced mushrooms
2½ cups **Green Giant Frozen French Style Green Beans**
2 tbsp. soy sauce
1 tbsp. vinegar
2 tbsp. sherry
½ cup water
2 tbsp. cornstarch

Slice chicken into bite-sized strips. Heat oil in large frypan or wok. Add garlic and chicken and stir fry until browned. Add carrots and onions and stir fry for 4 minutes. Add ginger, green or red pepper and mushrooms and cook for 3 minutes; stir in green beans. Combine soy sauce, vinegar, sherry, water and cornstarch. Add to pan. Cook just until sauce thickens and vegetables are tender-crisp. Serve with rice.
Serves 4

CHICKEN JAMBALAYA

1 8-oz. package **Green Giant Sweetlets Peas in Butter Sauce**
1 tbsp. vegetable oil
1 small onion, sliced
½ garlic clove, finely chopped
1½ cups cooked, cubed chicken
½ lb. Polish sausage, cut in ½″ slices and quartered
1 19-oz. can tomatoes, coarsely chopped
½ cup sliced celery
¼ cup sliced pitted green olives
½ tsp. Worcestershire sauce
¼ tsp. hot red-pepper sauce
1½ cups cooked rice

In bowl of warm water, thaw pea pouch for 20 minutes. In large skillet, heat oil; sauté onion and garlic about 3 minutes, until tender. Stir in chicken, sausage, tomatoes, celery, olives, Worcestershire sauce and hot red-pepper sauce. Bring mixture to boil; cover, reduce heat and simmer 20 minutes. Stir in thawed Peas in Butter Sauce and rice. Cover and continue cooking 5 minutes or until rice and peas are thoroughly heated.
Serves 4

FLANDERS WATERZOY

1 whole chicken, divided in 7 pieces
1 package **Le Gourmet Nantaise Vegetable Soupmix**
3½ cups cold water
1 cup cream
4 egg yolks, well beaten
3 tbsp. butter

Boil the chicken. Apart, mix the contents of Vegetable Soupmix with water and bring to boil. Simmer for 20 minutes and add cream, egg yolks and butter. Place the chicken in a soup tureen. Pour the sauce over it and serve.

EASY BAKE BARBECUE HONEY CHICKEN

3 lb. broiler chicken
¼ cup **Billy Bee Honey**
1¼ cups **Billy Bee Bar-B-Q Sauce**
½ tsp. garlic powder

Clean and cut up chicken. Season to taste. Mix together other ingredients and pour over the chicken. Marinate in refrigerator for 3 hours or overnight. Bake at 350°F in an open roasting pan for approximately 45 minutes. May also be barbecued.

SESAME CHICKEN WITH CUMBERLAND SAUCE

6 chicken breasts
1 envelope **Shake'n Bake Regular Coating Mix for Chicken**
1 tbsp. sesame seeds
1 cup red currant jelly
2 tbsp. port wine
1 tsp. Dijon mustard
1 tsp. grated orange rind
1 tsp. grated lemon rind
¼ tsp. ginger
1 tbsp. water
1 tbsp. cornstarch
hot, cooked, parsley rice

Coat chicken pieces with coating mix as directed on package. Place in a shallow baking pan. Sprinkle with sesame seeds. Bake at 400°F for 40 minutes. Meanwhile, combine jelly, wine, mustard, grated orange and lemon rind and ginger. Cook and stir over medium heat until jelly melts. Blend water and cornstarch. Slowly add to jelly mixture. Cook and stir over medium heat until thickened, about 5 minutes. Arrange chicken on parsley rice on serving platter. Spoon sauce over chicken.
Serves 4-6

CHICKEN PAILLARD

2 whole chicken breasts, boned, skinned and split
¼ cup **HP Sauce**
¼ cup dry white wine
2 tbsp. olive oil
½ tsp. **Lea & Perrins Worcestershire Sauce**
1 garlic clove, finely chopped

Place chicken breasts between 2 sheets of waxed paper. Pound gently to flatten to an even thickness of ¼". Place in a shallow glass or enamel pan. Combine HP Sauce, wine, olive oil, Worcestershire sauce and garlic. Pour over chicken. Cover and marinate for 4 hours in the refrigerator. Drain well, reserving marinade. Place on a lightly greased grill. Barbecue 6" over hot coals, basting frequently with marinade, for 8-10 minutes per side or until juice runs clear and chicken is tender. To Broil: Place marinated chicken breasts on foil-lined broiling rack. Broil 3"-4" from heat, basting frequently with reserved marinade, 6-8 minutes each side until chicken is tender and juices run clear.
Serves 4

TANDOORI CHICKEN KEBABS

12 small boiling onions, peeled
1 lb. boneless chicken breasts, skinned
1 green pepper
1 small unpeeled eggplant
¼ cup **Patak's Tandoori Paste**
¼ cup plain yogurt
¼ cup melted butter or margarine

Cook onions in boiling water until tender, about 10 minutes. Cut chicken, pepper and eggplant into 1" cubes. Combine tandoori paste, yogurt and melted butter. Alternate chicken and vegetables on 6 skewers. Brush with tandoori mixture. Broil or grill 4"-6" from heat for 20-30 minutes, turning occasionally and brushing with remaining tandoori mixture.
Serves 6

MEXICAN SEASONED CHICKEN

3 cups chicken, cooked, boned and cubed
1 cup sour cream
1 tbsp. lime juice
1 jalapeno pepper, finely minced
2-3 tbsp. finely minced green onions
1 tsp. cumin
1 lb. **Krinos Fillo Leaves**
½ lb. butter, melted for fillo

Marinate chicken in next 5 ingredients for a few hours. Then prepare fillo leaves according to package directions, fill and shape into triangles, rolls or squares. Bake in preheated 400°F oven for 15-20 minutes or until golden brown.

Sesame Chicken with Cumberland Sauce

SZECHUAN DRAGON CHICKEN STIR FRY

1 whole chicken breast, skinned and boned
4 tbsp. **Kikkoman Soy Sauce**, divided
1 tbsp. cornstarch
½ tsp. sugar
1 garlic clove, minced
4 tsp. cornstarch
¼-½ tsp. crushed red pepper
2 tbsp. vegetable oil, divided
2 carrots, cut in half lengthwise, then cut into diagonal chunks
1 onion, chunked and separated
2 small zucchini, cut in half lengthwise, then cut into diagonal chunks
¼ cup unsalted peanuts
hot cooked rice

Cut chicken into thin narrow strips. Combine 1 tbsp. soy sauce and next three ingredients; stir in chicken and set aside. Blend 4 tsp. cornstarch, remaining soy sauce, red pepper and 1 cup water; set aside. Heat 1 tbsp. oil in wok or large skillet over high heat. Add chicken and stir fry 2 minutes or until chicken is tender; remove. Heat remaining oil in same wok. Add carrots and onion; stir fry 3 minutes. Add zucchini; stir fry 2 minutes. Stir in chicken and soy-sauce mixtures; cook and stir until sauce boils and thickens. Just before serving, stir in peanuts. Serve immediately with rice if desired.
Serves 4-6

SUPREME OF CHICKEN WITH GRAND MARNIER

4 chicken breasts, deboned, skinless
2 tbsp. unsalted butter
juice of 1 orange
¼ cup **Crème de Grand Marnier Liqueur**
parsley and orange slices to garnish

Marinade:

¼ cup soy sauce
¼ cup **Grand Marnier Cordon Rouge Liqueur**
⅛ tsp. ground ginger
¼ tsp. freshly ground black pepper
zest of ½ orange, finely chopped
2 garlic cloves, minced

Mix the marinade ingredients together. Remove fat from chicken breasts, flatten and place in the marinade for at least 3 hours (for best results, overnight). In a frypan melt the butter. When hot, brown the chicken for 2-3 minutes on each side (do not burn the butter). Add the orange juice and 4 tsp. of the marinade (leftover marinade can be used for pork loin, pork chops or ham before grilling or roasting). Let simmer for a few minutes, then add Crème de Grand Marnier and let the sauce with the chicken reduce by one half. Place the breast on a serving dish, pour the sauce over, sprinkle with chopped parsley and garnish with orange slices. Serve with rice or pasta.
Serves 4

STUFFED ROCK CORNISH GAME HENS

4 Rock Cornish game hens
watercress to garnish

Stuffing:

½ cup finely sliced scallions
½ cup finely sliced mushrooms
4 tbsp. unsalted butter
giblets and livers from the game hens, chopped quite fine
2 cups cooked rice
1 tsp. salt
½ tsp. freshly ground black pepper
zest and juice of 1 orange
1 cup chicken stock
⅓ cup **Grand Marnier**
heavy cream

Sauté the scallions and mushrooms in butter until they are just limp. Add the chopped giblets and livers and toss them with the scallions and mushrooms. Add the rice, salt, pepper, orange zest and juice, chicken stock and Grand Marnier. Toss lightly to blend well. If the mixture seems dry, add 3-4 tbsp. heavy cream. Stuff the hens lightly and truss. Arrange them on a rack in a shallow roasting pan and rub with butter. Roast in a 400°F oven for 30-35 minutes. Remove and discard the strings, transfer to a bed of watercress on a hot platter and garnish with additional watercress.
Serves 4

Szechuan Dragon Chicken Stir Fry

TANDOORI CHICKEN

6 portions chicken
1 tsp. salt
juice of 1 lemon
1 sachet **Sharwood's Tandoori Barbecue Mix** (or 4 tbsp. from **Sharwood's Drum of Tandoori Mix**)
3 tbsp. oil
3 tbsp. vinegar
3 tbsp. natural yogurt
lettuce
lemon wedges

Remove chicken skin and slash flesh several times with a sharp knife. Sprinkle with salt and half the lemon juice. Set aside. Whisk together the Tandoori Barbecue Mix with oil, vinegar, remaining lemon juice and yogurt. Coat chicken with this marinade, cover and refrigerate a few hours, preferably overnight. Remove from the marinade, grill for 15-20 minutes each side. Serve with lettuce and lemon wedges. This recipe can also be used with lamb chops.
Serves 6

Tandoori Chicken

CHICKEN DIJON WITH SPICE AND WINE

2½ lb. chicken parts
2 tbsp. butter or margarine
salt and pepper to taste
1 medium garlic clove, minced
1 bay leaf
¼ tsp. marjoram
¼ tsp. thyme
¾ cup chicken broth
¾ cup dry white wine
12 small white onions
12 whole baby carrots
1 14-oz. can artichoke hearts
⅓ cup **Maille Dijon Mustard with White Wine**

In large skillet, brown chicken in butter. Sprinkle lightly with salt and pepper. Add garlic, bay leaf, marjoram, thyme, broth and wine. Cover and simmer stirring occasionally, 35 minutes. Add onions, carrots and artichokes. Cover and simmer 10 minutes or until vegetables are tender. Remove chicken and vegetables to heated serving dish. Add Dijon mustard to remaining liquid. Bring to boil. Thicken sauce with 1 tbsp. flour mixed in 2 tbsp. water, if desired. Spoon sauce over chicken and vegetables.
Serves 6

CRISPY FRIED CHICKEN

1 egg
2 tbsp. milk
1 tbsp. salt
¼ tsp. black pepper
¼ tsp. garlic powder
1 lb. **Humpty Dumpty Regular Chips**, crushed
1 lb. boneless chicken, sliced

In shallow bowl, whisk together egg, milk and seasonings. Dip chicken pieces in egg mixture, then in crushed Humpty Dumpty potato chips to coat. Place chicken in large shallow baking pan and cook in 350°F oven for 40 minutes (or until chicken is tender). Serve hot or cold. For delicious barbecued chicken use **Humpty Dumpty BBQ-flavored Chips** to coat.
Serves 6-8

STUFFED CHICKEN BREASTS

1 small onion, chopped
1 garlic clove, minced
2 tbsp. oil
1 celery stalk, chopped
1 small carrot, grated
6 oz. mushrooms, chopped
2 **Weetabix**, crushed
½ cup hot chicken stock
1 egg
salt and pepper
8 large chicken breasts, boned and skinned
¼ cup flour, seasoned with with salt, pepper and paprika
1 cup chili sauce
few drops hot red-pepper sauce
1 tsp. Worcestershire sauce
1 green pepper, in rings

Sauté onion and garlic in oil. Add celery, carrot and mushrooms, stirring until moist. Crush Weetabix in a bowl. Add stock and egg. Add vegetables, salt and pepper. Flatten the chicken breasts in the flour. Put 2 tbsp. of stuffing on each breast and roll up. Place seam-side-down in a greased baking dish. Mix chili sauce with hot red-pepper sauce and Worcestershire sauce. Pour over breasts. Bake in preheated oven at 350°F for 45 minutes, uncovered. Garnish with green pepper rings and bake 15 minutes more. Stuffing can be baked separately in a baking dish at 350°F for 45-60 minutes.
Serves 8

CHINESE POT ROAST CHICKEN

1 package **Noh Chinese Roast Chicken Seasoning Mix**
1 tbsp. water
1 lb. chicken, cut into bite-sized pieces
1 tbsp. cooking oil
1 onion, cut into ¼" slices
1 medium Chinese won bok cabbage, cut into 1" strips
1 cup bamboo shoots, cut into ¼" wedges

Combine Roast Chicken Seasoning Mix with water and blend well. Marinate chicken in this mixture. Add oil to saucepan and parcook chicken. Then add onion, Chinese cabbage and bamboo shoots. Simmer for 10 minutes and serve.

Pesto Chicken Gourmet

HONEYCUP CURRIED CHICKEN

1½ lb. boneless chicken breasts, cut into strips
¼ cup soy sauce
1½ tsp. cumin
1½ tsp. curry powder
1 tbsp. cornstarch
2 tbsp. **Honeycup Mustard**
2 tbsp. peanut oil
1 large onion, diced
2 large zucchini, sliced in rounds
1 cup green peas, defrosted
1 red pepper, cut into strips
1 green pepper, cut into strips
2 shallots, finely chopped
2 tbsp. finely chopped fresh, candied or preserved ginger
½ cup orange juice
dash hot red-pepper sauce (optional)

Stir the first 6 ingredients together and marinate in refrigerator for several hours or overnight. Sauté chicken in wok in hot peanut oil. Push aside and add onion, zucchini, peas, peppers, shallots and ginger. Stir fry for 3 minutes. Then stir in orange juice and hot red-pepper sauce to taste. Continue stir frying just until heated through. Serve on a bed of rice to which you have added roasted peanuts.
Serves 6

PESTO CHICKEN GOURMET

Pesto filling:
1 cup fresh parsley
¼ cup grated Parmesan cheese
¼ cup chopped walnuts
3 tbsp. **Mazola Corn Oil**
2 tsp. dried basil leaves
⅛ tsp. pepper
1 garlic clove, chopped

Chicken:
4 chicken breasts, skinned and boned
¼ cup flour
¼ tsp. salt
⅛ tsp. pepper
1 egg plus 1 tbsp. water
½ cup fine dry bread crumbs
½ cup **Mazola Corn Oil**

Prepare pesto: Process all ingredients in blender until smooth. Drop by tablespoonfuls onto cookie sheet and freeze. Makes 8 tbsp. To prepare chicken, pound each chicken breast to ¼" thickness. Combine flour, salt and pepper in shallow pan. Beat egg and water together in shallow pan. Place bread crumbs in another shallow pan. Place 2 tbsp. frozen pesto filling on each chicken breast. Roll up, tucking edges in. Secure with toothpick. Roll in seasoned flour, dip in egg wash and roll in bread crumbs. Refrigerate chicken. Pour oil into large skillet. Fry chicken over medium heat until browned and cooked throughout, turning after 10 minutes.
Serves 4

BIRYANI

- ½ box **Sharwood's Basmati Rice**, rinsed
- salt
- 3 tbsp. oil
- 1 medium onion, finely chopped
- 1 lb. skinned chicken meat, cut into bite-sized pieces
- ½ jar **Sharwood's Biryani Paste**
- 2 fresh tomatoes, sliced
- 2 tbsp. chopped fresh coriander (optional)
- 5 oz. natural yogurt
- flaked almonds and sliced onions to garnish

Boil rice in plenty of well salted water for 8 minutes and drain. Fry onion in oil. When softened add chicken and Biryani Paste. Cook briskly for 5 minutes and transfer to a casserole. Arrange the tomatoes and coriander on top, spread yogurt over, top with rice, tightly cover and bake 30-40 minutes at 375°F until chicken is cooked and rice is fluffy. Garnish with flaked almonds and sliced onion rings.

COCONUT CHICKEN

- 1 lb. skinned chicken meat
- 1 medium onion, finely chopped
- 1 small green pepper, sliced
- 3 tbsp. oil
- 2 tsp. puréed fresh ginger (optional)
- 3 tbsp. **Sharwood's Mild Madras Curry Powder**
- 2 oz. **Sharwood's Creamed Coconut**
- ½ cup hot water
- 3 tbsp. light cream
- salt to taste

Cut the chicken into bite-sized pieces. Fry the onion and green pepper in oil, when soft remove the pepper. Add the ginger purée and chicken, brown well. Add curry powder. Combine the creamed coconut with the hot water and add to the chicken. Simmer gently for approximately 15 minutes or until the chicken is cooked, stir in the cream to make a smooth sauce and season to taste. Add the cooked green pepper to garnish and serve.

Biryani (top right) and Coconut Chicken (bottom left)

CHICKEN CELESTINE WITH GRAND MARNIER

- 1 chicken
- flour
- salt
- pepper
- ⅓ cup butter
- 2 tbsp. **Grand Marnier**
- 3 tbsp. white stock
- 1 small carton whipping cream
- 2 tbsp. flaked almonds, roasted
- 4 small apples

Divide the chicken into 6 portions (2 legs, 2 wings, 2 portions from the breast). Flour and season and fry in very hot butter, first one side and then the other. When well colored, sprinkle with Grand Marnier, add the white stock, cover and simmer for 35 minutes. Remove the chicken to a serving dish. Make the sauce by adding some Grand Marnier (if required) to the stock in the pan, and gently stir in the cream. Add the roasted flaked almonds. Cover the chicken with this sauce and garnish with apple. To garnish, peel the apples and cut into cubes. Cook in the oven with a little butter until soft. To avoid mashing, do not stir.
Serves 6

CURRIED MANGO CHICKEN

- 8 chicken pieces (breasts or thighs)
- ¼ cup unsalted butter
- 1½ cups chopped onions
- 3 garlic cloves, chopped
- 1" piece ginger, finely chopped
- 1 tsp. ground cumin
- 1 tsp. turmeric
- 1 tsp. ground coriander
- ¼ tsp. ground fennel
- ½ cup water
- 1 jalapeno pepper, chopped
- 1 cup chopped fresh tomato
- 2 tbsp. finely chopped fresh coriander
- ½ cup plain yogurt
- salt to taste
- 1 tsp. garam masala
- ⅓ jar **Emelia Spiced Mango Preserve**

Sauté chicken in butter, remove; add onions, garlic and ginger. Fry until soft; reduce heat, add spices and water. Sauté 1 minute; stir in pepper, tomato, 1 tbsp. fresh coriander, yogurt and salt to taste. Raise heat, add chicken and juices. Sprinkle with garam masala, simmer 20 minutes. Stir in Spiced Mango Preserve. Serve on rice, sprinkled with fresh coriander and lemon juice.
Serves 8

SPANISH CHICKEN

1 lb. chicken parts
1 cup (about ¼ lb.) sliced fresh mushrooms
1 tbsp. shortening
salt
pepper
½ 10-oz. can **Campbell's Condensed Tomato Soup**
2 tbsp. Chablis or other dry white wine
1 medium bay leaf
1 medium garlic clove, minced
½ medium green pepper, cut in squares
1 tbsp. sliced pimento-stuffed olives

In frypan, brown chicken and mushrooms in shortening; pour off fat. Season with salt and pepper. Stir in remaining ingredients. Cover; cook over low heat 30 minutes or until done. Stir occasionally; remove bay leaf.
Serves 2

NOUVEAU CHICKEN AND VEGETABLE ENTRÉE

2 medium carrots
3 celery stalks
1 medium zucchini
6 boneless chicken breast halves
2 garlic cloves, minced
4 tbsp. **Mazola Corn Oil**
2½ cups chicken broth
1 tsp. dried thyme leaves
⅛ tsp. salt
¼ tsp. pepper
⅓ cup **Veloutine Light**

Cut carrots, celery and zucchini in ¼" x 2" sticks. Remove skin from chicken. In large skillet heat oil. Add carrot, celery, zucchini and garlic; stir fry 3-4 minutes or until tender-crisp. Remove vegetables and set aside. Brown chicken in hot oil on both sides. Lower heat and add chicken broth, thyme, salt and pepper. Cover and simmer 20 minutes or until cooked. Remove chicken and keep warm. Gradually sprinkle Veloutine into simmering liquid, stirring constantly. Boil 1 minute; return vegetables and chicken to sauce, stirring until hot. Serve chicken on a bed of vegetables with cooked rice or pasta.
Serves 6

Spanish Chicken (top)
Nouveau Chicken and Vegetable Entrée (bottom)

TANDOORI CHICKEN MASALA

4 chicken breasts
1 sachet **Sharwood Tandoori Barbecue Mix** (or 4 tbsp. from **Sharwood's Drum of Tandoori Mix**)
3 tbsp. oil
3 tbsp. vinegar
juice of ½ lemon
3 tbsp. natural yogurt
4 tbsp. melted butter
3 tbsp. oil
1 large onion, very finely chopped
1 tsp. **Sharwood's Garlic Purée**
1 tsp. puréed fresh ginger (optional)
1 tsp. **Sharwood's Hot Madras Curry Powder**
½ cup water
5 oz. light cream
salt to taste
fresh coriander to garnish

Remove chicken skin and slash flesh several times with a sharp knife. Set aside. Whisk together the Tandoori Barbecue Mix with 3 tbsp. oil, vinegar, lemon juice and yogurt. Coat chicken with this marinade and refrigerate a few hours, preferably overnight. Drain breasts, retaining marinade, and roast at 425°F for approximately 30 minutes, brushing occasionally with butter. Retain cooking juices. Fry onion, garlic and ginger in oil. When golden add curry powder and fry gently for 2 minutes. Add drained marinade, retained chicken juices, water and cream. Simmer 5 minutes. Slice chicken, add to sauce, salt to taste, simmer 10 minutes and serve garnished with fresh coriander.
Serves 4

SOUTH SEAS CHICKEN

1 envelope **Shake'n Bake Regular Coating Mix for Chicken**
1 tsp. curry powder
6 chicken pieces
¼ cup melted butter or margarine
1 cup **Baker's Angel Flake Coconut**

Empty coating mix into plastic shaker bag. Add curry powder; mix well. Coat chicken pieces with coating mix as directed on package. Bake at 400°F for 35 minutes. Meanwhile, combine melted butter and coconut. Place on top of chicken pieces and bake an additional 5 minutes, or until golden brown.
Serves 4-6

CHICKEN BREASTS WITH ARTICHOKE-CHEESE STUFFING

4 boneless, skinless chicken breast halves
¾ cup grated Monterey Jack or mild Cheddar cheese
¼ cup mayonnaise
2 tsp. chopped green onion
2 tsp. dried parsley flakes
½ tsp. Dijon mustard
1 6-oz. jar marinated artichoke hearts, drained
½ cup all-purpose flour
½ tsp. salt
pinch pepper
1 egg
1 tbsp. water
½ cup seasoned dry bread crumbs
⅓ cup **Crisco Oil**

Pound chicken breasts until ¼" thick. Set aside. Mix cheese, mayonnaise, onion, parsley flakes and mustard in small mixing bowl. Cut artichoke hearts into bite-sized pieces, stir into cheese mixture. Place ¼ of artichoke–cheese mixture at end of each chicken breast. Roll, folding in sides. Mix flour, salt and pepper in shallow dish. Combine egg and water in shallow dish. Place bread crumbs in a shallow dish. Dip chicken rolls in flour mixture to coat, in egg mixture and then in bread crumbs. Cover and refrigerate for 1 hour. Preheat oven to 350°F. Place Crisco Oil in 13" x 9" baking pan and heat in oven 10 minutes. Remove from oven. Carefully roll coated chicken breasts in hot Crisco Oil, using tongs. Arrange chicken in pan. Bake at 350°F for 35 minutes or until golden brown.
Serves 4

PEACH AND PEPPER CHICKEN

1 chicken, cut into 6 pieces
1 onion, sliced
6 celery green tops, chopped
3 carrots, cut in julienne strips
Glaze:
1 large garlic clove, finely chopped
½" piece ginger, grated
1 tbsp. tamari or soy sauce
1 tbsp. dry sherry
½ jar **Emelia Peach and Pepper Preserve** or **Red Pepper Jelly**

Preheat oven to 375°F. Scatter vegetables over the bottom of baking pan. Place chicken pieces on top and roast for 45 minutes. Combine glaze ingredients. Glaze chicken and roast for 30 minutes longer. Serve with rice pilaf and buttered dill carrots.
Serves 6

South Seas Chicken

CHICKEN HAWAIIAN

2 lb. chicken pieces
3 tbsp. oil
1 cup **Heinz Chili Sauce**
1 7½-oz. can **Heinz Tomato Sauce**
1 14-oz. can pineapple chunks, drained (reserve liquid)

Brown chicken in hot oil in skillet. Stir in chili sauce, tomato sauce and pineapple juice (add water to juice to make 1¼ cups). Simmer 30-35 minutes. Add pineapple chunks; heat through. Serve over noodles.
Serves 4

TERIYAKI CHICKEN

2 tbsp. soy sauce
2 tbsp. water
6 pieces chicken
1 envelope **Shake'n Bake Regular Coating Mix for Chicken**
½ tsp. ginger
¼ tsp. garlic powder
liquid honey

Combine soy sauce and water in large bowl. Dip chicken pieces in soy-sauce mixture and shake off excess liquid. Add ginger and garlic powder to coating mix; blend well. Shake chicken pieces in bag one at a time. Arrange chicken in a single layer on a microwave rack in a non-metal baking dish, placing the thickest part of each piece toward the outside of the dish. Microwave on high power 10 minutes. Rotate dish and microwave on high power 10 minutes more. Brush generously with honey. Microwave on high power 2 minutes. Cover and let stand 5 minutes before serving.
Serves 4-6

Chicken Hawaiian (top)
Teriyaki Chicken (bottom)

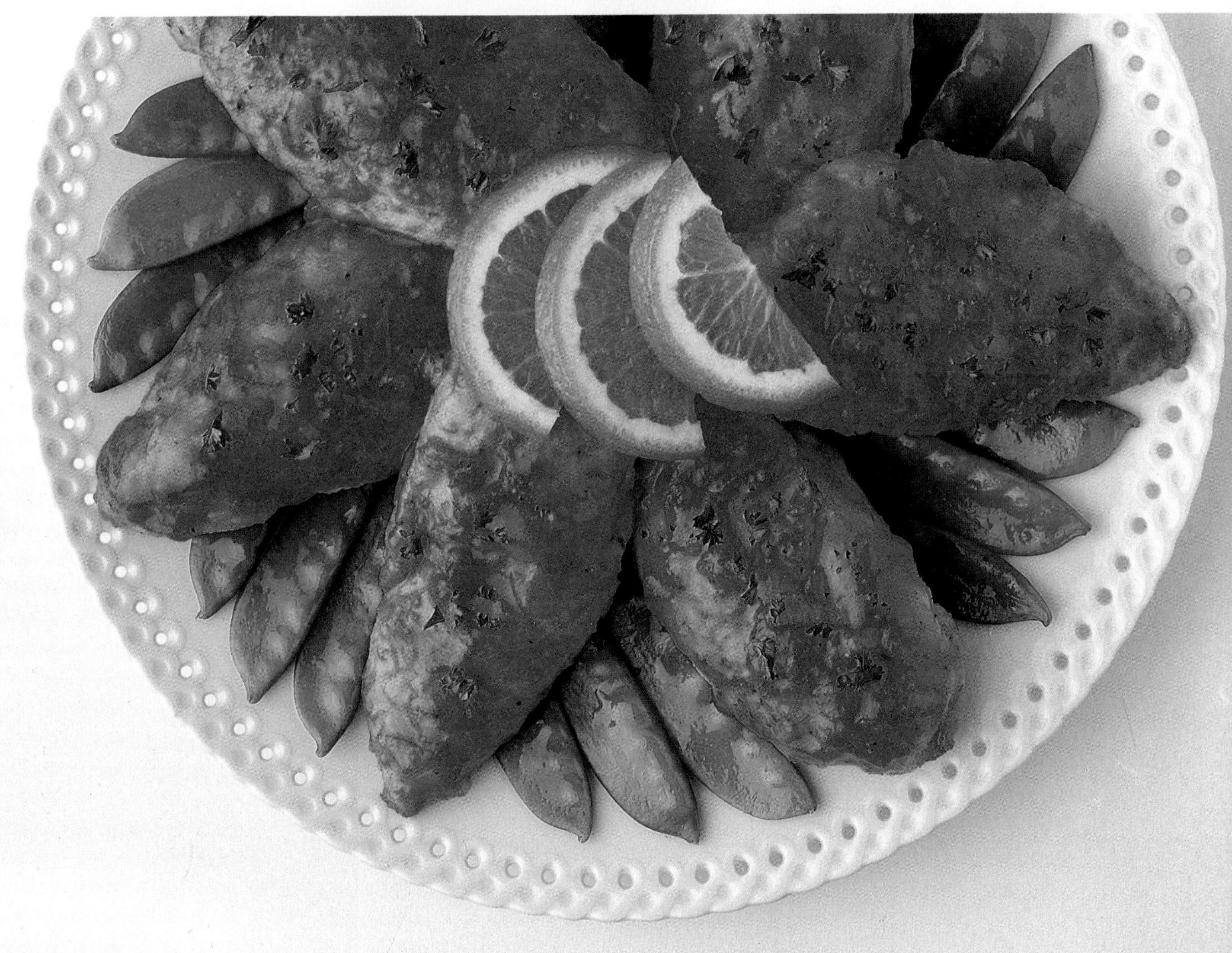

Zesty Glazed Chicken

TURKEY CORDON

2¼ lb. turkey, ground
1 egg, slightly beaten
1¼ tsp. salt
¼ tsp. black pepper
½ cup fresh bread crumbs
¼ cup milk
8 small slices Danish ham
Dijon mustard
8 thin slices **Danish Natural Tybo** or **Havarti Cheese**
fine, fresh bread crumbs
½ cup butter or margarine
parsley to garnish

In large mixing bowl, blend together ground turkey meat with egg, salt, pepper, bread crumbs and milk. Divide into 8 equal portions. Place slices of ham on a flat surface. Spread lightly with Dijon mustard. Top each with slices of Danish Tybo or Havarti cheese. Fold in half. Cover each ham and cheese portion with the turkey portion, patting the meat evenly to cover the ham and cheese. Coat each portion in bread crumbs. (This preparation may be done early in the day, refrigerated, but left out at room temperature 20 minutes before cooking.) Heat a large skillet to medium-hot. Melt about ¾ of the butter or margarine and when hot place the packets of turkey/ham/cheese in the skillet to slowly cook to a golden dark brown on one side. Turn, add remaining butter and brown other side. Place on a warm platter and garnish with parsley.
Serves 8

ZESTY GLAZED CHICKEN

6 chicken breasts, skinned and boned
1 tbsp. cornstarch
½ tsp. salt
¼ tsp. pepper
2 tbsp. vegetable oil
¼ cup orange juice
⅓ cup orange marmalade
¼ cup **Heinz Chili Sauce**
2 tsp. Dijon mustard
½ tsp. curry powder
2 tbsp. chopped parsley

Coat chicken with cornstarch, salt and pepper. Heat oil in frypan over medium heat. Cook chicken 20 minutes until brown. Turn occasionally. Drain fat. Combine orange juice, marmalade, chili sauce, mustard and curry. Stir into pan, glazing chicken. Heat through. Sprinkle with parsley.
Serves 4-6

MAIN DISHES AND CASSEROLES

Today's dining tastes tend to the eclectic. We may enjoy a pungent curry one evening, a crisp stir fry the next or perhaps a hearty meatless casserole on yet another.

With the abundance of fine imported foods so readily available, today's cook has the opportunity to create some truly world-class dishes.

Whether you prefer good down-home cooking or more exotic flavors, you'll find the recipes in this chapter are all wonderfully satisfying...and many can be prepared ahead of time and reheated at your convenience.

We hope some of these recipes will become fast favorites at your house.

Italian Enchiladas (see page 154)

Creamy Shepherd's Pie (left) and Chili Con Corny Butterflake Pie

CLARK BEAN CASSOULET

6 slices bacon, chopped
½ lb. chicken, cut in cubes
4 small onions, cut in half, then quartered
1 garlic clove, crushed
1 tbsp. dried parsley flakes
¼ tsp. salt
¼ tsp. pepper
¼ tsp. thyme
½ lb. Kielbasa sausage slices
1 bay leaf
2 14-oz. cans **Clark Beans with Pork and Tomato Sauce**
1 19-oz. can tomatoes

In a large saucepan, cook bacon until crisp; remove from pan and drain. Leave 2 tbsp. bacon fat in pan; add cubed chicken and cook until lightly browned. Add onion, garlic, parsley, salt, pepper and thyme. Cook over medium heat until onions are transparent. Add bacon, sausage slices, bay leaf, beans and tomatoes. Mix gently to combine. Pour mixture into 3-quart casserole dish. Bake at 375°F for 35-40 minutes or until thoroughly heated. Serve with **Pillsbury Refrigerated Buttermilk** or **Sweetmilk Biscuits**.
Serves 4-6

CREAMY SHEPHERD'S PIE

1 lb. ground beef
½ cup chopped onion
⅓ cup chopped celery
¼ tsp. salt
¼ tsp. pepper
1 10-oz. can cream of mushroom soup
1 10-oz. can **Green Giant Kitchen Sliced Cut Green Beans**, drained
1 7½-oz. can **Green Giant Niblets Whole Kernel Corn**, drained

Topping:
2½ cups mashed potatoes
½ tsp. salt
1 egg, beaten
¼ cup Parmesan cheese
½ cup grated Cheddar cheese
dash paprika

Heat oven to 350°F. Lightly grease a pie plate. In large skillet, brown ground beef, onion and celery; drain. Stir in salt, pepper and soup. Spread meat mixture in prepared pan. Spread green beans and corn over mixture. In medium bowl, mix mashed potatoes, salt, beaten egg and Parmesan cheese. Spread over vegetables, covering to edges of pie plate. Sprinkle grated cheese over potatoes; sprinkle with paprika. Bake at 350°F for 25-30 minutes.
Serves 4-6

CHILI CON CORNY BUTTERFLAKE PIE

1 lb. ground beef
½ cup chopped onion
1 tsp. chili powder
¼ tsp. garlic powder
⅛ tsp. pepper
1 12-oz. can **Green Giant Niblets Whole Kernel Corn**, drained
1 7½-oz. can tomato sauce
1 8-oz. can **Pillsbury Refrigerated Butterflake Dinner Rolls**
4 slices processed cheese

Heat oven to 350°F. Grease a pie plate. In large skillet, brown ground beef and onion, drain. Stir in chili powder, garlic powder, pepper, corn and tomato sauce. Simmer while preparing crust. Separate Butterflake Dinner Rolls into 10 rolls. Arrange rolls around sides in prepared pie plate. Spoon hot meat mixture into center. Bake at 350°F for 25 minutes. Cut each slice of cheese into 4 strips. Arrange in lattice on top of pie. Return to oven and bake for 5 minutes or until cheese begins to melt. Let stand 5 minutes before cutting.
Serves 4-6

SPRING GARDEN CASSEROLE

1 package **Uncle Ben's Florentine Rice**

2 cups water

1 tsp. butter or margarine

1 lb. broccoli flowerets, cut into bite-sized pieces

¼ cup butter or margarine

2 cups fresh mushrooms, sliced

1 cup diced red pepper

1 cup thinly sliced red onion

1 cup thinly sliced celery

1 garlic clove, minced

1 cup Cheddar cheese, grated

Prepare rice in water with butter according to package directions. Steam broccoli until tender-crisp and bright green in appearance (about 8-10 minutes). Preheat oven to 375°F and butter a shallow casserole dish. In a large frypan, sauté mushrooms, pepper, onion, celery and garlic. Stir in cooked rice. Arrange half of the rice mixture, broccoli flowerets and cheese in layers in the casserole dish. Repeat process ending with cheese. Cover tightly with aluminum foil. Bake about 15 minutes, until hot and bubbly and cheese is melted.

Serves 5-6

ORIENTAL DINNER

1 package **Uncle Ben's Oriental Rice Supreme**

2 cups water

1 tbsp. butter or margarine

2 eggs, slightly beaten

1 tbsp. cooking oil

½ lb. cooked beef, thinly sliced (or ham, pork, chicken, turkey or shrimp)

½ cup fresh bean sprouts (if using canned, drain well)

¼ cup thinly sliced water chestnuts

¼ cup thinly sliced green pepper

½ cup celery, sliced diagonally

1 tbsp. diced onion

1 tsp. salt

¼ tsp. black pepper

soy sauce (optional)

Prepare rice in water with butter according to package directions. Cook eggs in oil over low heat until set; remove and chop into small pieces. Add meat to pan (and more oil if needed) and brown. Stir in bean sprouts, chestnuts, green pepper, celery and onion and simmer 2-3 minutes. Then add salt, pepper, rice and eggs. Soy sauce may be added to suit your own taste. Simmer 2-3 minutes or until heated through. Serve.

Makes 4 1-cup portions

JAMBALAYA

½ cup chopped onion

½ cup chopped green pepper

2 tbsp. butter or margarine

1 large garlic clove, minced

½ tsp. ground seafood seasoning

dash pepper

1 10-oz. can **Campbell's Condensed Tomato Soup**

⅓ cup water

1 cup diced cooked ham

½ lb. small shrimp, cleaned

1½ cups cooked rice

In 2-quart shallow glass dish (12" x 8" x 2"), combine onion, green pepper, butter and seasonings. Cook in microwave oven 4 minutes or until vegetables are tender, stir once. Stir in remaining ingredients except rice. Cook 6 minutes, stir twice. Add rice, cook 6-8 minutes or until done, stir twice.

Serves 4-6

Spring Garden Casserole (top) and Oriental Dinner

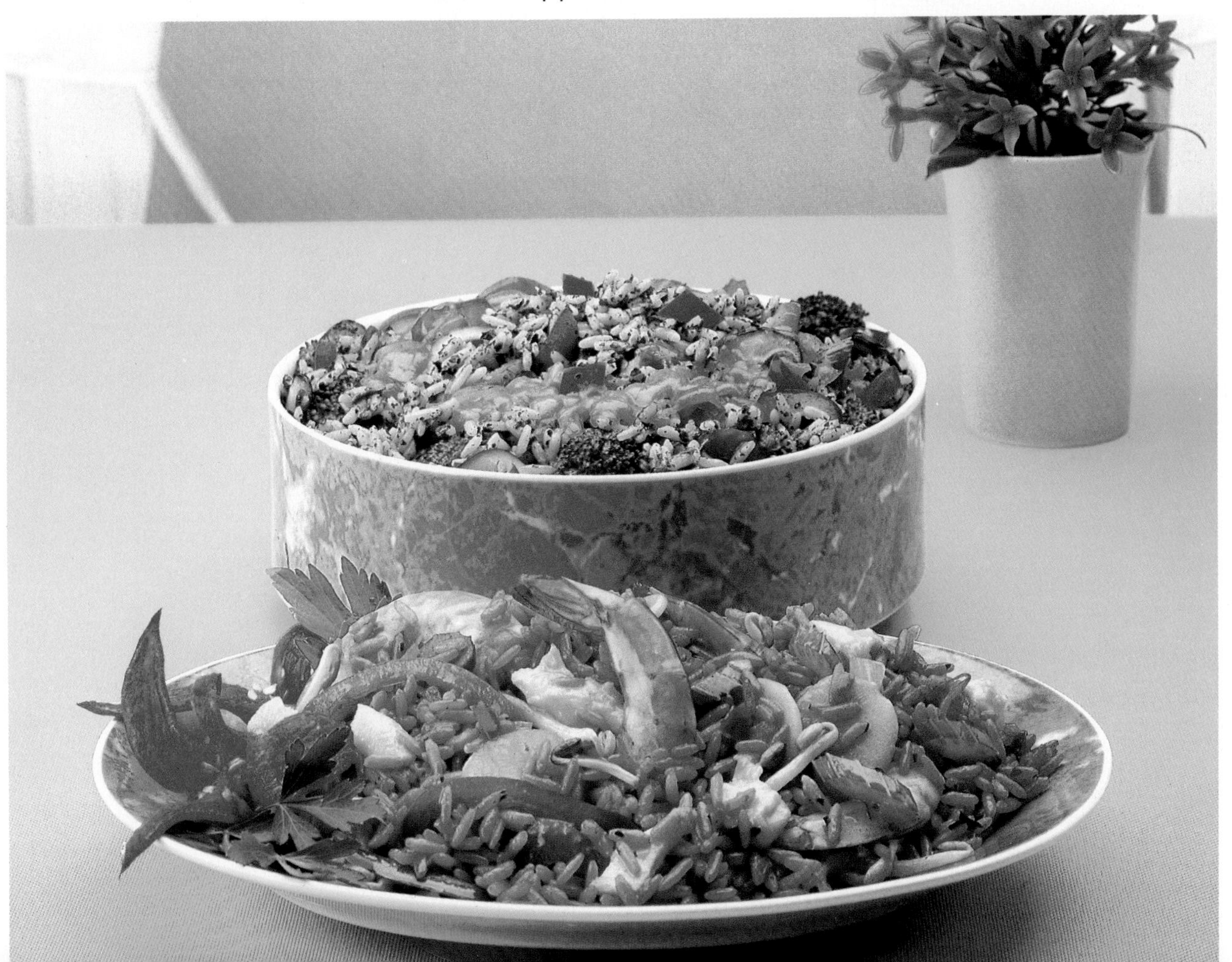

PASTICHO

1 onion, chopped fine
2 lb. ground lean beef
salt and pepper to taste
2 tbsp. tomato paste
1 lb. macaroni
¼ lb. melted butter
1 quart milk
4 eggs
2 lb. cottage cheese
¼ lb. feta cheese
8 **Krinos Fillo Leaves**

Sauté onion. Add meat and cook slowly until brown. Add seasonings and tomato paste. Simmer until liquid is almost evaporated. Remove from heat. Boil macaroni in salted water for about 15 minutes and then drain. Butter bottom of a 12" x 17" pan. Spread half the macaroni over entire bottom. Put meat over macaroni. Then spread the remainder of the macaroni over the meat. Now pour the milk, eggs and cheese mixture slowly over the top. Add 8 fillo leaves, buttering each. Poke a few air holes on the top with a fork. Sprinkle with water and bake for about 30 minutes in a preheated 375°F oven or until golden brown.

ITALIAN ENCHILADAS

1½ lb. bulk sausage
½ cup chopped onion
½ cup chopped green pepper
2 tbsp. flour
16 oz. cream-style cottage cheese
4 oz. mushrooms, drained and chopped
¼ tsp. basil leaves
¼ tsp. garlic powder
¼ tsp. cayenne pepper
1 15½-oz. jar pizza sauce
1 7½-oz. jar **Gerber Junior Mixed Vegetables**
1 11-oz. package large flour tortillas
2 cups shredded Mozzarella cheese

Preheat oven to 375°F. In skillet cook the sausage, onion and green pepper until brown. Drain fat. Stir in flour, cottage cheese, mushrooms and spices. In a bowl, add Mixed Vegetables to the pizza sauce. Stir ½ cup of the sauce mixture into the sausage mixture. Spoon about ⅓ cup meat onto each tortilla. Fold over in thirds. Place tortillas, seam-side-down, in 2 greased 8" x 8" x 2" baking pans. Pour remaining sauce over tortillas. Bake covered in 375°F oven for 35-40 minutes. Uncover and sprinkle with Mozzarella cheese. Bake uncovered 3 minutes or until cheese melts.
Makes 12 enchiladas

CHINESE EGG ROLLS FILLO STYLE

3 tbsp. vegetable oil
½ cup finely chopped celery
¾ cup shredded Chinese cabbage
½ cup chopped mushrooms (optional)
4 scallions, finely chopped
½ cup diced shrimp
½ cup diced cooked pork (optional)
½ cup drained, finely chopped water chestnuts (optional)
½ cup bean sprouts (optional)
1 garlic clove, minced
¼ cup soy sauce
dash of ground ginger
1 garlic clove, minced
¼ cup soy sauce
½ tsp. sugar
1 lb. **Krinos Fillo Leaves**
½ lb. unsalted butter, melted for fillo

Heat oil in skillet or wok. Add celery, cabbage, mushrooms and scallions and stir fry briefly. Add shrimp and pork and stir fry for 3 minutes. Add water chestnuts, bean sprouts, ginger, garlic, soy sauce and sugar. Stir fry for 5 minutes. Cool filling. Place 4 tbsp. on prepared fillo for rolls. Bake on a greased baking pan in a preheated 375°F oven for 20 minutes or until golden brown.

Country Kitchen Casserole

RICE TUNA CASSEROLE

1 cup **Uncle Ben's Converted Brand Rice**
3 tbsp. butter
2 cups finely diced (¼") stale bread
¼ cup chopped parsley
3 cups sliced mushrooms (about ¾ lb.)
¼ cup minced onion
4 tsp. all-purpose flour
2 cups low-fat milk
salt and pepper
1 cup frozen peas
1 6½-oz. can tuna, packed in water

In 2 cups boiling water, cook rice, covered, for 20 minutes or until water is absorbed. Fluff with fork and set aside. Meanwhile, in large skillet, melt butter and toss 2 tbsp. of it with bread cubes and parsley in small bowl; set aside. Add mushrooms and onion to remaining butter in skillet and cook over medium heat, stirring often, for 5 minutes. Sprinkle with flour and cook, stirring, for 1 minute. Gradually stir in milk; cook, stirring for 2-3 minutes or until thickened and bubbly. Season with salt and pepper to taste; stir in rice. Rinse peas under hot water and gently stir in. Drain and break up tuna slightly; gently stir into rice mixture and transfer to 8-cup shallow casserole. Sprinkle bread cube mixture evenly over top. (Recipe can be prepared to this point, covered and refrigerated for up to 6 hours.) Bake, uncovered, in 375°F oven for 20-30 minutes or until bubbly and top is golden brown.
Serves 4

COUNTRY KITCHEN CASSEROLE

1 10-oz. can **Campbell's Condensed Cream of Mushroom Soup**
¼ cup water
2 tsp. prepared mustard
1 tsp. Worcestershire sauce
1 cup shredded Cheddar cheese
2 cans small whole white potatoes, drained and sliced
1 10-oz. package frozen peas, cooked and drained
1 10-oz. package luncheon meat, cut in 6 slices

In bowl, combine soup, water, mustard, Worcestershire sauce and cheese; add potatoes and peas. Spoon into 1½-quart shallow baking dish; top with meat. Bake at 400°F for 25 minutes or until hot.
Serves 6

STUFFED CABBAGE ROLLS

8 large cabbage leaves
1 lb. ground beef
1 cup cooked rice
¼ cup chopped onion
1 egg, slightly beaten
1 tsp. salt
¼ tsp. pepper
1 10-oz. can **Campbell's Condensed Tomato Soup**

Cook cabbage leaves in boiling salted water a few minutes to soften; drain. Combine beef, rice, onion, egg, salt and pepper with 2 tbsp. soup. Divide meat mixture among cabbage leaves. Roll and secure with toothpicks or string. Place cabbage rolls in frypan; pour remaining soup over. Cover; cook over heat about 40 minutes. Stir often, spooning sauce over rolls.
Serves 4

MEXICAN RICE-SAUSAGE CASSEROLE

1 lb. Italian sausage (sweet or hot)
2 small zucchini, sliced
1 onion, chopped
1 7-oz. can whole kernel corn, drained
2 cups cooked **Uncle Ben's Converted Brand Rice**
1 14-oz. can tomatoes
1 tbsp. chili powder
dash **Tabasco** brand pepper sauce
1 cup shredded Cheddar cheese

Remove sausage from casings and microwave in deep 2-quart casserole on high for 3 minutes. Break up with spoon and microwave for 3 minutes longer. Remove with slotted spoon to drain on paper towels. In same casserole, microwave zucchini and onion on high for 3 minutes, stirring once. Remove to small bowl and stir in corn. Place half the sausage, then half the corn mixture back in casserole in layers. Add half the rice in a layer; then repeat. Partially drain tomatoes, chop coarsely and stir together with chili powder and Tabasco. Pour over top of layers and, without stirring, sprinkle with cheese. Microwave, uncovered, on high for 10-12 minutes or until cheese begins to form a crust.
Serves 4

EASY CABBAGE ROLL CASSEROLE

1 lb. lean ground beef
3 cloves garlic, minced
2 onions, chopped
¾ cup uncooked **Uncle Ben's Converted Brand Rice**
1 28-oz. can tomato sauce
⅓ cup cider vinegar
3 tbsp. brown sugar
1 tbsp. Worcestershire sauce
½ tsp. salt
¼ tsp. pepper
dash **Tabasco** brand pepper sauce
8 cups coarsely chopped cabbage

In large skillet over medium heat, cook beef with garlic and onions until meat is no longer pink. Stir in rice and set aside. In bowl, stir together tomato sauce, vinegar, sugar, Worcestershire sauce, salt, pepper and Tabasco pepper sauce. Layer ⅓ of the cabbage in bottom of 4-quart casserole. Arrange half the rice-beef mixture on top and drizzle with ⅓ of the tomato mixture. Repeat, ending with cabbage and remaining tomato mixture. Cover and bake in 350°F oven for 1 hour and 45 minutes without stirring.
Serves 6

PEROGIES

4 medium potatoes, boiled
2 eggs
2 tbsp. butter
2 tbsp. milk
salt and pepper to taste
½ lb. **Krinos Fillo Leaves**
½ stick butter, melted for fillo
½ cup shredded Cheddar cheese

Peel boiled potatoes and mash in a bowl. Add eggs, butter, milk, salt and pepper. Blend well. Prepare fillo leaves according to package directions and cut into strips. Spoon mashed potatoes on to ends of fillo strips and then a tsp. of shredded Cheddar cheese. Fold up into triangles. Bake in a preheated 375°F oven for 20 minutes or until golden brown. Bacon bits, chives and shredded meat may be added to mashed potatoes, in combinations or separately.

Ham and Cheese Strata

HAM AND CHEESE STRATA

6 slices bread
2 cups celery, cut in ½" slices
2 cups grated Cheddar cheese
1 6½-oz. can **Puritan Flaked Ham**, flaked with a fork
4 eggs, slightly beaten
2 cups milk
2 tbsp. minced onion
½ tsp. salt
⅛ tsp. pepper
¼ tsp. oregano

Cut a 2" round from each slice of bread. Crumble remainder into greased shallow 1½-quart baking dish and sprinkle with celery, cheese, ham and top with bread rounds. Mix remaining ingredients and pour over top. Cover and refrigerate at least 1 hour. Uncover and bake at 350°F for 1 hour or until set and lightly brown.
Serves 4-6

SOUFFLÉ VEGETABLE PIZZA

1 cup **KRAFT Real Mayonnaise**
½ cup grated **KRAFT Mozzarella Cheese**
½ cup **KRAFT Grated Parmesan Cheese**
1 tsp. dry mustard
½ tsp. garlic powder
2 egg whites
1 cup sliced mushrooms
1 small onion, thinly sliced
1 red pepper, thinly sliced
1 green pepper, thinly sliced
2 ready-made 12" prebaked pizza crusts

Mix mayonnaise, cheese, mustard and garlic powder. Beat egg whites until stiff peaks form; fold into mayonnaise mixture. Arrange half of the vegetables on each pizza crust. Spoon mayonnaise mixture over vegetables. Bake on ungreased baking sheet at 450°F about 10 minutes or until puffed and lightly browned.
Makes 2 12" pizzas

BEEF ENCHILADA FILLO ROLLS

½ lb. **Krinos Fillo Leaves**
1 stick butter, melted for fillo
2 onions, chopped
1 lb. grated sharp cheese

Sauce:
8 tbsp. flour
½ cup vegetable oil
2 tbsp. chili powder
1 tbsp. cumin
2 tsp. salt
2 garlic cloves, crushed
5½ cups hot water

Meat:
1 lb. lean ground beef
½ tsp. cumin
1 garlic clove, crushed
½ tsp. salt
2 tbsp. hot taco sauce
1 tbsp. water (if needed)

To make sauce, brown the flour in a pan in a 500°F oven about 20 minutes to look like cocoa. Place in large saucepan with oil and add all other ingredients except for water. Blend over low heat until smooth. Add the water slowly, stirring constantly. Simmer 2-3 hours or until fairly thick. Cool and refrigerate overnight. Brown meat. Add other meat ingredients and simmer 20-30 minutes. Prepare fillo leaves for rolls. Spoon on some meat mixture, a small amount of sauce, a sprinkle of onion and a tsp. of grated cheese. Roll all these ingredients in the fillo. Repeat this process for all rolls. Bake in preheated 350°F oven for 20-30 minutes or until golden brown. (Brush rolls with butter to help them brown, or sprinkle them with water.) Serve while hot with remaining sauce.

MADRAS CURRY

1 medium onion, finely chopped
1 tomato, finely chopped
1½ lb. uncooked meat or poultry
4 tbsp. **Patak's Madras Curry Paste**
1 tbsp. oil

Sauté onions in the oil for 3 minutes. Add the tomato and meat and cook for 15 minutes, stirring occasionally. Add Patak's Madras Curry Paste and simmer for 30 minutes. Garnish with spring onions or fresh coriander. Serve with pappadums, rice or bread. As an alternative, 1 cup of water may be added to give a gravy consistency.
Serves 4

FRENCH'S CHICKEN DIVAN WITH HORSERADISH MUSTARD

1 bunch broccoli, cut in flowerets
2 cups cooked, diced chicken
2 tbsp. butter
2 tbsp. flour
1 cup milk
1 cup shredded medium Cheddar cheese
¼ cup **French's Horseradish Mustard**
pinch **French's Cayenne Pepper**
pinch **French's Ground Black Pepper** (to taste)

Steam broccoli in large pot for about 2 minutes or until tender-crisp. Drain and set aside. Place chicken in a medium-sized casserole dish, placing broccoli on top. In a medium-sized saucepan over medium heat, melt butter, stir in flour and cook about 30 seconds. Slowly add milk, bringing the mixture to boil and reduce to low heat, stirring in the cheese, horseradish mustard and cayenne. Cook until cheese has melted and remove from heat. Add pepper to taste. Pour sauce over broccoli and chicken and bake in a preheated 350°F oven for approximately 25 minutes or until bubbly and heated through.
Serves 4

CHEDDAR BEEF FONDUE

3 tbsp. butter
3 tbsp. all-purpose flour
¾ cup beer or ale
¾ cup milk
2 tsp. Worcestershire sauce
1 tsp. dry mustard
½ tsp. paprika
dash cayenne
3 cups (12 oz.) shredded **Spring Farm Cheddar Cheese** (mild, medium, old or extra old)

In a heavy saucepan, melt butter and blend in flour. Gradually stir in combined beer and milk and cook over medium heat stirring constantly until thickened. Blend in Worcestershire sauce and spices. Remove saucepan from heat. Add cheese about ½ cup at a time to the hot mixture, stirring after each addition. Return to low heat stirring constantly until cheese is melted. If fondue is prepared in advance, refrigerate covered in a glass or ceramic bowl. Reheat in double boiler, over hot but not boiling water, stirring frequently. Serve warm in fondue pot or chafing dish.
Makes 3 cups

WEETABIX PIZZA PIZAZZ

Base:
1 cup warm water
½ tsp. sugar
1 package yeast
4 **Weetabix**, crushed
2 cups flour
1 tsp. salt

Sauce:
2 tbsp. oil
1 onion, chopped
1 garlic clove, chopped
1 celery stalk, chopped
1 28-oz. can Italian tomatoes, drained and chopped
½ tsp. dry basil
½ tsp. dry oregano
salt and freshly ground pepper

Toppings:
4 oz. Mozzarella cheese
1 oz. grated Parmesan
Choice of pepperoni, mushrooms, etc.

Stir sugar into warm water. Sprinkle on the yeast. Let stand for 10 minutes. Combine flour, Weetabix and salt. Stir yeast into flour and mix until dough is not sticky (more flour may be necessary). Place in oiled bowl, cover and let stand 1 hour or more. Divide dough in half and spread onto 2 pizza pans. Meanwhile, sauté the onion, garlic and celery in oil until golden. Add tomatoes and spices. Simmer 15 minutes or until most of the liquid has evaporated. Spread sauce over pizza base, add favorite toppings and cover with cheese. Bake at 400°F for 20 minutes. Serve.

ESCALOPES CORDON BLEU

4 turkey or chicken breasts, skinned and boned
black pepper
4 thin slices cooked ham
1 8-oz. package Swiss cheese, cut into 4 slices
1 10-oz. can **Sharwood's White Wine Sauce**
watercress to garnish

Place breasts in a shallow baking pan. Sprinkle with freshly ground black pepper. Lay a slice of ham, then a slice of cheese on top of each breast. Pour over White Wine Sauce, cover and bake at 350°F for 1¼ hours or until fork tender. Garnish with watercress.
Serves 4

GOULASH

2 tsp. butter and oil
3 onions, sliced
2 lb. beef, cut into 1" x 1½" cubes
2 tsp. paprika
pinch cayenne pepper
salt and pepper
1 bay leaf
1 tbsp. wine vinegar
beef bouillon
3 tbsp. butter
3 tbsp. flour
1 cup **Delisle Plain Yogurt**
1-2 pickles, chopped
6 cups cooked noodles

Heat fat and sauté onions. Remove onions and in same frypan, adding fat if needed, sauté beef cubes. Add paprika, cayenne pepper, salt, pepper, bay leaf, wine vinegar, onions and enough beef bouillon to cover meat. In a 2½-quart baking dish, cook at 350°F for 2 hours. Make beurre manié by blending butter and flour. Add to liquid in casserole. Simmer 1-2 minutes. Add yogurt. Mix thoroughly, add pickles and adjust seasoning. Serve on noodles. (Add beef bouillon if needed during cooking.)
Serves 8-10

KOFTA CURRY

½ lb. ground beef
1 small onion, minced
2 garlic cloves, minced
pinch ground cloves
pinch cinnamon
salt and pepper
1 egg, beaten
oil for frying
1 10-oz. can **Sharwood's Authentic Curry Sauce**
a few mint leaves, roughly chopped

Mix together ground beef, onion, garlic, spices and season with salt and pepper. Bind with beaten egg and shape into 8-10 meatballs. Fry in hot oil, either in a deep-fat fryer or large skillet until evenly browned. Drain well. Heat curry sauce in a large saucepan, diluting with a little water if necessary. Add meatballs and simmer for 15 minutes. Serve garnished with mint leaves.
Serves 2-3

PIZZA

Base:

3 cups self-rising flour

pinch salt

¼ cup margarine or butter

1 cup milk

Topping:

1 tbsp. salad oil

1 garlic clove, minced

1 medium onion, chopped

2 heaped tsp. **Sharwood's Madras Curry Powder**

¾ lb. ground beef

3 tbsp. tomato purée

½ lb. tomatoes, peeled and chopped

salt and pepper

5 oz. Mozzarella cheese, sliced

Garnish:

a few black and pimento-stuffed olives

a few anchovies

Mix flour and salt and rub in the margarine. Bind together with just enough milk to produce a soft dough. Roll out dough and shape into a 10" round. Place on a greased pizza pan and leave in a cool place while preparing topping. Soften onion and garlic in heated oil. Add curry powder and ground beef and cook for a further few minutes. Stir in tomato purée and tomatoes and season to taste. Simmer for 15 minutes, cool slightly, spread over the dough nearly to the edge. Top with cheese, decorate with olives and anchovies and bake at 425°F for 30 minutes, covered with foil if necessary to prevent over-browning.
Serves 4-6

HOT CHILI'N CHEESE

1 lb. lean ground beef

½ cup chopped green pepper

½ cup chopped onion

1-2 tbsp. chili powder

1 14-oz. can tomatoes, drained and chopped

1 19-oz. can red kidney beans, drained

CHEEZ WHIZ Process Cheese Spread (Mexican or Regular)

In large saucepan, brown meat. Add chopped pepper, onion and chili powder; cook until tender. Stir in tomatoes and beans; simmer 15 minutes. To serve, add two heaping tablespoonsful of cheese spread to each bowl. If preparing ahead, turn chili into a 6-cup casserole and refrigerate. To serve, bake at 350°F for 35 minutes. Spoon cheese spread evenly over top and return to oven for 10 minutes to finish heating.

Microwave Method: Crumble meat in an 8-cup casserole. Microwave on high for 5 minutes, stirring several times; drain. Stir in chopped pepper, onion and chili powder. Cover with vented plastic wrap and cook on high 1 minute. Stir in tomatoes and beans and continue to cook 5 minutes or until hot. To serve, add two heaping tablespoonsful of cheese spread to each bowl.
Serves 4-6

PARTY CHILI CHICKEN

8 oz. uncooked medium noodles

¼ cup chopped onion

1 tbsp. butter or margarine

1 10-oz. can **Campbell's Condensed Cream of Mushroom Soup**

2 tbsp. chopped pimento

1 tbsp. finely chopped green pepper

1½ cups cut-up cooked chicken or turkey

salt and pepper

3 oz. grated Cheddar cheese

Cook noodles as directed on package, drain. In large frypan cook onion in butter until tender, stir in soup, pimento and chopped green pepper. In a greased 2-quart casserole, layer ½ the noodles and ½ the chicken. Season with salt and pepper. Top with half the soup mixture and half the cheese. Repeat layers. Bake uncovered in 350°F oven for 45 minutes.
Serves 8-12

MEATBALLS AND SAUCE ROLLS

1 lb. ground round steak

1 small onion, chopped

4 medium mushrooms, chopped

1 tbsp. butter

2 tbsp. chicken broth or cream

1 egg

1 tbsp. grated Romano cheese

1 tsp. salt

¼ tsp. pepper

½ tsp. basil or marjoram

¼ tsp. oregano

1 tbsp. butter

2 cups tomato sauce

Krinos Fillo Leaves

½ cup grated Parmesan cheese for topping

Put ground round steak in a bowl. Sauté chopped onion and mushrooms in 1 tbsp. butter until limp. Add broth or cream and remove from heat. Pour over meat in bowl; mix thoroughly. Then beat in egg, grated cheese and seasonings. Form the meat into small balls of about a tsp. each and sauté in 1 tbsp. butter for about 10 minutes, shaking the pan and turning the meatballs so they are browned on all sides. Place in a baking pan and pour tomato sauce over the meatballs. Preheat oven to 400°F and bake for 15 minutes. Drain out all excess fat from meatballs and sauce. Prepare the fillos for rolls. Place 3 meatballs on each roll with a tsp. of sauce. Roll up in fillo. Place in a buttered baking pan and bake in oven (same temperature) for another 15 minutes or until golden brown. Sprinkle tops of rolls with water to make them brown and flaky. Serve hot with extra sauce and cheese.

CREAMY CORN SCALLOP

1 10-oz. can **Campbell's Condensed Cream of Celery, Chicken** or **Mushroom Soup**

1 tbsp. minced onion

dash pepper

1 14-oz. can whole kernel corn, drained

1 cup crumbled soda crackers

2 tbsp. butter or margarine

Combine soup, onion and pepper. In 1-quart casserole, arrange alternative layers of corn, soup mixture and crackers; dot with butter. Bake in a 400°F oven for 25 minutes.
Serves 6

FLORENTINE CHICKEN ROLLS

3 tbsp. **Kikkoman Lite In Salt Soy Sauce**
3 tbsp. dry white wine
3 large, whole chicken breasts, halved, boned and flattened to ½″ thickness
1 10-oz. package frozen chopped spinach, thawed and well drained
4 tbsp. sour cream, divided
2 tsp. **Kikkoman Lite In Salt Soy Sauce**
¼ tsp. ground nutmeg
2½ tsp. cornstarch

Combine 3 tbsp. soy sauce and wine in large shallow pan. Add chicken; turn to coat. Marinate 30 minutes; turn chicken once or twice. Meanwhile, combine spinach, 2 tbsp. sour cream, 2 tsp. soy sauce and nutmeg. Remove chicken from marinade; reserve marinade. Spoon equal amounts of spinach mixture lengthwise along center of each breast. Roll chicken over filling lengthwise and secure with string in 3 places. Place breasts seam-side-down, in single layer in lightly greased baking pan. Bake at 350°F 30 minutes or until chicken is tender; brush occasionally with reserved marinade. Remove chicken to serving platter; keep warm. Combine pan juices with remaining marinade; add enough water to measure ¾ cup. Combine mixture with cornstarch in saucepan. Bring to boil; cook and stir until slightly thickened. Remove from heat and stir in remaining sour cream. To serve, remove strings from chicken and cover with sauce.
Serves 4-6

BEEF AND RICE CASSEROLE

¼ cup uncooked rice
2½ cups frozen peas, cooked and drained
2 cups cubed, cooked beef
1 10-oz. can **Campbell's Condensed Cheddar Cheese Soup**
1 cup milk
¼ tsp. salt
dash pepper
⅓ cup croutons

Cook rice according to package directions. Combine rice, peas and beef in a shallow 2-quart casserole. Blend cheese soup with milk in a medium-sized bowl; add salt and pepper. Pour over rice mixture; toss lightly to mix. Arrange croutons around edge of dish. Bake in 375°F oven 30 minutes, or until sauce is bubbly and the top is lightly browned.
Serves 6-8

CHEESE-TOPPED BEEF PIE

1 9″ **Crisco Single-Crust Pastry** *(see Pies and Tarts)*
1 lb. lean ground beef
½ cup evaporated milk
½ cup ketchup
⅓ cup fine dry bread crumbs
¼ cup chopped onion
¾ tsp. salt
½ tsp. dried oregano, crushed
¼ tsp. pepper
1 cup shredded processed cheese
1 tsp. Worcestershire sauce
pickle slices (optional)

Preheat oven to 350°F. Line 9″ pie plate with pastry. In a bowl, combine ground beef, evaporated milk, ketchup, bread crumbs, onion, salt, crushed oregano and pepper. Turn meat into pastry shell. Bake at 350°F for 35-40 minutes. Toss cheese with Worcestershire sauce; sprinkle atop pie. Bake 10 minutes more. Remove from oven; let stand 10 minutes before serving. Trim with pickle slices, if desired.
Serves 6

TOMATO BASIL PIZZA WITH FRESH VEGETABLES

1 lb. bag of fresh or frozen pizza dough or 1 ready-made 12″ pizza crust
2 tbsp. cornmeal
1 cup shredded mozzarella cheese
4 ripe tomatoes, seeded and sliced
½ cup fresh basil leaves
½ tsp. **Tabasco** brand pepper sauce
olive oil
suggested toppings: snowpeas, cooked broccoli pieces, pineapple tidbits, green pepper chunks, beansprouts, etc.

Preheat oven to 425°F. Roll out pizza dough to create a 12″ crust. Dust crust with cornmeal. Distribute mozzarella cheese evenly over crust. Layer with tomato slices, basil leaves and choice of toppings. Drizzle with Tabasco pepper sauce and olive oil. Bake 15 minutes or until crust is golden brown.
Serves 2-4

Florentine Chicken Rolls

5-LAYER CHICKEN DIVAN

1 8-oz. package **Green Giant Frozen Rice Medley**

1 8-oz. package **Green Giant Broccoli Spears Frozen in Butter Sauce**

1 tbsp. butter or margarine

1 tbsp. all-purpose flour

½ cup milk

¼ cup salad dressing or mayonnaise

1 tbsp. sherry (optional)

½ tsp. lemon juice

¼ tsp. salt

2 cups cooked, cubed chicken

½ cup grated Cheddar cheese

Heat oven to 350°F. Cook rice pouch and broccoli pouch according to package directions. Meanwhile, in small saucepan, melt butter; stir in flour until well blended. Add milk. Cook until thickened, stirring constantly. Stir in salad dressing, sherry, lemon juice and salt. Empty rice from pouch into bottom of ungreased 8" square pan, spreading evenly to edges. Top with broccoli and chicken. Pour sauce evenly over chicken; sprinkle with cheese. Bake 30 minutes.
Serves 3-4

DEEP DISH PIZZA PIRAEUS

2 tbsp. olive oil

1 cup chopped onion

1 clove garlic, minced

1 10-oz. package frozen, chopped spinach, thawed and well-drained

1 cup sliced fresh mushrooms

½ tsp. **Tabasco** brand pepper sauce

1 9" frozen deep dish pie crust

½ cup sliced black olives

1 cup cherry tomatoes, cut in halves

1 cup crumbled feta cheese

1 cup shredded mozzarella cheese

In large skillet, heat oil; sauté onion and garlic until tender. Remove from heat. Stir in spinach, mushrooms and Tabasco pepper sauce. Spoon half the spinach mixture evenly into frozen pie crust. Sprinkle with half the black olives, tomatoes, feta cheese and mozzarella cheese. Repeat with spinach mixture followed by remaining olives, tomatoes and cheese. Bake in a 400°F oven 30-35 minutes or until crust is golden brown and cheese is melted and bubbling. Remove from oven and sprinkle with additional Tabasco pepper sauce, if desired.
Makes 1 9" deep dish pizza

COMPANY CASSEROLE

Bottom:

3 cups cooked macaroni, drained

2 eggs, lightly beaten

⅓ cup **KRAFT Grated Parmesan Cheese**

Filling:

1½ lb. lean ground beef

½ lb. mushrooms, sliced

1 medium onion, chopped

1 14-oz. can tomato sauce

1 tsp. garlic powder

1 tsp. dried oregano leaves

1 tsp. dried basil leaves

pinch of ground cinnamon

salt and pepper to taste

Topping:

⅓ cup **PARKAY Margarine** or butter

⅓ cup all-purpose flour

¼ tsp. salt

¼ tsp. ground nutmeg

3 cups milk

2 eggs, lightly beaten

1 cup grated **KRAFT Mozzarella Cheese**

⅓ cup **KRAFT Grated Parmesan Cheese**

garnishes: chopped fresh tomatoes, sliced pitted black olives, sliced green onions and crumbled feta cheese (as desired)

For bottom, combine macaroni, eggs and cheese. Spread over bottom of greased 13" x 9" x 2" baking dish. Set aside. For filling, in a large frypan, cook beef, mushrooms and onion until tender and browned. Drain off fat. Stir in tomato sauce and seasonings. Simmer, uncovered, while preparing topping. For topping, melt margarine in a large saucepan. Stir in flour, salt and nutmeg. Add milk; cook and stir until thickened and bubbly. Gradually stir into eggs, then return to saucepan. Cook over low heat 1 minute longer. To assemble, spread meat filling over macaroni. Spread topping over meat. Sprinkle with Mozzarella, then Parmesan cheese. Bake at 350°F for 35-40 minutes or until golden brown and bubbly. Arrange garnishes on top in diagonal rows or as desired.
Serves 8-10

Company Casserole

HERBED CHICKEN AND CHEESE

6 chicken breast halves
3 tbsp. butter, divided
1 tsp. salt
1 tsp. dried sweet basil, divided
¼ tsp. cayenne pepper
2 medium onions, cut in small wedges
10 cherry tomatoes, halved
1½ cups half and half cream
1 tbsp. cornstarch
2 cups shredded **Danish Havarti** or **Tybo Cheese**, loosely packed

Rinse chicken and pat dry. In a large skillet, brown chicken on all sides in 2 tbsp. butter over medium heat. Season with salt, ½ tsp. sweet basil and cayenne pepper. Remove to an ovenproof serving dish; reserve pan drippings. In same skillet, sauté onions; spoon over chicken. Arrange tomato halves on top. Bake in a 350°F oven for 45 minutes, until tender. In same skillet, melt remaining tbsp. butter, add remaining ½ tsp. sweet basil; let simmer. Mix half and half with cornstarch and add to skillet. Cook over medium heat, stirring, until thickened. Add shredded cheese, stirring until smooth. Spoon over chicken to serve.
Serves 6

DUTCH POTATO BAKE

6 slices bacon
1 10-oz. can **Campbell's Condensed Chicken Broth**
2 tbsp. flour
¼ cup vinegar
2 tbsp. brown sugar
2 tbsp. diced pimento
¼ cup diagonally sliced green onions
½ tsp. celery salt
¼ tsp. hot red-pepper sauce
6 cups sliced cooked potatoes

In frypan, cook bacon until crisp; remove. Pour off all but ¼ cup drippings. Gradually blend broth into flour until smooth; slowly stir into drippings. Add remaining ingredients except potatoes. Cook, stir until thickened. In 1½-quart shallow baking dish (10" x 6" x 2") arrange potatoes; pour broth mixture over potatoes. Cover; bake at 400°F for 30 minutes or until hot.
Garnish with bacon.
Makes 6 cups

CHEESE-CLOUD CASSEROLE

1 cup mayonnaise
1 cup sour cream
1 tbsp. lemon juice
1 tbsp. finely chopped onion
½ tsp. curry powder (or to taste)
⅛ tsp. cayenne pepper
1 cup frozen peas, thawed
6 cups cooked, cubed chicken, turkey or ham
5 cups (about 1 lb.) **Danish Fontina** or **Creamy Havarti Cheese**
6 egg whites
½ tsp. cream of tartar
parsley or watercress sprigs for garnish

In large bowl, blend mayonnaise, sour cream, lemon juice, onion, curry and cayenne pepper. Fold in peas, poultry and a little less than half of cheese. Spoon into buttered, shallow, oven-to-table dish; cover and bake in preheated 300°F oven for about 20 minutes, until warm. Remove dish from oven. Meanwhile, beat egg whites with cream of tartar until stiff peaks form. Gradually sprinkle and fold in remaining cheese. Spoon meringue onto warm mixture forming 6-8 mounds. Increase oven temperature to 400°F. Return dish to oven and bake 8-10 minutes or until meringue is golden brown. Garnish with parsley or watercress. Serve at once with crisp French bread.
Serves 6-8

CORNED BEEF AND CABBAGE CASSEROLE

1 10-oz. can **Campbell's Condensed Cream of Celery Soup**
½ cup chopped onion
1 tsp. dry mustard
1 cup diced cooked corned beef
4 cups coarsely shredded cabbage

Mix all ingredients in 1½-quart casserole. Cover; bake in a 375°F oven 45 minutes.
Serves 3-4

FETA-FONTINA-AND-SPINACH LOAF

1 10-oz. package frozen spinach
1 small onion, finely chopped
1 garlic clove, minced
3 tbsp. butter
1 cup crumbled **Danish Feta Cheese**
1 cup cubed **Danish Fontina Cheese**
2 eggs, lightly beaten
¼ cup heavy cream
½ tsp. dillweed
¼ tsp. salt
¼ tsp. pepper
½ tsp. cayenne
½ tsp. lemon juice
1 loaf French bread, about 16" long
4 hard-cooked eggs (optional)

Let spinach thaw until soft enough to cut into ½" cubes; set aside. In skillet, sauté onion and garlic in butter until tender. Add cubed spinach. Cook and stir over medium-high heat until spinach is completely thawed and liquid is absorbed, about 5 minutes. Remove from heat. With fork stir in cheeses, then the lightly beaten eggs. Add seasonings and lemon juice. Using serrated knife, hollow out bread, leaving 1"-thick shell (reserve crumbs for another purpose). Spoon spinach mixture into cavity and, if desired, press hard-cooked eggs into filling. Place loaf on cookie sheet and bake in 375°F oven 25-30 minutes or until custard has set. If softer crust is desired, wrap loaf in foil, leaving filling exposed. Let cool on rack 5 minutes. Cut into slices about 1" thick and serve at once.
Serves 4-6

For hors d'oeuvres: Use a slender baguette about 24" long instead of a French loaf. Halve it crosswise to fit onto cookie sheet. Slice halves across tops, leaving ½"-thick walls. Hollow out baguettes. Cut hard-cooked eggs lengthwise and reduce baking time by 5 minutes.
Makes approximately 24 bite-sized pieces

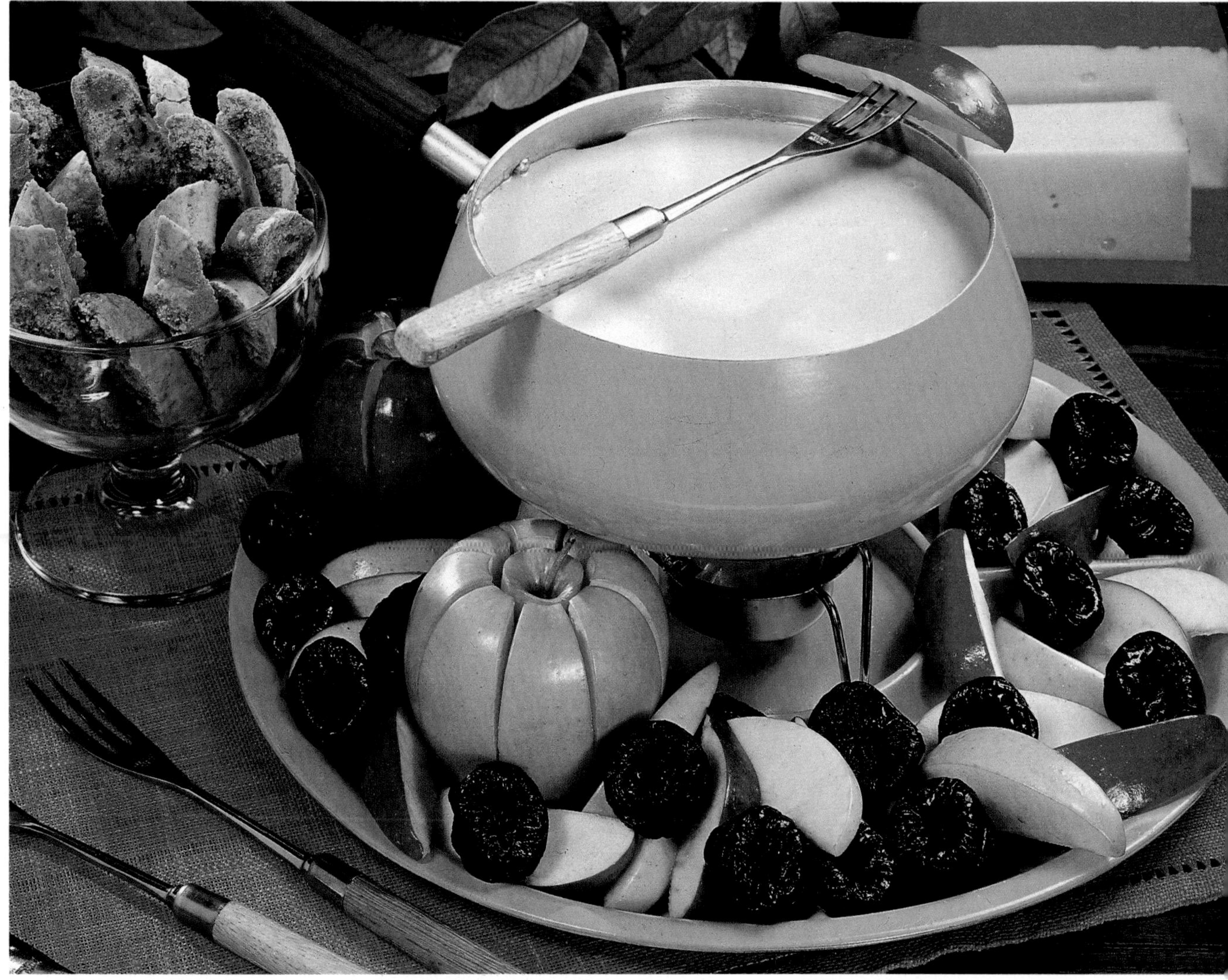

Easy Danish Cheese Fondue

EASY DANISH CHEESE FONDUE

1½ cups dry white wine (or 12-oz. beer)
1 garlic clove
4 cups shredded **Danish Cheese** (combine 2 of **Tybo**, **Danbo**, **Samsoe**, **Svenbo**, **Havarti**, **Esrom** or **Fontina**)
2 tbsp. cornstarch
1 tbsp. brandy or aquavit
dash white pepper
dash nutmeg
¼ tsp. baking soda

Pour wine or beer into a 2-quart saucepan. Add garlic. Heat gently until bubbles start to rise. Discard garlic. Toss cheese with cornstarch. Add the cheese by thirds to saucepan, stirring gently until all cheese is melted. Add brandy and spices. Just before serving, stir in baking soda.
Serves 4

CHILI CON CARNE

1 lb. ground beef
1 cup chopped onion
1 garlic clove, crushed
1 tbsp. chili powder
1 tsp. salt
½ tsp. pepper
1 19-oz. can tomatoes
1 5½-oz. can tomato paste
2 14-oz. cans **Clark Beans with Pork and Tomato Sauce**

In a large saucepan, cook ground meat until it is evenly browned. Add onion, garlic, chili powder, salt and pepper. Cook for 4 minutes over medium heat. Stir in tomatoes, tomato paste and beans. Simmer over low heat for 30 minutes.
Serves 4-6

CHICKEN AND AVOCADO IN YOGURT

6 boned chicken breasts
salt and pepper
2 tsp. butter and oil
1 shallot, chopped
½ lb. mushrooms, sliced
3 tbsp. Cognac
1 cup 35% cream
1 cup **Delisle Plain Yogurt**
1 avocado, cut in ½″ strips

Cut each chicken breast into 6 strips lengthwise. Salt and pepper. Heat fat and sauté chicken 3-4 minutes. Remove chicken from frypan and put aside, reserving hot fat. Add more fat if needed and sauté shallot and mushrooms. Sprinkle with Cognac, add cream and yogurt and cook a few minutes. Salt and pepper. Add avocado and cook a few minutes. Add chicken and heat through. Serve with curried rice.
Serves 6

DANISH CHEESE RICE BAKE

- 2 tbsp. butter
- 1 garlic clove, pressed
- ½ cup onion, finely chopped
- ½ tsp. dried oregano, crumbled
- 1 28-oz. can stewed tomatoes
- 3 cups rice, cooked
- 1 10-oz. package frozen chopped spinach, lightly cooked (or 1 bunch fresh spinach, lightly cooked and chopped)
- salt and pepper
- 2 cups shredded **Danish Tybo**, **Creamy Havarti** or **Danbo Cheese**
- ½ lb. sliced bacon, cut into 1½" pieces, then lightly browned

In large skillet, sauté garlic, onion and oregano in butter until onions are tender. Add stewed tomatoes and simmer about 5 minutes. Spoon cooked rice into an ovenproof dish. Cover with cooked spinach. Season lightly with salt and pepper. Sprinkle 1 cup of shredded cheese on top of spinach. Pour tomato mixture over cheese, top with bacon bits. Bake in a 325°F oven for approximately 20 minutes. Remove from oven; sprinkle with remaining cheese and place under broiler until cheese has melted, about 3 minutes.
Serves 4-6

HAM AND TURKEY CASSEROLE

- 2 cups ham strips
- 1 tsp. poultry seasoning
- 1 tbsp. butter or margarine
- 2 10-oz. cans **Campbell's Condensed Cream of Celery Soup**
- ⅔ cup milk
- 2 cups cubed, cooked turkey
- 1 16-oz. can small whole white onions, drained
- 1 10-oz. package frozen peas, cooked and drained
- 2 8-oz. packages refrigerated crescent rolls
- 1 8-oz. package sliced processed cheese (or ½ cup shredded Cheddar cheese)

In saucepan, brown ham in butter with poultry seasoning. In shallow baking dish (13" x 9" x 2"), combine ham with remaining ingredients except rolls and cheese. Bake at 400°F for 20 minutes or until hot. Meanwhile, cut cheese slices diagonally in half; separate rolls. Top each roll with cheese triangle; roll up as directed on package. Stir hot casserole; top with rolls. Bake 15-20 minutes more or until rolls are baked.
Serves 8

CHICKEN CACCIATORE

- ⅓ cup all-purpose flour
- 1 2½-3 lb. chicken, cut up
- ¼ cup **Crisco Oil**
- 1 medium onion, thinly sliced and separated into rings
- ½ cup chopped green pepper
- 2 garlic cloves, minced
- 1 16-oz. can whole tomatoes, undrained
- 1 8-oz. can tomato sauce
- 1 4-oz. can sliced mushrooms, drained
- ¾ tsp. salt
- ½ tsp. dried oregano leaves
- hot cooked noodles

Place flour in large plastic food storage bag. Add a few chicken pieces. Shake to coat. Remove chicken from bag. Repeat with remaining chicken. Heat oil in large frypan. Add chicken. Brown over medium-high heat. Remove chicken from frypan; set aside. Add onion, green pepper and garlic to frypan. Sauté over moderate heat until tender. Add tomatoes, tomato sauce, mushrooms, salt and oregano, stirring to break apart tomatoes. Place chicken pieces on top of tomato mixture. Cover. Reduce heat. Simmer 30-40 minutes, or until chicken is tender and meat near bone is no longer pink. Serve with noodles.
Serves 4

CHICAGO-STYLE DEEP DISH PIZZA

- 1½ lb. ground beef
- ½ cup chopped onion
- 1 7½-oz. can pizza sauce
- 2 tbsp. grated Parmesan cheese
- 1½ tsp. oregano
- ½ tsp. salt
- ½ tsp. pepper
- 1 8-oz. can **Pillsbury Buttermilk** or **Sweetmilk Biscuits**
- 1 cup sliced mushrooms
- 1 tomato, sliced
- 1 cup grated mozzarella cheese
- green pepper rings
- 3-4 pitted black olives, sliced (optional)

Heat oven to 350°F. Grease a 9" pie pan. Brown ground beef and onion; drain. Stir in pizza sauce, 1 tbsp. Parmesan cheese, oregano, salt and pepper. Simmer while preparing crust. Separate dough into 10 biscuits. Arrange biscuits in prepared pan; press over bottom and up sides to form crust. Spoon hot meat mixture into crust. Arrange mushroom and tomato slices over meat; top with mozzarella cheese. Arrange green pepper rings and olives, if desired, over cheese and sprinkle with remaining Parmesan cheese. Bake 20-25 minutes or until crust is deep golden brown. Cool 5 minutes before serving.
Serves 6

TACO DEEPDISH

- 1½ lb. ground beef
- 1½ tbsp. chili powder
- 1 tsp. cumin
- 1 tsp. oregano
- ¼ tsp. red pepper
- ½ tsp. salt
- 8 **Krinos Fillo Leaves**
- bread crumbs
- 3 medium, fresh tomatoes, chopped
- hot red-pepper sauce
- ⅓ cup chopped onion
- 1 cup grated Colby cheese
- ⅓ head lettuce, shredded
- ½ cup melted butter for fillo

In a skillet, brown beef and drain off excess fat. Add chili powder, cumin, oregano, red pepper and salt. Butter bottom of oblong baking dish and place 5 fillo leaves on the bottom of the pan, buttering and sprinkling bread crumbs after each leaf. Then place 3 additional leaves on the bottom of the pan (not on the sides and not in a smooth fashion as they must be bulky to add volume). Butter and sprinkle with bread crumbs again. Turn in the edges to finish. Butter edges. The remaining ingredients are to be placed in pan in the following order: beef mixture (press down slightly), tomatoes, hot red-pepper sauce and onion. Bake in preheated 375°F oven for 15 minutes. Then add the cheese (reserving a little for topping) and bake 10 more minutes. Remove from oven and sprinkle with shredded lettuce and cheese. Serve immediately with a handful of corn chips for character. Hint: Vegetarians make tacos by substituting refried beans for the meat.

Chicken Divan

CHICKEN DIVAN

½ cup mayonnaise

1 10-oz. can cream of chicken soup

1 10-oz. can cream of mushroom soup

1 tsp. lemon juice

2 10-oz. packages frozen whole broccoli

6 chicken breasts

1 envelope **Shake'n Bake Regular Coating Mix for Chicken**

¼ cup grated Parmesan cheese

Combine mayonnaise, soups, and lemon juice in 13" x 9" baking pan; mix well. Place broccoli on top of soup mixture. Coat chicken pieces with coating mix as directed on package. Place on top of broccoli. Sprinkle with cheese. Bake at 400°F for 40 minutes.
Serves 4-6

COQ AU VIN

1 3½ lb. chicken, cleaned and trussed

¼ cup butter

1 tbsp. oil

3 tbsp. brandy

1 10-oz. can **Sharwood's Red Wine Sauce**

1 garlic clove, minced

¼ lb. small white onions, sautéed

2 oz. small mushrooms, sautéed

chopped parsley

Heat the butter and oil in a large skillet, and brown the chicken all over. Transfer chicken to a large casserole. Warm the brandy, set it alight and pour it flaming over the chicken. As soon as the flames subside pour over red wine sauce and add garlic. Cover casserole and cook for 1 hour at 300°F until chicken is fork-tender. Remove chicken and divide into joints. Thicken sauce, if necessary, adjust seasoning and pour over the chicken. Serve garnished with sautéed onions and mushrooms and chopped parsley.
Serves 4

LUNCHEON CHICKEN TARTS

Crisco Pastry for 6 tart shells *(see Pies and Tarts)*

½ cup mayonnaise or salad dressing

½ cup sour cream

2 tbsp. chutney

½ tsp. curry powder

2 cups chopped cooked chicken

1 8-oz. can pineapple slices, drained and cut up

1 cup chopped celery

¼ cup toasted slivered almonds

Preheat oven to 425°F. Bake tart shells for 10-15 minutes or until golden brown. Cool. Remove from pans. Combine the mayonnaise, sour cream, chutney and curry powder. Add the chicken, cut-up pineapple and celery. Toss slightly. Spoon chicken mixture into tart shells just before serving. Sprinkle the almonds over the top.
Serves 6

MOO GOO GAI PAN

2 tbsp. cornstarch
2 tbsp. water
3 whole boneless chicken breasts, skinned and cut into 1" pieces
½ tsp. salt
⅛ tsp. pepper
¼ cup **Crisco Oil**
¼ cup chopped green onions
2 cups sliced fresh mushrooms
1 2-oz. jar sliced pimento, drained
1 tsp. ground ginger
1 14½-oz. can chicken broth
2 6-oz. packages frozen pea pods
hot cooked rice
toasted almonds
soy sauce

Blend cornstarch and water in small bowl until smooth. Set aside. Sprinkle chicken with salt and pepper. Heat oil in large frypan or wok. Add chicken. Stir fry over medium-high heat until no longer pink. Remove chicken from frypan. Add onion and stir fry over medium-high heat 1 minute. Stir in mushrooms, pimento and ginger. Cook, stirring constantly, 2-3 minutes, or until mushrooms are tender. Add chicken broth and pea pods. Heat to boiling, stirring to break apart pea pods. Add cornstarch mixture. Heat to boiling, stirring constantly. Boil 1 minute. Remove from heat. Stir in chicken. Serve with rice. Sprinkle with toasted almonds and serve with soy sauce, if desired.
Serves 6-8

PORK CHOP AND POTATO SCALLOP

4 pork chops (about 1 lb.)
1 10-oz. can **Campbell's Condensed Cream of Mushroom Soup**
½ cup sour cream
¼ cup water
2 tbsp. chopped parsley
4 cups thinly sliced potatoes
salt
pepper

Brown chops; blend soup, sour cream, water and parsley. In 2-quart casserole, alternate layers of potatoes, sprinkled with salt and pepper, and sauce. Top with chops; cover; bake in a 375°F oven for 1¼ hours.
Serves 3-4

CHICKEN CASSEROLE

2 bunches broccoli
3 tbsp. butter
3 tbsp. flour
1½ cups milk
1 10-oz. can cream of celery soup
¾ cup mayonnaise
2 tsp. Worcestershire sauce
½ tsp. nutmeg
¼ cup sherry
¾ cup **Delisle Plain Yogurt**
6 chicken breasts, cooked and boned
¾ cup bread crumbs
1 cup Parmesan cheese
dabs butter

Cook broccoli a few minutes in salted boiling water. Heat butter, add flour and cook for a few minutes. Remove from heat, add milk and mix thoroughly. Return to heat, cook and stir a few minutes. Add cream of celery soup, mayonnaise, Worcestershire sauce and nutmeg. Mix thoroughly. Add sherry and yogurt. Arrange broccoli in the bottom of an ovenproof baking dish. Top with chicken. Pour sauce over chicken. Sprinkle with bread crumbs and Parmesan cheese. Dab with butter. Bake at 400°F for 30 minutes or until very hot. (Note: Leftover cooked chicken and frozen broccoli may be used.)
Serves 6

CHUCKWAGON CASSEROLE

1 lb. bulk pork sausage
1 celery stalk, sliced
1 medium onion, chopped
1 garlic clove, minced
1 cup **KRAFT Regular Barbecue Sauce**
1 14-oz. can baked beans
1 19-oz. can red kidney beans

Place sausage, celery, onion and garlic in 3-quart microwaveable casserole. Cover with lid or vented plastic wrap and microwave on high 6-9 minutes, until sausage is no longer pink, stirring halfway through; drain. Combine sausage mixture, barbecue sauce and beans in same casserole. Cover with lid or vented plastic wrap and microwave on high 10 minutes; stir. Cover tightly and microwave on medium 15 minutes.
Serves 8

BEEF STROGANOFF

1½ lb. boneless sirloin, cut into bite-sized pieces
1 tbsp. oil
4 tbsp. butter
1 large onion, chopped
½ lb. mushrooms, chopped
½ cup beef stock
1 cup sour cream
1 tsp. dry mustard
1 tbsp. oregano
1 tsp. Worcestershire sauce
salt and pepper to taste
8 **Krinos Fillo Leaves**
½-1 stick butter, melted for fillo

In a skillet, brown beef in vegetable oil for 15 minutes. In a separate large skillet, sauté onion and mushrooms in butter until tender. Add beef stock, sour cream, mustard, oregano, Worcestershire sauce, salt and pepper. Simmer for 2 minutes and then add beef. Stir together well. Remove from heat and allow mixture to cool for 10 minutes. In the meantime, prepare fillo for crêpes *(see Chicken and Egg Crêpes in Crêpes and Pancakes)*. Spoon mixture onto crêpe shells, butter and place in baking pan. Bake in preheated 400°F oven for 20 minutes or until golden brown. When served, sour cream and chives as a topping adds a special touch to your meal.

SHRIMP CREOLE

1 medium onion, chopped
1 medium green pepper, chopped
1 stalk celery, chopped
1 tsp. garlic powder
1½ tsp. oil
¾ lb. shrimp, cleaned
1¼ cups water
1 cup stewed tomatoes
¼ tsp. salt
¼ tsp. pepper
1½ cups **Instant Brown MINUTE RICE**

Cook and stir vegetables and garlic powder in hot oil in large skillet until tender but not browned. Add shrimp, water, tomatoes, salt and pepper; bring to boil. Stir in rice. Return to boil. Cover, reduce heat and simmer 5 minutes. Remove from heat and stir. Cover and let stand 5 minutes.
Serves 4

GRAVIES AND SAUCES

Tasty sauces and gravies are simple additions that can be the crowning glory to any meat, fish or vegetable dish. They enhance the appearance and flavor of food and in many cases add to its nutritional value.

In this chapter you will find easy-to-prepare gourmet recipes which have been created and tested by food companies around the world.

Because sauces and gravies are a combination of many spices, herbs and seasonings, as well as basic ingredients, the art of sauce and gravy making appeals to amateurs and professionals alike. There is almost no limit to the imaginative variations you can create.

Ruby Sherried Meat Sauce (see page 170)

ZIPPY COLA MARINADE

½ cup ketchup
½ cup cola drink
3 garlic cloves, chopped
¾ tsp. **Tabasco** brand pepper sauce

Combine ingredients in large bowl or plastic bag. Mix well. Use to marinate 2 lb. of flank steak, 5 hours or overnight, before grilling.
Makes 1 cup

QUICK AND SASSY BAYOU SAUCE

1 cup mayonnaise or whipped salad dressing
1 tbsp. ketchup
1½ tsp. **Tabasco** brand pepper sauce
freshly cracked black pepper to taste

Combine ingredients in small bowl. Cover and refrigerate. Serve as a sauce or dip for seafood or vegetables.
Makes about 1 cup

BARBECUE SAUCE

1 8-oz. can tomato sauce
½ cup orange juice
2 tbsp. brown sugar
¼ cup **Maille Dijon Mustard**

In a small saucepan, combine the above ingredients. Bring to boil. Reduce heat. Simmer 5 minutes. Delicious on chicken and pork.

YOGURT CUCUMBER SAUCE

½ cup **Hellmann's or Best Foods Real Mayonnaise**
½ cup yogurt
1 tbsp. chopped green onion
½ tsp. curry powder
¼ tsp. salt
¼ tsp. dry mustard
⅛ tsp. white pepper
2 drops hot red-pepper sauce
1½ cups chopped cucumber

Combine mayonnaise, yogurt, green onion, curry powder, salt, mustard, pepper and hot red-pepper sauce and mix thoroughly. Stir in cucumber. Delicious with fish or as a salad dressing.
Makes 2 cups sauce

CALYPSO SAUCE

½ cup light brown sugar
¼ cup lime juice
2 tbsp. rum
1 tsp. ground ginger
2 garlic cloves, minced
¼ tsp. salt
¼ tsp. **Tabasco** brand pepper sauce
⅛ tsp. ground cloves

Combine ingredients in a 1-cup glass measure. Microwave on high 45 seconds to 1 minute. Serve with shrimp, pork or chicken.
Makes ¾ cup

TANGY TARTAR SAUCE

1 cup mayonnaise
¼ tsp. **Tabasco** brand pepper sauce
1 tsp. vinegar
1 tbsp. minced onion
1 tbsp. chopped parsley
1 tbsp. chopped capers
2 tbsp. chopped pickle

Mix ingredients well. Serve with fish or seafood.
Makes 1 cup

OLIVE, PEPPER AND WALNUT SAUCE FOR PASTA

¼ cup olive oil
1 red pepper, seeded and chopped
1 garlic clove, minced
½ cup ripe olives, pitted and chopped
½ cup chopped walnuts
⅓ cup chopped parsley
½ tsp. **Tabasco** brand pepper sauce
¼ tsp. salt

Heat olive oil in small saucepan. Stir in red pepper and garlic and cook until tender. Remove from heat and stir in olives, walnuts, parsley, Tabasco pepper sauce and salt. Serve on hot pasta.
Makes 2 cups

AVERY ISLAND BARBECUE SAUCE

2 tbsp. butter or margarine
1 cup chopped onion
½ cup diced celery with leaves
¼ cup diced green pepper
1 tbsp. minced fresh garlic
1 28-oz. can tomatoes, drained and coarsely chopped
1 5½-oz. can tomato paste
⅓ cup red wine vinegar
3 tbsp. molasses
2 lemon slices
2 tsp. **Tabasco** brand pepper sauce
2 tsp. dry mustard
1 bay leaf
½ tsp. ground cloves
½ tsp. ground allspice

Melt butter in a large heavy non-aluminum saucepan over medium heat. Add onion, celery, green pepper and garlic; sauté 6-7 minutes, stirring frequently, until tender. Stir in remaining ingredients and bring to boil over high heat. Reduce heat to low; cover and simmer 30 minutes, stirring occasionally, until sauce is thickened. Remove from heat. Remove and discard lemon slices and bay leaf. Process in a food processor or blender until smooth. Ladle sauce into clean jars. Keeps refrigerated up to 2 weeks.
Makes 2¼ cups

GREEN SAUCE

1 cup fresh parsley sprigs, packed
1 cup fresh watercress, packed
1 cup fresh basil leaves, packed
¼ cup pine nuts or toasted almonds
¼ cup fresh lime juice
¼ cup olive oil
2 garlic cloves, chopped
½ tsp. **Tabasco** brand pepper sauce

Blend ingredients in blender or food processor until smooth. Transfer to container, cover and chill for 24 hours to develop flavor. Serve with hot or cold meals, poultry or fish.
Makes 1 cup or enough for 16 servings

ONION GRAVY

1 pouch **Lipton Onion Recipe and Soup Mix**

2 cups water, divided

1-2 tbsp. flour

In medium saucepan, stir soup mix into 1½ cups boiling water. Reduce heat, cover and simmer for 5 minutes. Mix ½ cup cold water with flour. Stir flour mixture into soup. Cook for 2-3 minutes until thickened.

Makes about 2 cups

BILLY BEE TERIYAKI SAUCE

1 cup soy sauce

½ cup **Billy Bee Honey**

¼ cup vegetable oil

2 tbsp. lemon juice

2 tsp. ginger

¼ tsp. pepper

4 garlic cloves, minced

Combine all ingredients. Mix well. Refrigerate. Use to marinate shrimp, diced beef or pork.

RED PEPPER BARBECUE BASTE

1 large garlic clove

1 cup **Emelia Red Pepper Jelly**

1 tbsp. freshly grated ginger

2 tsp. soy sauce

1 tbsp. Sake or dry sherry

Finely chop garlic and combine with rest of ingredients. Stir well. Use as a broiling or roasting glaze or as a barbecue sauce. Delicious on shish kebab, chicken, pork chops, lamb chops, ham, turkey or meatloaf.

Makes 1 cup

TANDOORI CHUTNEY

4 oz. plain yogurt

1 tbsp. chopped fresh mint

1 tbsp. chopped fresh coriander

large pinch **Sharwood's Garam Masala**

salt to taste

Combine all ingredients and serve. Especially good with Indian meat dishes.

BÉARNAISE SAUCE

¼ cup dry white wine

2 tbsp. tarragon vinegar or white vinegar

1 tbsp. chopped onion

½ tsp. dried tarragon leaves

¼ tsp. salt

⅛ tsp. white pepper

2 egg yolks

⅔ cup **Mazola Corn Oil**

⅓ cup **Hellmann's or Best Foods Real Mayonnaise**

Combine wine, vinegar, onion, tarragon, salt, pepper and egg yolks in blender or food processor. Blend until light and lemon colored (8-10 seconds). Slowly add oil until blended. Pour into saucepan. Cook over low heat until mixture thickens, about 2 minutes. Remove from heat and stir in mayonnaise.

Makes 2 cups sauce

Béarnaise Sauce

CUMBERLAND SAUCE

1 cup **Emelia Red Currant, Raspberry and Cherry Preserve**
juice and rind of an orange
juice and rind of a lemon
1 green onion, finely chopped
1 tsp. mustard
2 large pinches ginger
2 large pinches cayenne
1 cup good port wine

Melt Emelia Preserve in a 2-cup non-metallic saucepan. For an elegant effect, julienne the orange and lemon rind. Add to preserves. Add green onion, mustard, ginger, cayenne and port. Heat for 1-2 minutes over low heat. Sauce is good with roast duck, goose or cold tongue.
Makes approximately 2 cups

PEPPERED BRANDY SAUCE

2 tbsp. **Mazola Corn Oil** or beef drippings
1 cup sliced mushrooms
1 cup beef broth
¼ cup brandy
¼ cup **Veloutine Dark**
2 tbsp. whipping cream
ground pepper

In small saucepan heat oil or drippings. Add mushrooms and sauté 2-3 minutes. Add beef broth and brandy. Bring to boil, sprinkle in Veloutine, stirring constantly. Boil 1 minute; reduce heat and stir in cream. Add pepper to taste. Serve over cooked steaks or roast beef.

TARTAR SAUCE

1 cup **Hellmann's or Best Foods Real Mayonnaise**
¼ cup finely chopped onion
¼ cup finely chopped sweet pickles
2 tbsp. chopped pimento
2 tsp. capers
1 tsp. lemon juice
¼ tsp. salt
⅛ tsp. pepper

Thoroughly combine all ingredients. This tartar sauce is good not only with fish but also as a sandwich spread when mixed with tuna or egg.
Makes 1½ cups sauce

FIERY ORANGE GINGER GLAZE

½ cup orange marmalade
¼ cup rice or red wine vinegar
¼ cup soy sauce
2 tbsp. sesame oil
6 cloves garlic, minced
1 3" piece gingerroot, peeled and finely grated, or 1½ tsp. ground ginger
1 cinnamon stick
½ tsp. **Tabasco** brand pepper sauce
4 whole cloves

Mix all ingredients in medium-sized saucepan. Bring to boil over high heat, stirring constantly. Reduce heat to medium and simmer 2-3 minutes, stirring until slightly thickened. Remove from heat and allow to cool to room temperature. Remove and discard cinnamon stick and cloves.
Makes 1 cup

QUICK SPAGHETTI SAUCE

3 slices bacon, cut in small pieces
1 medium onion, chopped
1 celery stalk, thinly sliced
1 garlic clove, minced
2 cups canned tomatoes
1 10-oz. can **Campbell's Condensed Tomato Soup**
1 tsp. salt
½ tsp. oregano
½ tsp. basil
¼ tsp. pepper
⅓ cup water

In 2-quart saucepan over medium heat, fry bacon until crisp. Add onion, celery and garlic; cook 5 minutes or until onion and celery are tender. Add water and remaining ingredients; heat to boiling. Reduce heat to low and simmer, stir occasionally, about 15 minutes.
Makes 1½ cups

BASIC COCKTAIL SAUCE

½ cup ketchup or chili sauce
2 tbsp. lemon juice
½ tsp. **Tabasco** brand pepper sauce
2 tsp. Worcestershire sauce
1 tbsp. horseradish

Mix ingredients, chill well and serve with seafood.
Makes ¾ cup

STROGANOFF SAUCE

¼ cup chopped onion
½ tsp. paprika
2 tbsp. butter or margarine
1 10-oz. can **Campbell's Condensed Golden Mushroom Soup**
¼ cup sour cream

In saucepan, cook onion with paprika in butter until tender. Stir in soup and sour cream; heat, stirring occasionally. Serve over sliced cooked beef, hamburgers, noodles, potatoes or rice.
Makes 1½ cups

RUBY SHERRIED MEAT SAUCE

½ cup **Hellmann's or Best Foods Real Mayonnaise**
2 tbsp. horseradish
2 tbsp. red currant jelly
1 tbsp. tarragon vinegar or white vinegar
1 tbsp. dry sherry
1 tsp. Dijon mustard
½ tsp. salt
2 drops hot red-pepper sauce
½ cup whipping cream, softly whipped

Combine mayonnaise and horseradish in medium bowl. Stir red currant jelly to soften. Add jelly, vinegar, sherry, mustard, salt and hot red-pepper sauce to mayonnaise and mix well. Fold in whipped cream.
Makes 1¾ cups sauce

CONFETTI CORN RELISH

1 12-oz. can whole kernel corn, drained
4 green onions, chopped
½ red pepper, chopped
⅓ cup **KRAFT CATALINA Dressing**

Mix ingredients; chill.
Makes 2 cups

HORSERADISH STEAK SAUCE

1 cup **KRAFT Regular Barbecue Sauce**
2 tbsp. horseradish

Combine ingredients. Use sauce as marinade for steaks and for basting while grilling.
Makes 1 cup

Onion Mushroom Gravy

ONION MUSHROOM GRAVY

1 pouch **Lipton Onion-Mushroom Recipe, Soup and Gravy Mix**

1-2 tbsp. flour

1¾ cups water

In a medium saucepan, combine soup mix, flour and water. Bring to boil, stirring occasionally. Reduce heat; cover and simmer for 5 minutes.

Makes about 2 cups

NO-COOK TOMATO SAUCE

1 lb. tomatoes, peeled, seeded and chopped or 1 28-oz. can well-drained tomatoes

1 green onion

⅛ tsp. **Club House Garlic Powder**

2 tsp. **Club House Italian Seasoning**

½ tsp. salt

½ tsp. **Club House Ground Black Pepper**

¼ tsp. **Club House Crushed Red Pepper**

1 tbsp. olive oil

1 tbsp. tomato paste

Combine all ingredients in food processor or blender and process until smooth. Cover and refrigerate. This is a great tomato sauce for pizza and pasta.

Makes about 1 cup

FRENCH'S SWEET'N TANGY MUSTARD BUTTER

½ cup butter, softened

¼ cup **French's Sweet'n Tangy Mustard**

1 tbsp. **French's Parsley Flakes**

Blend ingredients together. Place on waxed paper and form into a cylinder. Wrap well and keep refrigerated or frozen. Great on roast beef sandwiches, fish or vegetables.

Makes ¾ cup

Cheese Sauce

SOUR CREAM SAUCE

¼ cup chopped onion

1 tbsp. butter

1 10-oz. can **Campbell's Condensed Cream of Celery**, **Chicken** or **Mushroom Soup**

½ cup sour cream

dash paprika

Cook chopped onion in butter until tender. Stir in mixture of soup, sour cream and paprika. Heat; stir. Serve with cooked noodles, meats or poultry.
Makes 2 cups

HOLLANDAISE SAUCE

¾ cup **Hellmann's or Best Foods Real Mayonnaise**

⅓ cup milk

¼ tsp. dry mustard

¼ tsp. salt

1 tbsp. lemon juice

1 tsp. grated lemon rind

Whisk together mayonnaise, milk, mustard and salt in small saucepan. Warm over low heat, stirring constantly. Stir in lemon juice and rind. Serve with broccoli, cauliflower, asparagus or carrots.
Makes 1¼ cup sauce

CHEESE SAUCE

1 pouch **Lipton Cheddar Cheese Recipe, Soup and Sauce Mix**

1½ cups water

Prepare soup mix according to package directions and use to make one of the following variations if desired.

White Wine Sauce: Reduce water to 1¼ cups, add ¼ cup white wine.

Apple Juice Sauce: Reduce water to 1 cup, add ½ cup apple juice.

Fondue: Reduce water to 1 cup, add ¼ cup white wine or beer, ½ tsp. dry mustard. Serve with bread chunks or raw vegetable dippers.
Makes 1½ cups sauce

HERB SAUCE

1 10-oz. can **Campbell's Condensed Golden Mushroom Soup**
1/3 cup water
1/3 cup chopped onions or shallots
2 tbsp. butter
1/4 cup dry white wine
1 tbsp. chopped parsley
generous dash crushed chervil
generous dash tarragon

Combine soup and water in saucepan. Heat; stir. In another saucepan, cook onion in butter until tender. Add wine and simmer a few minutes. Stir in soup, parsley and herbs. Heat; stir. Serve over cooked meats, poultry or vegetables.
Makes 2 cups

BORDELAISE SAUCE

1 10-oz. can **Campbell's Condensed Golden Mushroom Soup**
1/3 cup water
1/4 cup chopped onion or shallots
2 tbsp. butter
1/4 cup dry red wine
1 tbsp. parsley

Combine soup and water in saucepan. Heat; stir. In another saucepan, cook onion in butter until tender. Add wine and simmer a few minutes. Stir in soup and parsley. Heat; stir. Serve over cooked meats, poultry or vegetables.
Makes 2 cups

TOMATO SAUCE

1 28-oz. can whole tomatoes (preferably in thick purée)
1 large onion, quartered
2 garlic cloves
2 tbsp. unsalted butter
zest of 1 orange
1/4 cup **Grand Marnier**

Combine the tomatoes, onion, garlic, butter and zest of orange in a 2-quart saucepan and simmer, uncovered, for 3-4 hours. Add the Grand Marnier and continue to simmer for an additional 1-1½ hours. Excellent with fish.

HERBED SPAGHETTI SAUCE

1/2 lb. ground beef
1/4 cup finely chopped onion
1/4 cup finely chopped green pepper
1 garlic clove, minced
1 10-oz. can **Campbell's Condensed Tomato Soup**
1 cup tomato sauce
1 12-oz. can mushroom stems and pieces, drained
1 bay leaf
1/4 tsp. salt
1/4 tsp. crushed dried oregano
1/4 tsp. crushed dried basil
dash crushed rosemary
dash crushed thyme
dash pepper
hot cooked spaghetti
grated Parmesan cheese

In frypan, cook ground beef, onion, green pepper and garlic until meat is brown; drain off excess fat. Stir in soup and tomato sauce. Stir in mushrooms, bay leaf, salt, oregano, basil, rosemary, thyme and pepper. Bring to boil; reduce heat. Cover and simmer about 30 minutes, stir occasionally; discard bay leaf. Serve over hot cooked spaghetti; top with Parmesan cheese.
Makes 3 cups

MUSHROOM GRAVY

2 tbsp. **Mazola Corn Oil** or beef drippings
1 cup sliced mushrooms
1 cup beef broth
1/4 cup sherry, red wine or beef broth
1½ tsp. Worcestershire sauce
1/8 tsp. thyme
2 tbsp. minced parsley
1/4 cup **Veloutine Dark**

In small saucepan heat oil or drippings. Add mushrooms and sauté 2-3 minutes. Add beef broth, sherry, Worcestershire sauce, thyme and parsley. Bring to boil; sprinkle in Veloutine, stirring constantly. Boil 1 minute. Serve hot on steaks or roast beef.
Makes about 1½ cups

ZESTY HOT SAUCE

1 cup ketchup
1/3 cup pickle relish, drained
1/4 cup **ReaLemon Reconstituted Lemon Juice**
2 tbsp. finely chopped onion
2 tbsp. prepared horseradish

In small bowl, combine ingredients. Refrigerate. Serve with your favorite fish or seafood.
Makes 1¾ cups

DANISH BLUE SAUCE

1 cup (about 4 oz.) **Danish Blue Cheese,** crumbled
1 cup sour cream, at room temperature
1/4 cup champagne or dry white wine
cooked vegetables such as cauliflower, broccoli, carrots, asparagus or green beans

Warm blue cheese in heavy saucepan over low heat, stirring constantly until melted. Add sour cream. Continue to stir over low heat until smooth and barely warm. Do not simmer. Stir in champagne or wine. Pour over cooked vegetable(s), or pass in sauce boat.
Makes about 1½ cups

ESPAGNOLE SAUCE

1 10-oz. can **Campbell's Condensed Golden Mushroom Soup**
1/3 cup water
1 slice bacon
1/3 cup chopped onion
1 small bay leaf
dash crushed thyme
1/3 cup tomato juice

Combine soup and water in saucepan. Heat; stir. In another saucepan, cook bacon until crisp, crumble and put aside. Add onion, bay leaf and thyme to drippings; cook until onion is tender. Stir in soup, tomato juice and reserved bacon. Heat; stir. Serve with cooked meats, poultry or vegetables.
Makes 2 cups

CAKES

When Marie Antoinette declared, “Let them eat cake”, did she mean chocolate or angel food? Maybe cupcakes were more what she had in mind. At any rate there are a great number of choices that can be made when it comes to favorite cakes. From chocolate cakes to cheesecakes, from tea cakes to tortes, they're all delicious.

We've gathered together some of the finest cake recipes around and we've added some wonderful, easy-to-mix frostings that you can use to add new sparkle to your own favorite recipes.

Any way you slice it, your family and friends will be coming back for more...make sure you save at least one piece for the cook.

Marble Cake à l'Orange (see page 176)

MARBLE CAKE À L'ORANGE

1¾ cups all-purpose flour
1½ cups sugar
1 tbsp. baking powder
1 tsp. salt
½ cup **Mazola Corn Oil**
5 eggs, separated
½ cup water
1 orange rind
¼ cup orange juice
2 squares semi-sweet chocolate, melted
½ tsp. cream of tartar

Chocolate Orange Glaze:

1 cup icing sugar
2 tbsp. orange liqueur
1 tbsp. orange juice
1 tsp. vanilla
2 squares semi-sweet chocolate, melted

Combine flour, sugar, baking powder and salt in large bowl. Make a well in center of flour mixture. Stir in oil, egg yolks, water, orange rind and juice. Beat together until well mixed. Divide batter between 2 large bowls. Beat melted chocolate into 1 bowl of batter. Beat egg whites until frothy. Add cream of tartar and continue beating until stiff. Carefully fold half of egg whites into each bowl of batter. Spoon about half the orange batter into ungreased 10" tube pan. In random fashion, spoon in chocolate batter and top with remaining orange batter. Run a knife, zigzag fashion, through batter to create marble effect. Bake at 350°F about 55 minutes or until done. Invert and cool. Loosen sides of cake and remove from pan. To make glaze, blend all ingredients until smooth. Spread over cake and let drizzle down sides. Garnish with grated orange rind if desired.

Makes 1 cake

APPLESAUCE CAKE

2 cups sifted all-purpose flour
1 tsp. **Cow Brand Baking Soda**
¾ tsp. salt
1 tsp. ground cinnamon
⅛ tsp. ground cloves
½ cup vegetable shortening
1 cup firmly-packed light brown sugar
1 egg
1 cup sweetened applesauce
1½ tsp. grated lemon peel
3 tbsp. vinegar
1 cup dark seedless raisins

Sift together flour, baking soda, salt and spices. Using an electric mixer, cream shortening until soft in large bowl; add sugar gradually, creaming until light and fluffy. Beat in egg. Stir together applesauce, lemon peel and vinegar; add alternately with dry ingredients to creamed mixture, beginning and ending with dry ingredients. Beat well after each addition. Stir in raisins. Turn into greased and floured 8" square baking pan. Bake in 350°F oven 55 minutes or until toothpick inserted in center of cake comes out clean. Cool in pan 10 minutes; remove from pan and cool on rack. Serve with whipped cream if desired.

Makes an 8" square cake

DESSERT GINGERBREAD

1½ cups sifted all-purpose flour
1 tsp. **Cow Brand Baking Soda**
1 tsp. ground ginger
¼ tsp. salt
⅓ cup vegetable shortening
½ cup sugar
1 egg
½ cup light molasses
¾ cup boiling water

Sift together flour, baking soda, ginger and salt. Using an electric mixer, cream shortening until light and fluffy in large bowl. Add sugar gradually, beating after each addition. Beat in egg thoroughly; blend in molasses. Gradually stir dry ingredients into creamed mixture. Beat thoroughly. Stir in water. Turn into greased and floured 8" square baking pan. Bake in 350°F oven 40 minutes or until toothpick inserted in center of cake comes out clean. Cool in pan 10 minutes; remove from pan and cool on rack.

Makes an 8" square cake

PUMPKIN TEA CAKE

2½ cups sifted all-purpose flour
3 tsp. baking powder
1½ tsp. salt
1 tsp. **Cow Brand Baking Soda**
1 tsp. ground cinnamon
½ tsp. ground nutmeg
½ tsp. ground ginger
¼ tsp. ground cloves
½ cup wheat germ
½ cup vegetable oil
2 eggs
1½ cups sugar
1½ cups canned pumpkin

Sift together flour, baking powder, salt, baking soda and spices. Stir in wheat germ. In large bowl, beat together oil, eggs and sugar until creamy. Blend in pumpkin. Add dry ingredients and stir until moistened. Spread smoothly into greased 13" x 9" x 2" pan. Bake in 350°F oven 30 minutes or until toothpick inserted in center comes out clean. Cool in pan. Serve with whipped cream or ice cream, if desired, or dust with icing sugar.

LEMON LOAF CAKE

2 cups sifted cake flour
½ tsp. **Cow Brand Baking Soda**
¼ tsp. salt
½ cup butter or margarine
1 cup sugar
2 eggs
½ cup milk
4½ tsp. lemon juice
1 tsp. grated lemon peel

Sift together flour, baking soda and salt. Using an electric mixer, cream butter until light and fluffy in large bowl. Add sugar gradually, beating after each addition. In separate bowl, beat eggs until thick and lemon colored. Slowly beat eggs into butter mixture. Combine milk and lemon juice. Alternately add dry ingredients and liquid to creamed mixture, beginning and ending with dry ingredients. After each addition, beat until smooth. Stir in lemon peel. Turn into greased and floured 8" square pan. Bake in 350°F oven 45 minutes or until toothpick inserted in center comes out clean. Cool in pan 10 minutes. Remove from pan and cool on rack.

Makes an 8" square cake

PUMPKIN CHEESECAKE

Base:

1½ cups **Nabisco 100% Bran Cereal**

1 tsp. ginger

2 tbsp. granulated sugar

½ cup **Blue Bonnet Margarine**, melted

Filling:

4 eggs

1 14-oz. can pumpkin

1 lb. cream cheese, softened

⅔ cup lightly packed brown sugar

½ cup **Nabisco 100% Bran Cereal**

½ tsp. nutmeg

½ tsp. cinnamon

Topping:

1 cup sour cream

2 tbsp. granulated sugar

½ tsp. vanilla

ground nutmeg and hazelnuts (filberts) for garnish

Process cereal in blender or food processor or roll between sheets of waxed paper, until it resembles fine crumbs. Combine with ginger, 2 tbsp. granulated sugar and margarine. Press into the bottom of a 9″ springform cake pan. Refrigerate. Beat eggs in a medium bowl; blend in pumpkin. Set aside. Beat cream cheese and brown sugar in large bowl, with an electric mixer, until smooth and creamy. Beat in cereal, spices and egg mixture. Pour filling into prepared crust. Bake at 325°F for 60-65 minutes or until set. Combine topping ingredients and spread carefully on top of hot cake. Cool completely. Refrigerate 4 hours or until well chilled. Remove ring, garnish with ground nutmeg and hazelnuts.

Serves 8

CHOCOLATE FROSTING ROYALE

⅓ cup butter or margarine

⅓ cup **Fry's Cocoa**

½ tsp. vanilla

3 cups sifted icing sugar

3 tbsp. milk

Melt butter in a saucepan. Remove from heat. Stir in cocoa and vanilla. Alternately blend in icing sugar and milk until frosting is smooth and of spreading consistency.

Cocoa Peppermint Frosting: Proceed as above, adding ¼ tsp. peppermint extract.

Makes 1⅔ cups

Pumpkin Cheesecake

STRAWBERRY ALMOND CHEESECAKE

1 cup graham cracker crumbs

¼ cup finely chopped almonds

¼ cup melted butter

½ lb. cream cheese, at room temperature

1 cup **Hellmann's or Best Foods Real Mayonnaise**

⅔ cup sugar

2 eggs

2 tsp. almond flavoring

½ tsp. vanilla

2 cups whole strawberries

¼ cup apple jelly, melted

Combine graham cracker crumbs, almonds and melted butter. Press into 9″ springform pan. Bake at 325°F 10 minutes. Beat together cream cheese, mayonnaise, sugar, eggs and flavorings until creamy. Pour onto baked crust. Bake at 350°F 40 minutes. Cool. One hour before serving, arrange berries over filling. Brush with melted apple jelly. Refrigerate.

Makes 1 cake

SOUR CREAM POUND CAKE

3 cups sifted all-purpose flour

¼ tsp. **Cow Brand Baking Soda**

¼ tsp. salt

3 cups sugar

1 cup butter or margarine

6 eggs

1 cup sour cream

1 tsp. vanilla or lemon extract

icing sugar

Sift together flour, baking soda and salt. Using an electric mixer, cream together sugar and butter until light and fluffy in large bowl; add eggs one at a time, beating after each addition. Stir in sour cream and extract. Gradually mix dry ingredients into egg mixture until completely blended. Turn into greased and floured 10″ tube pan. Bake in 350°F oven 1 hour and 25 minutes or until toothpick inserted in center comes out clean. Remove from pan and cool on rack. Before serving, sprinkle with icing sugar.

Makes a 10″ tube cake

Mix-Easy Chocolate Cake

MIX-EASY CHOCOLATE CAKE

⅓ cup vegetable oil
2 squares **Baker's Unsweetened Chocolate**
¾ cup water
1 cup sugar
1 egg
1¼ cups all-purpose flour
½ tsp. salt
½ tsp. baking soda
1 tsp. vanilla
1 cup **Baker's Semi-Sweet Chocolate Chips**
⅓ cup chopped nuts

Heat oil and chocolate in 8″ square cake pan, in 350°F oven for about 4 minutes. Add water, sugar, egg, flour, salt, baking soda and vanilla. Beat with fork until smooth, about 2 minutes. Spread evenly in pan. Sprinkle with chocolate chips and nuts. Bake at 350°F for 40 minutes, or until cake tester inserted in center comes out clean. Cool.

Makes 8 servings

MOIST CARROT CAKE

1 cup flour
4 **Weetabix**, crushed
2 tsp. baking powder
1½ tsp. baking soda
5 tsp. cinnamon
1 tsp. salt
1½ cups oil
2 cups sugar
1 tsp. vanilla
4 eggs
1 cup chopped walnuts
2 cups grated carrots
1 cup crushed pineapple and juice

Orange Glaze:

½ cup sugar
rind of 1 orange
orange juice

Stir together first six ingredients. Set aside. Beat together oil, sugar and vanilla. Add eggs one at a time, beating well after each addition. Mix in flour mixture. Stir in nuts, carrots and pineapple. Pour batter into greased 9″ x 13″ pan. Bake at 350°F for 30 minutes, then 325°F for 30 minutes. Cool on rack for 10 minutes. Remove from pan. Prepare orange glaze by combining sugar and rind, adding juice gradually until a pouring consistency. Pour orange glaze over cake while still warm.

Makes 1 cake

SWISS CAKE

1 cup all-purpose flour
1 tsp. baking powder
1 cup **Alpen Mixed Cereal**
½ cup margarine
½ cup fruit sugar
2 eggs
a little milk

Mix together flour, baking powder and Alpen. Blend in margarine. Add sugar and well beaten eggs. Add milk if necessary to make a smooth mixture. Place mixture in a well greased 6″ round cake pan. Bake in 350°F oven, 45 minutes to 1 hour until golden brown.

Makes 1 cake

FUNNY FACE CUPCAKES

1¼ cups all-purpose flour
¾ cup **Fry's Cocoa**
1 tbsp. baking powder
½ tsp. salt
½ cup softened butter
1⅓ cups sugar
3 eggs
⅔ cup milk
1 tsp. vanilla
assorted candies

Frosting:

⅓ cup butter
⅓ cup **Fry's Cocoa**
½ tsp. vanilla
3 cups sifted icing sugar
3 tbsp. milk

Set 22 large paper baking cups in muffin tins. Sift together flour, Fry's Cocoa, baking powder and salt. Cream butter; gradually beat in sugar. Add eggs one at a time, beating well after each addition. Add sifted dry ingredients to creamed mixture alternately with milk and vanilla, combining lightly after each addition. Divide batter evenly among baking cups. Bake in preheated 375°F oven 20-25 minutes. Cool and frost. To make frosting: Melt butter in a saucepan. Remove from heat. Stir in Fry's Cocoa and vanilla. Alternately blend in sifted icing sugar and milk until frosting is smooth and of spreading consistency. Use candies to make funny faces.
Makes 22 cupcakes

BUTTERSCOTCH APPLE CAKE

2 tbsp. butter
2-3 apples, peeled and cored
½ cup **Lynch Butterscotch Topping**
2 eggs, separated
2 tbsp. water
½ cup sugar
1 tsp. vanilla
½ cup all-purpose flour
¼ tsp. salt
½ tsp. baking powder
additional **Lynch Butterscotch Topping** for garnish
whipped topping for garnish

Melt butter and pour into 8" x 8" x 2" pan. Slice apples and arrange in butter on bottom of pan. Pour Butterscotch Topping over apple slices. Beat egg yolks with water. Gradually beat in sugar and vanilla. Sift dry ingredients together and add to egg-yolk mixture a little at a time until well mixed. In a separate bowl beat egg whites until stiff peaks form. Fold egg whites into cake batter. Pour batter over apples and butterscotch in pan. Bake at 350°F for 35-40 minutes until golden brown. Serve warm with additional Butterscotch Topping drizzled over top and a dollop of whipped topping.
Makes 12 2" squares

COCONUTTY PUMPKIN CAKE

¾ cup softened butter
1½ cups sugar
3 eggs
1½ cups canned pumpkin
1½ tsp. vanilla
3 cups all-purpose flour
3½ tsp. baking powder
1 tsp. baking soda
¾ tsp. salt
1½ tsp. ground cinnamon
¾ tsp. ground nutmeg
¼ tsp. ground ginger
¾ cup undiluted **Carnation Evaporated Milk**

Topping:

¼ cup melted butter
1 cup packed brown sugar
⅓ cup undiluted **Carnation Evaporated Milk**
⅔ cup dessicated coconut
½ cup chopped nuts

Cream butter and sugar until light. Add eggs, one at a time, beating well after each addition. Blend in pumpkin and vanilla. Stir together flour, baking powder, baking soda, salt and spices. Add dry ingredients to creamed mixture alternately with evaporated milk, beginning and ending with dry ingredients. Turn batter into greased 13" x 9" x 2" cake pan. Bake in preheated 350°F oven 45-50 minutes. Cool. Combine melted butter, brown sugar, ⅓ cup evaporated milk, coconut and nuts. Spread over cake. Broil until bubbly.
Makes 1 cake

BAKER'S BEST UPSIDE-DOWN CHOCOLATE PECAN CAKE

Pecan/Coconut Mixture:

¼ cup butter
½ cup firmly packed brown sugar
⅔ cup pecan halves
⅔ cup **Baker's Angel Flake Coconut**

Cake:

1½ cups cake and pastry flour, unsifted
1 cup granulated sugar
½ tsp. baking soda
½ tsp. baking powder
½ tsp. salt
⅓ cup butter, softened
¾ cup buttermilk or sour milk (to sour milk, place 2 tsp. vinegar in a measuring cup; fill with milk to ¾ cup level)
1 tsp. vanilla
4 squares **Baker's Sweet Chocolate**, melted and cooled
2 eggs

To prepare pecan/coconut mixture: Grease and line with waxed paper a 9" round cake pan. Melt butter in pan in oven; blend in brown sugar. Spread evenly in pan. Arrange pecan halves in a decorative pattern on sugar mixture; sprinkle with coconut. Set aside. To make cake: Sift flour with sugar, baking soda, baking powder and salt. Cream butter. Add flour mixture, ½ cup of the buttermilk, and the vanilla. Blend; then beat 2 minutes at medium speed of electric mixer. Add chocolate, eggs and remaining buttermilk. Beat 1 minute longer. Pour over pecan/coconut mixture in pan. Bake at 350°F for 45-50 minutes, or until cake springs back when lightly pressed. Remove from pan immediately. Remove waxed paper. Serve warm or cooled, topped with whipped cream, if desired.

SWISS ROLL

1 cup all-purpose flour
¼ cup **Fry's Cocoa**
1 tsp. baking powder
¼ tsp. salt
3 eggs
1 cup sugar
⅓ cup water
1 tsp. vanilla

Sift together flour, cocoa, baking powder and salt. Beat eggs in a small bowl until thick and lemon colored. Gradually beat in sugar. Stir in water and vanilla. Blend in sifted dry ingredients at lowest speed on mixer. Spread batter in a greased and waxed-paper-lined 15" x 10" x ¾" jelly roll pan. Bake in preheated 375°F oven 12 minutes. Invert cake immediately onto tea towel dusted with cocoa; peel off paper. Roll up cake and towel together, starting at short end. Cool on wire rack, seam-side-down. Unroll to fill and frost with Cocoa Whipped Cream, or fill and frost with Cocoa Buttercream and decorate as a Yule Log.

Ice Cream Roll: Proceed as above, filling Swiss Roll with 1 quart slightly softened ice cream. Freeze until firm. To serve, slice and top with Fudgey Chocolate Sauce.
Makes 1 jelly roll

COCOA BUTTERCREAM

2 cups icing sugar
½ cup **Fry's Cocoa**
1 cup butter (do not use margarine)
1½ tsp. vanilla
3 eggs

Sift together icing sugar and cocoa. Cream butter until light; beat in cocoa mixture and vanilla. Add eggs, one at a time, beating well after each addition.
Makes about 4 cups

COCOA WHIPPED CREAM

2 cups whipping cream
½ cup **Fry's Cocoa**
½ cup sugar

Combine whipping cream, cocoa and sugar. Cover and refrigerate at least 1 hour. Whip cream until softly stiff.

Crème de Cacao: Proceed as above, adding ¼ cup coffee or chocolate liqueur to whipping cream before whipping.
Makes about 4 cups

FUDGEY CHOCOLATE SAUCE

½ cup **Fry's Cocoa**
⅔ cup sugar
½ cup water
½ cup butter or margarine
1 tsp. vanilla

Combine cocoa and sugar in a saucepan. Stir in water. Cook over medium heat, stirring constantly, until mixture comes to boil. Reduce heat and boil gently 5 minutes. Remove from heat. Stir in butter and vanilla. Cool. Serve sauce warm or cooled over ice cream, cake or fruit.
Makes 1⅓ cups

SAINT-NICHOLAS CAKE

2½ cups **Robin Hood All-Purpose Flour** or 2½ cups **Instant Blending Flour** (or 2¾ cups **Robin Hood Velvet Cake and Pastry Flour**)
1¾ cups granulated sugar
2 tsp. baking powder
1 tsp. salt
1 cup softened butter
1 cup milk
2 tsp. rum or brandy extract
4 eggs
½ cup raisins
½ cup cut-up candied cherries
½ cup chopped pecans

Glaze:
2 cups sifted icing sugar
1 tbsp. soft butter
1 tsp. lemon juice or vanilla
2-3 tbsp. hot water

Remove 2 tbsp. flour and mix with fruits and nuts. Combine remaining flour, sugar, baking powder and salt in large mixing bowl. Stir well to blend. Add butter, milk and flavoring. Blend on low to mix, then 2 minutes on medium speed. Add eggs and beat 2 minutes more. Stir in floured fruit and nut mixture. Turn batter into greased and floured 12-cup Bundt pan or tube pan. Bake at 350°F for 55-60 minutes or until cake tests done. Cool 10 minutes in pan. Turn out on wire rack to cool completely. Frost with glaze or sprinkle with icing sugar. To make glaze: Combine glaze ingredients, adding enough water to make a thick glaze consistency.

Christmas Cupcakes: Prepare batter as above. Spoon into 24 large muffin cups, filling ¾ full. Bake at 350°F for 20-25 minutes.

HAZELNUT CAKE

1 lb. unsalted butter, at room temperature
1 lb. sugar
10 large eggs
1 lb. cake flour, sifted
1 tsp. baking powder
½ tsp. salt
½ tsp. nutmeg
½ cup finely chopped orange rind (fresh or candied)
2 cups finely chopped hazelnuts
2 tbsp. flour
½ cup **Grand Marnier**
1 tsp. vanilla

Butter and flour a 10" x 4" tube pan. Cream together the butter and sugar until light and fluffy. Add the eggs, one at a time, beating well after each addition. Sift together the flour, baking powder, salt and nutmeg. In a separate bowl, toss the orange rind and nuts with the 2 tbsp. flour. Add the Grand Marnier and vanilla to the prepared batter, then add ⅓ of the flour and ⅓ of the rind-nut mixture and combine well. Add another ⅓ of each of the mixtures, mix well, then add the remainder and mix thoroughly. Pour the batter into the prepared pan and level the top with a spatula. Bake on the lowest rack of a preheated 350°F oven for about 1 hour and 20 minutes, or until a knife inserted in the middle comes out clean. Remove the cake from the oven, allow it to cool for 10 minutes, then turn it out onto a rack to cool completely. For best flavor, allow the cake to rest for at least a day before serving.
Makes a 10" cake

LEMON CAKE

½ cup butter or margarine
grated rind of 1 lemon
½ cup fruit sugar
2 eggs
1 tbsp. lemon juice
1¼ cups all-purpose flour
1¼ tsp. baking powder
1 cup **Alpen Mixed Cereal**

Cream margarine, rind of lemon and sugar until light and fluffy. Whisk eggs and lemon juice, and gradually add to creamed mixture. Stir in sifted flour and baking powder, and lastly the Alpen. Place mixture in greased 6" round or 5" square cake pan. Bake in 300°F oven for 45-50 minutes, until golden brown.
Makes 1 cake

BAKER'S BEST NO-BAKE CHOCOLATE CHEESECAKE

1/3 cup chopped almonds, toasted
1 lb. cream cheese, softened
1 cup sugar
6 squares **Baker's Semi-Sweet Chocolate**, melted and cooled
1/4 cup cold water
1 envelope unflavored gelatin
1 cup whipping cream, whipped
melted chocolate and almonds for topping (optional)

Grease an 8½" springform pan. Sprinkle evenly with almonds. Beat cream cheese on lowest speed of electric mixer until smooth. Blend in sugar and chocolate; mix well. Sprinkle gelatin on top of cold water in saucepan. Let stand 5 minutes to soften. Stir mixture over low heat until gelatin is dissolved. Blend warm gelatin into cheese mixture. Fold cheese mixture into whipped cream. Pour into pan. Chill at least 3 hours. Drizzle with melted chocolate and press additional almonds onto sides of cake, if desired. Leftover cake may be frozen.
Makes 1 cake

BANANA CAKE

1¼ cups sifted cake flour
3/4 tsp. **Cow Brand Baking Soda**
1/2 tsp. salt
1/2 cup vegetable shortening
1 cup sugar
2 eggs
3/4 cup mashed bananas (about 2 medium)
1/2 cup buttermilk
icing sugar or whipped cream (optional)

Sift together flour, baking soda and salt. Using an electric mixer, cream shortening in large bowl; gradually add sugar and continue beating until light and fluffy. Add eggs, one at a time, beating after each addition. Blend in mashed bananas and buttermilk. Add dry ingredients to banana mixture and mix well. Turn into greased and floured 9" square pan. Bake in 350°F oven 35 minutes or until toothpick inserted in center comes out clean. Cool on rack. If desired, sift icing sugar over cake or top with whipped cream.
Makes a 9" square cake

NO-BAKE STRAWBERRY CHEESECAKE

1¼ cups graham wafer crumbs
1/4 cup sugar
1/4 cup melted butter or margarine
1 lb. cream cheese, softened
1 cup sugar
1/4 tsp. salt
2 tsp. lemon juice
2 tsp. vanilla
2 envelopes **Dream Whip Dessert Topping Mix**
2 cups fresh strawberries, halved

Combine crumbs, 1/4 cup sugar and melted butter. Press firmly in bottom of a 9" springform pan. Chill. Blend cream cheese, 1 cup sugar and salt until smooth and fluffy. Stir in lemon juice and vanilla. Prepare dessert topping mix as directed on package; fold in cheese mixture. Pour into crust. Chill at least 3 hours. Top with halved berries.
Serves 8-10

Baker's Best No-Bake Chocolate Cheesecake

TOMATO SOUP CAKE

2¼ cups cake flour (or 2 cups all-purpose flour)
1⅓ cups sugar
4 tsp. baking powder
1 tsp. baking soda
1½ tsp. allspice
1 tsp. cinnamon
½ tsp. ground cloves
1 10-oz. can **Campbell's Condensed Tomato Soup**
½ cup shortening
2 eggs
¼ cup water

Cream Cheese Frosting:

6 oz. cream cheese, softened
1 tbsp. milk
1 lb. confectioners' sugar, sifted
½ tsp. vanilla extract (optional)

Preheat oven to 350°F. Generously grease and flour 2 8"-9" round layer pans or an oblong pan 13" x 9" x 2". Measure dry ingredients into large bowl. Add soup and shortening. Beat at low to medium speed for 2 minutes scraping sides and bottom of bowl constantly. Add eggs and water. Beat 2 minutes more, scraping bowl frequently. Pour into pans. Bake 35-40 minutes. (For a 9" tube pan, prepare as above; bake 1 hour.) Let stand in pans 10 minutes; remove and cool on rack. To prepare frosting: Blend cream cheese with milk. Gradually add confectioners' sugar; blend well. Mix in vanilla extract, if desired.

Nut or Raisin Cake: After mixing, fold in 1 cup chopped nuts or 1 cup raisins. Bake 35-40 minutes.

Date and Nut Cake: After mixing, fold in 1 cup chopped walnuts and 1 cup chopped dates. (Use 1-2 tbsp. flour to sprinkle over dates while chopping them.) Bake in 9" layer pan or 13" x 9" x 2" pan for 40-45 minutes.

MAGNIFICENT MOCHA TORTE

Cake:

⅔ cup all-purpose flour
⅔ cup **Fry's Cocoa**
½ tsp. salt
5 eggs, separated
½ tsp. cream of tartar
1¼ cups sugar, divided
⅔ cup cold black coffee
½ tsp. vanilla

Filling:

2 cups whipping cream
½ cup **Fry's Cocoa**
½ cup sugar

For cake, sift together flour, cocoa and salt. Beat egg whites and cream of tartar until frothy. Gradually beat in ½ cup of the sugar; beat until stiff peaks form; set aside. Beat egg yolks and remaining ¾ cup sugar until very light. Stir in coffee and vanilla. Stir dry ingredients into egg-yolk mixture on low speed of mixer; fold into meringue. Divide batter between 2 ungreased 8" round layer-cake pans. Bake in preheated 325°F oven 35-40 minutes. Invert pans on wire racks; cool 10 minutes. Remove from pans; cool. Split each layer and fill with filling. To make filling, combine whipping cream, cocoa and sugar. Cover and refrigerate at least 1 hour. Whip cream until stiff. Makes about 4 cups filling.

Makes 1 cake

GUM DROP FRUIT CAKE

1 1-lb. package **McCormick's Baking Gums** (approximately 2⅓ cups)
1 lb. light seedless raisins
½ cup shortening
1 cup white sugar
2 eggs, beaten
2 cups sifted pastry flour
½ tsp. salt
1 tsp. cinnamon
1 tsp. nutmeg
1 tsp. baking powder
1 cup milk

Grease a 9" x 5" x 3" loaf pan. Line bottom and sides with double thickness of oiled brown paper. Cut gum drops quite finely with scissors. Mix gum drops and raisins. Cream shortening, sugar and eggs thoroughly. Beat well. Sift together dry ingredients. Sift about ⅓ cup dry ingredients over gum drops and raisins. Toss lightly. Add dry ingredients alternately with milk to shortening mixture. Add gum drops and raisins. Bake in slow 300°F oven for 2½ hours. Cool slightly before removing from pan. Then remove paper and complete cooling on rack. Wrap. Store in closely covered tin for several days before use. Cut as fruit cake. Will keep for at least 3 weeks. (Note: A dark cake may be made by using dark raisins and 1 cup whole wheat flour and 1 cup pastry flour.)

LITE AND LUSCIOUS PUMPKIN CHEESECAKE

1 cup gingersnap crumbs
¼ cup melted butter
2 envelopes unflavored gelatin
½ cup cold water
¾ lb. cream cheese, softened
1¼ cups sugar, divided
2 eggs, separated
2 cups canned pumpkin
½ tsp. salt
1 tsp. ground cinnamon
½ tsp. ground nutmeg
¼ tsp. ground ginger
1 tsp. vanilla
⅔ cup undiluted **Carnation 2% Evaporated Milk**
1 tbsp. orange juice

Combine crumbs and butter. Press onto bottom of a 9" springform pan; chill. Sprinkle gelatin over water; let stand 5 minutes to soften. Cook and stir over low heat until dissolved; cool. Cream cheese until smooth; beat in 1 cup of the sugar. Beat in egg yolks, pumpkin, salt, spices, vanilla and cooled gelatin. Gradually beat remaining ¼ cup sugar into egg whites; continue beating until stiff peaks form. Pour evaporated milk into 8" cake pan. Freeze until soft ice crystals form around edges of pan (10-15 minutes). Whip evaporated milk and orange juice in small mixing bowl until stiff (2-3 minutes). Fold meringue and whipped evaporated milk into pumpkin mixture. Pour over crust. Chill until firm.

Makes 1 cheesecake

TRIPLE CHOCOLATE ALMOND CAKE

Cake:

1 4-serving-size package **Jell-o Chocolate Instant Pudding**

1 2-layer-size package Devil's Food or chocolate cake mix

1 cup sour cream

½ cup vegetable oil

½ cup water

½ cup toasted chopped almonds

4 eggs

3 tbsp. almond liqueur

1 tsp. almond extract

1 cup **Baker's Semi-Sweet Chocolate Chips**

Glaze:

4 squares **Baker's Semi-Sweet Chocolate**

2 tbsp. butter

2 tbsp. almond liqueur

½ tsp. vegetable oil

Blend all ingredients for cake except chocolate chips, in large mixing bowl; then beat 4 minutes at medium speed of electric mixer. Blend in chocolate chips. Pour into greased and floured 10" tube or fluted tube pan. Bake at 350°F for 55-60 minutes or until cake springs bake when lightly pressed. Cool in pan for 15 minutes. Remove from pan and finish cooling on rack. For glaze, melt chocolate and butter over hot water. Add liqueur and oil. Spoon over cake. Garnish with toasted slivered almonds, if desired.

Makes 1 cake

Triple Chocolate Almond Cake

FUDGEY COCOA FROSTING

3 tbsp. butter or margarine

¼ cup **Fry's Cocoa**

½ tsp. vanilla

2 cups sifted icing sugar

¼ cup milk

Melt butter in a saucepan. Remove from heat. Stir in cocoa and vanilla. Alternately blend in icing sugar and milk until frosting is smooth and of spreading consistency.

Fudgey Orange Cocoa Frosting: Proceed as above, substituting ¼ cup orange juice for milk and adding 1 tsp. grated orange rind.

Fudgey Cherry Cocoa Frosting: Proceed as above, substituting ¼ cup maraschino cherry juice for milk and adding ¼ tsp. almond extract.

Makes 1 cup

LEMON BUTTER FROSTING

½ cup butter or margarine, softened

4 cups confectioners' sugar

⅛ tsp. salt

3-4 tbsp. **ReaLemon Reconstituted Lemon Juice**

In small mixing bowl, cream butter with about ⅓ of the sugar. Blend in salt, 3 tbsp. lemon juice and remaining sugar. Gradually stir in remaining lemon juice to desired spreading consistency. Use to frost cake or cupcakes.

Makes 2¼ cups (enough to frost a 2-layer cake or 36 cupcakes)

LEMON ICING

1½ cups confectioners' sugar

2 tbsp. water

1 tsp. **ReaLemon Reconstituted Lemon Juice**

⅛ tsp. ground nutmeg

Combine all ingredients; mix well. Spread on cooled cake or cookies.

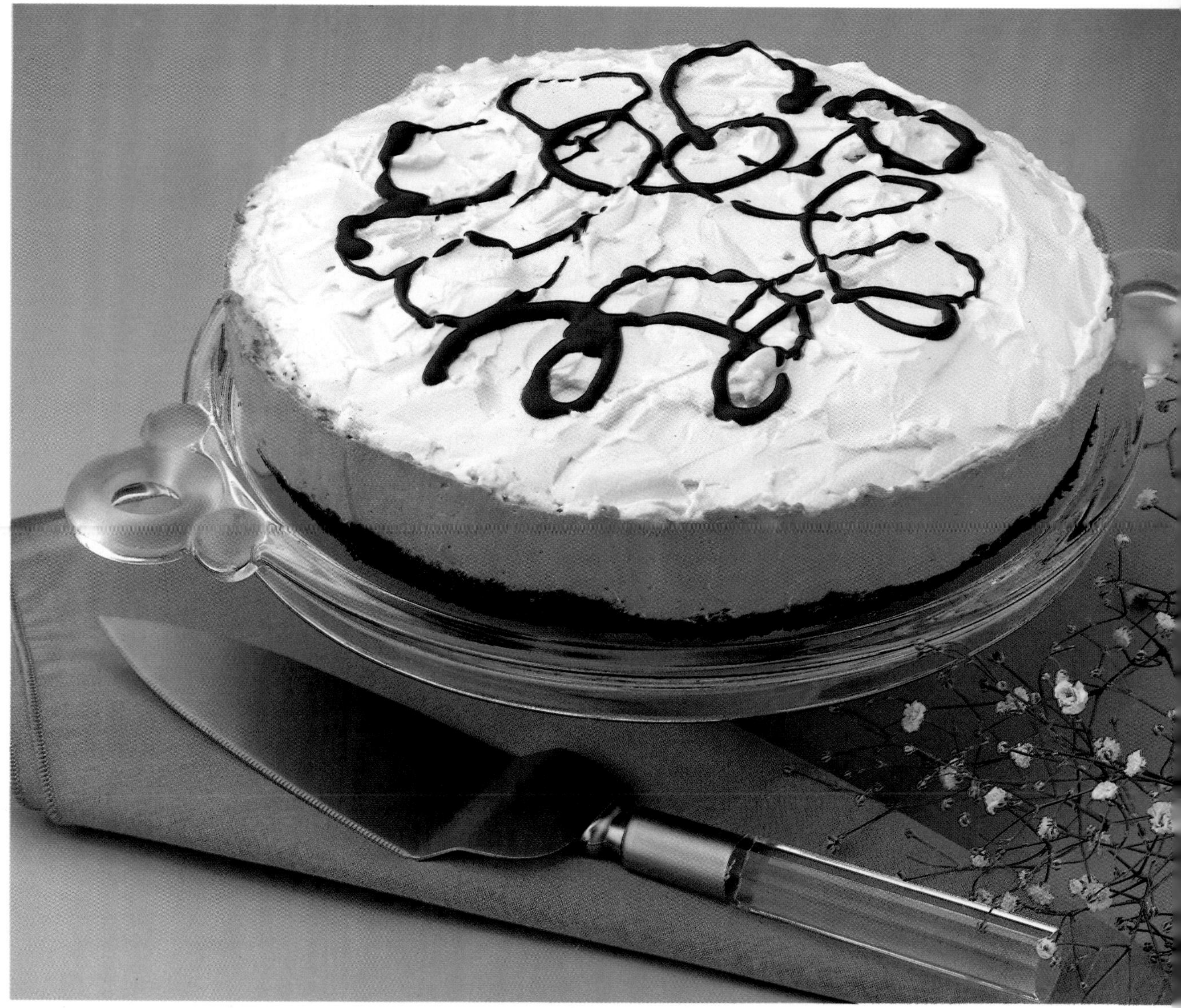

Chocolate Cheesecake

CHOCOLATE CHEESECAKE

Crust:

2 cups chocolate wafer crumbs

6 oz. **Nestlé Pure Thick Cream**, well shaken

¼ cup sugar

Filling:

½ lb. cream cheese, softened

1 15-oz. can **Nestlé Ready to Serve Chocolate Pudding**

6 oz. **Nestlé Pure Thick Cream**

⅓ cup sugar

2 tbsp. chocolate liqueur

Mix crust ingredients together and spread in the bottom of a 9" springform pan. Bake at 350°F for 25 minutes. Beat filling ingredients together and pour into prepared crust. Chill overnight.
Makes 1 cake

SPONGE CAKE WITH ORANGE GRAND MARNIER GLAZE

1¼ cups sifted cake flour

1½ cups sugar

½ tsp. salt

½ tsp. baking powder

½ cup egg yolks
(6 or more depending on size)

¼ cup cold orange juice

1 tsp. vanilla

1 tbsp. orange zest

½ cup egg whites
(about 4 depending on size)

¼ tsp. cream of tartar

Glaze:

1 cup sieved orange marmalade

4 tbsp. **Grand Marnier**

Sift the flour with 1 cup of the sugar, the salt and the baking powder in the bowl of an electric mixer. Put the egg whites in another bowl of the mixer, or into a large mixing bowl, and beat them until fluffy. Gradually beat in the remaining sugar and continue beating until very stiff peaks are formed. With the electric mixer on slow speed, beat the flour, egg yolk and flavoring mixture until well blended, about 1 minute. Fold this mixture into the egg whites, gently but thoroughly. Pour into an ungreased 10" tube pan. Bake in a 350°F oven for 40-50 minutes. If the cake springs back when pressed lightly in the center, it is done. It should also have begun to shrink from the sides of the pan. Immediately invert onto a wire rack and allow it to cool before removing it from the pan. Heat the orange marmalade in a saucepan until boiling. Stir in the Grand Marnier and pour the hot glaze over the cake.
Makes 8 servings

GERMAN SWEET CHOCOLATE CAKE

4 squares **BAKER'S Sweet Chocolate**
3/4 cup butter
1 1/2 cups sugar
3 eggs
1 tsp. vanilla
2 cups all-purpose flour
1 tsp. baking soda
1/2 salt
1 cup buttermilk

Melt chocolate and butter in small saucepan over very low heat or microwave chocolate and butter in large microwaveable bowl on high 2 minutes or until butter is melted. Stir until chocolate is completely melted. Stir in sugar until well blended. With electric mixer at low speed, beat in eggs, one at a time, until completely mixed. Add vanilla. Beat in 1/2 cup of the flour, the baking soda and salt. Beat in remaining flour alternately with buttermilk until well blended and smooth. Pour into 2 greased 9" round cake pans. Bake at 350°F for 30 minutes or until cake springs back when lightly pressed in center. Cool 15 minutes; remove from pans, finish cooling on racks. Spread Coconut Pecan Frosting between layers and over top of cake.
Makes 1 cake

COCONUT PECAN FROSTING

1 cup evaporated milk
1 cup sugar
3 slightly beaten egg yolks
1/2 cup butter
1 tsp. vanilla
1 1/2 cups **BAKER'S ANGEL FLAKE Coconut**
1 cup chopped pecans

Combine milk, sugar, egg yolks, butter and vanilla in saucepan. Bring to boil. Cook and stir over medium heat about 8-10 minutes or until golden. Remove from heat. Stir in coconut and nuts. Cool. Spread over cake as directed above.
Makes icing for 1 cake

BROWN VELVET CAKE

2 cups sifted cake flour
1 tsp. **Cow Brand Baking Soda**
3/4 tsp. salt
1/2 cup vegetable shortening
1 1/2 cups firmly packed light brown sugar
2 eggs
3 3-oz. squares unsweetened chocolate, melted
1 cup plus 2 tbsp. milk
1 tsp. vanilla extract
Fluffy White Frosting

Sift together flour, baking soda and salt. Using an electric mixer, beat shortening and sugar in large bowl. Beat in eggs until mixture is very light and fluffy; stir in chocolate. Combine milk and vanilla. Alternately add dry ingredients and liquid to beaten egg mixture, beginning and ending with dry ingredients. After each addition, beat until smooth. Pour into 2 greased and floured 9" layer-cake pans. Bake in 350°F oven 25 minutes or until toothpick inserted in center comes out clean. Cool in pan 10 minutes; remove from pan and cool thoroughly on rack. Spread Fluffy White Frosting between layers and on sides and top of cake.
Makes enough for a 2-layer cake

FLUFFY WHITE FROSTING

3/4 cup sugar
1/3 cup light corn syrup
3 tbsp. water
3 egg whites
1 tsp. vanilla extract

Combine sugar, syrup and water in small heavy saucepan. Stir and heat to boiling over medium heat. Boil without stirring until mixture reaches 240°F on candy thermometer (soft ball stage). As syrup boils, beat egg whites with electric mixer until stiff. Pour hot syrup very slowly into egg whites, beating constantly. Add vanilla and beat several minutes or until stiff. An ideal frosting for almost any cake.
Makes enough for a 2-layer cake

QUICK FUDGE FROSTING

1/2 cup granulated sugar
2 tbsp. unsweetened cocoa
2 tbsp. butter or margarine
1/4 cup milk
1 tbsp. light corn syrup
1/2-2/3 cup icing sugar
1/2 tsp. vanilla extract

Mix granulated sugar and cocoa in small heavy saucepan. Add butter, milk and syrup; heat to boiling, stirring frequently. Boil 3 minutes, stirring occasionally. Cool slightly. Beat in icing sugar and vanilla; continue beating until thick enough to spread.
Makes enough for an 8" or 9" square cake

BUTTERMILK CHOCOLATE CAKE

2 cups sifted cake flour
1 tsp. **Cow Brand Baking Soda**
1/4 tsp. salt
1/2 cup butter or margarine
1 cup sugar
2 eggs
2 2-oz. squares unsweetened chocolate, melted
1 cup buttermilk
1 tsp. vanilla extract
Quick Fudge Frosting

Sift together flour, baking soda and salt. Using an electric mixer, cream butter until light in large bowl. Gradually add sugar and continue beating until fluffy. Add eggs; beat well. Stir in melted chocolate. Combine buttermilk and vanilla. Alternately add dry ingredients and liquid to creamed mixture, beginning and ending with dry ingredients; beat after each addition. Turn into greased and floured 9" square pan. Bake in 325°F oven 45 minutes or until toothpick inserted in center comes out clean. Cool in pan 10 minutes; remove from pan and cool on rack. Spread Quick Fudge Frosting.
Makes a 9" square cake

INDIVIDUAL CHOCOLATE CHEESE CAKES

¾ cup graham cracker crumbs (about 8 crackers)
2 tbsp. sugar
3 tbsp. butter, melted
1 8-oz. package cream cheese
⅓ cup sugar
⅔ cup **Hershey's Canned Chocolate Syrup**
1 tsp. vanilla
2 eggs
sweetened whipped cream or topping and fresh or canned fruit for garnish

Combine graham crumbs, 2 tbsp. sugar and butter in a small bowl. Divide crumb mixture evenly (about 1 tbsp. per cup) between 12 paper-lined muffin cups (2½" in diameter); press firmly on bottom of cup. Set aside. Blend cream cheese and ⅓ cup sugar in small mixing bowl; add chocolate syrup, vanilla and eggs blending well. Pour mixture into muffin cups filling cups almost full. Bake at 375°F for 17-19 minutes or until set. Remove from oven onto wire rack. Cool slightly; remove from pans. Cool completely chill. Before serving, pipe cream or topping onto each cup using a rosette tip; garnish with fruit. Peel off papers, if desired.
Makes about 12 cheesecake cups

COUNTRY APPLE COFFEE CAKE

2 tbsp. butter or margarine, softened
1½ cups peeled, chopped apples
1 8-oz. can **Pillsbury Refrigerated Buttermilk** or **Sweetmilk Biscuits**
⅓ cup firmly packed brown sugar
¼ tsp. cinnamon
⅓ cup corn syrup
1½ tsp. whiskey (optional)
1 egg
½ cup pecan halves or pieces
Glaze:
⅓ cup icing sugar
¼ tsp. vanilla extract
1-2 tsp. milk

Heat oven to 350°F. Using 1 tbsp. butter, generously grease bottom and sides of 9" round or square cake pan. Spread 1 cup apples in prepared pan. Separate biscuit dough into 10 pieces; cut each into 4 pieces. Arrange biscuit pieces, point-side-up, over apples. Top with remaining apples. In a small bowl, combine 1 tbsp. butter, brown sugar, cinnamon, corn syrup, whiskey and egg; beat 2-3 minutes until sugar is partially dissolved. Stir in pecans; spoon over biscuit pieces. Bake for 35-45 minutes or until deep golden brown. Cool 5 minutes. In a small bowl, blend glaze ingredients until smooth; drizzle over warm coffee cake.
Serves 6-8

EGYPTIAN CAKE

2 large oranges (preferably seedless navels)
6 eggs
⅓ cup **Grand Marnier**
1½ cups very finely ground almonds
pinch of salt
1 cup sugar
1 tsp. baking powder
Garnish:
thin slices of peeled orange sprinkled with confectioners' sugar and a touch of cinnamon, or fresh raspberries

Wash the oranges and boil them in water to cover, without peeling, until very soft, about 30 minutes. Drain, cool, cut into quarters, and remove the seeds, if any. Process the oranges to a fairly fine purée in a blender or food processor or by putting them through a meat grinder. Don't chop too fine, however. The little bits of rind, which will not be at all bitter after the boiling, are pleasant to bite on. Beat the eggs in a bowl until thick, then add the Grand Marnier, ground almonds, salt, sugar, baking powder and orange purée and mix well. Pour the batter into a deep, round 9" cake pan that has been buttered and floured, and bake in a 400°F oven for 1 hour or longer, until firm to the touch when pressed with the tip of your finger. Remove the pan to a rack, allow the cake to cool completely, then turn it out of the pan and onto a serving dish. Serve the cake with whipped cream, if desired.
Makes 8 servings

Country Apple Coffee Cake

COFFEE BREAK CAKE

Streusal:
½ cup **Skippy Super Chunk Peanut Butter**
¼ cup brown sugar
¼ cup all-purpose flour
½ cup chopped peanuts

Cake:
¼ cup **Skippy Super Chunk Peanut Butter**
¼ cup butter
¾ cup sugar
2 eggs
1½ cups all-purpose flour
2 tsp. baking powder
¼ tsp. salt
1 cup sour cream

Thoroughly combine all streusal ingredients. Set aside. For cake, cream peanut butter and butter. Beat in sugar and then eggs, one at a time, beating well after each addition. Combine flour, baking powder and salt. Beat into creamed mixture alternately with sour cream, beginning and ending with flour. Pour ½ of batter into greased 9″ square pan. Spoon ½ of streusal mixture over batter. Pour on remaining batter and top with remaining streusal. Bake at 350°F 40 minutes or until done.
Makes 1 cake

PLUM AND ORANGE RIPPLE COFFEE CAKE

⅓ cup soft butter
¾ cup sugar
2 egg yolks
½ cup milk
½ tsp. almond extract
1½ cups unbleached all-purpose flour
2 tsp. baking powder
¼ tsp. salt
2 egg whites
½ cup **Emelia Plum and Orange Preserve**
2 tbsp. sugar
½ cup chopped pecans
2 tbsp. melted butter

Cream butter and sugar. Beat yolks, milk and extract with fork. Combine flour, baking powder and salt. Add to creamed butter alternately with yolks. Blend well. Beat whites until stiff. Fold into batter. Spoon into pan. Spoon preserve onto batter. Ripple with a knife. Combine sugar and pecans and sprinkle over preserve. Drizzle with melted butter. Bake at 375°F for 35 minutes in an 8″ square pan.
Makes 1 cake

Coffee Break Cake

HAWAIIAN CARROT CAKE

2 cups all-purpose flour
2 tsp. baking soda
2 tsp. cinnamon
½ tsp. nutmeg
½ tsp. salt
3 eggs
1½ cups sugar
¾ cup **Hellmann's or Best Foods Real Mayonnaise**
1 8-oz. can crushed pineapple, undrained
2½ cups shredded carrots
¾ cup chopped walnuts

Grease 9″ tube pan or 13″ x 9″ baking dish. Stir together first 5 ingredients. In large bowl beat eggs, sugar, mayonnaise and pineapple until well blended. Gradually beat in flour mixture. Stir in carrots and walnuts. Turn into pan. Bake in 350°F oven 60 minutes for tube pan, 50 minutes for baking dish, or until done. Cool, remove from pan. Frost with Cream Cheese Frosting *(see Tomato Soup Cake).*
Makes 1 cake

CARROT CAKE

1 cup oil
1 cup brown sugar
4 large eggs
3 cups grated carrots
1 tsp. vanilla
2 cups whole wheat flour
2 tsp. baking soda
2 tsp. baking powder
2 tsp. cinnamon
1 tsp. salt
½ cup chopped nuts

Icing:
1 lb. cream cheese, softened
1 tsp. vanilla
1 tsp. brandy
½-¾ cup icing sugar
pecan halves to garnish

Preheat oven to 350°F. Prepare 2 8″ round pans. Beat together oil and brown sugar. Add eggs, one at a time, and beat until fluffy. Add carrots and vanilla. Combine dry ingredients and add along with nuts. Bake for 45 minutes. Fill with ¾ jar **Emelia Spiced Gooseberries**. For icing: Whip all icing ingredients (except pecan halves) to a smooth, fluffy consistency. Ice cake and decorate with pecan halves.

Cheesecake Flan with Fruit Topping

GRAHAM CRACKER CAKE

1 tsp. baking powder
3 tbsp. flour
½ tsp. salt
2 cups **McCormick's Graham Cracker Crumbs**
½ cup butter or shortening
1 cup granulated sugar
1 egg
1 cup milk, at room temperature
1 cup fine coconut (flake coconut may be used)
1 tsp. vanilla

Mix together baking powder, flour, salt and Graham Cracker Crumbs. Cream butter and sugar well. Add egg and part of crumb mixture. Add half the milk and mix well. Add the rest of the crumbs and milk, fold in coconut and add vanilla. Bake at 325°F for about 45 minutes in a lightly greased 8" x 8" pan. Needs no icing. Best served the following day.

RED DEVILS CAKE

2 cups sifted cake flour
1¼ tsp. **Cow Brand Baking Soda**
¼ tsp. salt
½ cup butter or margarine
1 cup sugar
2 eggs
2 2-oz. squares unsweetened chocolate, melted
¾ cup buttermilk
1 tsp. vanilla extract
⅓ cup boiling water
Quick Fudge Frosting

Sift together flour, baking soda and salt. Using an electric mixer, cream butter until light in large bowl. Add sugar gradually, beating after each addition until fluffy. Beat in eggs; add chocolate. Combine buttermilk and vanilla. Alternately add the dry ingredients and liquid to chocolate mixture, beginning and ending with dry ingredients; beat well after each addition. Blend in water. Turn into 2 greased and floured 8" layer-cake pans. Bake in 350°F oven for 25 minutes or until toothpick inserted in center comes out clean. Cool on rack. Spread Quick Fudge Frosting between layers and on sides and top of cake.
Makes enough for a 2-layer cake

RUM-NUT PUDDING CAKE

1 cup chopped pecans or walnuts
1 2-layer-size package white or yellow cake mix
1 4-serving-size package **Jell-o Vanilla Instant Pudding**
4 eggs
½ cup cold water
¼ cup vegetable oil
⅓ cup dark rum
1 cup sugar
½ cup butter or margarine
¼ cup water
⅓ cup dark rum

Sprinkle nuts evenly in bottom of greased and floured 10" tube or fluted tube pan. Combine cake mix, pudding mix, eggs, ½ cup water, oil and ⅓ cup rum into large mixing bowl. Blend; then beat at medium speed of electric mixer for 4 minutes. Pour into pan. Bake at 350°F about 1 hour or until cake tester inserted in cake comes out clean. Cool in pan 15 minutes. Meanwhile, combine sugar, butter and ¼ cup water in saucepan. Cook and stir until mixture comes to a boil; boil 5 minutes, stirring constantly. Stir in ⅓ cup rum and bring just to a boil. Remove cake from pan onto serving plate and prick with cake tester or wooden pick. Carefully spoon warm syrup over warm cake. Cool.

CHEESECAKE FLAN WITH FRUIT TOPPING

½ lb. cream cheese, softened
1 egg
⅓ cup granulated sugar
⅓ cup sour cream
1 **Gainsborough Frozen Flan Shell**
sliced fruit for topping
¼ cup apricot jam

Beat cream cheese, egg, sugar and sour cream 2-3 minutes until smooth. Place frozen flan shell in foil pan on cookie sheet. Pour cream cheese mixture into shell. Bake at 350°F for 25-30 minutes or until set. Cool completely. Carefully remove from foil pan. Arrange sliced fruit on top of cheesecake. Glaze with apricot jam, softened over medium heat. Chill well.
Makes 1 cake

DELICIOUS CAKE

⅔ cup chocolate chips
½ cup boiling water
2½ cups pastry flour
1 tsp. baking soda
½ tsp. salt
1 cup butter
2 cups sugar
4 egg yolks
1 tsp. vanilla
1 cup **Delisle Plain Yogurt**
4 egg whites

Melt chocolate in boiling water. Sift and measure flour, add soda and salt. Cream butter, add sugar gradually, then egg yolks, 1 at a time, beating after each addition. Add chocolate and vanilla. Fold in flour alternately with yogurt. Beat egg whites and fold into flour mixture. Pour into 3 greased and floured 9" pans. Bake at 350°F for 30-35 minutes. Cool 10 minutes in pans. Remove from pans and cool completely on racks.

Makes 3 9" layers

SKIPPY 'N SPICE CAKE

Cake:

½ cup **Skippy Creamy Peanut Butter**
¼ cup butter
1 cup brown sugar
2 eggs
1½ cups all-purpose flour
2 tsp. baking powder
¼ tsp. salt
¼ tsp. nutmeg
¼ tsp. ground allspice
1 cup milk

Icing:

½ cup **Skippy Super Chunk** or **Creamy Peanut Butter**
2 tbsp. butter
1½ cups icing sugar
4 tbsp. milk or cream
1 tsp. vanilla

For cake, cream peanut butter and butter. Beat in brown sugar and then eggs, one at a time, beating well after each addition.

Skippy 'n Spice Cake

Combine flour, baking powder, salt, nutmeg and allspice. Beat into creamed mixture alternately with the milk, beginning and ending with flour. Pour into greased 9" square or round pan. Bake at 350°F 25-30 minutes or until done. Cool before icing. For icing, cream peanut butter and butter. Beat in icing sugar, milk and vanilla and continue beating until smooth. Spread on cooled cake. Garnish with chopped peanuts if desired.

Makes 1 cake

PIES AND TARTS

For more than two centuries, North American moms have been rolling out dough and filling up pie shells with apples, cherries, custards and, of course, lots of love. Pies, more recently, have also come to hold such unusual fillings as carrots or peanut butter! And moms aren't the only ones rolling them out.

Here is a collection of some scrumptious pies and tarts that have been developed using some of your favorite brand names. You'll also find pastry recipes you can make and fill with fresh fruits and berries in season.

One thing every good pie has in common is a great crust. While some of our pies call for ready-made or cracker-crumb crusts, here are two key points to keep in mind when preparing a standard pastry shell: Make sure your utensils and water are as cold as possible; and avoid overhandling or overmixing the ingredients.

Use your imagination and the tried-and-true recipes that follow to create some family traditions of your own.

Brandy Alexander Pie (see page 199)

VIENNESE MOCHA TORTE

Cake:

1 4-serving-size package **Jell-o Chocolate Instant Pudding**

1 2-layer-size package chocolate or devil's food cake mix

4 eggs

1 cup water

¼ cup vegetable oil

Frosting:

1 cup cold milk

1 cup cold prepared **Maxwell House Coffee**

1 envelope **Dream Whip Dessert Topping Mix**

1 6-serving-size package **Jell-o Chocolate Instant Pudding**

¼ cup cold prepared **Maxwell House Coffee**

1 cup apricot jam

Cake: Combine pudding mix, cake mix, eggs, water and oil in large mixing bowl. Blend; then beat at medium speed of electric mixer for 4 minutes. Pour into 2 greased and floured 9" layer pans. Bake at 350°F for 30-35 minutes, or until cake tester inserted in center comes out clean and cakes spring back when lightly pressed. Cool in pans about 15 minutes. Remove from pans and finish cooling on racks. Split cakes, making 4 layers. To make frosting: Pour milk and 1 cup coffee into deep narrow-bottom mixing bowl. Add dessert topping mix and pudding mix. Beat at low speed of electric mixer until well blended. Gradually increase beating speed to high and beat until mixture forms soft peaks, 4-6 minutes. Sprinkle each cake layer with 1 tbsp. of the remaining coffee. Spread half of the jam on one layer and top with 1 cup of the frosting. Add a second cake layer; spread with 1 cup of the frosting. Repeat with remaining layers. Garnish with chocolate curls, if desired. Chill. Store any leftover cake in refrigerator.

BUTTERSCOTCH PIE

⅓ cup butter or margarine, melted

1¼ cups **Alpen Mixed Cereal**

1 3¼-oz. package butterscotch instant pudding

2 cups milk

2 bananas

whipped cream

To prepare crust, combine melted butter or margarine and Alpen and press into bottom and sides of an 8" or 9" pie plate. Bake at 350°F for 8-10 minutes or microwave 1½-2 minutes at full power. Allow to cool. Prepare pudding according to package directions using the 2 cups milk. Peel and slice 1 of the bananas and stir into pudding. Pour filling into pie crust, chill until serving. To serve, garnish with whipped cream and remaining slices of bananas.
Serves 6-8

LIME CHIFFON PIE

Crust:

1⅓ cups crushed **Weetabix**

⅓ cup light brown sugar, packed

¾ cup melted butter

½ cup melted semi-sweet chocolate

Filling:

finely grated rind and juice of 4 limes (about ⅓ cup)

¾ cup sugar

2 tbsp. cornstarch

2 eggs, separated

2 drops green food coloring (optional)

sweetened whipping cream and lime slices to garnish

Crush the Weetabix and mix with the sugar, butter and chocolate. Press into the bottom and sides of a greased 9" pie plate. Chill for 30 minutes. Meanwhile, make the filling. Measure the juice and rind into a measuring cup and add enough water to make 1¼ cups. Mix the sugar and cornstarch together in a heavy saucepan. Add enough juice to form a paste. Stir in the yolks and the remaining juice and rind. Heat gently, stirring, until thick. Remove from heat and cool. Add the food coloring if desired. Beat the egg whites until stiff and fold into the filling. Pour into the shell and bake at 400°F for 15 minutes. Let cool, then chill. Garnish with whipped cream and lime slices.

LIME PARFAIT PIE

1 **Keebler Ready-Crust Butter-Flavored Pie Crust**

1 3-oz. package lime-flavored gelatin

1¼ cups boiling water

2 tbsp. lime juice

1 pint vanilla ice cream, softened

2 cups whipped cream or topping

Dissolve gelatin in boiling water. Stir in lime juice. Add ice cream by spoonfuls, stirring until completely melted. Pour into crust. Chill until firm, about 2 hours. Spread whipped cream or topping over gelatin layer.

Lemon Parfait: Substitute lemon gelatin and lemon juice. Add ½ tsp. grated lemon peel, if desired.

PEANUT BUTTER CREAM PIE

1½ cups whipping cream, chilled

1 7-7½-oz. jar marshmallow creme

½ cup chunky peanut butter

¼ cup milk

2 tbsp. brown sugar

1 **Keebler Ready-Crust Graham Cracker Pie Crust**

Using well-chilled beaters and bowl, whip cream until stiff. Using same beaters, mix marshmallow, peanut butter, milk and sugar until well blended. Fold whipped cream into marshmallow mixture. Spoon into crust. Chill until firm, about 4 hours. Garnish with additional whipped cream and chopped peanuts, if desired.

ROCKY ROAD TARTS

1 4-serving-size package instant chocolate pudding

2 cups milk

1 cup miniature marshmallows

⅓ cup salted peanuts

1 cup whipped cream or topping

1 package **Keebler Ready-Crust Graham Cracker Tart Crusts**

maraschino cherries

In medium mixing bowl, mix pudding and milk on low speed of electric mixer until thickened, about 2 minutes, scraping bowl occasionally. Chill until set, about 5 minutes. Stir marshmallows and peanuts into mixture. Fold in whipped cream or topping. Spoon into tart crusts. Garnish with cherries. Serve immediately or chill until needed.

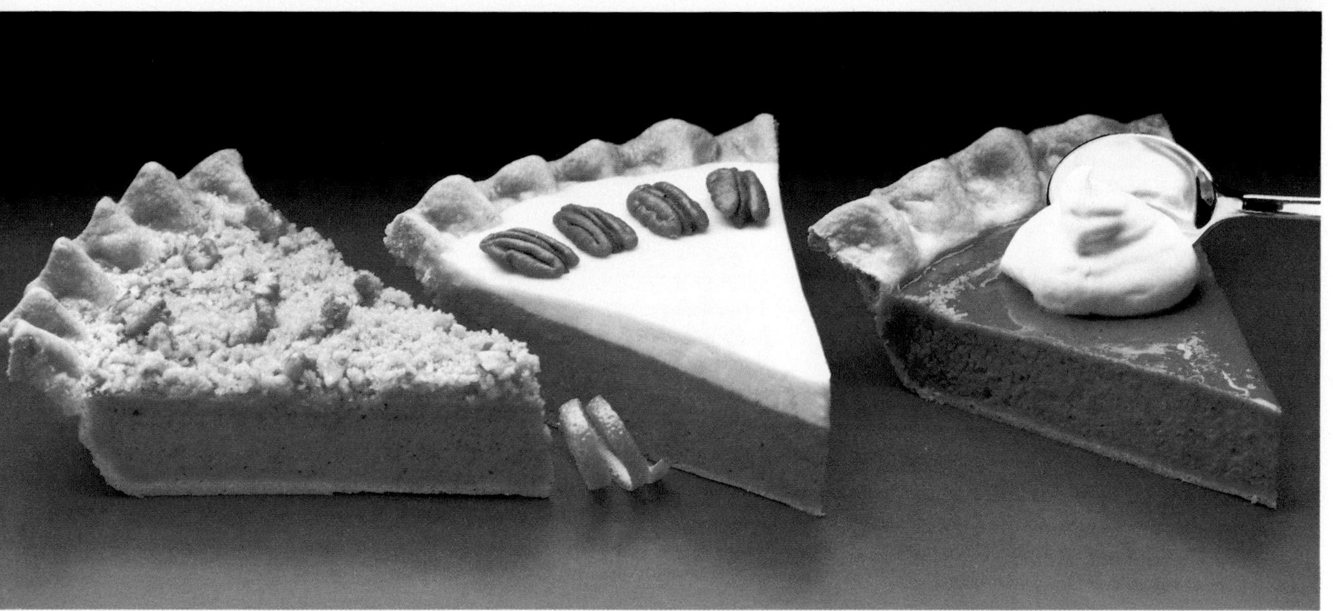

Traditional Pumpkin Pie

TRADITIONAL PUMPKIN PIE

1 9" unbaked pastry shell
1 14-oz. can pumpkin
1 can **Eagle Brand Sweetened Condensed Milk**
2 eggs
1 tsp. ground cinnamon
½ tsp. salt
½ tsp. ground ginger
½ tsp. ground nutmeg
whipped cream

Preheat oven to 425°F. In a large bowl, combine all ingredients except pastry shell and whipped cream; mix well. Pour into shell. Bake 15 minutes. Reduce oven to 350°F. Continue baking 25-30 minutes or until knife inserted 1" from edge comes out clean. Cool. Garnish with whipped cream, or with Streusal Topping or Sour Cream Topping as follows.

Streusal Topping: In medium mixing bowl, combine 6 tbsp. packed light brown sugar and 6 tbsp. all-purpose flour. Cut in 3 tbsp. cold butter until crumbly; stir in 3 tbsp. chopped nuts. After 30 minutes of baking the pie, sprinkle the streusal topping on top of the pie; bake 10 minutes longer.

Sour Cream Topping: In medium mixing bowl combine 1½ cups sour cream, 2 tbsp. sugar and 1 tsp. vanilla. After 30 minutes of baking the pie, spread mixture evenly over top of pie; bake 10 minutes longer and garnish as desired.

TRIFLE CREAM PIE

1 4-serving-size package instant vanilla pudding and pie filling
2 cups whipping cream
⅓ cup milk
3 tbsp. cream sherry
1 **Keebler Ready-Crust Graham Cracker Pie Crust**
¼ cup red raspberry preserves
½ cup sliced almonds, toasted
2 tbsp. powdered sugar
½ tsp. vanilla

In small mixing bowl, combine pie filling mix, 1 cup of whipping cream and milk. Blend on low speed of electric mixer; then increase speed to high and beat until mixture is very thick. Add sherry and beat again until thick. Layer ½ of pudding into crust. Carefully layer preserves evenly over pudding and sprinkle with ¼ cup of the nuts. Layer remaining pudding over the nuts. Chill until set, about 3 hours. In chilled bowl, beat remaining 1 cup whipping cream, powdered sugar and vanilla until stiff. Spread whipped cream over pudding; sprinkle with remaining ¼ cup toasted almonds.

ICE CREAM SUNDAE PIE

2 pints ice cream
1 **Keebler Ready-Crust Chocolate-Flavored Pie Crust**
1 cup hot fudge sauce, heated
¼ cup chopped nuts
whipped cream or topping
maraschino cherries

Try peppermint, pistashio nut, fruit-flavored or chocolate ice cream, or combine 2 flavors from chocolate and peppermint, mint-chocolate chip, fruit or nut ice creams. Allow ice cream to soften or stir with a spoon until pliable. Spoon into crust. Cover and freeze until firm, about 3 hours. Serve pie wedges with hot fudge sauce, nuts, whipped cream or topping and cherries.

CREAMY LEMON PIE

1 9″ graham wafer crumb crust

1 can **Eagle Brand Sweetened Condensed Milk**

½ cup **ReaLemon Reconstituted Lemon Juice**

few drops yellow food coloring

3 egg whites

¼ tsp. cream of tartar

whipped cream

In medium bowl, combine condensed milk, lemon juice and food coloring. Mix well. In small bowl, beat egg whites with cream of tartar until stiff but not dry. Gently fold into condensed milk mixture. Pour over prepared crust. Chill 3 hours. Garnish with whipped cream before serving.

Creamy Lemon Pie

BLACKCURRANT CREAM PIE

1½ cups graham cracker crumbs

¼ cup brown sugar

¼ cup butter, melted

½ pint whipping cream

½ cup **Lynch Blackcurrant Topping**

Combine graham cracker crumbs with brown sugar in a small bowl, pour in melted butter and mix evenly. Flatten crust into a 9″ round or 8″ x 8″ square pan reserving 2 tbsp. of crumbs for garnish. Refrigerate crust. Whip cream until stiff and fold in Lynch Blackcurrant Topping. Smooth the cream filling into the crust and refrigerate until served.

CRANBERRY PECAN PIE

1 jar **Emelia Cranberries and Pecans in Sherry**

⅓ cup water

1 9″ pie crust

¾ cup pecans

⅓ cup brown sugar

jigger or 2 bourbon

whipped cream

Preheat oven to 375°F. Combine Cranberries and Pecans in Sherry with water and pour into pie shell. Combine pecans, brown sugar and bourbon, and sprinkle evenly over cranberries. Bake for 30-40 minutes, or until pie crust is golden brown. Serve with whipped cream flavored with bourbon.
Serves 6-8

MANDARIN FLAN

¼ cup melted butter or margarine

3 tbsp. sugar

¾ cup **Alpen Mixed Cereal**

¼ cup raisins

½ cup whipping cream

1 10-oz. can mandarin oranges, drained

To prepare crust, combine melted butter or margarine, sugar, Alpen and raisins and press into 8″ or 9″ pie plate or flan pan. Chill. To serve, whip cream and spread over crust. Garnish with drained mandarin oranges.
Serves 6-8

PUMPKIN PIE ROLLS

1 can evaporated milk

2 eggs, beaten

1 18-oz. can pumpkin pie filling

1 lb. **Krinos Fillo Leaves**

¼ lb. butter, melted for fillo

Blend milk and eggs together. Stir in pumpkin pie filling and mix until stiff. Put in pan and bake at 375°F for about 15-20 minutes. The top will be a deep golden brown. Cool. Fold a strudel leaf in half and butter top. Fold in half again and butter top. Put 1 tbsp. of filling on center of leaf, 1″ from end. Fold from left side to center, then right side to center. Roll away from you. Place in buttered pan, with room between rolls. Put in preheated 400°F oven for 20 minutes or until golden brown.

PUMPKIN CHIFFON PIE

Filling:

1 envelope unflavored gelatin

¾ cup packed brown sugar, divided

½ tsp. salt

¾ tsp. ground nutmeg

½ tsp. ground cinnamon

¼ tsp. ground ginger

2 eggs, separated

1¼ cups undiluted **Carnation 2% Evaporated Milk**

1¼ cups canned pumpkin

Pie Shell:

1 egg white

1 tbsp. granulated sugar

¼ tsp. salt

1½ cups finely chopped pecans

For pie shell, beat egg white slightly. Add sugar, salt and pecans and press onto bottom and sides of a greased 9″ pie plate. Bake in 375°F oven 5-6 minutes. Cool completely. For filling, combine gelatin, ½ cup of the brown sugar, salt and spices in a saucepan; mix well. Beat egg yolks slightly; blend in evaporated milk and pumpkin. Stir into gelatin mixture. Cook and stir over low heat until gelatin is dissolved, about 10 minutes. Chill until mixture is the consistency of unbeaten egg white. Beat egg whites until soft peaks form. Beat in remaining ¼ cup brown sugar; continue beating until very stiff. Fold meringue into pumpkin mixture. Spoon onto pie shell. Garnish if desired. Chill at least 3 hours or until firm.

PEAR AND CHOCOLATE TART

Pâte Sucrée Tart Shell:

1¾ cups sifted flour

1 stick unsalted butter, firmly chilled, cut into small pieces

1 egg yolk, slightly beaten with 2 tbsp. ice water

1 tbsp. lemon juice

¼ tsp. salt

2 tbsp. sugar

1 egg yolk, beaten

Filling:

4-6 pears, peeled, halved and cored

2 cups water

1 cup sugar

1 tsp. vanilla extract

6 oz. semi-sweet chocolate

2 tbsp. butter

whipped cream to garnish

Glaze:

1 1-lb. jar orange marmalade

4 tbsp. **Grand Marnier**

To make pâte sucrée: Put the flour in a mixing bowl, make a well in the center, and put the butter in the well. Work the butter and flour together quickly with the fingertips until the mixture forms small, flaky granules, like oatmeal. Blend in the egg yolk mixture, lemon juice, salt and sugar. Cupping your hands tightly, gather the dough into a rough ball. Break off small pieces, about 2-3 tbsp. each, and smear them across a pastry board by pushing hard with the heel of your hand. This process, called the fraisage, ensures the complete blending of the butter and flour. Gather the dough together and form it into a ball; wrap in waxed paper and chill for 30 minutes or until firm, but not so firm that it cracks at the edges when rolled out. Roll out the pastry on a lightly floured board to a thickness of ¼", until you have a circle 11"-12" in diameter. Fit the pastry into a 9" tart pan. Trim the edges by rolling your rolling pin over the top. Prick the pastry lightly, line with foil, pressing it well into the pastry, then bake the shell in a 425°F oven for 14-16 minutes. Remove from the oven and discard the foil lining. Brush the bottom with beaten egg yolk, and return to the oven for 2-4 minutes, or until nicely browned. Chill before using. To prepare filling and glaze: Bring the water, sugar and vanilla to a boil in a heavy skillet and cook for 5 minutes to make a syrup. Poach the pears in the syrup until just cooked through but still firm. Do not overcook. Cool in the syrup, remove and drain them on paper towels. Melt the chocolate and butter in a small saucepan over low heat. Brush the bottom of the tart shell with the chocolate mixture and let it cool. Arrange the poached pear halves in the shell and prepare the glaze. Melt the orange marmalade in a pan and bring to a boil, stir in the Grand Marnier and boil for 1 minute. Brush the hot glaze over the pears. Cool. Before serving garnish the tart with whipped cream piped through a pastry bag with a #7 rosette tip.

TOURTIÈRE DE CRÈME GRAND MARNIER

Crust:

3 oz. butter, melted

1½ cups graham cracker crumbs

¼ cup sugar

Filling:

1 tbsp. unflavored gelatin

½ cup water

½ cup sugar

pinch salt

3 eggs, separated

½ cup **Grand Marnier**

1 cup heavy cream

whipped cream and chocolate curls to garnish

Mix the butter, crumbs and sugar in a bowl and press firmly into a 9" pie pan. Bake for 10 minutes in a 350°F oven. Remove to a wire rack to cool completely before filling. Sprinkle the gelatin over the water in a medium-sized saucepan. Stir over low heat until completely dissolved. Add ¼ cup of the sugar, salt and the egg yolks. Mix well and cook over low heat, stirring constantly, until thickened. Make sure it does not come to a boil or it will curdle. Remove the pan from the heat and add the Grand Marnier. Cool until partially set. Beat the egg whites until soft peaks form, add the remaining sugar and continue beating until the whites are stiff but not dry. Whip the cream in a chilled bowl until you have soft peaks. Place the Grand Marnier mixture in a large bowl, fold in the whites and whipped cream gently but thoroughly. Spoon the mixture into the prepared pie shell. Chill in the refrigerator for 4-5 hours. Before serving garnish the top with whipped cream and chocolate curls.

Serves 8

CRÈME DE GRAND MARNIER PIE

Crust:

3 oz. sweet butter, melted

1½ cups graham cracker crumbs

¼ cup sugar

Filling:

1 envelope unflavored gelatin

½ cup water

½ cup sugar

pinch salt

3 eggs, separated

¾ cup **Crème de Grand Marnier**

1 cup whipping cream

whipped cream and chocolate curls to garnish

Mix the butter, crumbs and sugar in a bowl and press firmly into a 9" pie pan. Bake for 10 minutes in a 350°F oven. Remove to a wire rack to cool completely before filling or use a ready made pie shell. Sprinkle the gelatin over the water in a medium-sized saucepan. Stir over low heat until completely dissolved. Add ¼ cup of the sugar, salt and the egg yolks. Mix well and cook over low heat, stirring constantly, until thickened. Make sure it does not come to a boil or it will curdle. Remove the pan from the heat and add the Grand Marnier. Cool until partially set. Beat the egg whites until soft peaks form, add the remaining sugar and continue beating until the whites are stiff but not dry. Whip the cream in a chilled bowl until you have soft peaks. Place the Grand Marnier mixture in a large bowl, fold in the whites and whipped cream gently but thoroughly. Spoon the mixture into the prepared pie shell. Chill in the refrigerator for 4-5 hours. Before serving garnish the top with whipped cream and chocolate curls.

BUTTERSCOTCH WALNUT TARTS

2 eggs

1 cup **Lynch Butterscotch Topping**

dash salt

½ tsp. vanilla

½ cup raisins

¼ cup walnut pieces

12 unbaked tart shells, 2½" in diameter

Beat eggs. Add Butterscotch Topping, salt and vanilla. Beat thoroughly. Divide raisins and walnuts among tart shells. Pour butterscotch mixture on top, filling shells ¾ full. Bake at 400°F for 20 minutes or until golden brown.

Makes 12 tarts

CHOCOLATE MOCHA PIE

1 tsp. unflavored gelatin
1 tbsp. cold water
½ pint whipping cream
½ cup **Lynch Chocolate Fudge Topping**
¼ cup white sugar
1 tsp. instant coffee dissolved in 1 tsp. cold water
1 can mandarin orange sections, well drained
1 tbsp. toasted almonds
1 9" baked pastry or graham cracker pie shell

Combine gelatin and cold water and let stand 5 minutes. Heat over boiling water until dissolved. Cool. Beat whipping cream to soft peaks. Add gelatin and continue beating until stiff. Fold in Lynch Chocolate Fudge Topping, white sugar, dissolved instant coffee and drained mandarin oranges. Pour into pie shell. Garnish with orange sections and toasted almonds. Refrigerate 2-3 hours before serving.

TARTE AUX CAROTTES

Pâte Sucrée Tart Shell *(see Pear and Chocolate Tart)*
2 cups finely shredded raw carrot
3 eggs
¼ cup sugar
¼ tsp. salt
⅛ tsp. nutmeg
½ cup heavy cream
½ cup **Grand Marnier**
whipped cream to garnish

Prepare the tart shell. Cook the carrots in boiling water for 10-15 minutes, or until very tender. Drain. Process in a food processor or in a blender to make a smooth purée. Lightly whisk the eggs in a mixing bowl. Add the purée, sugar, salt, nutmeg, cream and Grand Marnier. Whisk to combine thoroughly. Pour the filling into the shell and bake in a 350°F oven for 20-25 minutes, or until the filling appears set when the tart is shaken gently. Remove to a wire rack to cool. Before serving pipe rosettes of whipped cream around the edge of the tart.

CREAMY LEMON MERINGUE PIE

3 eggs, separated
1 14-oz. can sweetened condensed milk (not evaporated)
½ cup lemon juice
1 tsp. grated lemon peel
2-3 drops yellow food coloring
1 **Keebler Ready-Crust Butter-Flavored Pie Crust**
¼ tsp. cream of tartar
dash salt
⅓ cup sugar

Preheat oven to 350°F. In medium bowl, beat egg yolks; stir in sweetened condensed milk, lemon juice, peel and food coloring. Place crust on baking sheet. Pour lemon mixture into crust. In small bowl, beat egg whites with cream of tartar and salt until foamy; gradually add sugar, beating until stiff but not dry. Spread meringue on top of filling, sealing carefully to edge of crust. Bake on baking sheet at 350°F for 12-15 minutes or until golden brown. Cool several hours. Chill.

FUDGEY PECAN PIE

1 envelope **Robin Hood Flaky Pie Crust Mix**
4 squares **Baker's Semi-Sweet** or **Sweet Chocolate**
¼ cup butter
1 can **Eagle Brand Sweetened Condensed Milk**
½ cup hot water
2 eggs, beaten
1 tsp. vanilla extract
pinch salt
1¼ cups pecan halves or pieces
vanilla ice cream

Prepare pastry according to package directions for a 1-crust unbaked pie shell. Melt chocolate and butter in medium saucepan. Stir in sweetened condensed milk, hot water and beaten eggs, mixing until smoothly blended. Remove from heat; stir in vanilla, salt and nuts. Pour into pie shell. Bake at 350°F for 40-45 minutes or until set. Cool slightly. Serve warm or chilled with ice cream.

MAPLE WALNUT TARTS

1 envelope **Robin Hood Flaky Pie Crust Mix**
½ cup lightly packed brown sugar
¼ cup **Robin Hood All-Purpose Flour** or **Instant Blending Flour**
1 egg, beaten
¼ cup melted butter
½ tsp. maple extract
½ cup finely chopped walnuts
¼ cup raspberry jam

Maple Icing:

2 tbsp. butter, softened
1 cup sifted icing sugar
1 tsp. maple extract
1 tbsp. milk or cream

Prepare pastry according to package directions. Roll out on lightly floured surface to ⅛" thickness. Cut into rounds with floured cutter and fit into 24 small tart tins. Combine brown sugar, flour, egg, melted butter, extract and nuts. Mix well. Spoon about ½ tsp. jam into each tart shell. Cover with filling, dividing evenly. Bake at 375°F for 12-15 minutes, or until filling is set. Cool and remove from pan. To make icing: Combine all icing ingredients, mixing until smooth. Add more icing sugar as necessary to make a spreadable consistency. Spread Maple Icing over each tart and garnish with a walnut half if desired.
Makes 2 dozen tarts

FILLO APPLE PIE

1 can apple pie filling (enough for 1 pie)
8 **Krinos Fillo Leaves**
2 tbsp. melted butter for fillo

Preheat oven to 325°F. Follow directions on apple pie filling can. In a 9½" deep-dish pie plate, place 1 sheet of fillo so that edges hang over the side. Brush fillo inside pie plate with about ½ tsp. of the butter. Place another sheet of fillo on top of the first and butter. Repeat this process with two more sheets. Spoon apple mixture into pie plate. Cover with the remaining 4 sheets of fillo, buttering each layer separately. Form excess fillo dough into an edge by rolling it under toward the pie plate rim. If dough is dry and cracks, moisten with wet fingertips. With a sharp knife make 3 slits in top of pie. Bake 40-45 minutes until top of pie is golden brown.

Fresh Fruit Flan

STRAWBERRY KIWI SURPRISE

Pastry:
1½ cups sifted all-purpose flour
3 tbsp. sugar
½ tsp. salt
½ cup **Crisco Shortening**
3 tbsp. water
Filling:
1 lb. cream cheese, softened
2 eggs
⅔ cup granulated sugar
⅔ cup sour cream
1 tbsp. orange liqueur
Topping:
2 kiwi fruit, peeled and sliced
strawberries, sliced or whole
⅓ cup apricot jelly, heated

For pastry: Combine flour, sugar and salt in a bowl. Cut in shortening with a pastry blender until mixture resembles coarse crumbs. Sprinkle with water (1 tbsp. at a time) tossing with a fork to form dough. Press dough to fit 9" pie plate or springform pan. For Filling: Beat cream cheese, eggs, sugar, sour cream and orange liqueur 2-3 minutes or until smooth. Pour mixture into pastry-lined pan; place on cookie sheet. Bake at 350°F for 35-40 minutes or until set and slightly browned on top. Cool completely. Carefully remove from pan. Arrange sliced fruit on top of filling. Glaze with warm apricot jelly. Chill well before serving.

ORANGE TART

Sweet Pastry:
1 cup sifted flour
⅛ tsp. salt
¼ cup sugar
½ cup unsalted butter
1 egg
Syrup:
1⅛ cups sugar
5 oz. water
5 seedless oranges
Almond Cream Filling:
3 tbsp. **Grand Marnier**
3½ oz. softened butter
2 eggs
½ cup ground almonds

To make sweet pastry: Sift flour, salt and sugar into a bowl, add butter and egg and blend until well combined. Form into a ball and knead lightly with heels of hands against a smooth surface to mix butter thoroughly. Re-form into a ball, wrap in waxed paper and chill for at least 1 hour. Make a syrup with ⅝ cup of the sugar and the water, then peel the oranges and slice them into thin rounds. Put the slices in the syrup and allow to simmer softly for 15 minutes without stirring. Remove the orange slices and place in strainer to drain and bring the syrup to a boil. Cook for 8 minutes to thicken. Remove the saucepan from the heat, add 1½ tbsp. of the Grand Marnier. Keep syrup warm. Make the almond cream filling as follows: Mix the softened butter, ½ cup sugar and eggs (1 at a time), with the ground almonds and the remaining Grand Marnier. Beat well. Roll out the sweet pastry and line a tart tin. Spread the almond cream on the pastry base and cook for 20 minutes in a fairly hot oven, 425°F. Arrange the orange slices on the tart. Cover with the syrup and allow to cool.

FRESH FRUIT FLAN

1 4-serving-size package **JELL-O Vanilla Instant Pudding**
2 tbsp. almond liqueur
1 9" ready-made cake flan
3 cups fresh fruit and berries
⅓ cup **KRAFT Apricot Jam**
1 tbsp. water
sliced toasted almonds

Prepare pudding according to package directions, reducing milk to 1½ cups. Stir in liqueur. Let stand 5 minutes. Spread evenly over flan. Arrange fruit on top of pudding. Heat jam and water over low heat until melted; sieve. Cool slightly and brush or spoon over fruit. Garnish with sliced almonds. Chill about 30 minutes.
Serves 6-8

SHORT PEACH CRUST

6 cups flour
1½ tsp. salt
1 lb. shortening, chilled
¼ cup butter, chilled
½ cup **Emelia Peach and Lime Marmelo**
3-6 tbsp. lemon juice, cold
peach pie filling

Combine flour and salt. Cut shortening into flour until it reaches the consistency of cornmeal. Using a fork, toss in Peach and Lime Marmelo and 3-6 tbsp. lemon juice until it is moist enough to hold together in a solid mass. Chill for 15-30 minutes. Divide dough in 6. Roll out. Fill with peach pie filling. Bake in preheated 450°F oven for 20 minutes, reduce heat to 350°F and bake 40 minutes longer.
Makes 6 pie shells or 3 double-crust pies

PECAN PIE

1 9" **Crisco Single-Crust Pastry**
3 tbsp. **Crisco Shortening**
2 tsp. vanilla extract
½ cup granulated sugar
¼ cup packed brown sugar
3 eggs, well beated
½ cup chopped pecans
1 cup dark corn syrup
¼ tsp. salt
½ cup pecan halves

Line a 9" pie plate with pastry; set aside. Preheat oven to 450°F. Cream Crisco and vanilla extract. Gradually add sugars, beating well after each addition. Add beaten eggs in thirds, beating well after each addition. Thoroughly blend in chopped pecans, corn syrup and salt. Pour filling into unbaked pie shell. Bake at 450°F for 10 minutes; reduce heat to 350°F. Arrange pecan halves over top of filling. Continue baking for 30-35 minutes or until set. Cool thoroughly on a rack before cutting.

FRUIT FLAN

Filling:
1 lb. cream cheese, softened
2 eggs
⅔ cup granulated sugar
⅔ cup sour cream
1 tbsp. grated lemon rind
1 tbsp. fresh lemon juice
1 9" **Crisco Single-Crust Pastry**

Topping:
1 10-oz. can mandarin orange sections, drained
⅓ cup fresh blueberries
⅔ cup fresh raspberries
⅓ cup apple jelly, heated

Beat cream cheese, eggs, sugar, sour cream, lemon rind and lemon juice 2-3 minutes or until smooth. Pour filling into pastry-lined flan pan or pie plate; place on cookie sheet. Bake for 35-40 minutes at 350°F or until set and slightly browned on top. Cool completely. Arrange fruit on top of filling. Glaze with warm apple jelly. Chill well before serving.
Makes a 9" pie

DEEP-DISH PEACH PIE

10 cups sliced peaches
½ cup golden raisins
1 cup sugar
⅓ cup cornstarch
½ tsp. ground cinnamon
¼ tsp. nutmeg
pinch salt
3 tbsp. butter
1 9" **Crisco Double-Crust Pastry**

Place peaches and raisins in a large bowl. Combine sugar, cornstarch, cinnamon, nutmeg and salt. Add to peaches and raisins; mix until evenly coated. Place in 13" x 9" baking pan. Dot with butter. Preheat oven to 425°F. Roll pastry out on floured surface to fit over top of baking pan. Place pastry on top of fruit in pan and secure pastry to sides of pan. Cut vent holes in pastry. Bake for 15 minutes. Reduce heat to 325°F and bake for an additional 40-50 minutes or until crust is golden. Remove from oven and let cool 15 minutes before serving or serve cold.
Serves 12

RASPBERRY SOUR-CREAM PIE

2 eggs, slightly beaten
1 cup sour cream
1 cup sugar
⅓ cup all-purpose flour
1 tbsp. fresh lemon juice
1 tsp. lemon rind
4 cups fresh raspberries
1 9" **Crisco Single-Crust Pastry**

Topping:
½ cup brown sugar
½ cup all-purpose flour
½ cup chopped pecans
¼ cup butter, melted

Roll out pastry on floured surface to fit 9" pie plate. Flute edge. Combine beaten eggs, sour cream, sugar, flour, lemon juice and rind. Fold in 3 cups of raspberries. Reserve 1 cup. Pour mixture into prepared shell. Bake for 30 minutes at 400°F. Combine topping ingredients. Sprinkle topping on pie and bake for an additional 10 minutes. Remove from oven. Garnish pie with remaining raspberries. Cool before serving.
Makes a 9" pie

CRISCO PASTRY

2 cups sifted all-purpose flour
¾ tsp. salt
1 cup **Crisco**
4 tbsp. water

Combine flour and salt in mixing bowl. Cut Crisco into flour with two knives or a pastry blender until pieces are the size of large peas and mixture is fairly uniform. Do not over mix. Sprinkle cold water (1 tbsp. at a time) lightly mixing with a fork or spatula between each spoonful. Turn out onto floured surface, form into a firm ball with a minimum of handling, halve dough and roll out each half to ⅛" thickness. Avoid overworking dough. Recipe may be doubled and dough can be refrigerated or frozen until needed, either before or after rolling out. (Note: 2¼ cups cake and pastry flour may be substituted but use only ¾ cup Crisco.) Bake as required for your recipes.

Double-Crust Fruit Pies: Add filling to pastry-lined pie plate; cover with top crust, fold top edge under bottom crust and flute with fingers or fork. Prick top. Bake at 425°F for 40-50 minutes or as directed in filling recipe.

Baked Shells with Cooked Filling: Prick dough. Bake at 425°F for 12-15 minutes. Cool pastry before adding filling.

Unbaked Shells with Uncooked Filling: Do not prick dough. Add uncooked filling and bake at 450°F for 10 minutes then at 325-350°F for 30-40 minutes, or as directed in filling recipe.
Makes 1 9" double crust or 2 single shells or 6-8 tart shells

LAYERED LEMON PIE

1 9" **Crisco Single-Crust Pastry**
1 quart lemon sherbet, softened
1 quart vanilla ice cream, softened
1½ cups soft macaroon crumbs (about 4 large macaroons)

Line 9" pie plate with pastry; bake and cool. Spread ½ quart of softened sherbet in pastry shell; freeze until firm. Combine softened ice cream and macaroon crumbs; spread evenly over lemon layer and freeze until firm. Top with second ½ quart of sherbet, spreading evenly over ice cream. Freeze until firm. To serve, remove from freezer about 15 minutes before slicing.
Serves 12-15

BRANDY ALEXANDER PIE

1 envelope unflavored gelatin
⅓ cup sugar
⅛ tsp. salt
½ cup cold water
3 egg yolks, beaten
⅓ cup crème de cacao
2 tbsp. brandy
3 egg whites
⅓ cup sugar
1 envelope **Dream Whip Dessert Topping Mix**
1 9″ baked and cooled graham or chocolate crumb crust
chocolate curls or shaved chocolate to garnish

Combine gelatin, sugar and salt in saucepan. Add water and egg yolks. Cook and stir over low heat until gelatin dissolves and mixture thickens slightly. Remove from heat; add crème de cacao and brandy. Chill until slightly thickened. Beat egg whites until soft peaks form. Gradually add ⅓ cup sugar and beat until stiff peaks form. Fold gelatin mixture into egg whites. Prepare dessert topping mix as directed on package; fold into egg-white mixture. Pour into crust. Chill until set. Garnish with chocolate curls or shaved chocolate, if desired.

CINNAMON PEAR PIE

1 9″ **Crisco Single-Crust Pastry**
1¼ cups water
½ cup red cinnamon candies
⅓ cup sugar
3 tbsp. cornstarch
2 tbsp. lemon juice
3 14-oz. cans pear halves, well drained and halved
whipped cream cheese

Line 9″ pie plate with pastry; bake and cool. In saucepan, combine water and candies. Cook and stir until candies dissolve. Combine sugar and cornstarch; gradually stir in candy liquid. Cook and stir until mixture thickens and bubbles. Remove from heat; stir in lemon juice. Cool slightly. Gently spread ¼ cup glaze over bottom of pastry shell. Arrange half of the pears in pastry shell; spoon half of the remaining glaze over fruit. Repeat with remaining pears and glaze. Chill 3-4 hours. Garnish each serving with whipped cream cheese.

"CHRISTMAS IN JULY" MINCEMEAT PIE

Crust:
2 tbsp. butter
¾ cup flaked coconut
Filling:
⅔ cup **Lynch Old Style Mincemeat**
1 pint vanilla ice cream
¼ cup chopped maraschino cherries

To prepare crust: Preheat oven to 300°F. Spread butter evenly around sides and bottom of 9″ diameter pie plate. Press coconut evenly into butter. Bake 15-20 minutes or until evenly browned. Chill. To prepare filling: Warm mincemeat to soften suet and chill. Quickly mix chilled mincemeat, ice cream and cherries and spoon into coconut crust (mixture will be quite soft at this stage). Chill several hours in freezer until firm.
Serves 6-8

DREAMY ORANGE AND YOGURT PIE

35 vanilla wafers
1 envelope unflavored gelatin
2 tbsp. lemon juice
½ cup orange juice
½ tsp. grated orange rind
½ cup sugar
¾ cup orange-flavored yogurt
2 cups prepared **Dream Whip Dessert Topping**

Arrange wafers on bottom and sides of 9″ pie plate. Sprinkle gelatin over juices, rind and sugar in saucepan. Stir over low heat until gelatin dissolves. Cool. Stir in yogurt. Fold yogurt mixture into prepared dessert topping. Spoon into crust. Chill until set. Garnish with additional dessert topping and orange pieces.

Dreamy Orange and Yogurt Pie

Layered Lemon Cheese Pie (left) and Key Lime Pie

EASY BLUEBERRY FLAN

1 8-roll package refrigerated crescent dinner rolls

½ cup orange juice

2 tsp. grated orange rind

¼ cup sugar

1 10½-oz. package frozen, unsweetened blueberries

⅓ cup **Veloutine Light**

1 8-oz. package whipped cream cheese

whipped cream and grated orange rind to garnish (optional)

Line a 12" pizza pan with crescent rolls to form a crust. Pierce with fork; bake in 375°F oven for 10-12 minutes or until lightly browned. Cool about 5-10 minutes. If desired, transfer crust to large serving plate. In small saucepan combine juice, rind, sugar and thawed blueberries. Bring to boil; sprinkle in Veloutine, stirring constantly. Boil 1 minute. Cool. Spread whipped cream cheese over baked crust. Spread blueberry mixture over cheese. Chill 2-3 hours. Garnish.

LAYERED LEMON CHEESE PIE

1 4-serving-size package **JELL-O Lemon Pie Filling**

½ cup sugar

1¼ cups water

2 egg yolks

1 cup milk

¼ lb. cream cheese, softened

1 tbsp. butter or margarine

2 egg whites

¼ cup sugar

1 9" baked and cooled pie shell

Combine pie filling mix, sugar and ¼ cup of the water in saucepan. Blend in egg yolks. Add remaining water and milk. Cook and stir over medium heat until mixture comes to a full bubbling boil. Divide mixture in half. Beat cream cheese into one half and butter into remaining half. Beat egg whites until foamy throughout. Gradually beat in ¼ cup sugar and continue beating until mixture forms stiff shiny peaks. Fold in cream-cheese pie-filling mixture and pour into pie shell. Spoon remaining pie filling evenly over filling in pie shell. Chill 3 hours.

KEY LIME PIE

1 4-serving-size package **JELL-O Lemon Pie Filling**

1 cup sugar

2¼ cups water

2 egg yolks

3 tbsp. lime juice (bottled or fresh)

¾ tsp. grated lime rind

1 tbsp. butter or margarine

green food coloring

1 9" baked and cooled pie shell

2 egg whites

¼ cup sugar

Combine pie filling mix, 1 cup sugar and ¼ cup of water in saucepan. Blend in egg yolks. Add remaining 2 cups water. Cook and stir over medium heat until mixture comes to a full bubbling boil. Remove from heat; stir in lime juice, rind and butter. Add enough food coloring to tint light green. Pour into pie shell. Beat egg whites until foamy throughout. Gradually beat in ¼ cup sugar and continue beating until mixture forms stiff shiny peaks. Spread over pie filling, sealing well at edges. Bake at 425°F for about 5 minutes or until lightly browned. Cool for 3 hours.

PINK PEPPERMINT PIE

1 tsp. unflavored gelatin
2 tbsp. cold water
1½ cups cold whipping cream
1 7-oz. jar marshmallow crème
¼ tsp. peppermint extract
¼ tsp. vanilla
4-5 drops red food coloring
1 **Keebler Ready-Crust Chocolate-Flavored Pie Crust**
peppermint candies to garnish (optional)

In a small custard cup, soften gelatin in cold water. Place cup in pan of boiling water and stir until gelatin dissolves. Transfer mixture to a large mixing bowl. Using well chilled beaters and bowl, whip cream until stiff. Using same beaters, combine marshmallow crème and cooled gelatin, beating until smooth. Add peppermint extract and vanilla. Tint mixture pink with food coloring. Reserve 1 cup whipped cream for garnish. Fold remaining whipped cream into marshmallow mixture. Pour into crust. Chill until firm, about 3 hours. Garnish with reserved whipped cream. Decorate with peppermint candies, if desired.

STRAWBERRY YOGURT PIE

1 pint fresh strawberries
1 envelope (1 tbsp.) unflavored gelatin
½ cup sugar
2 eggs, separated
½ cup milk
1 8-oz. carton strawberry yogurt
1 tbsp. lemon juice
4 drops red food coloring (optional)
1 **Keebler Ready-Crust Butter-Flavored Pie Crust**

In blender or food processor, purée enough strawberries to equal ¾ cup; reserve whole strawberries for garnish. In medium saucepan, mix gelatin with ¼ cup sugar; blend in egg yolks beaten with milk. Let stand 1 minute. Stir over low heat until gelatin is dissolved, about 5 minutes. With wire whisk or electric mixer, blend in puréed strawberries, yogurt, lemon juice and food coloring. Chill, stirring occasionally, until mixture mounds slightly when dropped from spoon. In medium bowl, beat egg whites until soft peaks form; gradually add remaining sugar and beat until stiff. Fold into strawberry mixture. Pour into crust and chill until firm, about 4 hours. Garnish with remaining strawberries.

BAKER'S BEST CHOCOLATE PECAN PIE

1 cup corn syrup
½ cup sugar
4 squares **Baker's Semi-Sweet Chocolate**
3 tbsp. butter
1 tsp. **Maxwell House Instant Coffee**
1 tsp. vanilla
3 eggs
1 cup coarsely chopped pecans
1 9" unbaked pie shell

Combine corn syrup and sugar. Bring to boil over high heat. Reduce heat and boil gently for 2 minutes, stirring constantly. Remove from heat and stir in chocolate, butter, coffee and vanilla; mix well. Blend in eggs and pecans. Pour into pie shell. Bake at 375°F for 45-50 minutes. (The center will appear not set when shaken gently. To reduce cracking on surface be sure not to overbake pie.)

FLUFFY COFFEE PIE

1 4-serving-size package instant vanilla pudding and pie filling
1 1½-oz. envelope whipped topping mix
1¾ cups cold milk
1 tbsp. instant coffee
1 **Keebler Ready-Crust Chocolate-Flavored Crust**
whipped cream or topping

In medium mixing bowl, combine pie filling mix, whipped topping mix, milk and coffee. Blend at low speed of electric mixer until smooth. Increase speed to high and beat until very thick, about 3-4 minutes. Spoon into crust. Chill 3 hours or until firm. Garnish with whipped cream or topping.

STRAWBERRY-AND-RHUBARB CHIFFON PIE

½ pint whipping cream
1 jar **Emelia Strawberries and Rhubarb in Champagne**
1 9" graham-cracker crust, baked
fresh, sliced strawberries to garnish

Beat cream just until stiff. Reserve some whipped cream for trim. Fold in Strawberries and Rhubarb in Champagne. Spread in pie shell. Put in freezer for 4 hours. Trim with fresh, sliced strawberries and additional whipped cream.
Serves 6-8

EASY BLUEBERRY CREAM PIE

1 **Keebler Ready-Crust Butter-Flavored Pie Crust**
1-lb. 5-oz. can blueberry pie filling
2 cups whipped cream or topping
1 tsp. grated lemon peel
3 cups miniature marshmallows

Spoon blueberry pie filling into crust. Fold whipped cream and lemon peel into marshmallows. Spread marshmallow mixture over pie filling. Chill overnight.

BLACK FOREST PIE

1 cup cold whipping cream
1 7-oz. jar marshmallow crème
2 squares unsweetened chocolate, melted
1 tsp. vanilla
2 tbsp. maraschino cherry juice
½ cup quartered maraschino cherries
1 **Keebler Ready-Crust Chocolate-Flavored Pie Crust**

Using well-chilled beaters and bowl, whip cream until stiff. Using same beaters, combine marshmallow, chocolate and vanilla until well blended. Gradually add cherry juice blending until smooth. Fold in whipped cream and cherries. Pour into crust. Freeze until firm, about 2 hours. Garnish with additional cherries, if desired.

BAKED ALASKA TARTS

1 package **Keebler Ready-Crust Graham Cracker Tart Crusts**
3 cups ice cream (neopolitan, fudge swirl, etc.), softened
3 egg whites
¼ tsp. vanilla
¼ tsp. salt
½ cup sugar

Layer ½ cup ice cream into each tart. Freeze until firm, about 1 hour. In deep narrow bowl, beat egg whites, vanilla and salt on low speed of electric mixer until very foamy. Increase speed to high and add sugar gradually. Continue beating until meringue is stiff and glossy. Spread meringue over tarts, sealing to edge. Place tarts on baking sheet and bake at 500°F, about 2-3 minutes, or until browned. Serve immediately or hold in freezer until needed. (Tarts may be topped with meringue in advance, frozen and then browned as needed.)

DESSERTS

An 11-year-old informed us recently that he could cope with being sent to bed with no dinner, but that just the thought of missing out on dessert was enough to keep him on the straight and narrow.

Indeed, dessert equates with reward for many of us, regardless of our age.

Plain or fancy, light or rich, desserts should contain an element of fun or even surprise. In this chapter we present some simply wicked dessert creations which are sure to draw rave reviews from family and guests alike.

Strawberry Brulée **(see page 204)**

STRAWBERRY BRULÉE

1 4-serving-size package vanilla pudding and pie filling
1 cup milk
1 pouch **Lucky Whip Dessert Topping Mix**
¼ cup milk
¼ cup sherry (or 2 tsp. almond extract)
½ cup packed brown sugar
½ cup slivered almonds
2 cups sliced and whole strawberries

Cook pudding and pie filling with 1 cup milk according to package directions. Cover surface of pudding with plastic wrap and cool to room temperature. Whip dessert topping mix with ¼ cup milk and sherry (or with ¼ cup milk and almond extract) according to package directions. Fold into cooled pudding. Pour into a large ovenproof shallow baking dish. Sprinkle with brown sugar and almonds. Place 3" under a preheated broiler until sugar melts and bubbles and starts to brown, about 5 minutes. Watch closely to prevent sugar burning. Serve warm or cold with strawberries.
Serves 5-6

HUMPTY DUMPTY BANANA FRITTERS

4 firm bananas
2 tbsp. lemon juice
½ cup buttermilk baking mix
2 tbsp. sugar
dash nutmeg
¼ cup milk
1 egg
1 cup crushed **Humpty Dumpty Potato Chips**
oil for deep frying
powdered sugar
sweetened whipped cream

Peel and cut bananas into 2" chunks; brush with lemon juice. In small bowl combine baking mix, sugar, nutmeg, milk and egg, mix thoroughly. In deep saucepan heat 3" of oil to 375°F. Dip banana chunks into batter, drain, then coat lightly with chips. Fry about 2 minutes, just until browned. Drain on paper towels. Dust with powdered sugar. Serve hot with whipped cream.
Serves 4

Cherry Chocolate Whirl

BILLY BEE HONEY BAKED APPLES

For each serving, scoop out core of apple leaving a bit of apple and skin at blossom end. Fill with raisins and walnuts and drizzle 1 tbsp. **Billy Bee Honey** into the core hole. Wrap in aluminum foil and bake at 400°F about 30 minutes.

Microwave method: Place apple in glass dish, cover with lid or plastic wrap, microwave on high power for 2½-3 minutes.

CHERRY CHOCOLATE WHIRL

1 pouch **Knox Unflavored Gelatine**
½ cup milk, divided
¼ cup boiling water
¾ cup sugar
⅓ cup cocoa powder
2 tsp. vanilla
2 cups whipping cream
1 tbsp. cherry brandy

Sprinkle gelatin over ¼ cup milk in small bowl; allow to stand until gelatin is moistened. Add boiling water; stir constantly until gelatin is completely dissolved. Combine sugar and cocoa in mixing bowl; add remaining milk, vanilla, whipping cream and brandy. Beat at medium speed until soft peaks form. Slowly add gelatin mixture; beat at high speed until stiff peaks form. Spoon into serving dishes. Chill until set. Cocktail cherries and chocolate curls create the perfect accent.
Serves 5

MOCHA MOUSSE

4 tbsp. cold milk
1 tbsp. instant coffee
⅔ cup **Carnation Coffee-Mate**
¾ cup instant chocolate powder
2 egg whites
⅛ tsp. cream of tartar

Chill a small deep bowl and beaters in freezer for 15 minutes. Measure milk and instant coffee into chilled bowl. Stir to dissolve coffee. Using an electric mixer at low speed, beat in Coffee-Mate. At high speed whip until soft peaks form. Gradually beat in chocolate powder. In another bowl, beat egg whites until frothy. Add cream of tartar and beat until stiff. Fold in chocolate mixture. Store in freezer until ready to serve.
Serves 2-5

Classic Baked Rice Pudding

CLASSIC BAKED RICE PUDDING

½ cup **Uncle Ben's Converted Brand Rice**
1⅔ cups water
1½ tsp. butter or margarine
¼ tsp. salt
2 cups milk
2 eggs
⅓ cup sugar
1 tsp. vanilla
¼ cup raisins
cinnamon to taste (optional)
nutmeg to taste (optional)
whipped topping, as desired
1 tsp. chopped nuts
2 tbsp. rum sauce (optional)

Combine rice, water, butter or salt in a large saucepan. Bring to boil; cover and reduce heat to medium-low and boil gently until most of the water is absorbed (about 25 minutes). Preheat oven to 350°F. Add milk to cooked rice and boil gently, stirring occasionally until mixture thickens slightly (about 10 minutes). Beat eggs, sugar and vanilla together in a bowl. Gradually add to hot rice mixture, stirring constantly. Pour into a greased baking dish. If desired, stir in raisins and sprinkle cinnamon and/or nutmeg over top. Place in oven and bake uncovered for 45-50 minutes, or until knife inserted near center comes out clean. Serve warm or chilled, with whipped topping, chopped nuts and warm rum sauce if desired.
Makes 8 ½-cup portions

CHERRY TRUFFLE LIQUEUR

⅓ cup corn syrup
1½ tsp. granulated sugar
⅓ cup chocolate syrup
3 tbsp. milk
⅔ cup vodka
2 tbsp. cherry brandy
⅔ cup **Carnation Coffee-Mate**

In a saucepan, combine corn syrup and sugar. Heat until mixture bubbles and sugar dissolves. Stir in chocolate syrup and allow mixture to cool. In a bowl, combine milk, vodka, cherry brandy and Coffee-Mate. Stir thoroughly. Stir cooled syrup into alcohol mixture. Strain mixture through a fine sieve. Serve chilled over ice as a liqueur or drizzle over ice cream for dessert. Store in refrigerator.
Makes 15 1-oz. servings

CRUNCHY DIPPED BANANAS

12 oz. chocolate chips
4 bananas, cut into chunks
1 cup crushed **Humpty Dumpty Potato Chips**

Melt chocolate chips over hot water. Cool slightly. Using a fork or wooden skewer, dip chunks of banana into chocolate and then roll in crushed potato chips. Place on waxed-paper-lined baking sheet and chill until firm.
Serves 4

TOBLERONE CHOCOLATE FONDUE

1 14-oz. bar **Toblerone Milk Chocolate**
½ cup 35% cream
3-5 tbsp. liqueur (cognac, orange liqueur, brandy, coffee liqueur, or almond liqueur)
fruit

Break chocolate bar into separate triangles and melt in top of double boiler over simmering water. Stir until smooth. Add cream slowly, stirring constantly. Add liqueur 1 tbsp. at a time, stirring after each addition. Add more cream, 1 tbsp. at a time, if a thinner consistency is desired. Mixture should be thick enough to coat the fruit or pastry of your choice. Fresh strawberries, raspberries, firm pear and peach slices, banana chunks, pound cake (cut into 1" squares), pitted cherries, or apples are good with this chocolate coating.

BANANA FRAPPÉE

1 banana
½ cup orange juice
½ cup 10% cream or milk
1 tbsp. molasses
1 egg
3 oz. **Crème de Grand Marnier**

Mix at high speed in a blender and pour into dessert dishes.
Serves 3

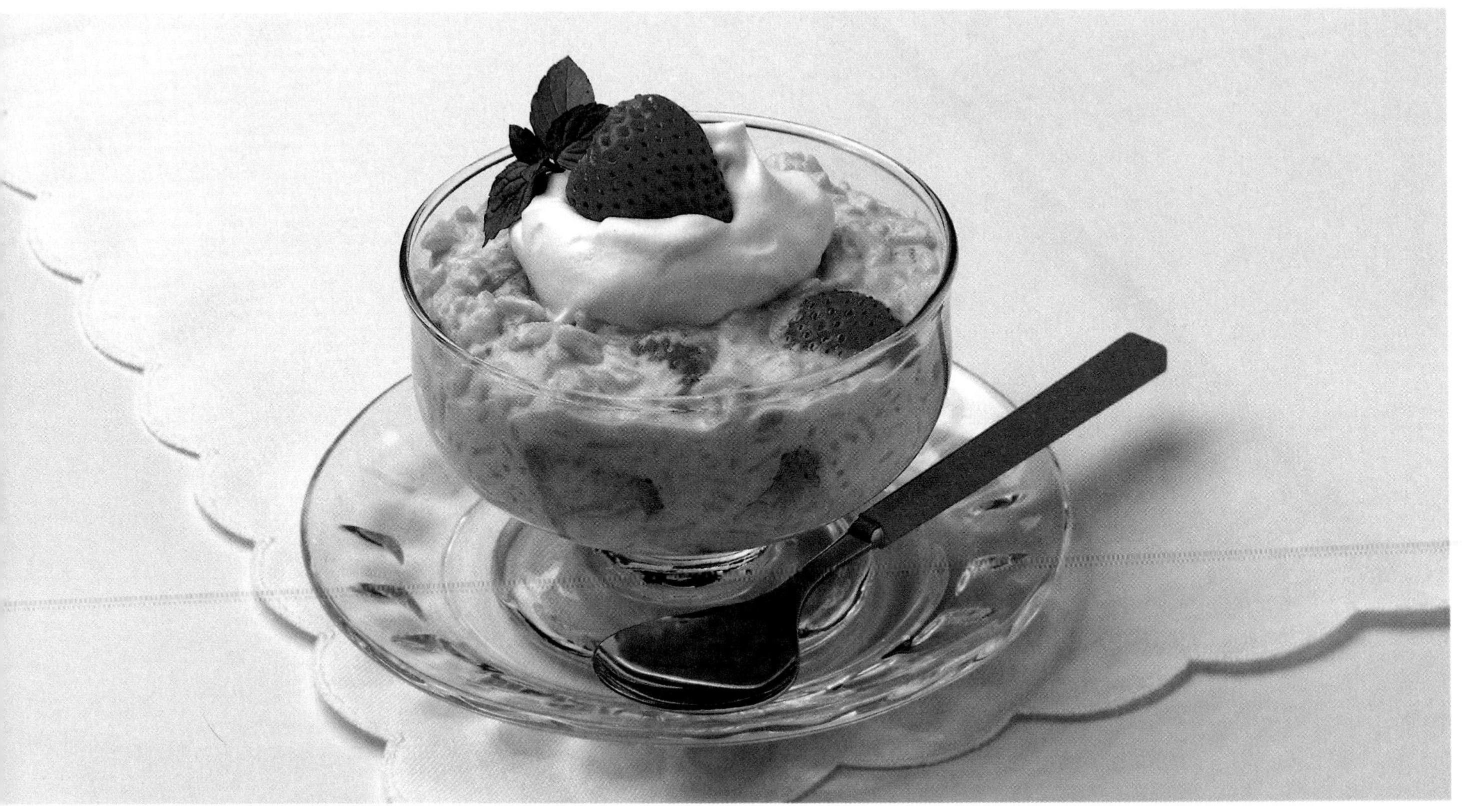

Strawberry Rice Swirl

CHOCOLATE MINT FONDUE

- 3/4 cup half-and-half cream
- 2 tbsp. **McCormick Mint Leaves**, crushed
- 8 squares semi-sweet chocolate
- 2 tbsp. icing sugar
- assorted dippers: strawberries, seedless grapes, pineapple chunks, cherries, peach slices, orange sections, melon chunks, dried apricots, marshmallows, angel food cake or pound cake cubes (ensure fruits are dry)

Combine cream and dried mint leaves in top of double boiler. Let stand 5 minutes. Add chocolate and sugar. Heat over hot, not boiling, water until melted and smooth, stirring occasionally. Pour into fondue pot and set over warmer. Serve with assorted dippers (if fondue becomes too thick, add a little more cream).
Serves 4-6

BAKLAVA

- 1 lb. walnuts or blanched almonds, chopped
- 1/2 cup sugar
- 1/2 tsp. cinnamon
- 1/8 tsp. cloves
- 2 lb. **Krinos Thin Fillo**
- 1 lb. sweet butter, melted

Syrup:

- 2 cups sugar
- 1 cup honey
- 2 cups water
- 1 lemon or orange rind

Combine chopped walnuts, 1/2 cup sugar, cinnamon and cloves. Brush 12" x 17" baking tray with melted butter. Place 8 fillo leaves at bottom, brushing each with melted butter. Spread half of walnut mixture on top of fillo leaves and repeat process. Place last fillo leaves on top and brush with remaining melted butter. With a pointed sharp knife, score top sheets in diamond square shapes in sizes yòu desire. Bake in moderate 375°F preheated oven for 1 hour or until golden brown. Let cool. To prepare syrup: Bring syrup ingredients to boil and simmer for 10 minutes. Strain and let cool slightly. Pour evenly over Baklava. Serve when cool.

STRAWBERRY RICE SWIRL

- 1 cup **Uncle Ben's Converted Brand Rice**
- 2 1/2 cups milk
- 1 tbsp. butter or margarine
- 1/3 cup sugar
- 2 cups strawberries, sliced and sweetened (fresh or frozen)
- 2 tbsp. sugar
- 2 tsp. cornstarch
- 1 cup milk
- 1/2 tsp. almond flavoring
- 1 cup whipped cream or dessert topping

In large saucepan, combine rice, milk, butter or margarine and sugar. Bring to boil over medium-high heat, stirring frequently. Cover and reduce heat to medium-low. Simmer for 20-25 minutes, until rice is tender, stirring occasionally. (Mixture will be thick and creamy.) At the end of this time, add the strawberries to the rice mixture. Continue cooking over medium-low heat. Combine sugar and constarch, add slowly to milk, stirring constantly. Add almond flavoring to milk mixture. Stir the milk mixture into the prepared rice mixture. Increase heat to medium and cook, stirring frequently, just until mixture begins to bubble. Remove from heat and cool. Chill for 1 hour. Place strawberry mixture in serving dish. Swirl whipped cream into the mixture with a spoon. Serve.
Makes 8 1/2-cup portions

CHOCOLATE-SYRUP SWIRL DESSERT

Crust:

2 cups vanilla-wafer or graham-cracker crumbs

1/3 cup melted butter or margarine

Vanilla Filling:

1 tsp. unflavored gelatin

1 tbsp. cold water

2 tbsp. boiling water

1 cup whipping cream

2 tbsp. sugar

1/2 tsp. vanilla

Chocolate Filling:

1 envelope unflavored gelatin

1/4 cup cold water

1 8-oz. package cream cheese

1/4 cup sugar

1 tsp. vanilla

3/4 cup **Hershey's Canned Chocolate Syrup**, chilled

3/4 cup milk

fresh fruit to garnish

For crust, combine vanilla-wafer or graham-cracker crumbs with melted butter or margarine. Press on bottom and 1½" up sides of a 9" springform pan or 10" pie pan. Chill. For vanilla filling, sprinkle gelatin onto cold water in a cup; let stand 1 minute to soften. Add boiling water and stir until gelatin is completely dissolved; cool slightly. Combine whipping cream, sugar and vanilla in small mixing bowl; beat until soft peaks form. Gradually add gelatin mixture; beat just until stiff peaks form. For chocolate filling, sprinkle gelatin over cold water in small saucepan; allow to soften. Place over low heat stirring to dissolve. Beat cream cheese with sugar and vanilla in large mixing bowl until creamy. Add chocolate syrup, gelatin mixture and milk blending well. Chill, stirring occasionally, until mixture mounds from a spoon. To assemble, spoon 1/2 chocolate filling into crust; top with 1/2 vanilla filling. Repeat procedure ending with dollops of vanilla filling on top. Gently swirl with spatula to give marbled effect. Chill several hours or overnight. Garnish with fresh fruit.
Serves 10-12

CHOCOLATE-SYRUP MINT MOUSSE

1 tsp. unflavored gelatin

1 tbsp. cold water

2 tbsp. boiling water

1 cup whipping cream

1/2 cup **Hershey's Canned Chocolate Syrup**, chilled

2-3 drops mint extract

sweetened whipped cream or topping and fresh fruit to garnish

Sprinkle gelatin onto cold water in a cup. Allow to sit a few minutes to soften. Blend in boiling water, stirring until gelatin is dissolved. Beat whipping cream in small mixing bowl until soft peaks form; gradually add gelatin mixture beating until stiff peaks form. Fold in chocolate syrup and mint extract. Spoon into individual serving dishes. Chill 20 minutes or until set. Garnish as desired.
Serves 4

EMPANADAS

Filling:

1 cup canned pumpkin

1/4 cup brown sugar

1 tsp. anise seed

1 tsp. pumpkin pie spice

dash of salt

Pastry:

2 **Krinos Fillo Leaves**

2 tbsp. milk

1/4 cup granulated sugar

Blend all filling ingredients and bring to boil. Lower heat and simmer for 10 minutes. Cool. To make pastry: Spread out 2 sheets of fillo. Cut in approximately 4" squares. In the center of each square, put a small spoonful of pumpkin filling. Fold the fillo to form a triangle. Moisten the edges with milk and seal. Moisten the top with milk and sprinkle lightly with granulated sugar. Bake at 375°F until edges of crust are lightly browned.

Chocolate-Syrup Swirl Dessert (top) and Chocolate-Syrup Mint Mousse

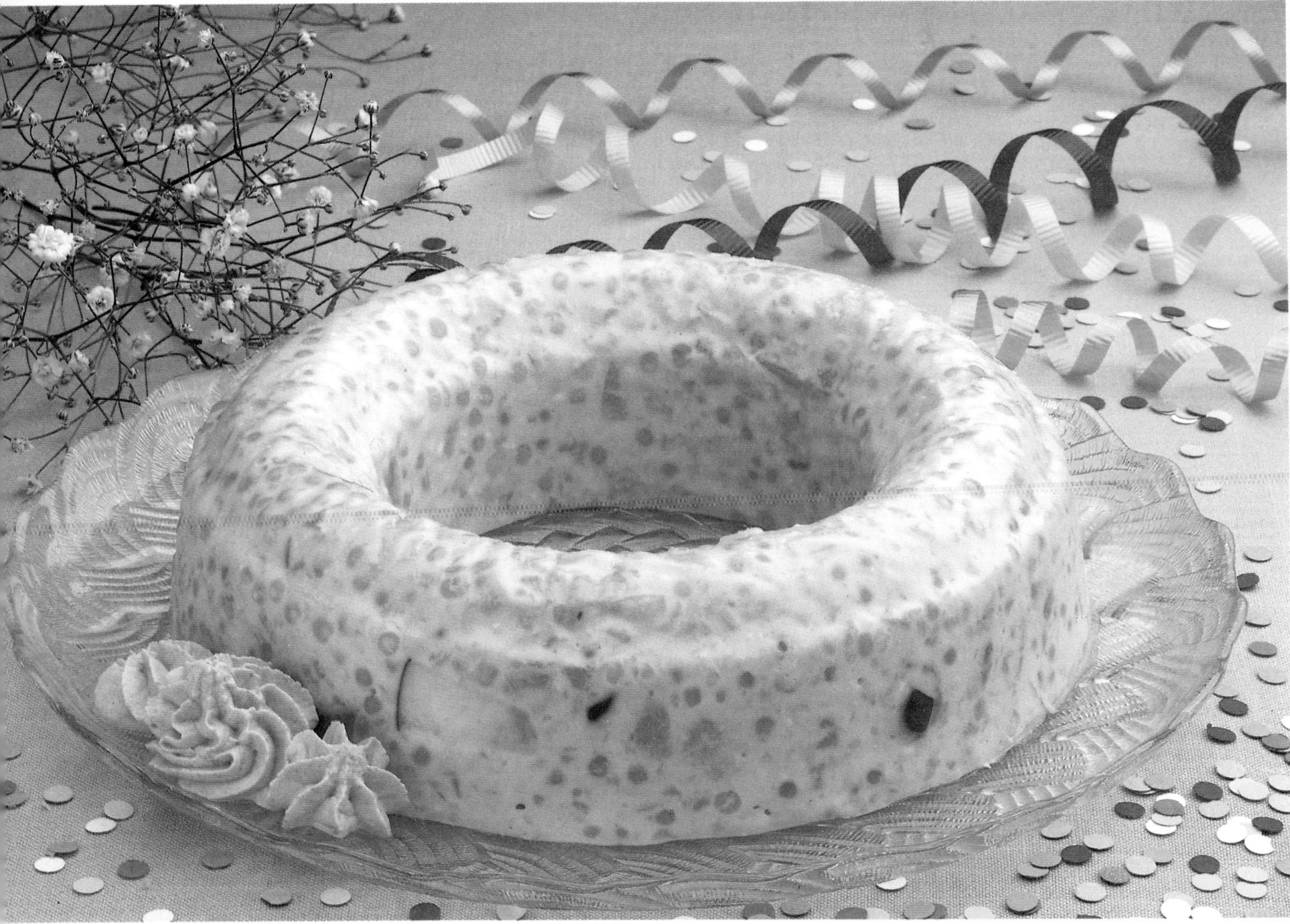

Tapioca Ring

TAPIOCA RING

1 14-oz. can apricots
2 envelopes unflavored gelatin
1 cup sugar
1 tsp. orange extract
1 14-oz. can fruit cocktail, drained
1 red apple, chopped
1 15-oz. can **Nestlé Ready-to-Serve Tapioca Pudding**
1 6-oz. can **Nestlé Pure Thick Cream**, well shaken

Drain apricots, reserving liquid. Purée apricots. Soften gelatin in ½ cup apricot syrup. Heat until melted, cool. Blend together apricots, gelatin, sugar, orange extract, fruit cocktail, apple, tapioca pudding and cream. Pour into a 6-cup ring mold. Chill 4-6 hours.
Serves 6-8

APPLE CREAM

4-5 medium cooking apples, peeled and sliced
2-3 tbsp. water
3 whole cloves
½ cup whipping cream
1 tbsp. honey
½ cup **Alpen Mixed Cereal**
2 tbsp. lemon juice
grated rind of ½ lemon
1 tbsp. **Alpen Mixed Cereal**, to garnish

Combine apples, water and cloves in medium saucepan. Cover and simmer over low heat until soft. Purée the apples in a food processor or blender or put through a sieve. Cool. Meanwhile whip cream. Then fold purée, honey, Alpen, lemon juice and rind into whipped cream. Spoon into individual serving glasses and garnish with remaining Alpen. Chill until served.
Serves 4

SAUCY HOT-FUDGE PUDDING

1 cup all-purpose flour
1½ cups sugar, divided
2 tsp. baking powder
¼ tsp. salt
½ cup melted butter
½ cup **Fry's Cocoa**, divided
½ cup milk
1 tsp. vanilla
½ cup chopped nuts
1½ cups hot water

In a 9″ square cake pan combine flour, ¾ cup of the sugar, baking powder and salt. Blend butter and ¼ cup of the cocoa; add to dry ingredients along with milk and vanilla; mix well with a fork. Combine remaining ¾ cup sugar, ¼ cup cocoa and nuts. Sprinkle over batter. Carefully pour hot water over all; do not stir. Bake in preheated 350°F oven 40-45 minutes. Serve warm with ice cream or whipped cream if desired.
Serves 6

FESTIVE MINCEMEAT TRIFLE

1½ cups **Lynch Olde Style Mincemeat**
1 14-oz. can peach halves
1 3-oz. package vanilla pudding mix
½ lb. golden pound cake
rum or brandy (optional)
1 pint whipping cream, whipped

Warm mincemeat to soften suet and chill. Chop peaches; mix with mincemeat, reserving a few peach pieces for garnish. Prepare vanilla pudding mix according to package directions; cover surface with waxed paper and chill, stirring occasionally. Crumble pound cake and spread half the crumbs in bottom of a 2-quart glass bowl. Sprinkle with peach juice, rum or brandy. Add one layer each of the mincemeat-peach mixture, vanilla pudding and whipped cream using half of each ingredient. Repeat all layers starting with cake crumbs. Garnish with reserved peach pieces and chill several hours or overnight.
Serves 10-12

FRENCH CHOCOLATE MOUSSE

1 envelope unflavored gelatin
3 tbsp. cold water
2 eggs
¼ cup sugar
½ cup **Lynch Chocolate Fudge Topping**
¼ tsp. rum flavoring
⅛ tsp. cinnamon
⅛ tsp. nutmeg
½ pint whipping cream
chopped nuts or grated chocolate to garnish

Combine gelatin and cold water and let stand 5 minutes. Heat over boiling water until dissolved. Cool. Beat eggs with sugar until very thick. Beat in fudge topping, rum flavoring, cinnamon and nutmeg. Beat whipping cream until stiff. Carefully fold in chocolate mixture. Pour into 6 dessert dishes. Garnish with chopped nuts or grated chocolate. Refrigerate before serving.
Serves 6

FROSTY LADYFINGER LOAF

1 3-oz. package unfilled ladyfingers, split
1 cup whipping cream
½ cup **Hershey's Canned Chocolate Syrup**, chilled
1 cup pecan or walnut pieces
½ tsp. vanilla
sweetened whipped cream or topping and fresh or canned fruit to garnish

Line 8½" x 4½" x 2 ⅝" loaf pan with 12 ladyfingers (cutting as needed to fit tightly). Beat whipping cream until stiff peaks form. Gently fold in chocolate syrup, nut pieces and vanilla; pour into prepared loaf pan. Cover; freeze several hours or overnight. To serve, unmold onto chilled plate. Garnish with cream or topping and fruit.
Makes 1 loaf

Frosty Ladyfinger Loaf

VIENNESE FILLO APPLE STRUDEL

½ cup dark seedless raisins
2 tbsp. brandy
2 cups pared, thinly sliced apples
½ cup chopped walnuts
¼ cup granulated sugar
2 tbsp. melted butter
1 tbsp. grated lemon peel
½ tsp. ground cinnamon
½ tsp. vanilla
2 tbsp. melted butter
½ cup fine bread crumbs or **Fillo Flakes**
½ cup apricot preserves
1 tbsp. brandy
6 **Krinos Fillo Leaves**
melted butter and powdered sugar for top of strudel

Soak raisins in 2 tbsp. brandy about 2 hours. Combine raisin mixture, apples, walnuts, granulated sugar, 2 tbsp. melted butter, lemon peel, cinnamon and vanilla in large bowl. Set aside. In a small skillet, melt 2 tbsp. butter and stir in bread crumbs. Cook until browned. In a small saucepan, heat apricot preserves over low heat until hot; stir in 1 tbsp. brandy. Heat oven to 350°F. Layer fillo leaves on kitchen towel, brushing each leaf with melted butter. Spread entire surface with hot apricot mixture; sprinkle with bread crumbs. Spoon apple mixture along longest end of leaves in a 3″ strip, leaving a ½″ border. Using the towel for assistance, lift to roll leaves over filling. This will form a jelly roll. Place strudel on lightly buttered jelly roll pan, 15½″ x 10½″ x 1″, seam-side-down. Brush with butter. Score strudel diagonally, through top few leaves, into 12-15 equal sections. Bake until apples are tender and strudel is brown and crisp, 45-50 minutes. Cool to lukewarm; sprinkle with powdered sugar. Cut into servings.

FASTASTIC CHOCOLATE SYRUP

1½ cups **Fry's Cocoa**
2½ cups sugar
2 cups water
2 tsp. vanilla

Mix cocoa and sugar in a saucepan. Add water. Cook and stir over medium heat until mixture comes to boil. Reduce heat and boil gently 5 minutes; stir occasionally. Cool. Add vanilla. Cover and store in refrigerator. Use for chocolate milk or as a dessert topping.

FUDGEY FROSTY POPS

1 envelope unflavored gelatin
¼ cup water
1½ cups marshmallow cream
1 cup Fastastic Chocolate Syrup *(see above)*
1 cup milk
10 paper cups
10 wooden stir sticks
¼ cup chopped nuts

Sprinkle gelatin over water; let stand 10 minutes to soften. Cook over low heat, stirring constantly, until dissolved; cool. Beat together marshmallow cream and chocolate syrup until smoothly combined. Gradually stir in milk and cooled gelatin. Divide mixture evenly among paper cups. Freeze until partially firm. Insert a wooden stick into center of each. Freeze until firm. To serve, peel off paper cups; dip ends in chopped nuts.
Makes 10 pops

CARIBBEAN BANANAS

4 large bananas
½ cup pineapple juice
⅔ cup **Alpen Mixed Cereal**
¼ cup brown sugar
1 tbsp. butter

Slice bananas in half lengthwise and in half crosswise. Arrange in a well buttered, broiler-proof dish. Combine pineapple juice and Alpen. Spread evenly over bananas. Sprinkle with brown sugar and dot with butter. Place under preheated broiler 5-10 minutes, or until golden brown. Serve with whipped or ice cream.
Serves 4

CHOCO-BANANA CREAM DELIGHT

¾ cup vanilla wafer crumbs
3 tbsp. **Fry's Cocoa**
3 tbsp. icing sugar
3 tbsp. melted butter
1 envelope unflavored gelatin
½ cup granulated sugar
¼ cup **Fry's Cocoa**
1¼ cups milk
1½ medium bananas
1 cup vanilla ice cream

Combine wafer crumbs, 3 tbsp. cocoa and icing sugar in a bowl. Add butter; toss well. Press mixture over bottom of an 8″ square cake pan. Bake in preheated 350°F oven 8-10 minutes; cool. Combine gelatin, granulated sugar and ¼ cup cocoa in a saucepan. Stir in milk. Cook over medium heat, stirring constantly until gelatin is dissolved. Peel and quarter bananas; process in blender until smooth. Add ice cream and banana purée to gelatin mixture; stir until ice cream is melted. Chill until mixture mounds from a spoon. Spread over baked chocolate crust. Chill until set.
Serves 6-8

LEMON CAKE PUDDING

¾ cup granulated sugar
2 tbsp. **Club House Potato Flour**
¼ tsp. salt
1½ tsp. grated lemon rind
¼ cup lemon juice
2 tbsp. vegetable oil
2 eggs, separated
1 cup milk

Combine sugar, potato flour and salt. Stir in lemon rind, lemon juice and vegetable oil. Lightly beat egg yolks; add milk. Add to lemon mixture and mix well. Beat egg whites until stiff peaks form; fold into lemon mixture. Pour into 1-quart baking dish. Place baking dish in larger pan containing 1″ hot water. Bake at 350°F for about 45 minutes or until cake is tender. (Two layers form, cake and pudding). Serve warm or cooled.
Serves 4-6

Rice Apple Crisp

APPLE CRISP

4 cups sliced apples (4 medium)
¾ cup packed brown sugar
½ cup all-purpose flour
½ cup oats
¾ tsp. ground cinnamon
¾ tsp. ground nutmeg
⅓ cup softened butter
⅓ cup **Fillo Flakes**

Heat oven to 375°F. Arrange apples in greased square pan, 8″ x 8″ x 2″. Mix remaining ingredients except for Fillo Flakes. Sprinkle over apples. Then sprinkle Fillo Flakes on top of all ingredients. Bake until topping is golden brown and apples are tender, about 30 minutes. Serve warm and, if desired, with cream or ice cream.

APPLE CRUMBLE

4 cups sliced apples
½ cup sugar
1 tbsp. lemon juice
⅓ cup butter or margarine
1 cup **Alpen Mixed Cereal**

Place sliced apples in buttered baking dish. Sprinkle with sugar and lemon juice. Melt butter in top of double boiler. Stir in Alpen with melted butter, mixing well. Spread mixture evenly over apples. Bake at 350°F for approximately 30 minutes. Serve hot with cream or ice cream.

Rhubarb Crumble: Substitute 4 cups chopped rhubarb for apples.

RICE APPLE CRISP

2 15-oz. cans **Nestlé Ready-to-Serve Rice Pudding**
¼ tsp. cinnamon
1 19-oz. can apple pie filling
½ cup brown sugar
¼ cup flour
¼ cup butter, softened
¼ tsp. cinnamon
½ cup chopped walnuts

Combine first 3 ingredients in an 8″ square baking dish. Blend together remaining ingredients to make a crumb topping. Sprinkle over rice and apple mixture. Bake at 400°F for 30 minutes.

ICE SOUFFLÉ WITH GRAND MARNIER

3 tbsp. water
5 tbsp. **Grand Marnier**
6 ladyfingers
1½ cups sweet cream
3 eggs
6 egg yolks
1 cup plus 2 tbsp. confectioners' sugar, sifted
a few almond halves or candied fruits for garnish

Preparation for the 2-quart soufflé dish: Cut a strip of waxed paper to a width of 2½"-3". Place the paper around the outside of the dish and secure with scotch tape, arranged so that the collar stands about 1½" above the rim. Add 3 tbsp. of the Grand Marnier to the water and soak the ladyfingers in the mixture. Beat the cream until thick and place in the refrigerator. Using a double boiler, heat the eggs, egg yolks and sugar until the mixture is lukewarm, and remove the top pan from the heat and continue to beat until the mixture is cool. Blend in the whipped cream and the remaining 2 tbsp. of Grand Marnier. Pour a layer of this mixture into a 2-quart soufflé dish and alternate with layers of ladyfingers and the mixture. Put the soufflé in the freezer to freeze for at least 4 hours. When ready to serve, decorate with the almonds or candied fruits and remove the paper collar.

GRAND MARNIER TRIFLE

10 ladyfingers
2 tbsp. **Grand Marnier**
3 oranges
2 cups milk
1 oz. prepared custard powder
½ cup sugar
½ cup whipping cream

Break ladyfingers in a large glass dish. Pour the Grand Marnier over them and allow to soak. Peel and break the oranges into segments and add to the dish, reserving a few for decoration. Make the custard, blending together milk, custard powder and sugar. Pour into the dish. Cool and chill in the refrigerator until set. Before serving, top with whipped cream. Garnish with the reserved orange segments.
Serves 6

ORANGE CHOCOLATE MOUSSE

12 oz. semi-sweet chocolate
⅜ cup **Grand Marnier**
2 tsp. vanilla
12 egg whites
pinch of salt
¾ cup superfine sugar
1½ tbsp. finely chopped orange rind
whipped cream, sliced almonds or chocolate curls to garnish

Melt the chocolate over low heat, then allow to cool. Add the Grand Marnier and vanilla and mix thoroughly. Beat the egg whites with the salt until soft peaks form, then slowly add the sugar, continuing to beat until the peaks are very stiff and glossy. Add the orange rind, then fold in the chocolate, gently but thoroughly, making sure that no large areas of white remain. Pour into a 2-quart serving dish and smooth the top with a spatula. Refrigerate the mousse for 2 hours before serving. Before serving, garnish with whipped cream, sliced almonds or chocolate curls.
Makes 12 servings

GRAND-MARNIER-FLAVORED DIPLOMAT

1 cup warm water
4 tbsp. **Grand Marnier**
30 ladyfingers
1 cup orange marmalade
1 cup apricot preserves
1 cup red currant preserves

Prepare overnight. Mix the warm water with 2½ tbsp. of the Grand Marnier. Dip the ladyfingers quickly, one by one, into the Grand Marnier mixture and line the bottom and sides of a 5" mold with enough ladyfingers to cover. Mix the orange marmalade and the apricot preserves together. Fill the ladyfinger-lined-mold with a layer of the preserves and alternate with layers of remaining soaked ladyfingers and the preserves. Finish with a top layer of ladyfingers. Place a plate on the top layer of ladyfingers and place a heavy weight on top of this to press the Diplomat. Put the Diplomat in the refrigerator for several hours, or overnight. Melt the red currant preserves over low heat and add the remaining 1½ tbsp. Grand Marnier. Remove the Diplomat from the mold. Pour the red-currant-Grand-Marnier sauce over it.
Serves 4

ICE CREAM CUP

2 bananas
½ tbsp. **Grand Marnier**
½ cup heavy cream
3 tbsp. confectioners' sugar
1 pint vanilla ice cream
4 pineapple rings
4 maraschino cherries
2 tbsp. **Grand Marnier**

Peel the bananas and cut into thin rounds. Sprinkle with ½ tbsp. of Grand Marnier. Whip the cream and confectioners' sugar until thick. Scoop the ice cream into 4 individual dessert dishes and top with the whipped cream. Place one ring of pineapple on each dish. Place a cherry on top, in the center of each ring. Surround the pineapple with banana slices. Pour the remaining Grand Marnier equally on the 4 dishes.
Serves 4

HOT SOUFFLÉ GRAND MARNIER

1¾ cups milk
5 oz. sugar
¼ cup unsalted butter
¼ cup sifted flour
2½ tbsp. **Grand Marnier**
5 egg yolks, lightly beaten
7 egg whites, beaten until thick

Bring the milk and sugar to a slow boil. Melt the butter and blend it with the flour in a separate saucepan. Slowly pour in the milk, stirring all the time, until a thick creamy consistency is obtained. Remove the saucepan from the heat and add the Grand Marnier and stir in the egg yolks, one by one. Fold in the thickly beaten egg whites. Butter and sugar a 2-quart soufflé dish. Pour in the soufflé mixture. Put into preheated 375°F oven to bake until puffed and golden brown, about 30-45 minutes. Do not open the oven door while baking. Serve immediately.
Serves 4-6

WATERMELON POND

½ medium watermelon, deseeded and scooped into balls
1 20-oz. can lychees, drained
3 pieces **Sharwood's Stem Ginger**, sliced
a few mint leaves and crushed ice to garnish

Arrange watermelon balls, lychees and ginger attractively in scooped out watermelon shell. Serve on crushed ice with leaves.

SAVARIN

¼ cup butter, softened
3 eggs
½ cup sugar
1 cup flour
2 tbsp. fresh cream
1 tsp. baking powder
Syrup:
just under 1 cup water
1 cup sugar
⅓ cup **Grand Marnier**
candied fruit or fresh fruit salad to garnish

Blend the softened butter, eggs and the sugar. Beat for some time. Add the flour all at once. Still beating, fold in the cream and the baking powder. Butter a ring mold and pour in the mixture, which should only half fill the mold. Cook for 30 minutes in medium oven, 350°F. After taking out of the oven, wrap the cake, still in the mold in a clean cloth. Boil the water and sugar for 3-4 minutes. Unwrap the cake and remove from mold. Add the Grand Marnier to the syrup. Cover the cake, which should be very hot, with the very hot syrup. Let cool before serving. The cake can be either decorated with candied fruit or fruit salad in the center hollow.
Serves 4-6

SABAYON

8 egg yolks
⅔ cup sugar
1 tbsp. orange zest
½ cup port
½ cup **Grand Marnier**
½ envelope unflavored gelatin, dissolved in 2 tbsp. water
1 pint heavy cream, whipped
whipped cream to garnish

In the top of a double boiler over simmering, not boiling, water, beat the egg yolks very well. Remove from heat. Add the sugar, orange zest, port and Grand Marnier. Place the top of the double boiler over slightly boiling water and continue beating until the mixture thickens. Transfer the top of the double boiler to a bowl of ice, add the dissolved gelatin, and whisk until cold. Fold in the whipped cream, spoon into individual custard dishes and freeze for several hours. Just before serving, garnish with a dollop of whipped cream.
Serves 6

CHOCOLATE MOUSSE WITH GRAND MARNIER

6 tbsp. strong coffee
¼ cup **Grand Marnier**
1 6-oz. package semi-sweet chocolate bits
¼ cup sugar
2 cups heavy cream
½ tsp. vanilla

Combine coffee, Grand Marnier and chocolate in top of a double boiler. Place over simmering water. Stir until chocolate is melted. Add sugar, continue to stir until very smooth and glossy. Cool. Whip cream with vanilla until very thick. Thoroughly blend chocolate mixture into cream. Spoon into glasses, cover and chill.
Serves 6

GRAND MARNIER CREAM

1¾ cups milk
½ cup confectioners' sugar
4 egg yolks
2½ tbsp. **Grand Marnier**

Over low heat, warm and blend the milk and confectioners' sugar. Beat the egg yolks until lemon colored and pour into the warming milk, stirring constantly. Pour the egg and milk mixture into top of double boiler and cook on moderate heat, stirring all the time until mixture thickens, but do not boil. Add the Grand Marnier and blend into mixture. Pour the Grand Marnier cream into small dessert dishes and allow to cool. Serve chilled.
Serves 4

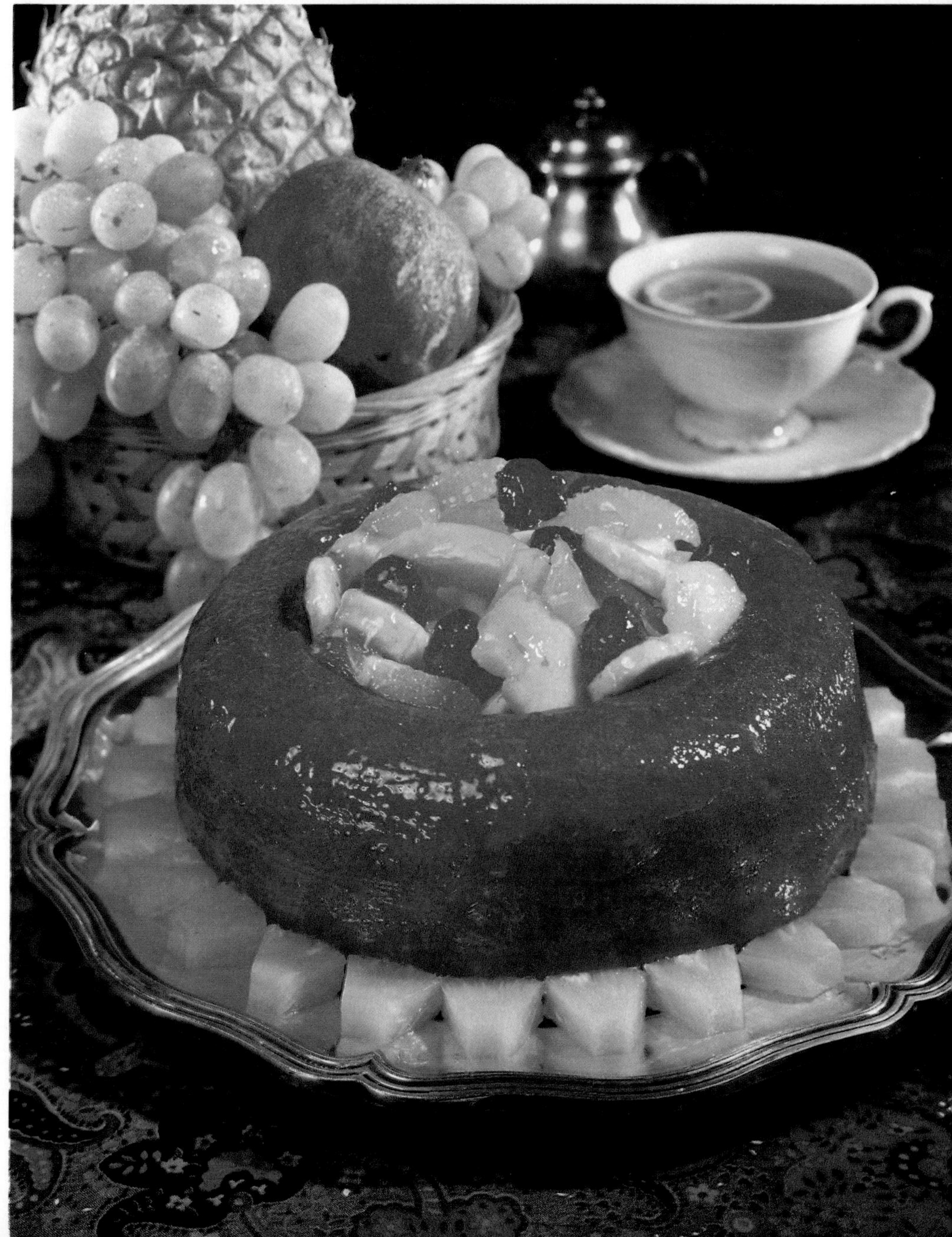

Savarin

MALMAISON CUP

2 seedless oranges
⅓ cup confectioners' sugar
2 tbsp. **Grand Marnier**
1 lb. fresh strawberries

Peel and slice 1 orange, slicing it into rounds. Cut each round in half. Squeeze the juice of the remaining orange; mix the juice with the sugar, and then add the Grand Marnier. Wash the strawberries and remove the hulls. Cut the larger ones in half and place in individual dessert dishes. Pour the Grand-Marnier-flavored orange juice over the strawberries. Garnish with the half slices of oranges.
Serves 4

PEACHES GRAND MARNIER

1 16-oz. can peaches, halved and drained
⅓ cup unsalted butter
⅓ cup confectioners' sugar
3 tbsp. **Grand Marnier**

After draining the syrup from the can, dry each peach half gently with paper towels. Warm the butter in a frypan. Slide in the peaches and heat for 2 minutes on 1 side. Turn over and heat the other side for 2 minutes. Sprinkle sugar over the peaches and continue heating until it browns lightly. Pour the Grand Marnier over the peaches and, when it is hot, ignite the Grand Marnier and serve.
Serves 4-6

SNOWBALL CORDON ROUGE

4 eggs
6 oz. sugar
1 orange
1 cup milk
2 tbsp. **Grand Marnier**

Separate egg yolks from the whites. Beat egg whites to a stiff meringue, adding 3 oz. of the sugar and the juice of the orange. Bring the milk to near boiling. Scoop the meringue, tbsp. by tbsp., into the hot milk; poach for 2 minutes each side. Remove meringues and reserve milk. In a bowl combine yolks, 3 oz. sugar and 2 tbsp. Grand Marnier. Pour reserved hot milk onto mixture; stir thoroughly and return mixture to saucepan. Cook gently until custard coats the back of a spoon. Pour egg custard into a serving dish, place poached meringue on the custard. Chill. Serve very cold, decorated with orange zest. Chill.
Serves 4-6

CRÈME DE GRAND MARNIER MOUSSE

6 egg yolks
2 cups whipping cream
½ cup sugar
2 tsp. vanilla extract
1 cup **Crème de Grand Marnier**

In a double boiler combine egg yolks, half the cream and sugar. Boil constantly mixing until thickened. Cool. Mix in vanilla and Crème de Grand Marnier. Whip the other half of the cream and combine with the mixture. Refrigerate.
Serves 6

FLORIDA CREAM

1 14-oz. can pineapple chunks, drained
1 8-oz. package cream cheese
⅓ cup confectioners' sugar
2 tbsp. **Grand Marnier**
4 maraschino cherries

Set aside a few chunks of pineapple and dice the rest. In a blender, or with electric hand beater, whip the cream cheese and confectioners' sugar. Add the Grand Marnier and the diced pineapple and blend well. Serve in dessert dishes with a garnish of pineapple chunks and the cherries.
Serves 4

Malmaison Cup

PINEAPPLE BAKLAVA

1 20-oz. can crushed pineapple
1 8-oz. package cream cheese, softened
1½ cups ricotta cheese
1½ cups sugar
3 egg yolks
1 tsp. grated lemon peel
1 tsp. vanilla
1 lb. **Krinos Fillo Leaves**
1 cup sweet butter, melted
½ cup water
2 tsp. lemon juice

Drain pineapple and save syrup. In mixer, combine cream cheese, ricotta cheese, ½ cup sugar, egg yolks, lemon peel and vanilla. Blend well together. Stir in drained pineapple. Place a leaf of fillo in a well greased 9" x 12" x 2" pan. Brush with melted butter and repeat with more leaves (about 8). Spoon on the pineapple-cheese mixture and spread evenly. Top with the remaining fillo leaves, brushing each leaf with melted butter as it is layered. Using a sharp knife, score the top of the Baklava into diamond or square shapes. Bake in preheated 375°F oven for 50-60 minutes or until golden brown. Combine reserved pineapple syrup, remaining cup of sugar, ½ cup water and lemon juice. Bring to boil and simmer for 10 minutes. Cool slightly. When Baklava is baked, spoon syrup evenly over top. Cool, then cut at markings.

BEAU RIVAGE CARAMEL CUSTARD

7 oz. sugar
1 tbsp. water
1½ cups milk
4 eggs
2½ tbsp. **Grand Marnier**

Heat half the sugar with the water and when the sugar turns brown, pour the caramel into 4 molds (each about 5 oz.). Boil the milk and pour into the eggs beaten with the remaining sugar, add ½ tbsp. Grand Marnier and fill the 4 molds. Place the molds in a pan of water in a medium oven for 20 minutes. Allow to cool and place in refrigerator. Turn custard out of molds. Pour remaining Grand Marnier over them before serving.
Serves 4

BANANA SPLIT

1 banana, peeled and cut lengthwise
2 scoops vanilla ice cream
1 oz. **Crème de Grand Marnier**
chopped almonds
dried apricots or orange peel
whipped cream, orange slice and maraschino cherry to garnish

Top the banana with ice cream. Pour Crème de Grand Marnier over top and sprinkle with almonds and apricots or orange peel. Decorate with whipped cream, orange slice and cherry.
Serves 1

APPLES ARDECHOISE STYLE

4 baking apples
8 chestnuts in syrup (or marron glacé)
2½ tbsp. **Grand Marnier**
1 cup chestnut spread
(not purée de marrons)

Peel and core the apples. Place a chestnut over each cavity. Place apples in buttered and sugared baking dish. Cook in 425°F oven, until apples are baked throughout. Mix the Grand Marnier with the chestnut spread and decorate the dish with this mixture, adding the 4 remaining chestnuts for garnish.
Serves 4

Apples Ardechoise Style

APRICOT PARFAIT

1 lb. cooked apricots, stones removed (or canned apricots, syrup drained and reserved)

3½ oz. cream cheese

7 tbsp. confectioners' sugar

¾ cup whipping cream

2½ tbsp. **Grand Marnier**

Set the temperature in freezer compartment at lowest temperature. Reserve 10 apricot halves and put the rest of the apricots into a blender to purée. Beat the purée with the cream cheese, the sugar and the cream until light and smooth. Pour the mixture into an ice-cream mold and put into the freezer for 3 hours. In a saucepan, boil the apricot syrup for 2 minutes and remove saucepan from the heat. Add the Grand Marnier and stir well. Remove the parfait from the mold. Decorate with the reserved apricot halves. Pour the Grand Marnier syrup over the parfait.
Serves 4

FRESH AND FRUITY DIP

2 cups plain low-fat yogurt

2 tbsp. **KRAFT Liquid Honey**

½ envelope **CRYSTAL LIGHT Orange, Lemonade** or **Berry Blend Low Calorie Drink Mix**

Mix yogurt, honey and drink mix in small bowl; chill. Serve with or over fresh fruit.
Makes 2 cups

BAKED BRIE

2 **KRAFT INTERNATIONALE Brie**

2 tbsp. **KRAFT Apricot Jam**

2 tbsp. toasted sliced almonds

sliced French stick

Slice top skin off Brie. Place on baking sheet. Spread jam over cheese; sprinkle with almonds. Bake at 300°F for 12-14 minutes. Serve hot on French stick.
Serves 4

PRIVILÈGE AU GRAND MARNIER

5 oz. butter

5 eggs

⅝ cup confectioners' sugar

¾ cup freshly ground almonds

¼ cup sifted flour

1½ tbsp. **Grand Marnier**

Decoration:

½ cup sifted confectioners' sugar (blended with 1 tbsp. milk and ⅛ tsp. almond extract)

½ tbsp. water

2 tbsp. **Grand Marnier**

a few almonds

10 maraschino cherries

Melt the butter. Separate the egg yolks from whites. Mix the yolks with 7 tbsp. of the confectioners' sugar until a creamy white consistency is obtained. Blend in the ground almonds, melted butter and flour. Beat the egg whites with 3 tbsp. of the sugar until thick, and fold into the cream mixture by gently raising the cream from the bottom of the mixing bowl to the top. Butter a baking mold, pour the batter in and place in a 375°F preheated oven. Bake for 30 minutes. Remove from the mold. Allow to cool and sprinkle the 1½ tbsp. of Grand Marnier over the cake. To prepare decoration: Mix the confectioners' icing, water and Grand Marnier. Spread smoothly over the top of the cake with the blade of a knife and decorate with almonds and cherries.
Serves 4-6

GLACE NEGRESCO

12 egg yolks

¾ cup sugar

1 quart milk

3 tbsp. instant espresso coffee

⅓ cup **Grand Marnier**

Combine the egg yolks and sugar in a heavy saucepan and beat until well blended. Bring the milk to boil and slowly pour into the egg-yolk mixture. Cook over low heat, stirring constantly, until thick and will coat the spoon when lifted. Remove from the heat and cool. Dissolve the coffee in the Grand Marnier and add to the egg-yolk mixture. Pour into the container of an ice-cream freezer and freeze. Serve with a chocolate sauce, if desired.
Makes 2 quarts

Privilège au Grand Marnier

CHOCOLATE BOMBE

¾ cup rice
2 cups milk
1 package unflavored gelatin, dissolved in ¼ cup water
1 tsp. vanilla
pinch salt
2 tbsp. orange zest
½ cup sugar
¼ cup **Grand Marnier**
3 eggs, separated

Chocolate Cream:

4 oz. confectioners' sugar
1 tsp. arrowroot
4 egg yolks
½ cup milk
½ cup cream
1 tbsp. **Grand Marnier**
1 oz. semi-sweet chocolate, melted
2 oz. unsweetened chocolate, melted
½ cup whipping cream, whipped, to garnish

Butter the bottom and sides of a 1½-quart round mold. Put the rice in a saucepan with water to cover. Bring to boil and boil for 5 minutes. Drain. Return the rice to the pan. Bring the milk to boil and pour over the rice. Add the gelatin, vanilla, salt, orange zest, sugar and Grand Marnier. Simmer over low heat, covered, for 45 minutes or until the rice is creamy and no longer grainy. Lightly beat the egg yolks and fold into the rice. Beat the egg whites until you have firm peaks. Fold them in and pour into the prepared mold. Refrigerate for 4-5 hours or until set. Remove from the refrigerator and rub the bottom and sides of the mold with a hot cloth, or dip the mold into hot water for 5 seconds. Invert and unmold onto a serving plate. Prepare the chocolate cream by combining the sugar, arrowroot and egg yolks in a saucepan. Beat with a wooden spatula until well blended. Bring the milk and cream to boil and pour into the yolk mixture. Stir over low heat until thickened. Add the Grand Marnier and chocolate and beat until smooth and creamy. Spread the chocolate cream over the molded rice rather thickly. When ready to serve garnish with a wreath of whipped cream using a pastry bag fitted with a #7 rosette tip.

Serves 6-8

PROFITEROLES MARQUISE

4 eggs
⅝ cup confectioners' sugar
¼ cup flour
1¾ cup milk
3 tbsp. **Grand Marnier**
16 small baked pastry balls
¼ cup sweet cream
½ cup dark chocolate, broken into pieces
slivered, blanched almonds to garnish

Mix the eggs, sugar and flour in a saucepan, over low heat. Add the milk gradually. Warm gently, stirring all the time, allow to boil for 1 minute. Remove from heat and allow to cool. Add 2 tbsp. of the Grand Marnier. Split the pastry balls half way through. Spoon 1 tsp. of the cream mixture into each pastry. In double boiler, boil the sweet cream and blend in broken pieces of the chocolate. When chocolate is melted into cream and well mixed, add the remaining 1 tbsp. of Grand Marnier and blend. Pile the filled pastry balls on a dish into a high mound. Cover with the hot chocolate sauce, sprinkle with the almonds and serve.

Serves 4-6

HOMEY CHEDDAR APPLE CRISP

6-8 large apples, cored, peeled and sliced
2 tbsp. lemon juice
½ cup brown sugar
2 tbsp. all-purpose flour
½ tsp. cinnamon
½ tsp. nutmeg
½ tsp. allspice
¾ cup large flake rolled oats
¾ cup brown sugar
¼ cup **PARKAY Margarine** or butter, melted
½ cup chopped nuts (optional)
1 cup grated **CRACKER BARREL Cheddar Cheese**

Combine apples, lemon juice, ½ cup brown sugar, flour and spices. Place mixture in greased 11" x 7" x 1½" baking dish or 6 individual baking dishes. Blend oats, ¾ cup brown sugar, margarine and nuts to make a crumbly mixture. Sprinkle over apple mixture. Bake at 350°F for 30 minutes. Sprinkle cheese over topping and bake 10 minutes more or until apples are soft and topping is golden.

Serves 6

Profiteroles Marquise

PRALINE PUMPKIN CUSTARDS

2 eggs, beaten
2/3 cup granulated sugar
1 cup canned pumpkin
1/4 tsp. salt
1/2 tsp. ground cinnamon
1/4 tsp. ground ginger
1/4 tsp. ground nutmeg
1 13½-oz. can undiluted **Carnation Evaporated Milk**
2 tbsp. melted butter
1/2 cup packed brown sugar
1/3 cup chopped nuts

Combine eggs, sugar, pumpkin, salt, spices and evaporated milk. Pour into 6 6-oz. custard cups. Place in pan about 2½" deep. Pour 1" hot water around custard cups. Bake in preheated 350°F oven about 35-40 minutes or until knife inserted in center comes out clean. Combine melted butter, brown sugar and nuts. Sprinkle evenly over baked custards. Broil until bubbly, about 1 minute. Serve warm or chilled.
Serves 6

CANDY CANE PARFAITS

1 envelope **Dream Whip Dessert Topping Mix**
1¼ lb. cream cheese, softened
1/4 cup sugar
1 tsp. vanilla
1 4-serving-size package **JELL-O Raspberry Jelly Powder**
1¼ cups boiling water
3 tbsp. sugar
2½ cups unsweetened individually frozen raspberries

Prepare dessert topping as directed on package. Beat cream cheese, ¼ cup sugar and vanilla until soft and smooth. Fold cream-cheese mixture into prepared dessert topping. Dissolve jelly powder in boiling water. Add remaining 3 tbsp. sugar and raspberries and stir until berries separate and jelly begins to thicken. Alternately layer dessert topping mixture and jelly mixture into parfait glasses or dessert dishes. Chill about 1 hour.
Serves 4

PINEAPPLE DELIGHT

2½ cups **McCormick's Graham Cracker Crumbs** (reserve ¼ cup for top)
1/2 cup soft butter or margarine
1/2 cup butter or margarine
1¼ cups icing sugar
2 eggs, unbeaten
1/2 pint whipping cream
1 14-oz. can crushed pineapple, well drained

Mix first 2 ingredients well. Press into 13" x 9" pan. Bake 15 minutes in 300°F oven. Cream next 3 ingredients together. Beat well. Spread over cooled crumb mixture. Beat whipping cream until stiff, then add pineapple. Spread over mixture in pan. Top with remaining ¼ cup graham-cracker crumbs. Store in refrigerator until ready to serve.

GALATORBOUREKO

8 cups milk
6-7 eggs
1½ cups farina (semolina)
2 cups sugar
1 tsp. vanilla flavoring (or 2 tbsp. grated orange rind)
pinch of salt
1/4 lb. **Krinos Fillo Leaves**
1 cup sweet butter, melted
Syrup:
3 cups sugar
3 cups water

Heat milk. Beat eggs well in bowl. Add farina, sugar, vanilla and pinch of salt. Pour 2 cups of hot milk, little by little, into mixture. Pour all the above into saucepan with the hot milk, stirring constantly until thick. In a buttered 9" x 13" pan, lay half the number of fillo leaves, buttering each as it is stacked. Spread the above mixture over all. Add the balance of the fillo, buttering each leaf as it is added. Score with sharp knife to desired size and shape. Bake in preheated 375°F oven for 45 minutes or until golden brown. While it is baking, prepare the syrup so it can be poured on as soon as pie is removed from oven. To prepare syrup: Dissolve sugar in water. Bring to boil. Boil for 20 minutes. Be careful not to burn the sugar solution. Allow pie to absorb syrup a little at a time. Let cool and cut before serving.

BREAD PUDDING ROYALE

3 English muffins, split
3 tbsp. butter or margarine, softened
1 13-oz. jar **Chambord Preserves**
6 eggs
1½ cups milk
1 cup whipping cream
1 tsp. vanilla
powdered sugar
Chambord Sauce:
3/4 cup **Chambord Black Raspberry Liqueur**
Chambord Preserves
3 tbsp. lemon juice
1 tbsp. cornstarch

Lightly toast muffin halves; spread with butter while warm. Spread 1½ tbsp. preserves on each half and cut into quarters; set aside. Preheat oven to 375°F. In bowl, combine next 4 ingredients. Beat to blend thoroughly, then pour into shallow 1½ to 2-quart baking dish. Arrange muffin quarters on top of egg mixture, preserves-sides-up. Set baking dish in larger shallow pan. Pour boiling water into pan to half the height of baking dish. Bake in center of oven 40-50 minutes, just until custard is set and knife inserted into center comes out clean. Cool. Meanwhile, prepare Chambord Sauce: In a 1-quart saucepan combine ¾ cup Chambord Liqueur and the preserves remaining from the pudding recipe; bring to a simmer, stirring to melt preserves. In a small bowl, mix the lemon juice with the cornstarch; stir into Chambord mixture. Simmer and stir 2-3 minutes until slightly thickened. Cool 5-10 minutes before serving. (If necessary, reheat sauce over low heat, stirring constantly.) Dust pudding with powdered sugar. Spoon warm pudding into dessert dishes. Pass warm Chambord Sauce separately.
Serves 8

PEANUT BUTTER ICE-CREAM SAUCE

3/4 cup **Skippy Super Chunk** or **Creamy Peanut Butter**
1/2 cup **Crown Brand** or **Karo Corn Syrup**
2 tbsp. butter
1 tsp. ground ginger
1 tbsp. lemon juice
ice cream

Stir all ingredients together in small saucepan. Heat over low heat 5 minutes. Serve over ice cream.

CAFÉ AU LAIT CHOCOLATE CUPS

Chocolate Cups:

8 squares **BAKER'S Semi-Sweet Chocolate**

Filling:

1 6-serving-size package **JELL-O Vanilla Pudding and Pie Filling**

2½ cups milk

1 tsp. **MAXWELL HOUSE Instant Coffee** granules

½ cup sour cream

1 tbsp. sherry or orange liqueur

maraschino cherries or grated chocolate

For chocolate cups, chop each square of semi-sweet chocolate into 8 pieces. Melt in bowl over hot, not boiling, water until ⅓ is still unmelted. Remove from water and stir until completely melted. Place 10 large aluminum foil baking cups in muffin pan. Using a teaspoon, spread chocolate mixture inside the cups, covering entire surface. Chill until firm. Carefully peel off foil. (Can be made ahead and kept refrigerated.) For filling, prepare pudding with milk as directed on package and add instant coffee granules. Cool, stirring occasionally, for 5 minutes. Stir in sour cream and sherry. Place plastic wrap on surface of pudding and chill for 30-40 minutes or until cool. Stir pudding and fill chocolate cups. Chill 2 hours or until serving time. Garnish with maraschino cherries or sprinkle with grated chocolate, if desired. (Chocolate cups can be prepared in miniature foil cups too.)
Serves 10

CINNAMON APPLE CRISP

6 cups peeled and sliced apples (or 2 19-oz. cans apple pie slices)

1 cup **Quaker Oats**, uncooked

½ cup firmly packed brown sugar

⅓ cup all-purpose flour

⅓ cup melted butter or margarine

1 tsp. cinnamon

½ tsp. salt

Spoon apples into 8″ x 8″ square baking dish. Combine remaining ingredients, mixing until crumbly. Sprinkle crumb mixture over apples. Bake in preheated 350°F oven about 30 minutes.

Cinnamon Peach Crisp: Substitute 6 cups sweetened fresh peach slices or 2 28-oz. cans drained peach slices, for apple slices.
Serves 6-8

Berries on a Cloud

BERRIES ON A CLOUD

2 cups strawberries, sliced, or 1 package frozen strawberries, thawed (omit sugar)

2 tbsp. icing sugar

1 tbsp. brandy (optional)

1 tbsp. orange liqueur (optional)

6 slices angel food or sponge cake

2 cups **COOL WHIP Whipped Topping**, thawed

Combine strawberries, sugar, brandy and liqueur. Toast cake slices under broiler until lightly browned. Place cake slices on individual serving plates. Top each with strawberries and whipped topping.
Serves 6

YOGURT FRUIT FLUFF

1 4-serving-size package **JELL-O Lemon or Peach Jelly Powder**

1 cup plain yogurt or sour cream

2 cups **COOL WHIP Whipped Topping**, thawed

2 cups fruit pieces: fresh melon, strawberries, raspberries, blueberries and mandarin oranges

Add dry jelly powder to yogurt and stir until well blended, about 1 minute. Fold topping into mixture. Layer with or fold in fruit. For fluffy dessert, serve immediately. For set texture, chill 30 minutes.
Serves 6

Chocolate Wafer Log

CHOCOLATE WAFER LOG

¾ cup cold milk
1 envelope **Dream Whip Dessert Topping Mix**
2 tbsp. sugar
½ tsp. peppermint or almond extract
7 oz. chocolate wafer cookies
chocolate curls, grated chocolate or candied cherries to garnish

Blend milk, dessert-topping mix, sugar and flavoring in deep narrow-bottom bowl. Prepare dessert topping as directed on package. Spread about 1 tbsp. dessert topping on each cookie and stack in groups of 6 cookies. Place cookie stacks end to end on a serving plate to form a log. Frost top and sides with remaining dessert topping. Decorate with chocolate curls, grated chocolate or candied cherries. Chill at least 4 hours. To serve, cut into diagonal slices. Refrigerate any leftover dessert.
Serves 8

CHOCOLATE MOUSSE

7½ squares **Baker's Semi-Sweet Chocolate**, melted and cooled
3 eggs
3 tbsp. icing sugar
1 cup whipping cream
½ square **Baker's Semi-Sweet Chocolate**, melted and cooled
rose leaves to garnish

Combine 7½ squares chocolate, 1 whole egg and 2 egg yolks; mix well. Beat 2 egg whites until foamy. Add icing sugar and beat until stiff shiny peaks form. Beat whipping cream until stiff peaks form. Fold into egg whites. Carefully fold chocolate mixture into egg-white mixture. Pour into 4-cup serving dish or individual dishes. Chill 3 hours. Use remaining ½ square to coat 4 rose leaves for garnish.

CRÈME CÉLESTE

1½ tsp. plain gelatin
3 tbsp. cold water
1 cup milk
½ cup sugar
1 cup sour cream
1 envelope **Dream Whip Dessert Topping Mix**
2 tbsp. brandy
1 small package frozen raspberries, thawed

Add gelatin to cold water to soften. Combine ½ cup milk, gelatin and sugar in a saucepan. Cook and stir over low heat until gelatin and sugar are dissolved. Cool. Add sour cream and beat until mixture is smooth. Prepare dessert-topping mix with remaining ½ cup milk as directed on package. Fold brandy and sour-cream mixture into whipped topping. Pour into a 1-quart mold. Chill until firm, about 4 hours. Unmold. Spoon raspberries over each serving.
Serves 6-8

STRAWBERRY SMOOTHIE

1 4-serving-size package **JELL-O Strawberry Jelly Powder** (or your favorite red flavor)

2 cups **COOL WHIP Whipped Topping**, thawed

sliced strawberries and whipped topping to garnish

Prepare jelly powder as directed on package using Quick Set Method. Blend into whipped topping with a wire whisk. Pour mixture into individual molds or dishes. Chill until set. To unmold, dip in very hot water for 10 seconds and invert onto serving plate. Garnish with sliced strawberries and whipped topping.
Serves 6

LIME TIME

1 4-serving-size package **JELL-O Lime Jelly Powder**

1 cup seedless green grapes, halved

½ cup sour cream or plain yogurt

Dissolve jelly powder as directed on package using Quick Set Method. Measure 1 cup of jelly into bowl; stir in grapes. Fold sour cream into remaining jelly. Spoon half of the fruit jelly into dessert dishes. Pour the creamy jelly on top. Chill for 10 minutes. Spoon remaining fruited jelly over creamy layer. Chill until set, about 30 minutes.
Serves 6

ORANGES TO GO

4 large oranges

1 4-serving-size package **JELL-O Orange Jelly Powder**

1 cup boiling water

2 cups vanilla ice cream

Cut oranges in half. Remove fruit from each half. Scrape shells clean with a sharp spoon. Chop fruit, removing membrane, and set aside. Dissolve jelly powder in boiling water. Add ice cream by spoonfuls, stirring until smooth. Fold in chopped fruit. Chill until mixture will mound. Spoon into orange shells. Chill until set, about 30 minutes.
Serves 4

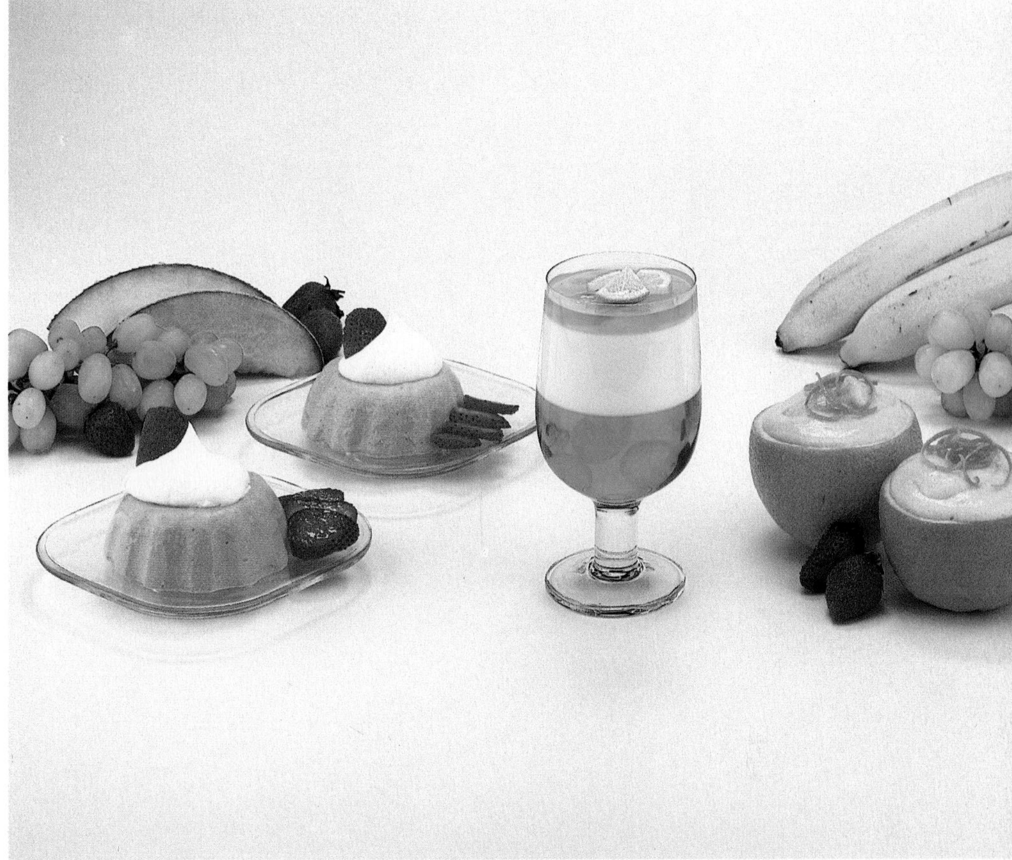

Strawberry Smoothie (left), Lime Time (center) and Oranges to Go

TRUFFLES ROYALE

⅓ cup whipping cream

2 tbsp. butter

2 tbsp. sugar

¼ tsp. vanilla

4 squares **Baker's Semi-Sweet Chocolate**, coarsely chopped

¾ cup chocolate or vanilla wafer crumbs or tinted or toasted coconut for coating

Combine cream, butter and sugar in a double boiler. Heat on high until cream just comes to a boil. Turn down heat and add vanilla and chocolate and continue to heat until chocolate is melted. Chill mixture until firm enough to handle, about 3-4 hours. Drop by teaspoonfuls into desired coating. Roll into balls. Store chilled in airtight container. If you prefer, you can coat these truffles in melted chocolate. Partially melt 4 squares of Baker's Semi-Sweet Chocolate over hot water; remove from heat and stir to finish melting. Then place chocolate over saucepan of lukewarm water (approx. 88°F). Dip chilled truffles in chocolate; place on waxed-paper-lined tray. Chill to set chocolate.
Makes about 2 dozen truffles

BANANA CRÈME DELUXE

1 4-serving-size package **JELL-O Vanilla Pudding and Pie Filling**

¼ cup firmly packed brown sugar

1 tbsp. butter or margarine

¼ cup water

1 tbsp. dark rum

½ tsp. vanilla

3 medium bananas

½ cup sour cream

Prepare pudding-and-pie-filling mix as directed on package. Cover surface of pudding with plastic wrap; chill. Combine brown sugar and butter in saucepan. Stir until butter melts and sugar is dissolved. Gradually add water, rum and vanilla; bring to boil. Continue boiling for 2 minutes. Remove from heat. Slice bananas diagonally in ½" slices. Add to hot syrup mixture and toss lightly. Add sour cream to pudding and beat until smooth. Spoon banana mixture into dessert dishes; top with pudding. Chill until serving time.
Serves 6

CHOCOLATE JUBILEE

1 4-serving-size package **JELL-O Chocolate Pudding and Pie Filling**

2 cups milk

2 tbsp. rum, brandy or fruit liqueur (optional)

1 19-oz. can cherry pie filling

Prepare pudding-and-pie-filling mix with milk following directions on the package. Cover surface of hot pudding with plastic wrap; cool 15 minutes. Stir well. Stir in rum. Spoon ⅓ cup cherry pie filling into 4 dessert dishes. Spoon pudding on top of cherry pie filling. Serve warm.
Serves 4

RASPBERRY CHANTILLY PARFAIT

1 4-serving-size package **JELL-O Vanilla Pudding and Pie Filling**

1 4-serving-size package **JELL-O Raspberry Jelly Powder**

2 cups water

1 envelope **Dream Whip Dessert Topping Mix**

1 cup fresh raspberries

sliced almonds for garnish (optional)

Combine pudding-and-pie-filling mix, jelly powder and water in saucepan. Cook and stir over medium heat until mixture comes to a full bubbling boil. Remove from heat; chill about 3 hours or until mixture is thickened. Prepare dessert-topping mix as directed on package; fold in chilled pudding mixture. Layer with raspberries in parfait glasses or dessert dishes. Decorate with sliced almonds, if desired.
Serves 6

STRAWBERRY SWIZZLE

1 4-serving-size package **JELL-O Jelly Powder** (any flavor)

assorted fruit pieces

Prepare jelly powder as directed on package using Quick Set Method. Arrange fruit on toothpicks for kebabs. Spoon slightly thickened jelly into dessert dishes. Partially insert fruit kebabs into jelly. Chill for 30 minutes.
Serves 4

Chocolate Jubilee (top)
Strawberry Swizzle (bottom)

FRUIT MEDLEY

1 4-serving-size package **JELL-O Lime Jelly Powder** (or your favorite flavor)

1½ cups fresh fruit (orange sections, sliced strawberries, blueberries, banana slices or melon cubes)

Dissolve jelly powder as directed on package using Quick Set Method. Pour into pan. Chill until set. Cut jelly into cubes. Alternately spoon jelly cubes and fruit into parfait dishes.
Serves 6

BANANAS ROYALE

1 4-serving-size package **JELL-O Orange Jelly Powder**

1 cup boiling water

1 cup ice cubes

1 medium banana, sliced

1 cup vanilla ice cream

1 tbsp. dark rum

Dissolve jelly powder in boiling water. Measure ½ cup of the jelly into another bowl and add ice cubes. Stir until the jelly begins to thicken; remove any unmelted ice. Stir banana into slightly thickened jelly. Spoon mixture into dessert dishes. Chill. Stir ice cream by spoonfuls into the remaining jelly. Blend until smooth. Add rum. Spoon over the fruited jelly layer.
Serves 6

STRAWBERRY CAKEWALK

Filling:

1 lb. cream cheese, softened

1 cup sugar

2 tsp. lemon juice

2 tsp. vanilla

2 envelopes **Dream Whip Dessert Topping Mix**

1 4-serving-size package **JELL-O Strawberry Jelly Powder**

2 cups fresh strawberries, halved

Crust:

1¼ cups graham wafer crumbs

¼ cup sugar

¼ cup melted butter or margarine

To prepare crust: Combine crumbs, sugar and melted butter. Press firmly on bottom of a 9" springform pan. Chill. For filling: Blend cream cheese and sugar until smooth and fluffy. Stir in lemon juice and vanilla. Prepare dessert-topping mix as directed on package; fold in cheese mixture. Pour into crust. Chill at least 4 hours. Prepare jelly powder as directed on package using Quick Set Method reducing ice cubes to 1½ cups. Spoon half of the jelly over cheesecake. Arrange berries in a decorative pattern on top and spoon remaining jelly over berries. Chill until set, about 3 hours.
Serves 8-10

Fruit Medley (left), Bananas Royale (center) and Strawberry Cakewalk

CROWN JEWEL DESSERT

1 4-serving-size package **JELL-O Orange Jelly Powder**

1 4-serving-size package **JELL-O Strawberry Jelly Powder**

1 4-serving-size package **JELL-O Lime Jelly Powder**

1 4-serving-size package **JELL-O Lemon Jelly Powder**

1 cup boiling water

½ cup canned pineapple juice

1½ cups graham wafer crumbs

⅓ cup melted butter or margarine

2 envelopes **Dream Whip Dessert Topping**, prepared as directed on package

Prepare the orange, strawberry and lime jelly powders separately, as directed on package, reducing cold water addition to ½ cup for each. Pour each into a separate 8" square pan. Chill until firm, about 3 hours or overnight. Cut into ½" cubes. Dissolve lemon jelly powder in boiling water; stir in pineapple juice. Chill until slightly thickened. Mix together crumbs and melted butter; press into bottom of 9" springform pan. Chill. Fold prepared dessert topping into slightly thickened lemon jelly. Fold in jelly cubes. Spoon over crumb crust. Chill until firm, about 4 hours or overnight.
Serves 12

Holiday Ring Mold

HOLIDAY RING MOLD

1 6-serving-size package **JELL-O Jelly Powder** (any red flavor)
2 cups boiling water
1 cup cold water
¼ tsp. cinnamon (optional)
⅛ tsp. ground cloves (optional)
1 14-oz. can peach slices, drained
½ cup seedless green grapes, halved
½ cup orange sections
½ cup pecan halves
2 cups **COOL WHIP Whipped Topping**, thawed

Dissolve jelly powder in boiling water. Add cold water. Pour ¾ cup into a 4 or 5-cup ring mold. Chill until partially set around edge, about 30 minutes. Add spices to remaining jelly and chill until slightly thickened. Meanwhile arrange some of the fruit and nuts in a decorative pattern on partially set jelly and press down gently, almost to bottom of mold. Chill until set but not firm. Fold remaining fruits and nuts into thickened jelly and spoon into mold. Chill until firm, about 4 hours. Unmold. To serve fill center with whipped topping.
Serves 8-10

TIPSY SQUIRE

1½ cups milk
3 tbsp. sweet sherry wine
1 4-serving-size **JELL-O Vanilla Instant Pudding**
6 ladyfingers, split
(or 12 3″ x 1″ sponge-cake strips)
⅔ cup **Baker's Angel Flake Coconut**, toasted
½ cup slivered almonds, toasted
1 14-oz. can sliced peaches or apricots, drained
2 kiwi fruit, peeled and sliced

Combine milk and sherry. Add pudding mix. Prepare according to package directions. Break ladyfingers into bite-sized pieces and place in serving bowl. Cover with alternate layers of coconut, almonds, peaches, kiwi and pudding, ending with a layer of coconut. Chill.
Serves 8

HOMEMADE APRICOT ICE CREAM

1 jar **Emelia French Apricot Preserve with Napoleon Brandy**
½ pint whipping cream
1 cup milk
1 tbsp. brandy
apricot halves
Emelia Pineapple and Apricot Preserve or **Emelia Plum and Orange Gourmet Sauce with Pecans** to garnish
fresh stemmed cherry to garnish

Add preserve, whipping cream and milk to processing container of ice cream maker. Process until ice cream is very thick. Remove paddle. Fold in brandy and freeze for at least 2 hours. Serve on apricot halves with Pineapple and Apricot Preserve as a sauce, or Plum and Orange Gourmet Sauce with Pecans. Garnish with cherry.
Serves 10-12

PEARS AU CHOCOLAT

Pears:
6 pears, peeled, halved and cored
⅓ cup fresh orange juice
1 tsp. grated orange rind
¼ cup firmly packed brown sugar
2 tbsp. butter or margarine
¼ cup water

Chocolate Sauce:
1 4-serving-size package **JELL-O Chocolate Pudding and Pie Filling**
½ cup sugar
1 cup water
2 tbsp. butter or margarine

To prepare pears: In a large shallow pan cover pears with orange juice, rind, sugar, butter and water. Simmer over low heat until tender, about 10-15 minutes. Remove pears from pan; bring remaining liquid to a boil over high heat and continue boiling until syrupy. Pour over pears. To prepare sauce: Combine pudding-and-pie-filling mix, sugar and water. Cook and stir over medium heat, until mixture comes to a full bubbling boil. Stir in butter. Spoon warm sauce over pears.
Serves 6

Peach Raspberry Melba

PEANUT BUTTER TRUFFLES

3 squares semi-sweet chocolate
½ cup **Skippy Creamy Peanut Butter**
¼ cup icing sugar
¼ cup ground almonds
1 tbsp. cream or almond liqueur
2 squares semi-sweet chocolate (or ½ cup icing sugar)

Melt 3 squares of chocolate in bowl over boiling water. Stir in peanut butter, ¼ cup icing sugar, almonds, and cream or almond liqueur. Shape into small balls. Dip balls in remaining 2 squares melted chocolate or roll in icing sugar instead. Place on waxed paper on plate in refrigerator while chocolate hardens. If rolling in icing sugar, roll once, set in refrigerator for 1 hour, then roll in icing sugar again. Store truffles covered in refrigerator.

Makes 24

PEACH RASPBERRY MELBA

1 6-serving-size package **JELL-O Peach Jelly Powder**
2 cups boiling water
2 cups vanilla ice cream
1 small package frozen raspberries, partially thawed
1 14-oz. can sliced peaches, drained

Dissolve jelly powder in boiling water. Measure 1 cup; set aside. Spoon ice cream into remaining jelly, stir until smooth. Spoon ice-cream mixture into parfait glasses or dessert dishes. Chill for 15 minutes. Meanwhile, add partially frozen raspberries to remaining jelly and stir until berries separate and jelly begins to thicken. Add peaches and spoon into glasses. Chill until set, about 15 minutes.

Serves 8

FROZEN PUDDING SANDWICHES

1½ cups milk
½ cup **KRAFT Peanut Butter**
1 4-serving-size package **JELL-O Chocolate Instant Pudding** or your favorite flavor
24 chocolate wafers or your favorite cookies

Add milk gradually to peanut butter in deep narrow-bottom bowl, blending until smooth. Add pudding mix. Beat slowly at lowest speed of electric mixer until well blended, about 2 minutes. Let stand 5 minutes. Spread filling about ½″ thick on 12 of the cookies. Top with remaining cookies, pressing lightly. Smooth around edges with spatula. Freeze until firm, about 3 hours.

Makes 12 sandwiches

PEARS IN WHITE CUSTARD SAUCE

1 28-oz. can pear halves
½ cup dry white wine
1 egg yolk
1 tbsp. lemon juice
1 tsp. lemon rind
⅓ cup **Veloutine Light**
½ cup whipping cream
2 tbsp. toasted almonds

Drain pears reserving 1 cup of juice. In small saucepan combine reserved pear juice, wine, egg yolk, lemon juice and rind; beat well with egg beater or whisk. Bring to boil; sprinkle in Veloutine, stirring constantly. Boil 1 minute. Cool and then cover the surface with plastic wrap. Chill. Just before serving, whip cream and fold into chilled sauce. Divide mixture evenly among dessert dishes. Place pears in custard. Garnish with almonds.
Serves 4-6

Fruit Topped Eggnog Ring

RHUBARB CRISP

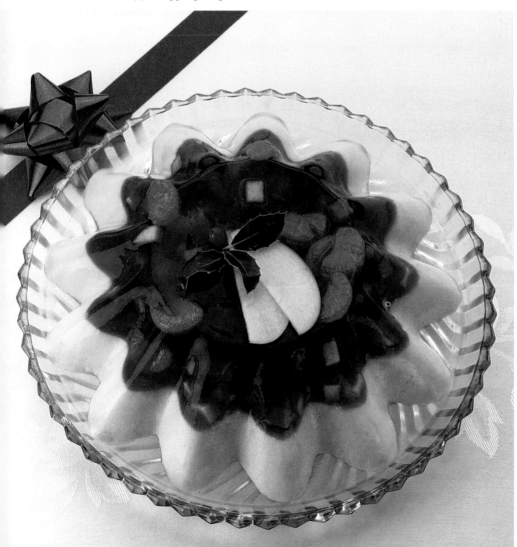

5 cups rhubarb (or other fruits like apples or peaches)
1 cup sugar
2 tbsp. minute tapioca
½ cup flour
pinch salt
1 tsp. cinnamon
½ cup rolled oats
¾ cup brown sugar
⅓ cup butter
1 cup **Delisle Plain Yogurt**
2 tbsp. icing sugar
½ tsp. vanilla

Wash rhubarb and cut into ¾" pieces. Add sugar and tapioca. Pour into a buttered 2-quart baking dish. Combine flour, salt, cinnamon, rolled oats and brown sugar. Add butter and blend. Spread over rhubarb. Bake at 375°F about 45 minutes. Mix yogurt, icing sugar and vanilla. Mix in blender, then chill. Serve rhubarb crisp hot with the yogurt sauce.
Serves 8

FRUIT TOPPED EGGNOG RING

1 4-serving-size package **JELL-O Cherry Jelly Powder**
1¾ cups boiling water
2 cups ice cubes
1 10-oz. can mandarin orange segments, drained
1 cup unpeeled chopped red apple
1 4-serving-size package **JELL-O Lemon Jelly Powder**
¾ cup eggnog
¼ cup cold water
1 tsp. rum (optional)
1 envelope **Dream Whip Dessert Topping Mix**

Dissolve cherry jelly powder in ¾ cup boiling water. Add ice cubes and stir until jelly begins to thicken, 3-5 minutes. Remove unmelted ice. Fold in mandarin oranges and apple. Spoon into 6-cup mold. Chill. Dissolve lemon jelly powder in remaining 1 cup boiling water. Add eggnog, cold water and rum; mix well. Chill until slightly thickened. Prepare dessert topping mix as directed on package; reserve 1 cup. Fold eggnog mixture into remaining prepared dessert topping. Spoon over fruit-jelly layer. Chill until set, about 4 hours or overnight. Unmold onto chilled serving plate. (To unmold, run tip of small knife around the edge of the mold. Dip mold in warm water, about 10 seconds, then invert onto serving plate.) Garnish with remaining dessert topping, if desired.
Serves 10

ZABAGLIONE

1 cup milk
1½ cups light cream
1 egg, separated
2 tbsp. sweet sherry
1 4-serving-size package **JELL-O Vanilla Instant Pudding**
2 tbsp. sugar
6 peach halves, peeled and pitted
raspberry jam

Combine milk, cream, egg yolk and sherry; add pudding mix and prepare as directed on package. Let stand 5 minutes. Beat egg white until foamy; gradually add sugar. Beat until mixture forms soft peaks. Fold into pudding. Divide mixture among dessert glasses. Just before serving, place an inverted peach half on each dessert. Garnish with a spoonful of raspberry jam.
Serves 6

Strawberries Romanoff (top) and Mocha Pots de Crème

WILD BLUEBERRY MOUSSE

1 jar **Emelia Wild Blueberry Gourmet Sauce**
1 envelope unflavored gelatin
½ cup water
2 tbsp. lemon juice
dash salt
1 tsp. vanilla
1 tbsp. cognac
½ pint whipping cream
crystallized violets

Gently heat the Blueberry Sauce. Soften gelatin in water and add to sauce. Heat to dissolve gelatin, but do not allow to boil. Add lemon juice, salt, vanilla and cognac. In cold bowl, beat whipping cream. Meanwhile cool blueberry sauce to room temperature. Fold blueberry sauce into cream (reserve ⅓ of cream to decorate). Refrigerate to set at least 1 hour. Pipe or spoon remaining cream to make a decorative border and use crystallized violets for the finishing touch.
Serves 8

STRAWBERRIES ROMANOFF

2 cups strawberries, washed and hulled
1 6-serving-size package **JELL-O Strawberry Jelly Powder**
2 cups boiling water
2 tbsp. brandy
1 tbsp. orange liqueur
½ cup cold water
2 cups prepared **Dream Whip Dessert Topping** (or 1 container **Frozen Cool Whip Whipped Topping**, thawed)
½ cup cold water

Halve berries. Dissolve jelly powder in boiling water. Measure ¾ cup of the jelly; add brandy, liqueur and ½ cup cold water. Chill until slightly thickened. Fold in prepared dessert topping. Pour into a 6-cup serving dish. Chill until set, but not firm. Add remaining ½ cup cold water to remaining jelly. Chill until slightly thickened. Stir in strawberries. Spoon over set layer in dish. Chill until firm, about 4 hours or overnight.
Serves 6

MOCHA POTS DE CRÈME

1 4-serving-size package **JELL-O Chocolate Pudding and Pie Filling**
2 cups light cream
2 squares **Baker's Semi-Sweet Chocolate**
1 tbsp. **Maxwell House Instant Coffee**
2 egg yolks, beaten
chocolate curls to garnish

Combine pudding-and-pie-filling mix, cream, chocolate and coffee. Cook as directed on package. Add a small amount of hot pudding mixture to egg yolks; blend well. Return egg mixture to saucepan and cook 2-3 minutes, stirring constantly. Do not boil. Pour into small individual dessert dishes or pots de crème cups. Chill. Garnish with chocolate curls if desired.
Serves 6

APPLESAUCE YOGURT DESSERT

1 4-serving-size package **JELL-O Light Raspberry Jelly Powder**

1 cup boiling water

¾ cup unsweetened applesauce

¼ tsp. cinnamon

½ cup plain yogurt

Dissolve jelly powder in boiling water. Measure ¾ cup of the jelly; add applesauce and cinnamon. Pour into 4 individual dessert dishes. Chill until set but not firm. Chill remaining jelly until slightly thickened, then blend in yogurt and spoon over applesauce mixture in dishes. Chill until firm, about 2 hours. Garnish with additional yogurt and cinnamon if desired.
Makes 4 ½-cup servings

APPLESTICK SNACK

1 4-serving-size package **JELL-O Light Strawberry Jelly Powder**

¾ cup boiling water

½ cup apple juice

ice cubes

1 medium unpeeled red, yellow or green apple, cut in matchstick pieces (about 1½ cups)

Dissolve jelly powder in boiling water. Combine juice and ice cubes to make 1¼ cups. Add to jelly and stir until slightly thickened; remove any unmelted ice. Add apple. Chill in bowl or individual dishes until set, about 2 hours.
Makes 5 ½-cup servings

TIPSY PARSON

24 ladyfingers (or 2 sponge-cake layers)

½ cup sherry or madiera

1 jar **Emelia Wild Blueberry and Apple Preserve**

nuts if desired

fresh or glacéed fruit if desired

2 cups custard

½ pint whipping cream

crystallized violets

Line a large deep glass bowl with ladyfingers or sponge cake (cut in strips). Sprinkle with sherry or madiera. Spread with preserve. Add nuts or fresh or glacéed fruit if desired. Cover with custard. Decorate with whipped cream and crystallized violets.
Serves 12

Applesauce Yogurt Dessert (top)
Applestick Snack (bottom)

STRAWBERRIES AND CREAM

1 can **Eagle Brand Sweetened Condensed Milk**

1½ cups cold water

1 4-serving-size package instant vanilla pudding mix

2 cups whipping cream, whipped

1 package frozen pound cake thawed and cubed (about ½-¾ lb.)

4 cups fresh strawberries, cleaned, hulled and sliced

½ cup strawberry jam

fresh strawberries and toasted slivered almonds to garnish

In large mixing bowl, combine sweetened condensed milk and water. Add pudding mix; beat well. Chill until set. Fold in whipped cream. Spoon 2 cups pudding mixture into 4-quart round glass serving bowl; top with half the cake cubes, half the strawberries, half the jam and half the remaining pudding mixture. Repeat layering, ending with pudding mixture. Garnish with more strawberries and almonds. Chill 4 hours or until set. Refrigerate leftovers.
Serves 10-12

WILLIAMETTE RASPBERRY SOUFFLÉ

4 egg yolks

1 tbsp. lemon juice

1 tbsp. grated orange rind

4 egg whites

dash salt

1 tsp. lemon juice

¼ cup sugar

½ jar **Emelia Williamette Raspberry Preserve**

Preheat oven to 350°F. Butter a 7" soufflé dish and dust with sugar. Add lemon juice to yolks and beat until thick. Add orange rind. Beat egg whites with a dash of salt, lemon juice and sugar until stiff moist peaks form. Fold whites into yolks. Pile half of mixture lightly into soufflé dish. Spoon strained preserve evenly over soufflé batter and cover with remaining batter. Bake for 30-35 minutes in a pan of hot, but not boiling water. This is baked quickly in the French way, still saucy in the center. Serve immediately.
Serves 4

Strawberries and Cream

PAVLOVA

4 egg whites

a few drops vinegar (as needed)

a few grains salt (as needed)

1 cup fruit sugar

½ tsp. vanilla

½ jar **Emelia Kiwi Fruit Preserve**

½ pint whipping cream

3 kiwi fruit

1 banana

Preheat oven to 250°F. Beat egg whites to froth stage, add vinegar and salt. Continue beating to a fine foam and gradually add sugar. Beat until all sugar is completely dissolved and foam forms stiff, unbending peaks. Fold in vanilla. Spoon or pipe into 9" circle on parchment paper, or a floured baking sheet. Bake 1-1½ hours or until dry and lightly colored. When cold, top with preserve, whipped cream and decorate with peeled kiwi fruit and sliced banana. Reserve a little cream for a piped border.
Serves 8

KIWI SHERBET

½ cup sugar
1 cup milk
3 tbsp. lemon juice
1 cup kiwi purée (about 6 kiwis)
2 egg whites
2 tbsp. sugar
1 cup **Delisle Plain Yogurt**
1 cup whipping cream
1 kiwi

Heat sugar and milk until sugar is dissolved. Add lemon juice and kiwi purée. Freeze 1 hour. Beat egg whites until frothy, adding sugar gradually. Whip yogurt and cream together. Fold egg whites, yogurt and cream into kiwi mixture. Mix gently. Return to freezer in a serving dish or cups or 6-cup mold. When serving decorate with kiwi slices.
Serves 12

FRUITY COTTAGE CHEESE

1 4-serving-size package **JELL-O Light Strawberry Jelly Powder** (or your favorite flavor)
¾ cup boiling water
½ cup cold water
ice cubes
1½ cups sliced or diced fresh or canned fruit
¾ cup lowfat cottage cheese
¾ cup lowfat yogurt
1 tsp. grated lemon rind

Dissolve jelly powder in boiling water. Combine cold water and ice cubes to make 1¼ cups. Add to jelly and stir until slightly thickened; remove any unmelted ice. Add fruit; set aside. Combine cheese, yogurt and lemon rind; spoon into individual dessert glasses. Top with the fruited jelly. Chill until set, about 2 hours.
Makes 8 ½-cup servings

Kiwi Sherbet (top)
Fruity Cottage Cheese (bottom)

NO-BAKE SUMMER DELIGHT

1 4-serving-size package **JELL-O Strawberry Jelly Powder** (or your favorite flavor)

¾ cup boiling water

2 cups ice cubes

2 cups **COOL WHIP Whipped Topping**, thawed

¾ cup set-style yogurt, plain or fruited

1 cup sliced fresh strawberries (or whole raspberries)

1 9" baked crumb crust

Dissolve jelly powder in boiling water. Add ice cubes and stir constantly until slightly thickened (2-3 minutes). Remove unmelted ice. Fold whipped topping and yogurt into jelly. Stir gently with a whisk until smooth. Fold in fruit. Chill until mixture will mound, 10-15 minutes. Spoon filling into crumb crust. Chill about 2 hours. For fast set, freeze about 30 minutes. Garnish with additional fruit if desired.

ORANGE BAVARIAN

1 tbsp. gelatin

¼ cup cold water

⅓ cup boiling water

1¼ cups sugar

¼ cup lemon juice

1 tsp. grated orange rind

1 cup orange juice

3 egg whites

½ cup **Delisle Plain Yogurt**

½ cup whipping cream

2 tsp. orange liqueur

Soften gelatin in cold water. Add boiling water and stir to dissolve. Add sugar, lemon juice, orange rind and orange juice. Chill until partially set. Beat egg whites, fold into gelatin mixture. Whip yogurt and cream. Fold into egg mixture, then add orange liqueur. Pour into 6 dishes or 1 4-cup mold. Chill.

Serves 6

No-Bake Summer Delight (top)
Orange Bavarian (bottom)

YOGURT FLUFF

¾ cup boiling water

1 4-serving-size package **JELL-O Light Strawberry Jelly Powder** (or your favorite flavor)

½ cup cold water

ice cubes

¾ cup plain yogurt

½ tsp. vanilla

Pour boiling water into blender container. Add jelly powder and blend at low speed until dissolved, about 1 minute. Combine cold water and ice cubes to make 1 cup. Add to jelly and stir until ice is almost melted, then blend in yogurt and vanilla. Chill in dessert dishes or bowl until set, about 1 hour.
Makes 5 ⅓-cup servings

MELON BUBBLE

1 4-serving-size package **JELL-O Light Orange Jelly Powder**

¾ cup boiling water

½ cup orange juice

ice cubes

1 cup melon balls or diced melon

Dissolve jelly powder in boiling water. Combine juice and ice cubes to make 1¼ cups. Add to jelly and stir until slightly thickened; remove any unmelted ice. Measure 1⅓ cups; add melon and pour into individual dishes. Beat remaining jelly at highest speed of electric mixer until fluffy and thick and about double in volume; spoon carefully over fruited layer in dishes. Chill until set, about 2 hours.
Makes 7 ½-cup servings

GUAVA SORBET

1 can **Sharwood's Guavas**, drained and puréed

2 oz. superfine granulated sugar

juice of 1 lemon

2 egg whites

Pass guava purée through a sieve to remove pips. Mix with the sugar and lemon and freeze for 1-1½ hours until slushy. Whisk the egg whites until stiff and gradually add to the guava mixture, whisking well each time, until the mixture is light and fluffy. Refreeze.

Yogurt Fluff (top)
Melon Bubble (bottom)

Rice Brulé

MANGO AND LIME MOUSSE

3 eggs, separated

4 oz. superfine granulated sugar

1 tbsp. gelatin

3 tbsp. hot water

juice and rind of 1 large fresh lime or lemon

1 can **Sharwood's Mango Slices**, drained and puréed

5 oz. whipping cream

Beat the egg yolks and sugar over a pan of boiling water until the sugar is dissolved and the mixture is light, creamy and thick. Remove from heat. Dissolve gelatin in the hot water and stir into the mixture. Add lime juice, rind and puréed mango; refrigerate. Meanwhile whisk the egg whites to form soft peaks. Add the cream to the mixture and fold in the egg whites. Leave to set in a refrigerator for at least 1 hour. Decorate with slices of mango and lime.

RICE BRULÉ

1 cup quick-cooking rice

1 6-serving-size package **JELL-O Vanilla Pudding and Pie Filling**

4 cups light cream

2 eggs lightly beaten

¼ cup firmly packed brown sugar

Combine rice, pudding-and-pie-filling mix, cream and eggs. Cook and stir over medium heat until mixture comes to a full bubbling boil. Remove from heat. Pour into ovenproof serving dish. Cover surface of pudding with plastic wrap. Chill 3 hours. Sprinkle brown sugar evenly over surface of pudding. Broil 6″ from preheated broiler until sugar caramelizes, about 1½ minutes. Serve when sugar hardens or chill again and serve cold.
Serves 10

COOKIES, SQUARES AND CANDIES

It has happened a hundred times. You are at a party and as you head toward a plate of baked goods you spy those enticing little delicacies made from "a secret family recipe".

As you munch away you try to conceive of how to pry this golden recipe away and make it your own.

Relax. On the pages ahead we think you'll find the "secret" recipes for a number of those irresistible treats. And, in addition, you'll find some new recipes your guests will soon be begging you to share.

Secret Truffles (see page 236)

Big Peanutty Chip Cookies

BIG PEANUTTY CHIP COOKIES

½ cup shortening
½ cup peanut butter, at room temperature
¾ cup firmly packed brown sugar
½ cup granulated sugar
2 eggs
1 tsp. vanilla
1¾ cups all-purpose flour
1 tsp. baking soda
½ tsp. salt
2 cups **Chipits Semi-Sweet Chocolate Jumbo Chips**
½ cup **Planters Blanched Peanuts**

Cream shortening, peanut butter and sugars until light and fluffy. Beat in eggs and vanilla. Combine flour, baking soda and salt; blend into creamed mixture. Stir in Chipits and peanuts. Drop from heaping tbsp. onto baking sheets; flatten slightly with a fork. Bake at 375°F for 10-12 minutes.
Makes about 2½ dozen large cookies

SECRET TRUFFLES

2 cups **Chipits Chocolate Mint Chips**, **Chocolate Orange** or **Semi-Sweet Chocolate Chips**
1 can sweetened condensed milk
Christie Chocolate Wafers, crushed (or finely chopped nuts or **Chipits Cocoa**)
1 **Chipits Semi-Sweet Chocolate Baking Square**, melted (optional, instead of frosting)

Frosting:
1 cup icing sugar
¼ tsp. almond extract
4 tsp. milk

Melt Chipits over hot water. Remove from heat. Stir in condensed milk until well blended. Chill until firm enough to handle, about 2 hours. Form into ½" balls and roll in wafer crumbs or chopped nuts or cocoa. Garnish with drizzled chocolate or frosting. Then store in covered container in refrigerator. To prepare frosting: Combine icing sugar, almond extract and milk, blending until smooth.
Makes about 5 dozen truffles

CHOCOLATE-CHIP PEANUT COOKIES

2¼ cups sifted all-purpose flour
1 tsp. **Cow Brand Baking Soda**
1 tsp. salt
½ cup butter or margarine
½ cup vegetable shortening
¾ cup firmly packed light brown sugar
¾ cup granulated sugar
1½ tsp. vanilla
2 eggs
1 6-oz. package semi-sweet chocolate chips
½ cup chopped dry roasted peanuts

Sift together flour, baking soda and salt. Using an electric mixer, cream together butter and shortening in large bowl. Gradually add sugars and vanilla; continue beating until light and fluffy. Beat in eggs. Gradually add sifted dry ingredients. Stir in chocolate chips and nuts. Drop by tsp. about 3" apart onto ungreased baking sheets. Bake in 375°F oven 8 minutes or until lightly browned. Cool on racks.
Makes about 6½ dozen cookies

CANDY CANE COOKIES

2½ cups **Robin Hood All-Purpose Flour**
1 tsp. baking powder
1 cup butter, softened
¾ cup granulated sugar
1 egg
1 tsp. vanilla
½ tsp. peppermint extract (optional)
¾ tsp. red or green food coloring

Combine flour and baking powder. Stir well to blend. Cream butter, sugar, egg, vanilla and peppermint extract until light and fluffy. Add flour mixture, beating until blended. Divide dough into 2 equal portions. Stir red or green food coloring into 1 portion. Beat or knead dough until color is thoroughly blended in. Shape 1 tsp. of each color of dough into a 5″-long rope. Place 1 colored rope and 1 white rope side by side; press together lightly and twist. Place on ungreased baking sheets. Curve 1 end of cookie down to form top of candy cane. Bake at 375°F for 8-10 minutes or until edges just begin to brown. Cool on wire racks.

Makes about 4 dozen cookies

NEOPOLITAN STRIPS

1 cup butter
½ cup granulated sugar
1 egg
1 tsp. vanilla
2¼ cups **Robin Hood All-Purpose Flour**
½ tsp. salt
1 square unsweetened chocolate, melted
⅓ cup finely chopped walnuts
⅓ cup finely chopped maraschino cherries
red food coloring

Cream butter, sugar, egg and vanilla together thoroughly. Stir in flour and salt. Mix well. Divide dough into 3 equal portions. Stir melted chocolate and nuts into 1 portion. Stir cherries and enough red coloring to make a pink dough into another portion. Leave remaining portion plain. Line an empty waxed paper box (about 12″ long and 2″ wide) with plastic wrap. Press chocolate dough evenly into box. Cover with plain then cherry dough. Wrap well and chill overnight or until firm, about 2 hours. Cut roll into ¼″-thick slices and place on ungreased baking sheets. Bake at 375°F for 7-10 minutes or until set.

Makes about 5 dozen cookies

PECAN CHEESECAKE SQUARES

1 cup **Robin Hood All-Purpose Flour**
¼ cup lightly packed brown sugar
⅓ cup butter
1 8-oz. package cream cheese
⅓ cup lightly packed brown sugar
1 egg
2 tsp. milk
½ tsp. vanilla
¼ cup chopped pecans

Combine flour and ¼ cup brown sugar. Cut in butter until mixture resembles coarse meal. Press into ungreased 8″ square cake pan. Bake at 350°F for 10 minutes. Set aside. Beat remaining ingredients except pecans on low speed of electric mixer for 1 minute, scraping bowl constantly. Beat on medium speed 1 minute. Spread cheese mixture over partially baked crust. Sprinkle with pecans. Bake at 350°F for 25 minutes or until edges are lightly browned. Cool, then refrigerate at least 2 hours before cutting into small squares.

Makes about 3 dozen squares

OATMEAL DATE SQUARES

Filling:
2 cups chopped dates
1 cup water
½ cup granulated sugar
juice of 1 lemon

Base and Topping:
1⅓ cups **Robin Hood All-Purpose Flour** (or 1½ cups **Robin Hood Velvet Cake & Pastry Flour**)
¼ tsp. baking soda
1¾ cups **Robin Hood** or **Old Mill Oats**
1 cup lightly packed brown sugar
¾ cup butter

Combine ingredients for filling in small saucepan. Cook over medium heat until thick and smooth, stirring constantly. Cool. Stir flour, baking soda, oats and brown sugar together until thoroughly blended. Cut in butter until mixture is crumbly. Press half the mixture into a lightly greased 9″ square cake pan. Spread with date filling. Sprinkle remaining oat mixture over top. Pat lightly. Bake at 375°F for 45 minutes or until golden. Cool and cut into squares.

Makes about 2 dozen squares

GINGER CRISPS

2 cups **Robin Hood All-Purpose Flour** (or 2¼ cups **Robin Hood Velvet Cake & Pastry Flour**)
½ tsp. baking soda
½ tsp. salt
2 tsp. ginger
½ cup butter
1⅓ cups lightly packed brown sugar
1 egg
2 tbsp. molasses

Combine flour, baking soda, salt and ginger. Stir well to blend. Cream butter, brown sugar, egg and molasses until light and fluffy. Add dry ingredients to creamed mixture. Mix well. Shape dough into a roll 2″ in diameter. Wrap in waxed paper and chill overnight or until firm, about 4 hours. Cut roll into ¼″-thick slices. Bake at 400°F on ungreased baking sheets for 6-8 minutes or until set.

Makes about 6 dozen cookies

CHOCOLATE TOFFEE BARS

2 cups **Robin Hood All-Purpose Flour**
½ cup lightly packed brown sugar
¾ cup butter
¼ cup **Robin Hood All-Purpose Flour**
½ tsp. baking powder
½ tsp. salt
2 eggs
1½ cups lightly packed brown sugar
1 tsp. vanilla
1 cup flaked coconut
1 cup raisins
¾ cup chopped walnuts
1½ cups chocolate chips

Combine 2 cups flour and ½ cup brown sugar in mixing bowl. Cut in butter until mixture is crumbly. Press into a greased 13″ x 9″ x 2″ cake pan. Bake at 350°F for 10 minutes. Blend together ¼ cup flour, baking powder and salt. Beat eggs until foamy. Stir in 1½ cups brown sugar and vanilla. Add dry ingredients. Mix well. Stir in remaining ingredients. Spread over partially baked base. Bake 20-25 minutes longer or until set. Cool and cut into bars.

Makes about 4 dozen bars

CHOCOLATE CHIP COOKIES

- 1 cup **Robin Hood All-Purpose Flour**
- ½ tsp. baking soda
- ½ tsp. salt
- ⅓ cup butter
- ½ cup granulated sugar
- ¼ cup lightly packed brown sugar
- 1 egg
- 1 tsp. vanilla
- 1 cup chocolate chips
- ½ cup chopped nuts (optional)

Combine flour, baking soda and salt. Stir well to blend. Cream butter, sugars, egg and vanilla together thoroughly. Add flour mixture to creamed mixture. Mix well. Stir in chocolate chips and nuts. Drop mixture by tsp. onto lightly greased baking sheets. Bake at 375°F for 8-10 minutes or until golden.
Makes about 40 cookies

RASPBERRY PINWHEELS

- 2 cups **Robin Hood All-Purpose Flour** (or 2¼ cups **Robin Hood Velvet Cake & Pastry Flour**)
- 1 tsp. baking powder
- ¼ tsp. salt
- ½ cup butter
- 1 cup granulated sugar
- 1 egg
- 1 tsp. vanilla
- ½ cup raspberry jam
- ½ cup shredded coconut
- ¼ cup finely chopped walnuts

Combine flour, baking powder and salt. Stir well to blend. Cream butter, sugar, egg and vanilla together thoroughly. Mix dry ingredients with creamed mixture. Refrigerate dough ½ hour. Roll dough between 2 sheets of waxed paper to a 12" x 9" rectangle. Combine jam, coconut and walnuts. Spread evenly over dough to within ½" of edges. Roll up tightly, jelly-roll fashion, starting from long side. Gently press edge to seal. Wrap in waxed paper and chill overnight. Cut into ¼"-thick slices and place on greased baking sheets. Bake at 375°F for 8-10 minutes or until golden.
Makes about 40 cookies

SWEDISH BUTTER BALLS

- 1 cup butter, softened
- ½ cup sifted icing sugar
- 1 tsp. vanilla
- 2½ cups **Robin Hood Velvet Cake & Pastry Flour** (or 2¼ cups **Robin Hood All-Purpose Flour**)
- 1 cup finely chopped pecans
- icing sugar

Cream butter, icing sugar and vanilla together thoroughly. Add flour. Mix well. Stir in nuts. Shape dough into 1" balls. Place on ungreased baking sheet. Bake at 400°F for 8-12 minutes or until very light golden. Cool on racks. Roll in sifted icing sugar.
Makes about 4 dozen cookies

COCONUT MACAROONS

- ½ cup **Robin Hood All-Purpose Flour**
- 1 cup granulated sugar
- ¼ tsp. salt
- 2 cups shredded coconut
- 4 egg whites
- ¼ cup granulated sugar
- ½ tsp. vanilla
- maraschino cherries, halved

Combine flour, 1 cup sugar, salt and coconut. Stir well to blend. Beat egg whites until foamy. Gradually add ¼ cup sugar beating until stiff peaks form. Add vanilla. Fold flour mixture, half at a time, into meringue. Drop rounded tsp. of mixture onto aluminum-foil-lined baking sheets. Top each with cherry half. Bake at 325°F for 20-25 minutes or until set. Cool cookies thoroughly before removing from foil.
Makes about 4 dozen cookies

COCOA MACAROONS

- ⅔ cup sweetened condensed milk
- ¼ cup **Fry's Cocoa**
- 1 tsp. vanilla
- 2 cups shredded coconut
- 30 maraschino cherry halves, drained

Combine condensed milk, cocoa and vanilla in a bowl until smooth. Add coconut and stir until well combined. Drop from small spoons onto greased cookie sheet. Top each with a cherry half. Bake in preheated 350°F oven 10-12 minutes. Remove immediately from pan; cool.
Makes about 2½ dozen macaroons

CHOCOLATE-DIPPED RASPBERRY ALMOND CRISPS

- 1 cup **Robin Hood All-Purpose Flour**
- 1 cup finely chopped blanched almonds
- ½ cup butter, softened
- 6 tbsp. granulated sugar
- 1½ tsp. vanilla
- ¼ cup raspberry, strawberry or apricot jam
- 2 squares semi-sweet chocolate, melted (optional)

Combine flour and almonds. Stir well to blend. Cream butter, sugar and vanilla together thoroughly. Stir in flour and almonds. Mix well. Use your hands to work mixture into a smooth dough. Shape dough into a roll 2" in diameter. Wrap in waxed paper and chill overnight or until firm, about 3 hours. Cut roll in ¼" thick slices and place on ungreased baking sheets. Bake at 350°F for 10-12 minutes or until golden. Cool. Spread half of the cookies with about ½ tsp. jam. Top with remaining cookies. Line baking sheet with waxed paper. Dip half of each filled cookie into melted chocolate, if desired. Place on waxed paper. Let stand until set. Store in refrigerator.
Makes about 25 cookies

LEMON BARS

Base:
- 2 cups **Robin Hood All-Purpose Flour** (or 2¼ cups **Robin Hood Velvet Cake & Pastry Flour**)
- ½ cup sifted icing sugar
- ¾ cup butter

Filling:
- 4 eggs
- 2 cups granulated sugar
- ⅓ cup lemon juice
- ¼ cup **Robin Hood All-Purpose Flour** or **Velvet Cake & Pastry Flour**
- 1 tsp. baking powder
- sifted icing sugar (optional)

For base, combine flour and icing sugar in mixing bowl. Stir well to blend. Cut in butter with pastry blender until mixture is crumbly. Press into greased 13" x 9" x 2" cake pan. Bake at 325°F for 15-20 minutes or until lightly browned. For filling, beat eggs, sugar, lemon juice, flour and baking powder together until smooth and light. Pour over partially baked crust. Bake at 325°F for 25-30 minutes or until set and golden. Cool. Before serving sprinkle with icing sugar, if desired, and cut in bars.
Makes about 4 dozen bars

FLYING SAUCERS

1 cup sugar
1¼ cups flour
¾ cup **Gerber Mixed Cereal**
¾ cup shortening
1 egg
¼ cup light molasses
1 tbsp. baking soda
1 tsp. cloves
1 tsp. ginger
1 tsp. cinnamon
½ tsp. salt
¼ cup sugar

Preheat oven to 350°F. Mix all of the ingredients, except ¼ cup sugar, in a large bowl with electric mixer. Shape into 1" balls, roll in ¼ cup sugar. Place sugared balls on an ungreased cookie sheet about 3" apart, and flatten with bottom of a glass. Bake at 350°F for 8-10 minutes. Cool on wire rack.
Makes 30 cookies

DATE SQUARES

1 cup all-purpose flour
¾ cup **Alpen Mixed Cereal**
¼ tsp. baking soda
pinch salt
½ cup butter or margarine
½ cup brown sugar
1 tbsp. honey
grated rind of ½ lemon
1 tbsp. lemon juice
1½ cups chopped dates
¾ cup water

Combine flour, Alpen, soda and salt. With hands, rub in butter or margarine, then brown sugar, until well blended. Press half Alpen mixture evenly into bottom of lightly greased 8" or 9" square baking pan. In a small saucepan combine remaining ingredients. Over medium heat cook, stirring constantly, until mixture has thickened, about 5 minutes. Cool slightly. Spread mixture evenly over base. Sprinkle remaining Alpen mixture and press down. Bake at 350°F for 35-45 minutes, or until golden brown. Cool and cut in squares.

Flying Saucers

HUMPTY DUMPTY POPCORN BALLS

½ cup sugar
1 cup molasses
1 tbsp. butter
pinch baking soda
½ tsp. vinegar
½ tsp. vanilla
2 quarts **Humpty Dumpty Popped Corn**

Cook sugar, molasses and butter until syrup hairs when dripped from spoon. Add soda, vinegar and vanilla. Pour slowly over the popped corn in a large bowl. Mix thoroughly. Butter hands and form mixture into balls.
Makes 15 2½" popcorn balls

MACKINTOSH TOFFEE SNACKING SQUARES

4 2-oz. packages **Rowntree Mackintosh Toffee Bars**
2 tbsp. milk
2 tbsp. butter
3 cups rice crisp cereal
¼ cup shredded coconut
¼ cup pecans or walnuts (optional)

Melt Toffee, milk and butter in double boiler. Add cereal, coconut and nuts, if desired, and stir until well coated with toffee mixture. Press mixture into lightly greased 9" x 13" pan. Cut into squares and serve.

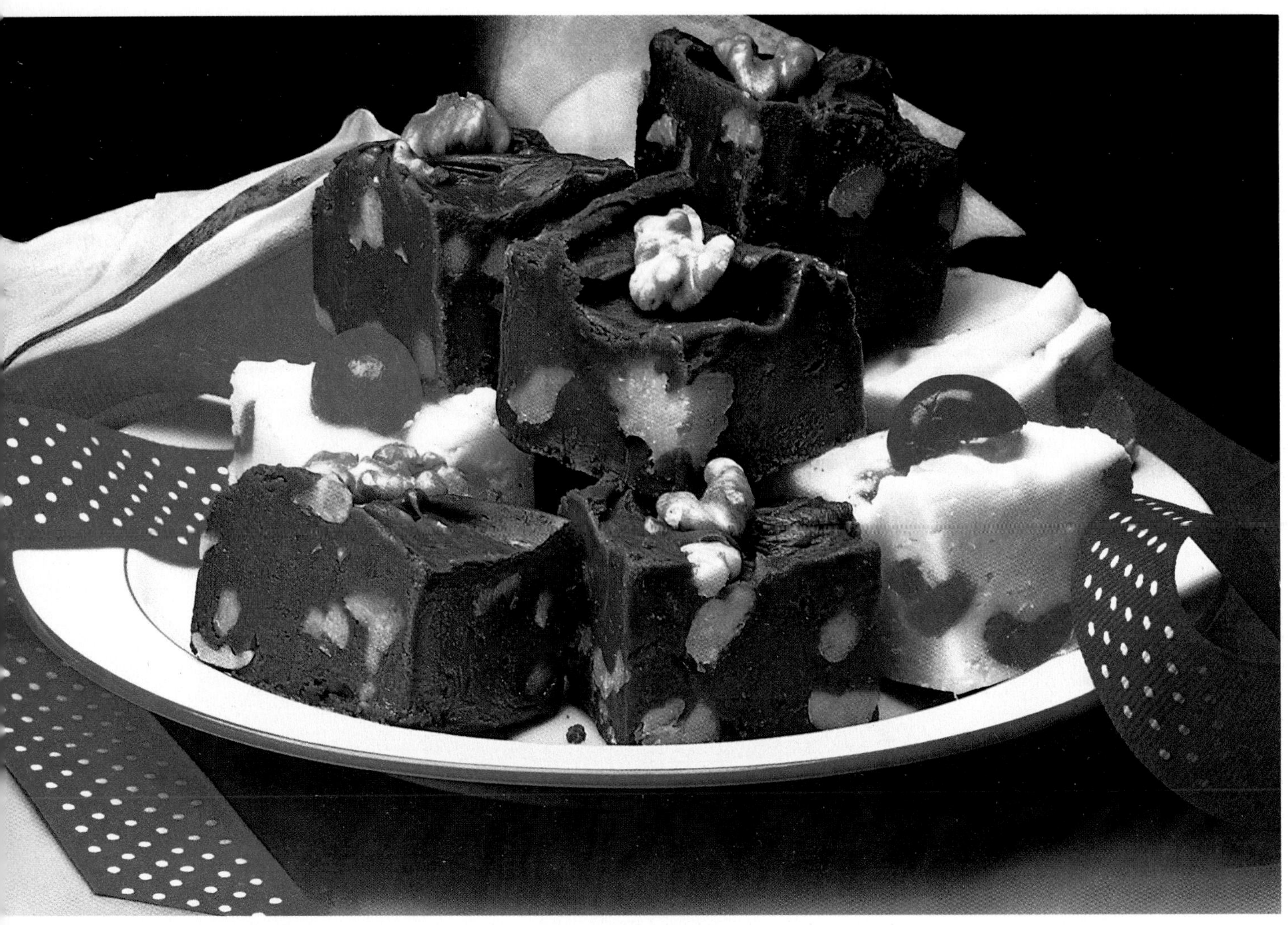

Chocolate Fudge

DROP SUGAR COOKIES

- 2½ cups sifted all-purpose flour
- ¾ tsp. salt
- ½ tsp. **Cow Brand Baking Soda**
- ½ cup butter or margarine
- ½ cup vegetable shortening
- 1 cup sugar
- 1 tsp. vanilla
- 1 egg
- 2 tbsp. milk

Sift together flour, salt and baking soda. Using an electric mixer, cream together butter and shortening in large bowl; gradually add sugar and continue beating until light and fluffy. Beat in vanilla and egg. Add flour mixture and beat until smooth; blend in milk. Drop by tsp. about 3" apart onto greased baking sheets. Flatten with bottom of glass that has been dipped in sugar. Bake in 400°F oven about 12 minutes or until edges are lightly browned. Cool on racks.
Makes about 5½ dozen 2" cookies

OLD-FASHIONED MOLASSES COOKIES

- 4 cups sifted all-purpose flour
- 2 tsp. **Cow Brand Baking Soda**
- 1½ tsp. ground ginger
- ½ tsp. ground cinnamon
- pinch salt
- 1½ cups molasses
- ½ cup lard, melted
- ¼ cup butter or margarine, melted
- ⅓ cup boiling water

Sift together flour, baking soda, spices and salt. Combine molasses, lard, butter and water in large bowl. Add dry ingredients to liquid and blend well. Cover and chill several hours or overnight. Turn onto well floured board. Using floured rolling pin, roll to ¼" thickness. Cut with 3½" floured cookie cutter. Sprinkle with sugar and place on ungreased baking sheets. Bake in 375°F oven 12 minutes. Cool on racks.
Makes about 3 dozen 3½" cookies

CHOCOLATE FUDGE

- 3 cups semi-sweet chocolate chips
- 1 can **Eagle Brand Sweetened Condensed Milk**
- 1¼ cups icing sugar
- pinch of salt
- 1½ tsp. vanilla
- ½ cup chopped nuts (optional)

In a heavy saucepan, over low heat, melt chocolate chips with Eagle Brand, stirring constantly. Remove from heat; stir in remaining ingredients. Spread evenly into waxed-paper-lined 8" square pan. Chill 2-3 hours or until firm. Turn fudge onto cutting board; peel off paper and cut into squares. Store loosely covered at room temperature.
Makes about 2 lb.

White Confetti Fudge: In a heavy saucepan, over low heat, melt 1½ lb. white chocolate with Eagle Brand, stirring constantly. Remove from heat. Stir in 1 cup chopped candied cherries, 1 tsp. vanilla and pinch of salt. Proceed as directed.
Makes about 2½ lb.

CREATE A CRITTER

3 cups **Robin Hood All-Purpose Flour** (or 3⅓ cups **Robin Hood Velvet Cake & Pastry Flour**)
1 tsp. baking powder
½ tsp. baking soda
¼ tsp. salt
½ cup butter
½ cup shortening
1 cup granulated sugar
2 eggs
1 square unsweetened chocolate, melted
mixed nuts, cereals and candies for decoration

Combine flour, baking powder, baking soda and salt. Stir well to blend. Cream butter, shortening, sugar and eggs together thoroughly. Stir in flour mixture. Mix well. Divide dough in half. Stir melted chocolate into 1 portion. Chill dough 30 minutes for easy handling. Create animals by placing mounds of plain and chocolate dough onto greased baking sheets. Mounds of dough should just touch. Place animals 3" apart. Decorate as desired. Bake at 375°F for about 12 minutes or until plain dough is light golden. Time will depend on size of cookie. Cool.
Makes about 3 dozen animal cookies

TOPPERS

1½ cups **Robin Hood All-Purpose Flour**
¼ tsp. baking soda
¼ tsp. salt
½ cup butter
½ cup lightly packed brown sugar
2 eggs
½ tsp. vanilla
3 cups pecan halves
1 cup chocolate chips, melted

Combine flour, baking soda and salt. Stir well to blend. Cream butter, brown sugar, 1 egg, 1 egg yolk and vanilla together thoroughly. Add dry ingredients; mix well. Chill 1 hour if necessary for easy handling. Arrange pecans on lightly greased baking sheet in groups of 4 with their ends touching. Shape dough into 1" balls. Dip bottom into unbeaten egg white and press lightly onto center of group of nuts so the tips show. Bake at 350°F for 10-13 minutes. Cool completely. Dip tops of cookies into melted chocolate. Chill to set chocolate.
Makes about 4 dozen toppers

FLORENTINE TRIANGLES

Crust:
1½ cups **Robin Hood All-Purpose Flour** (or 1⅔ cups **Robin Hood Velvet Cake & Pastry Flour**)
½ cup sifted icing sugar
½ cup butter
2 tbsp. whipping cream
2 tsp. vanilla

Topping:
¾ cup butter
½ cup granulated sugar
¼ cup whipping cream
½ cup chopped red candied cherries
½ cup chopped green candied cherries
½ cup chopped yellow candied pineapple
1 cup sliced blanched almonds
2 squares semi-sweet chocolate, melted

Combine flour and icing sugar in mixing bowl. Cut in butter until mixture is crumbly. Stir in cream and vanilla, mixing until dough clings together. Press dough evenly into greased 15" x 10" jelly roll pan. Chill. Combine butter, sugar and cream in medium-sized saucepan. Bring to boil, stirring often, then boil 1-2 minutes, stirring constantly until thickened. Remove from heat. Stir in remaining ingredients except chocolate. Spread evenly over chilled crust. Bake at 375°F for 15-20 minutes or until golden. Cool in pan. Drizzle with melted chocolate. Allow chocolate to set. Cut into strips, then cut strips into triangles. Store in refrigerator if desired.
Makes about 6 dozen florentines

SHORTBREAD

2 cups butter, softened
1 cup granulated sugar
¼ cup cornstarch
4 cups **Robin Hood All-Purpose Flour** (or 4½ cups **Robin Hood Velvet Cake & Pastry Flour**)

Cream butter and sugar until light. Stir in cornstarch and flour. Knead well with hands to blend in last of flour. Turn out onto a lightly floured surface and roll to ¼" thickness. Cut in desired shapes. Place on ungreased baking sheets. Sprinkle with colored sugar or decorate as desired with cherries, nuts, etc. Bake at 300°F for 15-20 minutes, or until very lightly browned. Time will depend on size of cookies.
Makes about 6 dozen cookies

BASIC REFRIGERATOR COOKIES

2½ cups **Robin Hood All-Purpose Flour** (or 2¾ cups **Robin Hood Velvet Cake & Pastry Flour**)
1 tsp. baking powder
½ tsp. baking soda
¼ tsp. salt
½ cup butter
½ cup shortening
1 cup granulated sugar
2 eggs
1 tsp. vanilla

Combine flour, baking powder, baking soda and salt. Stir well to blend. Cream butter, shortening, sugar, eggs and vanilla together thoroughly. Stir flour mixture into creamed mixture. Mix well. Shape dough into 2 rolls about 1½" in diameter. Wrap in waxed paper and chill overnight or until firm, about 3 hours. Cut into ¼" slices. Place on ungreased baking sheets. Bake at 375°F for 8-10 minutes or until golden.
Makes about 7 dozen cookies

Butterscotch Nut Cookies: Follow basic recipe above except substitute 1 cup lightly packed brown sugar for the granulated sugar. Mix ½ cup chopped nuts into dough.

Chocolate Nut Cookies: Follow basic recipe. Blend 3 squares unsweetened chocolate, melted and cooled and ½ cup chopped nuts into the creamed mixture.

Oatmeal Cookies: Follow basic recipe except reduce flour to 2 cups and substitute brown sugar for granulated sugar. Stir 1½ cups **Robin Hood** or **Old Mill Oats** into dough after flour has been added.

Fruit Cookies: Follow basic recipe. Mix in ¾ cup chopped candied fruit or cherries.

Spice Cookies: Follow basic recipe except add 1½ tsp. ginger and 1 tsp. cinnamon to flour. Blend ¼ cup molasses into the creamed mixture.

Orange Cookies: Follow basic recipe except add 1 tbsp. grated orange rind, 1 tsp. grated lemon rind and 1 tbsp. orange juice to the creamed mixture.

THUMBPRINT COOKIES

2 cups **Robin Hood All-Purpose Flour** (or 2¼ cups **Robin Hood Velvet Cake & Pastry Flour**)
¼ tsp. salt
1 cup butter, softened
½ cup lightly packed brown sugar
2 egg yolks
1 tsp. vanilla
2 egg whites, slightly beaten
1½ cups finely chopped nuts
raspberry jam or jelly

Combine flour and salt. Stir well to blend. Cream butter, brown sugar, egg yolks and vanilla together thoroughly on medium speed of electric mixer. Add flour to creamed mixture gradually. Mix well. Shape dough into ¾" balls. Dip in egg white and then in chopped nuts. Place on ungreased baking sheets. Make indentation in center of each cookie with thumb. Bake at 300°F for 5 minutes. Press center down again. Bake 10-15 minutes longer or until set. Cool and fill center with jam.
Makes about 5 dozen cookies

CHERRY BLOSSOMS

1 cup butter, softened
½ cup sifted icing sugar
1 tsp. vanilla
2½ cups **Robin Hood Velvet Cake & Pastry Flour** (or 2¼ cups **Robin Hood All-Purpose Flour**)
1 cup ground almonds
60 whole maraschino cherries, patted dry
granulated sugar

Cream butter, icing sugar and vanilla together thoroughly. Add flour. Mix well. Stir in almonds. Flatten a small amount of dough in palm of hand. Place a cherry in center and wrap dough around to enclose cherry completely. Shape into smooth ball. Place on ungreased baking sheet. Bake at 325°F for 10-15 minutes or until light golden. Roll balls in sugar while warm.
Makes about 5 dozen cookies

Nut Blossoms: Wrap dough around pecans or filberts instead of cherries and bake as directed.

COOKIE PIZZA

1½ cups **Robin Hood All-Purpose Flour**
2 tsp. baking soda
1 tsp. salt
2⅓ cups **Robin Hood** or **Old Mill Oats**
1 cup butter
1½ cups lightly packed brown sugar
2 eggs
½ tsp. vanilla
1½ cups shredded coconut
½ cup chopped walnuts
2 cups chocolate chips
1 cup colored candies
1 cup peanuts

Combine flour, baking soda, salt and oats. Stir well to blend. Cream butter, brown sugar, eggs and vanilla together thoroughly. Add flour mixture to creamed mixture. Mix well. Stir in ½ cup coconut and chopped walnuts. Spread dough evenly in 2 greased 10" pizza pans or press into 10" circles on greased baking sheets. Bake at 350°F for 10 minutes. Remove from oven. Sprinkle with chocolate chips, remaining 1 cup coconut, candies and peanuts. Bake for 5-10 minutes longer or until golden. Cool in pans on wire racks. Cut cooled cookie pizzas into wedges. (For 3" cookies, drop dough by tsp. onto lightly greased baking sheets. Flatten slightly with hands or floured fork. Bake at 350°F for 8-10 minutes or until golden.)
Makes 2 pizzas, 24 wedges, or 7 dozen cookies

GRANOLA BARS

3 cups **Robin Hood** or **Old Mill Oats**
1 cup chopped peanuts
1 cup raisins
1 cup sunflower seeds
1 cup semi-sweet chocolate chips
1 can sweetened condensed milk
½ cup melted butter

Line a 15" x 10" jelly roll pan with foil; grease. Combine all ingredients in large mixing bowl. Mix well. Press evenly into prepared pan. Bake at 325°F for 25-30 minutes or until golden brown. Cool slightly; remove from pan and peel off foil. Cut into bars. Store loosely covered at room temperature.
Makes 36 bars

GREAT BIG BROWN BEARS

2½ cups all-purpose flour
⅓ cup **Fry's Cocoa**
¼ tsp. baking soda
1 cup butter, softened
¾ cup packed brown sugar
½ cup corn syrup
1 egg
½ tsp. vanilla

Sift together flour, Fry's Cocoa and baking soda. Cream butter; beat in sugar. Stir in corn syrup. Beat in egg and vanilla. Blend in sifted dry ingredients. Shape dough into 2 rolls 1½" in diameter; wrap and chill well. Cut dough into ¼" slices. Use 7 slices for each bear. On an ungreased cookie sheet arrange 6 cookies in a pyramid fashion (3 on bottom), sides touching. For ears, cut seventh slice in half; place about ⅛" from head (top slice), curved sides out. Bake in preheated 350°F oven 12-14 minutes. Cool on cookie sheet 3-5 minutes. Remove from the sheet; cool. Decorate as desired.
Makes about 14 large cookies

COCONUT FUDGE BARS

Base:
1¼ cups **Robin Hood All-Purpose Flour** (or 1⅓ cups **Robin Hood Velvet Cake & Pastry Flour**)
⅔ cup granulated sugar
¼ cup cocoa
¼ tsp. salt
½ cup butter, softened
1 egg, beaten

Filling:
1 can sweetened condensed milk
¼ cup **Robin Hood All-Purpose Flour** (or **Velvet Cake & Pastry Flour**)
1 tsp. vanilla
⅔ cup chopped walnuts
½ cup flaked coconut
½ cup chocolate chips

For base, combine flour, sugar, cocoa and salt. Stir well to blend. Cut in butter until mixture is crumbly. Stir in egg. Press evenly into a greased 13" x 9" cake pan. Bake at 350°F for 10-12 minutes or until surface is dry. For filling, combine sweetened condensed milk, flour and vanilla. Stir in remaining ingredients. Spread mixture over hot crust and bake 20-25 minutes longer or until light golden. Cool and cut into bars.
Makes about 4 dozen bars

Chocolate Gourmandise

HONEY OATMEAL COOKIES

1 cup **Billy Bee Honey**
½ cup shortening
1 egg
1½ cups sifted flour
½ tsp. baking soda
½ tsp. salt
1⅔ cups oatmeal
4 tbsp. sour milk
1 cup raisins
½-1 cup chopped nuts

Cream honey and shortening. Add egg. Sift dry ingredients together and add oatmeal. Mix milk and flour mixture alternately into honey mixture. Stir in raisins and nuts. Drop by spoon onto cookie sheet and bake in moderate oven for 12-15 minutes.

CHOCO CRISP COOKIES

½ cup butter or margarine
½ cup semi-sweet chocolate chips
1⅓ cups **Weetabix** crumbs
⅓ cup brown sugar

Melt butter and chocolate chips together in a double boiler. Remove from heat. Stir in Weetabix crumbs and brown sugar. Mix well. Pour on 9" x 15" jelly roll pan. Spread evenly. Bake in preheated 350°F oven for 8 minutes. Remove and put on rack. Let sit for 1 minute. Cut into squares and let cool in pan on rack.
Makes approximately 40 cookies

CHOCOLATE GOURMANDISE

½ lb. Nutella
1 lb. **Brie de St-Eloi** (without rind)
slivered almonds, cocoa or sugar icing

Place Nutella in a saucepan, leave at room temperature. In small quantities at a time, mix Brie de St-Eloi and lukewarm Nutella in a blender. Blend the mixture until it has a smooth, pasty consistency. Refrigerate the mixture for a minimum of 4 hours. Shape the mixture into little balls and put back in the fridge. Before serving, add slivered almonds, cocoa or sugar icing.

Back Packer's Bars

BACK PACKER'S BARS

Base:

1/3 cup butter or margarine, softened
3/4 cup firmly packed brown sugar
1 egg
3/4 cup whole wheat flour
1/2 cup **Post Grape-Nuts Cereal**
1/2 tsp. baking powder
1/2 tsp. salt
1/8 tsp. baking soda
1 tsp. grated orange rind

Cereal/Fruit Topping:

3 eggs
1/4 cup firmly packed brown sugar
1/2 cup **Post Grape-Nuts Cereal**
1/2 cup dried apricots, halved
1/2 cup chopped dates
1/2 cup **Baker's Angel Flake Coconut**
1/2 cup whole unblanched almonds

For base, cream butter with brown sugar. Stir in egg, flour, cereal, baking powder, salt, baking soda and orange rind. Spread mixture evenly in 9" baking pan. For topping, combine eggs and brown sugar; mix well. Stir in cereal, apricots, dates, coconut and almonds; mix well. Pour over cereal mixture in pan. Bake at 350°F for 30-35 minutes or until golden brown. Cool thoroughly. Cut into bars. Store in airtight container.

CHOCOLATE FUDGE

1 1/3 cups sugar
2/3 cup **Delisle Plain Yogurt**
3 tbsp. butter
8 oz. semi-sweet chocolate, in small pieces
3 cups miniature marshmallows
1/2 cup nuts
1/2 cup candied cherries

In a saucepan, combine sugar, yogurt and butter. Cook about 8 minutes or to 227°F on a thermometer. Remove from heat, add chocolate and marshmallows. Stir until melted. Add nuts and cherries. Pour into a greased 8" square pan. Cool and cut into squares.

Makes about 24 squares

CHOICE CHEWS

1 cup **Skippy Super Chunk** or **Creamy Peanut Butter**
1 cup **Crown Brand** or **Karo Corn Syrup**
1/2 cup brown sugar
1/4 cup butter
1/2 tsp. nutmeg
3 cups flaked bran cereal
1 cup raisins
1 cup chopped walnuts
1 tsp. vanilla

In saucepan over medium heat, stir together peanut butter, corn syrup, brown sugar, butter and nutmeg until well blended. Remove from heat. Stir in cereal, raisins, walnuts and vanilla. Combine thoroughly. Press into greased 9" pan. Refrigerate to chill. Cut into squares. Store in refrigerator.

ALMOND CREAM-CHEESE COOKIES

1/2 cup **Crisco**
4 1/2 oz. cream cheese, softened
1/2 cup sugar
1/2 tsp. almond extract
1 cup sifted flour
2 tsp. baking powder
1/4 tsp. salt
1 cup crisp rice cereal
red and green candied cherries

In bowl, blend Crisco, cheese, sugar and extract until combined. Combine flour, baking powder and salt. Stir into creamed mixture until combined. Chill about 2 hours. Preheat oven to 350°F. Form dough into balls, using 1 tbsp. for each cookie. Roll in coarsely crushed cereal. Place on ungreased cookie sheet. Cut cherries in slivers. Top each ball with cherry piece, pressing in lightly. Bake for 12-14 minutes. Cool on rack.

Makes about 30 cookies

CHOCOLATE MARBLED BROWNIES

⅔ cup all-purpose flour
½ tsp. baking powder
¼ tsp. salt
½ cup butter
½ cup **Fry's Cocoa**
1 cup sugar
2 eggs
¾ tsp. vanilla

Cream Cheese Filling:

½ lb. cream cheese, softened
⅓ cup sugar
1 egg
½ tsp. vanilla

To prepare filling: Beat softened cream cheese. Gradually beat in sugar, egg and vanilla until smooth. To prepare brownie mixture: Stir together flour, baking powder and salt. Melt butter in medium saucepan. Remove from heat. Stir in Fry's Cocoa. Beat in sugar, eggs and vanilla. Blend in dry ingredients. Pour half the batter into a greased 9" square baking pan. Carefully spread Cream Cheese Filling on top. Spoon remaining chocolate batter over filling. Pull a knife through both batters to create a marbled effect. Bake in preheated 350°F oven 40-45 minutes. Cool.
Makes about 2 dozen brownies

CRUNCHY ALPEN COOKIES

½ lb. shortening
1 cup lightly packed brown sugar
2 cups **Alpen Mixed Cereal**
1 tsp. vanilla
1¾ cups all-purpose flour
½ tsp. salt
1 tsp. baking soda
¼ cup hot water

Cream shortening and blend in sugar. Add Alpen and vanilla. Sift flour with salt. Combine baking soda and hot water. Add flour to sugar mixture, alternately with soda and water, combining well. Break off dough in pieces about size of a walnut. Place about 1½" apart on lightly greased cookie sheets, flatten with floured fork. Bake in 350°F oven, about 10 minutes.
Makes approximately 5 dozen

CRISP CHOCOLATE COOKIES

1 cup soft butter or margarine
1½ cups all-purpose flour
1 cup icing sugar
⅓ cup **Fry's Cocoa**

Cream butter. Sift together flour, sugar and cocoa. Gradually blend dry ingredients into butter to form a soft dough. Use this dough to complete one of the following recipes:

Chocolate Pecan Shorties: Add 1 cup finely chopped pecans to cookie dough. Shape dough into 1" balls. Place on ungreased cookie sheet. Flatten to ⅛" with bottom of glass dipped in granulated sugar. Bake in preheated 300°F oven 20-25 minutes. Cool slightly before removing from pan.
Makes 3 dozen cookies

Chocolate Cherry Winks: Shape dough into 1" balls; flatten slightly. Roll in dry quick-cooking rolled oats. Place on ungreased cookie sheet. Press a candied cherry half into the center of each cookie. Bake as for Chocolate Pecan Shorties.
Makes 3 dozen cookies

Choco Mint Sandwiches: Shape dough into 1" balls. Flatten with a fork dipped in granulated sugar. Bake as for Chocolate Pecan Shorties; cool. To make sandwiches: Combine 3 tbsp. melted butter with ¼ cup Fry's Cocoa. Blend in ¼ cup milk, ½ tsp. vanilla, a few drops peppermint extract and 2 cups sifted icing sugar until smooth. Spread filling on half of the cookies. Top with remaining cookies to form sandwiches.
Makes 1½ dozen cookies

Chocolate Happy Faces: Roll dough, part at a time, on a lightly floured board to ⅛" thickness. Cut out 2½" rounds. Cut out eyes and mouths on half the cookies. Bake as for Chocolate Pecan Shorties; cool. To assemble: Cream ¼ cup butter or margarine with 1 cup sifted icing sugar and ¼ tsp. vanilla. Spread each plain cookie with an equal amount of butter mixture and top with a face cookie.
Makes 13 cookies

COCOA NUTTY CHEWS

1½ cups quick-cooking rolled oats
1 cup bran flake cereal
1 cup chopped peanuts
1 cup raisins
1 cup miniature marshmallows
½ cup honey
⅓ cup packed brown sugar
1 cup peanut butter
¼ cup butter
½ cup **Fry's Cocoa**
2 tsp. vanilla

Mix together oats, bran cereal, peanuts, raisins and marshmallows in a large bowl. Combine honey and sugar in a saucepan. Cook over medium heat, stirring constantly, until mixture comes to boil. Add peanut butter and butter; stir until melted and smooth; remove from heat. Stir in Fry's Cocoa and vanilla. Pour over cereal mixture; stir to combine. Shape mixture into balls; store in the refrigerator.
Makes about 4 dozen

ALPEN GINGER COOKIES

¾ cup all-purpose flour
⅔ cup **Alpen Mixed Cereal**
½ cup sugar
½ tsp. baking soda
½ tsp. ground ginger
⅓ cup butter or margarine
1 tbsp. milk
1 tbsp. honey

Preheat oven to 300°F. Combine flour, Alpen, sugar, soda and ginger. Melt the butter with milk and honey over low heat. Pour over Alpen mixture, blending well. Roll into small balls and arrange 4" apart on lightly greased cookie sheets. Bake 20-25 minutes at 300°F or until golden brown. Cool 2-3 minutes before removing from cookie sheets.
Makes about 20 cookies

Peanutty Tropical Treats (top), "No-No" Nanaimos (center) and "Worth the Effort" Crescents

PEANUTTY TROPICAL TREATS

½ cup **Skippy Super Chunk** or **Creamy Peanut Butter**
¼ cup butter
1 cup brown sugar
1 cup all-purpose flour
2 eggs
1 tsp. vanilla
½ tsp. baking powder
¾ cup flaked coconut
juice and rind of 1 lemon

Cream peanut butter and butter. Blend in ½ cup brown sugar and ⅔ cup flour. Turn into 8″ pan and press down evenly. Bake at 350°F 10 minutes. Meanwhile, beat together eggs, vanilla, remaining ½ cup brown sugar, remaining ⅓ cup flour and baking powder. Stir in coconut, lemon rind and juice. Pour over baked layer and return to oven. Bake 15-20 minutes until square is just set and golden brown.

"NO-NO" NANAIMOS

½ cup butter
¼ cup sugar
1 egg
1½ cups graham cracker crumbs
¾ cup flaked coconut
½ cup chopped peanuts
½ cup **Skippy Super Chunk Peanut Butter**
2 tbsp. softened butter
2 cups icing sugar
¼ cup milk
4 squares semi-sweet chocolate
1 tbsp. butter

Mix first 3 ingredients in medium saucepan. Cook over low heat, stirring constantly for 5 minutes until smooth and slightly thickened. In large bowl, mix graham cracker crumbs, coconut and peanuts. Pour butter-egg mixture over dry ingredients and combine thoroughly. Press into 9″ square pan. Chill 15 minutes. Beat together peanut butter, 2 tbsp. butter, 2 cups icing sugar and milk until smooth. Spread over crumb mixture. Chill 30 minutes. Melt chocolate and 1 tbsp. butter together over boiling water. Spread over icing layer. Refrigerate until firm.

"WORTH THE EFFORT" CRESCENTS

½ cup **Skippy Super Chunk** or **Creamy Peanut Butter**
½ cup butter
½ cup sour cream
1½ cups all-purpose flour
½ cup sugar
¼ cup raisins
¼ cup chopped walnuts
1 tsp. cinnamon

Cream peanut butter and butter in large bowl. Beat in sour cream and flour until well blended. Cover and chill dough 2 hours. Blend together sugar, raisins, walnuts and cinnamon. After chilling, divide dough into 3 balls. On floured board, roll one ball into 9″ circle. Spread circle with ⅓ of sugar mixture. Cut into 12 wedges. Roll up each wedge starting at widest point. Twist into crescent shape and place on cookie sheet. Repeat with remaining 2 balls of dough. Bake crescents at 375°F 12-15 minutes.
Makes 3 dozen

ALPEN TRUFFLES

2 tbsp. butter or margarine
3 tbsp. milk
¼ cup sugar
2 tbsp. cocoa
⅔ cup **Alpen Mixed Cereal**
¾ cup coconut
½ tsp. vanilla or rum flavoring
chocolate flavored or cocoa decorations

Melt the butter with milk over low heat. Stir in sugar and cocoa. Add Alpen, coconut and vanilla or rum flavoring, stirring until well blended. Allow to cool. Shape into small balls (about 20) and roll in chocolate decorations or cocoa. Place on waxed paper until set.
Makes about 20 truffles

FRY'S FUDGEY BROWNIES

1⅓ cups all-purpose flour
1 tsp. baking powder
½ tsp. salt
1 cup butter or margarine
1 cup **Fry's Cocoa**
2 cups sugar
4 eggs
1½ tsp. vanilla
1 cup chopped nuts

Mix together flour, baking powder and salt. Melt butter in a large saucepan. Remove from heat. Stir in cocoa. Blend in sugar, eggs and vanilla. Blend in dry ingredients and nuts. Pour batter into a greased 9" x 13" x 2" rectangular pan. Bake in preheated 350°F oven 30-35 minutes. Cool completely. Frost with Fudgey Cocoa Frosting *(see Cakes).*

Peanut Butter Brownies: Proceed as above reducing butter to ½ cup and adding ½ cup peanut butter. Use 1 cup chopped salted peanuts. Frost with Fudgey Cocoa Frosting *(see Cakes)* and top with chopped peanuts.

Orange Date and Nut Brownies: Proceed as above reducing sugar to ¾ cup. Add ¾ cup finely chopped dates to melted butter. Add 1 tbsp. grated orange rind to batter and reduce nuts to ½ cup. Frost with Fudgey Orange Cocoa Frosting *(see Cakes for Fudgey Cocoa Frosting).*

Cherry Coconut Brownies: Proceed as above reducing nuts to ½ cup and adding ½ cup well drained, chopped maraschino cherries and ½ cup flaked coconut to batter. Frost with Fudgey Cherry Cocoa Frosting *(see Cakes for Fudgey Cocoa Frosting).*

CRISP CHOCOLATE SQUARES

Base:
¼ cup butter or margarine, melted
¾ cup **Alpen Mixed Cereal**
¼ cup firmly packed brown sugar

Cake:
1¼ cups all-purpose flour
3 tbsp. cocoa
1½ tsp. baking powder
½ tsp. salt
½ cup butter or margarine
¾ cup firmly packed brown sugar
2 eggs
1 tbsp. milk
1 tsp. vanilla

Preheat oven to 375°F. To prepare base, combine melted butter or margarine, Alpen and sugar. Spread evenly over bottom of lightly greased 8" or 9" square baking pan. Combine flour, cocoa, baking powder and salt. Cream butter or margarine with sugar until fluffy. Beat in eggs, 1 at a time. Stir dry mixture into creamed mixture with milk and vanilla. Spread batter over Alpen base. Bake 35-50 minutes at 375°F. Cool on wire rack. When cool, cut in squares.

PEANUTTY COCOA COOKIES

½ cup all-purpose flour
½ cup **Fry's Cocoa**
½ tsp. baking soda
½ tsp. salt
½ cup peanut butter
½ cup shortening
½ cup granulated sugar
½ cup firmly packed brown sugar
1 egg
3 tbsp. milk
1 cup chopped salted peanuts

Sift together flour, cocoa, baking soda and salt. Cream peanut butter and shortening together; beat in granulated sugar and brown sugar. Beat in egg. Add sifted dry ingredients alternately with milk. Stir in peanuts. Drop from small spoon onto ungreased cookie sheet. Bake in preheated 375°F oven for 12-14 minutes. Cool.
Makes about 3 dozen cookies

ALPEN FLORENTINES

½ cup butter or margarine
½ cup sugar
¾ cup **Alpen Mixed Cereal**
¼ cup chopped walnuts
2 tbsp. chopped glacé cherries
2 tbsp. mixed peel
2 tbsp. flour
1 tbsp. milk
3 squares semi-sweet chocolate, melted

Preheat oven to 350°F. In a medium saucepan over low heat, melt butter then stir in sugar until dissolved. Boil 1 minute. Add remaining ingredients, except chocolate, blending well. Drop by tsp. about 4" apart on lightly greased cookie sheets. Bake at 350°F for 10-15 minutes, or until golden brown. Remove and cool on wire racks. Frost cookies with melted chocolate.
Makes 10-12 biscuits

CHOCOLATE OATMEAL SQUARES

1½ cups quick-cooking rolled oats
1¼ cups all-purpose flour
½ tsp. salt
½ tsp. baking soda
½ cup butter, softened
1 cup packed brown sugar
2 eggs
1 10-oz. can sweetened condensed milk
½ cup **Fry's Cocoa**
½ cup chopped nuts
2 tsp. vanilla

Stir together oats, flour, salt and baking soda. Cream butter; gradually beat in sugar. Add eggs, 1 at a time, beating well after each addition. Add dry ingredients and mix until combined. Gradually stir condensed milk into Fry's Cocoa. Stir in nuts and vanilla. Spread ⅔ of the oat mixture in bottom of ungreased 9" square cake pan. Pour cocoa mixture on top. Drop small spoonfuls of remaining oat mixture over all. Bake in preheated 350°F oven 40-45 minutes. Cool.
Makes about 24 squares

CHEWY CHOCOLATEY BROWNIES

½ cup butter
3 squares unsweetened chocolate
1¼ cups granulated sugar
1 tsp. vanilla
3 eggs
⅔ cup **Robin Hood All-Purpose Flour**
½ tsp. baking powder
½ tsp. salt
½ cup chopped nuts
chocolate icing (optional)

Melt butter and chocolate in saucepan on low heat, stirring until smoothly blended. Remove from heat and add sugar, vanilla and eggs. Beat well. Combine flour, baking powder and salt. Add to chocolate mixture, stirring until well blended. Stir in nuts. Spread in greased 9″ square cake pan. Bake at 350°F for 25-30 minutes. Cool. Frost if desired and cut into squares.
Makes about 25 brownies

OATMEAL RAISIN COOKIES

2 cups **Robin Hood All-Purpose Flour** (or 2¼ cups **Robin Hood Velvet Cake & Pastry Flour**)
2 cups **Robin Hood** or **Old Mill Oats**
1 tsp. baking soda
1 tsp. salt
1 cup butter
¾ cup granulated sugar
¾ cup lightly packed brown sugar
2 eggs
1½ tsp. vanilla
1 cup raisins

Combine flour, oats, baking soda and salt. Stir well to blend. Cream butter, sugars, eggs and vanilla together until light and fluffy. Add dry ingredients to creamed mixture, mixing thoroughly. Stir in raisins. Drop dough by tbsp. onto lightly greased baking sheets. Bake at 375°F for 10-12 minutes or until light golden.
Makes about 4 dozen cookies

CHINESE FORTUNE COOKIES

1 cup **Robin Hood All-Purpose Flour**
½ cup granulated sugar
2 tbsp. cornstarch
½ tsp. salt
½ cup oil
4 egg whites
1 tbsp. water
2 tsp. vanilla

Write fortunes on ½″ x 3″ strips of paper. Place near oven for convenience. Also, have ready a straight-sided bowl and a muffin pan for cooling the cookies in. Combine flour, sugar, cornstarch and salt. Add oil, egg whites, water and vanilla; beat until smooth. Drop batter by level tbsp. onto a well greased sheet and spread out evenly with the back of a spoon into 5″ circles. Bake only 1 or 2 per sheet. Bake at 300°F for 11-14 minutes or until lightly golden. (Don't underbake or cookies will tear during shaping.) Using a wide spatula, remove 1 cookie at a time from oven. Flip cookies over from spatula into your hand protected with an oven mitt. Hold prepared fortune in center of cookie while you fold it in half; work quickly. Grasp ends of cookie and draw gently over the edge of a bowl to crease in the traditional fortune cookie shape. Ensure cookies hold their shape by cooling, ends down, in a muffin pan. (If cookie hardens too fast, you can restore flexibility by returning it to the oven for about 1 minute.) Repeat for remaining batter, using a cold greased baking sheet for each batch. Store in airtight container.
Makes 18 large cookies

SWISS DELIGHT CHOCOLATE BARK

8 squares **Baker's Semi-Sweet Chocolate**
½ cup whole blanched toasted almonds, (peanuts or hazelnuts)
½ cup raisins

Partially melt chocolate over hot water. Remove from heat and continue stirring until completely melted. Stir in nuts and raisins. Spread on waxed-paper-lined baking sheet. Chill until firm. Break into pieces. Store in refrigerator.
Makes about 12 oz. candy

BUTTER TART SQUARES

1 cup **Robin Hood All-Purpose Flour**
¼ cup granulated sugar
½ cup butter
2 eggs, lightly beaten
1 cup lightly packed brown sugar
2 tbsp. **Robin Hood All-Purpose Flour**
½ tsp. baking powder
¼ tsp. salt
½ tsp. vanilla
1 cup raisins
½ cup coarsely chopped pecans

Combine 1 cup flour and granulated sugar. Cut in butter until mixture resembles coarse meal. Press into greased 9″ square cake pan. Bake at 350°F for 12-15 minutes or until light golden. Beat together eggs, brown sugar, 2 tbsp. flour, baking powder, salt and vanilla. Stir in raisins and nuts. Pour over partially baked base. Bake at 350°F for 25 minutes or until filling is almost set. Cool and cut into squares.
Makes about 2 dozen squares

HOMEMADE FUDGE BROWNIE MIX

Mix:
2 cups sugar
1⅓ cups sifted flour
1 cup unsweetened cocoa powder
1¼ tsp. baking powder
1¼ tsp. salt
1 cup **Crisco**

Brownies:
2 eggs
1 tsp. vanilla
3 cups Mix
½ cup chopped nuts
icing sugar

To prepare mix: In bowl, combine dry ingredients. Cut in Crisco until it resembles coarse cornmeal. Store in covered container up to 6 weeks at room temperature. Freeze for longer storage. To measure, lightly spoon into measuring cup; level off. Makes about 6 cups. To make brownies: Preheat oven to 350°F. Beat eggs with vanilla. Add Mix; stir until nearly smooth. Stir in chopped nuts. Spread in greased 8″ x 8″ x 2″ baking pan. Bake about 30 minutes. Cool. Sift icing sugar over top. Cut.
Makes 16 brownies

THE BAKER'S CLASSIC BROWNIE

- 2 squares **Baker's Unsweetened Chocolate**
- ⅓ cup butter
- ⅔ cup all-purpose flour
- ½ tsp. baking powder
- ¼ tsp. salt
- 2 eggs
- 1 cup sugar
- 1 tsp. vanilla
- ½ cup chopped nuts

Melt chocolate with butter over hot water; cool. Sift flour with baking powder and salt. Beat eggs. Gradually add sugar, beating until well blended. Blend in chocolate mixture and vanilla. Stir in flour mixture. Fold in nuts. Spread into greased and floured 8" square pan. Bake at 350°F for 25-30 minutes or until brownies begin to pull away from sides of pan. Cool in pan on wire rack.

Gloriously Glazed Classic Brownie: Melt 1 square **Baker's Unsweetened Chocolate** with 1 tbsp. butter and ¼ cup milk; blend until smooth. Add 1¼ cups icing sugar; blend well. Spread over cooled brownies.

Really Rocky Road Classic Brownie: Sprinkle still-warm brownies with 2 cups miniature marshmallows. Broil under preheated broiler until marshmallows are golden brown. Drizzle with 1 square melted chocolate.

The Baker's Classic Brownie

QUAKER OATMEAL RAISIN COOKIES

- 1 cup shortening at room temperature
- 2 cups packed brown sugar
- 2 tsp. vanilla
- 1½ cups all-purpose flour
- 1 tsp. baking soda
- 1 tsp. salt
- 1 tsp. cinnamon
- 1½ cups raisins, dates or chocolate chips
- 3 cups **Quaker Oats**
- ½ cup water

Cream shortening and sugar, add vanilla. Sift together flour, baking soda, salt and cinnamon, blend in raisins. Add dry ingredients to the shortening-sugar mixture and stir well. Add oats and water. Mix until oats are well blended. Drop well rounded teaspoonfuls onto a greased cookie sheet. Bake at 350°F for 12-15 minutes.

Makes about 4 dozen cookies

QUAKER OAT BRAN COOKIES

- ¾ cup butter or margarine
- 1 cup white sugar
- ½ cup packed brown sugar
- 1 egg, slightly beaten
- 1 cup flour
- ¼ cup **Quaker Oats**
- 1 cup **Quaker Oat Bran**
- ¾ cup coconut
- 1 tsp. baking powder
- 1 tsp. baking soda
- 1 cup raisins

Cream butter or margarine, sugars and egg together. Combine all dry ingredients and stir in gradually to the butter-sugar-egg mixture. Mix until all ingredients are well incorporated. Drop by tsp. onto greased cookie sheet. Bake at 350°F for 12-15 minutes.

Makes about 4 dozen cookies

CHOCOLATE-TOPPED CRUNCHIES

- ⅓ cup firmly packed brown sugar
- 3 tbsp. corn syrup
- 2 tbsp. crunchy peanut butter
- 2 tbsp. melted butter
- ½ tsp. vanilla
- 2 cups **Post Bran Flakes**
- 4 squares **Baker's Semi-Sweet Chocolate**
- ⅓ cup crunchy peanut butter

Combine brown sugar, corn syrup, 2 tbsp. peanut butter, butter and vanilla; mix well. Add cereal; mix well. Press into greased 8" square pan. Bake at 375°F for 5 minutes. Melt chocolate and ⅓ cup peanut butter over hot water. Spread evenly over baked layer. Cool and store in refrigerator.

Makes 32 2" x 1" bars

CALIFORNIA DREAM BARS

¾ cup **Mazola Corn Oil**
½ cup sugar
rind of 1 orange
2 eggs
¼ cup **Crown Brand** or **Karo Corn Syrup**
1½ cups all-purpose flour
2 tsp. baking powder
1 tsp. cinnamon
½ tsp. nutmeg
½ tsp. allspice
¼ tsp. salt
6 tbsp. orange juice
1 cup raisins
½ cup chopped walnuts

Orange Frosting:
2¼ cups icing sugar
2 tbsp. **Mazola Corn Oil**
rind of 1 orange
3 tbsp. orange juice

Beat together, in large bowl, oil, sugar and orange rind. Beat in eggs, 1 at a time, and corn syrup. In second bowl, blend flour, baking powder, cinnamon, nutmeg, allspice and salt. Add dry ingredients to large bowl, alternately with orange juice. Beat well. Stir in raisins and walnuts. Pour into greased 9" x 13" pan. Bake at 350°F 30 minutes. Cool. To prepare frosting: Beat together all frosting ingredients until smooth. Spread over cake. Store in refrigerator. At serving time, cut into bars.

CHOCOLATE DOUBLEHEADERS

2 cups semi-sweet chocolate chips
2 cups all-purpose flour
½ tsp. baking soda
¼ tsp. salt
2 eggs
¾ cup sugar
½ cup **Hellmann's or Best Foods Real Mayonnaise**
1 tsp. vanilla
1 cup chopped nuts

Melt 1 cup chocolate chips. In medium bowl, blend flour, baking soda and salt. In large bowl, beat together eggs, sugar, mayonnaise and vanilla. Beat in melted chocolate. Stir in flour mixture, remaining chocolate chips and nuts. Drop by tsp. onto greased cookie sheet. Bake at 375°F for 10 minutes.
Makes 5 dozen cookies

SLICE-AND-BAKE OATMEAL COOKIES

1 cup **Crisco**
1 cup granulated sugar
1 cup packed brown sugar
2 eggs
1 tsp. vanilla
1½ cups sifted flour
1 tsp. baking soda
1 tsp. salt
1 tsp. ground cinnamon
1½ cups quick-cooking rolled oats
½ cup finely chopped walnuts

In mixing bowl, cream together Crisco, granulated sugar and brown sugar till light and fluffy. Add eggs, 1 at a time, beating well after each; add vanilla. Combine the flour, baking soda, salt and cinnamon; stir into creamed mixture. Stir in oats and walnuts. Shape dough into 2 8" rolls. Wrap in waxed paper or clear plastic wrap. Chill thoroughly, about 3 hours. Preheat oven to 350°F. Cut dough into ¼" slices. Place on greased cookie sheet. Bake for 8-10 minutes. Cool on rack.
Makes about 60 cookies

SIMPLY DELICIOUS PECAN SQUARES

Squares:
¼ cup **Mazola Corn Oil**
1 cup brown sugar
2 eggs
¼ cup chopped pecans
1 tsp. vanilla
¾ cup all-purpose flour
1 tsp. baking powder
½ tsp. salt

Topping:
½ cup brown sugar
2 tbsp. **Mazola Corn Oil**
1 tbsp. milk or cream
½ cup chopped pecans

To make squares: Beat together, in large bowl, oil and brown sugar. Beat in eggs, 1 at a time. Add pecans and vanilla. In second bowl, blend flour, baking powder and salt. Stir dry ingredients into large bowl and mix well. Pour into greased 8" square cake pan. Bake at 350°F 20 minutes. For topping, stir together ingredients; spread over cake and broil until top is bubbly.

GLAZED LEMON BARS

Bottom Layer:
1 cup sifted all-purpose flour
¼ cup icing sugar
¼ tsp. salt
½ cup **Crisco Shortening**

Filling:
2 cups sugar
¼ cup all-purpose flour
1 tsp. baking powder
¼ tsp. salt
4 eggs, slightly beaten
¼ cup lemon juice
2 tsp. grated lemon peel

Glaze:
½ cup icing sugar
2 tbsp. lemon juice
1 tbsp. **Crisco Shortening**

To make bottom layer: Combine flour, icing sugar and salt in a bowl. Cut in shortening until mixture resembles crumbs. Turn dough into a 9" square pan; press into an even layer. Bake at 325°F for 12-15 minutes or until lightly browned. To prepare filling: Combine sugar, flour, baking powder and salt in a large bowl. Add eggs, lemon juice and peel; mix thoroughly. Remove baked layer from oven and pour filling over bottom layer. Return to oven and bake 25 minutes or until golden. Combine glaze ingredients until smooth. Remove pan from oven, cool slightly; spread glaze over filling. Cool thoroughly before cutting.
Makes 2 dozen bars

COCONUT FUDGE BROWNIES

1 cup bran flakes
¾ cup all-purpose flour
¾ cup coconut
½ tsp. baking powder
¼ tsp. salt
1 cup semi-sweet chocolate chips
2 eggs
½ cup **Hellmann's or Best Foods Real Mayonnaise**
½ cup sugar
1 tsp. vanilla

Mix together the first 5 ingredients. Melt chocolate chips. Beat eggs, melted chocolate, mayonnaise, sugar and vanilla until well blended. Stir flour mixture into egg mixture. Pour into greased 9" square pan. Bake at 350°F for 25 minutes.

Monster Cookies

MONSTER COOKIES

1 cup **Skippy Super Chunk** or **Creamy Peanut Butter**
¾ cup **Mazola Corn Oil**
1 cup brown sugar
1 cup white sugar
2 eggs
1 tsp. vanilla
1¼ cups quick-cooking rolled oats
¾ cup all-purpose flour
1 tsp. baking soda
1 cup peanuts
1 cup chocolate chips
½ cup raisins

Beat together, in large bowl, peanut butter, oil, brown sugar, white sugar, eggs and vanilla. Combine rolled oats, flour, baking soda, peanuts, chocolate chips and raisins in second bowl. Stir dry ingredients into large bowl and mix well. Drop by large spoonfuls onto greased cookie sheet. Bake at 350°F 10-12 minutes.
Makes 3½ dozen large cookies

MIDNIGHT MADNESS BARS

½ cup **Skippy Super Chunk** or **Creamy Peanut Butter**
½ cup butter
¾ cup brown sugar
½ cup milk
1 cup quick-cooking rolled oats
1 cup all-purpose flour
½ tsp. baking soda
½ tsp. salt
½ tsp. cinnamon
1 cup chocolate chips, melted

Cream peanut butter and butter. Beat in brown sugar. Pour milk over rolled oats. Combine flour, baking soda, salt and cinnamon. Stir into creamed mixture. Stir in rolled oats and milk. Spread ½ the batter in greased 8″ square pan. Cover with all but 1 tbsp. melted chocolate chips. Top with remaining batter. Drizzle remaining chocolate in lines over top of batter. Bake at 350°F 30 minutes. Cool; cut into squares.

SKIPPY CHIP COOKIES

1 cup **Skippy Super Chunk** or **Creamy Peanut Butter**
1 cup butter
¾ cup sugar
¾ cup brown sugar
2 eggs
1 cup all-purpose flour
1 cup whole wheat flour
1 tsp. baking soda
½ cup chocolate chips

Cream peanut butter and butter in large bowl. Gradually beat in sugar, brown sugar and eggs. Combine all-purpose flour, whole wheat flour and baking soda. Stir in creamed mixture. Stir in chocolate chips. Drop by spoonfuls onto cookie sheet. Flatten with fork. Bake at 350°F 10 minutes.
Makes 4 dozen cookies

BAKED PEANUT-BUTTER POPCORN

3 quarts freshly popped popcorn

1 cup sugar

⅔ cup **Crown Brand** or **Karo Corn Syrup**

⅔ cup **Skippy Super Chunk Peanut Butter**

1 tsp. vanilla

½ tsp. baking soda

Place popcorn in a large shallow roasting pan. In heavy saucepan, stir together sugar and corn syrup. Place over medium heat. Stirring constantly, cook until mixture boils. Stir in peanut butter. Continue cooking, without stirring, 5 minutes. Remove from heat. Stir in vanilla and baking soda (mixture will foam up). Pour peanut-butter mixture over popcorn. Stir to coat well. Bake at 275°F 45 minutes. During the 45 minutes, remove pan from oven every 15 minutes and stir to coat popcorn with syrup mixture. Turn onto 2 foil-lined baking sheets to cool spreading out with wooden spoon.
Makes 3 quarts

HINT-OF-ORANGE SPICE COOKIES

1 cup **Skippy Super Chunk** or **Creamy Peanut Butter**

¾ cup butter

1 cup brown sugar

2 eggs

2½ cups all-purpose flour

1 tsp. baking soda

½ tsp. cinnamon

¼ tsp. nutmeg

rind of 1 orange, grated

Cream peanut butter and butter in large bowl. Gradually beat in brown sugar and eggs. Combine flour, baking soda, cinnamon, nutmeg and orange rind. Stir into creamed mixture. Drop by spoonfuls onto cookie sheet. Flatten with fork, pressing down once, then a second time at right angles to first imprint. Bake at 350°F 10 minutes.
Makes 5 dozen cookies

SKIPPY GRANOLA BARS

1¼ cups quick-cooking rolled oats

¼ cup sesame seeds

¾ cup **Skippy Super Chunk Peanut Butter**

¼ cup **Crown Brand** or **Karo Corn Syrup**

¼ cup brown sugar

2 tbsp. softened butter

1 egg

1 tsp. vanilla

½ cup raisins

½ cup coconut

½ cup chopped peanuts

¼ cup wheat germ

Toast rolled oats and sesame seeds together on cookie sheet at 350°F 10 minutes until just golden brown. Mix peanut butter, corn syrup, brown sugar, butter, egg and vanilla together in large bowl. Mix raisins, coconut, peanuts and wheat germ together in second bowl. Add dry ingredients to peanut butter mixture and combine thoroughly. Stir in rolled oats and sesame seeds. Spoon into greased 8" square pan and press down evenly. Bake at 350°F 20 minutes.

CHERRY JUBILEES

½ cup **Skippy Creamy Peanut Butter**

¼ cup softened butter

½ cup graham cracker crumbs

½ cup icing sugar

¼ cup chopped walnuts

2 tbsp. **Crown Brand** or **Karo Corn Syrup**

½ cup shredded coconut

12 maraschino cherries, halved

Cream peanut butter and butter in medium bowl. Beat in graham cracker crumbs, icing sugar, walnuts and corn syrup. Shape into small balls and roll in coconut. Top each ball with cherry half and flatten slightly. Chill.
Makes 24 cookies

S'MORES

milk chocolate candy bar

KRAFT Marshmallows

graham cracker squares

Place 2 squares of candy bar and 1 large marshmallow on graham cracker. Place on napkin. Microwave on high power 15 seconds for 1 S'more or 25 seconds for 2 S'mores. Top with graham cracker. Rest 1 minute to melt chocolate.
Serves 1 or 2

PEANUT BUTTER AND JAM COOKIES

1 cup **Skippy Super Chunk** or **Creamy Peanut Butter**

¾ cup butter

1 cup sugar

1 egg

1½ cups all-purpose flour

½ tsp. baking soda

¼ tsp. salt

½ cup strawberry or raspberry jam

Cream peanut butter and butter in large bowl. Gradually beat in sugar and then egg. Combine flour, baking soda and salt. Stir into creamed mixture. Drop by spoonfuls onto cookie sheet. Press down the center of each cookie using thumb. Bake at 350°F 10 minutes. Fill indentation with jam.
Makes 5 dozen cookies

COUNTRY HOEDOWN COOKIES

½ cup **Skippy Super Chunk Peanut Butter**

½ cup butter

1 cup brown sugar

1 egg

½ tsp. vanilla

¾ cup all-purpose flour

¾ cup quick-cooking rolled oats

½ tsp. baking soda

½ cup raisins

Cream peanut butter and butter in large bowl. Gradually beat in brown sugar, egg and vanilla. Combine flour, rolled oats, baking soda and raisins. Stir into creamed mixture. Drop by spoonfuls onto cookie sheet. Flatten with fork dipped in flour. Bake at 350°F for 10 minutes.
Makes 3 dozen cookies

CRUNCHY MUNCHIES

1 cup butterscotch chips

½ cup **Skippy Super Chunk Peanut Butter**

1½ cups chow mein noodles

1 cup miniature marshmallows

½ cup peanuts

Melt butterscotch chips over boiling water. Remove from heat, add peanut butter and stir until smooth. Combine noodles, marshmallows and peanuts. Pour melted butterscotch chips and peanut butter over dry ingredients. Stir until all are coated. Using a tsp. form cookies and place on cookie sheet. Chill until firm. Store in refrigerator.
Makes 4 dozen

Strawberry Ribbon Squares

STRAWBERRY RIBBON SQUARES

1 cup unsifted all-purpose flour
¼ cup sugar
⅔ cup butter or margarine, softened
1 4-serving-size package **Jell-o Vanilla Instant Pudding**
1¾ cups milk
1 envelope **Dream Whip Dessert Topping Mix**
1 4-serving-size **Jell-o Strawberry Jelly Powder**
1 cup boiling water
1 15-oz. package frozen sliced strawberries
1 tbsp. lemon juice

Combine flour and sugar, cut in butter until mixture resembles fine crumbs. Press evenly on bottom of a 13″ x 9″ x 2″ baking pan. Bake at 350°F for 12-15 minutes or until lightly browned. Cool. Prepare instant pudding as directed on package, using 1¾ cups milk. Prepare dessert-topping mix as directed on package; fold 1 cup into prepared pudding. Spread on baked crust. Dissolve jelly powder in boiling water. Add frozen strawberries, breaking apart with a fork. Stir until slightly thickened, 3-5 minutes. Add lemon juice. Spoon evenly over pudding layer. Chill until firm. To serve, cut in squares. Garnish with remaining prepared dessert topping.

Serves 16

WALNUT SQUARES

Bottom crust:
1 cup **McCormick's Graham Cracker Crumbs**
½ cup flour
½ cup butter
1 tbsp. brown sugar

Topping:
1½ cups brown sugar
2 beaten eggs
½ cup coconut
1 cup walnuts, chopped
1 cup dates or mixed fruit
½ tsp. baking powder
1 tsp. vanilla
⅛ tsp. salt

Mix Graham Cracker Crumbs, flour, butter and sugar until crumbly. Pack down well in 8″ buttered pan and bake at 250°F for 10 minutes. Mix topping ingredients together and pour over bottom crust. Bake 300°F for a few minutes to start, then 250°F for 30 minutes. Ice with butter icing, if desired, and cut in squares.

SPICED PEAR AND CARROT COOKIES

½ cup butter
½ cup sugar
1 egg
½ cup **Emelia Spiced Pear and Lime Marmelo**
1 cup grated raw carrot
2 cups whole wheat flour
½ tsp. salt
½ tsp. baking soda
½ tsp. orange rind
⅓ cup raisins
⅓ cup nuts

Cream butter and sugar. Add egg and beat. Add Spiced Pear and Lime Marmelo and carrot. Combine dry ingredients and add, along with rind, raisins and nuts. Drop by tsp. onto cookie sheet. Bake at 350°F for 12-15 minutes.

Makes 2 dozen cookies

GUMDROP BALLS

1 can sweetened condensed milk

dash salt

3 cups coarsely crushed corn flakes

1½ cups **McCormick's Gum Drops**, finely cut up

1 tsp. vanilla

¼ tsp. almond extract

flaked coconut

Put condensed milk and salt in the top of a double boiler. Set over simmering water and heat, stirring occasionally, until very thick and caramel colored, about 1 hour. Stir in corn flakes, gum drops, vanilla and almond extract. Drop mixture by small spoonfuls into flaked coconut and roll them around to coat on all sides. Put on waxed paper to set.

Makes about 7 dozen balls

APRICOT PECAN CRESCENTS

1 cup butter or **PARKAY Margarine**

2 cups all-purpose flour

1 egg yolk, beaten

½ cup sour cream

½ cup **KRAFT Apricot Jam**, divided

½ cup **BAKER'S ANGEL FLAKE Coconut**

¼ cup finely chopped pecans

granulated sugar

Cut butter into flour until mixture resembles fine crumbs. Combine egg yolk and sour cream; blend into flour mixture. Chill dough several hours or overnight. Divide dough into 4 equal portions, keeping each part refrigerated until ready to use. Roll each part into a 10" circle on lightly floured surface. Spread with 2 tbsp. apricot jam, sprinkle with 2 tbsp. coconut and 1 tbsp. nuts. Cut circle into 12 wedges. Starting from wide end, roll each wedge into a crescent. Sprinkle with sugar. Place on ungreased cookie sheet. Bake at 350°F for 15 to 20 minutes or until lightly browned. Cool on rack. Repeat with remaining pastry.

Makes 4 dozen

BUTTERSCOTCH MALLOW SQUARES

Base:

⅓ cup **PARKAY Margarine**

1 cup lightly packed brown sugar

1 egg

1 tsp. vanilla

¾ cup all-purpose flour

1 tsp. baking powder

¼ tsp. salt

½ cup chopped pecans

Filling:

2½ cups **KRAFT Miniature Marshmallows**

Frosting:

¼ cup **PARKAY Margarine**

½ cup packed brown sugar

2 tbsp. milk

2 cups sifted icing sugar

32 pecan halves (optional)

For base, melt margarine in saucepan. Stir in brown sugar, egg and vanilla. Blend together flour, baking powder and salt. Stir dry ingredients into margarine mixture along with pecans. Spread batter in greased 8" square pan. Bake at 350°F for 20-30 minutes or until toothpick inserted in center comes out clean. Immediately scatter marshmallows over entire surface of hot cake. Press gently to flatten. For frosting, melt margarine in saucepan. Add brown sugar and simmer over low heat, stirring constantly for 2 minutes. Add milk, stirring until mixture returns to boil. Remove from heat; cool. Gradually add icing sugar, beating with a wooden spoon after each addition. If necessary, thin icing with additional few drops of milk. Spread over top of marshmallows. Garnish with pecans, if desired. Cool before cutting into squares.

Makes 20 squares

CHOCOLATE WHEELS

26 **McVitie's Digestive Biscuits**

13 marshmallows

5 oz. plain chocolate, melted

Place 13 McVitie's Digestive Biscuits on a baking tray. In the center of each put a marshmallow and put in the oven at a low heat until the marshmallow has melted just enough to flatten. Remove from the oven, spread with a knife, place another McVitie's Digestive on top. Dip the biscuits into melted chocolate and spread evenly with a knife. Decorate with sweets.

DIGESTIVE COCONUT CRISP

2 oz. margarine

1 level tbsp. corn syrup

1 oz. soft brown sugar

2-3 heaped tbsp. crushed cornflakes

2-3 heaped tbsp. desiccated coconut

McVitie's Digestive Biscuits

Melt the margarine, syrup and sugar, then add all the other ingredients. Spread over the Digestive biscuits, this quantity is sufficient to cover about 12-15 biscuits. Place the biscuits under a moderate grill until the topping is golden brown. Leave to cool.

Makes about 12-15

DAINTY SLICES

32 marshmallows

½ cup chopped walnuts

½ cup cut-up dates

½ cup sweetened condensed milk

¼ cup boiling water

2 cups **McCormick's Graham Cracker Crumbs**

Blend marshmallows, walnuts, dates, sweetened condensed milk, boiling water and 1¼ cups Graham Cracker Crumbs (mixture will be sticky). Form into 2 rolls about 1½" in diameter. Roll in remaining crumbs to coat, wrap in waxed paper or foil and chill until ready to serve. Slice with serrated knife.

Makes 3-4 dozen slices

ROCKY ROAD FUDGE

4 squares **BAKER'S Unsweetened Chocolate**

3 tbsp. butter or **PARKAY Margarine**

3 cups icing sugar

¼ tsp. salt

⅓ cup hot milk

1 tsp. vanilla

1½ cups **KRAFT Miniature Marshmallows**

1 cup chopped walnuts

½ cup **BAKER'S Miniature Chocolate Chips**

Melt chocolate and butter in a saucepan over medium heat; stir until smooth. Add icing sugar, salt, milk and vanilla; mix well. Fold in marshmallows, nuts and chocolate chips. Spread in 9" × 5" loaf pan lined with waxed paper. Chill until firm.

Microwave Method: In a large microwaveable bowl, melt unsweetened chocolate and butter on medium for 3-4 minutes; stir until smooth. Continue as directed above.

Makes 32 pieces

Magic Cookie Bars

MAGIC COOKIE BARS

½ cup butter

1½ cups graham wafer crumbs

1 can **Eagle Brand Sweetened Condensed Milk**

1 cup semi-sweet chocolate chips

1¼ cups flaked coconut

1 cup chopped nuts

Preheat oven to 350°F or 325°F for glass dish. In 13" x 9" baking pan, melt butter in oven. Sprinkle crumbs over butter; mix together and press into pan. Pour sweetened condensed milk evenly over crumbs. Sprinkle with chips, then coconut and nuts; press down firmly. Bake 25-30 minutes or until lightly browned. Cool well before cutting. Store loosely covered at room temperature.
Makes 24 bars

MOCHA ALMOND BUTTER BARS

Base:

1 cup sifted all-purpose flour

¼ cup granulated sugar

2 tsp. **MAXWELL HOUSE Instant Coffee** granules

½ cup butter

Topping:

⅓ cup sifted all-purpose flour

½ tsp. baking powder

1 tsp. **MAXWELL HOUSE Instant Coffee** granules

¼ tsp. salt

½ tsp. cinnamon

3 eggs

1 cup firmly packed brown sugar

1 tsp. almond extract

1½ cups sliced blanched almonds

For base, combine flour, sugar and 2 tsp. instant coffee. Cut in butter until mixture resembles fine crumbs. Press into an 8" square pan. Bake at 350°F for 20 minutes. For topping, sift together flour, baking powder, 1 tsp. instant coffee, salt and cinnamon; set aside. Beat eggs well. Gradually add brown sugar, almond extract and flour mixture; blend. Stir in almonds. Spread over base. Bake for 25 minutes. Cool on wire rack and cut into bars.
Makes 32 bars

PEANUTTY OATMEAL CHOCOLATE CHUNK COOKIES

1½ cups **KRAFT Smooth** or **Crunchy Peanut Butter**

½ cup butter or margarine, softened

¾ cup sugar

⅔ cup packed brown sugar

2 eggs

1½ tsp. vanilla

1 cup rolled oats

¾ cup all-purpose flour

½ tsp. baking soda

8 squares **BAKER'S Semi-Sweet Chocolate**, each square cut into 8 pieces

In mixing bowl, cream together peanut butter and butter. Gradually beat in sugars. Blend in eggs and vanilla. Add oats, flour and baking soda. Blend into creamed mixture, just to combine. Stir in chocolate chunks. Drop by tablespoonfuls onto greased cookie sheets. Bake at 350°F for 10-12 minutes or until centers are still soft to touch. Cool 3 minutes; move to rack.
Makes about 3½ dozen cookies

EASY GINGERBREAD COOKIES

1 6-serving-size package **JELL-O Butterscotch Pudding and Pie Filling**

¾ cup **PARKAY Margarine**

¾ cup firmly packed brown sugar

1 egg

2¼ cups all-purpose flour

1 tsp. baking soda

3 tsp. ginger

1½ tsp. cinnamon

Cream pudding and pie filling with margarine and sugar. Add egg and blend well. Combine flour, baking soda, ginger and cinnamon; blend into pudding mixture. Chill dough until firm, about 5-10 minutes. Roll on a floured board to about ¼" thickness and cut with cookie cutter. Place on greased baking sheets and use a straw to make a hole in the top of each cookie for hanging on the tree. Bake at 350°F for 10-12 minutes. Cool on wire rack and decorate as desired.
Makes 16-18 cookies

HOT AND COLD BEVERAGES

Nothing seems to set the mood quite like the perfect beverage. The right drink can pick you up, get your party started, or relax and calm you after a long hard day.

This chapter invites you to try a wide range of thirst-quenching concoctions. Our recipes range from aromatic, warm beverages, to frosty coolers and non-alcoholic favorites.

Whether you're planning to entertain or simply spend a quiet evening around the fireplace, the perfect beverage awaits.

Cheers!

Bright's Quick Thick Apple Breakfast (left, see page 261) and Hot Mulled Apple Toddy (see page 260)

MULLED RICH BLEND

2 cups apple juice
2 cups water
½ cup brown sugar
1 cinnamon stick
16 whole cloves
dash ground nutmeg
2 tbsp. **Nescafé Rich Blend Coffee**
4 cinnamon sticks to garnish

In a large saucepan, combine all ingredients except Nescafé Rich Blend Coffee and cinnamon sticks. Cover and simmer for 20 minutes. Stir in Nescafé Rich Blend Coffee. Ladle into mugs and garnish with a cinnamon stick. (Also delicious with Nescafé Viva Decaffeinated or Nescafé Colombia.)
Makes 4 8-oz. servings

MEXICANA COFFEE

¼ cup butter or margarine
¾ cup **Fry's Cocoa**
⅓ cup corn syrup
½ cup coffee liqueur
1 cup whipping cream
5 cups hot coffee

Melt butter in a small saucepan. Remove from heat. Blend in cocoa and corn syrup. Stir in liqueur. Chill. Whip cream until softly stiff; fold in chocolate mixture. Store in refrigerator. To serve, fill 8-oz. mugs half full with chocolate mixture. Add enough hot coffee to fill mugs. Stir to blend. Serve immediately.
Serves 8

COFFEE LIQUEUR

2 cups boiling water
2 cups white sugar
5 tbsp. **Camp Coffee**
1 tsp. vanilla
26 oz. generic-brand alcohol from your liquor store

Combine the first 4 ingredients above. Let cool, then add the alcohol. Sterilize whatever bottle you are going to use. Bottle and let stand for about 2-3 weeks. Shake occasionally. Tastes similar to Tia Maria.
Makes approximately 1½ bottles.

Mulled Rich Blend

COFFEENOG

3 eggs, separated
2½ tbsp. **Taster's Choice Coffee** (regular, decaffeinated or continental blend)
¾ cup sugar
¾ cup cold water
3 tsp. vanilla
3 cups milk
¾ cup brandy
⅓ cup sugar
1½ cups whipping cream, whipped

In a medium-sized bowl, beat the egg yolks, Taster's Choice and sugar together until smooth. Add water, vanilla, milk and brandy; blend thoroughly. Pour into a punch bowl. In a separate bowl, beat egg whites until soft peaks form. Gradually beat in ⅓ cup sugar and beat until stiff peaks form. Fold whipped cream and egg whites into coffee mixture in the punch bowl. Keep chilled until serving time.
Makes 12 4-oz. servings

IRISH CREAM

1-2½ oz. whiskey or brandy
1 can sweetened condensed milk
1 pint half and half cream
3 tbsp. **Camp Coffee**
1 tbsp. **Coco Lopez Cream of Coconut**, well blended

Blend the above for 3-4 minutes. Pour into sterilized bottles. Keep refrigerated for 1-2 weeks. Serve and enjoy.
Makes approximately 1½ bottles

CHOCOLATE ICE-CREAM SODA

2-3 tbsp. **Hershey's Brown Cow**
¼ cup gingerale or club soda, chilled
2 scoops vanilla ice cream
additional club soda, chilled
strawberry or cherry to garnish

Mix Brown Cow and ¼ cup club soda in a tall glass; add scoops of vanilla ice cream. Fill glass with additional club soda. Garnish with strawberry or cherry. Serve with long-handled spoon and straw.
Makes 12 oz.

MOTT'S CLAMATO CAESAR

celery salt
ice cubes
dash hot red-pepper sauce
2 dashes Worcestershire sauce
salt and pepper to taste
Mott's Clamato Juice or **Extra-Spicy Clamato**
vodka (optional)
celery stalk and slice of lime to garnish

Rim large glass with celery salt. Over ice cubes, add hot red-pepper sauce, Worcestershire sauce, salt and pepper to taste. Fill to the brim with Mott's Clamato. (Or, if desired, make with 4 parts Mott's Clamato and 1 part vodka.) Stir. Garnish with celery stalk and slice of lime.
Serves 1

ROSE'S DAIQUIRI

1½ oz. rum
1 oz. **Rose's Lime Cordial**
½ tsp. sugar
ice cubes

Combine rum, Rose's Lime Cordial, sugar and ice cubes in cocktail shaker. Cover and shake well. Strain into cocktail glass.
Serves 1

SWISS BEER PUNCH

3 bottles **Birell Non-Alcoholic Beer**
¼ cup domestic sherry
¼ cup domestic brandy
dash nutmeg
1 tbsp. sugar
3 tbsp. lemon juice
few pieces of lemon peel

Mix ingredients and pour over crushed ice.
Serves 6

SWEET LASSI

1 cup plain yogurt
1 cup milk
½ cup crushed ice
½ tsp. ground cardamom seeds
few drops of rose water (optional)

Blend all ingredients together. Pour into tall glasses. Sprinkle cardamom on top.

Mango Lassi: Purée a 15-oz. can of **Sharwood's Mango Slices** with their juice and use in the above recipe to replace milk.

COOL WHINER

Mix equal measures of wine and your choice of **Canada Dry Club Soda**, **Wink**, **Bitter Lemon** or **Lime Rickey** in a wine glass. Top with a lemon or lime wedge.
Serves 1

GIN COOLER

1¼ oz. gin
¼ oz. orange liqueur
½ oz. lime juice

Mix in a tall glass with cracked ice. Fill with **Canada Dry Club Soda.**
Serves 1

GIN AND WINK COOLERS

1½ oz. gin or vodka
5 oz. **Canada Dry Wink**
½ oz. any fruit liqueur

Mix together in a tall glass, over ice.
Serves 1

VODKA COOLER

1½ oz. vodka
2 oz. lemon juice

Mix in a tall glass with cracked ice. Fill with **Canada Dry Bitter Lemon.**
Serves 1

VODKA WINE COOLER

1½ oz. vodka
4 oz. white or red wine
4 oz. **Canada Dry Wink** or **Bitter Lemon**

Mix together in a tall glass. Serve with ice.
Serves 1

VELVET RICH BANANA WHIP

2 bananas, cut up
⅓ cup **ReaLemon Reconstituted Lemon Juice**
1 can **Eagle Brand Sweetened Condensed Milk**
2 cups crushed ice
maraschino cherries (optional)

In blender container, combine all ingredients except cherries in order listed; blend until smooth. If desired, garnish with maraschino cherries. (Mixture stays thick and creamy in the refrigerator.)
Makes 1 quart

CAROL JAMIESON'S CHAMPAGNE TEA PUNCH

3½ cups triple strength **Fruit-Flavored Smith & Jamieson Tea**
½ cup brandy
¼ cup orange liqueur
1 bottle champagne
sugar to taste
lemon and lime slices

Make tea and allow it to cool. Fill a large punch bowl ⅓ full with ice. Add tea, brandy, orange liqueur and champagne. Stir, taste and add sugar if desired. Float slices of lemon and lime on top. (Smith & Jamieson Tea comes in Wild Strawberry, Apricot, Earl Grey, Black Currant, Raspberry, Spice, Blackberry, Wild Cherry, Tropical Fruit, Lemon, Sweet Orange and Peppermint.)
Makes about 7 cups

THICK STRAWBERRY WHIP

1 pint fresh strawberries, cleaned and hulled (reserve several for garnish, if desired) or 2 cups frozen strawberries
¼ cup **ReaLemon Reconstituted Lemon Juice**
1 can **Eagle Brand Sweetened Condensed Milk**
2 cups crushed ice

In blender container, combine all ingredients in order listed; blend until smooth. If desired, garnish with reserved strawberries. (Mixture stays thick and creamy in the refrigerator.)
Makes 4 cups

WINK SHANDY

3 parts beer or ale
1 part **Canada Dry Wink**
1 part soda

Mix in a tall glass and add ice.
Serves 1

RUBY SPRITZER

4 oz. **Ocean Spray Cranberry Cocktail**
club soda
lemon wedge

Pour Cranberry Cocktail over ice in a large wine glass. Add a splash of club soda. Garnish with lemon wedge. (If desired, 1½ oz. of wine may be added before club soda.)
Serves 1

MARNISSIMO

1 coffeespoon powdered sugar
1½ tbsp. **Grand Marnier**
a good cup of coffee
whipped cream, lightly whipped

Put the coffeespoon of powdered sugar in a glass. Add hot Grand Marnier and then approximately twice the amount of coffee. Stir. Top with the lightly whipped cream. Be careful not to mix while serving.
Serves 1

MIDNIGHT SIN

2 parts vodka
2 parts **Grand Marnier Liqueur**
1 part lemon juice
cherries or lemon twists to garnish

Shake well with cracked ice, strain into glasses. Decorate with cherries or lemon twists.

MIMOSA

6 oz. chilled dry champagne
1 oz. **Grand Marnier Liqueur**
3 oz. chilled orange juice

All ingredients should be very cold. Combine in a pitcher, mix gently using a long-handled spoon. Pour in glasses and serve at once.
Serves 2

CAFÉ MARNIER

1 tsp. powdered sugar
2 tbsp. **Grand Marnier Liqueur**
1 cup (6 oz.) strong brewed coffee
whipped cream

Stir together in a glass, sugar, Grand Marnier and good strong coffee. Top lightly with whipped cream. Be careful not to mix while serving.
Serves 1

GRAND MARNIER PLUS

1 oz. **Grand Marnier**
1 oz. **Cognac Marnier-Lapostolle**

Mix and serve in a snifter. If preferred cold, served iced.
Serves 1

GRAND MARNIER "SOUR"

1 oz. **Grand Marnier**
juice of ½ lemon
1 slice orange

Mix in cocktail shaker with ice. Strain into a tall glass. Decorate with slice of orange. Enjoy over ice.

ORANGE CHAMPAGNE

6 parts iced dry champagne
1 part **Grand Marnier**
3 parts very cold orange juice

Mix in a jug, first the champagne, then the Grand Marnier followed by the orange juice. Pour into glasses and serve.

RED LION

1 part dry gin
1 part **Grand Marnier**
1 part orange juice
dash lemon juice

Prepare in advance. Mix all together in a jug. Stir. Cool, then serve.

THE BEAUTIFUL

1 oz. **Grand Marnier**
1 oz. **Marnier Lapostolle V.S.O.P. Cognac**

Mix and serve in a snifter.
Serves 1

MOGUL

1 mug hot chocolate
1-1½ oz. **Grand Marnier**
whipped cream
bitter chocolate shavings

To a mug of hot chocolate add the Grand Marnier. Top with two mounds (moguls!) of whipped cream, then sprinkle with bitter chocolate shavings.

BILLY BEE DAIQUIRI

1½-2 oz. light rum
½ oz. lime juice
½-1 tsp. **Billy Bee Honey**
½ cup crushed ice

Put all ingredients in a blender and blend at a low speed 10-15 seconds.
Serves 1

HOT MULLED APPLE TODDY

1 48-oz. can **Bright's Pure Apple Juice**
½ cup brown sugar
½ tsp. ground cinnamon
⅛ tsp. ground cloves
⅛ tsp. mace
dash nutmeg
½ medium lemon, sliced
1 medium orange, sliced
4 spiced apple rings (optional)
8 cinnamon sticks (optional)

In large saucepan, combine juice, brown sugar, spices and fruit slices; cover. Simmer over low heat for 1 hour to allow flavors to blend. Serve warm, garnished with cinnamon sticks, if desired.
Serves 8

CRANBERRY COLLINS

4 oz. **Ocean Spray Cranberry Cocktail**
1 tsp. sweetened lime juice
club soda

In a tall glass, pour Cranberry Cocktail and lime juice over ice cubes. Top with club soda. Stir.
Serves 1

HOT TODDY

2 tbsp. **Lynch Butterscotch Topping**
6 oz. boiling water
1-1½ oz. rum or brandy (more or less to taste)
1 strip lemon peel
1 whole clove
1 cinnamon stick or a pinch of cinnamon

Preheat a mug with hot water. Stick clove in lemon peel. Combine all ingredients together in the heated mug. Stir and serve.
Makes 8 oz.

BEEF BROTH CHABLIS

1 10-oz. can **Campbell's Condensed Beef Broth**
10 oz. water
2 tbsp. Chablis or other dry white wine

Combine all ingredients. Place in refrigerator for at least 4 hours. Serve in chilled cups or glasses.
Makes 3 servings

BRÛLOT MARNIER

4 oz. good quality red wine
pinch of cinnamon
1 oz. **Grand Marnier**

When wine is hot, add cinnamon. Pour into small toddy mug. Then heat 1 oz. Grand Marnier in large spoon. Light Grand Marnier and pour flaming Grand Marnier over wine. Sweeten to taste.
Serves 1

GRAND MARNIER TONIC

1 part **Grand Marnier**
1 slice lemon
3-4 parts tonic water

Fill a large glass with ice, add the Grand Marnier and the slice of lemon. Top up with tonic water. Serve.
Serves 1

BRIGHT'S QUICK THICK APPLE BREAKFAST

½ cup partially skimmed plain yogurt
1 tbsp. liquid honey
¾ cup **Bright's Pure Apple Juice**
1 medium banana, sliced

In blender container, combine all ingredients. Cover and blend at high power until smooth. Serve chilled.
Serves 2

BRIGHT'S APPLE SHANTY COCKTAIL

3 cups **Bright's Pure Apple Juice**, chilled
1 bottle (3 cups) gingerale, chilled
1 tsp. lemon juice

In large pitcher, combine all ingredients. Stir to blend. Serve chilled.
Serves 8-10

FRUITED APPLE TEA

1 48-oz. can **Bright's Pure Apple Juice**
3 tea bags
10 whole cloves
¼ tsp. cinnamon
½ tsp. sugar
3 tbsp. lemon juice
⅓ cup orange juice
1 medium orange, sliced

In a large saucepan, heat apple juice to boiling; remove from heat. Add tea bags, cloves and cinnamon. Cover and let steep for 5 minutes. Remove tea bags and stir in sugar, lemon juice and orange juice. Heat over low heat until hot. Serve warm with orange slices.
Serves 8

BRIGHT'S QUICK APPLE SHAKE

1 cup **Bright's Pure Apple Juice**
½ cup vanilla ice cream
1 egg
dash cinnamon

In blender container, combine all ingredients. Cover and blend at high power until smooth. Serve chilled. Sprinkle each serving with cinnamon.
Serves 2

BRIGHT'S APPLE NOG

4 eggs, separated
2 tbsp. sugar
2 cups vanilla ice cream
2 cups **Bright's Pure Apple Juice**
dash nutmeg

In large bowl, beat egg yolks until thick. Add sugar, ice cream and apple juice; mix until blended. In medium bowl, beat egg whites with electric mixer until soft peaks form; fold into apple juice mixture. Serve chilled. Sprinkle each serving with nutmeg.
Serves 6-8

BILLY BEE BUZZ

1 oz. gin
juice of ¼ lemon
1 tsp. **Billy Bee Honey**

Shake with crushed ice, strain and serve.
Serves 1

Grand Marnier Tonic

CHOCO-BANANA SHAKE

1 cup milk

¼ cup Fastastic Chocolate Syrup *(see Desserts)*

¼ cup peanut butter

2 large scoops vanilla ice cream

Combine all ingredients in a blender container. Cover and blend until smooth.
Makes 2 servings

P'NUTTY CHOCOLATE SHAKE

1 cup milk

¼ cup Fastastic Chocolate Syrup *(see Desserts)*

¼ cup peanut butter

2 large scoops vanilla ice cream

Combine all ingredients in a blender container. Cover and blend until smooth.
Makes 2 servings

BLITHE SPIRITED GROG

1 can **Eagle Brand Sweetened Condensed Milk**

2½ cups water

1 cup brandy

½ cup dark rum

2 egg whites

nutmeg

In small punch bowl or pitcher, combine sweetened condensed milk and water; stir in brandy and rum. Set aside. In small bowl, beat egg whites to very soft peaks, stir into milk mixture. Chill. Garnish with nutmeg.
Makes 1 quart

BREAKFAST EXPRESS

1 cup milk

2 tbsp. **TANG Orange Flavour Crystals**

1 egg

⅓ cup sliced fresh strawberries or 1 small banana

Combine milk, crystals, egg and fruit in blender jar or food processor. Blend on high speed until smooth. Serve immediately.

Variations: Add any of the following ingredients to the basic recipe: 1 peeled sliced kiwi fruit, 1 tsp. honey or ¼ cup yogurt. For a hot breakfast nog—heat milk with 1 tbsp. *each* honey and wheat germ before adding to other ingredients.
Makes 1 breakfast shake

FIRESIDE APPLE TODDY

4 10-oz. cans **Campbell's Condensed Beef Broth**

20 oz. apple juice

10 oz. water

¼ cup brandy

¼ tsp. ground cinnamon

¼ tsp. ground cloves

¼ tsp. ground nutmeg

orange slices

In a saucepan, combine all ingredients except orange slices. Bring to boil; reduce heat. Simmer a few minutes to blend flavor. Serve in mugs; garnish with orange slices.
Makes 8-9 cups

NUTMEG MUG

1 10-oz. can **Campbell's Condensed Green Pea Soup**

10 oz. water or milk

⅛-¼ tsp. ground nutmeg

orange slices, cut in quarters

Combine soup, water or milk and nutmeg. Heat; stir occasionally. Serve in mugs or cups; garnish with orange slices.
Makes 2-3 servings

BERRY BERRY DAIQUIRI

½ cup **CRYSTAL LIGHT Berry Blend Concentrate***

4-5 fresh whole strawberries

¼ cup white rum or vodka

½ cup crushed ice

Combine concentrate, strawberries, rum and crushed ice in blender container. Blend at high speed until smooth. Pour ½ cup of concentrate over crushed ice in brandy snifter. Garnish with twisted orange slice and whole strawberry on cocktail pick. Serve with straw.

*To prepare concentrate, empty 1 pouch CRYSTAL LIGHT Berry Blend Low Calorie Drink Mix into plastic container. Add 3 cups cold water; stir to dissolve crystals. Store covered in refrigerator.
Makes 1 cocktail

BRAZILIAN COFFEE

⅓ cup cocoa

1 tsp. salt

1 tsp. ground cinnamon

1 can **Eagle Brand Sweetened Condensed Milk**

5 cups water

1⅓ cups strong coffee

In 3-quart saucepan, combine cocoa, salt and cinnamon. Add sweetened condensed milk; mix well. Over medium heat, slowly stir in water and coffee; heat thoroughly but do not boil.
Makes 8 cups

EXQUISITE EGG NOG

4 eggs, separated

1 can **Eagle Brand Sweetened Condensed Milk**

1 cup brandy (optional)

1 tsp. vanilla

4 cups homogenized milk

¼ tsp. salt

nutmeg

In large bowl, beat egg yolks until thick and light. Gradually beat in sweetened condensed milk, brandy, vanilla, milk and salt. In small bowl, beat egg whites to soft peaks; gently fold into milk mixture. Chill. Pour into chilled bowl or serving cups. Garnish with nutmeg.
Makes 7 cups

AMBROSIAL APRICOT PUNCH

1 can **Eagle Brand Sweetened Condensed Milk**

¼ cup honey

1 48-oz. can apricot nectar, chilled

26 oz. club soda, chilled

vanilla ice cream

mint leaves (optional)

In medium punch bowl, combine sweetened condensed milk and honey. Slowly stir in apricot nectar. Just before serving add club soda and scoops of ice cream. If desired, garnish with mint leaves.
Makes 2 quarts

CAFÉ BRÛLOT

1 cup **MAXWELL HOUSE Ground Coffee**
3 sticks cinnamon
1 tbsp. whole cloves
4 cups cold water
¼ cup sugar
½ cup brandy (optional)
peel of 1 orange, cut in strips
peel of 1 lemon, cut in strips

Place coffee, cinnamon and cloves in basket of coffee maker. Brew coffee as usual; let stand in carafe 10 minutes. Meanwhile, heat sugar, brandy and peel in large saucepan, stirring until sugar dissolves. Slowly add coffee and heat through. Ladle into small cups.
Serves 8

VERY MELLOW RUM TODDY

2 tbsp. butter or **PARKAY Margarine**
1 cup firmly packed brown sugar
½ tsp. each cinnamon, nutmeg, allspice and cloves
4 tsp. **MAXWELL HOUSE Instant Coffee** granules
3 cups boiling water
2 tbsp. rum
½ cup light cream
strips of orange peel

Spice Mix: Cream butter with sugar; blend in spices. Store in jar with tight-fitting cover in refrigerator. Makes 1 cup mix or enough for 16 servings.

For 4 servings: Place instant coffee in coffee pot or carafe. Add boiling water; stir well. Add 4 tbsp. spice mix, rum and cream. Garnish with strips of orange peel, if desired.
Makes about 4 cups

SUPER CREAMY COCOA

½ cup cocoa
1 tsp. salt
1 can **Eagle Brand Sweetened Condensed Milk**
6½ cups water
marshmallows (optional)

In 3-quart saucepan, combine cocoa and salt. Add sweetened condensed milk; mix well. Over medium heat, slowly stir in water; heat thoroughly but do not boil. If desired, serve with marshmallows.
Makes 8 cups

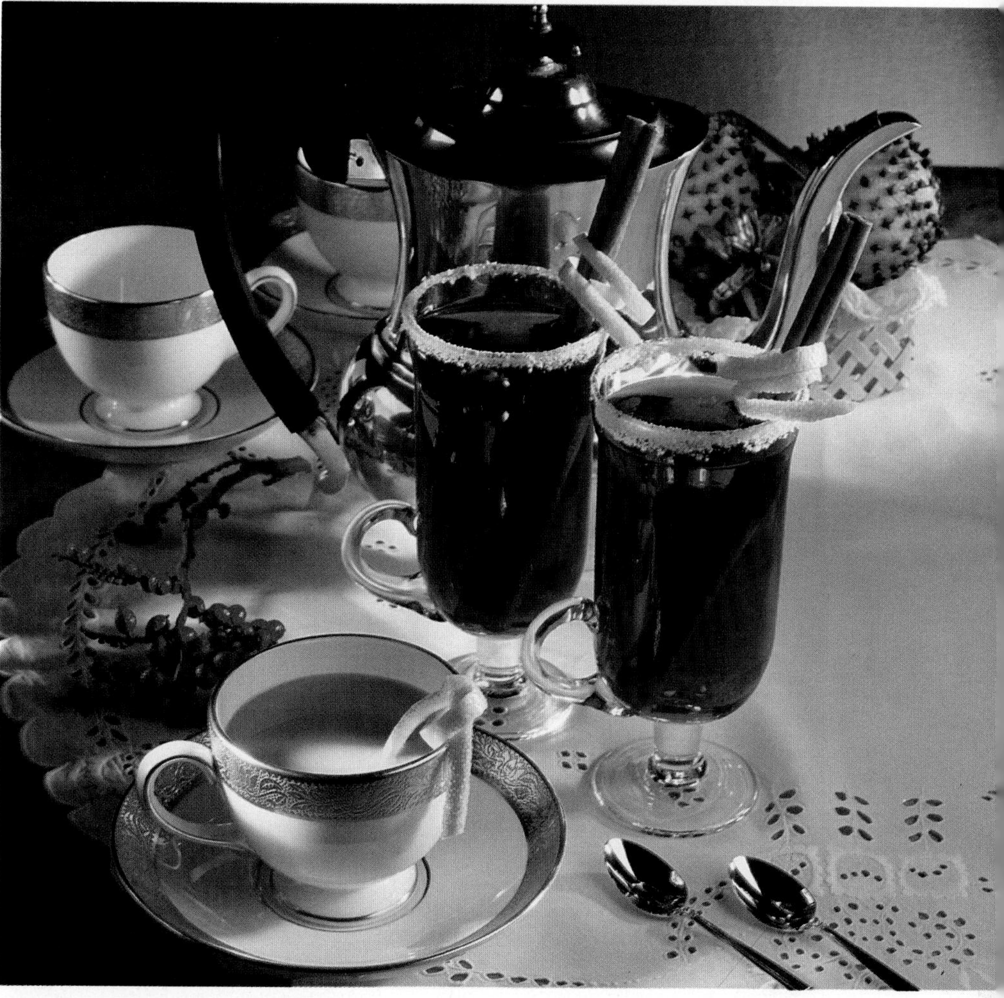

Café Brûlot and Very Mellow Rum Toddy

SPICED FRIENDSHIP COFFEE

1 medium orange
1 cup **MAXWELL HOUSE Ground Coffee**
2 cinnamon sticks
3 whole cloves
2 cardamom seeds
4 cups water
¼ cup orange liqueur

Remove rind from orange in strips. Place coffee, rind strips and spices in basket of coffeemaker. Brew coffee with water. Stir in orange liqueur. Pour into cups. Serve with a cinnamon stick, if desired.
Serves 8

WAKE-UP CARDAMOM COFFEE

¾ cup **MAXWELL HOUSE Ground Coffee**
½ tsp. ground cardamom
6 cups cold water

Place coffee and cardamom in filter basket of coffeemaker. Brew as usual.
Serves 8

COFFEE EGG NOG

2 egg yolks
1½ cups milk
1 cup 18% cream
¼ cup light corn syrup
4 tsp. **MAXWELL HOUSE Instant Coffee** granules
¼ cup brandy
2 egg whites

Beat egg yolks slightly in saucepan. Stir in milk, cream and corn syrup. Scald over low heat, stirring often. Remove from heat. Dissolve coffee in a small amount of the egg yolk mixture and blend with remaining egg yolk mixture in saucepan. Stir in brandy. In a serving bowl, beat egg whites until soft peaks form. Fold in yolk mixture. Beat with rotary beater or wire whisk until thoroughly blended. Sprinkle with nutmeg. Serve warm in punch cups or demitasse cups.
Serves 10

CRYSTAL LIGHT SPORTS QUENCHER

1 cup prepared double-strength **CRYSTAL LIGHT Orange, Berry Blend** or **Fruit Punch Low Calorie Drink Mix**

1 cup cold skim milk

2 tbsp. plain low-fat yogurt

6 ice cubes

2 mint sprigs for garnish

Place all ingredients except mint sprigs in a blender container. Blend until well mixed and frothy. Pour into 2 serving glasses. Garnish with mint sprigs.
Serves 2

CRYSTAL LIGHT MELONADE

1 cup prepared **CRYSTAL LIGHT Orange** or **Lemonade Low Calorie** beverage

1/3 small ripe cantaloupe

Peel and slice melon. Place beverage and melon in blender container. Process on high speed until smooth. Serve over ice if desired.
Serves 2

ICED TEA WITH LIME

1 pouch **CRYSTAL LIGHT Iced Tea Low Calorie Drink Mix**

3 cups water

3 cups crushed ice

3 tbsp. lime juice

Dissolve drink mix in water. In blender, place 1 cup of this mixture, 1 cup crushed ice and 1 tbsp. lime juice. Blend until smooth, then pour into a tall glass. Repeat twice more.
Serves 3

LEMON-LIME COOLER

1 pouch **CRYSTAL LIGHT Lemon-Lime Low Calorie Drink Mix**

3/4 cup peach schnapps

ice cubes

peach slices

Prepare drink mix according to package directions. Stir in peach schnapps. Pour into tall glasses filled with ice.
Serves 6

CRYSTAL LIGHT BERRY SLIM

1 cup prepared **CRYSTAL LIGHT Berry Blend Low Calorie** beverage

1/2 ripe banana or 1/3 cup sliced strawberries, peaches or papaya

2 tbsp. plain yogurt

For each serving, place beverage, fruit and yogurt in blender container. Process on high speed until smooth.
Makes 1 1/2 cups

HAWAIIAN DELIGHT

1 cup pineapple juice

1 cup milk

2 cups crushed ice

1 tsp. **Club House Banana Extract**

1/2 tsp. **Club House Coconut Extract**

1/2 tsp. **Club House Rum Extract**

Mix all ingredients in a blender or food processor and serve.
Makes 4 cups

PEACH SMOOTHIE

3 fresh peaches (unpeeled, pitted)

1/2 cup sparkling mineral water

2 cups crushed ice

1/2 tsp. **Club House Orange Extract**

1/4 tsp. **Club House Coconut Extract**

Mix all ingredients in a blender or food processor and serve.
Makes 3 cups

TANG SUPER SHAKE

2 tbsp. **TANG Mixed Fruit Flavour Crystals**

1 cup milk

2 scoops ice cream or fruit sherbet

Combine ingredients in blender container. Blend on high speed until smooth. Fresh fruit may be added before blending, if desired.
Serves 1

KOOL-AID SHAKES

1 cup **KOOL-AID**, your favorite flavor

1 1/2 cups vanilla ice cream

Place ingredients in blender container. Blend until smooth and frothy.

Smoothie Variation: Blend in 1/2 cup each chopped fruit or berries and plain yogurt.
Makes 1 large shake

SIMPLE GRAPE SODAS

1 envelope **QUENCH Grape Flavour Crystals**

1 cup water

2 12 1/2-oz. cans club soda

vanilla ice cream

Dissolve crystals in water. Stir in soda. Place one scoop of ice cream in each of 4 1-cup glasses. Pour in soda mixture. Stir.
Makes 4 servings

PEACH SLUSH

1 pouch **QUENCH Peach Flavour Crystals**

4 cups crushed ice

1 1/2 cups water

Place all ingredients in blender container; blend well. Serve in a tall glass with a straw.
Makes 4 1-cup servings

HOT MULLED LEMONADE

1 pouch **QUENCH Lemonade Flavour Crystals**

3 sticks cinnamon

5 whole allspice

10 whole cloves

5 cups water

2 tbsp. honey

1 orange, sliced

Place all ingredients except orange in medium saucepan. Bring to boil; simmer 10 minutes, stirring occasionally. Add orange slices and simmer 5 minutes more. Ladle into mugs or glasses.
Makes 6 3/4-cup servings

CREAMSICLE SHAKE

2 cups milk

1 pouch **QUENCH Orange Flavour Crystals**

4 ice cubes

8 scoops vanilla ice cream

Place all ingredients in blender container. Blend on high speed until smooth. Pour into 4 tall glasses.
Makes 4 1-cup servings

Index

L

T